The Sundance Reader

The Sundance Reader

Mark Connelly
Milwaukee Area Technical College

Harcourt Brace College Publishers

Fort Worth Philadelphia San Diego New York Orlando Austin San Antonio
Toronto Montreal London Sydney Tokyo

ACQUISITIONS EDITOR	Michael Rosenberg
DEVELOPMENTAL EDITOR	Tia Black
PROJECT EDITOR	Sandy Walton
PRODUCTION MANAGER	Eddie Dawson
MARKETING MANAGER	Ilse Wolf West
ART DIRECTOR	Scott Baker
COPY EDITOR	Kay Kaylor
PROOFREADER	Deanna Johnson
COMPOSITOR	G&S Typesetters
TEXT TYPE	11/13 Caslon 540 Roman

Address for Editorial Correspondence
Harcourt Brace College Publishers, 301 Commerce Street, Suite 3700, Fort Worth, TX 76102

Address for Orders
Harcourt Brace College Publishers, 6277 Sea Harbor Drive, Orlando, FL 32887

1-800-782-4479, or 1-800-433-0001 (in Florida)

Harcourt Brace College Publishers will provide complimentary supplements or supplement packages to those adopters qualified under our adoption policy. Please contact your sales representative to learn how you may qualify. If as an adopter or potential user you receive supplements you do not need, please return them to your sales representative or send them to:

ATTN: Returns Department
Troy Warehouse
465 South Lincoln Drive
Troy, MO 63379

ISBN: 0-15-503169-4

Library of Congress Catalog Card Number: 96-77465

Printed in the United States of America

9 0 1 2 3 4 5 6 016 10 9 8 7 6 5

To Stanley Felber

PREFACE

The Sundance Reader contains over ninety readings drawn from a range of academic disciplines and professions. The collection of essays and articles organized by rhetorical modes includes both classic and contemporary authors such as George Orwell, E. B. White, Alice Walker, Cornel West, and Terry Tempest Williams. In addition to writing from the disciplines of law, medicine, and science by writers such as Joseph Biden, Oliver Sacks, Jane Goodall, and Carl Sagan, *The Sundance Reader* offers students practical advice on resumé writing and job interviews. Applied readings at the end of each chapter demonstrate how writers use the rhetorical modes beyond the classroom. Entries such as "The Reconstructed Logbook of the *Titanic*," "Interrogation of Lee Harvey Oswald," and "The Heimlich Maneuver" illustrate various writing tasks students will face in future courses and in their careers.

The Sundance Reader's wide variety of topics on the environment, culture, social issues, and business make the textbook suitable for thematic courses. Individual chapters include self-contained units on current issues, and the thematic contents lists a number of topics that can be explored in depth.

With its wealth of readings and a four-part questioning strategy following each entry, *The Sundance Reader* provides students a unique perspective on how writing is shaped in different contexts.

The Sundance Reader has several features that make it a useful teaching tool for college instructors:

- ***A range of readings*** Each chapter opens with brief, readable entries which clearly demonstrate the rhetorical mode, followed by longer, more challenging essays. Each chapter highlights a model "blending" the modes showing how writers often use several methods of development to tell a story or explain a process. Samples of applied writing appear at the end, illustrating how writers use the mode in different professions. Instructors have flexibility in assigning readings best suited to their student populations.
- ***Brief entries suitable for in-class reading*** Many of the essays are short enough to be read in class and used as writing prompts, reducing the need for handouts.
- ***An emphasis on writing*** *The Sundance Reader* moves students from *reading* to *writing.* Chapters open with reading questions and conclude with writing guidelines and lists of suggested topics. Each chapter ends with a checklist of common writing problems.

- ***Writers on writing*** The readings include William Zinsser's "The Transaction" and Peter Elbow's "Desperation Writing" which examine writing as both a process and a product. Fran Martin's "Documentation Tips" explains how nurses should word reports to prevent malpractice suits. In "Resumes That Rate a Second Look," Anne Weisbord demonstrates the importance of writing skills to job seekers.
- ***An emphasis on critical thinking*** *The Sundance Reader* stresses critical thinking by including James Austin's article about the role of chance in scientific research and S. I. Hayakawa's "Reports, Inferences, and Judgments" analyzing the way language shapes meaning. Samuel Scudder's essay "Take This Fish and Look at It" dramatizes the importance of detailed observation. Darrell Huff's "How to Lie with Statistics" and John Allen Paulos's "Innumeracy" heighten student awareness of how statistics are misused and manipulated.
- ***Pro and con entries*** Instructors have found that presenting essays with contrasting viewpoints can stimulate class discussion and prompt writing activities. *The Sundance Reader* presents pairs of pro and con articles on three critical issues: global warming, gender differences, and bilingualism.
- ***Focus on diversity*** Over a third of the selections are written by women. African-American, Asian, Hispanic, and Native-American writers are well-represented. In addition to social commentaries by Gloria Steinem and Martin Luther King, women and minorities are featured in nontraditional areas such as science, technology, and advertising.
- ***Writing across the curriculum*** *The Sundance Reader* demonstrates how each mode is developed by writers working in several disciplines, including law, medicine, psychology, history, law enforcement, and business.
- ***Writing beyond the classroom*** Each chapter includes a section illustrating how writers use the modes in "the real world." Advertisements, brochures, government documents, and a resumé introduce elements of business and technical writing to composition students. In addition, several of the entries taken from academic journals are reproduced with full documentation.
- ***Collaborative writing*** Writing suggestions following the readings include directions for collaborative writing activities. The introduction provides useful guidelines for successful group writing.
- ***Advice on the job search*** *The Sundance Reader* contains articles offering students practical advice on writing resumés, succeeding in job interviews, and evaluating job offers. Other articles provide recommendations for entrepreneurs and business managers.

Above all, *The Sundance Reader* has been designed to encourage students to read and develop confidence as writers.

ACKNOWLEDGMENTS

I would like to thank the following reviewers for their critiques and recommendations:

Michel de Benedictus, Miami Dade Community College; Iris Rose Hart, Santa Fe Community College; Donna Hickey, University of Richmond; Janice Hunter, Valencia Community College; Kimberlie A. Johnson, Seminole Community College; Steve Katz, State Technical Institute; David L. Miller, Fayetteville Technical Community College; Jack Miller, Normandale Community College; Anne Myers, State University of New York College of Technology, Cobleskill; Jack Pate, Ozarka Technical College; Blair Ray, Polk Community College; Wendolyn Tetlow, DeVry Technical Institute; Albert Wilhelm, Tennessee Technical University.

All books are a collaborative effort. My special thanks goes to Michael Rosenberg at Harcourt Brace for his perception, editorial judgment, and enthusiasm for *The Sundance Reader*. His guidance was critical in determining the final table of contents. Tia Black provided valuable advice in developing the final draft of the book and crafting the apparatus. In addition I would like to thank the talented Harcourt Brace Production team: production manager, Eddie Dawson; project editor, Sandy Walton; art director, Scott Baker; marketing manager, Ilse Wolfe West; copy editor, Kay Kaylor; and proofreader, Deanna Johnson.

Contents

THEMATIC CONTENTS

ART AND ENTERTAINMENT

AUTOBIOGRAPHY

BIOGRAPHY

BUSINESS AND ECONOMICS

CHILDHOOD

CIVIL RIGHTS

COMMUNITY AND CULTURE

CRITICAL THINKING

DIVERSITY

EDUCATION

ENVIRONMENT

HEALTH AND MEDICINE

HISTORY

JOB INTERVIEWS

LANGUAGE

LAW AND CRIME

POLITICS

PSYCHOLOGY AND HUMAN BEHAVIOR

WOMEN AND MEN

WORK AND CAREER

WRITING

1

Introduction

HOW WE WRITE

In the summer of 1939 scientist Leo Szilard was worried. As Americans enjoyed the New York World's Fair, the exiled physicist followed events in Europe with growing anxiety. His experiments proved that a nuclear chain reaction could create an atomic bomb. German scientists had split the atom, and the Nazis had seized rich deposits of uranium in Czechoslovakia. As a Jew who had escaped on the last train out of Nazi Germany, Szilard was horrified at the prospect of Hitler obtaining nuclear weapons. Now living in New York, he tried to warn the American government, but officials in Washington were unwilling to fund atomic research. A refugee without resources or political contacts, Szilard sought help from his old friend Albert Einstein, a Nobel Prize winner with an international reputation. Szilard hoped the government would listen to Einstein. Although the idea of a nuclear chain reaction had never occurred to him, Einstein quickly grasped its implications and suggested writing President Roosevelt. Einstein dictated a letter and asked Szilard to revise it. Szilard wrote a new version then telephoned Einstein, who requested another meeting. Accompanied by fellow physicist Edward Teller, Szilard met Einstein at a summer cottage to discuss the letter. The scientists soon became frustrated. Einstein realized their abstract theories would be difficult to explain to a nonscientist. Equally frustrating was the fact that English was a second language to all three scientists. Einstein dictated a new draft to Edward Teller in German. Leo Szilard wrote two more letters in English and mailed them to Einstein. After reviewing them carefully, Einstein selected the longer version and signed it. Just eight paragraphs long, the letter began with a simply worded declaration of Einstein's concerns:

> Sir:
>
> Some recent work by E. Fermi and L. Szilard, which has been communicated to me in manuscript, leads me to expect that the element uranium may be turned into a new and important source of energy in the immediate future. Certain aspects of the situation which has arisen seem to call for watchfulness and, if necessary, quick action on the part of the Administration. I believe therefore that it is my duty to bring to your attention the following facts and recommendations:

This letter (see page 676 for the full version) was presented to President Roosevelt and helped launch the Manhattan Project and the nuclear age.

The story behind Einstein's letter demonstrates important elements about writing. Writing is a complex process and does not occur in a vacuum. It takes place in a *context* formed by three factors:

1. The writer's purpose and role
2. The knowledge base, attitudes, needs, expectations, and biases of the reader
3. The conventions, history, and culture of a particular discipline, profession, organization, publication, situation, or community

Writing, as the creation of Einstein's letter shows, is often *collaborative*, a product of a group activity. Writing may reflect the ideas of more than one person. Einstein's letter also illustrates a common dilemma writers face in a technological society. Experts frequently have to communicate with readers outside their discipline, people with little understanding or appreciation of the writers' subjects.

Context explains why a newspaper article about an airplane crash differs from a Federal Aviation Administration (FAA) report or the airline's condolence letter to the victims' families. Stated simply and printed in narrow columns for easy skimming, a newspaper account briefly describes current events for general readers. An FAA report detailing the causes of a plane crash runs hundreds of pages and includes extensive data and testimony of witnesses and survivors. Directed to aviation safety experts, the report is stated in technical language largely incomprehensible to the average reader. The airline's letter to victims' families addresses people enduring confusion, grief, and anger. Carefully worded, it attempts to inform readers without appearing callous or falsely sympathetic.

You may have noticed how context affects your own writing. The notes you take in class for personal use look very different from the in-class essay you submit for a grade. The words you choose when adding a line to a birthday card for your seven-year-old cousin differ from those used on a job application or in a note to your roommate. Almost unconsciously, you alter the way you write depending on your purpose, reader, and circumstances. To be an effective writer in college and in your future career, it is important to increase your understanding of the three elements that form a writing context.

QUESTIONS

1. Can you recall writing situations where you had difficulty expressing your ideas because you were unsure how your reader would react? Did you have problems finding the right words or just "getting your thoughts on paper"?
2. Have you found that teachers and professors have different attitudes about what constitutes "good writing"? How is writing a paper in English literature different from writing a paper in psychology or economics?
3. Have you observed that magazines often have strikingly different writing styles? What do articles in *Cosmopolitan*, *Car and Driver*, or *The Wall Street Journal* reveal about their intended readers?

THE WRITER

All writing has a goal. A shopping list serves to refresh your memory. A memo informs employees of a policy change. Research papers demonstrate students' knowledge and skills. Résumés encourage employers to call applicants for job interviews. Even essays written for self-expression must contain more than random observations. To be effective an essay must arouse interest, provide readers with information they can understand, and offer proof to support the writer's thesis.

The Writer's Purpose

Students and professionals in all fields face similar writing tasks. The way they present their ideas, the language they use, and even the physical appearance of the finished document are determined in part by their purpose. Although every writing assignment forms a unique context, most writing tasks can be divided into basic modes or types:

narration *To relate a series of events, usually in chronological order.* Biographies, histories, and novels use narration. Business and government reports often include sections called *narratives* that provide a historical overview of a problem, organization, or situation. Letters to friends usually consist of narratives detailing recent events or experiences.

description *To create a picture or impression of a person, place, object, or condition.* Description is a basic element in all writing and usually serves to provide support for the writer's main goal. Descriptions may be wholly factual and objective, as in an accident report or parts catalog. Others contain personal impressions emphasizing what the writer saw, thought, or felt. A novelist describing a city is more likely to focus on his or her "feel" of the streets and people rather than on statistics and census figures.

definition *To explain a term, condition, topic, or issue.* In many instances definitions are precise and standard, such as a state's definition of second-degree murder or a biology book's definition of a virus. Other definitions, such as the definition of a good parent or an ideal teacher, may be based on a writer's personal observation, experience, and opinion.

comparision/contrast *To examine the similarities and differences between two or more subjects.* Textbooks often employ comparison/contrast to discuss different scientific methods, theories, or subjects. Comparisons can be made to distinguish topics or to recommend one subject as superior to others. Consumer magazines frequently use comparison to highlight differences among competing products.

analysis *To evaluate a subject and identify its essential elements, impact, effectiveness, or qualities.* Writers of a formal analysis can follow a standard method. Stockbrokers, medical examiners, building inspectors, archaeologists, botanists, criminologists, and other professionals generally use uniform methods of studying subjects and presenting their conclusions. Essayists and newspaper columnists, on the other hand, analyze issues from an entirely personal perspective, relying on anecdotal evidence and individual observation. Movie reviews, a sports writer's column about a coach's performance, and a pollster's view on the president's popularity are examples of personal analysis.

division *To name subgroups or divisions in a broad class.* Writers seek to make a large or complex topic understandable or workable by dividing it into smaller units. Insurance can be divided into life, health, homeowner's, and auto policies. A zoology text divides animals into fish, birds, mammals, and reptiles.

classification *To place objects into different classes or levels according to a single measurement.* Writers classify with a scale to grade subjects. Homicides are classified first-, second-, or third-degree according to circumstances and premeditation. Burns are classified first-, second-, or third-degree based on the severity of tissue damage.

Like analysis, division and classification can be based on professional standards or personal evaluation. A financial adviser might rate mutual funds by risk and performance using commonly accepted criteria. A movie critic, however, could grade films on a one-to-five-star scale based solely on his or her tastes.

process *To explain how something occurs or to demonstrate how to accomplish a specific task.* A nuclear power plant, the human heart, and inflation can be described as processes. By examining each stage, a writer can make a complex mechanism or event easier to understand. A recipe, the owner's manual of a computer, and a first-aid book offer step-by-step instructions to complete specific tasks.

cause and effect *To trace the reasons for or results of an occurrence.* A writer can list causes for an increase in crime, for the return of an endangered species, or for the success or failure of an advertising campaign. Similarly, he or she could list the effects crime has on a community, the response to rescued wildlife, or the impact of television commercials. Physicians refer to medical books that explain the causes of disease and the effects of drugs.

persuasion and argumentation *To influence reader opinion, attitudes, and actions.* Writers persuade with logical appeals based on factual evidence, with ethical appeals based on values or beliefs, or with emotional appeals that arouse feelings to support their views. A fund-raising letter persuades readers to donate money to a charity. An engineer's report presents an argument why a building should be condemned or an engine redesigned. Essayists and columnists try to influence readers to accept their opinions on topics ranging from abortion to welfare reform.

QUESTIONS

1. Consider how you have organized papers in the past. Did any assignments lend themselves to one of the modes? Could following one of these methods make it easier to present and organize your ideas?
2. Do you use modes such as *comparison, classification,* or *cause and effect* in organizing your thoughts and solving problems? Do you *compare* apartments before deciding which one to rent or *classify* courses you want to take next semester by difficulty or desirability?

The way writers achieve their goals depends greatly on the other two elements of context: their readers and the discipline. Each chapter of *The Sundance Reader* focuses on one of these modes, illustrating how writers use it in different contexts.

A Note about Modes

Modes refer to the writer's basic goal. Often writing cannot be neatly labeled. Few writing tasks call for the use of a single mode. A dictionary entry is pure definition, and a parts catalog offers simple product descriptions. But a movie review *analyzing* a new release will first *describe* the film and possibly *compare* it to the director's previous work. It might use *narration* to explain elements of the plot and *classification* to rank it with other films in its genre. Some writing can easily fit two or more categories. The Declaration of Independence, for instance (page 608), is an example of both *cause and effect* and *persuasive writing.*

The Writer's Role

An important aspect of context is the writer's role. As a student your role is much like that of a freelance writer. Your essays, reports, and research papers are expected to reflect only your own efforts. In general, your work is judged independently. A low grade on a first paper should not affect your chances of earning a higher grade later in the semester. What you write in psychology has no influence on your grades in English. Your comments on controversial issues are not likely to be raised at future job interviews.

Outside of academics, however, your role is more complicated. Often you act as an agent of a larger organization, corporation, or profession. Business letters, memos, and reports are assumed to express the views of the employer, not a single employee. Expressing personal views that conflict with corporate practices or administrative policy can jeopardize your position. Frequently, you will have an ongoing relationship with your readers. Comments made in one letter or report affect how readers will respond to your ideas in the future.

Probably the most obvious aspect of a writer's role concerns *perspective,* or the writer's position in the paper. Writing in a newspaper's sports section, a columnist may be free to offer personal opinion: "Given poor ticket sales and the age of the stadium, I predict this town will lose its ball club within two years." A front-page article, however, would be weakened by the use of first person. A reporter would express the same view in more objective terms: "The decline in ticket sales and the age of the stadium indicate the city is in danger of losing its baseball team."

When writing as a member of a group or as an agent of an organization, remember that the ideas you express will be considered the ideas of the group. Refrain from stating anything that would alienate other members or expose your organization to liability. If you state personal views, make sure you clearly identify them as being your opinions.

In many instances your profession will dictate a role that will greatly shape what is expected in your writing. Police officers and nurses, for example, are required to provide objective and impersonal records of their observations. Fashion consultants, decorators, and advertising executives, who are esteemed for their creativity, are more likely to offer personal insights and make first-person statements.

QUESTIONS

1. Consider the jobs you have had and businesses you have worked for. What writing style would be appropriate for professionals in these fields? Is objective reporting required, or are employees free to offer personal impressions and suggest innovations?
2. What type of writing do you expect to confront in your career? How does writing in engineering and accounting differ from writing in public relations, sales, or nonprofit charities? Does your future profession demand adherence to governmental regulations and industry standards, or does it allow for individual expression?

THE READER

Writing is more than self-expression; it is an act of communication. To be effective your message must be understood. The content, form, and tone of your writing is largely shaped by the needs and expectations of your readers. A medical researcher announcing a new treatment for AIDS would word an article for *Immunology* very differently from one for *Newsweek* or *Redbook*. Each magazine represents a different audience, a different knowledge base, and a different set of concerns. Fellow immunologists would be interested in the author's research methods and would demand detailed proof of his or her claims. These readers would expect to see extensive data and precise descriptions of experiments and testing methods. Most readers of nonmedical publications would require definitions of scientific terms and would expect brief summaries of data they would be unable to evaluate. Readers of *Newsweek* could be concerned with issues such as cost, government policy, and insurance coverage. Subscribers to a women's magazine might wonder if the treatment works equally well for both sexes or if the treatment would be suitable for pregnant women with HIV.

Audiences often differ within a discipline. The medical researcher writing for the *New England Journal of Medicine* would be addressing practicing physicians, not laboratory researchers. Doctors would be interested in the practical aspects of the treatment. What drugs does it interact with? What are the side effects? Which patients should receive the drug and in what doses? An article in *Nursing* would focus on the concerns of nurses who closely monitor patients for reactions. What effect does the treatment have on a patient's physical and psychological well-being? Are there special considerations for patients with unrelated disorders, such as hypertension and diabetes?

As a writer you will have to determine how much knowledge your readers have about your subject. Do technical terms have to be defined? Does your writing include historical or biographical references requiring explanation? Do you use concepts that general readers might misunderstand or find confusing? In addition to your readers' level of understanding, you must consider your readers' needs and expectations in relation to your own goal. What information do your readers want from you? Is your audience reading for general interest, curiosity, or entertainment? Or do your readers demand specific information in order to make decisions or plan future actions?

It is also important to take into account how your readers will respond to your ideas. Is your audience likely to be favorable or hostile to you, your ideas, or the organization you might represent? Defense attorneys and prosecutors have different attitudes toward illegally obtained evidence. Environmentalists and real estate developers have conflicting philosophies of land use. Liberals and conservatives have opposing concepts of the proper role of government regulation. When presenting ideas to audiences with undefined or differing attitudes, you will have to work hard to overcome their natural resistance, biases, and suspicions.

Individual Readers

The papers you write in high school and college are usually read by a single teacher or professor evaluating your work in the context of a particular course. Instructors form a special audience because they are counted on to read your work and remain objective. Beyond the classroom, however, you may have to persuade someone to read your résumé or proposal. Few of these readers will even attempt objectivity. Unlike the papers you write for instructors, your reports and letters seek more than a grade. In many instances, you will ask an employer for a job or persuade a client to buy a product. In accepting your ideas, your reader may be investing substantial resources on your behalf, conceivably placing his or her career in your hands. In writing to these individuals, you will have to analyze their needs and concerns very carefully.

Extended Readerships

Many contexts involve two audiences: the immediate person or persons who receive your document and a second, extended readership. When you write as a student, most of your work is returned to you. In most jobs your correspondence, reports, and publications are retained for future reference. The safety inspection report you write in April may be routinely skimmed by your supervisor, filed, and forgotten. But if a serious accident occurs in May, this report will be retrieved and closely examined by state inspectors, insurance investigators, and attorneys. If you engage in a dispute with a customer or another employee, your writing may be reviewed by a supervisor or, in the case of litigation, introduced into court as evidence. Many professionals practice "defensive writing," precisely wording their thoughts and observations, understanding that whatever they write may be examined by adversaries. In court, police officers and physicians are often asked to explain and defend comments they have written months or years before.

When you write outside of academics, bear in mind who else may see your writing. This is a critical consideration whenever you are writing as an employee or agent of others. Think carefully before making remarks that might be misunderstood out of context.

The Perceptual World

To learn how readers respond to ideas, it is helpful to understand what communications researchers call the *perceptual world*, the context in which people perceive new information and experiences. As individuals or groups, readers base their reactions on a number of factors that have varying significance and often operate simultaneously:

- **Past experiences** influence how people respond to new information and situations. Readers who have lost money in the stock market will be more skeptical of an investment offer than those who have enjoyed substantial returns. A labor union with a harmonious relationship with management will view contract offers differently from a union with a history of stalled talks, bitter negotiations, and strikes.
- **Education,** both formal and informal, affects people's reading ability, background knowledge, and understanding of terminology. Training in specific

disciplines also will influence how readers evaluate the evidence writers present as support. Scientists and mathematicians may be more skeptical of advertising claims using statistics than the general public.

- **Professional experience,** along with training and job responsibilities, shapes people's attitudes. An economics professor with tenure may exhibit a greater ability to be objective about a new tax policy than a small-business owner struggling to meet a weekly payroll. Police officers and emergency-room doctors may be less sympathetic to drunken drivers than people who rarely see the harm they cause.
- **Status** or amount of investment influences people's response to potential change. An entry-level employee is less likely to be concerned about a change in pension plans than is one nearing retirement. Homeowners have more invested in their neighborhoods than renters and may show greater interest in crime or pollution.
- **Values,** whether religious, political, or cultural, help shape readers' responses. Often these values are unspoken but deeply held. People's attitudes about money, sexual conduct, drug use, child rearing, and the role of government affect how they react to new ideas.
- **Reference groups** include people or institutions readers respect and defer to. A physician who is unsure about prescribing a new drug may base his or her decision on the opinion of the American Medical Association. A student thinking of changing his or her major might seek advice from parents and friends.
- **Social roles,** such as being a parent, civic leader, or property owner influence how a person evaluates ideas. A thirty year old with two small children will have different concerns from someone of the same age without children. A shop steward plays a special role and may be expected to react differently than other employees.
- **Age** affects reader attitudes in two ways. People are products of the times they have lived through. Men and women who came of age during World War II have different views than those who grew up during the Vietnam War. In general, older readers have more invested in existing institutions than younger readers and may be more cautious about change.

Other aspects of the perceptual world include gender, ethnic background, and income. In determining your readers' perceptual world, it is important to avoid basing assumptions on common stereotypes. Not all older people are conservative, and not all African Americans endorse Affirmative Action. Many elements of the perceptual world are unconscious and cannot be easily ascertained. No doubt you have been surprised by the reactions of friends you believed you knew very well.

QUESTIONS

1. How would you describe the perceptual world of your parents, coworkers, or friends? How do their common experiences, values, roles, and education affect their attitudes? How would they respond to a letter urging them to donate money to the homeless, to support a handgun ban, or to picket an abortion clinic? Which issues would be difficult to present to them? Why?
2. Have you ever tried to understand someone you hoped to influence in some way? In practicing a presentation, preparing for a job interview, or seeking the right words to discuss a difficult issue with a friend or family member, did you consider how that person might react? Is understanding people's perceptual worlds something we engage in every day?

THE DISCIPLINE

The communication between writer and reader occurs within a particular discipline, setting, culture, publication, or situation. Each academic discipline has a unique history. Some disciplines, such as literature and mathematics, have slowly evolved over thousands of years. Students still read *Oedipus* and study Euclid's principles of geometry. In contrast, the fields of computer science and bioengineering are so new that many of their founders are still actively developing the nature of the discipline.

Every discipline has its own communications style and methods of measuring data, weighing results, and presenting conclusions. In the humanities, research is generally oriented to examining specific works. Whether the researcher is studying Bach, Shakespeare, or Georgia O'Keeffe, the artist's work is the central focus. Disciplines often contain several schools of thought or types of criticism. In literature, for example, some scholars interpret a novel in light of the author's life and thoughts. Other critics would analyze the book in terms of its historical position or political message. Some critics specialize in feminist or Marxist interpretations of literature. But no matter what their approach, literary critics essentially present an educated opinion based on interpretations of the text.

In the sciences, such as biology, chemistry, and physics, scholars base their evaluations on the principles of laboratory research and experiments. Scholars making new assertions in these fields must demonstrate where they obtained their data and prove that other scientists can repeat their experiments and obtain the same results. Although the sciences can seem exact, personal opinion can play a significant role in setting up experiments and interpreting data.

The social sciences of psychology, sociology, criminology, political science, and economics blend some of the features of the humanities and sciences. Although psychologists and criminologists can conduct experiments and often use scientific evidence, many of their conclusions are based on data that can be collected and interpreted in a number of ways.

As a college student you can appreciate the nature of each discipline by examining your textbooks, particularly introductory chapters that often provide a history of the field.

Each profession forms its own context of historical experience, technical training, areas of concern, responsibilities, and political and social outlooks. Corporate executives charged with obtaining investor capital for expansion and research develop different attitudes toward capital-gains taxes than social workers assisting low-income families. The medical profession has a strict tradition of relying on standardized treatment and research methods. Physicians tend to be skeptical of anyone claiming to have a cure for a disease unless the claims can be clearly supported by research and not anecdotal endorsements. Professions measure success differently, praising creativity, sales, or communications skills. Law enforcement officers approach a case of suspected child abuse with the goal of determining if evidence indicates a crime has been committed. A mental health professional is more interested in the child's well-being, whether the situation meets the definitions of legal abuse or not. To a therapist even an imagined incident would be treated seriously if it caused the child distress.

The discipline, profession, or situation creates different methods of using and looking at writing. David Ogilvy, a noted advertising executive, devoted his career to writing ad copy, coming up with snappy, creative, innovative ways of grabbing consumers' attention and boosting sales of his clients' products. For him, writing is a tool to project an image, gain attention, and, above all, sell:

> Always try to inject *news* into your headlines, because the consumer is always on the lookout for new products, or new ways to use an old product, or new improvements in an old product.

> The two most powerful words you can use in a headline are FREE and NEW. You can seldom use FREE, but you can almost always use NEW—if you try hard enough.

Fran Martin, a nurse who serves as an expert witness in medical malpractice trials, offers a very different kind of writing advice to nurses. Unlike ad writers whose success depends on creativity or originality, nurses are counted on to maintain precise records:

> You communicate with other health care providers through the chart and, obviously, incorrect data doesn't give an accurate picture of your patient's condition. That could lead to life-threatening errors. It also raises the specter of fraud, which could make your actions appear not just negligent, but also criminal.

Writing Contexts

The contexts writers operate in are limitless, but a few general patterns follow:

1. **Expert to general reader:** Most books and articles are written by experts to people reading for information or enjoyment. An attorney preparing a university brochure on date rape would have to anticipate that most student attitudes have been largely formed by the media. He or she might have to dispel common misconceptions and explain terms and legal procedures.
2. **Expert to expert within a discipline:** Law reviews, medical journals, and trade magazines are largely read by professionals within a specific field. Writers for these periodicals can assume readers will understand basic concepts and terminology. Advanced textbooks in biology or criminal law rarely provide the introductory material found in first-year books. The letters, reports, and documents generated within a corporation or government agency may adopt a unique style and format that almost become a code few outsiders can understand. But writers in these situations should always keep an extended readership in mind. An audit, budget review, or investigation could circulate as a memo or letter to a wider audience.
3. **Expert to expert in different disciplines:** This is perhaps one of the most challenging contexts writers face. Einstein's letter to Roosevelt is a classic example of this context—a world-famous scientist attempting to explain a discovery to a powerful leader with minimal knowledge of

physics. How does an engineer explain the practical difficulties to a designer interested in style and creativity? How does an economist persuade a politician facing reelection to raise taxes or cut benefits? In communicating with professionals in different disciplines, it is important for writers to establish trust, to address their readers' concerns, and to explain unfamiliar concepts clearly.

THE WRITING PROCESS

Writing is a process as well as a product. Good writing respects each of the three elements of context. When you plan a writing project, determine your purpose, evaluate your readers, and follow the conventions of your discipline. Many college instructors provide requirements for writing assignments. In a professional situation you can benefit from examining samples of the writing tasks you are undertaking.

Prewriting

Writing is not only a means of preparing a finished document but also a way of thinking and exploring. You can use a number of planning techniques to discover topics, define your thesis, and list needed items.

Freewriting records thoughts and impressions without interruption and without any concern for spelling, grammar, or punctuation. Freewriting should not be confused with writing a rough draft. Freewriting is like talking to yourself. It may have no direction, it may skip from topic to topic, and it may contradict itself. Freewriting is a bit like making a series of fast sketches before determining the subject matter of a large painting. The goal of freewriting is not writing a "paper" but simply discovering possible topics.

Overhearing a claim that the government was behind the influx of drugs in the inner city, a student sat at her computer and rapidly recorded a stream of thoughts on the topic of conspiracy theories:

The CIA is behind the drug epidemic. The US government pays South Koreans to set up grocery stores in the inner city. Every president since Nixon has lied about MIA's held captive in Southeast Asia. The airforce lies about UFO sitings. The number of conspiracy theories is limitless. The lumber industry is against legalizing marijuana because hemp makes better paper than woodpulp. Roosevelt knew the Japanese were going to bomb Pearl Harbor but let it happen. Conspiracies are endless. They are populair. They sell a lot of newspapers and create a lot of TV shows & employ an army of theoriests who move from talk show to talk show touting their books and their latest proof that the CIA or blacks or the Fortune 500 is responsible for some horrible deed or social threat. No doubt some mad scienist in a govt lab created AIDS and loosed it on the world. No doubt someone has cured cancer and has been kidnapped or killed so millions of doctors and thousands of drug companies won't go out of business. Why? Why do people love these theories?

Some people to need to believe that no lone assassin could have killed JFK. They cling to this belief, no matter what the evidence. Why? Maybe we need to believe in conspiracy theories. It makes the evil in the world less frightening. We are not victims of random chaos, but evil people who can theoretically be located and exposed. To abandon conspiracy theories means accepting chaos. Also it allows us to escape blame. If we blame all our problems on mysterious forces beyond our control, then we can dodge personnal responsibility.

Although this freewriting is loose, repetitive, and misspelled, it moves from listing conspiracy theories to speculating why people need to believe in them. The student now has something to focus on and a possible title: "Why We Need Conspiracy Theories."

Brainstorming is another prewriting process that can help you generate ideas and identify possible topics for further writing. As in freewriting, list your ideas as quickly as possible. Do not bother to worry if your ideas are repetitive or irrelevant. Again, your purpose is not to outline a paper but simply to develop ideas.

Brainstorming can be used to discover a topic for an essay or to help a professional identify details needed to be included in a business letter or report. A composition student assigned a comparison/contrast essay might list as many ideas as possible in hopes of discovering a topic:

high school teachers/college professors
male/female attitudes about first dates
American/Japanese ideas about privacy
Puerto-Ricans vs. Mexican-Americans
Mexican-born vs. 1st generation Mex-Americans
English only vs. Bilingual
Mexican-born English/1st gen. Mex-Am attitudes

Through brainstorming or listing, the student has run through a number of ideas before focusing on a topic suited for a short paper comparing the attitudes of Mexican-born Americans and their children toward English.

Even when the topic is defined, brainstorming can help writers identify what they should include. The third-shift supervisor of a warehouse planning a report following a forklift accident could use brainstorming to make sure he or she produces a complete report, so managers can examine the firm's legal liability, safety policies, employee training, and equipment use:

time/date/location of accident.
Injured personnel--Alex Bolton, Sara Lopez
    (Medical Status)
911 call--get time from dispatcher
Bolton's forklift--last inspection (service log)
forklift load--stability (check manual)
Use of helmets, earplugs
surveillance cameras (tapes)
accident witnesses

From this list, the supervisor identifies the information needed to meet the needs of the readers.

WRITING ACTIVITIES

1. *Freewriting:* Select one of the following topics, and write for at least ten minutes. Do not worry about making sense or maintaining logical connections between ideas. Remember, this is not the rough draft of a paper but an attempt to develop ideas and discover topics.

your worst job	blind dates	television talk shows
job interviews	marriage	capital punishment
recycling	censorship	student loans
campus housing	car repair	media images of women

2. *Brainstorming:* Select one of the columns of ideas and build on it, adding your own ideas. Jot down your thoughts as quickly as possible. Do not worry if some of your ideas are off the topic.

men/women	success/money	vacation plans
dating	careers	plane/car
expectations	salary/income	hotel/meals
conflicts	risk/reward	budget/costs

Clustering represents a more visual method of developing ideas. Instead of complete sentences or listed ideas, topics are grouped in circles and boxes. Visual markers such as arrows, question marks, and ink color can be used to organize and link ideas. A student writing about the information superhighway clustered the following topics:

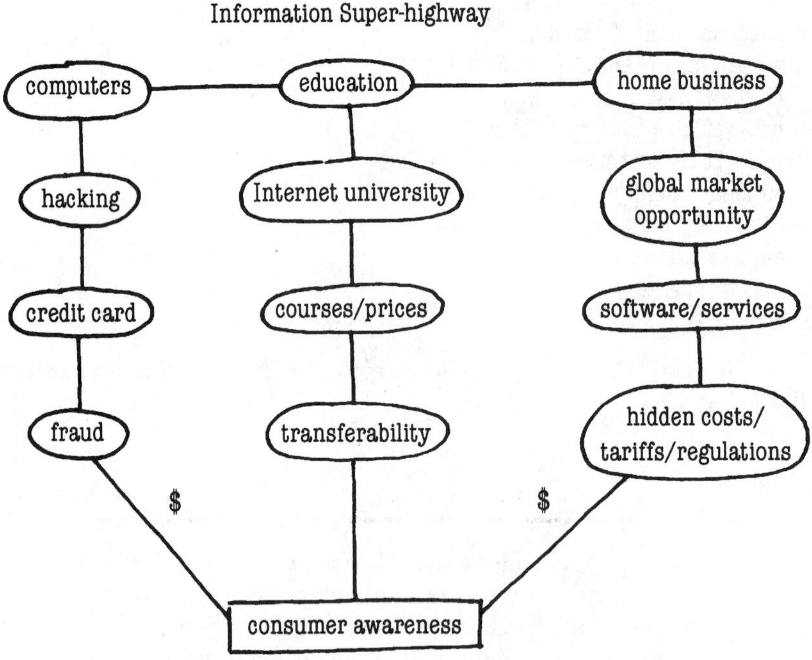

Drawing clusters helps the student focus on a topic: consumer awareness and the Internet.

Asking questions is a method used by reporters and investigators to help identify critical information. For generations newspaper reporters have been trained to ask the "Five Ws": Who? What? When? Where? Why? Asking questions can help you identify topics and narrow your focus. A student considering writing a paper about Arthur Miller's *Death of a Salesman* might list the following questions to help identify a topic for a short analytical paper:

Death of a Salesman

What are Willy's values?
Is Willy a victim of society or of his own delusions?
What role does Uncle Ben play?
Is Willy's suicide caused by despair or a last attempt at success?

What impact does Willy's infidelity have?
Biff steals a suit and a fountain pen. What do these objects represent?
Linda knows Willy has lost his salary but does not confront him about it. Why?
Why does Miller pose Willy and Biff next to Uncle Charlie and Bernard?
Is the play an attack on the American dream?
Why does Willy refuse to take a job from Charlie?
This play is world famous but the hero is abusive, selfish, and short-tempered. Why is the play so popular?
What is the purpose of the requiem at the end?
How would the play be different without it?

By posing lists of questions, you can often identify key issues and provoke critical thinking that will lead to developing a thesis.

WRITING ACTIVITIES

1. *Clustering:* Select one of the following topics. Use a large piece of paper to record and arrange your ideas. Group related ideas with circles or squares. Use arrows to connect ideas. You may use different colors, switch from pen to pencil, or mark major ideas with a highlighter. Whatever method you use, do not allow your artwork to overshadow your goal of developing ideas for a paper.

year-round school	computer hacking	nutrition
gay rights	the American dream	women in combat
airports	working out	childless couples
aging	being laid off	divorce

2. *Asking questions:* Select one of the following topics, and write a list of questions. Write as quickly as possible, and do not worry about being repetitive. Try to ask as many questions as you can to explore as many avenues as possible.

recent hit movie	gangs	television violence
day care	welfare reform	suburbs
role models	teen pregnancy	corporate downsizing
labor unions	singles' bars	drunk driving

Moving from Topic to Thesis

A paper is never "about" something; it must make a clear statement. The student who begins writing "about *Death of a Salesman*" may find himself or herself facing an endless number of issues or end up creating nothing more than a plot summary. Writing should have a focus, a direction. The word *thesis* refers to the writer's main idea. A good thesis makes a clear point that is supported by the body of the writing. In some writing the thesis is the central idea or controlling statement. In argumentative writing the thesis is clearly articulated. In descriptive or narrative writing, the thesis can be implied. A writer who offers a powerful description of the homeless may assume readers will be moved to take action.

A thesis makes a strong statement about a topic:

Topic: Consumers and the Internet
Thesis: Users of the Internet unknowingly expose themselves to consumer fraud.

Topic: Conspiracy theories
Thesis: Like ancient mythology, today's conspiracy theories serve to explain the unexplainable and reduce fear of chaos.

Topic: *Death of a Salesman*
Thesis: Willy Loman commits what psychologists call altruistic suicide.

Once you have determined your thesis, you can begin writing. Writers work in many different ways. Some make elaborate outlines and carefully write a draft, perfecting each paragraph or section until they complete a text ready for proofreading. Others make few plans but write several complete drafts, writing and revising key areas over and over again.

Many writers go through a five-stage process that helps improve their writing and save time. As a beginning writer you can benefit from following these guidelines. With experience, you can personalize your method of writing.

HOW TO WRITE AN ESSAY

1. **Plan—establish context.** Once you have established your goal and thesis, determine how you will develop your paper in light of your readers' needs and the conventions of the discipline. Develop an outline listing the items needed to achieve your goal. Your opening should attract attention, announce the topic, and prepare readers for main ideas presented in the body of the work. The conclusion should bring the paper to a logi-

cal end, using a final observation, quote, or question to make a strong impression.

2. **Write—get your ideas on paper.** After reviewing your plans, write as much as possible without stopping. Writing the first draft can be considered controlled freewriting. As you write, new ideas may occur to you. Record *all* your thoughts. Do not pause to check spelling or look up a fact because it may break your train of thought. Underline words you think are misspelled or sentences that contain grammatical errors. Leave gaps for missing details. Place question marks next to items you want to double-check.
3. **Cool—put your writing aside.** It is difficult to evaluate your work immediately after writing because much of what you wish to say is still fresh in your mind. Set your work aside. Work on other assignments, read, watch television, or take a walk to clear your mind. Afterward, you can return to your writing with greater objectivity.
4. **Revise—review your writing in context.** Before searching your paper for misspelled words or grammatical errors, examine it holistically. Review your goal and plan. Examine any instructions you have received. Then read your paper. Does it clearly express your goal and support your thesis? Is it properly directed to your audience? Does it violate any principles in the discipline? Revision can mean rewriting the entire paper or merely reworking certain details.
5. **Edit—correct mechanical errors and polish style.** When you have a completed paper, examine your writing for missing words, grammatical errors, and misspelled words. In addition, review your diction. Eliminate wordy phrases and reduce repetition. Make sure ideas flow evenly and smoothly. *Reading a paper aloud can help identify errors and awkward sentences.*

These five stages are not neatly isolated. Writing, according to current research, is *recursive*—the steps overlap and occur simultaneously. As you write you will find yourself brainstorming, editing, correcting, spelling, and freewriting.

WRITING THE WHOLE COMPOSITION

The stages of the writing process are illustrated here by a student developing a paper for a freshman composition class. Having read and discussed several essays concerning criminal justice, the class was instructed to turn in a short commentary debating the merits of a current legal issue.

Prewriting

The student began exploring topics through prewriting. Note that her work blends several techniques, including brainstorming, freewriting, and clustering:

Topics: Criminal justice (issues)
capital punishment pro/con
gun control
Courtroom TV
What is the impact of televised trials?
Do TV trials educate the public?
How does media attention affect juries?
Victims and crime—are they forgotten?
Who speaks for victims?
Do prosecutors properly speak for victims?

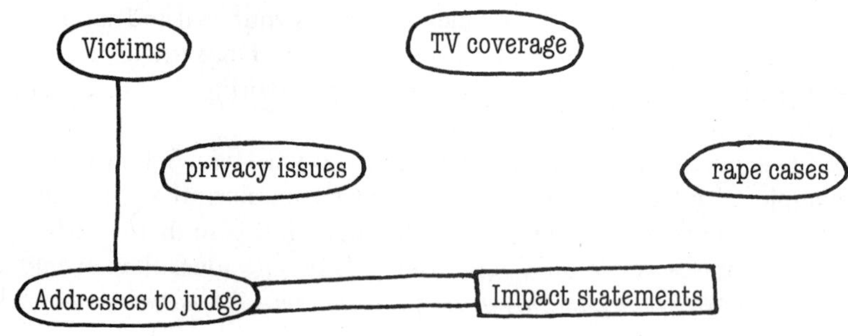

Victim impact statements are increasingly a feature of modern trials as people are allowed to state their feelings about the crime and the criminal after he/she is convicted. Judges can consider the impact of the crime on the victim in sentencing. Sometimes victims ask for harsh punishment and sometimes they even ask for leniency and give the criminal, especially a young person a 2nd chance........

Who is most impressive?
What about victims who can't speak well or don't know English?
What about families of homicide victims?
Victims without mourners? Less important?

Topic: Victim impact statements
Thesis: Although victim impact statements are supposed to empower the victims of crime, they may serve only to further marginalize the most helpless among us.

Planning

Victim Impact Statements

INTRO: Background of impact statements
Definition

PRO: -- empowers victims who feel forgotten
-- helps heal victims by addressing criminal
-- helps people regain control over their lives & move on
-- makes the human cost of a crime part of the sentencing decision.

CON: Question?
Whose impact is more effective?
Middle class professional vs. Welfare mom

END: Question, helpful or hurtful to victims?

First Draft

Across America today more and more victims of crime are being allowed to address the court in terms of making what is called a victim impact statment. This written or oral presentation to the court allows victims to express their feelings to the judge after someone has been convicted of a crime.

Advocates of victim impact statements point to key advantages. First, these statements give victims' a voice. For years, victims have felt helpless. Prosecutors represent the state, not the crime victim. Victims have been dismayed when prosecutors have aranged plea bargains without their knowledge. Some victims are still recovering from their injuries when they learn the person who hurt them has plead to a lesser charge and received probation.

Therapists who work with victims also say that being able to adress the court helps with the healing process. Victims of violent crime can feel powerless and vulnerable. Instead of suffering in silence, they are given the chance to address the criminal, to clear their chests, and get on with the rest of their lives.

Impact statements allows judges to consider what sentences are appropriate. In one case a judge who planned to fine a teenager for shoplifting accepted the store owner's suggestion of waving the fine if the defendant completed his GED.

But giving victims a chance to speak raises some issues. What about the victim who is not articulate, who doesn't even speak English? In murder cases the victim's relatives are given a chance to speak? Does this mean that a middle class professional victim with a circle grieving friends and family members will be granted more significance than the homeless murder victim who leaves no one behind?

Victim impact statements may help empower victims who are educated, personally impressive, and socially promient. But they may also allow forgotten victims to remain voiceless.

After completing the first draft, the student set the paper aside for several hours before returning to examine it. As a rough draft it clearly captured the writer's main ideas, but it could be improved to make a greater impression on readers. Note the student's marginal comments; "SP" refers to a misspelling. The editing process is still incomplete in this stage.

Revision

wordy SP — Across America today more and more victims of crime are being allowed to address the court in terms of making what is called a victim impact statment. This written or oral presentation to the court allows victims to express their feelings to the judge after someone has been convicted of a crime.

Advocates of victim impact statements point to key advantages. First, these statements give victims a voice. For years, victims have felt helpless. Prosecutors represent the state, not the crime victim. Victims have been dismayed when prosecutors have aranged plea bargains without their knowledge. Some victims are still recovering from their injuries when they learn the person who hurt them has plead to a lesser charge and received probation. (SP)

Therapists who work with victims also say that being able to adress the court helps with the healing process. Victims of violent crime can feel powerless and vulnerable. Instead of suffering in silence, they are given the chance to address the criminal, to clear their chests, and get on with the rest of their lives. (SP; cliché)

Impact statements allows judges to consider what sentences are appropriate. In one case a judge who planned to fine a teenager for shoplifting accepted the store owner's suggestion of waving the fine if the defendant completed his GED. (SP)

But giving victims a chance to speak raises some issues. What about the victim who is not articulate, who doesn't even speak English? In murder cases the victim's relatives are given a chance to speak? Does this mean that a middle class professional victim with a circle grieving friends and family members will be granted more significance than the homeless murder victim who leaves no one behind? (weak)

Victim impact statements may help empower victims who are educated, personally impressive, and socially promient. But they may also allow forgotten victims to remain voiceless. (SP)

Revision Notes

Needs better opening -- needs attention-getter
Sharper definition
Clearer examples
Tighter conclusion

Second Draft

The courtroom scene was riveting. One by one, the survivors of a deadly commuter-train shooting took the stand and addressed the man who had maimed them. Their voices quivering with emotion, they told the court how the gunman's actions changed their lives forever. Spouses and parents of the dead spoke of loss. There were tears, moments of intense anger, and quiet despair. Victim impact statements have become a common feature of criminal proceedings. Spoken in court or submitted in writing, these statements provide an opportunity for victims to be heard before sentencing.

Advocates of victim impact statements believe these declarations give victims a voice, an opportunity to be heard. Traditionally, victims have appeared in court only as witnesses subject to cross-examination. Prosecutors, victims soon learn, represent the state and not individuals. Still hospitalized after a brutal beating, a New Jersey restaurant owner learned from reading a newspaper that his assailants had plea-bargained to a lesser charge and received probation. Joining with other victims, he became an advocate for victims' rights, including impact statements.

Therapists who counsel victims of crime believe that addressing the court and taking an active role in the legal process instead of remaining a passive witness helps people recover from a sense of helplessness and regain a measure of self-respect.

Impact statements allow judges to consider appropriate sentences. In a Florida case, a judge who intended to fine a teenager for shoplifting agreed with the store owner's suggestion that the fine be waived if the defendant completed his GED.

But giving victims a chance to speak has led to ugly courtroom scenes which seem inappropriate in a democracy. In Milwaukee a sister of a young man murdered by Jeffrey Dahmer wailed and shrieked in contortions of pure rage. The relative of another murder victim shouted that he would execute the killer himself. Bailiffs had to restrain him as he begged the judge, "Just gimme five minutes with him!" Defense attorneys argue these harangues are unnecessary. What need is there to heap abuse upon a person about to lose his or her life or liberty? Can anger and harassment be considered healing?

But even restrained, well-reasoned impact statements raise troubling questions. What about the victim who is too impaired, too frightened, or too wounded to speak? Is his or her absence judged as indifference? What about those whose English is limited? What of those without friends or family? Should the drunk driver who kills a young professional missed by friends, family, and colleagues receive a tougher sentence than the drunk driver who kills a homeless man who dies unmourned, unmissed, and uncounted? Do we really want our courts and society to suggest that some lives are more significant than others?

Victim impact statements may help empower victims, especially the educated, the personally impressive, and the socially prominent. But these statements, unintentionally, may also further marginalize the most helpless among us, allowing forgotten victims to remain voiceless.

QUESTIONS

1. What have you found most challenging or difficult about writing? Discovering ideas? Getting started? Revising?
2. What comments have instructors made about your writing? Does a pattern exist? Have they suggested areas for improvement?
3. What writing habits do you have? What could aid you in improving your work and meeting deadlines? What ideas in this chapter might you adopt to write more effectively?

COLLABORATIVE WRITING

Writing often occurs in groups. Even when produced by a single person, writing may have to reflect the views of many people. Thomas Jefferson wrote the Declaration of Independence, but a committee including Jefferson, John Adams, Benjamin Franklin, and two others made forty-seven changes. Franklin replaced Jefferson's original phrase (in italics) "we hold these rights to be *sound and undeniable*" to "*self-evident.*" More changes occurred when the declaration was presented to the entire Continental Congress. Jefferson's impassioned attack on slavery was eliminated to appease southern representatives. In all, eighty-seven alterations were made to Jefferson's declaration before it was unanimously accepted. By the time John Hancock stepped forward to sign the Declaration of Independence, a quarter of Jefferson's original draft had been changed or deleted.

As a college student, you may be called on to work in a writing group. More and more professors are teaching collaborative writing because writing in groups is common in business and industry. Most professionals work in groups or committees. The partners of a small software company seeking a new personnel director have to agree on the wording of a want ad. The sales team introducing a new product must determine what language to use in its brochures. Volunteers seeking government funding for a day care center must work together on a proposal.

Working in groups poses additional challenges in the writing process. The writing must reflect the ideas of different people. Viewpoints and personalities may clash. Even scheduling time for the group to meet may be difficult. Because people regard their writing as personal expression and are accustomed to working alone, it can be difficult for them to accept criticism.

But whether you are writing alone or in a group, the basic process remains the same. The writing must address the issue, meet the needs of the readers, and respect the conventions of the discipline or discourse community. To be effective, writing groups must achieve the "Three Cs" of group dynamics: *cohesion*, *cooperation*, and *compromise.* Members must have a clearly defined goal or task. They must be willing to meet and to work outside the group. Finally, and often most difficult, individuals must be willing to accept that their opinions may not prevail and be willing to drop or alter ideas they greatly value.

Guidelines for Collaborative Writing

1. **Work to establish cohesion by stressing the goals, intended readers, and requirements of the writing project.** It is important for members of a writing group to feel trust so they can share ideas. In addition, they must be willing to offer and accept criticism.
2. **Keep the group focused on the task by creating a timeline.** People enjoy talking. Discussions can easily become generalized forums for spirited debate or the latest gossip. A target timeline can help keep the group on track by outlining expected outcomes and reminding members of the deadline. The timeline should reflect stages in the writing process.
3. **Make meetings productive by setting goals and assigning tasks.** Meetings can easily degenerate into a series of discussion sessions, which, though interesting, may not help produce the needed writing. Members should be assigned specific responsibilities: gathering research, conducting interviews, writing sample drafts. Each meeting should open with a goal statement of what is to be achieved. Meetings should end with a summary of what has been completed and an announcement of what must be accomplished at the next meeting.
4. **Designate one member to serve as a moderator or recorder.** One member of the group should serve as chair or recorder to document the progress of the group and serve as secretary to exchange messages between meetings.
5. **Avoid personalizing disagreements.** It is important to discuss opposing viewpoints in neutral terms. Avoid attaching ideas to individuals, which can lead to "*us* against *them*" conflicts.
6. **Take advantage of technology.** Students often have trouble finding common times to meet for social activities, let alone assignments. Consider

how the group can maintain links through telephone conferences, fax machines, and the Internet.

READING CRITICALLY

As a student you are accustomed to reading to gain information. Cramming for a history exam, you read a textbook, hoping to extract the dates, facts, and concepts that will appear on the test. Reading a novel, you may allow yourself to be swept away by an exciting plot or an intriguing character. But as a writer, you need to read critically; you need to read with a "writer's eye."

While most diners savor a new gourmet item, a cook wants to know the recipe. Visitors to a new office tower may marvel at the atrium, but an architect analyzes the support structure. Moviegoers gasp at an exciting car chase as film students review the director's editing technique. As a writer, you need to look at writing in much the same way. In addition to figuring *what* an essay says, it is important to determine *how* it is organized, how the writer overcame problems, and how language and detail contribute to its effect.

How to Read an Essay

When you pick up a magazine, you rarely read every article. You flip through the pages, letting your eyes guide you. A headline, a photograph, a chart, or a familiar name makes you pause and begin reading. If bored, you skip to the next article. While reading your textbooks, you often skim, moving over familiar material so you can devote more time to items that are new to you. If you read *The Great Gatsby* in high school, for a college literature course you will probably find yourself reviewing it rather than reading it.

In this course, however, you should read *all* the assigned selections carefully. Reading with a writer's eye, you will examine familiar works differently from readers seeking information. Critical reading, like writing, occurs best in stages.

1. **Look ahead and skim entries.** Do not wait until the night before to examine assigned readings. Check your syllabus and skim through future

readings to get a general impression. Often, if you think about the authors and their issues, you can approach an essay more critically. The more you bring to the reading, the more effective your analysis will be.

2. **Study the headnote and introduction.** Consider the author, the issue, and the context of the reading.
3. **For the first reading, read the entire work.** Just as in writing the first draft, it is important to complete the entire essay. Do not bother to look up unfamiliar words. Instead, try to get the "big picture" and understand the writer's main goal.
4. **Read with a pencil or pen in your hand.** Make notes and underline sentences that strike you as interesting, odd, offensive, or troubling. Reading while holding a writing tool will prompt you to write, to be an active reader rather than a passive consumer of words.
5. **For the first reading, focus on understanding the author's meaning.** Summarize, in your own words, what the essay is about. Identify the thesis and the main types of support.
6. **For the second reading, begin with the questions following the essay.** Considering the questions can help you focus on a closer, analytical reading of the work. The questions are arranged in three groups:

Understanding Meaning What is the author's purpose? What is the thesis? What is the author trying to share with his or her readers?

Evaluating Strategy How does the author make his or her point? What support is used? How does the writer organize ideas?

Appreciating Language How does the writer use words? What does the language reveal about the intended reader? Does the language reflect the writer's attitudes?

7. **Summarize your responses in a point or two for class discussion.** Consider how you will express your opinions of the essay to fellow students. Be prepared to back up your remarks by citing passages in the text.
8. **Most important, focus on what this essay can teach you about writing.** How can this writer's style, way of organizing ideas, or word choice enrich your own writing? Though you may not want to imitate everything you see, you can pick up techniques to broaden your personal array of skills.
9. **Think of how writers wrestle with the same problems you face.** If you have trouble making an outline and organizing ideas, study how the essays in this book are arranged. If your instructor returns papers with comments about vague theses and a lack of focus, examine how the writers in this book state their theses.
10. **Above all, read to learn.**

Read the following essay by Cornel West, and study how it has been marked during a critical reading. West is a highly organized writer who blends the use of several modes in this comparison essay on the current state of African American political leadership.

CORNEL WEST

Cornel West was a religion professor and Director of Afro-American Studies at Princeton University before he was appointed to the faculty at Harvard University. The author of Keeping Faith, Prophetic Fragments, *and other books, West has specialized on writing on race in America.*

Black Political Leadership

"Black Political Leadership" appeared in West's best-selling 1994 book Race Matters. *In this section, West compares the current generation of black political leaders with leaders of the Civil Rights era. Although West's purpose is to compare, he uses a number of modes to develop his ideas.*

1 Black political leadership reveals the tame and genteel face of the black middle class. The black dress suits with white shirts worn by Malcolm X and Martin Luther King, Jr., signified the seriousness of their deep commitment to black freedom, whereas today the expensive tailored suits of black politicians symbolize their personal success and individual achievement. Malcolm and Martin called for the realization that black people are somebodies with which America has to reckon, whereas black politicians tend to turn our attention to *their* somebodiness owing to *their* "making it" in America.

thesis/ opening

clothes as symbolic

compare

note use of italics

2 This crude and slightly unfair comparison highlights two distinctive features of black political leaders in the post–Civil Rights era: the relative lack of authentic anger and the relative absence of genuine humility. What stood out most strikingly about Malcolm X, Martin Luther King, Jr., Ella Baker, and Fannie Lou Hamer was that they were almost always visibly upset about the condition of black America. When one saw them speak or heard their voices, they projected on a gut level that the black situation was urgent, in need of immediate attention. One even gets the impression that their own stability and sanity rested on how soon the black predicament could be improved. Malcolm, Martin, Ella, and Fannie were angry about the state of black America, and this anger fueled their boldness and defiance.

division

provides examples

shift/ transition · *use of repetitive wording for emphasis* · *contrast*

3 In stark contrast, most present-day black political leaders appear too hungry for status to be angry, too eager for acceptance to be bold, too self-invested in advancement to be defiant. And when they do drop their masks and try to get mad (usually in the presence of black audiences), their bold rhetoric is more performance than personal, more play-acting than heartfelt. Malcolm, Martin, Ella, and Fannie made sense of the black plight in a poignant and powerful manner, whereas most contemporary black political leaders' oratory appeals to black people's sense of the sentimental and sensational.

supplies personal definition · *cause and effect*

4 Similarly, Malcolm, Martin, Ella, and Fannie were examples of humility. Yes, even Malcolm's aggressiveness was accompanied by a common touch and humble disposition toward ordinary black people. Humility is the fruit of inner security and wise maturity. To be humble is to be sure of one's self and one's mission that one can forego calling excessive attention to one's self and status. And, even more pointedly, to be humble is to revel in the accomplishments or potential of others—especially those with whom one identifies and to whom one is linked organically. The relative absence of humility in most black political leaders today is a symptom of the status-anxiety and personal insecurity pervasive in black middle-class America. In this context, even a humble vesture is viewed as a cover for some sinister motive or surreptitious ambition.

division · *definition*

5 Present-day black political leaders can be grouped under three types: race-effacing managerial leaders, race-identifying protest leaders, and race-transcending prophetic leaders. The first type is growing rapidly. The Thomas Bradleys and Wilson Goodes of black America have become a model for many black leaders trying to reach a large white constituency and keep a loyal black one. This type survives only sheer political savvy and thrives on personal diplomacy. This kind of candidate is the lesser of two evils in a political situation where the only other electoral choice is a conservative (usually white) politician. Yet this type of leader tends to stunt progressive development and silence the prophetic voices in the black community by casting the practical mainstream as the only game in town.

analysis

6 The second type of black political leader—race-identifying protest leaders—often view themselves in the tradition of Malcolm X, Martin Luther King, Jr., Ella Baker, and Fannie Lou Hamer. Yet they are usually self-deluded. They actually operate more in the tradition of Booker T. Washington, by confining themselves to the black turf, vowing to protect their leadership status over it, and serving as power

brokers with powerful nonblack elites (usually white economic or political elites, though in Louis Farrakhan's case it may be Libyan) to "enhance" this black turf. It is crucial to remember that even in the fifties, Malcolm X's vision and practice were international in scope, and that after 1964 his project was transracial—though grounded in the black turf. King never confined himself to being solely the leader of black America—even though the white press attempted to do so. And Fannie Lou Hamer led the National Welfare Rights Organization, not the Black Welfare Rights Organization. In short, race-identifying protest leaders in the post–Civil Rights era function as figures who white Americans must appease so that the plight of the black poor is overlooked and forgotten. When such leaders move successfully into elected office—as with Marion Barry—they usually become managerial types with large black constituencies, flashy styles, flowery rhetoric, and Booker T. Washington–like patronage operations within the public sphere.

7 Race-transcending prophetic leaders are rare in contemporary black America. Harold Washington was one. The Jesse Jackson of 1988 was attempting to be another—yet the opportunism of his past weighed heavily on him. To be an elected official and prophetic leader requires personal integrity and political savvy, moral vision and prudential judgment, courageous defiance and organizational patience. The present generation has yet to produce such a figure. We have neither an Adam Clayton Powell, Jr., nor a Ronald Dellums. This void sits like a festering sore at the center of the crisis of black leadership—and the predicament of the disadvantaged in the United States and abroad worsens.

examples

final effects

USING *THE SUNDANCE READER*

The Sundance Reader is organized into nine chapters focusing on writers' goals. The readings in each section illustrate how writers achieve their purpose in different contexts. Each chapter opens with an explanation of the goal or mode. The first few readings in each chapter are brief, clear-cut examples of the mode and can serve as models for many of your composition assignments. The middle readings are longer and more complex and demonstrate writing tasks in a range of disciplines and writing situations. Each chapter ends with samples of applied writings taken from business, industry, and government to illustrate how writing is used beyond the classroom.

When reading entries, keep these general questions in mind:

1. **What is the writer's purpose?** Even writers pursuing the same goal—to tell a story or explain a process—have slightly different intentions. What is the purpose of the story—to raise questions, to motivate the reader to take action, or to change his or her point of view?
2. **What is the writer's thesis?** Does a clear thesis statement exist that you can highlight, or is it implied? Can you restate the thesis in your own words?
3. **Who are the intended readers?** Note the source of the article. What does it tell you about the readers? Does the writer direct it to a specific group or a general audience? What assumptions does the writer seem to make about the reader? What terms or references are defined? What knowledge does the writer expect his or her audience to possess?
4. **What evidence does the writer use to support the thesis?** Does the writer provide personal observation, statistics, studies, or the testimony of others to support his or her views?
5. **What is the nature of the discipline, profession, or writing situation?** What discipline is the writer addressing? Is he or she working within a discipline or addressing readers in another discipline? Is the writer addressing general readers? Do special circumstances guide the way the writer develops the thesis, presents ideas, and designs the physical appearance of the writing?
6. **How successful is this writing—in context?** Does the writer achieve his or her goals while respecting the needs of the reader and the conventions of the discipline or situation? Do special circumstances explain why some aspects of the writing appear to "break" the rules of what most English courses consider "good writing"?

2

NARRATION

RELATING EVENTS

WHAT IS NARRATION?

Narration seeks to answer the basic question What happened? The goal of narration is to tell a story. The Bible, Greek myths, Native American fables, novels, short stories, diaries, autobiographies, and history books are examples of narration. Narrative writing forms the heart of most newspaper articles. Narration is also probably one of the most common types of professional writing. Physicians write narration to record a patient's history or outline a course of treatment. Attorneys use narrative writing to relate the details of a crime or explain the rationale for a lawsuit. Government reports, grant proposals, sales brochures, and business plans generally include a section labeled "narrative" that provides the history of an organization or a summary of a current project.

The Writer's Purpose

Narration can be subjective or objective, depending on the writer's goal and context. Subjective narration focuses on personal impressions, thoughts, insights, and feelings. Often the writer is at the center of the narrative, either as a principal character or key witness. In "The Lesson" (page 47) Nathan McCall relates his first encounter with racism while attending a previously segregated school:

> It was the beginning of my sixth-grade school year, and I was walking down the hall, searching for my new class, when a white boy timed my steps, extended his foot, and tripped me. The boy and his friends nudged each other and laughed as I stumbled into a locker, spilling books and papers everywhere. "Hey, nigger," the boy said. "You dropped something."

McCall's purpose is to share a deeply personal experience of pain and humiliation, impressing readers with what he thought and felt. His emotional reactions form the core of the narrative:

> I was sitting on the gym floor with the rest of the student body, watching a school assembly program, when a group of rowdy white upperclassmen began plucking my head and ridiculing me. I got confused. *What should I do?* To turn around and say something to them would start another fight. To get up and leave would require me to wade through a sea of hostile white students to reach the nearest exit. With nowhere to go, I sat there and took the humiliation until I broke. Tears welled in my eyes and started running, uncontrollably, down my face. I sat silently through the remainder of the assembly program with my vision blurred and my spirit broken. That was the only time, then or since, that I've been crushed so completely.

Objective narration, on the other hand, is usually stated in the third person to give the writer's views a sense of neutrality. In objective narration, the author is not a participant but a collector and presenter of facts. In "Final Warning" (page 63) Dr. Robert Peter Gale and Thomas Hauser relate the chain of events that led to the nuclear disaster at Chernobyl in a purely objective tone. Like the authors of a textbook or a newsmagazine article, they write in the third person with no reference to themselves or their personal views. Their goal is to state the facts:

> At one A.M., the reactor's power level was lowered to prepare for the test. Then, over the next twenty-four hours, technicians systematically disconnected power regulation and emergency cooling systems which would have automatically shut the reactor down and interfered with the test. Finally, at 1:23 on the morning of April 26, 1986—twenty-four hours after preparation for the test had begun—the flow of steam to the turbine was halted. Almost immediately, the cooling pumps slowed, diminishing the flow of cooling water to the reactor core. Normally, at this

> point, the reactor would have shut down, but the automatic shutdown system was one of six safety mechanisms that had been deliberately disconnected. Within seconds, there was a massive heat buildup in the reactor core, triggering an uncontrolled chain reaction. Power surged. At 1:23 A.M., the Unit Number 4 reactor exploded.

Authors do use first person in objective narration, particularly when they have directly participated in or witnessed events. However, unlike Nathan McCall, who focused on his *internal reactions* to situations, a scientist like Jane Goodall stresses *external events.* In "First Observations" (page 68) Goodall tells her story of studying chimpanzee behavior in Africa. Although she admits being "delighted" with her discoveries, her main concern is accurately reporting what she saw:

> Quickly focusing my binoculars I saw that it was a single chimpanzee, and just then he turned in my direction. I recognized David Graybeard.
>
> Cautiously I moved around so that I could see what he was doing. He was squatting beside the red earth mound of a termite nest, and as I watched I saw him carefully push a long grass stem down into a hole in the mound. After a moment he withdrew it and picked something from the end with his mouth. I was too far away to make out what he was eating, but it was obvious that he was actually using a grass stem as a tool.

Goodall focuses less on her feelings than on her professional actions as a scientist and researcher. When she discusses herself, most of the commentary is limited to recounting her methods, the location, and the problems she encountered observing her subjects.

In an effort to create a greater sense of objectivity, many writers avoid using the first person by documenting personal actions in passive voice. Instead of stating, "I took photographs of the crash site," they report, "Photographs of the crash site were taken." Rhetoricians, English instructors, and editors often object to passive voice because it is wordy and less precise. Passive voice deletes the actor from the action, in this case failing to state who took the photographs. Still, many writers insist on using passive voice to deliberately avoid personalizing their narratives.

Focus

Related to the writer's purpose is the narrative's focus. A biography of Abraham Lincoln can be a general account of his entire life or a psychological study of his problem with depression during the Civil War. A book about World War II could concentrate on military activities or on the role of women in the defense industry. An article on recycling may provide a survey of national trends or an in-depth study of a single city's program.

Focus determines the kinds of details the writer includes in the narrative and the types of evidence he or she relies on. In writing a popular history about the sinking of the *Titanic,* Walter Lord based much of his narrative on memories of the survivors. This gave his book human interest and created a tense series of dramas as he recounted the ship's last hours. A nautical engineer writing a technical article explaining the sinking of the "unsinkable" luxury liner would pay attention to mechanical details, specific measurements, and statistics.

Chronology

Chronology or time is a central organizing element in narrative writing. Writers do not always relate events in a straight timeline. A biography, for instance, does not have to begin with birth and childhood. Writers often alter the time sequences of their stories to dramatize events or limit their topic. A biographer of Franklin Roosevelt might choose to highlight a key event or turning point in his life. The narrative might open with his polio attack, flash back to his childhood and early political career, then flash forward to his recovery and election to the presidency. Other writers find it more dramatic to begin a narrative at the end and then explain what led to this final event. The first chapter of a book about Czar Nicholas II could describe his execution and then flash back to the events leading to his downfall and death.

Each method of organizing a narrative has distinct advantages and disadvantages:

- **Beginning at the beginning** creates an open-ended narrative, providing readers with little direction to later events. Writers who relate complex stories with many possible causes can use a straight chronology to avoid highlighting a single event. Using a direct beginning-to-end approach is the most traditional method of telling a story. One of the difficulties can be determining exactly when the narrative should start. Often the beginning of a story consists of incidental background information that readers may find uninteresting.

- **Beginning at the middle or a turning point** can arouse reader interest by opening with a dramatic scene. This method of organization can focus the chain of events, persuading readers to concentrate on a particular issue. This is a common pattern in nonfiction articles, biographies, and histories written for a general readership. Critics, however, can view this alteration of chronology as distorting. Not all historians, for instance, may agree that Roosevelt's illness was the "turning point" of his life. Some biographers might feel that focusing on his physical disability ignores his intellectual development or downplays his political role.
- **Beginning at the end** serves to dramatize the final event. Organizing a narrative in this way can suggest that the conclusion was inevitable. When everything is presented in flashback, readers see events, actions, and thoughts in hindsight. The elements of suspense and randomness are removed, providing a stronger sense of cause and effect. Some readers will object to this method because it implies the final outcome was inevitable, when, in fact, events just as easily could have led to alternative endings.

READING NARRATION

When reading the narrations in this chapter, keep these questions in mind.

Meaning

1. What is the author's narrative purpose—to inform, enlighten, share a personal experience, or provide information required by the reader?
2. What is the writer's role? Is the author a participant or direct witness? Is he or she writing in a personal context, focusing on internal responses, or a professional context, concentrating on external events?
3. What readership is the narration directed toward—general or specific? How much knowledge does the author assume readers have?
4. What is the nature of the discipline, discourse community, or writing situation? Is the narration objective or subjective? Does the original source of the narrative (newsmagazine, scientific journal, or government document) reveal anything about the context?

Strategy

1. What details does the writer select to highlight? Are some items summarized or ignored?

2. What kind of support does the writer use—personal observation or factual documentation?
3. What is the sequence of events? How is the narration organized? Does the writer begin at the beginning, the end, or a midpoint?
4. Does the writer use flashbacks and flash-forwards?
5. What transitional devices does the writer use to advance the narrative? Does the author use time references such as "later that day" or "two months later"?

Language

1. What does the level of language suggest about the writer's role, intended readers, and the nature of the discipline or writing situation?
2. How does the writer use words to create tone and style? What do word choices suggest about the writer's attitude toward the subject?

SAMUEL SCUDDER

Samuel Scudder (1837–1911) was born in Boston and attended Williams College. In 1857 he entered Harvard, where he studied under the noted professor Louis Agassiz. Scudder held various positions and helped found the Cambridge Entomological Club. He published hundreds of papers and developed a comprehensive catalog of three centuries of scientific publications in mathematics and the natural and physical sciences. While working for the United States Geological Survey, he named more than a thousand species of fossil insects. Although later scientists would question some of his conclusions, much of Scudder's work is still admired for its attention to detail.

Take This Fish and Look at It

Today educators stress critical thinking, which begins with close observation. In this famous essay, Scudder relates the lesson in observation he learned under Professor Agassiz, whose teaching method was simple. Instead of lecturing, he directed his young student to "look again, look again."

1 It was more than fifteen years ago that I entered the laboratory of Professor Agassiz, and told him I had enrolled my name in the Scientific School as a student of natural history. He asked me a few questions about my object in coming, my antecedents generally, the mode in which I afterwards proposed to use the knowledge I might acquire, and, finally, whether I wished to study any special branch. To the latter I replied that, while I wished to be well grounded in all departments of zoology, I purposed to devote myself specially to insects.

2 "When do you wish to begin?" he asked.

3 "Now," I replied.

4 This seemed to please him, and with an energetic "Very well!" he reached from a shelf a huge jar of specimens in yellow alcohol. "Take this fish," he said, "and look at it; we call it a haemulon; by and by I will ask what you have seen."

5 With that he left me, but in a moment returned with explicit instructions as to the care of the object entrusted to me.

6 "No man is fit to be a naturalist," said he, "who does not know how to take care of specimens."

7 I was to keep the fish before me in a tin tray, and occasionally moisten the surface with alcohol from the jar, always taking care to replace the stopper tightly. Those were not the days of ground-glass stoppers and elegantly shaped exhibition jars; all the old students will recall the huge neckless glass bottles with their leaky, wax-besmeared corks, half eaten by insects, and begrimed with cellar dust. Entomology was a cleaner science than ichthyology, but the example of the Professor, who had unhesitatingly plunged to the bottom of the jar to produce the fish, was infectious; and though this alcohol had a "very ancient and fishlike smell," I really dared not show any aversion within these sacred precincts, and treated the alcohol as though it were pure water. Still I was conscious of a passing feeling of disappointment, for gazing at a fish did not commend itself to an ardent entomologist. My friends at home, too, were annoyed when they discovered that no amount of eau-de-Cologne would drown the perfume which haunted me like a shadow.

8 In ten minutes I had seen all that could be seen in that fish, and started in search of the Professor—who had, however, left the Museum; and when I returned, after lingering over some of the odd animals stored in the upper apartment, my specimen was dry all over. I dashed the fluid over the fish as if to resuscitate the beast from a fainting fit, and looked with anxiety for a return of the normal sloppy appearance. This little excitement over, nothing was to be done but to return to a steadfast gaze at my mute companion. Half an hour passed—an hour—another hour; the fish began to look loathsome. I turned it over and around; looked it in the face—ghastly; from behind, beneath, above, sideways, at three-quarters' view—just as ghastly. I was in despair; at an early hour I concluded that lunch was necessary; so, with infinite relief, the fish was carefully replaced in the jar, and for an hour I was free.

9 On my return, I learned that Professor Agassiz had been at the Museum, but had gone, and would not return for several hours. My fellow-students were too busy to be disturbed by continued conversation. Slowly I drew forth that hideous fish, and with a feeling of desperation again looked at it. I might not use a magnifying-glass; instruments of all kinds were interdicted. My two hands, my two eyes, and the fish: it seemed a most limited field. I pushed my finger down its throat to feel how sharp the teeth were. I began to count the scales in the different rows, until I was convinced that was nonsense. At last a happy thought struck me—I would draw the fish; and now with sur-

prise I began to discover new features in the creature. Just then the Professor returned.

10 "That is right," said he; "a pencil is one of the best of eyes. I am glad to notice, too, that you keep your specimen wet, and your bottle corked."

11 With these encouraging words, he added: "Well, what is it like?"

12 He listened attentively to my brief rehearsal of the structure of parts whose names were still unknown to me: the fringed gill-arches and movable operculum; the pores of the head, fleshy lips and lidless eyes; the lateral line, the spinous fins and forked tail; the compressed and arched body. When I finished, he waited as if expecting more, and then, with an air of disappointment:

13 "You have not looked very carefully; why," he continued more earnestly, "you haven't even seen one of the most conspicuous features of the animal, which is plainly before your eyes as the fish itself; look again, look again!" and he left me to my misery.

14 I was piqued; I was mortified. Still more of that wretched fish! But now I set myself to my task with a will, and discovered one new thing after another, until I saw how just the Professor's criticism had been. The afternoon passed quickly; and when, towards its close, the Professor inquired:

15 "Do you see it yet?"

16 "No," I replied, "I am certain I do not, but I see how little I saw before."

17 "That is next best," said he, earnestly, "but I won't hear you now; put away your fish and go home; perhaps you will be ready with a better answer in the morning. I will examine you before you look at the fish."

18 This was disconcerting. Not only must I think of my fish all night, studying, without the object before me, what this unknown but most visible feature might be; but also, without reviewing my discoveries, I must give an exact account of them the next day. I had a bad memory; so I walked home by Charles River in a distracted state, with my two perplexities.

19 The cordial greeting from the Professor the next morning was reassuring; here was a man who seemed to be quite as anxious as I that I should see for myself what he saw.

20 "Do you perhaps mean," I asked, "that the fish has symmetrical sides with paired organs?"

21 His thoroughly pleased "Of course! of course!" repaid the wakeful hours of the previous night. After he had discoursed most happily and

enthusiastically—as he always did—upon the importance of this point, I ventured to ask what I should do next.

22 "Oh, look at your fish!" he said, and left me again to my own devices. In a little more than an hour he returned, and heard my new catalogue.

23 "That is good, that is good!" he repeated; "but that is not all; go on"; and so for three long days he placed that fish before my eyes, forbidding me to look at anything else, or to use any artificial aid. "Look, look, look," was his repeated injunction.

24 This was the best entomological lesson I ever had—a lesson whose influence has extended to the details of every subsequent study; a legacy the Professor had left to me, as he has left it to so many others, of inestimable value which we could not buy, with which we cannot part.

25 A year afterward, some of us were amusing ourselves with chalking outlandish beasts on the Museum blackboard. We drew prancing starfishes; frogs in mortal combat; hydra-headed worms; stately crawfishes, standing on their tails, bearing aloft umbrellas; and grotesque fishes with gaping mouths and staring eyes. The Professor came in shortly after, and was as amused as any at our experiments. He looked at the fishes.

26 "Haemulons, every one of them," he said; "Mr. ____ drew them."

27 True; and to this day, if I attempt a fish, I can draw nothing but haemulons.

28 The fourth day, a second fish of the same group was placed beside the first, and I was bidden to point out the resemblances and differences between the two; another and another followed, until the entire family lay before me, and a whole legion of jars covered the table and surrounding shelves; the odor had become a pleasant perfume; and even now, the sight of an old, six-inch worm-eaten cork brings fragrant memories.

29 The whole group of haemulons was thus brought in review; and, whether engaged upon the dissection of the internal organs, the preparation and examination of the bony framework, or the description of the various parts, Agassiz's training in the method of observing facts and their orderly arrangement was ever accompanied by the urgent exhortation not to be content with them.

30 "Facts are stupid things," he would say, "until brought into connection with some general law."

31 At the end of eight months, it was almost with reluctance that I left these friends and turned to insects; but what I had gained by this outside experience has been of greater value than years of later investigation in my favorite groups.

Understanding Meaning

1. What is the purpose of Scudder's narrative? What is he trying to impress on his reader? What makes this essay more than a simple "first day of school" story?
2. Why did the professor prevent Scudder from using a magnifying glass? What did Professor Agassiz mean when he said "a pencil is one of the best of eyes"?
3. What did Scudder find frustrating about Dr. Agassiz's teaching method?
4. *Critical Thinking:* How effective was Professor Agassiz's nineteenth-century teaching method? By directing a new student to "look again, look again," did he accomplish more than if he had required Scudder to attend a two-hour lecture on the importance of observation? Is close observation a discipline most of us lack? Can you consider detailed observation the first level of critical thinking?

Evaluating Strategy

1. How does Scudder focus his narrative? What details does he leave out?
2. Do his personal reactions to the smell and his frustrations dramatize an extremely passive event? How can a writer create action in a story where the events are mental or emotional?
3. How does Scudder re-create his sense of boredom and frustration?
4. *Other Modes:* How does Scudder use *description* of the fish, the specimen bottles, and the smells to provide readers with a clear impression of the laboratory?

Appreciating Language

1. Review Scudder's narrative. How much scientific language does he use in relating his story? What does this say about his readers?
2. This story has little action. Essentially, it is a story about a man interacting with a dead fish. What words add drama or humor to the narrative?

Connections across the Disciplines

1. Scudder is a scientist writing to a general reader. How do you compare his writing style and vocabulary with Jane Goodall's (page 68) and Oliver Sacks's (page 75)?
2. *Critical Thinking:* Consider Professor Agassiz's statement, "Facts are stupid things until brought into connection with some general law." What does this say about instructors who teach facts and give multiple-choice tests based on rote memory?

Writing Suggestions

1. Apply Professor Agassiz's technique to a common object you might use every day. Spend five minutes carefully examining a clock radio, your watch, or a can of your favorite soft drink. Then write a brief *description* of what you have observed. List the features you have never noticed before.
2. Professor Agassiz gave his student little direction beyond a simple command. Write an essay relating an experience in which a parent, teacher, superior officer, or boss left you to act on your own. What problems did you encounter? Were you frustrated, afraid, or angry? Was it a learning experience?
3. *Collaborative Writing:* Working with three or four other students, select an object unfamiliar to the group. Allow each member to study the object and make notes. *Compare* your findings, and work to create a single *description* of it. Pay attention to the words you select to create an accurate, objective picture of the object. Notice the details you overlooked that others observed.

NATHAN McCALL

Nathan McCall grew up in Portsmouth, Virginia, where he attended both black and integrated public schools. In 1975 he was convicted of armed robbery and sentenced to eight years in prison. After serving three years, McCall was released and studied journalism at Norfolk State University. He became a reporter for the Virginian Pilot-Ledger Star *and later moved to* The Atlanta Journal-Constitution. *He covered the 1988 Republican National Convention in New Orleans and accompanied Andy Young on a European trade mission. In 1989 he joined the staff of* The Washington Post. *McCall's autobiography* Makes Me Wanna Holler *was published in 1995.*

The Lesson

In this passage of his autobiography, McCall relates his experience as one of the first African American students bused to a previously all-white public school in Virginia. His goal in this narrative is to share with readers the emotional trauma caused by racial hatred.

1 My harshest introduction to the world of white folks came in September 1966, when my parents sent me to Alford J. Mapp, a white school across town. It was the beginning of my sixth-grade school year, and I was walking down the hall, searching for my new class, when a white boy timed my steps, extended his foot, and tripped me. The boy and his friends nudged each other and laughed as I stumbled into a locker, spilling books and papers everywhere. "Hey, nigger," the boy said. "You dropped something."

2 The word sounded vile coming from his white mouth. When I regained my footing, I tore into that cat and tried to take his head off. Pinning him against a locker, I punched him in the face and kept on punching him until his two buddies jumped in to help him out. While other white students crowded around and cheered them on, we scuffled there in the hall until the bell rang, signaling the start of the next class period. Like combatants in a prizefight, we automatically stopped throwing punches and separated at the sound of the bell. The white boys went their way down the hall, calling me names along the way

and threatening to retaliate. I gathered my papers, straightened my clothes, and reeled toward my next class, dazed, trying to figure out what had just happened to me.

3 My parents sent me to Mapp in 1966 because that was the first year that blacks in Portsmouth were able to attend school wherever they wanted. The U.S. Supreme Court had long before ruled against the notion of separate but equal schools; still, Virginia, one of the states that had resisted desegregation, was slow in putting together a busing plan. Without a plan to ship black students to schools across town, over the years blacks and whites in Portsmouth had simply remained in separate schools. I could have gone to W. E. Waters, a junior high school that had just been built in our neighborhood, but, like many blacks then, my parents figured I could get a better education at the white school across town.

4 I was proud of their decision and held it out teasingly to my brothers as proof that I was the smart one in the family, that I held more academic promise than them. Billy had flunked the second grade, and Dwight and Junnie never showed much interest in books. My less studious brothers would attend their regular, all-black high school, but I was going to a *white* school, which made me feel special.

5 My parents didn't talk with me beforehand about the challenge I would face as one in the first wave of blacks to integrate Mapp. We had all seen TV news footage of police in riot gear escorting black students through hostile, jeering crowds to enroll in all-white high schools and colleges across the country, but for various reasons my parents saw no cause for alarm at Mapp. It was only a junior high school, which seemed far less menacing than the racially torn high schools and college campuses we heard about. Besides, there were no warning signals in Portsmouth to tip off my parents, no public protests by white citizens or high-profile white supremacist politicians like Alabama governor George Wallace threatening to buck the school integration plan.

6 At Mapp, I was the only African American in most of my classes. When I walked into one room and sat down, the students near me would get up and move away, as if my dark skin were dirty and hideous to them. Nobody talked directly to me. Instead, they shot daggers to each other that were intended for me. "You know, I hate niggers," they would say. "I don't understand why they're always following white people everywhere. We can't seem to get away from them. Why don't they just stay in their own schools?"

7 It wasn't much better dealing with white teachers. They avoided eye contact with me as much as possible and pretended not to see or hear white student hecklers. It was too much for an eleven-year-old to challenge, and I didn't try. Instead, I tried to become invisible. I kept to myself, remained quiet during class discussions, and never asked questions in or after class. I kept my eyes glued to my desk or looked straight ahead to avoid drawing attention to myself. I staggered, numb and withdrawn, through each school day and hurried from my last class, gym, without showering so that I wouldn't miss the only bus headed home. Students who missed the first school bus had to walk through the white neighborhood to the main street to catch the city bus. Mapp was located in a middle-class section of town called Craddock, where the whites were as hateful as the poor whites in Academy Park.

8 The daily bus ride home brought its own set of fears. A group of white boys got on our bus regularly for the sole purpose, it seemed, of picking fights. I was scared to death of them. With older brothers to fight at home, I was confident I could whip any white boy my age and size, but many of the white guys who got on that bus were eighth graders, and they looked like giants to me. Others were older, white, leather-jacket-wearing hoods who I was certain were high school dropouts.

9 When we boarded the bus, blacks automatically moved to the rear, as if Jim Crow laws were still in effect. The white boys would board last, crowd into the aisles, and start making racial slurs when the bus pulled away from school. "I hate the smell of niggers. They sure do stink. Don't you think niggers stink, Larry?"

10 "They sure do, man. They smell bad."

11 Before long, fists flew, girls screamed, and people tussled in the aisles. Few of the black guys on the bus were big and bad enough to beat the tough white boys, who outnumbered us seven to one. I never joined in to help the black guys out. I huddled in the far corner at the rear of the bus, tense, scared as hell, hoping the fighting wouldn't reach that far before the driver broke it up.

12 Children have an enormous capacity to adapt to insanity. I took my lumps in school and tried as much as possible to shrug it off when I went home. Billy, Dwight, and Junnie came home most days full of stories about the fun they were having at pep rallies and football games at their all-black high school. I envied them because I couldn't match their stories with tales of my own about fun times at Mapp. I

savored every minute of my weeknights at home and used weekends to gather the heart to face Mapp again. Monday mornings, I rose and dutifully caught the school bus back to hell.

13 The harassment never let up. Once, when my English teacher left the room, a girl sitting near me drew a picture of a stickman on a piece of paper, colored it black, scribbled my name below it, and passed it around the classroom for others to see. I lost my temper, snatched it from her, and ripped it up. She hit me. I hit her back, then the whole class jumped in. When the teacher returned, I was standing up, punching one guy while another was riding my back and hitting me in the head. The teacher demanded, "What's going on here?"

14 The white kids cried out in unison, "That *black* boy started a fight with us!"

15 Without another word, the teacher sent me to the principal's office and I was dismissed from school. The weeklong suspension alerted my parents that something was wrong. Mama sat me down and tried to talk to me about it. "Why were you fighting in school?"

16 "It wasn't my fault, Mama. That girl drew a picture of me and colored it black."

17 "That's no reason to fight. What's the matter with you? Your grades are falling and now you get into a fight. Don't you like your school?"

18 I tried to explain, then choked up and broke down in tears. Seeing that, my parents sought and got approval to transfer me to the neighborhood school, W. E. Waters.

19 But it wasn't over yet. One day, before the transfer went through, I was sitting on the gym floor with the rest of the student body, watching a school assembly program, when a group of rowdy white upperclassmen began plucking my head and ridiculing me. I got confused. *What should I do?* To turn around and say something to them would start another fight. To get up and leave would require me to wade through a sea of hostile white students to reach the nearest exit. With nowhere to go, I sat there and took the humiliation until I broke. Tears welled in my eyes and started running, uncontrollably, down my face. I sat silently through the remainder of the assembly program with my vision blurred and my spirit broken. That was the only time, then or since, that I've been crushed so completely. When it was over, I collected myself, went to the boys' bathroom, and boohooed some more.

20 There was no greater joy than that last bus ride home from Mapp. I sat near a window and stared out, trying to make sense of those past few

months. Everything that had happened to me was so contrary to all I'd been taught about right and wrong. Before Mapp, every grudge I had ever held against a person could be traced to some specific deed. I couldn't understand someone hating me simply for being black and alive. I wondered, *Where did those white people learn to hate so deeply at such a young age?* I didn't know. But, over time, I learned to hate as blindly and viciously as any of them.

Understanding Meaning

1. Why did McCall's parents send him to a white school?
2. How did the white students respond to his presence?
3. How was McCall treated by the white faculty?
4. What impact did the students' reactions have on the author?
5. Why did McCall envy his brothers, who attended all-black schools?
6. What lesson did McCall learn?
7. *Critical Thinking:* McCall makes the observation that "Children have an enormous capacity to adapt to insanity." Can you think of current incidents or examples from your own life that support this view? Is this a universal phenomenon?

Evaluating Strategy

1. How does McCall blend a series of separate incidents into a single narrative?
2. What objective facts does McCall introduce into the narrative? Why are they important?
3. *Other Modes:* How does McCall use *description* and *comparison* to develop his narrative?

Appreciating Language

1. McCall uses the terms *black* and *African American* interchangeably. Does this appear inconsistent, or does it simply help the writer avoid repetition?
2. McCall states that the word *nigger* sounded "vile" coming from a white student. Is he suggesting that the race of the user determines the meaning of a word most people view as a term of contempt?
3. *Critical Thinking:* At one point McCall states that he wished to be "invisible." Why does this word have special meaning for African Americans?

Connections across the Disciplines

1. Consider Carl T. Rowan's account of his black teacher in "Unforgettable Miss Bessie" (page 122). Does McCall's account suggest that many students are better served in black schools with black teachers?
2. How does McCall's experience compare to that of Ramón Pérez (page 58)? Do their experiences give them a sense of being alien?

Writing Suggestions

1. Write a short essay about an incident in which you learned something about your status in society. Think of a time in which people responded to you not as an individual but as a member of a group. Have you ever been seen as one of *them* and labeled by others who have a fear or hatred for people who are different? What occurred, and how did people's reactions make you feel? Choose words carefully to express how the incident made you feel.
2. *Collaborative Writing:* Discuss McCall's narrative with a group of students. Ask members of the group to respond to McCall's "lesson." Work together to write a brief *description* of how children learn to hate others.

MOLLY IVINS

Molly Ivins worked as a reporter for The New York Times *before becoming a columnist for the* Dallas Times Herald. *She has published numerous articles in* Ms., The Nation, The Progressive, Texas Observer, *and other magazines. Many of her pieces were published in her 1992 collection,* Molly Ivins Can't Say That, Can She? *Her witty and often sarcastic commentaries have covered a range of topics, including politics, country music, fashion, religion, and National Football League cheerleaders.*

A Short Story about the Vietnam War Memorial

Ivins is best noted for satiric social commentary. But in this column, published shortly after the Vietnam War Memorial was dedicated, Ivins uses fictional techniques to create a moving narrative. She impresses readers with the memorial's significance by demonstrating the emotions of a single visitor.

1 She had known, ever since she first read about the Vietnam War Memorial, that she would go there someday. Sometime she would be in Washington and would go and see his name and leave again.

2 So silly, all that fuss about the memorial. Whatever else Vietnam was, it was not the kind of war that calls for some *Raising the Flag at Iwo Jima* kind of statue. She was not prepared, though, for the impact of the memorial. To walk down into it in the pale winter sunshine was like the war itself, like going into a dark valley and damned if there was ever any light at the end of the tunnel. Just death. When you get closer to the two walls, the number of names start to stun you. It is terrible, there in the peace and the pale sunshine.

3 The names are listed by date of death. There has never been a time, day or night, drunk or sober, for thirteen years that she could not have told you the date. He was killed on August 13, 1969. It is near the middle of the left wall. She went toward it as though she had known beforehand where it would be. His name is near the bottom. She had to kneel to find it. Stupid clichés. His name leaped out at her. It was like being hit.

4 She stared at it and then reached out and gently ran her fingers over the letters in the cold black marble. The memory of him came back so strong, almost as if he were there on the other side of the stone, she could see his hand reaching out to touch her fingers. It had not hurt for years and suddenly, just for a moment, it hurt again so horribly that it twisted her face and made her gasp and left her with tears running down her face. Then it stopped hurting but she could not stop the tears. Could not stop them running and running down her face.

5 There had been a time, although she had been an otherwise sensible young woman, when she had believed she would never recover from the pain. She did, of course. But she is still determined never to sentimentalize him. He would have hated that. She had thought it was like an amputation, the severing of his life from hers, that you could live on afterward but it would be like having only one leg and one arm. But it was only a wound. It healed. If there is a scar, it is only faintly visible now at odd intervals.

6 He was a biologist, a t.a. at the university getting his Ph.D. They lived together for two years. He left the university to finish his thesis but before he lined up a public school job—teachers were safe in those years—the draft board got him. They had friends who had left the country, they had friends who had gone to prison, they had friends who had gone to Nam. There were no good choices in those years. She thinks now he unconsciously wanted to go even though he often said, said in one of his last letters, that it was a stupid, f---in' war. He felt some form of guilt about a friend of theirs who was killed during the Tet offensive. Hubert Humphrey called Tet a great victory. His compromise was to refuse officer's training school and go as an enlisted man. She had thought then it was a dumb gesture and they had a half-hearted quarrel about it.

7 He had been in Nam less than two months when he was killed, without heroics, during a firefight at night by a single bullet in the brain. No one saw it happen. There are some amazing statistics about money and tonnage from that war. Did you know that there were more tons of bombs dropped on Hanoi during the Christmas bombing of 1972 than in all of World War II? Did you know that the war in Vietnam cost the United States $123.3 billion? She has always wanted to know how much that one bullet cost. Sixty-three cents? $1.20? Someone must know.

8 The other bad part was the brain. Even at this late date, it seems to her that was quite a remarkable mind. Long before she read C. P.

Snow, the ferociously honest young man who wanted to be a great biologist taught her a great deal about the difference between the way scientists think and the way humanists think. Only once has she been glad he was not with her. It was at one of those bizarre hearings about teaching "creation science." He would have gotten furious and been horribly rude. He had no patience with people who did not understand and respect the process of science.

9 She used to attribute his fierce honesty to the fact that he was a Yankee. She is still prone to tell "white" lies to make people feel better, to smooth things over, to prevent hard feelings. Surely there have been dumber things for lovers to quarrel over than the social utility of hypocrisy. But not many.

10 She stood up again, still staring at his name, stood for a long time. She said, "There it is," and turned to go. A man to her left was staring at her. She glared at him. The man had done nothing but make the mistake of seeing her weeping. She said, as though daring him to disagree, "It was a stupid, f---in' war," and stalked past him.

11 She turned again at the top of the slope to make sure where his name is, so whenever she sees a picture of the memorial she can put her finger where his name is. He never said goodbye, literally. Whenever he left he would say, "Take care love." He could say it many different ways. He said it when he left for Vietnam. She stood at the top of the slope and found her hand half-raised in some silly gesture of farewell. She brought it down again. She considered thinking to him, "Hey, take care, love" but it seemed remarkably inappropriate. She walked away and was quite entertaining for the rest of the day, because it was expected of her.

12 She thinks he would have liked the memorial. He would have hated the editorials. He did not sacrifice his life for his country or for a just or noble cause. There just were no good choices in those years and he got killed.

Understanding Meaning

1. What impact did the memorial have on the visitor?
2. What attitude did the woman's lover have toward the war?
3. Why did she view his refusal to attend officers' training school as a "dumb gesture"?
4. What assumptions did the woman make about how the man's loss would affect her?

5. *Critical Thinking:* Ivins remarks that there were "no good choices in those years." Could this apply to soldiers in other wars, perhaps in all wars? Do wars ever provide people with "good choices"?

Evaluating Strategy

1. Does the title suggest that the story is purely fictional? Why should journalists clearly mark imaginative work to avoid allegations of falsification?
2. Ivins does not provide the people with names. What effect does this have? How would the story be different if the woman were called Jane, Kim, Juanita, or Siobhan?
3. *Critical Thinking:* Does a nonfiction writer such as a columnist or social commentator risk compromising his or her position by publishing what appears to be fiction in a newspaper column? Will readers assume that future articles may contain material that is "made up"?

Appreciating Language

1. What words does Ivins use to describe the monument?
2. Ivins compares the woman's grief to an "amputation." How effective is this image in describing an emotion?

Connections across the Disciplines

1. Would Nathan McCall's plight (page 47) of attending either possibly inferior black schools or hostile integrated schools suggest a similar lack of good choices?
2. Compare Ivins's unnamed visitor to Ellen Goodman's "company man" (page 185). What techniques do these writers use to develop symbolic characters?

Writing Suggestions

1. Write a short narrative with a fictional character. Your story may be serious, humorous, or satirical. Develop an unnamed character who embodies a typical student or employee. Have the character engage in a simple act, such as walking to class or answering the telephone at work.
2. Write a dramatic story about a person experiencing something momentous such as facing an angry boss, confronting an unfaithful lover,

approaching a clinic to be tested for HIV, or taking a final examination. Focus on the emotions and memories this confrontation evokes.

3. *Collaborative Writing:* Working with a group of students, discuss Ivins's comments about people who have "no good choices." Have each student write a brief narrative or description about a person facing limited options. At a second meeting have each student read his or her paper to the group. Determine which narrative best illustrates the dilemma of choice.

RAMON "TIANGUIS" PÉREZ

Ramon "Tianguis" Pérez is an undocumented alien and does not release biographical information.

The Fender-Bender

This narrative, taken from Pérez's book Diary of an Undocumented Immigrant, *illustrates how even a minor incident can affect the precarious existence of an undocumented alien. For Pérez a few pieces of paper stand between a life in America and deportation.*

1 One night after work, I drive Rolando's old car to visit some friends, and then head towards home. At a light, I come to a stop too late, leaving the front end of the car poking into the crosswalk. I shift into reverse, but as I am backing up, I strike the van behind me. Its driver immediately gets out to inspect the damage to his vehicle. He's a tall Anglo-Saxon, dressed in a deep blue work uniform. After looking at his car, he walks up to the window of the car I'm driving.

2 "Your driver's license," he says, a little enraged.

3 "I didn't bring it," I tell him.

4 He scratches his head. He is breathing heavily with fury.

5 "Okay," he says. "You park up ahead while I call a patrolman."

6 The idea of calling the police doesn't sound good to me, but the accident is my fault. So I drive around the corner and park at the curb. I turn off the motor and hit the steering wheel with one fist. I don't have a driver's license. I've never applied for one. Nor do I have with me the identification card that I bought in San Antonio. Without immigration papers, without a driving permit, and having hit another car, I feel as if I'm just one step away from Mexico.

7 I get out of the car. The white man comes over and stands right in front of me. He's almost two feet taller.

8 "If you're going to drive, why don't you carry your license?" he asks in an accusatory tone.

9 "I didn't bring it," I say, for lack of any other defense.

10 I look at the damage to his car. It's minor, only a scratch on the paint and a pimple-sized dent.

11 "I'm sorry," I say. "Tell me how much it will cost to fix, and I'll pay for it; that's no problem." I'm talking to him in English, and he seems to understand.

12 "This car isn't mine," he says. "It belongs to the company I work for. I'm sorry, but I've got to report this to the police, so that I don't have to pay for the damage."

13 "That's no problem," I tell him again. "I can pay for it."

14 After we've exchanged these words, he seems less irritated. But he says he'd prefer for the police to come, so that they can report that the dent wasn't his fault.

15 While we wait, he walks from one side to the other, looking down the avenue this way and that, hoping that the police will appear.

16 Then he goes over to the van to look at the dent.

17 "It's not much," he says. "If it was my car, there wouldn't be any problems, and you could go on."

18 After a few minutes, the long-awaited police car arrives. Only one officer is inside. He's a Chicano, short and of medium complexion, with short, curly hair. On getting out of the car, he walks straight towards the Anglo.

19 The two exchange a few words.

20 "Is that him?" he asks, pointing at me.

21 The Anglo nods his head.

22 Speaking in English, the policeman orders me to stand in front of the car and to put my hands on the hood. He searches me and finds only the car keys and my billfold with a few dollars in it. He asks for my driver's license.

23 "I don't have it," I answered in Spanish.

24 He wrinkles his face into a frown, and casting a glance at the Anglo, shakes his head in disapproval of me.

25 "That's the way these Mexicans are," he says.

26 He turns back towards me, asking for identification. I tell him I don't have that, either.

27 "You're an illegal, eh?" he says.

28 I won't answer.

29 "An illegal," he says to himself.

30 "Where do you live?" he continues. He's still speaking in English.

31 I tell him my address.

32 "Do you have anything with you to prove that you live at that address?" he asks.

33 I think for a minute, then realize that in the glove compartment is a letter that my parents sent to me several weeks earlier.

34 I show him the envelope and he immediately begins to write something in a little book that he carries in his back pocket. He walks to the back of my car and copies the license plate number. Then he goes over to his car and talks into his radio. After he talks, someone answers. Then he asks me for the name of the car's owner.

35 He goes over to where the Anglo is standing. I can't quite hear what they're saying. But when the two of them go over to look at the dent in the van, I hear the cop tell the Anglo that if he wants, he can file charges against me. The Anglo shakes his head and explains what he had earlier explained to me, about only needing for the police to certify that he wasn't responsible for the accident. The Anglo says that he doesn't want to accuse me of anything because the damage is light.

36 "If you want, I can take him to jail," the cop insists.

37 The Anglo turns him down again.

38 "If you'd rather, we can report him to Immigration," the cop continues.

39 Just as at the first, I am now almost sure that I'll be making a forced trip to Tijuana. I find myself searching my memory for my uncle's telephone number, and to my relief, I remember it. I am waiting for the Anglo to say yes, confirming my expectations of the trip. But instead, he says no, and though I remain silent, I feel appreciation for him. I ask myself why the Chicano is determined to harm me. I didn't really expect him to favor me, just because we're of the same ancestry, but on the other hand, once I had admitted my guilt, I expected him to treat me at least fairly. But even against the white man's wishes, he's trying to make matters worse for me. I've known several Chicanos with whom, joking around, I've reminded them that their roots are in Mexico. But very few of them see it that way. Several have told me how when they were children, their parents would take them to vacation in different states of Mexico, but their own feeling, they've said, is, "I am an American citizen!" Finally, the Anglo, with the justifying paper in his hands, says goodbye to the cop, thanks him for his services, gets into his van and drives away.

40 The cop stands in the street in a pensive mood. I imagine that he's trying to think of a way to punish me.

41 "Put the key in the ignition," he orders me.

42 I do as he says.

43 Then he orders me to roll up the windows and lock the doors.

44 "Now, go on, walking," he says.

45 I go off taking slow steps. The cop gets in his patrol car and stays there, waiting. I turn the corner after two blocks and look out for my car, but the cop is still parked beside it. I begin looking for a coat hanger, and after a good while, find one by a curb of the street. I keep walking, keeping about two blocks away from the car. While I walk, I bend the coat hanger into the form I'll need. As if I'd called for it, a speeding car goes past. When it comes to the avenue where my car is parked, it makes a turn. It is going so fast that its wheels screech as it rounds the corner. The cop turns on the blinking lights of his patrol car and leaving black marks on the pavement beneath it, shoots out to chase the speeder. I go up to my car and with my palms force a window open a crack. Then I insert the clothes hanger in the crack and raise the lock lever. It's a simple task, one that I'd already performed. This wasn't the first time that I'd been locked out of a car, though always before, it was because I'd forgotten to remove my keys.

Understanding Meaning

1. How serious is the accident?
2. Why does the van driver insist on calling the police?
3. What makes this incident a dangerous one for Pérez?
4. How does Pérez attempt to prevent the van driver from summoning the police?
5. Pérez answers the Chicano patrolman in Spanish. Was this a mistake? How did the officer treat Pérez?
6. *Critical Thinking:* Pérez implies that Chicanos have been offended when he has alluded to their Mexican roots; they insist on being seen as American citizens. What does this say about assimilation and identity? Does the Chicano officer's comments about Mexicans reveal contempt for immigrants? Have other ethnic groups—Jews, Italians, the Irish—resented the presence of unassimilated new arrivals from their homelands?

Evaluating Strategy

1. Why is a minor incident like a fender bender a better device to explain the plight of the undocumented immigrant than a dramatic one?
2. How does Pérez use dialogue to advance the narrative?

Appreciating Language

1. What words does Pérez use to minimize the damage caused by the accident?
2. What word choices and images stress the importance of paper documents in the lives of aliens?

Connections across the Disciplines

1. Compare Armando Rendón's attitude (page 667) toward his Spanish heritage with that of the Chicanos Pérez describes. How are they different? How common is the issue of embracing or rejecting one's ethnic origins?
2. How does Pérez's situation differ from Nathan McCall's (page 47)?

Writing Suggestions

1. Write a short narrative essay detailing a minor event that provided insight into your life or social conditions. Perhaps you discovered our dependence on energy when your apartment lost power, and you could not use your computer, watch television, or even open the garage door to get your car. A simple interaction with a homeless person may have caused you to question your assumptions about the poor.
2. *Collaborative Writing:* Working with a group of students, discuss your views on immigration and undocumented or "illegal" aliens. Take notes and write a brief statement outlining your views. If major differences of opinion exist, split the group into subgroups, and draft pro and con opinion statements.

DR. ROBERT PETER GALE AND THOMAS HAUSER

In April 1986 monitors at a Swedish nuclear power plant registered a high level of radioactivity. Operators checked their equipment and then realized the radioactivity was not being emitted from their facility but was in the atmosphere. They had discovered the first evidence of the worst nuclear disaster in history. Technicians at the Chernobyl reactor in the Soviet Union had made a series of errors that caused the plant to explode, releasing more radiation than the Hiroshima bombing. Scores of people were killed, and hundreds of thousands were contaminated. Today the reactor is encased in tons of concrete, but the hastily constructed cover called the Sarcophagus is already crumbling. The fuel inside will be lethal for thousands of years. The undamaged Chernobyl units are still in use.

Final Warning

Gale and Hauser wrote this brief narrative as part of the preface of their book Final Warning, *a collection of memoirs by Chernobyl survivors. The goal of this brief history is to give readers a basic chronology of the events behind one of the greatest human dramas of the nuclear age.*

1 During World War II, the United States and Germany were not alone in considering the potential of atomic weapons. As early as 1939, Russian physicists had recognized the possibility of harnessing a nuclear chain reaction. Three years later, Joseph Stalin ordered that high priority be given to investigating the military applications of nuclear fission, and in 1949 the Soviets successfully detonated an atomic explosion. Nuclear parity between the superpowers followed, and thereafter the Soviet government moved to implement an energy policy based in significant part on nuclear fission. By 1984, 10 percent of all electricity generated in the Soviet Union came from nuclear sources, and officials were targeting a 50 percent figure for the year 2000.

2 The pride of the Soviet nuclear program was a planned six-unit complex at Chernobyl. Chernobyl Unit Number 1 went into service in 1977, and was followed by Units 2, 3, and 4 in 1978, 1981, and 1983 respectively. Units 5 and 6 were scheduled to come on line in 1988. The

Chernobyl reactors were similar to one another in design, but differed from units in the United States in two significant respects. First, rather than using water as a moderator, the Chernobyl units employed graphite. And as a consequence of this and several other design features, chain reactions within the reactor were more likely to run out of control in the event of a loss-of-coolant accident. And second, while the Chernobyl units were protected by strong walls, they were housed in buildings which lacked reinforced concrete domes typical of Western containment structures. Whether either of these factors contributed to the scope of the disaster which ultimately occurred is subject to dispute, given the magnitude of the Chernobyl explosion.

3 The chain of events leading to disaster began on the morning of April 25, 1986. Unit Number 4 was scheduled to be taken out of service for routine maintenance, and the plant's electrical engineers wanted to conduct a test to determine how long the turbine-generators would continue to produce electricity to run the water pumps necessary to cool the reactor after the normal electrical supply had been interrupted.

4 At one A.M., the reactor's power level was lowered to prepare for the test. Then, over the next twenty-four hours, technicians systematically disconnected power regulation and emergency cooling systems which would have automatically shut the reactor down and interfered with the test. Finally, at 1:23 on the morning of April 26, 1986—twenty-four hours after preparation for the test had begun—the flow of steam to the turbine was halted. Almost immediately, the cooling pumps slowed, diminishing the flow of cooling water to the reactor core. Normally, at this point, the reactor would have shut down, but the automatic shutdown system was one of six safety mechanisms that had been deliberately disconnected. Within seconds, there was a massive heat buildup in the reactor core, triggering an uncontrolled chain reaction. Power surged. At 1:23 A.M., the Unit Number 4 reactor exploded.

5 There were two blasts, three seconds apart. The first was caused by steam, the second by steam or hydrogen which had formed when the fuel-rod cladding began to melt and interacted with water in the pressure vessel. The reactor core was torn apart. Its thousand-ton cover-plate was propelled upward, causing the building roof above the reactor to collapse. A deadly plume of radioactive material—more than was released at Hiroshima and Nagasaki—shot into the air, forming a fiery image above the roof before dispersing into the atmosphere. Exposed to intense heat and open air, the graphite moderator began to

burn. Radioactive water gushed into the reactor hall. Hot chunks of fuel and metal landed on what was left of the building roof and the roofs of adjacent buildings. Thirty fires began to burn.

6 Within minutes, the nuclear plant's firefighting unit was on the scene—twenty-eight men under the command of Major Leonid Telyatnikov. "You had the impression you could see the radiation," Telyatnikov said later. "There were flashes of light springing from place to place, substances glowing, luminescent, a bit like sparklers."

7 Telyatnikov ordered a "stage three" alarm, the highest for Soviet firefighters, summoning 250 reserves from as far away as Kiev. Then he and the few men available began working desperately to halt the fires. Their primary concern was that Unit Number 4 shared a ventilation system with, and was housed in the same reactor hall as, Unit Number 3. If the fire spread and Unit 3 went up in flames, the disaster would double in magnitude.

8 A dozen firemen in the Unit 3 reactor block attacked the blaze with hand-held extinguishers. As that struggle progressed, Telyatnikov led six men up a hundred-foot ladder to the collapsed roof of the reactor hall. Because of the heat, what was left of the asphalt roof had begun to melt. With each step, the firemen's boots sunk into the bitumen, and they had to strain to pull free. Poisonous fumes made breathing difficult; visibility was near zero. Water that was poured on the flames turned instantly to scalding radioactive steam.

9 Firefighting units from nearby towns began to arrive at three-thirty A.M. Still, the fires raged. "We knew about the radiation," Telyatnikov said later. "We were trying to get the fire before the radiation got us. We are firemen. This is what we were trained for. We are supposed to fight fires. We knew we must stay to the end. That was our duty."

10 Shortly before dawn, all fires except one in the Unit 4 reactor core (which would burn for weeks) had been extinguished. The reactor hall was in shambles. Of the seven men who fought the blaze on the building roof, all but Telyatnikov (who was hospitalized for three months) would die as a result of radiation exposure.

Understanding Meaning

1. Gale and Hauser's account of a complex disaster is quite short. Does it explain the main events and capture the scope of the events? Is their narrative totally objective?

2. What audience does this narrative seem to be directed to? Do Gale and Hauser assume readers have a basic knowledge of science and nuclear energy?
3. This narrative was written as part of a preface for a much longer work. How does an introductory narrative emphasizing times and events assist readers in following complex stories later in the book?
4. *Critical Thinking:* What implications does this story have for the United States, which had its own nuclear accident at Three Mile Island? How safe is nuclear power?

Evaluating Strategy

1. How do the authors arrange events? How important is the chronology?
2. Do the writers create a sense of tension and drama in a narrative that primarily involves machines rather than people? How can an objective narrative create an emotional impact? Can facts truly "speak for themselves"?
3. The writers quote Major Leonid Telyatnikov, who commanded the firefighters. Do his comments about his firefighters add a human element to the narrative?
4. *Critical Thinking:* Because the timing of events is critical in this narrative, should the authors have supplied a simple time line such as Walter Lord's log book for the *Titanic* (page 92)?

Appreciating Language

1. The writers do not bother to explain certain terms, such as *fuel-rod cladding* and *graphite moderator*. Does a reader need to know these terms to understand the significance of the main events? Would footnotes help or distract readers?
2. Do nontechnical expressions like "hot chunks of fuel" help dramatize events and provide graphic *description* of the disaster? What other phrases can you locate that help dramatize the event?

Connections across the Disciplines

1. What distinguishes this objective narrative from Scudder's subjective account of his experiences (page 41)?
2. Relate this account to Monika Bauerlein's article about nuclear waste (page 128). What do these articles say about humanity's relationship with the environment?

Writing Suggestions

1. Write a brief essay *analyzing* what the Chernobyl disaster reveals about the perils of technology.
2. Write a moment-by-moment narrative of an event you witnessed or participated in. You may add statements people made at the time.
3. *Collaborative Writing:* Working with at least three other students, draft a short, factual narrative of a recent event. Focus on having your group select the main events. How can a simple item like determining the time of an event be critical or even controversial?

JANE GOODALL

Jane Goodall (1934–) was born in London but has lived in Africa since the 1950s, when she began assisting the noted anthropologist Dr. Louis Leakey. In the 1960s she started her extensive studies on chimpanzees, viewing them both in groups and as individuals. Her work has made her a world-respected expert in chimpanzee behavior. "First Observations" documents her discovery that chimpanzees make and use tools, thus challenging the long-accepted notion that toolmaking was exclusively a human attribute.

First Observations

In attempting to observe and document chimpanzee behavior, Jane Goodall dramatizes the dilemma faced by many researchers—can one get close enough to study a subject without causing disruption in the process? She also deals with another problem humans have in studying animals. Can people view animals without making inferences about behavior that strikes them as being "human"?

1 For about a month I spent most of each day either on the Peak or overlooking Mlinda Valley where the chimps, before or after stuffing themselves with figs, ate large quantities of small purple fruits that tasted, like so many of their foods, as bitter and astringent as sloes or crab apples. Piece by piece, I began to form my first somewhat crude picture of chimpanzee life.

2 The impression that I had gained when I watched the chimps at the msulula tree of temporary, constantly changing associations of individuals within the community was substantiated. Most often I saw small groups of four to eight moving about together. Sometimes I saw one or two chimpanzees leave such a group and wander off on their own or join up with a different association. On other occasions I watched two or three small groups joining to form a larger one.

3 Often, as one group crossed the grassy ridge separating the Kasekela Valley from the fig trees on the home valley, the male chimpanzee, or chimpanzees, of the party would break into a run, sometimes moving in an upright position, sometimes dragging a fallen branch, sometimes stamping or slapping the hard earth. These charging displays were always accompanied by loud pant-hoots and afterward the

chimpanzee frequently would swing up into a tree overlooking the valley he was about to enter and sit quietly, peering down and obviously listening for a response from below. If there were chimps feeding in the fig trees they nearly always hooted back, as though in answer. Then the new arrivals would hurry down the steep slope and, with more calling and screaming, the two groups would meet in the fig trees. When groups of females and youngsters with no males present joined other feeding chimpanzees, usually there was none of this excitement; the newcomers merely climbed up into the trees, greeted some of those already there, and began to stuff themselves with figs.

4 While many details of their social behavior were hidden from me by the foliage, I did get occasional fascinating glimpses. I saw one female, newly arrived in a group, hurry up to a big male and hold her hand toward him. Almost regally he reached out, clasped her hand in his, drew it toward him, and kissed it with his lips. I saw two adult males embrace each other in greeting. I saw youngsters having wild games through the treetops, chasing around after each other or jumping again and again, one after the other, from a branch to a springy bough below. I watched small infants dangling happily by themselves for minutes on end, patting at their toes with one hand, rotating gently from side to side. Once two tiny infants pulled on opposite ends of a twig in a gentle tug-of-war. Often, during the heat of midday or after a long spell of feeding, I saw two or more adults grooming each other, carefully looking through the hair of their companions. . . .

5 One day, when I was sitting by the trickle of water in Buffalo Wood, pausing for a moment in the coolness before returning from a scramble in Mlinda Valley, I saw a female bushbuck moving slowly along the nearly dry streambed. Occasionally she paused to pick off some plant and crunch it. I kept absolutely still, and she was not aware of my presence until she was little more than ten yards away. Suddenly she tensed and stood staring at me, one small forefoot raised. Because I did not move, she did not know what I was—only that my outline was somehow strange. I saw her velvet nostrils dilate as she sniffed the air, but I was downwind and her nose gave her no answer. Slowly she came closer, and closer—one step at a time, her neck craned forward—always poised for instant flight. I can still scarcely believe that her nose actually touched my knee; yet if I close my eyes I can feel again, in imagination, the warmth of her breath and the silken impact of her skin. Unexpectedly I blinked and she was gone in a flash, bounding away with loud barks of alarm until the vegetation hid her completely from my view.

6 It was rather different when, as I was sitting on the Peak, I saw a leopard coming toward me, his tail held up straight. He was at a slightly lower level than I, and obviously had no idea I was there. Ever since arrival in Africa I had had an ingrained, illogical fear of leopards. Already, while working at the Gombe, I had several times nearly turned back when, crawling through some thick undergrowth, I had suddenly smelled the rank smell of cat. I had forced myself on, telling myself that my fear was foolish, that only wounded leopards charged humans with savage ferocity.

7 On this occasion, though, the leopard went out of sight as it started to climb up the hill—the hill on the peak of which I sat. I quickly hastened to climb a tree, but halfway there I realized that leopards can climb trees. So I uttered a sort of halfhearted squawk. The leopard, my logical mind told me, would be just as frightened of me if he knew I was there. Sure enough, there was a thudding of startled feet and then silence. I returned to the Peak, but the feeling of unseen eyes watching me was too much. I decided to watch for the chimps in Mlinda Valley. And, when I returned to the Peak several hours later, there, on the very rock which had been my seat, was a neat pile of leopard dung. He must have watched me go and then, very carefully, examined the place where such a frightening creature had been and tried to exterminate my alien scent with his own.

8 As the weeks went by the chimpanzees became less and less afraid. Quite often when I was on one of my food-collecting expeditions I came across chimpanzees unexpectedly, and after a time I found that some of them would tolerate my presence provided they were in fairly thick forest and I sat still and did not try to move closer than sixty to eighty yards. And so, during my second month of watching from the peak, when I saw a group settle down to feed I sometimes moved closer and was thus able to make more detailed observations.

9 It was at this time that I began to recognize a number of different individuals. As soon as I was sure of knowing a chimpanzee if I saw it again, I named it. Some scientists feel that animals should be labeled by numbers—that to name them is anthropomorphic—but I have always been interested in the *differences* between individuals, and a name is not only more individual than a number but also far easier to remember. Most names were simply those which, for some reason or other, seemed to suit the individuals to whom I attached them. A few chimps were named because some facial expression or mannerism reminded me of human acquaintances. . . .

10 One day I arrived on the Peak and found a small group of chimps just below me in the upper branches of a thick tree. As I watched I saw that one of them was holding a pink-looking object from which he was from time to time pulling pieces with his teeth. There was a female and a youngster and they were both reaching out toward the male, their hands actually touching his mouth. Presently the female picked up a piece of the pink thing and put it to her mouth: it was at this moment that I realized the chimps were eating meat.

11 After each bite of meat the male picked off some leaves with his lips and chewed them with the flesh. Often, when he had chewed for several minutes on this leafy wad, he spat out the remains into the waiting hands of the female. Suddenly, he dropped a small piece of meat, and like a flash the youngster swung after it to the ground. Even as he reached to pick it up the undergrowth exploded and an adult bushpig charged toward him. Screaming, the juvenile leaped back into the tree. The pig remained in the open, snorting and moving backward and forward. Soon I made out the shapes of three small striped piglets. Obviously the chimps were eating a baby pig. The size was right and later, when I realized that the male was David Graybeard, I moved closer and saw that he was indeed eating piglet.

12 For three hours I watched the chimps feeding. David occasionally let the female bite pieces from the carcass and once he actually detached a small piece of flesh and placed it in her outstretched hand. When he finally climbed down there was still meat left on the carcass; he carried it away in one hand, followed by the others.

13 Of course I was not sure, then, that David Graybeard had caught the pig for himself, but even so, it was tremendously exciting to know that these chimpanzees actually ate meat. Previously scientists had believed that although these apes might occasionally supplement their diet with a few insects or small rodents and the like they were primarily vegetarians and fruit eaters. No one had suspected that they might hunt larger mammals.

14 It was within two weeks of this observation that I saw something that excited me even more. By then it was October and the short rains had begun. The blackened slopes were softened by feathery new grass shoots and in some places the ground was carpeted by a variety of flowers. The Chimpanzees' Spring, I called it. I had had a frustrating morning, tramping up and down three valleys with never a sign or sound of a chimpanzee. Hauling myself up the steep slope of Mlinda Valley I headed for the Peak, not only weary but soaking wet from

crawling through dense undergrowth. Suddenly I stopped, for I saw a slight movement in the long grass about sixty yards away. Quickly focusing my binoculars I saw that it was a single chimpanzee, and just then he turned in my direction. I recognized David Graybeard.

15 Cautiously I moved around so that I could see what he was doing. He was squatting beside the red earth mound of a termite nest, and as I watched I saw him carefully push a long grass stem down into a hole in the mound. After a moment he withdrew it and picked something from the end with his mouth. I was too far away to make out what he was eating, but it was obvious that he was actually using a grass stem as a tool.

16 I knew that on two occasions casual observers in West Africa had seen chimpanzees using objects as tools: one had broken open palm-nut kernels by using a rock as a hammer, and a group of chimps had been observed pushing sticks into an underground bees' nest and licking off the honey. Somehow I had never dreamed of seeing anything so exciting myself. . . .

17 On the eighth day of my watch David Graybeard arrived again, together with Goliath, and the pair worked there for two hours. I could see much better: I observed how they scratched open the sealed-over passage entrances with a thumb or forefinger. I watched how they bit the end off their tools when they became bent, or used the other end, or discarded them in favor of new ones. Goliath once moved at least fifteen yards from the heap to select a firm-looking piece of vine, and both males often picked three or four stems while they were collecting tools, and put the spares beside them on the ground until they wanted them.

18 Most exciting of all, on several occasions they picked small leafy twigs and prepared them for use by stripping off the leaves. This was the first recorded example of a wild animal not merely *using* an object as a tool, but actually modifying an object and thus showing the crude beginnings of tool*making*.

19 Previously man had been regarded as the only toolmaking animal. Indeed, one of the clauses commonly accepted in the definition of man was that he was a creature who "made tools to a regular and set pattern." The chimpanzees, obviously, had not made tools to any set pattern. Nevertheless, my early observations of their primitive toolmaking abilities convinced a number of scientists that it was necessary to redefine man in a more complex manner than before. Or else, as Louis Leakey put it, we should by definition have to accept the chimpanzee as Man.

Understanding Meaning

1. What is Goodall's purpose in relating this narrative? What does she want her readers to understand about chimpanzee behavior?
2. What did Goodall consider her major discoveries?
3. How did her view of chimpanzees evolve over time?
4. Why do many scientists argue that animal subjects should be labeled by number and not granted names? Why does Goodall give the chimpanzees names?
5. *Critical Thinking:* Goodall describes chimpanzees by relating their actions to human behavior. Does this suggest a link among different species? Could seeing human traits in animals be misleading? Can humans easily misinterpret the cause or meaning of a gesture if it appears familiar? Could what looks like a handshake simply be an accidental movement, for example, and not a significant gesture?

Evaluating Strategy

1. What role does Goodall play in the narrative?
2. How does Goodall use transitional statements to demonstrate the passage of time and advance the narrative?
3. *Other Modes:* How does Goodall use *comparison* to draw distinctions between chimpanzees and human behavior? How does she employ *description* to provide details about chimpanzees and their society?

Appreciating Language

1. How much technical terminology does Goodall include in her narrative? What does this suggest about her readers?
2. Study the names she gives the individual chimpanzees. Do these names indicate a simple way of labeling chimpanzees based on their appearance, or do they imply a kind of humanization of the subjects?
3. Does Goodall's language suggest a desire to be objective?
4. What does "anthropomorphic" (par 9) mean?

Connections across the Disciplines

1. Does Goodall appear to practice the kind of close observation espoused by Dr. Agassiz in Samuel Scudder's essay, "Take This Fish and Look at It" (page 41)?
2. How does Goodall's role as observer compare with that of Oliver Sacks's role as physician (page 75)?

Writing Suggestions

1. In a few paragraphs describe the behavior of an animal you have observed. You might describe a single incident involving a family pet or a common behavior you notice in the birds, dogs, or wildlife in your area. What do your observations reveal about how animals adapt to human-influenced environments?
2. *Critical Writing:* Goodall mentions that the chimpanzees slowly became accustomed to her presence. Write a response to the argument that it is impossible to achieve an objective understanding of an environment if the observer's presence alters it in any way.
3. *Collaborative Writing:* Working with at least three other students, draft a brief *analysis* of how Goodall's findings challenge prevailing *definitions* of human behavior. Discuss how her conclusions could influence the animal rights movement.

OLIVER SACKS

Oliver Sacks (1933–) was born in London and studied in Oxford before coming to the United States to complete his education. A professor of neurology, he has written several accounts of his patients who suffer from baffling and often disturbing neurological disorders. His 1974 book Awakenings *told the stories of patients recovering from comas and served as the basis of a motion picture. This section, taken from a book of the same title, tells the story of Dr. P., who developed prosopagnosia, an inability to connect perceptions with understanding.*

The Man Who Mistook His Wife for His Hat

In this "tale"—a term he uses to describe his patients' histories—Sacks first describes *a set of odd symptoms exhibited by a professor of music. He then recalls his own astonishment as the highly educated artist found it difficult to identify common objects. As you read notice how Sacks uses* comparison, analysis, definition, *and* cause and effect *to develop his narrative.*

1 Dr. P. was a musician of distinction, well-known for many years as a singer, and then, at the local School of Music, as a teacher. It was here, in relation to his students, that certain strange problems were first observed. Sometimes a student would present himself, and Dr. P. would not recognise him; or, specifically, would not recognise his face. The moment the student spoke, he would be recognised by his voice. Such incidents multiplied, causing embarrassment, perplexity, fear—and, sometimes, comedy. For not only did Mr. P. increasingly fail to see faces, but he saw faces when there were no faces to see: genially, Magoo-like, when in the street he might pat the heads of water hydrants and parking meters, taking these to be the heads of children; he would amiably address carved knobs on the furniture and be astounded when they did not reply. At first these odd mistakes were laughed off as jokes, not least by Dr. P. himself. Had he not always had a quirky sense of humour and been given to Zen-like paradoxes and jests? His musical powers were as dazzling as ever; he did not feel ill—he had never felt better; and the mistakes were so ludicrous—and so

ingenious—that they could hardly be serious or betoken anything serious. The notion of there being "something the matter" did not emerge until some three years later, when diabetes developed. Well aware that diabetes could affect his eyes, Dr. P. consulted an ophthalmologist, who took a careful history and examined his eyes closely. "There's nothing the matter with your eyes," the doctor concluded. "But there is trouble with the visual parts of your brain. You don't need my help, you must see a neurologist." And so, as a result of this referral, Dr. P. came to me.

2 It was obvious within a few seconds of meeting him that there was no trace of dementia in the ordinary sense. He was a man of great cultivation and charm who talked well and fluently, with imagination and humour. I couldn't think why he had been referred to our clinic.

3 And yet there *was* something a bit odd. He faced me as he spoke, was oriented towards me, and yet there was something the matter—it was difficult to formulate. He faced me with his *ears,* I came to think, but not with his eyes. These, instead of looking, gazing, at me, "taking me in," in the normal way, made sudden strange fixations—on my nose, on my right ear, down to my chin, up to my right eye—as if noting (even studying) these individual features, but not seeing my whole face, its changing expressions, "me," as a whole. I am not sure that I fully realised this at the time—there was just a teasing strangeness, some failure in the normal interplay of gaze and expression. He saw me, he *scanned* me, and yet . . .

4 "What seems to be the matter?" I asked him at length.

5 "Nothing that I know of," he replied with a smile, "but people seem to think there's something wrong with my eyes."

6 "But *you* don't recognise any visual problems?"

7 "No, not directly, but I occasionally make mistakes."

8 I left the room briefly to talk with his wife. When I came back, Dr. P. was sitting placidly by the window, attentive, listening rather than looking out. "Traffic," he said, "street sounds, distant trains—they make a sort of symphony, do they not? You know Honegger's *Pacific 234?*"

9 What a lovely man, I thought to myself. How can there be anything seriously the matter? Would he permit me to examine him?

10 "Yes, of course, Dr. Sacks."

11 I stilled my disquiet, his perhaps, too, in the soothing routine of a neurological exam—muscle strength, coordination, reflexes, tone. . . . It was while examining his reflexes—a trifle abnormal on the left

side—that the first bizarre experience occurred. I had taken off his left shoe and scratched the sole of his foot with a key—a frivolous-seeming but essential test of a reflex—and then, excusing myself to screw my ophthalmoscope together, left him to put on the shoe himself. To my surprise, a minute later, he had not done this.

12 "Can I help?" I asked.

13 "Help what? Help whom?"

14 "Help you put on your shoe."

15 "Ach," he said, "I had forgotten the shoe," adding, *sotto voce,* "The shoe? The shoe?" He seemed baffled.

16 "Your shoe," I repeated. "Perhaps you'd put it on."

17 He continued to look downwards, though not at the shoe, with an intense but misplaced concentration. Finally his gaze settled on his foot: "That is my shoe, yes?"

18 Did I mis-hear? Did he mis-see?

19 "My eyes," he explained, and put a hand to his foot. "*This* is my shoe, no?"

20 "No, it is not. That is your foot. *There* is your shoe."

21 "Ah! I thought that was my foot."

22 Was he joking? Was he mad? Was he blind? If this was one of his "strange mistakes," it was the strangest mistake I had ever come across.

23 I helped him on with his shoe (his foot), to avoid further complication. Dr. P. himself seemed untroubled, indifferent, maybe amused. I resumed my examination. His visual acuity was good: he had no difficulty seeing a pin on the floor, though sometimes he missed it if it was placed to his left.

24 He saw all right, but what did he see? I opened out a copy of the *National Geographic Magazine* and asked him to describe some pictures in it.

25 His responses here were very curious. His eyes would dart from one thing to another, picking up tiny features, individual features, as they had done with my face. A striking brightness, a colour, a shape would arrest his attention and elicit comment—but in no case did he get the scene-as-a-whole. He failed to see the whole, seeing only details, which he spotted like blips on a radar screen. He never entered into relation with the picture as a whole—never faced, so to speak, *its* physiognomy. He had no sense whatever of a landscape or scene.

26 I showed him the cover, an unbroken expanse of Sahara dunes.

27 "What do you see here?" I asked.

28 "I see a river," he said. "And a little guest-house with its terrace on the water. People are dining out on the terrace. I see coloured parasols here and there." He was looking, if it was "looking," right off the cover into mid-air and confabulating nonexistent features, as if the absence of features in the actual picture had driven him to imagine the river and the terrace and the coloured parasols.

29 I must have looked aghast, but he seemed to think he had done rather well. There was a hint of a smile on his face. He also appeared to have decided that the examination was over and started to look around for his hat. He reached out his hand and took hold of his wife's head, tried to lift if off, to put it on. He had apparently mistaken his wife for a hat! His wife looked as if she was used to such things.

30 I could make no sense of what had occurred in terms of conventional neurology (or neuropsychology). In some ways he seemed perfectly preserved, and in others absolutely, incomprehensibly devastated. How could he, on the one hand, mistake his wife for a hat and, on the other, function, as apparently he still did, as a teacher at the Music School?

31 I had to think, to see him again—and to see him in his own familiar habitat, at home.

32 A few days later I called on Dr. P. and his wife at home, with the score of the *Dichterliebe* in my briefcase (I knew he liked Schumann), and a variety of odd objects for the testing of perception. Mrs. P. showed me into a lofty apartment, which recalled fin-de-siècle Berlin. A magnificent old Bösendorfer stood in state in the centre of the room, and all around it were music stands, instruments, scores. . . . There were books, there were paintings, but the music was central. Dr. P. came in, a little bowed, and, distracted, advanced with outstretched hands to the grandfather clock, but, hearing my voice, corrected himself, and shook hands with me. We exchanged greetings and chatted a little of current concerts and performances. Diffidently, I asked him if he would sing.

33 "The *Dichterliebe!*" he exclaimed. "But I can no longer read music. You will play them, yes?"

34 I said I would try. On that wonderful old piano even my playing sounded right, and Dr. P. was an aged but infinitely mellow Fischer-Dieskau, combining a perfect ear and voice with the most incisive musical intelligence. It was clear that the Music School was not keeping him on out of charity.

35 Dr. P.'s temporal lobes were obviously intact: he had a wonderful musical cortex. What, I wondered, was going on in his parietal and occipital lobes, especially in those areas where visual processing occurred? I carry the Platonic solids in my neurological kit and decided to start with these.

36 "What is this?" I asked, drawing out the first one.

37 "A cube, of course."

38 "Now this?" I asked, brandishing another.

39 He asked if he might examine it, which he did swiftly and systematically: "A dodecahedron, of course. And don't bother with the others—I'll get the icosahedron, too."

40 Abstract shapes clearly presented no problems. What about faces? I took out a pack of cards. All of these he identified instantly, including the jacks, queens, kings, and the joker. But these, after all, are stylised designs, and it was impossible to tell whether he saw faces or merely patterns. I decided I would show him a volume of cartoons which I had in my briefcase. Here, again, for the most part, he did well. Churchill's cigar, Schnozzle's nose: as soon as he had picked out a key feature he could identify the face. But cartoons, again, are formal and schematic. It remained to be seen how he would do with real faces, realistically represented.

41 I turned on the television, keeping the sound off, and found an early Bette Davis film. A love scene was in progress. Dr. P. failed to identify the actress—but this could have been because she had never entered his world. What was more striking was that he failed to identify the expressions on her face or her partner's, though in the course of a single torrid scene these passed from sultry yearning through passion, surprise, disgust, and fury to a melting reconciliation. Dr. P. could make nothing of any of this. He was very unclear as to what was going on, or who was who or even what sex they were. His comments on the scene were positively Martian.

42 It was just possible that some of his difficulties were associated with the unreality of a celluloid, Hollywood world; and it occurred to me that he might be more successful in identifying faces from his own life. On the walls of the apartment there were photographs of his family, his colleagues, his pupils, himself. I gathered a pile of these together and, with some misgivings, presented them to him. What had been funny, or farcical, in relation to the movie, was tragic in relation to real life. By and large, he recognised nobody: neither his family, nor

his colleagues, nor his pupils, nor himself. He recognised a portrait of Einstein because he picked up the characteristic hair and moustache; and the same thing happened with one or two other people. "Ach, Paul!" he said, when shown a portrait of his brother. "That square jaw, those big teeth—I would know Paul anywhere!" But was it Paul he recognised, or one or two of his features, on the basis of which he could make a reasonable guess as to the subject's identity? In the absence of obvious "markers," he was utterly lost. But it was not merely the cognition, the *gnosis,* at fault; there was something radically wrong with the whole way he proceeded. For he approached these faces—even of those near and dear—as if they were abstract puzzles or tests. He did not relate to them, he did not behold. No face was familiar to him, seen as a "thou," being just identified as a set of features, an "it." Thus, there was formal, but no trace of personal, gnosis. And with this went his indifference, or blindness, to expression. A face, to us, is a person looking out—we see, as it were, the person through his *persona,* his face. But for Dr. P. there was no *persona* in this sense—no outward *persona,* and no person within.

43 I had stopped at a florist on my way to his apartment and bought myself an extravagant red rose for my buttonhole. Now I removed this and handed it to him. He took it like a botanist or morphologist given a specimen, not like a person given a flower.

44 "About six inches in length," he commented. "A convoluted red form with a linear green attachment."

45 "Yes," I said encouragingly, "and what do you think it *is,* Dr. P.?"

46 "Not easy to say." He seemed perplexed. "It lacks the simple symmetry of the Platonic solids, although it may have a higher symmetry of its own. . . . I think this could be an inflorescence or flower."

47 "Could be?" I queried.

48 "Could be," he confirmed.

49 "Smell it," I suggested, and he again looked somewhat puzzled, as if I had asked him to smell a higher symmetry. But he complied courteously, and took it to his nose. Now, suddenly, he came to life.

50 "Beautiful!" he exclaimed. "An early rose. What a heavenly smell!" He started to hum "*Die Rose, die Lillie . . .*" Reality, it seemed, might be conveyed by smell, not by sight.

51 I tried one final test. It was still a cold day, in early spring, and I had thrown my coat and gloves on the sofa.

52 "What is this?" I asked, holding up a glove.

53 "May I examine it?" he asked, and, taking it from me, he proceeded to examine it as he had examined the geometrical shapes.

54 "A continuous surface," he announced at last, "infolded on itself. It appears to have"—he hesitated—"five outpouchings, if this is the word."

55 "Yes," I said cautiously. "You have given me a description. Now tell me what it is."

56 "A container of some sort?"

57 "Yes," I said, "and what would it contain?"

58 "It would contain its contents!" said Dr. P., with a laugh. "There are many possibilities. It could be a change purse, for example, for coins of five sizes. It could . . . "

59 I interrupted the barmy flow. "Does it not look familiar? Do you think it might contain, might fit, a part of your body?"

60 No light of recognition dawned on his face.[1]

61 No child would have the power to see and speak of "a continuous surface . . . infolded on itself," but any child, any infant, would immediately know a glove as a glove, see it as familiar, as going with a hand. Dr. P. didn't. He saw nothing as familiar. Visually, he was lost in a world of lifeless abstractions. Indeed, he did not have a real visual world, as he did not have a real visual self. He could speak about things, but did not see them face-to-face. Hughlings Jackson, discussing patients with aphasia and left-hemisphere lesions, says they have lost "abstract" and "propositional" thought—and compares them with dogs (or, rather, he compares dogs to patients with aphasia). Dr. P., on the other hand, functioned precisely as a machine functions. It wasn't merely that he displayed the same indifference to the visual world as a computer but—even more strikingly—he construed the world as a computer construes it, by means of key features and schematic relationships. The scheme might be identified—in an "identi-kit" way—without the reality being grasped at all.

62 The testing I had done so far told me nothing about Dr. P.'s inner world. Was it possible that his visual memory and imagination were still intact? I asked him to imagine entering one of our local squares from the north side, to walk through it, in imagination or in memory,

[1] Later, by accident, he got it on, and exclaimed, "My God, it's a glove!" This was reminiscent of Kurt Goldstein's patient "Lanuti," who could only recognise objects by trying to use them in action.

and tell me the buildings he might pass as he walked. He listed the buildings on his right side, but none of those on his left. I then asked him to imagine entering the square from the south. Again he mentioned only those buildings that were on the right side, although these were the very buildings he had omitted before. Those he had "seen" internally before were not mentioned now; presumably, they were no longer "seen." It was evident that his difficulties with leftness, his visual field deficits, were as much internal as external, bisecting his visual memory and imagination.

63 What, at a higher level, of his internal visualisation? Thinking of the almost hallucinatory intensity with which Tolstoy visualises and animates his characters, I questioned Dr. P. about *Anna Karenina.* He could remember incidents without difficulty, had an undiminished grasp of the plot, but completely omitted visual characteristics, visual narrative, and scenes. He remembered the words of the characters but not their faces; and though, when asked, he could quote, with his remarkable and almost verbatim memory, the original visual descriptions, these were, it became apparent, quite empty for him and lacked sensorial, imaginal, or emotional reality. Thus, there was an internal agnosia as well.[2]

64 But this was only the case, it became clear, with certain sorts of visualisation. The visualisation of faces and scenes, of visual narrative and drama—this was profoundly impaired, almost absent. But the visualisation of *schemata* was preserved, perhaps enhanced. Thus, when I engaged him in a game of mental chess, he had no difficulty visualising the chessboard or the moves—indeed, no difficulty in beating me soundly.

65 Luria said of Zazetsky that he had entirely lost his capacity to play games but that his "vivid imagination" was unimpaired. Zazetsky and Dr. P. lived in worlds which were mirror images of each other. But the saddest difference between them was that Zazetsky, as Luria said, "fought to regain his lost faculties with the indomitable tenacity of the damned," whereas Dr. P. was not fighting, did not know what was lost,

[2] I have often wondered about Helen Keller's visual descriptions, whether these, for all their eloquence, are somehow empty as well? Or whether, by the transference of images from the tactile to the visual, or, yet more extraordinarily, from the verbal and the metaphorical to the sensorial and the visual, she *did* achieve a power of visual imagery, even though her visual cortex had never been stimulated, directly, by the eyes? But in Dr. P.'s case it is precisely the cortex that was damaged, the organic prerequisite of all pictorial imagery. Interestingly and typically he no longer dreamed pictorially—the "message" of the dream being conveyed in nonvisual terms.

did not indeed know that anything was lost. But who was more tragic, or who was more damned—the man who knew it, or the man who did not?

66 When the examination was over, Mrs. P. called us to the table, where there was coffee and a delicious spread of little cakes. Hungrily, hummingly, Dr. P. started on the cakes. Swiftly, fluently, unthinkingly, melodiously, he pulled the plates towards him and took this and that in a great gurgling stream, an edible song of food, until, suddenly, there came an interruption: a loud, peremptory rat-tat-tat at the door. Startled, taken aback, arrested by the interruption, Dr. P. stopped eating and sat frozen, motionless, at the table, with an indifferent, blind bewilderment on his face. He saw, but no longer saw, the table; no longer perceived it as a table laden with cakes. His wife poured him some coffee: the smell titillated his nose and brought him back to reality. The melody of eating resumed.

67 How does he do anything? I wondered to myself. What happens when he's dressing, goes to the lavatory, has a bath? I followed his wife into the kitchen and asked her how, for instance, he managed to dress himself. "It's just like the eating," she explained. "I put his usual clothes out, in all the usual places, and he dresses without difficulty, singing to himself. He does everything singing to himself. But if he is interrupted and loses the thread, he comes to a complete stop, doesn't know his clothes—or his own body. He sings all the time—eating songs, dressing songs, bathing songs, everything. He can't do anything unless he makes it a song."

68 While we were talking my attention was caught by the pictures on the walls.

69 "Yes," Mrs. P. said, "he was a gifted painter as well as a singer. The School exhibited his pictures every year."

70 I strolled past them curiously—they were in chronological order. All his earlier work was naturalistic and realistic, with vivid mood and atmosphere, but finely detailed and concrete. Then, years later, they became less vivid, less concrete, less realistic and naturalistic, but far more abstract, even geometrical and cubist. Finally, in the last paintings, the canvasses became nonsense, or nonsense to me—mere chaotic lines and blotches of paint. I commented on this to Mrs. P.

71 "Ach, you doctors, you're such Philistines!" she exclaimed. "Can you not see *artistic development*—how he renounced the realism of his earlier years, and advanced into abstract, nonrepresentational art?"

72 "No, that's not it," I said to myself (but forbore to say it to poor Mrs. P.). He had indeed moved from realism to nonrepresentation to

the abstract, yet this was not the artist, but the pathology, advancing—advancing towards a profound visual agnosia, in which all powers of representation and imagery, all sense of the concrete, all sense of reality, were being destroyed. This wall of paintings was a tragic pathological exhibit, which belonged to neurology, not art.

73 And yet, I wondered, was she not partly right? For there is often a struggle, and sometimes, even more interestingly, a collusion between the powers of pathology and creation. Perhaps, in his cubist period, there might have been both artistic and pathological development, colluding to engender an original form; for as he lost the concrete, so he might have gained in the abstract, developing a greater sensitivity to all the structural elements of line, boundary, contour—an almost Picasso-like power to see, and equally depict, those abstract organisations embedded in, and normally lost in, the concrete. . . . Though in the final pictures, I feared, there was only chaos and agnosia.

74 We returned to the great music room, with the Bösendorfer in the centre, and Dr. P. humming the last torte.

75 "Well, Dr. Sacks," he said to me. "You find me an interesting case, I perceive. Can you tell me what you find wrong, make recommendations?"

76 "I can't tell you what I find wrong," I replied, "but I'll say what I find right. You are a wonderful musician, and music is your life. What I would prescribe, in a case such as yours, is a life which consists entirely of music. Music has been the centre, now make it the whole, of your life."

77 This was four years ago—I never saw him again, but I often wondered about how he apprehended the world, given his strange loss of image, visuality, and the perfect preservation of a great musicality. I think that music, for him, had taken the place of image. He had no body-image, he had body-music: this is why he could move and act as fluently as he did, but came to a total confused stop if the "inner music" stopped. And equally with the outside, the world . . .[3]

78 In *The World as Representation and Will,* Schopenhauer speaks of music as "pure will." How fascinated he would have been by Dr. P., a man who had wholly lost the world as representation, but wholly preserved it as music or will.

---

[3] Thus, as I learned later from his wife, though he could not recognise his students if they sat still, if they were merely "images," he might suddenly recognise them if they *moved.* "That's Karl," he would cry. "I know his movements, his body-music."

79 And this, mercifully, held to the end—for despite the gradual advance of his disease (a massive tumor or degenerative process in the visual parts of his brain) Dr. P. lived and taught music to the last days of his life.

Understanding Meaning

1. How does Sacks *describe* Dr. P.'s initial symptoms? What led Dr. P. to seek medical help?
2. What is prosopagnosia? How does Sacks demonstrate its effects?
3. What is Sacks trying to tell readers about how the brain connects perceptions to meaning? Does he use the plight of one patient to demonstrate how our brains operate normally?
4. What did the glove test reveal about Dr. P.'s condition?
5. How does Sacks explain how a person who failed to distinguish his hat from his wife or his shoe from his foot could continue to teach a complex subject like music?
6. *Critical Thinking:* On page 79 Sacks presented "with some misgivings" family pictures for Dr. P. to identify. Why was he reluctant to administer this test? Does this suggest that even doctors, like family members, prefer to deny the seriousness of a patient's condition?

Evaluating Strategy

1. Sacks organizes his writing in a format standard to scientific and medical discourse. He *describes* symptoms, and then provides an *analysis.* Is this method easy for general readers to follow?
2. What role does Sacks play in the narrative?
3. *Other Modes:* What parts of the narrative include *description, comparison, analysis, definition,* and *cause and effect?* What does the use of these modes reveal about the scientific methods Sacks employs to examine a patient and determine his condition?

Appreciating Language

1. What reaction did you have to Sacks's level of language? Did you find his use of scientific terminology a barrier to meaning, or could you understand much of it through context?
2. Look up the words *dementia, parietal lobe, opthalmologist, gnosis,* and *persona.*

3. Can a reader understand the *thesis* of Sacks's narrative without knowing the definitions of *ophthalmoscope, fin-de-siècle,* or *empirical?*
4. In explaining some of Dr. P.'s baffling observations, Sacks describes them as being "Martian." How does this metaphor help a general reader grasp the effect of this disorder?

Connections across the Disciplines

1. How does Sacks's role as doctor compare to the role Jane Goodall plays in "First Observations" (page 68)? Do they both strive to objectively observe their subjects?
2. What role does close observation play in the narrative? How does Sacks embody the "look again, look again" approach described by Samuel Scudder (page 41)?

Writing Suggestions

1. Write a few paragraphs relating an incident in which you observed or encountered someone's puzzling behavior. Use detailed observations to share with readers the actions and statements you found intriguing, bizarre, or frightening.
2. *Critical Writing:* Sacks tells his patient he cannot find out what is wrong and urges him to accept what is right and make music the whole of his life. Did Sacks fail as a physician because he could not "cure" Dr. P.? Write a short paper in response to the assertion that people expect too much from doctors.
3. *Collaborative Writing:* Work with other students to generate a one-paragraph *definition* of prosopagnosia based on the information provided in Sacks's article. Read the paragraph aloud to the group, and have each member comment on its accuracy.

FEDERAL BUREAU OF INVESTIGATION

At 12:30 P.M. on November 22, 1963, President John F. Kennedy was assassinated in Dallas, Texas. An hour and a half later a twenty-four-year-old man named Lee Harvey Oswald was arrested following a scuffle in a movie theater. Oswald was suspected of murdering the president and a Dallas police officer. Witnesses reported seeing Oswald taking a long package into the Texas School Book Depository, the building where he was employed, overlooking the site of the assassination. In the early hours of November 23, Oswald was charged with murder and interrogated by Federal Bureau of Investigation (FBI) agents.

Interrogation of Lee Harvey Oswald

This FBI report records statements made by Lee Harvey Oswald in response to questions and summarizes his account of his movements on November 22. Notice that the writer uses simple, direct language free of figurative expressions or personal responses to create an objective, fact-driven account.[1]

1 LEE HARVEY OSWALD was interviewed by Captain J. W. FRITZ, Homicide and Robbery Bureau, Dallas Police Department. OSWALD was advised of the identity of SA JAMES W. BOOKHOUT, and his capacity as a Special Agent of the Federal Bureau of Investigation. He was informed of his right to an attorney, that any statement he might make could be used against him in a court of law, and that any statement which he might make must be free and voluntary. He furnished the following information in the presence of T. J. NULLY, U.S. Secret Service; DAVID B. GRANT, Secret Service; ROBERT I. NASH, United States Marshall; and Detectives BILLY L. SENKEL and FAY M. TURNER of the Homicide and Robbery Bureau, Dallas Police Department.

[1] This document contains neither recommendations nor conclusions of the FBI. It was recorded by Special Agent James W. Bookhout in Dallas, Texas on November 23, 1963 and dictated on November 24, 1963.

2 Following his departure from the Texas School Book Depository, he boarded a city bus to his residence and obtained transfer upon departure from the bus. He stated that officers at the time of arresting him took his transfer out of his pocket.

3 OSWALD advised that he had only one post office box which was at Dallas, Texas. He denied bringing any package to work on the morning of November 22, 1963. He stated that he was not in the process of fixing up his apartment and he denied telling WESLEY FRAZIER that the purpose of his visit to Irving, Texas, on the night of November 21, 1963, was to obtain some curtain rods from MRS. RUTH PAINE.

4 OSWALD stated that it was not exactly true as recently stated by him that he rode a bus from his place of employment to his residence on November 22, 1963. He stated actually he did board a city bus at his place of employment but that after about a block or two, due to traffic congestion, he left the bus and rode a city cab to his apartment on North Beckley. He recalled that at the time of getting into the cab, some lady looked in and asked the driver to call her a cab. He stated that he might have made some remarks to the cab driver merely for the purpose of passing the time of day at that time. He recalled that his fare was approximately 85 cents. He stated that after arriving at his apartment, he changed his shirt and trousers because they were dirty. He described his dirty clothes as being a reddish colored, long sleeved, shirt with a button-down collar and gray colored trousers. He indicated that he had placed these articles of clothing in the lower drawer of his dresser.

5 OSWALD stated that on November 22, 1963, he had eaten lunch in the lunch room at the Texas School Book Depository, alone, but recalled possibly two Negro employees walking through the room during this period. He stated possibly one of these employees was called "Junior" and the other was a short individual whose name he could not recall but whom he would be able to recognize. He stated that his lunch had consisted of a cheese sandwich and an apple which he had obtained at MRS. RUTH PAINE'S residence in Irving, Texas, upon his leaving for work that morning.

6 OSWALD stated that MRS. PAINE receives no pay for keeping his wife and children at her residence. He stated that their presence in MRS. PAINE'S residence is a good arrangement for her because of her language interest, indicating that his wife speaks Russian and MRS. PAINE is interested in the Russian language.

7 OSWALD denied having kept a rifle in MRS. PAINE'S garage at Irving, Texas, but stated that he did have certain articles stored in her

garage, consisting of two sea bags, a couple of suitcases, and several boxes of kitchen articles and also kept his clothes at MRS. PAINE'S residence. He stated that all of the articles in MRS. PAINE'S garage had been brought there about September, 1963, from New Orleans, Louisiana.

8 OSWALD stated that he has had no visitors at his apartment on North Beckley.

9 OSWALD stated that he has no receipts for purchase of any guns and has never ordered any guns and does not own a rifle nor has he ever possessed a rifle.

10 OSWALD denied that he is a member of the Communist Party.

11 OSWALD stated that he purchased a pistol, which was taken off him by police officers November 22, 1963, about six months ago. He declined to state where he had purchased it.

12 OSWALD stated that he arrived about July, 1962, from USSR and was interviewed by the FBI at Fort Worth, Texas. He stated that he felt they overstepped their bounds and had used various tactics in interviewing him.

13 He further complained that on interview of RUTH PAINE by the FBI regarding his wife, that he felt that his wife was intimidated.

14 OSWALD stated that he desired to contact Attorney ABT, New York City, indicating that ABT was the attorney who had defended the Smith Act case about 1949–1950. He stated that he does not know Attorney ABT personally. Captain FRITZ advised OSWALD that arrangements would be immediately made whereby he could call Attorney ABT.

15 OSWALD stated that prior to coming to Dallas from New Orleans he had resided at a furnished apartment at 4706 Magazine Street, New Orleans, Louisiana. While in New Orleans, he had been employed by WILLIAM B. RILEY Company, 640 Magazine Street, New Orleans.

16 OSWALD stated that he has nothing against President JOHN F. KENNEDY personally; however in view of the present charges against him, he did not desire to discuss this phase further.

17 OSWALD stated that he could not agree to take a polygraph examination without the advice of counsel. He added that in the past he has refused to take polygraph examinations.

18 OSWALD stated that he is a member of the American Civil Liberties Union and added that MRS. RUTH PAINE was also a member of same.

19 With regard to Selective Service card in the possession of OSWALD bearing photograph of OSWALD and the name of ALEX

JAMES HIDELL, OSWALD admitted that he carried this Selective Service card but declined to state that he wrote the signature of ALEX J. HIDELL appearing on same. He further declined to state the purpose of carrying same or any use he has made of same.

20 OSWALD stated that an address book in his possession contains the names of various Russian immigrants residing in Dallas, Texas, whom he has visited with.

21 OSWALD denied shooting President JOHN F. KENNEDY on November 22, 1963, and added that he did not know that Governor JOHN CONNALLY had been shot and denied any knowledge concerning this incident.

Understanding Meaning

1. What is the writer's goal in this narrative?
2. Does the writer seek to imply OSWALD's guilt in any way? What attitude, if any, does the writer project toward his subject?
3. *Critical Thinking: Analyze* this report in light of your own knowledge of the Kennedy assassination. How is looking at an actual document different from reading a narrative written by a historian or journalist?

Evaluating Strategy

1. How does the writer structure the narrative?
2. What does the agent do to create as much objectivity as possible?
3. *Other Modes:* Where does the agent use *description* in his report to create a picture of Lee Harvey OSWALD? How objective is it?
4. *Critical Thinking:* How is writing an internal document to a specific reader different from addressing a general audience in a book or magazine article?

Appreciating Language

1. At first glance this report appears to break all the "rules" of good writing. It is flat, colorless, and repetitive. Why is this kind of writing acceptable in this context? Why would the use of lively, colorful imagery defeat the purpose of the report?
2. *Critical Thinking:* Examine this report the way a prospective defense attorney might, looking for evidence of prejudice against the accused. Can you find any examples?

Connections across the Disciplines

1. In "First Observations" (page 68) and "The Man Who Mistook His Wife for His Hat" (page 75) professionals record observations of subjects. Would their notes or academic reports to colleagues likely read much like this one?
2. Does the text of this report by a law enforcement officer bear similarities to scientific observations made by Dr. Robert Peter Gale and Thomas Hauser (page 63)?

Writing Suggestions

1. Imagine you are writing a highly factual novel based on the Kennedy assassination. Rewrite a passage from this report using dialogue, gestures, descriptions. Add the agent's tone of voice, describe OSWALD's facial expression, tell readers about the furniture in the room, and create a sense of tension, fatigue, or anger.
2. *Collaborative Writing:* Working with three or four students, write a purely objective report of the incident Nathan McCall describes during the assembly (page 47). Imagine your report will be read by the school board and several attorneys. Eliminate McCall's personal reflections, and state simply and directly what occurred in objective terms. Read the text aloud, and ask group members to identify statements that are subjective or make judgments without proof.

WALTER LORD

Walter Lord (1917–) was born in Baltimore and studied history at Princeton University. He entered Yale Law School, but his studies were interrupted by World War II. After serving with the Office of Strategic Services, he returned to law school. He served as editor in chief of a business information service but soon turned to writing history. He tracked down and interviewed the sixty-three living survivors of the Titanic *and studied the ship's records to produce* A Night to Remember, *a minute-by-minute account of the doomed luxury liner. Lord's style of blending fact with tense human drama made his book a best seller. His later books include* Day of Infamy, *about the Japanese attack on Pearl Harbor, and* Incredible Victory, *which tells the story of the Battle of Midway.*

The Reconstructed Logbook of the *Titanic*

A Night to Remember *tells the dramatic story of the famous liner that sank on its maiden voyage in 1912. Considered "unsinkable" by its builders, the* Titanic *had only twenty lifeboats for its 2,207 passengers. Rescuers located 705 survivors, many of them picked up in half-empty boats. To assist readers in following the chronology of events, Lord placed a reconstructed logbook of the ship in the appendix of his book.*

April 10, 1912	
12 noon	Leaves Southampton dock; narrowly escapes collision with American liner *New York*.
7:00 P.M.	Stops at Cherbourg for passengers.
9:00 P.M.	Leaves Cherbourg for Queenstown.
April 11, 1912	
12:30 P.M.	Stops at Queenstown for passengers and mail. One crewman deserts.
2:00 P.M.	Leaves Queenstown for New York, carrying 1316 passengers and 891 crew.
April 14, 1912	
9:00 A.M.	*Caronia* reports ice Latitude 42°N from Longitude 49° to 51° W.
1:42 P.M.	*Baltic* reports ice Latitude 41°51′N from Longitude 49°52′W.
1:45 P.M.	*Amerika* reports ice Latitude 41°27′N, Longitude 50°8′W.

7:00 P.M.	Temperature 43°.
7:30 P.M.	Temperature 39°.
7:30 P.M.	*Californian* reports ice Latitude 42°3′N, Longitude 49°9′W.
9:00 P.M.	Temperature 33°.
9:30 P.M.	Second Officer Lightoller warns carpenter and engine room to watch fresh water supply—may freeze up; warns crow's-nest to watch for ice.
9:40 P.M.	*Mesaba* reports ice Latitude 42°N to 41°25′N, Longitude 49° to 50°30′W.
10:00 P.M.	Temperature 32°.
10:30 P.M.	Temperature of sea down to 31°.
11:00 P.M.	*Californian* warns of ice, but cut off before she gives location.
11:40 P.M.	Collides with iceberg Latitude 41°46′N, Longitude 50° 14′W.
April 15, 1912	
12:05 A.M.	Orders given to uncover the boats, muster the crew and passengers.
12:15 A.M.	First wireless call for help.
12:45 A.M.	First rocket fired.
12:45 A.M.	First boat, No. 7, lowered.
1:40 A.M.	Last rocket fired.
2:05 A.M.	Last boat, Collapsible D, lowered.
2:10 A.M.	Last wireless signals sent.
2:18 A.M.	Lights fail.
2:20 A.M.	Ship founders.
3:30 A.M.	*Carpathia's* rockets sighted by boats.
4:10 A.M.	First boat, No. 2, picked up by *Carpathia*.
8:30 A.M.	Last boat, No. 12, picked up.
8:50 A.M.	*Carpathia* heads for New York with 705 survivors.

Understanding Meaning

1. What is the goal of presenting events in a time line?
2. How does this log assist readers to follow events in a complex story such as a disaster involving hundreds of people?
3. Why would this log be valuable to a board of inquiry investigating the disaster?
4. *Critical Thinking:* According to the log, it took forty minutes to launch the first lifeboat. Although the crew had more than two and one-half hours to evacuate the ship, fifteen hundred people were lost. Do these facts alone raise suspicion of incompetence?

Evaluating Strategy

1. Can such a log as this distort events by emphasizing time relationships instead of causal relationships?
2. How does a writer deal with events that do not have a clear time reference?

Appreciating Language

1. Why is word choice important in brief notations such as those in a log?
2. Can you locate any words that are not objective?

Connections across the Disciplines

1. How is Lord's time line similar to the FBI report on Lee Harvey Oswald?
2. Would a time line assist readers in understanding narratives such as Dr. Robert Peter Gale and Thomas Hauser's "Final Warning" (page 63)? Why or why not?

Writing Suggestions

1. Reconstruct a log of the actions you took yesterday. Consider the problems that arise in attempting to explain events that did not occur in a specific time frame.
2. *Collaborative Writing:* Working with a group of students, read the log and discuss your impressions. Should a luxury liner be able to safely evacuate its passengers in two hours? Write a paragraph summarizing your group's discussion.

GUIDELINES FOR WRITING NARRATION

1. **Determine your purpose.** Does your narrative have a goal beyond simply telling a story? What details or evidence do readers need to accept your point of view?
2. **Define your role.** As a narrator you can write in first person, either as the major participant in or a witness to events. You can use third person for greater objectivity, inserting personal opinions if desired.
3. **Consider your audience.** What are your readers' needs and expectations? How much background material will you have to supply? Which events will the audience find most impressive?
4. **Review the discipline or writing situation.** If you are writing a narrative report as an employee or agent of an organization, study samples to determine how you should present your story.
5. **Identify the beginning and end of your narrative.** You may find it helpful to place background information in a separate forward or introduction and limit comments on the ending to an afterward. This can allow the body of the paper to focus on a specific chain of events.
6. **Select a chronological pattern.** After reviewing the context of the narrative, determine which pattern would be most effective for your purpose—using a straight chronology, opening with a mid- or turning point, or presenting the final events first.
7. **Make use of transitional statements.** To prevent readers from becoming confused, make clear transitional statements to move the narrative. Statements such as "later that day" or "two weeks later" can help readers follow the passage of time. Clear transitions are important if you alter chronological order with flashbacks and flash-forwards.

SUGGESTED TOPICS FOR WRITING NARRATION

General Assignments

Write a narrative on any of the following topics. Your narrative may contain passages making use of other modes, such as definition or comparison. Choose your narrative structure carefully, and avoid including minor details that add little to the story line. Use flashbacks and flash-forwards carefully. Transitional statements, paragraphing, and line breaks can help clarify changes in the chronology.

1. Your first job interview
2. Moving into your first dorm room or apartment

3. The events that led you to take a major action—quit a job, end a relationship, or join an organization
4. A sporting event you played in or observed—you may wish to limit the narrative to a single play.
5. A first date
6. An event that placed you in danger
7. An experience that led you to change your opinion about a friend or family member
8. A typical day at school or your job
9. The worst day of your college career
10. An accident or medical emergency—focus on creating a clear, minute-by-minute chronology.

Writing in Context

1. Imagine you are participating in an experiment. Psychologists ask you to write a journal recording your experiences in college. Specifically, the researchers are interested in measuring stressors students face—deadlines, lack of sleep, conflicts with jobs, financial pressures. Write a diary for a week, detailing instances when you experience stress. Be as objective as possible.
2. Write a letter to a friend relating the events of a typical day in college. Select details your friend will find humorous or interesting.
3. Preserve on paper a favorite story told by your grandparents or other relatives. Include background details and identify characters.
4. You are accused of committing a crime last Tuesday. Create a detailed log to the best of your recollection of the day's events and your movements to establish an alibi.

NARRATION CHECKLIST

1. Does the narrative have a clear focus?
2. Can readers follow the chronology of events?
3. Do you write in a consistent tense or time? Does your paper contain illogical shifts from past to present?
4. Does the narrative flow evenly, or is it bogged down with unnecessary detail?
5. Does your narrative maintain a consistent point of view? Do you switch from first to third person without reason?
6. Does your narrative suit your purpose, reader, discipline, or situation?

3

DESCRIPTION

PRESENTING IMPRESSIONS

WHAT IS DESCRIPTION?

Description captures the essence of a person, place, object, or condition through sensory details. Nearly all writing requires description. Before you can narrate events, compare, classify, or analyze, you must provide readers with a clear picture of your subject. Dramatists open plays with set and character descriptions. Homicide detectives begin reports with descriptions of crime scenes. Before proposing expanding an airport, the writers of a government study must first describe congestion in the existing facility.

The way writers select and present details depends on context. Carl T. Rowan's article "Unforgettable Miss Bessie" (page 122), published in *Reader's Digest,* describes an influential teacher to a general audience reading for human interest:

> She was only about five feet tall and probably never weighed more than 110 pounds, but Miss Bessie was a towering presence in the classroom. She was the only woman tough enough to make me read *Beowulf* and think for a few foolish days that I liked it. From 1938 to 1942, when I attended Bernard High School in McMinnville, Tenn., she taught me English, history, civics—and a lot more than I realized.

Rowan's description includes details about the teacher's height and weight, the courses she taught, and the name of the school. But Rowan's focus is her "presence" and the impact she had in shaping his life. Writing in the first person, Rowan places himself in the essay to build rapport with his readers.

This intimate portrait contrasts sharply with the description of Lee Harvey Oswald included in an FBI report:

> OSWALD was advised questions were intended to obtain his complete physical description and background. Upon repetition of the question as to his present employment, he furnished same without further discussion.

Race	White
Sex	Male
Date of Birth	October 18, 1939
Place of Birth	New Orleans, Louisiana
Height	5′9″
Weight	140
Hair	Medium brown, worn medium length, needs haircut
Eyes	Blue-gray

Aside from noting that Oswald needed a haircut, the FBI agent never offers personal impressions and presents his observations in cold, factual statements. Unlike Rowan, who is writing to a general audience reading for entertainment, the FBI agent is preparing a report for a specialized reader who will use this information in a criminal investigation. The writer's statements will be scrutinized by investigators and attorneys. The introduction of any personal impressions or colorful phrases would be unprofessional and subject to challenge.

The differences between the descriptions of Miss Bessie and Lee Harvey Oswald illustrate the differences between *objective* and *subjective* description.

Objective and Subjective Description

The purpose of *objective* description is to inform readers by accurate reporting of factual details. Its language attempts to provide photographic realism of what people, places, things, and conditions are like. Research papers, business and government reports, and newspaper accounts of current events are objective. Objective description is effective when the writer's purpose is to present readers with information required to make an evaluation or decision. In many instances, it does not attempt to arouse a reader's interest since it is often written in response to reader demand.

Objective description focuses on facts and observable detail. *The New Illustrated Columbia Encyclopedia,* for example, offers readers this description of Chicago:

> The second largest city in the country and the heart of a metropolitan area of almost 7 million people, it is the commercial, financial, industrial, and cultural center for a vast region and a great midcontinental shipping port. It is a port of entry; a major Great Lakes port, located at the junction of the St. Lawrence Seaway with the Mississippi River system; the busiest air center in the country; and an important rail and highway hub.

In contrast to objective description, *subjective* description creates impressions through sensory details and imagery. Short stories, novels, essays, and opinion pieces use highly personal sensory details to create an individual sense of the subject. Instead of photographic realism, subjective description paints scenes, creates moods, or generates emotional responses. Providing accurate information is less important than giving readers a "feel" for the subject. In a subjective description of a car, the color, shape, ride, and the memories it evokes for the writer are more important than facts about horsepower, base price, and fuel efficiency.

Attempting to capture his view of Chicago, John Rechy compares the city to an expectant mother:

> You get the impression that once Chicago was like a constantly pregnant woman, uneasy in her pregnancy because she has miscarried so often. After its rise as a frontier town, plush bigtime madams, adventurers, and soon the titanic rise of the millionaires, the city's subsequent soaring population—all gave more than a hint that Chicago might easily become America's First City. But that title went unquestionably to New York. Brazenly, its skyscrapers, twice as tall as any in the Midwest city, symbolically invaded the sky. Chicago, in squat self-consciousness, bowed out. It became the Second City . . .

Rechy uses imagery and unconventional syntax to create a highly personalized view of the city. In the context of this essay written for a literary magazine, impression is more important than accuracy. Exact number and date statistics are irrelevant to his purpose. The writer's purpose in subjective description is to share a vision, not provide information.

Many writers blend the realism of objective description with the impressionistic details of subjective description to create striking portraits, such as Russell Miller's depiction of Chicago's State Street:

> Summer 1983. State Street, "that great street," is a dirty, desolate, and depressing street for most of its length. It runs straight and potholed from the Chicago city line, up through the black ghettos of the South Side, an aching wasteland of derelict factories pitted with broken windows, instant slum apartment blocks, vandalized playgrounds encased in chain-linked fencing, and vacant lots where weeds sprout gamely from the rubble and from the rusting hulks of abandoned automobiles. Those shops that remain open are protected by barricades of steel mesh. One or two men occupy every doorway, staring sullenly onto the street, heedless of the taunting cluster of skyscrapers to the north.

In this passage, details such as "vandalized playgrounds" are interwoven with expressions granting human emotions to inanimate objects so wastelands are "aching" and skyscrapers "taunting." Blended descriptions such as this one are useful in strengthening subjective views with factual details. This style of writing is used by journalists and freelance authors writing to audiences who may be reading for both enjoyment and information.

Whether objective or subjective, all descriptive writing communicates through detail—through a careful selection and clear presentation of facts or impressions that serve the writer's purpose and impress readers.

The Language of Description

Words have power. The impact descriptive writing makes depends on *diction*, the writer's choice of words. Whether your description is objective, subjective, or a blend, the words you select should be accurate, appropriate, and effective. In choosing words, consider your purpose, readers, and discipline.

Use Words Precisely

Many words are easily confused. Should a patient's heart rate be monitored "continually"—meaning at regular intervals such as once an hour, or "continuously"—meaning without interruption? Is the city council planning to "adapt" or "adopt" a handgun ban? Some of the numerous pairs of frequently misused words follow:

allusion An indirect reference
illusion A false or imaginary impression

infer To interpret
imply To suggest

conscience A sense of moral or ethical conduct
conscious To be awake or aware of something

principle Basic law, rule, or concept
principal Something or someone important, as in school principal

When writing, consult a dictionary or review the usage section of a handbook to ensure you are using the correct word.

Use Concrete Words

Concrete words are direct and understandable. They communicate more information and make clearer impressions than vague, abstract words:

ABSTRACT	CONCRETE
motor vehicle	pickup truck
modest suburban home	three-bedroom colonial
human resources contingent	employees
protective headgear	helmet
residential rental unit	apartment

Eliminate Unnecessary Words

Avoid cluttering your description with words that add little or no meaning:

WORDY	IMPROVED
at this point in time	now
few in number	few
consensus of opinion	consensus
strike situation	strike
thunderstorm activity	thunderstorms
winter months	winter

Avoid Diluted Verbs

Verbs convey action. Do not dilute their meaning by turning them into wordy phrases that weaken their impact and obscure the action they describe:

DILUTED VERB	IMPROVED
achieve purification	purify
render an examination of	examine
are found to be in agreement	agree
conduct an analysis	analyze

Avoid Clichés and Inflated Phrases

Description uses figurative language such as *similes* (comparisons using *like* or *as*) and *metaphors* (direct comparisons). To be effective, figurative language should create fresh and appropriate impressions. Avoid *clichés* (overly used expressions) and inflated phrases that distort through exaggeration:

CLICHE/INFLATED	IMPROVED
crack of dawn	dawn
pretty as a picture	attractive

straight from the shoulder	direct
as plain as day	obvious
terrible disaster	disaster
in the whole world today	today

Understand the Roles of Denotation and Connotation

All words *denote* or indicate a particular meaning. The words *home, residence,* and *domicile* all refer to where a person lives. Each has the same basic meaning or denotation, but the word *home* evokes personal associations of family, friends, and favorite belongings. *Domicile,* on the other hand, has a legalistic and official sound devoid of personal associations.

Connotations are implied or suggested meanings. Connotations often reflect the writer's purpose and opinion. A resort cabin can be described as a "rustic cottage" or a "seedy shack" depending on a person's point of view. The person who spends little money and shops for bargains can be praised for being "frugal" or ridiculed for being "cheap."

The following pairs of words have the same basic meaning or denotation, but their connotations create different impressions:

young	inexperienced
traditional	old-fashioned
brave	reckless
casual	sloppy
the homeless	bums
residential care facility	nursing home
unintended landing	plane crash

Connotations shape meaning and in many contexts can be used to express opinion and influence readers. Depending on your point of view, graffiti can be seen as a "prank" or an "act of vandalism."

Be Conscious of Ethical Issues with Connotation Words can be selected to dramatize or minimize an event or situation. This raises ethical issues. Because words like *accident* and *explosion* might alarm the public, nuclear regulations substitute the terms *event* and *rapid disassembly.* When the space shuttle *Challenger* exploded in midair, the National Aeronautics and Space Administration (NASA) referred to a "major malfunction." Writers in all disciplines have to weigh the moral implications of the words they choose.

READING DESCRIPTIONS

While reading the descriptions in this chapter, keep these questions in mind.

Meaning

1. What is the author's goal—to inform, enlighten, share personal observations, or provide information demanded by others? What is the writer's role? Is he or she writing from a personal or professional perspective?
2. What is the intended audience—general or specific readers? How much knowledge does the author assume his or her readers have? Are technical terms defined? Does the description appear to have a special focus?
3. What is the nature of the discipline, discourse community, or writing situation? Is the description objective or subjective? Does the original source of the description (newsmagazine, scientific journal, or government document) reveal something about context?

Strategy

1. What details does the writer select? Does he or she seem to ignore or minimize some details?
2. Does the description seek to establish a dominant impression? Which details support this impression?
3. How are details organized? Does the author use a particular method of grouping observations?

Language

1. What level of language does the writer employ? Are technical terms used without explanation?
2. Does the language include connotations that shade reader reaction to the subject?

TRUMAN CAPOTE

Truman Capote (1924–1985) was born in New Orleans and first gained prominence as a writer of short stories. At age twenty-four he produced his first novel, Other Voices, Other Rooms, *which achieved international attention. His other works include* Breakfast at Tiffany's *and* A Tree of Night. *In 1965 he published* In Cold Blood, *which became an immediate best seller. Based on extensive research and interviews,* In Cold Blood *told the story of a 1959 mass murder of a Kansas farm family and the fate of the killers. Although nonfiction, Capote's book read much like a novel.* In Cold Blood *helped shape a new school of journalism that uses the stylistic touches of fiction to relate wholly factual events.*

Out There

The opening pages of In Cold Blood *describe the small town of Holcomb, Kansas, where the murders occurred. Capote spent a great deal of time in Holcomb and describes it almost as if it had been his own hometown.*

1 The village of Holcomb stands on the high wheat plains of western Kansas, a lonesome area that other Kansans call "out there." Some seventy miles east of the Colorado border, the countryside, with its hard blue skies and desert-clear air, has an atmosphere that is rather more Far Western than Middle West. The local accent is barbed with a prairie twang, a ranch-hand nasalness, and the men, many of them, wear narrow frontier trousers, Stetsons, and high-heeled boots with pointed toes. The land is flat, and the views are awesomely extensive; horses, herds of cattle, a white cluster of grain elevators rising as gracefully as Greek temples are visible long before a traveler reaches them.

2 Holcomb, too, can be seen from great distances. Not that there is much to see—simply an aimless congregation of buildings divided in the center by the main-line tracks of the Santa Fe Railroad, a haphazard hamlet bounded on the south by a brown stretch of the Arkansas (pronounced "Ar-kan-sas") River, on the north by a highway, Route 50, and on the east and west by prairie lands and wheat fields. After rain, or when snowfalls thaw, the streets, unnamed, unshaded, unpaved, turn from the thickest dust into the direst mud. At one end of

the town stands a stark old stucco structure, the roof of which supports an electric sign—Dance—but the dancing has ceased and the advertisement has been dark for several years. Nearby is another building with an irrelevant sign, this one in flaking gold on a dirty window—Holcomb Bank. The bank closed in 1933, and its former counting rooms have been converted into apartments. It is one of the town's two "apartment houses," the second being a ramshackle mansion known, because a good part of the local school's faculty lives there, as the Teacherage. But the majority of Holcomb's homes are one-story frame affairs, with front porches.

3 Down by the depot, the postmistress, a gaunt woman who wears a rawhide jacket and denims and cowboy boots, presides over a falling-apart post office. The depot itself, with its peeling sulphur-colored paint, is equally melancholy; the Chief, the Super Chief, the El Capitan go by every day, but these celebrated expresses never pause there. No passenger trains do—only an occasional freight. Up on the highway, there are two filling stations, one of which doubles as a meagerly supplied grocery store, while the other does extra duty as a café—Hartman's Café, where Mrs. Hartman, the proprietress, dispenses sandwiches, coffee, soft drinks, and 3.2 beer. (Holcomb, like all the rest of Kansas, is "dry.")

4 And that, really, is all. Unless you include, as one must, the Holcomb School, a good-looking establishment, which reveals a circumstance that the appearance of the community otherwise camouflages: that the parents who send their children to this modern and ably staffed "consolidated" school—the grades go from kindergarten through senior high, and a fleet of buses transport the students, of which there are usually around three hundred and sixty, from as far as sixteen miles away—are, in general, a prosperous people. Farm ranchers, most of them, they are outdoor folk of very varied stock—German, Irish, Norwegian, Mexican, Japanese. They raise cattle and sheep, grow wheat, milo, grass seed, and sugar beets. Farming is always a chancy business, but in western Kansas its practitioners consider themselves "born gamblers," for they must contend with an extremely shallow precipitation (the annual average is eighteen inches) and anguishing irrigation problems. However, the last seven years have been years of droughtless beneficence. The farm ranchers in Finney County, of which Holcomb is a part, have done well; money has been made not from farming alone but also from the exploitation of plentiful natural-

gas resources, and its acquisition is reflected in the new school, the comfortable interiors of the farmhouses, the steep and swollen grain elevators.

Until one morning in mid-November of 1959, few Americans—in fact, few Kansans—had ever heard of Holcomb. Like the waters of the river, like the motorists on the highway, and like the yellow trains streaking down the Santa Fe tracks, drama, in the shape of exceptional happenings, had never stopped there. The inhabitants of the village, numbering two hundred and seventy, were satisfied that this should be so, quite content to exist inside ordinary life—to work, to hunt, to watch television, to attend school socials, choir practice, meetings of the 4-H Club. But then, in the earliest hours of that morning in November, a Sunday morning, certain foreign sounds impinged on the normal nightly Holcomb noises—on the keening hysteria of coyotes, the dry scrape of scuttling tumbleweed, the racing, receding wail of locomotive whistles. At the time not a soul in sleeping Holcomb heard them—four shotgun blasts that, all told, ended six human lives. But afterward the townspeople, theretofore sufficiently unfearful of each other to seldom trouble to lock their doors, found fantasy re-creating them over and again—those somber explosions that stimulated fires of mistrust in the glare of which many old neighbors viewed each other strangely, and as strangers.

Understanding Meaning

1. How much of Capote's description can be considered objective, and how much appears subjective?
2. Capote includes a great deal of factual detail—names of highways, the number of students in the high school, and Holcomb's population. What do these facts add to the description?
3. What does Capote attempt to capture in his description of Holcomb?

Evaluating Strategy

1. *Critical Thinking:* A key element in the opening of any book is to get people's attention and motivate them to continue reading. How does Capote generate interest in describing a nondescript town?
2. What responses do the closing lines in this section of the story create?

Appreciating Language

1. How does the language of Capote's description differ from that of an encyclopedia or newspaper article?
2. *In Cold Blood* has sold millions of copies. What elements in Capote's style make his story about a crime in a small Kansas town so popular? What phrases strike you as being colorful or interesting?

Connections across the Disciplines

1. How does Capote's description of a small town compare with Luis Alberto Urrea's "Border Story" (page 109)? What attitudes do the writers have toward their subjects? What "feel" do they give the landscapes they describe?
2. Does Edward Abbey's "First Morning" (page 139) suggest a different view of nature and open spaces than Capote's "Out There"?

Writing Ideas

1. Rewrite a recent article from the local newspaper, adding subjective details to arouse human interest for a national audience. Include details about your community to give readers a feel for the location.
2. Using Capote's description of Holcomb as a resource, write a purely objective, one-paragraph description of the town. Include as much factual detail as possible.

LUIS ALBERTO URREA

Luis Alberto Urrea was born in Tijuana to a Mexican father and American mother. He grew up in San Diego and attended the University of California. After graduation and a brief career as a movie extra, Urrea worked with a volunteer organization that provides food, clothing, and medical supplies to the poor of northern Mexico. In 1982 he taught writing at Harvard. His most recent novel, In Search of Snow, *was published in 1994.*

Border Story

In this description of the Mexican-American border from Across the Wire: Life and Hard Times on the Mexican Border *(1993), Urrea uses the device of second person to place his reader in the scene. By making "you," the "illegal," he seeks to dramatize and humanize the plight of the poor seeking a new life in the United States.*

1 At night, the Border Patrol helicopters swoop and churn in the air all along the line. You can sit in the Mexican hills and watch them herd humans on the dusty slopes across the valley. They look like science fiction crafts, their hard-focused lights raking the ground as they fly.

2 Borderlands locals are so jaded by the sight of nightly people-hunting that it doesn't even register in their minds. But take a stranger to the border, and she will *see* the spectacle: monstrous Dodge trucks speeding into and out of the landscape; uniformed men patrolling with flashlights, guns, and dogs; spotlights; running figures; lines of people hurried onto buses by armed guards; and the endless clatter of the helicopters with their harsh white beams. A Dutch woman once told me it seemed altogether "un-American."

3 But the Mexicans keep on coming—and the Guatemalans, the Salvadorans, the Panamanians, the Colombians. The seven-mile stretch of Interstate 5 nearest the Mexican border is, at times, so congested with Latin American pedestrians that it resembles a town square.

4 They stick to the center island. Running down the length of the island is a cement wall. If the "illegals" (currently, "undocumented workers"; formerly, "wetbacks") are walking north and a Border Patrol

vehicle happens along, they simply hop over the wall and trot south. The officer will have to drive up to the 805 interchange, or Dairy Mart Road, swing over the overpasses, then drive south. Depending on where this pursuit begins, his detour could entail five to ten miles of driving. When the officer finally reaches the group, they hop over the wall and trot north. Furthermore, because freeway arrests would endanger traffic, the Border Patrol has effectively thrown up its hands in surrender.

5 It seems jolly on the page. But imagine poverty, violence, natural disasters, or political fear driving you away from everything you know. Imagine how bad things get to make you leave behind your family, your friends, your lovers; your home, as humble as it might be; your church, say. Let's take it further—you've said good-bye to the graveyard, the dog, the goat, the mountains where you first hunted, your grade school, your state, your favorite spot on the river where you fished and took time to think.

6 Then you come hundreds—or thousands—of miles across territory utterly unknown to you. (Chances are, you have never traveled farther than a hundred miles in your life.) You have walked, run, hidden in the backs of trucks, spent part of your precious money on bus fare. There is no AAA or Travelers Aid Society available to you. Various features of your journey north might include police corruption; violence in the forms of beatings, rape, murder, torture, road accidents; theft; incarceration. Additionally, you might experience loneliness, fear, exhaustion, sorrow, cold, heat, diarrhea, thirst, hunger. There is no medical attention available to you. There isn't even Kotex.

7 Weeks or months later, you arrive in Tijuana. Along with other immigrants, you gravitate to the bad parts of town because there is nowhere for you to go in the glittery sections where the *gringos* flock. You stay in a run-down little hotel in the red-light district, or behind the bus terminal. Or you find your way to the garbage dumps, where you throw together a small cardboard nest and claim a few feet of dirt for yourself. The garbage-pickers working this dump might allow you to squat, or they might come and rob you or burn you out for breaking some local rule you cannot possibly know beforehand. Sometimes the dump is controlled by a syndicate, and goon squads might come to you within a day. They want money, and if you can't pay, you must leave or suffer the consequences.

8 In town, you face endless victimization if you aren't streetwise. The police come after you, street thugs come after you, petty crimi-

nals come after you; strangers try your door at night as you sleep. Many shady men offer to guide you across the border, and each one wants all your money now, and promises to meet you at a prearranged spot. Some of your fellow travelers end their journeys right here—relieved of their savings and left to wait on a dark corner until they realize they are going nowhere.

9 If you are not Mexican, and can't pass as *tijuanense,* a local, the tough guys find you out. Salvadorans and Guatemalans are routinely beaten up and robbed. Sometimes they are disfigured. Indians—Chinantecas, Mixtecas, Guasaves, Zapotecas, Mayas—are insulted and pushed around; often they are lucky—they are merely ignored. They use this to their advantage. Often they don't dream of crossing into the United States: a Mexican tribal person would never be able to blend in, and they know it. To them, the garbage dumps and street vending and begging in Tijuana are a vast improvement over their former lives. As Doña Paula, a Chinanteca friend of mine who lives at the Tijuana garbage dump, told me, "This is the garbage dump. Take all you need. There's plenty here for *everyone!*"

10 If you are a woman, the men come after you. You lock yourself in your room, and when you must leave it to use the pestilential public bathroom at the end of your floor, you hurry, and you check every corner. Sometimes the lights are out in the toilet room. Sometimes men listen at the door. They call you "good-looking" and "bitch" and "*mamacita,*" and they make kissing sounds at you when you pass.

11 You're in the worst part of town, but you can comfort yourself—at least there are no death squads here. There are no torturers here, or bandit land barons riding into your house. This is the last barrier, you think, between you and the United States—*los Yunaites Estaites.*

12 You still face police corruption, violence, jail. You now also have a wide variety of new options available to you: drugs, prostitution, white slavery, crime. Tijuana is not easy on newcomers. It is a city that has always thrived on taking advantage of a sucker. And the innocent are the ultimate suckers in the Borderlands.

Understanding Meaning

1. Urrea has called the border a "battlefield." How does his description illustrate this view?
2. What problems do the undocumented aliens face in their attempt to cross the border?

3. How are non-Mexican refugees treated in Tijuana?
4. What is the plight of refugee women on the border?
5. *Critical Thinking:* Urrea quotes a Dutch woman who used the term "un-American" to describe the border patrols. What is un-American about fences and helicopter patrols? Does this response to immigration clash with the Statue of Liberty's promise to welcome the tired and poor?

Evaluating Strategy

1. How effective is the use of the second person? Does it really put "you" in the scene? Does it help dramatize the plight of people many readers might choose to ignore?
2. What details does Urrea use to dramatize conditions along the border?

Appreciating Language

1. Throughout the description, Urrea uses lists—"beatings, rape, murder, torture, road accidents. . . ." How effective are they? Can listing words become tedious?
2. Select the words that create the most powerful images of the border. Why do they make strong impressions?

Connections across the Disciplines

1. How does Urrea's attempt to introduce his reader to the border compare with Truman Capote's description of Holcomb (page 105)?
2. Does the poverty and violence immigrants face in Mexico suggest a reason why some of their descendants, such as the Chicano police officer in "The Fender-Bender" (page 58), reject their heritage?

Writing Suggestions

1. Write an essay describing a place that highlights a social problem. Select a location you have personal knowledge of, and try to convey the conditions residents face through lists of details.
2. *Collaborative Writing:* Ask a group of fellow students to respond to Urrea's account. Consider the issues his description of the border raises. Ask members to suggest how conditions could be improved, and then draft a short *persuasion* essay outlining your ideas.

JOAN DIDION

Joan Didion (1934–) was born in Sacramento and attended the University of California at Berkeley. After graduating in 1956, Didion became an associate editor for Vogue. *Didion achieved prominence in the 1960s for articles commenting on American life and society. Her novels* Play It As It Lays *and* A Book of Common Prayer *were published in the 1970s. She also has written nonfiction accounts of her travels to Central America. Her book* Miami *examines problems faced by Florida's Cuban population. She has collaborated with her husband John Gregory Dunne on a number of screenplays, including* A Star Is Born *and* True Confessions.

The Metropolitan Cathedral in San Salvador

Joan Didion traveled to El Salvador in the early 1980s, when the country was torn by a bitter civil war. In this description from her book El Salvador, *Didion offers a view of a cathedral which became a powerful political statement.*

1 During the week before I flew down to El Salvador a Salvadoran woman who works for my husband and me in Los Angeles gave me repeated instructions about what we must and must not do. We must not go out at night. We must stay off the street whenever possible. We must never ride in buses or taxis, never leave the capital, never imagine that our passports would protect us. We must not even consider the hotel a safe place: people were killed in hotels. She spoke with considerable vehemence, because two of her brothers had been killed in Salvador in August of 1981, in their beds. The throats of both brothers had been slashed. Her father had been cut but stayed alive. Her mother had been beaten. Twelve of her other relatives, aunts and uncles and cousins, had been taken from their houses one night the same August, and their bodies had been found some time later, in a ditch. I assured her that we would remember, we would be careful, we would in fact be so careful that we would probably (trying for a light touch) spend all our time in church.

2 She became still more agitated, and I realized that I had spoken as a *norteamericana:* churches had not been to this woman the neutral ground they had been to me. I must remember: Archbishop Romero killed saying mass in the chapel of the Divine Providence Hospital in San Salvador. I must remember: more than thirty people killed at Archbishop Romero's funeral in the Metropolitan Cathedral in San Salvador. I must remember: more than twenty people killed before that on the steps of the Metropolitan Cathedral. CBS had filmed it. It had been on television, the bodies jerking, those still alive crawling over the dead as they tried to get out of range. I must understand: the Church was dangerous.

3 I told her that I understood, that I knew all that, and I did, abstractly, but the specific meaning of the Church she knew eluded me until I was actually there, at the Metropolitan Cathedral in San Salvador, one afternoon when rain sluiced down its corrugated plastic windows and puddled around the supports of the Sony and Phillips billboards near the steps. The effect of the Metropolitan Cathedral is immediate, and entirely literary. This is the cathedral that the late Archbishop Oscar Arnulfo Romero refused to finish, on the premise that the work of the Church took precedence over its display, and the high walls of raw concrete bristle with structural rods, rusting now, staining the concrete, sticking out at wrenched and violent angles. The wiring is exposed. Fluorescent tubes hang askew. The great high altar is backed by warped plyboard. The cross on the altar is of bare incandescent bulbs, but the bulbs, that afternoon, were unlit: there was in fact no light at all on the main altar, no light on the cross, no light on the globe of the world that showed the northern American continent in gray and the southern in white; no light on the dove above the globe, *Salvador del Mundo.* In this vast brutalist space that was the cathedral, the unlit altar seemed to offer a single ineluctable message: at this time and in this place the light of the world could be construed as out, off, extinguished.

4 In many ways the Metropolitan Cathedral is an authentic piece of political art, a statement for El Salvador as *Guernica* was for Spain. It is quite devoid of sentimental relief. There are no decorative or architectural references to familiar parables, in fact no stories at all, not even the Stations of the Cross. On the afternoon I was there the flowers laid on the altar were dead. There were no traces of normal parish activity. The doors were open to the barricaded main steps, and down the

steps there was a spill of red paint, lest anyone forget the blood shed there. Here and there on the cheap linoleum inside the cathedral there was what seemed to be actual blood, dried in spots, the kind of spots dropped by a slow hemorrhage, or by a woman who does not know or does not care that she is menstruating.

5 There were several women in the cathedral during the hour or so I spent there, a young woman with a baby, an older woman in house slippers, a few others, all in black. One of the women walked the aisles as if by compulsion, up and down, across and back, crooning loudly as she walked. Another knelt without moving at the tomb of Archbishop Romero in the right transept. "LOOR A MONSEÑOR ROMERO," the crude needlepoint tapestry by the tomb read, "Praise to Monsignor Romero from the Mothers of the Imprisoned, the Disappeared, and the Murdered," the *Comité de Madres y Familiares de Presos, Desaparecidos, y Asesinados Politicos de El Salvador.*

6 The tomb itself was covered with offerings and petitions, notes decorated with motifs cut from greeting cards and cartoons. I recall one with figures cut from a Bugs Bunny strip, and another with a pencil drawing of a baby in a crib. The baby in this drawing seemed to be receiving medication or fluid or blood intravenously, through the IV line shown on its wrist. I studied the notes for a while and then went back and looked again at the unlit altar, and at the red paint on the main steps, from which it was possible to see the guardsmen on the balcony of the National Palace hunching back to avoid the rain. Many Salvadorans are offended by the Metropolitan Cathedral, which is as it should be, because the place remains perhaps the only unambiguous political statement in El Salvador, a metaphorical bomb in the ultimate power station.

Understanding Meaning

1. What warnings did Didion and her husband receive before traveling to El Salvador?
2. How did Didion's concept of churches differ from the Salvadoran woman's?
3. What images does Didion provide of the church? What does it look like? How does the physical appearance of the church relate to its social or political significance?

4. Didion focuses on the offerings and notes left behind by worshippers. Why are they significant?
5. *Critical Thinking:* What does Didion mean by calling the cathedral a "metaphorical bomb in the ultimate power station"? How does the unfinished look of the church add to this metaphor?

Evaluating Strategy

1. What is the impact of the opening paragraph?
2. Didion makes a reference to Picasso's painting *Guernica* without explaining it. What does this suggest about her intended readers?
3. Didion does not offer an explanation of the political causes of the violence. Why not?
4. *Other Modes:* How does Didion use *narration* in developing her essay? How do these stories establish the significance of the cathedral?

Appreciating Language

1. Didion calls the effect of the cathedral "entirely literary." What does she mean by this statement?
2. Didion uses words like *brutalist* and *ineluctable.* What impact does this level of vocabulary have? Would simpler words communicate more clearly?

Connections across the Disciplines

1. How does Didion's depiction of the cathedral as a monument compare to Molly Ivins's description of the Vietnam War Memorial (page 53)?
2. How does Didion's role as observer differ from Truman Capote's (page 105) or Annie Dillard's (page 258)?

Writing Suggestions

1. Write a short essay describing a building you see as a monument or political statement. It could be a new office tower rising above the slums, your old high school, an abandoned factory, or your first home. Use details to highlight the social or political issues the structure embodies.

2. *Collaborative Writing:* Working with a group of students, select a structure everyone is familiar with and agrees has some social significance. Have each member write a list of its principal characteristics and provide a brief statement about its importance. Compare notes and work together to write a brief descriptive essay. Avoid including unnecessary details about the building's address, year of construction, or physical dimensions.

JOSÉ ANTONIO BURCIAGA

José Antonio Burciaga (1940–) grew up in a synagogue in El Paso, where his father worked as a custodian. Burciaga served in the U.S. Air Force and then attended the University of Texas, where he earned a fine arts degree. Pursuing both art and literature, Burciaga also has been active in Chicano affairs. His artwork was first exhibited in 1974. Two years later he published a collection of poetry called Restless Serpents.

My Ecumenical Father

This essay, which first appeared in Drink Cultura, *describes Burciaga's father, a man who maintained his ties to Mexican culture while taking pride in his American citizenship and developing a fierce devotion to the Jewish faith.*

1 ¡Feliz Navidad! Merry Christmas! Happy Hanukkah! As a child, my season's greetings were tricultural—Mexicano, Anglo and Jewish.

2 Our devoutly Catholic parents raised three sons and three daughters in the basement of a Jewish synagogue, Congregation B'nai Zion in El Paso, Texas. José Cruz Burciaga was the custodian and *shabbat goy.* A shabbat goy is Yiddish for a Gentile who, on the Sabbath, performs certain tasks forbidden to Jews under orthodox law.

3 Every year around Christmas time, my father would take the menorah out and polish it. The eight-branched candleholder symbolizes Hanukkah, the commemoration of the first recorded war of liberation in that part of the world.

4 In 164 B.C., the Jewish nation rebelled against Antiochus IV Epiphanes, who had attempted to introduce pagan idols into the temples. When the temple was reconquered by the Jews, there was only one day's supply of oil for the Eternal Light in the temple. By a miracle, the oil lasted eight days.

5 My father was not only in charge of the menorah but for 10 years he also made sure the Eternal Light remained lit.

6 As children we were made aware of the differences and joys of Hanukkah, Christmas and Navidad. We were taught to respect each celebration, even if they conflicted. For example, the Christmas carols

taught in school. We learned the song about the twelve days of Christmas, though I never understood what the hell a partridge was doing in a pear tree in the middle of December.

7 We also learned a German song about a boy named Tom and a bomb—*O Tannenbaum.* We even learned a song in the obscure language of Latin, called "Adeste Fideles," which reminded me of, *Ahh! d'este fideo,* a Mexican pasta soup. Though 75% of our class was Mexican-American, we never sang a Christmas song in *Español.* Spanish was forbidden.

8 So our mother—a former teacher—taught us "Silent Night" in Spanish: *Noche de paz, noche de amor:* It was so much more poetic and inspirational.

9 While the rest of El Paso celebrated Christmas, Congregation B'nai Zion celebrated Hanukkah. We picked up Yiddish and learned a Hebrew prayer of thanksgiving. My brothers and I would help my father hang the Hanukkah decorations.

10 At night, after the services, the whole family would rush across the border to Juarez and celebrate the *posadas,* which takes place for nine days before Christmas. They are a communal re-enactment of Joseph and Mary's search for shelter, just before Jesus was born.

11 To the posadas we took candles and candy left over from the Hanukkah celebrations. The next day we'd be back at St. Patrick's School singing, "I'm dreaming of a white Christmas."

12 One day I stopped dreaming of the white Christmases depicted on greeting cards. An old immigrant from Israel taught me Jesus was born in desert country just like that of the West Texas town of El Paso.

13 On Christmas Eve, my father would dress like Santa Claus and deliver gifts to his children, nephews, godchildren and the little kids in orphanages. The next day, minus his disguise, he would take us to Juarez, where we delivered gifts to the poor in the streets.

14 My father never forgot his childhood poverty and forever sought to help the less fortunate. He taught us to measure wealth not in money but in terms of love, spirit, charity and culture.

15 We were taught to respect the Jewish faith and culture. On the Day of Atonement, when the whole congregation fasted, my mother did not cook, lest the food odors distract. The respect was mutual. No one ever complained about the large picture of Jesus in our living room.

16 Through my father, leftover food from B'nai B'rith luncheons, Bar Mitzvahs and Bat Mitzvahs, found its way to Catholic or Baptist churches or orphanages. Floral arrangements in the temple that

surrounded a Jewish wedding ***huppah*** canopy many times found a second home at the altar of St. Patrick's Cathedral or San Juan Convent School. Surplus furniture, including old temple pews, found their way to a missionary Baptist Church in *El Segundo Barrio.*

17 It was not uncommon to come home from school at lunch time and find an uncle priest, an aunt nun and a Baptist minister visiting our home at the same time that the Rabbi would knock on our door. It was just as natural to find the president of B'nai Zion eating beans and tortillas in our kitchen.

18 My father literally risked his life for the Jewish faith. Twice he was assaulted by burglars who broke in at night. Once he was stabbed in the hand. Another time he stayed up all night guarding the sacred Torahs after anti-Semites threatened the congregation. He never philosophized about his ecumenism, he just lived it.

19 Cruz, as most called him, was a man of great humor, a hot temper and a passion for dance. He lived the Mexican Revolution and rode the rails during the Depression. One of his proudest moments came when he became a U.S. citizen.

20 September 23, 1985, sixteen months after my mother passed away, my father followed. Like his life, his death was also ecumenical. The funeral was held at Our Lady of Peace, where a priest said the mass in English. My cousins played mandolin and sang in Spanish. The president of B'nai Zion Congregation said a prayer in Hebrew. Members of the congregation sat with Catholics and Baptists.

21 Observing Jewish custom, the cortege passed by the synagogue one last time. Fittingly, father was laid to rest on the Sabbath. At the cemetery, in a very Mexican tradition, my brothers, sisters and I each kissed a handful of dirt and threw it on the casket.

22 I once had the opportunity to describe father's life to the late, great Jewish American writer Bernard Malamud. His only comment was, "Only in America!"

Understanding Meaning

1. What is a *shabbat goy?*
2. How did the author's family show respect to the congregation?
3. How did the author's family manage to blend respect for several cultures?
4. Burciaga points out that though he learned German and Latin songs in school, he was not allowed to sing in Spanish. What does this reveal about the educational system?

5. Why is the description of his father's funeral central to Burciaga's story?
6. *Critical Thinking:* What values does the ecumenical father represent? Are these values rare in our society? What lesson could this essay teach?

Evaluating Strategy

1. Would Bernard Malamud's comment, "Only in America," make a good title for this essay? Why or why not?
2. Burciaga offers an explanation of Hanukkah. What does this suggest about his intended audience?
3. *Other Modes:* Can this *description* be seen as an extended *definition* of *ecumenical?*

Appreciating Language

1. How did Burciaga's father define "wealth"?
2. Read through Burciaga's description and highlight his use of non-English words and phrases. How does he define them? What impact do all these unfamiliar words have?

Connections across the Disciplines

1. How does Burciaga's multicultural upbringing differ from the childhoods described by Nathan McCall (page 47) or Richard Rodriguez (page 673)?
2. How does Burciaga's description of a person he admired compare to that of Carl T. Rowan's account of Miss Bessie (page 122)? Do they use similar techniques? How do they bring their characters to life? What details do they include?

Writing Suggestions

1. Burciaga builds his description largely through details about his father's actions and behavior. Write a few paragraphs describing a person you know well. Try to capture what you consider the person's principal attributes by describing actions that reveal their values.
2. *Collaborative Writing:* Discuss this essay with a group of other students. What do readers find most striking about this Mexican immigrant? Are his attitudes valuable to society? Is multiculturalism a trend today? Have each member write a few paragraphs explaining the significance of this essay. Read the responses aloud, and work to blend as many as possible in a short *analysis* of this essay.

CARL T. ROWAN

Carl T. Rowan (1925–) was born in Tennessee and received degrees from Oberlin College and the University of Minnesota. He worked for years as a columnist for the Minneapolis Tribune *and the* Chicago Sun Times, *expressing his views on a variety of issues, especially race relations. Rowan also served as the director of the United States Information Agency and was the ambassador to Finland.*

Unforgettable Miss Bessie

This article describing a schoolteacher originally appeared in Reader's Digest, *where Rowan serves as an editor. Rowan's account is personal, and much of his description focuses on the impact this teacher had on him and other disadvantaged students.*

1 She was only about five feet tall and probably never weighed more than 110 pounds, but Miss Bessie was a towering presence in the classroom. She was the only woman tough enough to make me read *Beowulf* and think for a few foolish days that I liked it. From 1938 to 1942, when I attended Bernard High School in McMinnville, Tenn., she taught me English, history, civics—and a lot more than I realized.

2 I shall never forget the day she scolded me into reading *Beowulf.*

3 "But Miss Bessie," I complained, "I ain't much interested in it."

4 Her large brown eyes became daggerish slits. "Boy," she said, "how dare you say 'ain't' to me! I've taught you better than that."

5 "Miss Bessie," I pleaded, "I'm trying to make first-string end on the football team, and if I go around saying 'it isn't' and 'they aren't,' the guys are gonna laugh me off the squad."

6 "Boy," she responded, "you'll play football because you have guts. But do you know what *really* takes guts? Refusing to lower your standards to those of the crowd. It takes guts to say you've got to live and be somebody fifty years after all the football games are over."

7 I started saying "it isn't" and "they aren't," and I still made first-string end—and class valedictorian—without losing my buddies' respect.

8 During her remarkable 44-year career, Mrs. Bessie Taylor Gwynn taught hundreds of economically deprived black youngsters—includ-

ing my mother, my brother, my sisters and me. I remember her now with gratitude and affection—especially in this era when Americans are so wrought-up about a "rising tide of mediocrity" in public education and the problems of finding competent, caring teachers. Miss Bessie was an example of an informed, dedicated teacher, a blessing to children and an asset to the nation.

9 Born in 1895, in poverty, she grew up in Athens, Ala., where there was no public school for blacks. She attended Trinity School, a private institution for blacks run by the American Missionary Association, and in 1911 graduated from the Normal School (a "super" high school) at Fisk University in Nashville. Mrs. Gwynn, the essence of pride and privacy, never talked about her years in Athens; only in the months before her death did she reveal that she had never attended Fisk University itself because she could not afford the four-year course.

10 At Normal School she learned a lot about Shakespeare, but most of all about the profound importance of education—especially, for a people trying to move up from slavery. "What you put in your head, boy," she once said, "can never be pulled out by the Ku Klux Klan, the Congress or anybody."

11 Miss Bessie's bearing of dignity told anyone who met her that she was "educated" in the best sense of the word. There was never a discipline problem in her classes. We didn't dare mess with a woman who knew about the Battle of Hastings, the Magna Carta and the Bill of Rights—and who could also play the piano.

12 This frail-looking woman could make sense of Shakespeare, Milton, Voltaire, and bring to life Booker T. Washington and W. E. B. DuBois. Believing that it was important to know who the officials were that spent taxpayers' money and made public policy, she made us memorize the names of everyone on the Supreme Court and in the President's Cabinet. It could be embarrassing to be unprepared when Miss Bessie said, "Get up and tell the class who Frances Perkins is and what you think about her."

13 Miss Bessie knew that my family, like so many others during the Depression, couldn't afford to subscribe to a newspaper. She knew we didn't even own a radio. Still, she prodded me to "look out for your future and find some way to keep up with what's going on in the world." So I became a delivery boy for the Chattanooga *Times*. I rarely made a dollar a week, but I got to read a newspaper every day.

14 Miss Bessie noticed things that had nothing to do with schoolwork, but were vital to a youngster's development. Once a few classmates made fun of my frayed, hand-me-down overcoat, calling me "Strings."

As I was leaving school, Miss Bessie patted me on the back of that old overcoat and said, "Carl, never fret about what you *don't* have. Just make the most of what you *do* have—a brain."

15 Among the things that I did not have was electricity in the little frame house that my father had built for $400 with his World War I bonus. But because of her inspiration, I spent many hours squinting beside a kerosene lamp reading Shakespeare and Thoreau, Samuel Pepys and William Cullen Bryant.

16 No one in my family had ever graduated from high school, so there was no tradition of commitment to learning for me to lean on. Like millions of youngsters in today's ghettos and barrios, I needed the push and stimulation of a teacher who truly cared. Miss Bessie gave plenty of both, as she immersed me in a wonderful world of similes, metaphors and even onomatopoeia. She led me to believe that I could write sonnets as well as Shakespeare, or iambic-pentameter verse to put Alexander Pope to shame.

17 In those days the McMinnville school system was rigidly "Jim Crow," and poor black children had to struggle to put anything in their heads. Our high school was only slightly larger than the once-typical little red schoolhouse, and its library was outrageously inadequate—so small, I like to say, that if two students were in it and one wanted to turn a page, the other one had to step outside.

18 Negroes, as we were called then, were not allowed in the town library, except to mop floors or dust tables. But through one of those secret Old South arrangements between whites of conscience and blacks of stature, Miss Bessie kept getting books smuggled out of the white library. That is how she introduced me to the Brontës, Byron, Coleridge, Keats and Tennyson. "If you don't read, you can't write, and if you can't write, you might as well stop dreaming," Miss Bessie once told me.

19 So I read whatever Miss Bessie told me to, and tried to remember the things she insisted that I store away. Forty-five years later, I can still recite her "truths to live by," such as Henry Wadsworth Longfellow's lines from "The Ladder of St. Augustine":

20 The heights by great men reached and kept
Were not attained by sudden flight.
But they, while their companions slept,
Were toiling upward in the night.

21 Years later, her inspiration, prodding, anger, cajoling and almost osmotic infusion of learning finally led to that lovely day when Miss Bessie dropped me a note saying, "I'm so proud to read your column in the Nashville *Tennessean*."

22 Miss Bessie was a spry 80 when I went back to McMinnville and visited her in a senior citizens' apartment building. Pointing out proudly that her building was racially integrated, she reached for two glasses and a pint of bourbon. I was momentarily shocked, because it would have been scandalous in the 1930s and '40s for word to get out that a teacher drank, and nobody had ever raised a rumor that Miss Bessie did.

23 I felt a new sense of equality as she lifted her glass to mine. Then she revealed a softness and compassion that I had never known as a student.

24 "I've never forgotten that examination day," she said, "when Buster Martin held up seven fingers, obviously asking you for help with question number seven, 'Name a common carrier.' I can still picture you looking at your exam paper and humming a few bars of 'Chattanooga Choo Choo.' I was so tickled, I couldn't punish either of you."

25 Miss Bessie was telling me, with bourbon-laced grace, that I never fooled her for a moment.

26 When Miss Bessie died in 1980, at age 85, hundreds of her former students mourned. They knew the measure of a great teacher: love and motivation. Her wisdom and influence had rippled out across generations.

27 Some of her students who might normally have been doomed to poverty went on to become doctors, dentists and college professors. Many, guided by Miss Bessie's example, became public-school teachers.

28 "The memory of Miss Bessie and how she conducted her classroom did more for me than anything I learned in college," recalls Gladys Wood of Knoxville, Tenn., a highly respected English teacher who spent 43 years in the state's school system. "So many times, when I faced a difficult classroom problem, I asked myself, *How would Miss Bessie deal with this?* And I'd remember that she would handle it with laughter and love."

29 No child can get all the necessary support at home, and millions of poor children get *no* support at all. This is what makes a wise, educated, warm-hearted teacher like Miss Bessie so vital to the minds, hearts and souls of this country's children.

Understanding Meaning

1. What is Rowan's purpose in describing Miss Bessie? What makes this teacher significant to a middle-aged man?
2. What qualities of Miss Bessie does Rowan admire?
3. Does Rowan offer Miss Bessie as a role model? How does he demonstrate that she is an "asset to the nation"?

Evaluating Strategy

1. Rowan opens his essay with a physical description of Miss Bessie. Why are these details important to his purpose?
2. Why would this article appeal to readers of *Reader's Digest?* What values does it reinforce?
3. *Critical Thinking:* Would some people object to Rowan's article as being sentimental? Why or why not? Does this article suggest simple solutions to complex problems? Would a Miss Bessie be able to succeed in a modern urban high school?

Appreciating Language

1. Study the words Rowan uses in describing Miss Bessie. Which words have the most impact?
2. Rowan includes dialogue in his article. What do you notice about Miss Bessie's language? What does this add to the description?

Connections across the Disciplines

1. Consider William Raspberry's article "The Handicap of Definition" (page 320). Would Miss Bessie be a figure that resists such a handicap?
2. *Critical Thinking:* Compare Rowan's experience in a black high school with Nathan McCall's experience in "The Lesson" (page 47). Do African American students from disadvantaged communities benefit from integration or from participation in black schools with black teachers like Miss Bessie?

Writing Suggestions

1. Write a brief description of a teacher, employer, or coworker who greatly influenced your development. Provide specific examples of the lessons you learned.

2. *Collaborative Writing:* Working with three or four other students, discuss Miss Bessie's statement, "What you put in your head, boy, can never be pulled out by the Ku Klux Klan, the Congress or anybody." Use this quote as the headline of a poster urging people to read. Keep your message short. Read it aloud to hear how it sounds.

MONIKA BAUERLEIN

Monika Bauerlein is currently the managing editor of City Pages, *an alternative weekly newspaper in Minneapolis. She first became aware of the nuclear waste problem when Minnesota's Northern States Power Company announced plans to store radioactive material forty miles from St. Paul. This article, published in the* Utne Reader, *was voted one of the "25 Most Censored" stories of 1992 by Project Censored.*

Plutonium Is Forever: Is There Any Sane Place to Put Nuclear Waste?

Asserting that "nuclear waste is probably the toughest garbage problem known to humanity," Bauerlein alerts her readers to the challenge of storing toxic material that will be deadly for thousands of years.

1 Back in the 1950s, when nuclear energy was new, one of its few critics came up with a biting metaphor for an overlooked problem: "Nuclear waste is like getting on a plane, and in mid-air you ask the pilot, how are we going to land? He says, we don't know—but we'll figure it out by the time we get there." This sensible criticism was ignored; governments around the world were bent on pushing atomic technology for both civilian and military purposes.

2 Four decades later, our nuclear plane is preparing for a crash landing. During those 40 years, nuclear power has come and gone as a boiling political issue; in the past ten years it faded from the headlines almost completely. But now, starting with small communities wrestling with nuclear waste sites and reaching all the way into international negotiations, the nuclear waste issue is back—and it's more controversial than ever before.

3 A recent report by Nicholas Lenssen, a researcher at the Washington-based Worldwatch Institute (*Worldwatch Paper 106*, Dec. 1991), estimates the worldwide volume of high-level nuclear waste at more than 80,000 tons; the world's 413 commercial reactors produced 9,500 tons in 1990. And that's not even counting the tens of thousands of tons from weapons programs and medical and industrial uses.

4 Highly toxic nuclear waste is probably the toughest garbage problem known to humanity. Lenssen writes that in 1989 alone, U.S. reactors produced about 67 times the plutonium it would take to give everyone on earth lung cancer.

5 Most of the world's high-level nuclear waste is spent fuel from nuclear reactors. While it's possible to "reprocess" uranium rods and use them for another fuel cycle, it takes huge amounts of energy to do so and creates additional waste; the same is true for "transmutating" the waste into something less hazardous, an experimental technology with unknown risks. If you can't recycle it and you can't transmutate it, there's only one thing left to do with nuclear waste: Store it someplace where it won't endanger people or the environment.

6 The U.S. Department of Energy (DOE) selected Yucca Mountain, Nevada, as the national "permanent repository for nuclear waste." But after 10 years of research and more than $1 billion dollars, DOE still hasn't drilled a single hole into Yucca Mountain—mostly because of opposition from Nevadans and their state government, who have been able to show potential risks in the project. By now, DOE has pushed back its deadline for the dump from 1998 to 2010, and many believe Yucca Mountain will never open.

7 Meanwhile, nuclear waste keeps piling up at the country's 110 nuclear reactors, mostly in indoor water pools originally designed to hold small quantities for a few years. As the Minneapolis-St. Paul weekly *City Pages* (Jan. 29, 1992) reports, utility organizations estimate that within the next 10 years, about half of the nation's nuclear power plants will have to find another place to put their waste or shut down; as a result, power companies have begun to create their own on-site nuclear waste dumps. The preferred technology is called "dry-cask storage," which means keeping the waste in giant outdoor steel cans.

8 The first three dry-cask facilities—all located on the East Coast—provoked little public debate, but that changed when Minnesota's Northern States Power Company (NSP) announced that it wanted to put dry casks right next to the Prairie Island Mdewakanton Sioux community, a small reservation near the scenic Mississippi River bluffs 40 miles south of St. Paul. The Prairie Island community, which had long felt nervous about the neighboring nuclear plant, mounted a high-profile legal and political fight, and as of this writing the Indian tribe has convinced a state administrative law judge to issue a recommendation against the dump.

9 Even if dozens of reactors put up dry casks, however, DOE will still have to wrestle with finding a long-term dump; after all, the federal

government decades ago promised utilities that it would start taking their waste by 1998. The deadline looms even larger considering that—as Bill Breen reports in the environmental bi-monthly *Garbage* (March/April 1992)—at least 67 of the nation's current 110 nuclear plants will have to close and be dismantled within the next 30 years, adding uncounted tons of radioactive debris to the nuclear waste stream. The Bush administration is trying to avoid the problem by proposing that most reactors get "relicensed" for another 30 years beyond their original lifespan, but that idea carries its own set of safety and environmental problems.

10 So, since a safe, permanent nuclear waste site looks ever more unlikely, DOE has revived a concept Congress told it to forget at least until Yucca Mountain was built: monitored retrievable storage sites, or MRS sites. As Tony Davis puts it in the Rocky Mountain regional paper *High Country News* (Jan. 27, 1992), spent reactor fuel would be shipped in and stored in above-ground bunkers at the regional MRS sites until a permanent dump is ready.

11 When it started looking for an MRS host community, DOE sent out a "nuclear waste negotiator" with a package of promises considered irresistible to many impoverished rural communities. Communities willing to consider the waste dump were promised "500 to 1,000 jobs to pay salaries of up to $45,000 [and] additional payments of $5 million to $10 million a year," Davis reports.

12 By early this year, seven communities had applied for a $100,000 MRS "study grant"—two were rural counties in North Dakota and Wyoming, the other five were Native American tribes. Mordecai Specktor reports in the Minneapolis-St. Paul–based Indian monthly *The Circle* (Feb. 1992) that there's some evidence that DOE specifically targeted tribes, in part because of their sovereign status—which means state governments often can't interfere with the project—and in part because of their desperate economic straits.

13 In each community, announcements that local officials were considering the MRS proposal inevitably set off a firestorm. In Grant County, North Dakota, voters threw out a majority of the county commissioners who had voted for the MRS study. New Mexico's Mescalero Apache tribe, meanwhile, seems to be the farthest along the MRS road, though tribal chairman Wendell Chino says he would place the dump on off-reservation land that would be acquired and then declared tribal property.

14 Wherever MRS sites eventually go, if there are any at all, plenty of questions remain about environmental and health effects. At Prairie

Island, the tribe discovered that NSP's 48 dry casks (peanuts compared to the thousands envisioned for a regular MRS site) would emit radiation between 6 and 23 times higher than levels set by the state safety guidelines. The information won't do them much good, however, since the federal government has reversed authority to regulate all things nuclear, and therefore state guidelines don't apply.

15 In the meantime, a growing number of people support "intermediate storage" for 50 or 100 years or however long it takes to find another disposal method. Intermediate storage could mean "mothballing" waste and the decommissioned plants on site, thus avoiding risky dismantling and transportation (the British government plans to mothball dead reactors for at least 130 years).

16 This method of dealing with the problem would force governments, power companies, and the public to face up to just how daunting a dilemma nuclear waste has become. And then, it might be hard to escape the next logical conclusion: If we got ourselves into this mess, at least let's stop producing any more. There is, of course, always the alternative of keeping on at the rate we're going now—which means, notes the Worldwatch Institute, that we'll have to open at least one nuclear waste dump every two years for decades to come.

Understanding Meaning

1. The article opens with a brief story criticizing nuclear power. What does this say about Bauerlein's purpose and her intended audience?
2. How does Bauerlein describe the basic problem posed by waste from nuclear reactors?
3. Bauerlein's article contains facts and statistics. Does she make these details understandable to a general reader?
4. What issues does she raise about the future?

Evaluating Strategy

1. Bauerlein uses a question as a subtitle to her article. How does this advance her purpose?
2. *Critical Thinking:* Bauerlein includes citations to document her article. But many of her sources—*City Pages*, *Garbage*, and *High Country News*—are either alternative or regional publications. Does using sources as these strengthen or weaken a writer's position? Why is it better to cite more recognized sources?

3. *Other Modes:* How does Bauerlein use *comparison* to explain a highly technical issue to a general readership? How much of her description contains elements of *persuasion?*

Appreciating Language

1. Bauerlein defines DOE and MRS—what does this suggest about her intended audience's knowledge of the issue?
2. Locate places where Bauerlein's choice of words indicates her position on nuclear waste disposal. What connotations do these words have?

Connections across the Disciplines

1. What do Bauerlein's article and Dr. Robert Peter Gale and Thomas Hauser's "Final Warning" (page 63) suggest about nuclear power? Have scientists and engineers adequately designed reactors to avoid accidents? Did anyone in the industry appear to have given thought to the inevitable problem of waste disposal?
2. *Critical Thinking:* Review Einstein's letter to President Roosevelt (page 676). After the bombing of Hiroshima, Einstein regretted his actions, stating that the world was not ready for atomic power. How does Bauerlein's article suggest that even peaceful uses of nuclear energy reveal an inability to handle this force responsibly?

Writing Suggestions

1. Write a short essay describing an environmental problem in your area. Include as many factual details as you can. Focus on ramifications for the future. Perhaps a potentially valuable piece of property cannot be developed because of toxic waste. Does your campus have environmental problems? Do older buildings contain asbestos?
2. *Collaborative Writing:* Review Bauerlein's article with other students, and, using the information for support, write the text of a persuasive letter to the editor urging further research in nuclear waste. Read the letter aloud to the group, and evaluate its factual support and use of connotations. Your letter should arouse attention but avoid alarmist statements that cannot be supported by facts.

N. SCOTT MOMADAY

Navarre Scott Momaday (1934–) was born in Oklahoma and graduated from the University of New Mexico in 1958. He received a doctorate in English from Stanford University. Momaday is a literature professor, poet, artist, and frequent contributor to The New Yorker. *A Native American, he has published a collection of Kiowa folktales and edited* American Indian Authors. *His other books have included* The Gourd Dancer, *an illustrated children's book, and* House Made of Dawn, *a novel that received a Pulitzer Prize.*

The Way to Rainy Mountain

This essay first appeared in The Reporter. *Momaday later revised it and used it as an introduction to a book of the same title.*

1 A single knoll rises out of the plain in Oklahoma, north and west of the Wichita Range. For my people, the Kiowas, it is an old landmark, and they gave it the name Rainy Mountain. The hardest weather in the world is there. Winter brings blizzards, hot tornadic winds arise in the spring, and in summer the prairie is an anvil's edge. The grass turns brittle and brown, and it cracks beneath your feet. There are green belts along the rivers and creeks, linear groves of hickory and pecan, willow and witch hazel. At a distance in July or August the steaming foliage seems almost to writhe in fire. Great green-and-yellow grasshoppers are everywhere in the tall grass, popping up like corn to sting the flesh, and tortoises crawl about on the red earth, going nowhere in the plenty of time. Loneliness is an aspect of the land. All things in the plain are isolate; there is no confusion of objects in the eye, but *one* hill or *one* tree or *one* man. To look upon that landscape in the early morning, with the sun at your back, is to lose the sense of proportion. Your imagination comes to life, and this, you think, is where Creation was begun.

2 I returned to Rainy Mountain in July. My grandmother had died in the spring, and I wanted to be at her grave. She had lived to be very old and at last infirm. Her only living daughter was with her when she died, and I was told that in death her face was that of a child.

3 I like to think of her as a child. When she was born, the Kiowas were living that last great moment of their history. For more than a hundred years they had controlled the open range from the Smoky Hill River to the Red, from the headwaters of the Canadian to the fork of the Arkansas and Cimarron. In alliance with the Comanches, they had ruled the whole of the southern Plains. War was their sacred business, and they were among the finest horsemen the world has ever known. But warfare for the Kiowas was preeminently a matter of disposition rather than of survival, and they never understood the grim, unrelenting advance of the U.S. Cavalry. When at last, divided and ill-provisioned, they were driven onto the Staked Plains in the cold rains of autumn, they fell into panic. In Palo Duro Canyon they abandoned their crucial stores to pillage and had nothing then but their lives. In order to save themselves, they surrendered to the soldiers at Fort Sill and were imprisoned in the old stone corral that now stands as a military museum. My grandmother was spared the humiliation of those high gray walls by eight or ten years, but she must have known from birth the affliction of defeat, the dark brooding of old warriors.

4 Her name was Aho, and she belonged to the last culture to evolve in North America. Her forebears came down from the high country in western Montana nearly three centuries ago. They were a mountain people, a mysterious tribe of hunters whose language has never been positively classified in any major group. In the late seventeenth century they began a long migration to the south and east. It was a long journey toward the dawn, and it led to a golden age. Along the way the Kiowas were befriended by the Crows, who gave them the culture and religion of the Plains. They acquired horses, and their ancient nomadic spirit was suddenly free of the ground. They acquired Tai-me, the sacred Sun Dance doll, from that moment the object and symbol of their worship, and so shared in the divinity of the sun. Not least, they acquired the sense of destiny, therefore courage and pride. When they entered upon the southern Plains, they had been transformed. No longer were they slaves to the simple necessity of survival; they were a lordly and dangerous society of fighters and thieves, hunters and priests of the sun. According to their origin myth, they entered the world through a hollow log. From one point of view, their migration was the fruit of an old prophecy, for indeed they emerged from a sunless world.

5 Although my grandmother lived out her long life in the shadow of Rainy Mountain, the immense landscape of the continental interior

lay like memory in her blood. She could tell of the Crows, whom she had never seen, and of the Black Hills, where she had never been. I wanted to see in reality what she had seen more perfectly in the mind's eye, and traveled fifteen hundred miles to begin my pilgrimage.

6 Yellowstone, it seemed to me, was the top of the world, a region of deep lakes and dark timber, canyons and waterfalls. But, beautiful as it is, one might have the sense of confinement there. The skyline in all directions is close at hand, the high wall of the woods and deep cleavages of shade. There is a perfect freedom in the mountains, but it belongs to the eagle and the elk, the badger and the bear. The Kiowas reckoned their stature by the distance they could see, and they were bent and blind in the wilderness.

7 Descending eastward, the highland meadows are a stairway to the plain. In July the inland slope of the Rockies is luxuriant with flax and buckwheat, stonecrop and larkspur. The earth unfolds and the limit of the land recedes. Clusters of trees and animals grazing far in the distance cause the vision to reach away and wonder to build upon the mind. The sun follows a longer course in the day, and the sky is immense beyond all comparison. The great billowing clouds that sail upon it are shadows that move upon the grain like water, dividing light. Farther down, in the land of the Crows and Blackfeet, the plain is yellow. Sweet clover takes hold of the hills and bends upon itself to cover and seal the soil. There the Kiowas paused on their way; they had come to the place where they must change their lives. The sun is at home in the plains. Precisely there does it have the certain character of a god. When the Kiowas came to the land of the Crows, they could see the dark lees of the hills at dawn across the Bighorn River, the profusion of light on the grain shelves, the oldest deity ranging after the solstices. Not yet would they veer southward to the caldron of the land that lay below; they must wean their blood from the northern winter and hold the mountains a while longer in their view. They bore Tai-me in procession to the east.

8 A dark mist lay over the Black Hills, and the land was like iron. At the top of a ridge I caught sight of Devil's Tower upthrust against the gray sky as if in the birth of time the core of the earth had broken through its crust and the motion of the world was begun. There are things in nature that engender an awful quiet in the heart of man; Devil's Tower is one of them. Two centuries ago, because they could not do otherwise, the Kiowas made a legend at the base of the rock. My grandmother said:

9 Eight children were there at play, seven sisters and their brother. Suddenly the boy was struck dumb; he trembled and began to run upon his hands and feet. His fingers became claws, and his body was covered with fur. Directly there was a bear where the boy had been. The sisters were terrified; they ran, and the bear after them. They came to the stump of a great tree, and the tree spoke to them. It bade them climb upon it, and as they did so, it began to rise into the air. The bear came to kill them, but they were just beyond its reach. It reared against the tree and scored the bark all around with its claws. The seven sisters were borne into the sky, and they became the stars of the Big Dipper.

10 From that moment, and so long as the legend lives, the Kiowas have kinsmen in the night sky. Whatever they were in the mountains, they could be no more. However tenuous their well-being, however much they had suffered and would suffer again, they had found a way out of the wilderness.

11 My grandmother had a reverence for the sun, a holy regard that now is all but gone out of mankind. There was a wariness in her, and an ancient awe. She was a Christian in her later years, but she had come a long way about, and she never forgot her birthright. As a child she had been to the Sun Dances; she had taken part in those annual rites, and by them she had learned the restoration of her people in the presence of Tai-me. She was about seven when the last Kiowa Sun Dance was held in 1887 on the Washita River above Rainy Mountain Creek. The buffalo were gone. In order to consummate the ancient sacrifice—to impale the head of a buffalo bull upon the medicine tree—a delegation of old men journeyed into Texas, there to beg and barter for an animal from the Goodnight herd. She was ten when the Kiowas came together for the last time as a living Sun Dance culture. They could find no buffalo; they had to hang an old hide from the sacred tree. Before the dance could begin, a company of soldiers rode out from Fort Sill under orders to disperse the tribe. Forbidden without cause the essential act of their faith, having seen the wild herds slaughtered and left to rot upon the ground, the Kiowas backed away forever from the medicine tree. That was July 20, 1890, at the great bend of the Washita. My grandmother was there. Without bitterness, and for as long as she lived, she bore a vision of deicide.

12 Now that I can have her only in memory, I see my grandmother in the several postures that were peculiar to her: standing at the wood stove on a winter morning and turning meat in a great iron skillet; sitting at the south window, bent above her beadwork, and afterwards,

when her vision had failed, looking down for a long time into the fold of her hands; going out upon a cane, very slowly as she did when the weight of age came upon her; praying. I remember her most often at prayer. She made long, rambling prayers out of suffering and hope, having seen many things. I was never sure that I had the right to hear, so exclusive were they of all mere custom and company. The last time I saw her she prayed standing by the side of her bed at night, naked to the waist, the light of a kerosene lamp moving upon her dark skin. Her long, black hair, always drawn and braided in the day, lay upon her shoulders and against her breasts like a shawl. I do not speak Kiowa, and I never understood her prayers, but there was something inherently sad in the sound, some merest hesitation upon the syllables of sorrow. She began in a high and descending pitch, exhausting her breath to silence; then again and again—and always the same intensity of effort, of something that is, and is not, like urgency in the human voice. Transported so in the dancing light among the shadows of her room, she seemed beyond the reach of time. But that was illusion; I think I knew then that I should not see her again.

Understanding Meaning

1. How does Momaday describe Rainy Mountain? How do its physical characteristics differ from its importance to the Kiowas?
2. How does Momaday describe his grandmother? What were the dominant features of her life and her home?
3. What is the significance of the Kiowa legend about the seven sisters?
4. *Other Modes:* How does Momaday use *narration* and *comparison* to develop his description?
5. *Critical Thinking:* Momaday states that he did not speak his grandmother's language and did not understand her prayers. Does this loss of an ancestral language by a man interested in his past illustrate Jamaica Kincaid's (page 147) observation that Americans are "impatient with memory"?

Evaluating Strategy

1. Most descriptions focus on visual images. How does Momaday use sounds to describe his subject?
2. How does Momaday introduce historical background into a highly personal essay? What transitions does he use?

Appreciating Language

1. Momaday discusses his grandmother's reverence for the sun. What connotation does the word *sun* have?
2. Focus on Momaday's word choices. How does he refer to the beliefs of the ancient Native Americans? What do his connotations reveal about his attitudes toward their faith?

Connections across the Disciplines

1. How does Momaday's role as tribal member returning home compare to Armando Rendón's discovery of his roots in "Kiss of Death" (page 667)? Does a difference exist between immigrant and Native American culture? Is one harder to maintain or preserve?
2. How does Momaday's description of people and places compare with Truman Capote's "Out There" (page 105)? Do they pay similar attention to detail? Are their attitudes different? Does one writer seem more of an outsider?

Writing Suggestions

1. Write an essay describing an ancestral figure in your own past. Choose a relative, family friend, or neighbor who embodied a sense of your family, community, or culture. Choose words carefully to share with readers your attitudes toward this person.
2. *Collaborative Writing:* Discuss the role of grandparents in current society with several students. Select observations you agree on, and write a few paragraphs presenting your main points. Has the role of grandparents changed? On the one hand, are they discredited because our society emphasizes youth? On the other hand, are they often more influential since many take an active role in raising grandchildren?

EDWARD ABBEY

Edward Abbey (1927–1989) was born in Pennsylvania and first traveled to the West in 1948 to attend the University of New Mexico. Initially impressed with the romance of the cowboy, he later became concerned about the use of public lands and the environmental damage caused by development. Abbey worked as a park ranger for fifteen years. In 1968 he published Desert Solitaire, *which he called "not a travel guide but an elegy." His later works include* The Monkey Wrench Gang, Abbey's Road, *and* Down by the River.

The First Morning

Abbey opens this essay from Desert Solitaire *with a bold assertion: "This is the most beautiful place on earth." Abbey uses rich imagery and sensory details to get his reader to share his awe for a landscape empty of people.*

1 This is the most beautiful place on earth.

2 There are many such places. Every man, every woman, carries in heart and mind the image of the ideal place, the right place, the one true home, known or unknown, actual or visionary. A houseboat in Kashmir, a view down Atlantic Avenue in Brooklyn, a gray gothic farmhouse two stories high at the end of a red dog road in the Allegheny Mountains, a cabin on the shore of a blue lake in spruce and fir country, a greasy alley near the Hoboken waterfront, or even, possibly, for those of a less demanding sensibility, the world to be seen from a comfortable apartment high in the tender, velvety smog of Manhattan, Chicago, Paris, Tokyo, Rio or Rome—there's no limit to the human capacity for the homing sentiment. Theologians, sky pilots, astronauts have even felt the appeal of home calling to them from up above, in the cold black outback of interstellar space.

3 For myself I'll take Moab, Utah. I don't mean the town itself, of course, but the country which surrounds it—the canyonlands. The slickrock desert. The red dust and the burnt cliffs and the lonely sky—all that which lies beyond the end of the roads.

4 The choice became apparent to me this morning when I stepped out of a Park Service housetrailer—my caravan—to watch for the first

time in my life the sun come up over the hoodoo stone of Arches National Monument.

5 I wasn't able to see much of it last night. After driving all day from Albuquerque—450 miles—I reached Moab after dark in cold, windy, clouded weather. At park headquarters north of town I met the superintendent and the chief ranger, the only permanent employees, except for one maintenance man, in this particular unit of America's national park system. After coffee they gave me a key to the housetrailer and directions on how to reach it; I am required to live and work not at headquarters but at this one-man station some twenty miles back in the interior, on my own. The way I wanted it, naturally, or I'd never have asked for the job.

6 Leaving the headquarters area and the lights of Moab, I drove twelve miles farther north on the highway until I came to a dirt road on the right, where a small wooden sign pointed the way: Arches National Monument Eight Miles. I left the pavement, turned east into the howling wilderness. Wind roaring out of the northwest, black clouds across the stars—all I could see were clumps of brush and scattered junipers along the roadside. Then another modest signboard:

7 WARNING: QUICKSAND
DO NOT CROSS WASH
WHEN WATER IS RUNNING

8 The wash looked perfectly dry in my headlights. I drove down, across, up the other side and on into the night. Glimpses of weird humps of pale rock on either side, like petrified elephants, dinosaurs, stone-age hobgoblins. Now and then something alive scurried across the road: kangaroo mice, a jackrabbit, an animal that looked like a cross between a raccoon and a squirrel—the ringtail cat. Farther on a pair of mule deer started from the brush and bounded obliquely through the beams of my lights, raising puffs of dust which the wind, moving faster than my pickup truck, caught and carried ahead of me out of sight into the dark. The road, narrow and rocky, twisted sharply left and right, dipped in and out of tight ravines, climbing by degrees toward a summit which I would see only in the light of the coming day.

9 Snow was swirling through the air when I crossed the unfenced line and passed the boundary marker of the park. A quarter-mile beyond I found the ranger station—a wide place in the road, an informa-

tional display under a lean-to shelter, and fifty yards away the little tin government housetrailer where I would be living for the next six months.

10 A cold night, a cold wind, the snow falling like confetti. In the lights of the truck I unlocked the housetrailer, got out bedroll and baggage and moved in. By flashlight I found the bed, unrolled my sleeping bag, pulled off my boots and crawled in and went to sleep at once. The last I knew was the shaking of the trailer in the wind and the sound, from inside, of hungry mice scampering around with the good news that their long lean lonesome winter was over—their friend and provider had finally arrived.

11 This morning I awake before sunrise, stick my head out of the sack, peer through a frosty window at a scene dim and vague with flowing mists, dark fantastic shapes looming beyond. An unlikely landscape.

12 I get up, moving about in long underwear and socks, stooping carefully under the low ceiling and the lower doorways of the house-trailer, a machine for living built so efficiently and compactly there's hardly room for a man to breathe. An iron lung it is, with windows and venetian blinds.

13 The mice are silent, watching me from their hiding places, but the wind is still blowing and outside the ground is covered with snow. Cold as a tomb, a jail, a cave; I lie down on the dusty floor, on the cold linoleum sprinkled with mouse turds, and light the pilot on the butane heater. Once this thing gets going the place warms up fast, in a dense unhealthy way, with a layer of heat under the ceiling where my head is and nothing but frigid air from the knees down. But we've got all the indispensable conveniences: gas cookstove, gas refrigerator, hot water heater, sink with running water (if the pipes aren't frozen), storage cabinets and shelves, everything within arm's reach of everything else. The gas comes from two steel bottles in a shed outside; the water comes by gravity flow from a tank buried in a hill close by. Quite luxurious for the wilds. There's even a shower stall and a flush toilet with a dead rat in the bowl. Pretty soft. My poor mother raised five children without any of these luxuries and might be doing without them yet if it hadn't been for Hitler, war and general prosperity.

14 Time to get dressed, get out and have a look at the lay of the land, fix a breakfast. I try to pull on my boots but they're stiff as iron from the cold. I light a burner on the stove and hold the boots upside down

above the flame until they are malleable enough to force my feet into. I put on a coat and step outside. In the center of the world, God's navel, Abbey's country, the red wasteland.

15 The sun is not yet in sight but signs of the advent are plain to see. Lavender clouds sail like a fleet of ships across the pale green dawn; each cloud, planed flat on the wind, has a base of fiery gold. Southeast, twenty miles by line of sight, stand the peaks of the Sierra La Sal, twelve to thirteen thousand feet above sea level, all covered with snow and rosy in the morning sunlight. The air is dry and clear as well as cold; the last fogbanks left over from last night's storm are scudding away like ghosts, fading into nothing before the wind and the sunrise.

16 The view is open and perfect in all directions except to the west where the ground rises and the skyline is only a few hundred yards away. Looking toward the mountains I can see the dark gorge of the Colorado River five or six miles away, carved through the sandstone mesa, though nothing of the river itself down inside the gorge. Southward, on the far side of the river, lies the Moab valley between thousand-foot walls of rock, with the town of Moab somewhere on the valley floor, too small to be seen from here. Beyond the Moab valley is more canyon and tableland stretching away to the Blue Mountains fifty miles south. On the north and northwest I see the Roan Cliffs and the Book Cliffs, the two-level face of the Uinta Plateau. Along the foot of those cliffs, maybe thirty miles off, invisible from where I stand, runs U.S. 6-50, a major east-west artery of commerce, traffic and rubbish, and the main line of the Denver-Rio Grande Railroad. To the east, under the spreading sunrise, are more mesas, more canyons, league on league of red cliff and arid tablelands, extending through purple haze over the bulging curve of the planet to the ranges of Colorado—a sea of desert.

17 Within this vast perimeter, in the middle ground and foreground of the picture, a rather personal demesne, are the 33,000 acres of Arches National Monument of which I am now sole inhabitant, usufructuary, observer and custodian.

18 What are the Arches? From my place in front of the housetrailer I can see several of the hundred or more of them which have been discovered in the park. These are natural arches, holes in the rock, windows in stone, no two alike, as varied in form as in dimension. They range in size from holes just big enough to walk through to openings large enough to contain the dome of the Capitol building in Washington, D.C. Some resemble jug handles or flying buttresses,

others natural bridges but with this technical distinction: a natural bridge spans a watercourse—a natural arch does not. The arches were formed through hundreds of thousands of years by the weathering of the huge sandstone walls, or fins, in which they are found. Not the work of a cosmic hand, nor sculptured by sand-bearing winds, as many people prefer to believe, the arches came into being and continue to come into being through the modest wedging action of rainwater, melting snow, frost, and ice, aided by gravity. In color they shade from off-white through buff, pink, brown and red, tones which also change with the time of day and the moods of the light, the weather, the sky.

19 Standing there, gaping at this monstrous and inhuman spectacle of rock and cloud and sky and space, I feel a ridiculous greed and possessiveness come over me. I want to know it all, possess it all, embrace the entire scene intimately, deeply, totally, as a man desires a beautiful woman. An insane wish? Perhaps not—at least there's nothing else, no one human, to dispute possession with me.

20 The snow-covered ground glimmers with a dull blue light, reflecting the sky and the approaching sunrise. Leading away from me the narrow dirt road, an alluring and primitive track into nowhere, meanders down the slope and toward the heart of the labyrinth of naked stone. Near the first group of arches, looming over a bend in the road, is a balanced rock about fifty feet high, mounted on a pedestal of equal height; it looks like a head from Easter Island, a stone god or a petrified ogre.

21 Like a god, like an ogre? The personification of the natural is exactly the tendency I wish to suppress in myself, to eliminate for good. I am here not only to evade for a while the clamor and filth and confusion of the cultural apparatus but also to confront, immediately and directly if it's possible, the bare bones of existence, the elemental and fundamental, the bedrock which sustains us. I want to be able to look at and into a juniper tree, a piece of quartz, a vulture, a spider, and see it as it is in itself, devoid of all humanly ascribed qualities, anti-Kantian, even the categories of scientific description. To meet God or Medusa face to face, even if it means risking everything human in myself. I dream of a hard and brutal mysticism in which the naked self merges with a nonhuman world and yet somehow survives still intact, individual, separate. Paradox and bedrock.

22 Well—the sun will be up in a few minutes and I haven't even begun to make coffee. I take more baggage from my pickup, the grub box and cooking gear, go back in the trailer and start breakfast. Simply

breathing, in a place like this, arouses the appetite. The orange juice is frozen, the milk slushy with ice. Still chilly enough inside the trailer to turn my breath to vapor. When the first rays of the sun strike the cliffs I fill a mug with steaming coffee and sit in the doorway facing the sunrise, hungry for the warmth.

23 Suddenly it comes, the flaming globe, blazing on the pinnacles and minarets and balanced rocks, on the canyon walls and through the windows in the sandstone fins. We greet each other, sun and I, across the black void of ninety-three million miles. The snow glitters between us, acres of diamonds almost painful to look at. Within an hour all the snow exposed to the sunlight will be gone and the rock will be damp and steaming. Within minutes, even as I watch, melting snow begins to drip from the branches of a juniper nearby; drops of water streak slowly down the side of the trailerhouse.

24 I am not alone after all. Three ravens are wheeling near the balanced rock, squawking at each other and at the dawn. I'm sure they're as delighted by the return of the sun as I am and I wish I knew the language. I'd sooner exchange ideas with the birds on earth than learn to carry on intergalactic communications with some obscure race of humanoids on a satellite planet from the world of Betelgeuse. First things first. The ravens cry out in husky voices, blue-black wings flapping against the golden sky. Over my shoulder comes the sizzle and smell of frying bacon.

25 That's the way it was this morning.

Understanding Meaning

1. What does Abbey mean by the "one true home"?
2. How would you *define* Abbey's concept of a "homing sentiment"?
3. How comfortable is Abbey's home? Does this conflict with our usual concept of the ideal home? What makes this place more of a home to Abbey than a suite at a resort hotel?
4. What are the most striking features of this location? What draws Abbey to this spot? Why is it the "most beautiful place on earth" in his eyes?
5. How does Abbey respond to his environment? What reactions does he wish to suppress?
6. *Critical Thinking:* How does Abbey's solitary confrontation with "inhuman" nature alter his perceptions and his sense of self? Does something draw people to experience or contemplate the desert, a mountain, or the sea in isolation? Can one achieve greater insights away from civilization?

Evaluating Strategy

1. How effective is the opening statement? Does a bold statement arouse attention, or can it appear too cliché?
2. How does Abbey view his role in nature?
3. *Other Modes:* Locate places where Abbey uses *narration* and *comparison* in creating a description of his favorite place. Is his real goal to describe or to tell a story?

Appreciating Language

1. Abbey uses words such as "iron lung," "tomb," "jail," and "cave" to describe his trailer. What is his intent in using these connotations? Would the essay have a different focus if he sentimentalized his home as a "snug cabin"? Would it alter the role of nature in the essay?
2. What words does Abbey use to describe the arches? Would his language impress an urban reader?

Connections across the Disciplines

1. Does Abbey share a similar view of nature with Gretel Ehrlich (page 199)? Do they share a sense of awe?
2. *Critical Thinking:* Consider Betsy Hilbert's concern that people inadvertently affect the environment even when motivated by good intentions (page 324). Does Abbey appear to suggest that any human intrusion into the landscape is bound to have a negative effect? Can this "most beautiful place on earth" be shared by more than one person, by a group, by tourists? Do people have to alter their environment?

Writing Suggestions

1. Write a short essay describing your "most beautiful place on earth." Review Abbey's opening paragraph, in which he states that even a waterfront alley in Hoboken can be beautiful. If you choose an unconventional location, use imagery to explain why you find beauty here. You may wish to focus as much on your own feelings as on the place itself.
2. *Collaborative Writing:* Discuss Abbey's essay with a group of students. Ask members to agree or disagree with this statement:

> Abbey's love of nature implies a dislike of human beings. He seems to suggest that people are inherently dangerous to the environment as if they were alien creatures and not inhabitants of the same planet as the ravens he wishes he could speak to. Something is disturbing about someone who craves isolation, as if he alone can appreciate the natural world.

Record comments and develop a common reaction to this suggestion. If members disagree, they may develop group pro and con statements.

BLENDING THE MODES

JAMAICA KINCAID

Jamaica Kincaid (1949–) was born Elaine Richardson in Antigua, an island in the Antilles. Kincaid attended Princess Margaret School on the island. At seventeen she came to America to work for a New York family. After a series of odd jobs, she began writing. Her articles appeared in Rolling Stone, The Paris Review, *and* The New Yorker, *where she became a staff writer in 1976. In 1984 her collection of stories,* At the Bottom of the River, *was published. In 1990 she published* Lucy, *a novel based on her immigrant experiences.*

Alien Soil

This article, which first appeared in The New Yorker, *describes the European legacy that left its impression on Antigua, a British possession until 1981. Notice the role* comparison, analysis, *and* cause and effect *play in her depiction of her homeland.*

1 Whatever it is in the character of the English people that leads them to obsessively order and shape their landscape to such a degree that it looks like a painting (tamed, framed, captured, kind, decent, good, pretty), while a painting never looks like the English landscape, unless it is a bad painting—this quality of character is blissfully lacking in the Antiguan people. I make this unfair comparison (unfair to the Antiguan people? unfair to the English people? I cannot tell, but there is an unfairness here somewhere) only because so much of the character of the Antiguan people is influenced by and inherited, through conquest, from the English people. The tendency to shower pity and cruelty on the weak is among the traits the Antiguans inherited, and so is a love of gossip. (The latter, I think, is responsible for the fact that England has produced such great novelists, but it has not yet worked to the literary advantage of the Antiguan people.) When the English were a presence in Antigua—they first came to the island as slaveowners, when a man named Thomas Warner established a settlement there in 1632—the places where they lived were surrounded by severely trimmed hedges of plumbago, topiaries of willow (casuarina), and frangipani and hibiscus; their grass was green (odd, because water

was scarce; the proper word for the climate is not "sunny" but "drought-ridden") and freshly cut; they kept trellises covered with roses, and beds of marigolds and cannas and chrysanthemums.

2 Ordinary Antiguans (and by "ordinary Antiguans" I mean the Antiguan people, who are descended from the African slaves brought to this island by Europeans; this turns out to be a not uncommon way to become ordinary), the ones who had some money and could live in houses of more than one room, had gardens in which only flowers were grown. This made it even more apparent that they had some money, in that all their outside space was devoted not to feeding their families but to the sheer beauty of things. I can remember in particular one such family, who lived in a house with many rooms (four, to be exact). They had an indoor kitchen and a place for bathing (no indoor toilet, though); they had a lawn, always neatly cut, and they had beds of flowers, but I can now remember only roses and marigolds. I can remember those because once I was sent there to get a bouquet of roses for my godmother on her birthday. The family also had, in the middle of their small lawn, a willow tree, pruned so that it had the shape of a pine tree—a conical shape—and at Christmastime this tree was decorated with colored lights (which was so unusual and seemed so luxurious to me that when I passed by this house I would beg to be allowed to stop and stare at it for a while). At Christmas, all willow trees would suddenly be called Christmas trees, and for a time, when my family must have had a small amount of money, I, too, had a Christmas tree—a lonely, spindly branch of willow sitting in a bucket of water in our very small house. No one in my family and, I am almost certain, no one in the family of the people with the lighted-up willow tree had any idea of the origins of the Christmas tree and the traditions associated with it. When these people (the Antiguans) lived under the influence of these other people (the English), there was naturally an attempt among some of them to imitate their rulers in this particular way—by rearranging the landscape—and they did it without question. They can't be faulted for not asking what it was they were doing; that is the way these things work. The English left, and most of their landscaping influence went with them. The Americans came, but Americans (I am one now) are not interested in influencing people directly; we instinctively understand the childish principle of monkey see, monkey do. And at the same time we are divided about how we ought to behave in the world. Half of us believe in and support strongly a bad thing our government is doing, while the other half do

not believe in and protest strongly against the bad thing. The bad thing succeeds, and everyone, protester and supporter alike, enjoys immensely the results of the bad thing. This ambiguous approach in the many is always startling to observe in the individual. Just look at Thomas Jefferson, a great American gardener and our country's third president, who owned slaves and strongly supported the idea of an expanded American border, which meant the extinction of the people who already lived on the land to be taken, while at the same time he was passionately devoted to ideas about freedom—ideas that the descendants of the slaves and the people who were defeated and robbed of their land would have to use in defense of themselves. Jefferson, as president, commissioned the formidable trek his former secretary, the adventurer and botany thief Meriwether Lewis, made through the West, sending plant specimens back to the president along the way. The *Lewisia rediviva*, state flower of Montana, which Lewis found in the Bitterroot River valley, is named after him; the clarkia, not a flower of any state as far as I can tell, is named for his co-adventurer and botany thief, William Clark.

3 What did the botanical life of Antigua consist of at the time another famous adventurer—Christopher Columbus—first saw it? To see a garden in Antigua now will not supply a clue. I made a visit to Antigua this spring, and most of the plants I saw there came from somewhere else. The bougainvillea (named for another restless European, the sea adventurer Louis-Antoine de Bougainville, first Frenchman to cross the Pacific) is native to tropical South America; the plumbago is from southern Africa; the croton (genus *Codiaeum*) is from Malay Peninsula; the *Hibiscus rosa-sinensis* is from Asia and the *Hibiscus schizopetalus* is from East Africa; the allamanda is from Brazil; the poinsettia (named for an American ambassador, Joel Poinsett) is from Mexico; the bird of paradise flower is from southern Africa; the Bermuda lily is from Japan; the flamboyant tree is from Madagascar; the casuarina is from Australia; the Norfolk pine is from Norfolk Island; the tamarind tree is from Africa; the mango is from Asia. The breadfruit, the most Antiguan (to me) and starchy food, the bane of every Antiguan child's palate, is from the East Indies. This food has been the cause of more disagreement between parents and their children than anything else I can think of. No child has ever liked it. It was sent to the West Indies by Joseph Banks, the English naturalist and world traveler and the head of Kew Gardens, which was then a clearinghouse for all the plants stolen from the various parts of the world where the

English had been. (One of the climbing roses, *Rosa banksiae*, from China, was named for Banks's wife.) Banks sent tea to India; to the West Indies he sent the breadfruit. It was meant to be a cheap food for feeding slaves. It was the cargo that Captain Bligh was carrying to the West Indies on the ship *Bounty* when his crew so rightly mutinied. It's as though the Antiguan child senses intuitively the part this food has played in the history of injustice and so will not eat it. But, unfortunately for her, it grows readily, bears fruit abundantly, and is impervious to drought. Soon after the English settled in Antigua, they cleared the land of its hardwood forests to make room for the growing of tobacco, sugar, and cotton, and it is this that makes the island drought-ridden to this day. Antigua is also empty of much wildlife natural to it. When snakes proved a problem for the planters, they imported the mongoose from India. As a result there are no snakes at all on the island—nor other reptiles, other than lizards—though I don't know what damage the absence of snakes causes, if any.

4 What herb of beauty grew in this place then? What tree? And did the people who lived there grow anything beautiful for its own sake? I do not know; I can only make a straightforward deduction: the frangipani, the mahogany tree, and the cedar tree are all native to the West Indies, so these trees are probably indigenous. And some of the botany of Antigua can be learned from medicinal folklore. My mother and I were sitting on the steps in front of her house one day during my recent visit, and I suddenly focused on a beautiful bush (beautiful to me now; when I was a child I thought it ugly) whose fruit I remembered playing with when I was little. It is an herbaceous plant that has a red stem covered with red thorns, and emerald-green, simple leaves, with the same red thorns running down the leaf from the leafstalk. I cannot remember what its flowers looked like, and it was not in flower when I saw it while I was there with my mother, but its fruit is a small, almost transparent red berry, and it is this I used to play with. We children sometimes called it "china berry," because of its transparent, glassy look—it reminded us of china dinnerware, though we were only vaguely familiar with such a thing as china, having seen it no more than once or twice—and sometimes "baby tomato," because of its color, and to signify that it was not real; a baby thing was not a real thing. When I pointed the bush out to my mother, she called it something else; she called it cancanberry bush, and said that in the old days, when people could not afford to see doctors, if a child had thrush they would make a paste of this fruit and rub it inside the child's

mouth, and this would make the thrush go away. But, she said, people rarely bother with this remedy anymore. The day before, a friend of hers had come to pay a visit, and when my mother offered her something to eat and drink the friend declined, because, she said, she had some six-sixty-six and maidenblush tea waiting at home for her. This tea is taken on an empty stomach, and it is used for all sorts of ailments, including to help bring on abortions. I have never seen six-sixty-six in flower, but its leaves are a beautiful ovoid shape and a deep green—qualities that are of value in a garden devoted to shape and color of leaf.

5 People who do not like the idea that there is a relationship between gardening and wealth are quick to remind me of the cottage gardener, that grim-faced English person. Living on land that is not his own, he has put bits and pieces of things together, things from here and there, and it is a beautiful jumble—but just try duplicating it; it isn't cheap to do. And I have never read a book praising the cottage garden written by a cottage gardener. This person—the cottage gardener—does not exist in a place like Antigua. Nor do casual botanical conversation, knowledge of the Latin names for plants, and discussions of the binomial system. If an atmosphere where these things could flourish exists in this place, I am not aware of it. I can remember very well the cruel Englishwoman who was my botany teacher, and that, in spite of her cruelty, botany was one of my two favorite subjects in school. (History was the other.) With this in mind I visited a bookstore (the only bookstore I know of in Antigua) to see what texts are now being used in the schools and to see how their content compares with what was taught to me back then; the botany I had studied was a catalogue of the plants of the British Empire, the very same plants that are now widely cultivated in Antigua and are probably assumed by ordinary Antiguans to be native to their landscape—the mango, for example. But it turns out that botany as a subject is no longer taught in Antiguan schools; the study of plants is now called agriculture. Perhaps that is more realistic, since the awe and poetry of botany cannot be eaten, and the mystery and pleasure in the knowledge of botany cannot be taken to market and sold.

6 And yet the people of Antigua have a relationship to agriculture that does not please them at all. Their very arrival on this island had to do with the forces of agriculture. When they (we) were brought to this island from Africa a few hundred years ago, it was not for their pottery-making skills or for their way with a loom; it was for the free labor they

could provide in the fields. Mary Prince, a nineteenth-century African woman who was born in Bermuda and spent part of her life as a slave in Antigua, writes about this in an autobiographical account, which I found in *The Classic Slave Narratives*, edited by Henry Louis Gates, Jr. She says:

7 My master and mistress went on one occasion into the country, to Date Hill, for change of air, and carried me with them to take charge of the children, and to do the work of the house. While I was in the country, I saw how the field negroes are worked in Antigua. They are worked very hard and fed but scantily. They are called out to work before daybreak, and come home after dark; and then each has to heave his bundle of grass for the cattle in the pen. Then, on Sunday morning, each slave has to go out and gather a large bundle of grass; and, when they bring it home, they have all to sit at the manager's door and wait till he come out: often they have to wait there till past eleven o'clock, without any breakfast. After that, those that have yams or potatoes, or fire-wood to sell, hasten to market to buy . . . salt fish, or pork, which is a great treat for them.

Perhaps it makes sense that a group of people with such a wretched historical relationship to growing things would need to describe their current relationship to it as dignified and masterly (agriculture), and would not find it poetic (botany) or pleasurable (gardening).

8 In a book I am looking at (to read it is to look at it: the type is as tall as a doll's teacup), *The Tropical Garden*, by William Warren, with photographs by Luca Invernizzi Tettoni, I find statements like "the concept of a private garden planted purely for aesthetic purposes was generally alien to tropical countries" and "there was no such tradition of ornamental horticulture among the inhabitants of most hot-weather places. Around the average home there might be a few specimens chosen especially because of their scented flowers or because they were believed to bring good fortune. . . . Nor would much, if any, attention be paid to attractive landscape design in such gardens: early accounts by travellers in the tropics abound in enthusiastic descriptions of jungle scenery, but a reader will search in vain for one praising the tasteful arrangement of massed ornamental beds and contrasting lawns of well-trimmed grass around the homes of natives." What can I say to that? No doubt it is true. And no doubt contrasting lawns and massed ornamental beds are a sign of something, and that is that

someone—someone other than the owner of the lawns—has been humbled. To give just one example: on page 62 of this book is a photograph of eight men, natives of India, pulling a heavy piece of machinery used in the upkeep of lawns. They are without shoes. They are wearing the clothing of schoolboys—khaki shorts and khaki short-sleeved shirts. There is no look of bliss on their faces. The caption for the photograph reads, "Shortage of labour was never a problem in the maintenance of European features in large colonial gardens; here a team of workers is shown rolling a lawn at the Gymkhana Club in Bombay."

9 And here are a few questions that occur to me: what if the people living in the tropics, the ones whose history isn't tied up with and contaminated by slavery and indenturedness, are contented with their surroundings, are happy to observe an invisible hand at work and from time to time laugh at some of the ugly choices this hand makes; what if they have more important things to do than make a small tree large, a large tree small, or a tree whose blooms are usually yellow bear black blooms; what if these people are not spiritually feverish, restless, and full of envy?

10 When I was looking at the book of tropical gardens, I realized that the flowers and the trees so familiar to me from my childhood do not now have a hold on me. I do not long to plant and be surrounded by the bougainvillea; I do not like the tropical hibiscus; the corallita (from Mexico), so beautiful when tended, so ugly when left to itself, which makes everything around it look rusty and shabby, is not a plant I like at all. I returned from my visit to Antigua, the place where I was born, to a small village in Vermont, the place where I choose to live. Spring had arrived. The tulips I had planted last autumn were in bloom, and I liked to sit and caress their petals, which felt disgustingly delicious, like scraps of peau de soie. The dizzy-making yellow of dandelions and cowslips was in the fields and riverbanks and marshes. I like these things. (I do not like daffodils, but that's a legacy of the English approach: I was forced to memorize the poem by William Wordsworth when I was a child.) I transplanted to the edge of a grove of pine trees some foxgloves that I grew from seed in late winter. I found some Virginia bluebells in a spot in the woods where I had not expected to find them, and some larches growing grouped together, also in a place I had not expected. On my calendar I marked the day I would go and dig up all the mulleins I could find and replant them to a very sunny spot across from the grove of pine trees. This is to be my forest of mulleins,

though in truth it will appear a forest only to an ant. I marked the day I would plant the nasturtiums under the fruit trees. I discovered a clump of Dutchman's-breeches in the wildflower bed that I inherited from the man who built and used to own the house in which I now live, Robert Woodworth, the botanist who invented time-lapse photography. I waited for the things I had ordered in the deep cold of winter to come. They started to come. Mr. Pembroke, who represents our village in the Vermont legislature, came and helped me dig some of the holes where some of the things I wanted to put in were to be planted. Mr. Pembroke is a very nice man. He is never dressed in the clothing of schoolboys. There is not a look of misery on his face; on his face is the complicated look of an ordinary human being. When he works in my garden, we agree on a price; he sends me a bill, and I pay it. The days are growing longer and longer, and then they'll get shorter again. I am now used to that ordered progression, and I love it. But there is no order in my garden. I live in America now. Americans are impatient with memory, which is one of the things order thrives on.

Understanding Meaning

1. What is the thesis of Kincaid's description?
2. What does Kincaid's description of the botany and landscaping of the island reveal about its history and cultural development?
3. How many Antiguan plants originate from other parts of the world?
4. What relationship does Kincaid see between wealth and gardening? How does she explain the English cottage garden?
5. How does Kincaid *analyze* the meaning of the photograph of men in India laboring with a massive lawn roller in a colonial garden? What does this signify?
6. Consider the last line of the essay, "Americans are impatient with memory, which is one of the things order thrives on." Are Americans "impatient with memory"? Do Americans suffer from an amnesia about their past?
7. *Critical Thinking:* Does the English garden, often admired for its neatly trimmed hedges and groomed lawns, symbolize something sinister? What does Kincaid intend the garden to symbolize?

Evaluating Strategy

1. What impact does the title have? For whom is the soil "alien"?
2. What *comparison* does Kincaid use to open her essay? Why does she consider it "unfair"?

3. Locate places where Kincaid uses *cause and effect* to show the effect of British landscaping on the island.
4. How much of the description is based on a series of *comparisons?*

Appreciating Language

1. What language does Kincaid use to describe Antigua? What connotations do her words contain?
2. How does Kincaid *define* "ordinary Antiguans"?
3. Kincaid uses the phrase "botany thief" to describe Lewis and Clark. What meaning does this word choice have?

Connections across the Disciplines

1. Does Kincaid see nature the way Edward Abbey does (page 139)? Do they both see the same effects of human development on the land?
2. Kincaid states that she now considers herself an American. Compare her views of her culture with those of N. Scott Momaday (page 133) and Armando Rendón (page 667). Does becoming an American always entail a loss of a previous culture?

Writing Suggestions

1. Study the landscape of your community, campus, or workplace. Write a brief description, and *analyze* what it suggests about the people who designed it.
2. *Collaborative Writing:* Review Kincaid's description of Thomas Jefferson with several students. How does her description compare with the usual view of Jefferson as the author of the Declaration of Independence (page 608)? Is Kincaid's view honest, cynical, or simply an alternative interpretation? Record the comments made by the group and draft a common response. If members disagree, consider writing group pro and con statements.

WRITING BEYOND THE CLASSROOM

FRANK PILIPP AND CHARLES SHULL

Abstracts are brief summaries describing articles and reports. The fields of chemistry, biology, law, medicine, literature, and psychology each have specialized abstracts that serve as a valuable source to students and researchers. Most abstracts are now available on computer. This abstract describes an article analyzing how the subject of AIDS has been treated by TV movies. Other abstracts describe articles on everything from solar power to plastic surgery. As you review this entry, consider how abstracts can help students locate sources for research papers and skim current scholarship. *See page 386 for the full article.*

TV Movies of the First Decade of AIDS (Abstract)

1 Database: Expanded Academic Index
Subject: aids (disease) in motion pictures

2 TV movies of the first decade of AIDS. (American Values and Images)

3 Journal of Popular Film and Television, Spring 1993 v21 n1 p19(8).

4 Author: Frank Pilipp and Charles Shull

5 Abstract: The decade of 1983–1993 has produced several full-length feature films which respond to the AIDS epidemic. Three of them, 'As Is,' 'Andre's Mother,' and 'An Early Frost' undoubtedly portray the virus as non-partisan when it comes to gender, color, or sexual orientation, although they fail to destroy the image of AIDS as being a purely homosexual disease. The disease instead is viewed as punishment inflicted on the main characters and their families for their violation of middle-class norms and values.

6 Subjects: Gays—Portrayals, depictions, etc.
Motion pictures—Criticism, interpretation, etc.
AIDS (Disease) in motion pictures—Criticism, interpretation, etc.

7 Features: illustration; photograph

8 AN: 14558418

Understanding Meaning

1. What information is contained in the abstract? How helpful would it be if you were researching the way television has responded to AIDS?
2. Is the abstract objective?

Evaluating Strategy

1. What problems does an abstract writer have in reducing an eight-page article to a single paragraph?
2. Should an abstract writer inject subjective opinion?

Appreciating Language

1. How objective is the language of the abstract?
2. Should an abstract be devoid of figurative language?

Connections across the Disciplines

1. At the library locate abstracts in your field and review summaries of several articles. How would they be helpful in doing research?
2. Read the full article (page 386). How successfully does this abstract summarize Pilipp and Shull's article?

Writing Suggestions

1. Select one of the articles in this book and draft an abstract. Try to capture the writer's thesis and main support in a single paragraph.
2. *Collaborative Writing:* Discuss this abstract with a number of students who have read the full article. How effective is this summary? What points do students feel have been omitted?

THE TIMES-PICAYUNE, JULY 31, 1994

Want ads describe the ideal candidate for a job opening. This ad, which appeared in the New Orleans Times-Picayune, *presents a job description for a sales representative.*

3M Pharmaceutical Sales Representative Want Ad

Sales Representative

Pharmaceutical Products

3M Pharmaceuticals has an immediate need for an experienced sales professional to represent our products to physicians, pharmacies, hospitals and managed care facilities. These products include prescription medications related to the treatment of arthritic, cardiovascular and pulmonary conditions. This position will be based in New Orleans and will require overnight travel.

We prefer a college degree and 2+ years successful outside sales experience. Medical sales experience is preferred. Excellent communications and interpersonal skills are required. We provide base salary plus bonus, company car, complete business expenses and an attractive benefits package.

For confidential consideration, send two (2) copies of your resume to the below address by August 16, 1994. Candidates selected for consideration will be notified by September 2, 1994. No telephone inquiries or employment agency referrals please.

NAS REPLY SERVICE

Dept #7MP1089 One Appletree Square Minneapolis, MN 55425

We Are An Equal Opportunity Employer M/F/D/V

Understanding Meaning

1. What are the requirements for this position?
2. What does this ad suggest about the reader 3M hopes to reach?
3. *Critical Thinking:* What are the limits of any want ad? Can a job be fully described in a few paragraphs? Why can't employers address all their interests and concerns?

Evaluating Strategy

1. Why does the ad first describe the job and then list the requirements?
2. Why is it important for an employer to promise applicants "confidential consideration"?

Appreciating Language

1. What words does the ad use to describe the ideal candidate?
2. Some ads promise applicants "huge commissions" and demand "hard charging" people. What does the absence of this kind of language suggest about this employer?

Connections across the Disciplines

1. Study want ads in your local newspaper. What common words stand out? How do employers describe the positions and the desired candidates? Do you see trends in the job market?

Writing Suggestions

1. Write a want ad for a job you once had. Try to model yours after ones you have seen in the newspaper. Keep your ad as short as possible.
2. *Collaborative Writing:* Work with a group of students and write a want ad together. Imagine you are hiring a part-time employee to act as secretary for your writing group. Determine the skills needed, the major duties, and how the ad should be worded. If members have differences of opinion, craft more than one ad, and ask other students to choose the most effective ad.

MONICA RAMOS

Monica Ramos was born in New Orleans and worked as a nurse before entering advertising sales. Although she has never sold pharmaceuticals, she prepared this résumé to apply for the position advertised by 3M (page 158). Given her sales ability and experience working in a hospital, Ramos feels she is qualified for the position. Notice that her résumé uses bulleted lists of specific accomplishments to provide details that are easily read or skimmed.

The Résumé of Monica Ramos

1 MONICA RAMOS
1455 Josephine Street #12
New Orleans, Louisiana 70118
(504) 524-6580

2 OBJECTIVE Pharmaceutical Sales

3 OVERVIEW Three years experience in outside sales. Proven ability to secure new accounts in competitive markets. Five years experience in cardiac and pulmonary patient care. Knowledgeable in cardiac medications. Skilled in communicating with physicians and hospital staff.

4 EXPERIENCE
1993–Present

CRESCENT CITY MAGAZINE,
New Orleans, LA
Account representative selling advertising space in upscale magazine with 50,000 circulation.

* Developed 300 active accounts including hospitals, nursing homes, HMO's, clinics, and drug stores.
* Personally developed restaurant/ entertainment section, selling ads to

100 area restaurants worth $200,000 annually.
* Consistently rank in top 3 of 15 sales reps.
* Generated 65 new accounts in first three months.
* Directly assisted vice president of Charity Hospital in design of four-page insert.

5 1989–1993 TULANE UNIVERSITY MEDICAL CENTER, New Orleans, LA
Nurse in 25 bed intensive care unit specializing in critical cardiac and pulmonary care.
* Worked directly with physicians, cardiologists, and cardiovascular surgeons.
* Administered full range of cardiac medications.
* Attended inservice seminars presented by pharmaceutical representatives.
* Represented hospital on regional and state planning committees.

6 EDUCATION LOUISIANA STATE UNIVERSITY MEDICAL CENTER—NEW ORLEANS
B.S. Nursing, 1989

7 SALES TRAINING 1994–95 SALES MANAGEMENT INSTITUTE, New Orleans, LA
* Attended seminars on networking, presentation skills, and closing strategies.

8 VOLUNTEER WORK GREATER NEW ORLEANS YWCA
Conduct cardiac health/stress management workshops

9 References Available on Request

Understanding Meaning

1. Compare this résumé to the 3M want ad (page 158). Does it address the employer's needs?
2. What skills and experiences does Monica Ramos highlight? What are her important attributes?

Evaluating Strategy

1. One study revealed that the average executive devotes nine seconds to each résumé on initial screening. Does this résumé communicate its main points in a few seconds? Would it make a reader stop skimming and start reading?
2. How is the information arranged? Is it clear and easy to follow?

Appreciating Language

1. What is the tone of the résumé? How do the words portray the applicant?
2. What device does Monica Ramos use to convey a sense of action?

Connections across the Disciplines

1. Review this résumé after reading the article "Resumes That Rate a Second Look" (page 510). How does this résumé rate?

Writing Suggestions

1. Write your own résumé, either a current one or one as if you were prepared to graduate this semester.
2. *Collaborative Writing:* Meet with a group of students and have each member supply a résumé. Discuss the merits of each résumé you review. Talk about problems you have encountered. Take notes to improve your own résumé. Your library or placement office may offer guides and computer programs to help you develop your résumé.

GUIDELINES FOR WRITING DESCRIPTION

1. **Determine your purpose.** What is your goal—to entertain a general audience or to provide information to colleagues, employees, superiors, or customers? What are the most important details needed to support your purpose?
2. **Define your role.** If you are expressing personal opinion, you are free to add subjective elements to your writing. You may wish to include yourself in the piece of writing by making personal references and writing in the first person. If you are writing as a representative of a larger body, objective language is usually more appropriate.
3. **Consider your audience.** Which type of description would best suit your readers—subjective impressions or objective facts? What needs and expectations does your audience have? What details, facts, statistics, or descriptions will influence readers the most?
4. **Review the discipline or writing situation.** Determine if you should use technical or specialized terminology. If you are writing for a profession, academic discipline, government agency, or corporation, use standard methods of developing ideas.
5. **Select details.** Having determined the context, select details that emphasize your purpose, impress your audience, and follow any guidelines in your discipline. Descriptions should have focus. Eliminate details that may be interesting in themselves but do not serve your purpose.
6. **Organize details in an effective manner.** Good description is more than a collection of details. To be effective, your writing should be logically organized. You may organize details spatially by describing a house room by room or a city neighborhood by neighborhood. You may organize details in order of importance. If you use objective and subjective description, these details can alternate or be placed in separate sections.
7. **Avoid unnecessary detail or mechanical organization.** Descriptions have focus. A description of your apartment does not have to list every piece of furniture, explain how each room is decorated, or provide dimensions. In general avoid writing descriptions that draw unnecessary attention to mechanical arrangements:

> *On the left-hand wall* is a bookcase. *To the right of the bookcase* is a stereo. *Around the corner of the stereo* stands an antique aquarium filled with tropical fish. *Above the aquarium* is a large seascape painting. Model ships line the window sill. A cabinet *to the right of the window* is filled with seashells.

8. **Allow details to create a dominant impression.** A subjective description of a room can focus on a single theme:

Although I live hundreds of miles from the ocean, my apartment has a seagoing motif. Beneath a sweeping seascape, a large antique aquarium dominates the living room, its colorful tropical fish flashing among rocks and shells I collected in Florida. Miniature schooners, windjammers, and ketches line the windowsill. The ornate glass cabinet intended for china houses my prize collection of Hawaiian seashells.

SUGGESTED TOPICS FOR DESCRIPTIVE WRITING

General Assignments

Write a description on any of the following topics. Your description may contain passages demonstrating other modes, such as comparison or cause and effect. Select details carefully. Determine whether your description should rely on factual, objective support or subjective impressions. In choosing diction, be aware of the impact of connotation.

- Your first apartment
- The people who gather in a place you frequent—a coffee shop, store, tavern, library, or student union
- Your boss or professor
- The most desirable/least desirable place to live in your community
- The most dangerous situation you have faced
- The type of man/woman you find attractive
- The type of relationship you find most desirable
- The most serious environmental problem in your area
- The most interesting or most unconventional person you have met in the past year
- The best/worst party you have attended

Writing in Context

1. Imagine that your college has asked you to write a description of the campus for a brochure designed to recruit students. Your depiction should be easy to read and create a favorable impression.
2. Assume you write a column for an alternative campus newspaper. Develop a sarcastic description of the campus, the college administration, the faculty, or the student body.
3. Write an open letter to the student body of your high school describing what college life is like.
4. Imagine you are trying to sell your car. Write two brief ads, one designed for a campus flyer and the other for a newspaper.

DESCRIPTION CHECKLIST

1. Have you limited your topic?
2. What kind of support will best communicate to your readers—objective facts or sensory impressions?
3. Does your word choice suit your topic, purpose, and audience?
4. Have you avoided needless detail, clichés, and awkward constructions?
5. Does sensory detail include more than sight? Could you add sounds, smells, or tastes?
6. Do you include words or expressions your audience might find objectionable?
7. Read your paper aloud. How does it sound? Do any sections need expansion? Can irrelevant details be eliminated?

4

DEFINITION

ESTABLISHING MEANING

WHAT IS DEFINITION?

Effective communication requires that writers and readers have a shared language. Words and ideas must be *defined* clearly to eliminate confusion and misinterpretation. Definitions limit or explain the meaning of a term or concept. As a college student you have probably devoted much of your time to learning new words and their definitions. Fields such as chemistry, psychology, sociology, economics, law, and anatomy have technical terms that must be mastered in order to communicate within the discipline.

Clearly stated definitions play a critical role in professional and business writing. In order to prevent confusion, conflict, and litigation, many union contracts, insurance policies, sales agreements, and leases include definitions so all parties will share a common understanding of important terms. Government documents and business proposals contain glossaries to familiarize readers with new or abstract terms. Failing to understand a definition can be costly. A tenant who does not understand a landlord's definition of "excessive noise" may face eviction. The car buyer who misinterprets the manufacturer's definition of "normal use" can void his or her warranty.

The term *definition* leads most people to think of a dictionary. But defining entails more than looking something up. Definitions are not always precise or universally accepted. Distinctly different types of definitions exist. To be an effective writer in college and your future profession, it is important to appreciate the range of definitions:

- **Standard definitions** are universally accepted and rarely subject to change. Words such as *tibia, dolphin, uranium, felony, turbine,* and *rifle* have exact meanings that are understood and shared by scholars, professionals, and the general public. Doctors, nurses, paramedics, and football coaches, for example, all recognize *tibia* as a specific bone in the body. Though different state legislatures might disagree on which specific crime constitutes a *felony,* they all accept its general concept.
- **Regulatory definitions** are officially designated terms and are subject to change. The National Football League, Internal Revenue Service (IRS), Federal Aviation Administration, and Federal Communications Commission, school boards, labor organizations, the Catholic Church, and insurance companies issue definitions to guide policy, control operations, and make decisions. The IRS definition of *deductible meal allowance* can change yearly. One health insurance company may pay for a liver transplant while another carrier refuses, defining the procedure *experimental.* Regulatory definitions may be universally accepted, but they can change or be limited to a specific region or discipline. The building codes of New York and San Francisco may have varying definitions of what buildings are *structurally sound.* The medical definition of *insanity* varies greatly from the court-accepted, legal definition.
- **Evolving definitions** reflect changes in community attitudes, social values, governmental policy, and scientific research. In the nineteenth century corporal punishment was a routine feature of public school discipline. Today the same actions would be defined as *child abuse.* The term *date rape* defines incidents that generations ago would not be viewed as criminal assaults. Decades ago medical and psychology texts defined *homosexuality* as a mental disorder. Evolving definitions track social change and rarely shift as abruptly as regulatory definitions.
- **Qualifying definitions** limit meanings of words or concepts that are abstract or subject to dispute. How does one define an *alcoholic?* At what point do doctors label a patient *obese* or *senile?* Which young people are labeled *juvenile delinquents?* How does one define *genius?* In some fields organizations provide definitions. The American Medical Association may offer a definition of *alcoholism.* But unlike a regulatory term, physicians and researchers are free to dispute it and apply a different meaning altogether. Some definitions are hotly debated. Researchers, politicians, and social commentators continually argue whether drug addiction and alcoholism should be defined as a *disability,* which would entitle people to receive benefits.
- **Cultural definitions** are shaped by the history, values, and attitudes of a national, ethnic, or religious group. Just as evolving definitions alter over time, cultural definitions differ from group to group. In some countries it is customary to offer cash gifts to officials as a *tribute.* In the United States the

same action would be defined as an illegal *bribe*. People around the world embrace *freedom* but define it very differently. For most Americans *freedom* is defined in personal terms, meaning freedom of individual movement and expression. In other countries, people may define *freedom* in national terms, as protecting the independence and security of their homeland even if it means censorship and restricted personal liberties.

- **Personal definitions** are used by writers to express individual interpretations of words or ideas. Your concept of a good parent would be a personal definition. A writer can frame an entire essay in terms of a personal definition, such as John Ciardi's "What is Happiness?" (page 194), or simply establish a series of personal definitions at the outset of a narrative or persuasive paper. Writers often use personal definition as a method of stating their opinions.

Methods of Definition

Definitions can be established using a number of techniques:

1. **Defining through synonyms** is the simplest method of providing meaning for a word. Glossaries and dictionaries customarily define technical terms or foreign words with synonyms. *Costal* refers to *ribs*. A *siesta* can be translated as a *nap*. A *casement* can be explained as a *window*.
2. **Defining by description** provides details about a word or subject and gives readers a sense of what it might look, feel, taste, smell, or sound like. Defining a *costrel* as *a small flask with a loop or loops that is suspended from a belt* provides readers with a clear picture. Descriptive definitions also can demonstrate how something operates. An *airbag* can be defined as *a rapidly inflated cushion designed to protect automobile passengers in a collision.*
3. **Defining by example** provides specific illustrations to establish meaning. A *felony* can be defined as *a serious crime such as murder, rape, or burglary*. Examples can establish meaning through identification. Telling a fourth-grade class that an *adjective is a word that modifies a noun* will not be as effective as providing examples children can easily recognize—*red, fast, tall, silly, old-fashioned, hot*. Complex or abstract concepts are easier to comprehend if defined by example. Income tax instructions include numerous examples to define what is and is not deductible.
4. **Defining by comparison** uses analogies readers can understand to provide meaning to something less familiar. A television reporter covering a space mission defined NASA terminology using comparisons viewers would readily understand. To explain the term *power down*, she remarked that the astronauts were *conserving power by turning off nonessential electrical*

devices, much like switching off the radio and windshield wipers on a car. Because they can oversimplify complex ideas, comparative definitions must be used carefully.

5. **Extended definitions** qualify or limit the meaning of abstract, disputed, or highly complex words or concepts. Words such as *sin, love,* and *racism* cannot be adequately explained through synonyms, brief descriptions, or examples. A full description may require several paragraphs. Michael Korda devotes several pages to define a *leader* (page 189). The *yucca* can be defined as a *spear-leafed desert plant,* but, to explain its significance to the Navajo, Terry Tempest Williams writes an entire essay (page 205).

The Purpose of Definition

Definitions generally serve to establish meaning, to provide a common or shared understanding. But they also can be persuasive. Evolving definitions frequently indicate a break with past beliefs and suggest alternative interpretations. The first psychiatrists who defined *homosexuality* in terms of *sexual orientation* rather than as *deviancy, mental disorder,* or *sexual perversion* were clearly trying to persuade their readers to change their attitudes. In "Deafness as Culture" (page 214) Edward Dolnick explains that many deaf people prefer to define themselves as members of a distinct *culture* rather than as people sharing a *handicap.* Senator Joseph Biden uses a persuasive definition for the title of his law review article: "Domestic Violence: A Crime, Not a Quarrel" (page 651).

To transform public attitudes, writers frequently urge readers to redefine something, to change their perceptions and see striking a child as *abuse* instead of *spanking* or to accept graffiti as *street art* and not *vandalism.* Definitions can play a critical role in shaping opinions and making arguments. Drug addicts, for instance, can be defined in legalistic terms and viewed as *criminals* who should be imprisoned or depicted in medical terms as *sufferers* needing treatment.

Definition in Context

The way writers define subjects depends greatly on context. In defining *depression* for a marketing brochure, a psychotherapist directs an explanation to prospective clients:

> Depression is an internal state—a feeling of sadness, loss, "the blues," deep disappointment. *When it is more severe, you may have feelings of irritability, touchiness, guilt, self-reproach, loss of self-esteem, worthlessness, hopelessness, helplessness, and even thoughts of death and suicide.*

The definition is addressed to the reader, using the word "you," and focuses on personal "feelings" stated in general terms. In contrast, Jessica Kuper's *Encyclopedia of Psychology* offers a definition for mental health professionals:

> *Depression* is a term used to describe a mood, a symptom, and syndromes of affective disorders. As a mood, it refers to a transient state of feeling sad, blue, forlorn, cheerless, unhappy, and/or down. As a symptom, it refers to a complaint that often accompanies a group of biopsychosocial problems. In contrast, the depressive syndromes include a wide spectrum of psychobiological dysfunctions that vary in frequency, severity, and duration.

The inclusion of words such as "affective disorders" and "biopsychosocial" indicate that this definition is intended for a specialized audience familiar with technical terms.

READING DEFINITIONS

In reading the definition entries in this chapter, keep these questions in mind.

Meaning

1. Which type of definition is the author developing—standard, regulatory, evolving, qualifying, cultural, or personal?
2. What is the author's purpose—to provide a definition to establish common ground, to explain a complex issue, or to persuade readers to alter their opinions?
3. What audience is the writer addressing—a general reader or a specialist? Does the audience need to know the definitions in order to base decisions or guide future actions?
4. What is the nature of the discipline or writing situation? Is the writer working within a strictly regulated profession or the general marketplace of ideas?

Strategy

1. How does the writer define the word, object, or concept—through synonyms, descriptions, examples, or comparisons?
2. Is the definition limited to a specific incident or context, or can it be applied generally? Is the writer defining a particular person or a personality trait that could be shared by millions?
3. Does the writer supply personal examples, or does he or she rely on official sources to establish the definition?

Language

1. What role do word choice and connotation play in establishing the definition?
2. What do the tone and level of language reveal about the writer's purpose and intended audience?

EILEEN SIMPSON

Eileen Simpson is a psychotherapist who struggled for years to overcome dyslexia, a reading disorder that affects more than 20 million Americans. She is the author of several books, including Poets in Their Youth, *a memoir of her marriage to the poet John Berryman. Other books based on her personal experiences explored problems of children growing up without parents. This section comes from her 1979 book* Reversals: A Personal Account of Victory over Dyslexia.

Dyslexia

Simpson provides a standard definition of an existing term by examining its Greek and Latin roots and then demonstrates the effects dyslexia has on its victims. Notice that she supplies examples to help readers fully appreciate the implications of a widely misunderstood disorder.

1 Dyslexia (from the Greek, *dys*, faulty + *lexis*, speech, cognate with the Latin *legere*, to read), developmental or specific dyslexia as it's technically called, the disorder I suffered from, is the inability of otherwise normal children to read. Children whose intelligence is below average, whose vision or hearing is defective, who have not had proper schooling, or who are too emotionally disturbed or brain-damaged to profit from it belong in other diagnostic categories. They, too, may be unable to learn to read, but they cannot properly be called dyslexics.

2 For more than seventy years the essential nature of the affliction has been hotly disputed by psychologists, neurologists, and educators. It is generally agreed, however, that it is the result of a neurophysiological flaw in the brain's ability to process language. It is probably inherited, although some experts are reluctant to say this because they fear people will equate "inherited" with "untreatable." Treatable it certainly is: not a disease to be cured, but a malfunction that requires retraining.

3 Reading is the most complex skill a child entering school is asked to develop. What makes it complex, in part, is that letters are less constant than objects. A car seen from a distance, close to, from above, or below, or in a mirror still looks like a car even though the optical image

changes. The letters of the alphabet are more whimsical. Take the letter *b*. Turned upside down it becomes a *p*. Looked at in a mirror, it becomes a *d*. Capitalized, it becomes something quite different, a *B*. The *M* upside down is a *W*. The *E* flipped over becomes Ǝ. This reversed *E* is familiar to mothers of normal children who have just begun to go to school. The earliest examples of art work they bring home often have I LOVƎ YOU written on them.

4 Dyslexics differ from other children in that they read, spell, and write letters upside down and turned around far more frequently and for a much longer time. In what seems like a capricious manner, they also add letters, syllables, and words, or, just as capriciously, delete them. With palindromic words (was-saw, on-no), it is the order of the letters rather than the orientation they change. The new word makes sense, but not the sense intended. Then there are other words where the changed order—"sorty" for story—does not make sense at all.

5 The inability to recognize that g, *g*, and *G* are the same letter, the inability to maintain the orientation of the letters, to retain the order in which they appear, and to follow a line of text without jumping above or below it—all the results of the flaw—can make of an orderly page of words a dish of alphabet soup.

6 Also essential for reading is the ability to store words in memory and to retrieve them. This very particular kind of memory dyslexics lack. So, too, do they lack the ability to hear what the eye sees, and to see what they hear. If the eye sees "off," the ear must hear "off" and not "of," or "for." If the ear hears "saw," the eye must see that it looks like "saw" on the page and not "was." Lacking these skills, a sentence or paragraph becomes a coded message to which the dyslexic can't find the key.

7 It is only a slight exaggeration to say that those who learned to read without difficulty can best understand the labor reading is for a dyslexic by turning a page of text upside down and trying to decipher it.

8 While the literature is replete with illustrations of the way these children write and spell, there are surprisingly few examples of how they read. One, used for propaganda purposes to alert the public to the vulnerability of dyslexics in a literate society, is a sign warning that behind it are guard dogs trained to kill. The dyslexic reads:

9 Wurring
Guard God
Patoly

for

10 Warning
Guard Dog
Patrol

and, of course, remains ignorant of the danger.

11 Looking for a more commonplace example, and hoping to recapture the way I must have read in fourth grade, I recently observed dyslexic children at the Educational Therapy Clinic in Princeton, through the courtesy of Elizabeth Travers, the director. The first child I saw, eight-year-old Anna (whose red hair and brown eyes reminded me of myself at that age), had just come to the Clinic and was learning the alphabet. Given the story of "Little Red Riding Hood," which is at the second grade level, she began confidently enough, repeating the title from memory, then came to a dead stop. With much coaxing throughout, she read as follows:

> 12 Grandma you a top. Grandma [looks over at picture of Red Riding Hood]. Red Riding Hood [long pause, presses index finger into the paper. Looks at me for help. I urge: Go ahead] the a [puts head close to the page, nose almost touching] on Grandma

for

> 13 Once upon a time there was a little girl who had a red coat with a red hood. Etc.

14 "Grandma" was obviously a memory from having heard the story read aloud. Had I needed a reminder of how maddening my silences must have been to Miss Henderson, and how much patience is required to teach these children, Anna, who took almost ten minutes to read these few lines, furnished it. The main difference between Anna and me at that age is that Anna clearly felt no need to invent. She was perplexed, but not anxious, and seemed to have infinite tolerance for her long silences.

15 Toby, a nine-year-old boy with superior intelligence, had a year of tutoring behind him and could have managed "Little Red Riding

Hood" with ease. His text was taken from the *Reader's Digest's Reading Skill Builder*, Grade IV. He read:

16 A kangaroo likes as if he had but truck together warm. His saw neck and head do not . . . [Here Toby sighed with fatigue] seem to feel happy back. They and tried and so every a tiger Moses and shoots from lonesome day and shouts and long shore animals. And each farm play with five friends . . .

17 He broke off with the complaint, "This is too hard. Do I have to read any more?"

18 His text was:

19 A kangaroo looks as if he had been put together wrong. His small neck and head do not seem to fit with his heavy back legs and thick tail. Soft eyes, a twinkly little nose and short front legs seem strange on such a large strong animal. And each front paw has five fingers, like a man's hand.

20 An English expert gives the following bizarre example of an adult dyslexic's performance:

21 An the bee-what in the tel mother of the biothodoodoo to the majoram or that emidrate eni eni Krastrei, mestriet to Ketra lotombreidi to ra from treido as that.

22 His text, taken from a college catalogue the examiner happened to have close at hand, was:

23 It shall be in the power of the college to examine or not every licentiate, previous to his admission to the fellowship, as they shall think fit.

24 That evening when I read aloud to Auntie for the first time, I probably began as Toby did, my memory of the classroom lesson keeping me close to the text. When memory ran out, and Auntie did not correct my errors, I began to invent. When she still didn't stop me, I may well have begun to improvise in the manner of this patient—

anything to keep going and keep up the myth that I was reading—until Auntie brought the "gibberish" to a halt.

Understanding Meaning

1. What basic definition does Simpson provide? What misinterpretation does she note can occur if a condition is considered "inherited"?
2. How does Simpson summarize controversies in the field of research? What do scientists from different disciplines agree on?
3. What is the implication to dyslexics and their parents that dyslexia is "not a disease to be cured, but a malfunction that requires retraining"?
4. *Critical Thinking:* How can this disorder affect a child's development if it is not detected?

Evaluating Strategy

1. Why is it effective to provide an etymology of the word *dyslexia* at the opening? Does this help satisfy reader curiosity about a term many people have heard but do not fully understand?
2. How does Simpson's introduction of personal experience affect the definition? Does this add a human dimension to her definition, or does it detract from its objectivity? Would the inclusion of personal experience be appropriate in a textbook?
3. Do the examples of dyslexic reading dramatize the effects of this disorder? Would an explanation alone suffice to impress readers with the crippling effects of a reading disorder?
4. *Other Modes:* How does Simpson use *description* and *narration* to develop her definition? What role can stories or case studies provide readers seeking to understand a complex subject?

Appreciating Language

1. Simpson is defining a complex disorder. How does her language indicate that she is seeking to address a general audience? Would the vocabulary differ in a definition written for psychology students?
2. Simpson cites an example of a dyslexic reading a warning sign as "propaganda." Does the use of this word weaken her argument that dyslexia is a serious condition? Why or why not?
3. How does Simpson define the term "palindromic"?

Connections across the Disciplines

1. Simpson describes a disorder from the standpoint of a patient. How does her account differ from Oliver Sacks's account as a physician (page 75)?
2. *Compare* this article about a reading disorder with Edward Dolnick's commentary about deafness (page 214). What do they say about how people with disorders *define* themselves and how they function in a society designed by people with different abilities?

Writing Suggestions

1. Write a concisely worded definition of dyslexia in your own words.
2. *Critical Writing:* Write an essay expressing your view on how dyslexics should be graded in college. Should students with dyslexia be allowed more time on essay tests, be offered special tutorial services, or be given alternative assignments and examinations? Can students with disabilities be accommodated while maintaining academic standards?
3. *Collaborative Writing:* Working with several other students, craft a brief explanation of dyslexia to be incorporated into a brochure for parents of children with learning impairments. Keep your audience in mind, and avoid making negative comments that might upset parents.

JOHN ALLEN PAULOS

John Allen Paulos received his doctorate in mathematics from the University of Wisconsin. Currently teaching at Temple University in Philadelphia, Paulos has become an advocate for mathematics education and awareness. He has published several books for the general public, including Mathematics and Humor *and* I Think, Therefore I Laugh. *In 1990 he published* Innumeracy: Mathematical Illiteracy and its Consequences. *Although the book makes use of humor, the subject is serious. Paulos demonstrates that people without a knowledge of mathematics are incapable of critical thinking.*

Innumeracy

In this article based on his book, Paulos defines a term he invented. People who cannot understand letters are called illiterate; *people who cannot understand numbers, he asserts, are* innumerate. *Although people will go to great lengths to camouflage an inability to read, many will actually boast about their deficiencies in mathematics. As Paulos points out, ignorance of mathematics is no laughing matter.*

1 "Math was always my worst subject." . . . "A million dollars, a billion, a trillion, whatever. It doesn't matter as long as we do something about the problem." . . . "Jerry and I aren't going to Europe, what with all the terrorists."

2 You hear these types of statements all the time. They stem from an inability to deal comfortably with the fundamental notions of number and chance—a problem called Innumeracy.

3 This problem plagues far too many otherwise knowledgeable citizens. The same people who cringe when words such as "imply" and "infer" are confused react without a trace of embarrassment to even the most egregious of numerical solecisms. Unlike other failings, which are hidden, mathematical illiteracy is often flaunted: "I can't even balance my checkbook." "I'm a people person, not a numbers person." Or "I always hated math."

4 Part of the reason for this perverse pride in mathematical ignorance is the consequences are not usually as obvious as are those of other weaknesses. However, there are many real-world examples of

innumeracy—stock scams, diet and medical claims, the risk of terrorism and lotteries, for example.

5 Some of the blocks to dealing comfortably with numbers and probabilities are due to quite natural psychological responses to uncertainty, to coincidence or to how a problem is framed. Others can be attributed to anxiety, or to romantic misconceptions about the nature and importance of mathematics.

6 However, a particularly ominous aspect is the gap between scientists' assessments of various risks and the popular perceptions of those risks, a gap that threatens—eventually to lead either to unfounded and crippling public anxieties or to impossible and economically paralyzing demands for risk-free guarantees. Politicians are seldom a help in this regard, since they deal with public opinion and are therefore loath to clarify the likely hazards and trade-offs associated with almost any policy.

BIG NUMBERS, SMALL PROBABILITIES

7 I am always amazed and depressed when I encounter students who have no idea what the population of the United States is, or the approximate distance from coast to coast, or roughly what percentage of the world is Chinese. I sometimes ask them as an exercise to estimate how fast human hair grows in miles per hour, or approximately how many people die on earth each day, or how many cigarettes are smoked annually in this country. Despite some initial reluctance (one student maintained that hair just doesn't grow in miles per hour), they often improve their feeling for numbers dramatically.

8 Without some appreciation of common large numbers, it's impossible to react with the proper scepticism to terrifying reports that more than a million kids are kidnapped each year, or with the proper sobriety to a warhead carrying a megaton of explosive power—the equivalent of a million tons (or two billion pounds) of TNT.

9 If you don't have some feeling for probabilities, automobile accidents might seem a relatively minor problem of local travel, whereas being killed by terrorists might seem to be a major risk when going overseas. As often observed, however, the 45,000 people killed annually on American roads are approximately equal in number to all American dead in the Vietnam War. On the other hand, the 17

Americans killed by terrorists in 1985 were among the 28 million of us who traveled abroad that year—that's one chance in 1.6 million of becoming a victim. Compare that with these annual rates in the United States: one chance in 68,000 of choking to death; one chance in 75,000 of dying in a bicycle crash; one chance in 20,000 of drowning; and one chance in only 5,300 of dying in a car crash.

10 Confronted with these large numbers and with the corresponding small probabilities associated with them, the innumerate will inevitably respond with the non sequitur, "Yes, but what if you are that one," and then nod knowingly, as if they've demolished your argument with their penetrating insight. This tendency to personalize is a characteristic of many people who suffer from innumeracy. Equally typical is a tendency to equate the risk from some obscure and exotic malady with the chances of suffering from heart and circulatory disease, from which about 12,000 Americans die each week.

11 Slipping between millions and billions or between billions and trillions should in this sense be funny, but it isn't, because we too often lack an intuitive feeling for these numbers. Many educated people have little grasp for these numbers and are even unaware that a million is 1,000,000; a billion is 1,000,000,000; and a trillion, 1,000,000,000,000.

BLOODS, MOUNTAINS AND BURGERS

12 In a *Scientific American* column on innumeracy, the computer scientist Douglas Hofstadre cites the case of the Ideal Toy Company, which stated on the package of the original Rubik cube that there were more than three billion possible states the cube could attain. Calculations show that there are more than 4×10^{19} possible states, 4 with 19 zeros after it. What the package says isn't wrong; there are more than three billion possible states. The understatement, however, is symptomatic of a pervasive innumeracy which ill suits a technologically based society. It's analogous to having a sign at the entrance to the Lincoln Tunnel stating: New York, population more than 6; or McDonald's proudly announcing that they've sold more than 120 hamburgers.

13 The number 4×10^{19} is not exactly common-place, but numbers like ten thousand, one million, and a trillion are. Examples of collections each having a million elements, a billion elements, and so on, for quick comparison. For example, knowing that it takes only about

eleven and a half days for a million seconds to tick away, whereas almost thirty-two years are required for a billion seconds to pass, gives one a better grasp of the relative magnitudes of these two common numbers. What about trillions? Modern Homo sapien man is probably less than 10 trillion seconds old; and the complete disappearance of the Neanderthal version of early Homo sapiens occurred only a trillion or so seconds ago. Agriculture has been in use for approximately 300 billion seconds (10,000 years), writing for about 150 billion seconds, and rock music has been around for only about one billion seconds.

14 More common sources of such large numbers are the trillion-dollar federal budget and our burgeoning weapons stockpiles. Given a U.S. population of about 250 million people, every billion dollars in the federal budget translates into $4 for every American. Thus, an annual Defense Department budget of almost a third of a trillion dollars amounts to approximately $5,000 per year for a family of four. What have all these expenditures bought over the years? The TNT equivalent of all the nuclear weapons in the world amounts to 25,000 megatons, or 50 trillion pounds, or 10,000 pounds for every man, woman and child on earth. (One pound of TNT in a car, incidentally, demolishes the car and kills everyone in it.) The nuclear weapons on board just one of our Trident submarines contain eight times the firepower expended in all of World War II.

15 To cite some happier illustrations for smaller numbers, the standard I use for the lowly thousand is a section of Veterans Stadium in Philadelphia which I know contains 1,008 seats and, for me, is easy to picture. The north wall of a garage near my house contains almost exactly ten thousand narrow bricks. For one hundred thousand, I generally think of the number of words in a good-sized novel.

16 To get a handle on big numbers, it's useful to come up with one or two collections such as the above corresponding to each power of ten, up to maybe 13 or 14. The more personal you can make these collections, the better. It's also good practice to estimate whatever quantity piques your curiosity.

17 These estimates are generally quite easy and often suggestive. For example, what is the volume of all the human blood in the world? The average adult male has about six quarts of blood, adult women slightly less, children considerably less. Thus, if we estimate that on average each of the approximately 5 billion people in the world has about one gallon of blood, we get about 5 billion (5×10^9) gallons of blood in the world. Since there are about 7.5 gallons per cubic foot, there are

approximately 6.7 × 108 cubic feet of blood. The cube root of 6.7 × 108 is 870. Thus, all the blood in the world would fit into a cube 870 feet on a side, less than 1/200th of a cubic mile.

18 Central Park in New York has an area of 840 acres, or about 1.3 square miles. If walls were built about it, all the blood in the world would cover the park to a depth of something under 20 feet. The Dead Sea on the Israel-Jordan border has an area of 390 square miles. If all of the world's blood were put into the Dead Sea, it would add only three-fourths of an inch to its depth. Even without any particular context, these figures are surprising; there isn't that much blood in the world! Compare this with the volume of all the grass, or of all the leaves, or of all the algae in the world, and man's marginal status among life forms, at least volume-wise, is vividly apparent.

19 There are many harmful social effects that result from this innumeracy. Most consider some form of trade-off or balancing of conflicting concerns because it contributes to the relative invisibility of these trade-offs, or sometimes to seeing them where they aren't.

20 There's a strong human tendency to want everything, and to deny that trade-offs are usually necessary. Because of their positions, politicians are often more tempted than most to indulge in this magical thinking. Trade-offs between quality and price, between speed and thoroughness, between approving a possibly bad drug and rejecting a possibly good one, between liberty and equality, etc., are frequently muddled and covered with a misty gauze, and this decline in clarity is usually an added cost for everyone.

21 For example, when the recent decisions by a number of states to raise the speed limit on certain highways to 65 mph and not to impose stiffer penalties on drunk driving were challenged by safety groups, the limits were defended with the patently false assertion that there would be no increase in accident rates, instead of with a frank acknowledgment of economic and political factors which outweighed the likely extra deaths. Dozens of other incidents, many involving the environment and toxic wastes (money vs. lives), could be cited.

22 People taking this approach make a mockery of the usual sentiments about the pricelessness of every human life. Human lives are priceless in many ways, but in order to reach reasonable compromises, we must, in effect, place a finite economic value on them. Too often when we do this, however, we make a lot of pious noises to mask how low that value is. I'd prefer less false piety and a considerably higher economic value placed on human lives. Ideally, this value should be

infinite, but when it can't be, let's hold the saccharine sentiments. If we're not keenly aware of the choices we're making, we're not likely to work for better ones.

Understanding Meaning

1. How does Paulos define "innumeracy?" What examples does he use to illustrate the problem?
2. Paulos offers an example of a person joking about being unable to balance a checkbook. Why would the same person not joke about being unable to read a newspaper? Do we take math less seriously than reading?
3. Do people quote statistics without asking their source or understanding their meaning?
4. *Critical Thinking:* Why is mathematics important to nonmath students? Can one develop critical thinking skills or even be a wise consumer without a working knowledge of numbers and their relationships?

Evaluating Strategy

1. Why does Paulos provide so many examples? Is this necessary to arouse reader interest and understanding?
2. *Other Methods:* Where does Paulos use *cause and effect* to develop his definition?

Appreciating Language

1. How does Paulos manage to discuss his subject without using an excessive amount of technical language?
2. Paulos knows many people are frightened by mathematics. Do his references to common items such as hamburgers and auto accidents make his ideas more accessible?
3. Look up *neologism* in the dictionary. Can *innumeracy* be defined as a *neologism?*

Connections across the Disciplines

1. How does innumeracy help account for the mathematical errors Christina Hoff Sommers discusses in "Figuring Out Feminism" (page 348)?

2. How does Paulos's method of developing his invented definition compare with Eileen Simpson's definition of an accepted term (page 172)?

Writing Suggestions

1. Following Paulos's example, invent and define a new word to describe a common condition—"blind datism," "laundry denial syndrome," or "talk show dependency." Use examples to support your definition.
2. *Collaborative Writing:* Working with three or four other students, brainstorm to develop examples of innumeracy you have encountered. Have you or someone you have known lost money or had consumer problems because of a failure to understand numbers, prices, statistics, or probabilities? Select three or four examples, and develop a brief essay *defining* the dangers of innumeracy.

ELLEN GOODMAN

Ellen Goodman (1941–) was born in Massachusetts and graduated from Radcliffe College. She worked for Newsweek *and* The Detroit Free Press *before joining* The Boston Globe *in 1967. Her column "At Large" has been widely syndicated since 1976. As an essayist and television commentator, Goodman has discussed feminism, changes in family life, sexual harassment, and male and female relationships. Her essays have been collected in several books, including* Close to Home, At Large, *and* Turning Points.

The Company Man

Instead of using a number of illustrations to develop a definition, Goodman uses a single, extended example of a person who fits her personal view of what constitutes a workaholic in this essay from Close to Home.

1 He worked himself to death, finally and precisely, at 3:00 A.M. Sunday morning.

2 The obituary didn't say that, of course. It said that he died of a coronary thrombosis—I think that was it—but everyone among his friends and acquaintances knew it instantly. He was a perfect Type A, a workaholic, a classic, they said to each other and shook their heads—and thought for five or ten minutes about the way they lived.

3 This man who worked himself to death finally and precisely at 3:00 A.M. Sunday morning—on his day off—was fifty-one years old and a vice-president. He was, however, one of six vice-presidents, and one of three who might conceivably—if the president died or retired soon enough—have moved to the top spot. Phil knew that.

4 He worked six days a week, five of them until eight or nine at night, during a time when his own company had begun the four-day week for everyone but the executives. He worked like the Important People. He had no outside "extracurricular interests," unless, of course, you think about a monthly golf game that way. To Phil, it was work. He always ate egg salad sandwiches at his desk. He was, of course, overweight, by 20 or 25 pounds. He thought it was okay, though, because he didn't smoke.

5 On Saturdays, Phil wore a sports jacket to the office instead of a suit, because it was the weekend.

6 He had a lot of people working for him, maybe sixty, and most of them liked him most of the time. Three of them will be seriously considered for his job. The obituary didn't mention that.

7 But it did list his "survivors" quite accurately. He is survived by his wife, Helen, forty-eight years old, a good woman of no particular marketable skills, who worked in an office before marrying and mothering. She had, according to her daughter, given up trying to compete with his work years ago, when the children were small. A company friend said, "I know how much you will miss him." And she answered, "I already have."

8 "Missing him all these years," she must have given up part of herself which had cared too much for the man. She would be "well taken care of."

9 His "dearly beloved" eldest of the "dearly beloved" children is a hard-working executive in a manufacturing firm down South. In the day and a half before the funeral, he went around the neighborhood researching his father, asking the neighbors what he was like. They were embarrassed.

10 His second child is a girl, who is twenty-four and newly married. She lives near her mother and they are close, but whenever she was alone with her father, in a car driving somewhere, they had nothing to say to each other.

11 The youngest is twenty, a boy, a high-school graduate who has spent the last couple of years, like a lot of his friends, doing enough odd jobs to stay in grass and food. He was the one who tried to grab at his father, and tried to mean enough to him to keep the man at home. He was his father's favorite. Over the last two years, Phil stayed up nights worrying about the boy.

12 The boy once said, "My father and I only board here."

13 At the funeral, the sixty-year-old company president told the forty-eight-year-old widow that the fifty-one-year-old deceased had meant much to the company and would be missed and would be hard to replace. The widow didn't look him in the eye. She was afraid he would read her bitterness and, after all, she would need him to straighten out the finances—the stock options and all that.

14 Phil was overweight and nervous and worked too hard. If he wasn't at the office, he was worried about it. Phil was a Type A, a heart-attack natural. You could have picked him out in a minute from a lineup.

15 So when he finally worked himself to death, at precisely 3:00 A.M. Sunday morning, no one was really surprised.

16 By 5:00 P.M. the afternoon of the funeral, the company president had begun, discreetly of course, with care and taste, to make inquiries about his replacement. One of the three men. He asked around: "Who's been working the hardest?"

Understanding Meaning

1. How does Goodman define a workaholic? Why does she assert that his heart attack was directly related to his job?
2. What does her definition imply about Phil's life? What does she suggest was lacking?
3. What, if anything, seems to have driven Phil?
4. Goodman mentions that Phil provided well for his widow. Is Phil, a hard-working vice president who cares for his family, an ideal man in the eyes of many women? If Phil were an African American or Hispanic, would he be viewed as a "role model"? Would a "company woman" be viewed as a feminist?
5. *Critical Thinking:* Americans have long admired hard workers. Franklin, Edison, Henry Ford, and John Kennedy became legendary for their accomplishments. On the other hand, Americans long for more leisure time. Is this a double standard? Do we want to spend more time with friends and family but expect our doctor, lawyer, contractor, or stockbroker to work overtime, meet deadlines, and always remain a phone call away?

Evaluating Strategy

1. Would Goodman's definition be stronger if she included more than one example?
2. What impact does the final paragraph have? How does this reinforce her point?

Appreciating Language

1. Goodman places certain phrases in quotation marks—"well taken care of" and "dearly beloved." What is the effect of highlighting these terms?
2. What does the term "company man" suggest? Would "church man" or "charity man" provoke different responses?

Connections across the Disciplines

1. How does Goodman's strategy in developing a definition of a "workaholic" differ from Michael Korda's definition of a "leader" (page 189)?
2. How does the fate of a workaholic relate to observations made in Juliet Schor's "The Overworked American" (page 377)?

Writing Suggestions

1. Develop your own definition of *workaholic.* Can it be defined in hours worked, or should it be measured in stress? Does a writer working eighty hours a week on a novel fit the category of workaholic? Is a mother with young children by definition a workaholic?
2. *Collaborative Writing:* Speak with fellow students, and write a short statement in response to the question "What do we owe employers?"

MICHAEL KORDA

Michael Korda (1933–) was born in London. Following service in the Royal Air Force, he entered Oxford University. In 1956 he interrupted his studies to aid the Hungarian uprising against the Russian invasion. He returned to Oxford and graduated in 1958. Korda moved to New York and worked at a number of odd jobs, including reading television scripts for Columbia Broadcasting System (CBS), before becoming an assistant editor at Simon & Schuster. As an executive editor, Korda was instrumental in publishing several best-sellers. He has written a number of popular books, including Power, Male Chauvinism, Charmed Lives, *and* Queenie. *His works have included biographies and social commentary.*

What Makes a Leader?

Korda uses a number of historical examples to define the qualities of leadership. Leaders, he asserts, must be able to simplify issues and use power with deft control. This essay first appeared in Newsweek.

1 Not every President is a leader, but every time we elect a President we hope for one, especially in times of doubt and crisis. In easy times we are ambivalent—the leader, after all, makes demands, challenges the status quo, shakes things up.

2 Leadership is as much a question of timing as anything else. The leader must appear on the scene at a moment when people are looking for leadership, as Churchill did in 1940, as Roosevelt did in 1933, as Lenin did in 1917. And when he comes, he must offer a simple, eloquent message.

3 Great leaders are almost always great simplifiers, who cut through argument, debate and doubt to offer a solution everybody can understand and remember. Churchill warned the British to expect "blood, toil, tears and sweat"; FDR told Americans that "the only thing we have to fear is fear itself"; Lenin promised the war-weary Russians peace, land and bread. Straightforward but potent messages.

4 We have an image of what a leader ought to be. We even recognize the physical signs: leaders may not necessarily be tall, but they must have bigger-than-life, commanding features—LBJ's nose and ear

lobes; Ike's broad grin. A trademark also comes in handy: Lincoln's stovepipe hat, JFK's rocker. We expect our leaders to stand out a little, not to be like ordinary men. Half of President Ford's trouble lay in the fact that, if you closed your eyes for a moment, you couldn't remember his face, figure or clothes. A leader should have an unforgettable identity, instantly and permanently fixed in people's minds.

5 It also helps for a leader to be able to do something most of us can't: FDR overcame polio; Mao swam the Yangtze River at the age of 72. We don't want our leaders to be "just like us." We want them to be like us but better, special, more so. Yet if they are *too* different, we reject them. Adlai Stevenson was too cerebral. Nelson Rockefeller, too rich.

6 Even television, which comes in for a lot of knocks as an image-builder that magnifies form over substance, doesn't altogether obscure the qualities of leadership we recognize, or their absence. Television exposed Nixon's insecurity, Humphrey's fatal infatuation with his own voice.

7 A leader must know how to use power (that's what leadership is about), but he also has to have a way of showing that he does. He has to be able to project firmness—no physical clumsiness (like Ford), no rapid eye movements (like Carter).

8 A Chinese philosopher once remarked that a leader must have the grace of a good dancer, and there is a great deal of wisdom to this. A leader should know how to appear relaxed and confident. His walk should be firm and purposeful. He should be able, like Lincoln, FDR, Truman, Ike and JFK, to give a good, hearty, belly laugh, instead of the sickly grin that passes for good humor in Nixon or Carter. Ronald Reagan's training as an actor showed to good effect in the debate with Carter, when by his easy manner and apparent affability, he managed to convey the impression that in fact he was the President and Carter the challenger.

9 If we know what we're looking for, why is it so difficult to find? The answer lies in a very simple truth about leadership. *People can only be led where they want to go.* The leader follows, though a step ahead. Americans *wanted* to climb out of the Depression and needed someone to tell them they could do it, and FDR did. The British believed that they could still win the war after the defeats of 1940, and Churchill told them they were right.

10 A leader rides the waves, moves with the tides, understands the deepest yearnings of his people. He cannot make a nation that wants

peace at any price go to war, or stop a nation determined to fight from doing so. His purpose must match the national mood. His task is to focus the people's energies and desires, to define them in simple terms, to inspire, to make what people already want seem attainable, important, within their grasp.

11 Above all, he must dignify our desires, convince us that we are taking part in the making of great history, give us a sense of glory about ourselves. Winston Churchill managed, by sheer rhetoric, to turn the British defeat and the evacuation of Dunkirk in 1940 into a major victory. FDR's words turned the sinking of the American fleet at Pearl Harbor into a national rallying cry instead of a humiliating national scandal. A leader must stir our blood, not appeal to our reason. . . .

12 A great leader must have a certain irrational quality, a stubborn refusal to face facts, infectious optimism, the ability to convince us that all is not lost even when we're afraid it is. Confucius suggested that, while the advisors of a great leader should be as cold as ice, the leader himself should have fire, a spark of divine madness.

13 He won't come until we're ready for him, for the leader is like a mirror, reflecting back to us our own sense of purpose, putting into words our own dreams and hopes, transforming our needs and fears into coherent policies and programs.

14 Our strength makes him strong; our determination makes him determined; our courage makes him a hero; he is, in the final analysis, the symbol of the best in us, shaped by our own spirit and will. And when these qualities are lacking in us, we can't produce him; and even with all our skill at image-building, we can't fake him. He is, after all, merely the sum of us.

Understanding Meaning

1. What elements of leadership does Korda view as being beyond a leader's control?
2. List the key personality traits Korda associates with leadership. Are many of these superficial, such as physical appearance or trademarks?
3. What does Korda mean with his italicized statement, "*People can only be led where they want to go*"? Can you think of exceptions? By stating that leaders can only "match the national mood," does Korda imply that leadership is really only managing or directing the flow?
4. *Critical Thinking:* Many of the attributes Korda describes are visual. Does this suggest that leadership is more a matter of style, public relations, and

image rather than vision and determination? Can leadership be projected by staged events and photo opportunities?

Evaluating Strategy

1. Korda's title asks a question. Does a writer risk appearing insecure or indecisive by using a question instead of a simple declarative statement?
2. How effective are his examples? Does it matter that he mixes examples of democratically elected leaders such as Churchill, Reagan, Kennedy, and Carter with dictators like Lenin and Mao?
3. Korda states his thesis, that the leader is the sum of his or her followers, at the end of the essay. Is this effective? Would this be better placed at the opening?

Appreciating Language

1. Underline the words Korda uses to *describe* a leader. What do these words imply?
2. How effective is Korda's use of quotes? Why does allowing leaders to speak for themselves help define them?

Connections across the Disciplines

1. Can you *contrast* the qualities of leadership with those of Ellen Goodman's company man (page 185)? Is one a born leader and the other a born follower?
2. Bruce Catton's "Grant and Lee" (page 252) compares two famous generals. According to Catton's description, did both men embody the qualities of leadership Korda outlines?

Writing Suggestions

1. Write an essay *describing* a leader you admire. This person may be a national figure or someone you know personally. Try to *define* the qualities you consider central to his or her leadership ability.
2. *Collaborative Writing:* Develop a definition of a leader with three or four other students. Support your definition with examples. Your group may wish to respond to this observation:

Americans admire "role models" because they do not trust "leaders." Proud of their individuality and independence, they resist seeing themselves as followers. A leader demands obedience. But a role model merely exists to be admired and imitated by people seeking to improve themselves. Those who follow a leader are passive, but those who imitate role models see themselves as active, enhancing themselves in another's image.

JOHN CIARDI

John Ciardi (1916–1986) was a poet, literary critic, and translator. After teaching at Harvard, Rutgers, and the University of Kansas, he left academics to pursue a full-time literary career. As poetry editor for the Saturday Review *for two decades, he attempted to make poetry accessible to a wide audience. Ciardi's most ambitious work was a translation of Dante Alighieri's work, which took him sixteen years. As a poet, critic, and professor, Ciardi was a student of language. For many years he was a guest commentator on National Public Radio, where he offered listeners interesting and amusing anecdotes about the origins and histories of everyday words.*

What Is Happiness?

In this essay, which first appeared in Saturday Review, *Ciardi tries to define the elusive concept of happiness. In developing his definition, Ciardi* analyzes *the role of advertising and the nature of materialism in American life.*

1 The right to pursue happiness is issued to Americans with their birth certificates, but no one seems quite sure which way it ran. It may be we are issued a hunting license but offered no game. Jonathan Swift seemed to think so when he attacked the idea of happiness as "the possession of being well-deceived," the felicity of being "a fool among knaves." For Swift saw society as Vanity Fair, the land of false goals.

2 It is, of course, un-American to think in terms of fools and knaves. We do, however, seem to be dedicated to the idea of buying our way to happiness. We shall all have made it to Heaven when we possess enough.

3 And at the same time the forces of American commercialism are hugely dedicated to making us deliberately unhappy. Advertising is one of our major industries, and advertising exists not to satisfy desires but to create them—and to create them faster than any man's budget can satisfy them. For that matter, our whole economy is based on a dedicated insatiability. We are taught that to possess is to be happy, and then we are made to want. We are even told it is our duty to want. It was only a few years ago, to cite a single example, that car dealers

across the country were flying banners that read "You Auto Buy Now." They were calling upon Americans, as an act approaching patriotism, to buy at once, with money they did not have, automobiles they did not really need, and which they would be required to grow tired of by the time the next year's models were released.

4 Or look at any of the women's magazines. There, as Bernard DeVoto once pointed out, advertising begins as poetry in the front pages and ends as pharmacopoeia and therapy in the back pages. The poetry of the front matter is the dream of perfect beauty. This is the baby skin that must be hers. These, the flawless teeth. This, the perfumed breath she must exhale. This, the sixteen-year-old figure she must display at forty, at fifty, at sixty, and forever.

5 Once past the vaguely uplifting fiction and feature articles, the reader finds the other face of the dream in the back matter. This is the harness into which Mother must strap herself in order to display that perfect figure. These, the chin straps she must sleep in. This is the salve that restores all, this is her laxative, these are the tablets that melt away fat, these are the hormones of perpetual youth, these are the stockings that hide varicose veins.

6 Obviously no half-sane person can be completely persuaded either by such poetry or by such pharmacopoeia and orthopedics. Yet someone is obviously trying to buy the dream as offered and spending billions every year in the attempt. Clearly the happiness-market is not running out of customers, but what is it trying to buy?

7 The idea "happiness," to be sure, will not sit still for easy definition: The best one can do is to try to set some extremes to the idea and then work in toward the middle. To think of happiness as acquisitive and competitive will do to set the materialistic extreme. To think of it as the idea one senses in, say, a holy man of India will do to set the spiritual extreme. That holy man's idea of happiness is in needing nothing from outside himself. In wanting nothing, he lacks nothing. He sits immobile, rapt in contemplation, free even of his own body. Or nearly free of it. If devout admirers bring him food he eats it; if not, he starves indifferently. Why be concerned? What is physical is an illusion to him. Contemplation is his joy and he achieves it through a fantastically demanding discipline, the accomplishment of which is itself a joy within him.

8 Is he a happy man? Perhaps his happiness is only another sort of illusion. But who can take it from him? And who will dare say it is more illusory than happiness on the installment plan?

9 But, perhaps because I am Western, I doubt such catatonic happiness, as I doubt the dreams of the happiness-market. What is certain is that his way of happiness would be torture to almost any Western man. Yet these extremes will still serve to frame the area within which all of us must find some sort of balance. Thoreau—a creature of both Eastern and Western thought—had his own firm sense of that balance. His aim was to save on the low levels in order to spend on the high.

10 Possession for its own sake or in competition with the rest of the neighborhood would have been Thoreau's idea of the low levels. The active discipline of heightening one's perception of what is enduring in nature would have been his idea of the high. What he saved from the low was time and effort he could spend on the high. Thoreau certainly disapproved of starvation, but he would put into feeding himself only as much effort as would keep him functioning for more important efforts.

11 Effort is the gist of it. There is no happiness except as we take on life-engaging difficulties. Short of the impossible, as Yeats put it, the satisfactions we get from a lifetime depend on how high we choose our difficulties. Robert Frost was thinking in something like the same terms when he spoke of "The pleasure of taking pains." The mortal flaw in the advertised version of happiness is in the fact that it purports to be effortless.

12 We demand difficulty even in our games. We demand it because without difficulty there can be no game. A game is a way of making something hard for the fun of it. The rules of the game are an arbitrary imposition of difficulty. When the spoilsport ruins the fun, he always does so by refusing to play by the rules. It is easier to win at chess if you are free, at your pleasure, to change the wholly arbitrary rules, but the fun is in winning within the rules. No difficulty, no fun.

13 The buyers and sellers at the happiness-market seem too often to have lost their sense of the pleasure of difficulty. Heaven knows what they are playing, but it seems a dull game. And the Indian holy man seems dull to us, I suppose, because he seems to be refusing to play anything at all. The Western weakness may be in the illusion that happiness can be bought. Perhaps the Eastern weakness is in the idea that there is such a thing as perfect (and therefore static) happiness.

14 Happiness is never more than partial. There are no pure states of mankind. Whatever else happiness may be, it is neither in having nor in being, but in becoming. What the Founding Fathers declared for us as an inherent right, we should do well to remember, was not happi-

ness but the *pursuit* of happiness. What they might have underlined, could they have foreseen the happiness-market, is the cardinal fact that happiness is in the pursuit itself, in the meaningful pursuit of what is life-engaging and life-revealing, which is to say, in the idea of *becoming.* A nation is not measured by what it possesses or wants to possess, but by what it wants to become.

By all means let the happiness-market sell us minor satisfactions and even minor follies so long as we keep them in scale and buy them out of spiritual change. I am no customer for either puritanism or asceticism. But drop any real spiritual capital at those bazaars, and what you come home to will be your own poorhouse.

Understanding Meaning

1. How does the view "whoever dies with the most toys wins" fit with Ciardi's thoughts on materialism?
2. What seems to be Ciardi's purpose in this essay? How much of this definition is *persuasive?* What does he mean by the comment that "a nation is not measured by what it possesses or wants to possess, but by what it wants to become"?
3. How does Ciardi *compare* the Eastern mystic's concept of happiness with that of most Americans? Can happiness be achieved by being free of possessions or by owning them all?
4. How does advertising exploit the public hunger for happiness? Does advertising suggest, in Ciardi's view, that happiness can be purchased instead of earned?
5. *Critical Thinking:* Although he criticizes what he calls "the happiness-market," Ciardi does not condemn it. However, he advises readers to be cautious consumers. What does he warn readers against? What does he mean by his comment about dropping "any real spiritual capital"?

Evaluating Strategy

1. Ciardi admits that happiness is not easy to define, noting "the best one can do is to try to set some extremes to the idea and then work in toward the middle." Is this an effective method of defining abstract or elusive concepts?
2. Throughout the essay, Ciardi quotes Swift, Bernard DeVoto, and Frost. Is this an effective way of working toward the definition of a difficult subject? Does this add credibility to Ciardi's view?

3. *Other Modes:* How does Ciardi use *comparison* and *analysis* to develop his definition?

Appreciating Language

1. Ciardi uses simple but abstract words—*happiness, possessions, dream, illusion*. How does he define these terms and give them personal meaning?
2. How does Ciardi paraphrase the language of advertising to reveal its appeals to consumers?

Connections across the Disciplines

1. Review George Orwell's essay "Pleasure Spots" (page 551). Where does the pursuit of happiness lead people?
2. Does Ciardi construct his definition of *happiness* the same way Michael Korda does in "What Makes a Leader?" (page 189)?

Writing Suggestions

1. Use Ciardi's technique of setting extremes and then working toward the middle to define an elusive or complex subject such as love, friendship, success, wealth, or beauty in a short essay.
2. *Critical Writing:* Write an essay based on Ciardi's observation that the founding fathers did not promise a right to happiness but a right to the *pursuit* of happiness. Do Americans today seem to believe they have a *right* to happiness? Discuss whether Americans feel cheated if they are not happy and whether this partly explains the epidemic of drug abuse and violence.
3. *Collaborative Writing:* Discuss Ciardi's essay with a group of students, and then write a few paragraphs reflecting the group's viewpoint on happiness. You may wish to address a single observation made by Ciardi, such as the partial nature of happiness or the idea that it must derive from a challenge met.

GRETEL EHRLICH

Gretel Ehrlich (1946–) was born in Santa Barbara, California, and studied at the University of California, Los Angeles, film school and the New School of Social Research in New York. Ehrlich first visited Wyoming in 1976 to produce a film and made the state her home. She married a rancher and now lives near the Bighorn Mountains. She has published several books set in Wyoming, including Heart Mountain, *a novel about the internment camps established to house Japanese Americans during World War II. Her work has earned her several awards, including a Guggenheim Fellowship in 1989.*

A Storm, the Cornfield, and Elk

This essay, which appeared in her collection The Solace of Open Places, *provides a personal definition of autumn. Like much of her work, the essay explores the relationship between people and places and the role of nature in shaping our lives.*

1 Last week a bank of clouds lowered itself down summer's green ladder and let loose with a storm. A heavy snow can act like fists: Trees are pummeled, hay- and grainfields are flattened, splayed out like deer beds; field corn, jackknifed and bleached blond by the freeze, is bedraggled by the brawl. All night we heard groans and crashes of cottonwood trunks snapping. "I slept under the damned kitchen table," one rancher told me. "I've already had one of them trees come through my roof." Along the highway electric lines were looped to the ground like dropped reins.

2 As the storm blows east toward the Dakotas, the blue of the sky intensifies. It inks dry washes and broad grasslands with quiet. In their most complete gesture of restraint, cottonwoods, willows, and wild rose engorge themselves with every hue of ruddiness—russet, puce, umber, gold, musteline—whose spectral repletion we know also to be an agony, riding oncoming waves of cold.

3 The French call the autumn leaf *feuille morte*. When the leaves are finally corrupted by frost they rain down into themselves until the tree, disowning itself, goes bald.

4 All through autumn we hear a double voice: One says everything is ripe; the other says everything is dying. The paradox is exquisite. We feel what the Japanese call "aware"—an almost untranslatable word meaning something like "beauty tinged with sadness." Some days we have to shoulder against a marauding melancholy. Dreams have a hallucinatory effect: in one, a man who is dying watches from inside a huge cocoon while stud colts run through deep mud, their balls bursting open, their seed spilling into the black ground. My reading brings me this thought from the mad Zen priest Ikkyu: "Remember that under the skin you fondle lie the bones, waiting to reveal themselves." But another day, I ride in the mountains. Against rimrock, tall aspens have the graceful bearing of giraffes, and another small grove, not yet turned, gives off a virginal limelight that transpierces everything heavy.

5 Fall is the end of a rancher's year. Third and fourth cuttings of hay are stacked; cattle and sheep are gathered, weaned, and shipped; yearlings bulls and horse colts are sold. "We always like this time of year, but it's a lot more fun when the cattle prices are up!" a third-generation rancher tells me.

6 This week I help round up their cows and calves on the Big Horns. The storm system that brought three feet of snow at the beginning of the month now brings intense and continual rain. Riding for cows resembles a wild game of touch football played on skis: Cows and cowboys bang into each other, or else, as the calves run back, the horse just slides. Twice today my buckskin falls with me, crushing my leg against a steep sidehill, but the mud and snow, now trampled into a gruel, is so deep it's almost impossible to get bruised.

7 When the cattle are finally gathered, we wean the calves from the cows in portable corrals by the road. Here, black mud reaches our shins. The stock dogs have to swim in order to move. Once, while trying to dodge a cow, my feet stuck, and losing both boots in the effort to get out of the way, I had to climb the fence barefooted. Weaning is noisy; cows don't hide their grief. As calves are loaded into semis and stock trucks, their mothers—five or six hundred of them at a time—crowd around the sorting alleys with outstretched necks, their squared-off faces all opened in a collective bellowing.

8 On the way home a neighboring rancher who trails his steers down the mountain highway loses one as they ride through town. There's a high-speed chase across lawns and flower beds, around the general store and the fire station. Going at a full lope, the steer ducks behind the fire truck just as Mike tries to rope him. "Missing something?" a

friend yells out her window as the second loop sails like a burning hoop to the ground.

9 "That's nothing," one onlooker remarks. "When we brought our cattle through Kaycee one year, the minister opened the church door to see what all the noise was about and one old cow just ran in past him. He had a hell of a time getting her out."

10 In the valley, harvest is on but it's soggy. The pinto bean crops are sprouting, and the sugar beets are balled up with mud so that one is indistinguishable from the other. Now I can only think of mud as being sweet. At night the moon makes a brief appearance between storms and laces mud with a confectionary light. Farmers whose last cutting of hay is still on the ground turn windrows to dry as if they were limp, bedridden bodies. The hay that has already been baled is damp, and after four inches of rain (in a county where there's never more than eight inches a year) mold eats its way to the top again.

11 The morning sky looks like cheese. Its cobalt wheel has been cut down and all the richness of the season is at our feet. The quick-blanch of frost stings autumn's rouge into a skin that is tawny. At dawn, mowed hay meadows are the color of pumpkins, and the willows, leafless now, are pink and silver batons conducting inaudible river music. When I dress for the day, my body, white and suddenly numb, looks like dead coral.

12 After breakfast there are autumn chores to finish. We grease head gates on irrigation ditches, roll up tarp dams, pull horseshoes, and truck horses to their winter pasture. The harvest moon gives way to the hunter's moon. Elk, deer, and moose hunters repopulate the mountains now that the livestock is gone. One young hunting guide has already been hurt. While he was alone at camp, his horse kicked him in the spleen. Immobilized, he scratched an SOS with the sharp point of a bullet on a piece of leather he cut from his chaps. "Hurt bad. In pain. Bring doctor with painkiller," it read. Then he tied the note to the horse's halter and threw rocks at the horse until it trotted out of camp. When the horse wandered into a ranch yard down the mountain, the note was quickly discovered and a doctor was helicoptered to camp. Amid orgiastic gunfire, sometimes lives are saved.

13 October lifts over our heads whatever river noise is left. Long carrier waves of clouds seem to emanate from hidden reefs. There's a logjam of them around the mountains, and the horizon appears to drop seven thousand feet. Though the rain has stopped, the road ruts are

filled to the brim. I saw a frog jump cheerfully into one of them. Once in a while the mist clears and we can see the dark edge of a canyon or an island of vertical rimrock in the white bulk of snow. Up there, bull elk have been fighting all fall over harems. They charge with antlered heads, scraping the last of the life-giving velvet off, until one bull wins and trots into the private timber to mount his prize, standing almost humanly erect on hind legs while holding a cow elk's hips with his hooves.

14 In the fall, my life, too, is timbered, an unaccountably libidinous place: damp, overripe, and fading. The sky's congestion allows the eye's iris to open wider. The cornfield in front of me is torn parchment paper, as brittle as bougainvillea leaves whose tropical color has somehow climbed these northern stalks. I zigzag through the rows as if they were city streets. Now I want to lie down in the muddy furrows, under the frictional sawing of stalks, under corncobs which look like erections, and out of whose loose husks sprays of bronze silk dangle down.

15 Autumn teaches us that fruition is also death; that ripeness is a form of decay. The willows, having stood for so long near water, begin to rust. Leaves are verbs that conjugate the seasons.

16 Today the sky is a wafer. Placed on my tongue, it is a wholeness that has already disintegrated; placed under the tongue, it makes my heart beat strongly enough to stretch myself over the winter briliances to come. Now I feel the tenderness to which this season rots. Its defenselessness can no longer be corrupted. Death is its purity, its sweet mud. The string of storms that came across Wyoming like elephants tied tail to trunk falters now and bleeds into a stillness.

17 There is neither sun, nor wind, nor snow falling. The hunters are gone; snow geese waddle in grainfields. Already, the elk have started moving out of the mountains toward sheltered feed-grounds. Their great antlers will soon fall off like chandeliers shaken from ballroom ceilings. With them the light of these autumn days, bathed in what Tennyson called "a mockery of sunshine," will go completely out.

Understanding Meaning

1. Why does Ehrlich see autumn as a season of paradox?
2. What does the opening paragraph reveal about the power of nature?
3. What does fall symbolize to the rancher?

4. What is the significance of the story of the hunting guide who uses the horse that nearly killed him to carry his message to summon help? What does it reveal about the interaction of people and the natural world?
5. *Critical Thinking:* Can this essay be seen as a commentary about death? Is Ehrlich's purpose to define autumn as a time of death so her readers will accept it as something natural?

Evaluating Strategy

1. What figurative language does Ehrlich use to develop her essay about autumn?
2. How does Ehrlich use quotations and dialogue to introduce ideas in her essay?
3. What methods does Ehrlich employ to arrange her thoughts on the nature of autumn?
4. *Other Modes:* How does Ehrlich use *comparison* and *narration* to develop her essay?

Appreciating Language

1. Ehrlich compares elements of the natural world with artificial objects such as paper and chandeliers. How effective are these similes and metaphors in explaining nature to a largely urban audience?
2. Underline the most striking images you find in the essay. What makes them memorable? How do they help define Ehrlich's perception of autumn?

Connections across the Disciplines

1. How does Ehrlich's view of people's interaction with nature compare to that of Terry Tempest Williams's (page 205)?
2. How does Ehrlich's role of observer compare to that of Jane Goodall's (page 68)?

Writing Suggestions

1. Write a brief essay that defines the human significance of a natural event. You might write about tornadoes, floods, blizzards, the change of seasons, the migration of wildlife, or shooting stars. What lessons about life, the fragility of civilization, or our perceptions of reality can nature teach us?

2. *Collaborative Writing:* Working with a group of students, select a season or a natural event that is common in your location. Have each member suggest an idea of what this season or event teaches. Compare ideas and try to combine them in a single brief essay.

TERRY TEMPEST WILLIAMS

Terry Tempest Williams (1955–) was born in Utah, where her ancestors had lived for more than a century and a half. She received degrees in English and science education from the University of Utah, where she now teaches in a women's studies program. Williams also serves as Naturalist-in-Residence at the Utah Museum of Natural History in Salt Lake City. Her concern for nature is evident in her writing, which includes children's books, short stories about Utah, and two nonfiction books blending natural history and personal experience.

Yucca

This essay from Pieces of White Shell: A Journey to Navajoland *provides a personal definition of a plant, emphasizing its importance to the Navajo people of the Southwest. Notice how Williams blends several modes to demonstrate the significance of a common desert plant.*

1 One night the stars pulled me into a dream. A basket sat before me, coiled: around and around and around and around. It was striped with persimmon. I should not touch it. This much I knew. I knelt down closely and saw a woman's long black hair curled between stitches. I picked up a sprig of salt bush and rattled it above the hair strand. Suddenly, the woven bowl began to pulsate, writhe, until a snake uncoiled herself slowly. This is what I heard:

2 Sha-woman, Sha-woman, hiss
Sha-woman, Sha-woman, hiss
Tongue, rattle, hiss
Tongue, rattle, hiss
Sha-woman, Sha-woman, hiss

3 She stopped. She raised her head and blew upward. I watched the breezes pull her vertically until she became a white desert torch. Yucca.

4 In the Navajo account of yucca's birth, Tracking Bear was a monster from whom there was no escape. He lived in a cave in the mountains. Monster Slayer, pursued by Tracking Bear, climbed a sheer wall. As he did so he grasped a fruit of the yucca in his left hand, and in his right a twig of hard oak. The monster feared these medicine rattles. Monster Slayer killed Tracking Bear and cut off his claws and large canine teeth, taking the gall and windpipe as trophies. He then cut the head into three pieces: One became the broad-leaved yucca, one the narrow-leaved yucca, and one the mescal.

5 And so yucca appears evenly spaced across the land. They stand as sentinels with their flowering stalks rising from vegetative swords. They are shields for creatures who live near. Sundown strikes yucca. Desert candles flame.

6 I remember peering into a yucca flower at dusk and seeing a tiny moth scraping pollen from within. The little white-robed pilgrim rolled the pollen into a tight ball and carried it to another blossom. There I watched her pierce the ovary wall with her long ovipositor and lay a clutch of eggs among the ovules, much as a farmer in the spring scatters seeds along his furrows. She packed the sticky mass of pollen through the openings of the stigma. Moth larvae and seeds would now develop simultaneously, with the larvae feeding on developing yucca. She walked to the edge of the petals. With her last bit of strength, she glided into the darkness, carried away by grace. The larvae would eventually gnaw their way through the ovary wall and lower themselves to the ground to pupate until the yuccas bloomed again. Circles. Cycles. Yucca and moth.

7 Perhaps the moth was on her way to pollinate the Navajo mind as well, for yucca and Navajo are relatives. Yucca is the single most important noncultivated plant to Indian peoples in the Southwest. It has been plaited into baskets, woven into mats, and wrapped around bundles. Early peoples walked with yucca bound around their feet. Sandals. Imagine the care extended to plants when they mean your survival.

8 In days of painted language, yucca leaves were soaked in warm water to soften. They were then beaten against the rocks for further pliancy. Fibers finely peeled—like corn silk, only stronger—were twisted into cordage with organic tension. This same process can be tried today with patience.

9 The children know yucca, *tsá-ászi'*, intimately. On the banks of the San Juan River we stood in a circle with yucca at the center.

10 "What is this?" I asked.

11 "Yucca!" they sang out in unison.

12 "And what story does it tell?"

13 I heard as many responses as there are yucca blossoms. But one common strand connecting their stories was soap.

14 "We call it soapweed because there's soap under there. . . . "

15 "Yes?"

16 "Yes. You find the root under here—they pointed to the body of the plant—cut off a piece, and slice it into four strips. Then you pound it with your hands and add warm water until it lathers up."

17 "Then what do you do?"

18 "We wash our hair with the suds."

19 Before I knew what was happening, two boys pulled the plant out from the sand. They cut off the root, sliced it into four strips, placed it on the sandstone, and began pounding it with a rock—just as they had said. It worked: The root was frothing with suds.

20 The boys didn't stop there. They moved to a desert pothole that was holding rainwater. Loren bent over the basin as Bryan washed his hair. The rest of the children gathered. This was a familiar sight and they laughed.

21 "Loren, you better watch out—tomorrow you'll come to school with hair hanging down your back!"

22 The lore of yucca supports this teasing. The Navajo say a yucca shampoo will make your hair long, shiny, and black. If there are doubts as to yucca magic, just look at the children.

23 On another occasion, the children warned me against using yucca.

24 "Why not?" I asked. My curiosity was up.

25 "Because it might give you warts." A wave of giggles rushed over them.

26 But on this day, things were different. After the boys had finished their demonstration, they handed me a fresh section of the root.

27 "Try it."

28 The girls disappeared and returned with a brush they had made from a bunch of rice grass. They began combing my hair. I sat toward the wind, unable to speak.

29 The ritual of bathing with yucca suds is woven into the Navajo Way. It has been said that the mound of earth upon which the basket for water and suds is placed commemorates the visit of two children to Changing Woman's home, where they witnessed her rejuvenation. Blessed yucca suds have the power to transform—to change the

30 profane to sacred, the doubtful to controlled, the contaminated to the purified.

31 One of the Navajo ceremonies associated with yucca washings is *Kinaaldá,* Changing Woman's puberty rites. *Kinaaldá* is part of the Blessing Way, a Navajo rite that maintains harmony for the people by attracting the goodness and power of benevolent Holy People. Most Navajo use the word *kinaaldá* to refer to the "first menses," alluding to the ceremonial rather than the physical event.

32 *Kinaaldá* ushers the adolescent Navajo girl into womanhood and invokes blessings upon her, ensuring her health, prosperity, and well-being. It is a festive occasion where the accounts of Changing Woman and her *Kinaaldá* are retold and reenacted.

> 33 The *Kinaaldá* started when White Shell Woman first menstruated. Nine days after her *Kinaaldá,* Changing Woman gave birth to twin boys: Monster Slayer and Child-of-the-waters. They were placed on the earth to kill the monsters. As soon as they had done this, their mother, Changing Woman, who was then living at Governador Knob, left and went to her home in the west, where she lives today.
>
> 34 After she moved to her home in the west, she created the Navajo people. When she had done this, she told these human beings to go to their original home, which was Navajo country. Before they left, she said, "After this, all the girls born to you will have periods at certain times when they become women. When the time comes, you must set a day and fix the girl up to be *Kinaaldá;* you must have these songs sung and do whatever else needs to be done at that time. After this period, a girl is a woman and will start having children.
>
> 35 That is what Changing Woman told the people she made in the west. She told them to go to their own country and do this.

36 And so *Kinaaldá* continues. A *Kinaaldá* may last anywhere from three to five days depending on the circumstances. Today, many families cannot afford this ceremony as it has become too expensive to hire a medicine man and provide food for friends and family. Even so, many young Navajo women have participated in this celebration. Traditionally, the singer or medicine man conducting the ceremony asks the mentoring woman, usually the girl's mother or aunt, to set out the basket containing the yucca roots. This is done usually before dawn of the last day of the ceremony. The roots have been carefully unearthed with two rocks found close by to aid in the crushing. The older woman

ritualistically shreds the roots and pulverizes them. She then pours water into the basket, creating yucca suds so that the girl can bathe her hair. But first, the woman washes all the girl's jewelry—beads, bracelets, rings, and concha belt—and sets them on a blanket to dry. Then the girl kneels before the water, unfastens her hair tie, and begins to wash her hair with the same lather. The woman helps her, making certain she receives a good shampoo. All during the washing ritual "Songs of Dawn" are being sung and a ritual cake is being prepared.

37 The older woman takes the basket of soapweed water, *tálâwosh*, to the west and empties it in a northerly direction. As soon as the singing stops, the young woman in *Kinaaldá* wrings out her hair and begins her last run to the east before dawn. Younger sisters and friends may follow her.

38 The breeze coming from her as she runs
The breeze coming from her as she runs
The breeze coming from her as she runs is beautiful.

39 The breeze coming from her as she runs
The breeze coming from her as she runs
The breeze coming from her as she runs is beautiful.

40 How many times have Navajo hands asked for the release of this root from the earth? How many times have these beaten roots been rubbed between flesh in warm water until heavy lather appeared? This source of soap, containing the compound saponin, has bathed skeins of yarn and skeins of hair, leaving both to glisten in desert sunlight.

41 Yucca is also edible. The children call yucca fruit "Navajo bananas." When boiled, it tastes much like summer squash, slightly sweet but with a twist of bitterness. But most of the yucca fruit is left in the heat to dry and wither. I have cut into its flesh many times and found exquisite symmetry. Six windows—once panes for seeds—become a chartreuse kaleidoscope.

42 The children look through yucca and see each other playing the ball and stick game, traditionally known as the "moccasin game."

43 "You play the game like this," they said. "You make a ball out of the yucca root with your hands, then everyone takes off their shoes

and lines them up on either side of the yucca. One side takes the ball and hides it inside one of the shoes. The other team has to guess which shoe it's in. If they guess right it's their turn to hide the ball, but if they're wrong, the other side gets to cut off a yucca leaf. The side with the most yucca sticks at the end of the game wins."

44 Another story is told. A long, long time ago all creatures on earth, including insects, spoke as human beings. The Animal People gathered around the yucca and said, "Let's have a shoe game." A great hoopla rose from the crowd as everyone showed his favor for such an event.

45 "But how will we keep score?" asked a small beast.

46 "We will use the blades of yucca as counters," spoke another. And one hundred and two yucca sticks were pulled. A ball from the root of yucca was shaped, along with a stick for pointing.

47 "We will have the shoe game at a place called Tse´yaa Hodilhil," they said. And everyone ran, jumped, flew and crawled to the designated site.

48 Gopher dug two shallow furrows on either side. Four moccasins were placed in each groove and then covered with sand. Then it was asked among the herds, swarms, and flocks, "What shall we bet?"

49 A great stirring occurred in the animal assemblage as everyone offered opinions. Finally, all the diurnal beings said, "We will bet the earth to have continual sunlight."

50 The nocturnal beings stepped forward and said, "We will bet the sky to have perpetual darkness."

51 And so the bets were placed between day and night.

52 There were many, many Animal People on both sides. The diurnal creatures on the south, the nocturnal creatures on the north. Anticipation for the contest grew like midsummer corn.

53 The game began with one side hiding the ball in one of the four moccasins, then covering the moccasins up with sand. The other side began guessing with the indicator stick which shoe the ball was in. They were given three chances. If they guessed correctly it became their turn to hide the ball. If they were fooled, the opponents took a yucca counter. Back and forth, back and forth it went, with lots of laughter and singing.

54 The Animal People became so immersed in the shoe game that no one realized morning had come. They continued to play throughout the day and into the night placing their bets high, with neither side ever quite winning all one hundred and two yucca sticks.

55 They did things then just as people do today. Once they started something, they would not stop. The wager between day and night still continues.

56 The shoe game is played by Navajos with delight. Some call it Navajo gambling. But those who know the stories say it keeps Sun and Moon in balance.

57 After all the children have shared their own versions of the game, they are quick to tell you that "you must only play this game in winter." A botanist will tell you winter is the dormant season for yucca. Earth wisdom.

58 I brought out my pouch and took a slice, a circle of yucca. It had been aged by Sun. Once supple, now shriveled. Bitter, hard. What could this be? I mused over the possibilities. If I were home, it could be cucumber, zucchini, even eggplant. But here it could be peyote or datura, any number of powerful medicines. Where could they take me? I closed my eyes and slipped the yucca slice into my mouth. From a far-off place I could smell the smoke of piñyon.

59 Yucca. Plants. Navajo. Plants yield their secrets to those who know them. They can weep the colors of chokecherry tears, purplish-brown, into a weaver's hands. They can be backbones for baskets holding the blessings of *Kinaaldá.* Cedar bark and sage can purify; Indian paintbrush soothes an ailing stomach. Juniper ash water creates blue cornmeal. Petals of larkspur are sprinkled in ceremony. Native plants are a repository. They hold our health. A Navajo medicine man relies on plants as we rely on pharmacies.

60 Edward S. Ayensu, director of the Office of Biological Conservation at the Smithsonian Institution, tells a story about an African herbalist who told his students to pay attention to the natural world, to listen and observe the behavior of animals such as lizards, snakes, birds, rodents, and insects.

61 To stress his point, the herbalist narrated a fight between two chameleons. As Ayensu describes it:

> 62 At the climax of the fight one of the chameleons passed out. The other quickly dashed into a thicket and came back with a piece of a leaf in its mouth. It forcibly pushed the leaf into the mouth of the unconscious lizard. In a matter of two or three minutes the defeated chameleon shook its body and took off.

63 The specific plant that saved the life of the chameleon was not disclosed to me. When I insisted on knowing, the teacher smiled and said, "This is a trade secret. It is a plant that can spring a dying person to life. Unless you became one of us I cannot tell you."

64 This is earth medicine, and it is all around us, delivered into the hands that trust it. What do we know?

65 Yucca. The desert torch burns and returns its ashes to crimson sand. A snake slithers across the way and recoils itself under a slickrock slab. This is what I heard:

66 Sha-woman, Sha-woman, hiss
Sha-woman, Sha-woman, hiss
Tongue, rattle, hiss
Tongue, rattle, hiss
Sha-woman, Sha-woman, hiss

67 Silence. A basket sits before me, coiled: around and around and around and around. It is striped with persimmon.

Understanding Meaning

1. What are the principal characteristics of the yucca plant?
2. How was the yucca plant created, according to Navajo legend?
3. Why is the plant so important to the Native Americans of the Southwest?
4. What traditions do the children reenact?
5. What special role does the yucca plant play in the lives of Navajo women?
6. *Critical Thinking:* Williams makes the statement that "yucca and Navajo are relatives." Could a similar essay define the importance of the potato to the prefamine Irish or rice to the Chinese? Can American urban civilization be defined by oil or electricity?

Evaluating Strategy

1. Williams opens the essay with a dream. How does this help introduce the spiritual importance of yucca to the Navajo?
2. What role does Williams play in the essay? How does she use dialogue?

3. Near the end of her essay, Williams introduces comments by an official of the Smithsonian Institution. Is the inclusion of outside scientific authorities essential to her essay?
4. *Other Modes:* How does Williams blend *narration* and *description* into creating a definition of the yucca plant?

Appreciating Language

1. Underline the metaphors Williams uses to describe the yucca plant. How do they aid in creating a definition?
2. Look up the terms *nocturnal* and *diurnal.*

Connections across the Disciplines

1. How does Williams's role in the essay compare with that of Gretel Ehrlich's in "A Storm, the Cornfield, and Elk" (page 199)?
2. Does Williams's detailed observation of the yucca follow Dr. Agassiz's admonition to "look again, look again" in Samuel Scudder's essay (page 41)?

Writing Suggestions

1. Write a brief essay defining an element central to the lives of a group of people. You might define a computer as the heart of a small business or coffee as the lifeblood of students during exam week. Provide details to illustrate the significance of this object or substance.
2. *Collaborative Writing:* Working with several students, ask each member to select an item that is central to a group they know. If the yucca plant defines the Navajo, what would define students on your campus—soda, pizza, computer disks, sweatshirts? Ask each member of the group to supply a brief definition.

BLENDING THE MODES

EDWARD DOLNICK

Edward Dolnick wrote this article for the September 1993 issue of The Atlantic Monthly, *a magazine specializing in the arts and public affairs. In this article he discusses how numerous deaf people refuse to see deafness as a "disability" but define it as a "culture."*

Deafness as Culture

Edward Dolnick uses several modes to develop his essay about deafness. The act of defining can be persuasive, *altering public perceptions and social policy. Notice how* comparison, cause and effect, description, *and* narration *play important roles in the article.*

1 In 1773, on a tour of Scotland and the Hebrides Islands, Samuel Johnson visited a school for deaf children. Impressed by the students but daunted by their predicament, he proclaimed deafness "one of the most desperate of human calamities." More than a century later Helen Keller reflected on her own life and declared that deafness was a far greater hardship than blindness. "Blindness cuts people off from things," she observed. "Deafness cuts people off from people."

2 For millennia deafness was considered so catastrophic that very few ventured to ease its burdens. Isolation in a kind of permanent solitary confinement was deemed inevitable; a deaf person, even in the midst of urban hubbub, was considered as unreachable as a fairy-tale princess locked in a tower. The first attempts to educate deaf children came only in the sixteenth century. As late as 1749 the French Academy of Sciences appointed a commission to determine whether deaf people were "capable of reasoning." Today no one would presume to ignore the deaf or exclude them from full participation in society. But acknowledging their rights is one thing, coming to grips with their plight another. Deafness is still seen as a dreadful fate.

3 Lately, though, the deaf community has begun to speak for itself. To the surprise and bewilderment of outsiders, its message is utterly contrary to the wisdom of centuries: Deaf people, far from groaning

under a heavy yoke, are not handicapped at all. Deafness is not a disability. Instead, many deaf people now proclaim, they are a subculture like any other. They are simply a linguistic minority (speaking American Sign Language) and are no more in need of a cure for their condition than are Haitians or Hispanics.

4 That view is vehemently held. "The term 'disabled' describes those who are blind or physically handicapped," the deaf linguists Carol Padden and Tom Humphries write, "not Deaf people." (The uppercase *D* is significant: It serves as a succinct proclamation that the deaf share a culture rather than merely a medical condition.) So strong is the feeling of cultural solidarity that many deaf parents cheer on discovering that their baby is deaf. Pondering such a scene, a hearing person can experience a kind of vertigo. The surprise is not simply the unfamiliarity of the views; it is that, as in a surrealist painting, jarring notions are presented as if they were commonplaces.

5 The embrace of what looks indisputably like hardship is what, in particular, strikes the hearing world as perverse, and deaf leaders have learned to brace themselves for the inevitable question. "No!" Roslyn Rosen says, by shaking her head vehemently, she *wouldn't* prefer to be able to hear. Rosen, the president of the National Association of the Deaf, is deaf, the daughter of deaf parents, and the mother of deaf children. "I'm happy with who I am," she says through an interpreter, "and I don't want to be 'fixed.' Would an Italian-American rather be a WASP? In our society everyone agrees that whites have an easier time than blacks. But do you think a black person would undergo operations to become white?"

6 The view that deafness is akin to ethnicity is far from unanimously held. "The world of deafness often seems Balkanized, with a warlord ruling every mountaintop," writes Henry Kisor, the book editor for the *Chicago Sun-Times* and deaf himself. But the "deaf culture" camp—Kisor calls it the "New Orthodoxy"—is in the ascendancy, and its proponents invoke watchwords that still carry echoes of earlier civil-rights struggles. "Pride," "heritage," "identity," and similar words are thick in the air.

7 Rhetoric aside, however, the current controversy is disorientingly unfamiliar, because the deaf are a group unlike any ethnic minority: 90 percent of all deaf children are born to hearing parents. Many people never meet a deaf person unless one is born to them. Then parent and child belong to different cultures, as they would in an adoption across racial lines. And deaf children acquire a sense of cultural identity from

their peers rather than their parents, as homosexuals do. But the crucial issue is that hearing parent and deaf child don't share a means of communication. Deaf children cannot grasp their parents' spoken language, and hearing parents are unlikely to know sign language. Communication is not a gift automatically bestowed in infancy but an acquisition gained only by laborious effort.

8 This gulf has many consequences. Hearing people tend to make the mistake of considering deafness to be an affliction that we are familiar with, as if being deaf were more or less like being hard of hearing. Even those of us with sharp hearing are, after all, occasionally unable to make out a mumbled remark at the dinner table, or a whispered question from a toddler, or a snatch of dialogue in a movie theater.

9 To get a hint of blindness, you can try making your way down an unfamiliar hall in the dark, late at night. But clamping on a pair of earmuffs conveys nothing essential about deafness, because the earmuffs can't block out a lifetime's experience of having heard language. That experience makes hearing people ineradicably different. Because antibiotics have tamed many of the childhood diseases that once caused permanent loss of hearing, more than 90 percent of all deaf children in the United States today were born deaf or lost their hearing before they had learned English. The challenge that faces them—recognizing that other peoples' mysterious lip movements *are* language, and then learning to speak that language—is immeasurably greater than that facing an adult who must cope with a gradual hearing loss.

10 Learning to speak is so hard for people deaf from infancy because they are trying, without any direct feedback, to mimic sounds they have never heard. (Children who learn to speak and then go deaf fare better, because they retain some memory of sound.) One mother of a deaf child describes the challenge as comparable to learning to speak Japanese from within a soundproof glass booth. And even if a deaf person does learn to speak, understanding someone else's speech remains maddeningly difficult. Countless words look alike on the lips, though they sound quite different. "Mama" is indistinguishable from "papa," "cat" from "hat," "no new taxes" from "go to Texas." Context and guesswork are crucial, and conversation becomes a kind of fast and ongoing crossword puzzle.

11 "Speechreading is EXHAUSTING. I hate having to depend on it," writes Cheryl Heppner, a deaf woman who is the executive director of the Northern Virginia Resource Center for Deaf and Hard of

Hearing Persons. Despite her complaint, Heppner is a speech-reading virtuoso. She made it through public school and Pennsylvania State University without the help of interpreters, and she says she has never met a person with better speech-reading skills. But "even with peak conditions," she explains, "good lighting, high energy level, and a person who articulates well, I'm still guessing at half of what I see on the lips." When we met in her office, our conversation ground to a halt every sentence or two, as if we were travelers without a common language who had been thrown together in a train compartment. I had great difficulty making out Heppner's soft, high-pitched speech, and far more often than not my questions and comments met only with her mouthed "Sorry." In frustration we resorted to typing on her computer.

12 For the average deaf person, lip-reading is even less rewarding. In tests using simple sentences, deaf people recognize perhaps three or four words in every ten. Ironically, the greatest aid to lip-reading is knowing how words sound. One British study found, for example, that the average deaf person with a decade of practice was no better at lip-reading than a hearing person picked off the street.

13 Unsurprisingly, the deaf score poorly on tests of English skills. The average deaf sixteen-year-old reads at the level of a hearing eight-year-old. When deaf students eventually leave school, three in four are unable to read a newspaper. Only two deaf children in a hundred (compared with forty in a hundred among the general population) go on to college. Many deaf students write English as if it were a foreign language. One former professor at Gallaudet, the elite Washington, D.C., university for the deaf, sometimes shows acquaintances a letter written by a student. The quality of the writing, he says, is typical. "As soon as you had lend me $15," the letter begins, "I felt I must write you to let you know how relievable I am in your aid."

14 Small wonder that many of the deaf eagerly turn to American Sign Language, invariably described as "the natural language of the deaf." Deaf children of deaf parents learn ASL as easily as hearing children learn a spoken language. At the same age that hearing babies begin talking, deaf babies of parents who sign begin "babbling" nonsense signs with their fingers. Soon, and without having to be formally taught, they have command of a rich and varied language, as expressive as English but as different from it as Urdu or Hungarian.

15 At the heart of the idea that deafness is cultural, in fact, is the deaf community's proprietary pride in ASL. Even among the hearing the discovery of ASL's riches has sometimes had a profound impact. The

most prominent ally of the deaf-culture movement, for example, is the Northeastern University linguist Harlan Lane, whose interest in the deaf came about through his study of ASL. When he first saw people signing to one another, Lane recalls, he was stunned to realize that "language could be expressed just as well by the hands and face as by the tongue and throat, even though the very definition of language we had learned as students was that it was something spoken and heard." For a linguist, Lane says, "this was astonishing, thrilling. I felt like Balboa seeing the Pacific."

16 Until the 1960s critics had dismissed signing as a poor substitute for language, a mere semaphoring of stripped-down messages ("I see the ball"). Then linguists demonstrated that ASL is in fact a full-fledged language, with grammar and puns and poems, and dignified it with a name. Anything that can be said can be said in ASL. In the view of the neurologist and essayist Oliver Sacks, it is "a language equally suitable for making love or speeches, for flirtation or mathematics."

17 ASL is the everyday language of perhaps half a million Americans. A shared language makes for a shared identity. With the deaf as with other groups, this identity is a prickly combination of pride in one's own ways and wariness of outsiders. "If I happened to strike up a relationship with a hearing person," says MJ Bienvenu, a deaf activist speaking through an interpreter, "I'd have considerable trepidation about my [deaf] parents' reaction. They'd ask, 'What's the matter? Aren't your own people good enough for you?' and they'd warn, 'They'll take advantage of you. You don't know what they're going to do behind your back.'"

18 Blind men and women often marry sighted people, but 90 percent of deaf people who marry take deaf spouses. When social scientists ask people who are blind or in wheelchairs if they wish they could see or walk, they say yes instantly. Only the deaf answer the equivalent question no. The essence of deafness, they explain, is not the lack of hearing but the community and culture based on ASL. Deaf culture represents not a denial but an affirmation.

19 Spokespeople for deaf pride present their case as self-evident and commonsensical. Why should anyone expect deaf people to deny their roots when every other cultural group proudly celebrates its traditions and history? Why stigmatize the speakers of a particular language as disabled? "When Gorbachev visited the U.S., he used an interpreter to talk to the President," says Bienvenu, who is one of the

directors of an organization called The Bicultural Center. "Was Gorbachev disabled?"

UNEASY ALLIES

20 Despite the claims made in its name, though, the idea that deafness is akin to ethnicity is hardly straightforward. On the contrary, it is an idea with profound and surprising implications, though these are rarely explored. When the deaf were in the news in 1988, for instance, protesting the choice of a hearing person as president of Gallaudet, the press assumed that the story was about disabled people asserting their rights, and treated it the same as if students at a university for the blind had demanded a blind president.

21 The first surprise in the cultural view of deafness is that it rejects the assumption that medical treatment means progress and is welcome. Since deafness is not a deprivation, the argument runs, talk of cures and breakthroughs and technological wizardry is both inappropriate and offensive—as if doctors and newspapers joyously announced advances in genetic engineering that might someday make it possible to turn black skin white.

22 Last fall, for example, *60 Minutes* produced a story on a bright, lively little girl named Caitlin Parton. "We don't remember ever meeting [anyone] who captivated us quite as much as this seven-year-old charmer," it began. Caitlin is deaf, and *60 Minutes* showed how a new device called a cochlear implant had transformed her life. Before surgeons implanted a wire in Caitlin's inner ear and a tiny receiver under her skin, she couldn't hear voices or barking dogs or honking cars. With the implant she can hear ordinary conversation, she can speak almost perfectly, and she is thriving in school. *60 Minutes* presented the story as a welcome break from its usual round of scandal and exposé. Who could resist a delightful child and a happy ending?

23 Activists in the deaf community were outraged. Implants, they thundered in letters to *60 Minutes*, are "child abuse" and "pathological" and "genocide." The mildest criticism was that Caitlin's success was a fluke that would tempt parents into entertaining similar but doomed hopes for their own children. "There should have been parades all across America," Caitlin's father lamented months later. "This is a miracle of biblical proportions, making the deaf hear. But we keep

hearing what a terrible thing this is, how it's like Zyklon B, how it has to be stopped."

24 The anger should have been easy to anticipate. The magazine *Deaf Life*, for example, runs a question-and-answer column called "For Hearing People Only." In response to a reader's question well before *60 Minutes* came along, the editors wrote, "An implant is the ultimate invasion of the ear, the ultimate denial of deafness, the ultimate refusal to let deaf children be Deaf. . . . Parents who choose to have their children implanted, are in effect saying, 'I don't respect the Deaf community, and I certainly don't want my child to be part of it. I want him/her to be part of the hearing world, not the Deaf world.'"

25 The roots of such hostility run far deeper than the specific fear that cochlear implants in children are unproved and risky. More generally, the objection is that from the moment parents suspect their child is deaf, they turn for expert advice to doctors and audiologists and speech therapists rather than to the true experts, deaf people. Harlan Lane points to one survey that found that 86 percent of deaf adults said they would not want a cochlear implant even if it were free. "There are many prostheses from eyeglasses and artificial limbs to cochlear implants," Lane writes. "Can you name another that we insist on for children in flagrant disregard of the advice of adults with the same 'condition'?"

26 The division between the deaf community and the medical one seems to separate two natural allies. Even more surprising is a second split, between deaf people and advocates for the disabled. In this case, though, the two sides remain uneasy partners, bound as if in a bad marriage. The deaf community knows that whatever its qualms, it cannot afford to cut itself off from the larger, savvier, wealthier disability lobby.

27 Historically, advocates for every disabled group have directed their fiercest fire at policies that exclude their group. No matter the good intentions, no matter the logistical hurdles, they have insisted, separate is not equal. Thus buildings, buses, classes, must be accessible to all; special accommodations for the disabled are not a satisfactory substitute. All this has become part of conventional wisdom. Today, under the general heading of "mainstreaming," it is enshrined in law and unchallenged as a premise of enlightened thought.

28 Except among the deaf. Their objection is that even well-meaning attempts to integrate deaf people into hearing society may actually imprison them in a zone of silence. Jostled by a crowd but unable to

communicate, they are effectively alone. The problem is especially acute in schools, where mainstreaming has led to the decline of residential schools for the disabled and the deaf and the integration of many such students into ordinary public schools. Since deafness is rare, affecting one child in a thousand, deaf students are thinly scattered. As a result, half of all deaf children in public school have either no deaf classmates at all or very few.

29 "Mainstreaming deaf children in regular public-school programs," the prominent deaf educator Leo Jacobs writes, will produce "a new generation of educational failures" and "frustrated and unfulfilled adults." Another deaf spokesman, Mervin Garretson, is even harsher. The danger of mainstreaming, he contends, is that deaf children could be "educationally, vocationally, and emotionally mutilated."

THE CASE FOR ASL

30 In his brilliant and polemical book *The Mask of Benevolence*, Harlan Lane, the chief theoretician of the deaf-culture movement, makes his case seem as clear-cut as a proposition in formal logic. Deaf children are biologically equipped to do everything but hear, he argues; spoken language turns on the ability to hear; therefore spoken language is a poor choice for deaf children. For good measure, Lane throws in a corollary: Since an alternative language, ASL, is both available and easy for the deaf to learn, ASL is a better choice for a first language. QED.

31 For the parents of a deaf child, though, matters are far from simple. (Lane is childless.) Parents have crucial decisions to make, and they don't have the luxury of time. Children who learn a language late are at a lifelong disadvantage. Deafness is, in one scholar's summary, "a curable, or rather a preventable, form of mental retardation."

32 Osmond and Deborah Crosby's daughter was born in July of 1988. "Dorothy Jane Crosby," the birth announcement began. "Stanford class of 2009, track, academic all-American, B.S. in pre-astronautics, Cum Laude. 2008 Olympics (decathlon), Miss Florida, Senate hopeful."

33 "You can chuckle about that announcement," Oz Crosby says now, "but we all have expectations for our kids. That card was a message from my unconscious—these are the kinds of things I'd like to see, that would make me proud, in my child. And the first thing that happened after DJ's deafness was diagnosed was that I felt that child had

died. That's something you hear a lot from parents, and it's that blunt and that real."

34 Crosby, fifty, is tall and athletic, with blond hair and a small, neat moustache. A timber executive who now lives in the suburbs of Washington, D.C., he is a serious and intelligent man who had scarcely given deafness a thought before it invaded his household. Then he plunged into the deafness literature and began keeping a journal of his own.

35 He found that every path was pocked with hazards. The course that sounds simplest, keeping the child at home with her parents and teaching her English, can prove fantastically difficult. Even basic communication is a constant challenge. In a memoir called *Deaf Like Me,* a man named Thomas Spradley tells of raising a deaf daughter, Lynn. One Saturday morning shortly after Lynn had begun school, Spradley and his wife, Louise, found her outdoors, waiting for the school bus. Lynn stood at the end of the driveway, scanning the street every few seconds. After half an hour she gave up and came indoors. For weeks Lynn repeated the same futile wait every Saturday and Sunday, until her parents finally managed to convey the concept of "weekday" and "weekend." Words like "car" and "shoes" were easy; abstractions and relationships were not. The Spradleys knew Lynn loved her grandparents, for instance, but they had no idea if she knew who those devoted elderly people were. When Lynn once had to undergo a spinal tap, her parents could not explain what the painful test was for.

36 As much trouble as Thomas and Louise Spradley had in talking with their daughter, she was just as frustrated in trying to communicate with them. "How do you tell Mommy that you don't like your cereal with that much milk on it?" Spradley writes. "How do you ask Daddy to swing you upside down when all he seems to understand is that you want to be held? How do you tell them that you want to go to other people's houses like [her older brother]? How do you make them understand you want the same kind of Kool-Aid that you had two weeks ago at your cousin's house and just now remembered? How do you say, 'I forgot what I wanted'?"

37 Making matters more frustrating still, no one seems able to tell parents how successful their child will be in speaking and understanding English. "I'd ask, 'What's the future for us?'" Crosby says, "and they'd say, 'Every deaf child is different.'" Though given to measured, even pedantic, phrasing, Crosby grows angry as he recalls the scene. "It seemed like such a cop-out. I wanted to grab them by the throat and shout, 'Here's the bloody audiogram. How's she going to talk?'"

38 The truth, Crosby has reluctantly come to concede, is that only a few generalizations are possible. Children who are born deaf or who lose their hearing before learning to speak have a far harder time than those deafened later. Children with a profound hearing loss have a harder time than children with a mild loss. Children who cannot detect high-pitched sounds have problems different from those of children who cannot detect low pitches. Finally, and unaccountably, some deaf children just happen to have an easier time with spoken English than others.

39 Hence few overall statistics are available. Those few are not encouraging. In one study, for example, teachers of the deaf, evaluating their own pupils, judged the speech of two thirds of them to be hard to understand or unintelligible. Timothy Jaech, the superintendent of the Wisconsin School for the Deaf, writes, "The vast majority of deaf children will never develop intelligible speech for the general public." Jaech, who is deaf, speaks and reads lips. "To gamble 12 to 15 years of a deaf child's life is almost immoral," he says. "[My sister] and I were among the lucky ones. What of the other 99 percent?"

40 Still, it is indisputable that many profoundly deaf adults participate fully and successfully in the hearing world, as lawyers and engineers and in dozens of other roles. Do these examples show what parents might expect for their own child? Or are they inspiring but irrelevant tales that have as little bearing on the typical deaf child as Michael Jordan's success has on the future of a ten-year-old dreaming of NBA glory?

41 The case for ASL has problems of its own. ASL is certainly easier for the deaf child to learn, but what of the rest of the family? How can parents say anything meaningful to their child in a foreign language they have only begun to study? Moreover, many hearing parents point out, even if deaf culture is rich and vital, it is indisputably not the majority culture. Since spoken language is the ticket to the larger world, isn't giving a child ASL as a first language a bit risky?

42 The choices are agonizing. "I understand now how people choosing a cancer therapy for their child must feel," Crosby says, "You can't afford to be wrong." To illustrate the dilemma, Crosby wrote what he calls a parable:

43 Suppose that your one-year-old, who has been slow to walk, has just been diagnosed with a rare disorder of the nervous system. The prognosis is

44 for great difficulty in muscular control of the arms and legs due to tremors and impaired nerve pathways. With the help of special braces, physical therapy, and lots of training, she will be able to walk slowly, climb stairs haltingly, and use her hands awkwardly. In general, she will be able to do most of the things other kids do, although not as easily, smoothly, or quickly. Some children respond to this therapy better than others, but all can get around on their legs after a fashion. Even though they will never run or play sports, they will have complete mobility at a deliberate, shuffling pace.

45 There *is* an alternative, however. If her legs are amputated right away, the tremors will cease, and the remaining nerve pathways will strengthen. She will be able to use a wheelchair with ease. She can even be a wheelchair athlete, "running" marathons, playing basketball, etc., if she desires. Anywhere a wheelchair can go is readily available to her. There is easy access to a world that is geographically smaller. On the other hand, she can't climb simple stairs, hike trails slowly, or even use public transportation without special assistance.

46 "Now, Mr. and Mrs. Solomon," Crosby concluded, "which life do *you* choose for your child?"

CUED SPEECH

47 Crosby and his wife have chosen a compromise, a controversial technique called cued speech, in which spoken English is accompanied by hand signals that enable a deaf person to distinguish between words that look alike on the lips. The aim is to remove the guesswork from lip-reading by using eight hand shapes in different positions near the face to indicate that the word being spoken is, say, "bat" rather than "pan."

48 The technique, which is spread by a tiny but zealous group of parents with deaf children, has several advantages. It's easy to learn, for one thing, taking only twenty or so hours of study. A parent who sets out to learn American Sign Language, in contrast, must devote months or years to the project, as he would have to do in order to learn any foreign language. And since cued speech is, essentially, English, parents can bypass the stilted, often useless phrases of the beginning language student. Instead of stumbling over "*la plume de ma tante,*" they can talk to their deaf child from the beginning about any subject in the world.

49 Moreover, because cued speech is simply English transliterated, rather than a new language, nothing has to be lost in translation. A deaf child who learns cued speech learns English, along with its slang and jargon and idioms and jokes, as his native language. "It's a way to embrace English, the language your whole country runs on, instead of trying to pretend it doesn't exist," says Judy Weiss, a woman in Washington, D.C., who has used cued speech with her son since he lost his hearing as a ten-month-old.

50 This method, which was invented at Gallaudet in 1965–1966, is nonetheless out of favor with the deaf community. It's seen as a slap at ASL and as just a new version of the despised "oralism," in which deaf students were forced for hour upon hour to try to pronounce English words they had never heard. But the proponents of cued speech insist that these objections are political and unfounded. They point to a handful of small studies that conclude that deaf children who learn cued speech read as well as hearing students, and they mention a small group of highly successful deaf students who rely on cuing. Perhaps the most accomplished of all is a Wellesley undergraduate named Stasie Jones. Raised in France by an American mother and a British father, she speaks French and English and is now studying Russian and Spanish.

51 But the system is no godsend. "The trap I see a lot of cuing families fall into," Crosby says, "is to say, 'Johnny understands everything we say, we understand everything he says, he's getting *A*s at school—what's the problem?' The problem is, Johnny can't talk to someone he meets on the street and Johnny can't order a hamburger at McDonald's."

TOTAL COMMUNICATION

52 Cued speech is used only in a relative handful of schools. By far the most common method of teaching the deaf today is called "total communication." The idea is that teachers use any and all means of communication with their students—speech, writing, ASL, fingerspelling. Total communication was instituted in the 1970s as a reaction to a century of oralism, in which signing was forbidden and the aim was to teach the deaf child to speak and lip-read.

53 Oralism still has zealous adherents, but today it is used mainly with hard-of-hearing students and only rarely with deaf ones. Its dominance began with the Congress of Milan, an international meeting of educators in 1880, which affirmed "the incontestable superiority of speech over sign" and voted to banish sign language from deaf education. The ban, notorious to this day among the deaf, was effective. In 1867 every American school for the deaf taught in ASL; by 1907 not a single one did.

54 When total communication came along, the two rival camps in deaf education accepted it warily. Those who favored English reasoned that at least teachers would be speaking to their students; those who preferred ASL were pleased that teachers would be signing. Today hardly anyone is pleased, and one of the few points of agreement in the present debate is that deaf education is distressingly bad. The Commission on Education of the Deaf, for example, which reported to the President and Congress in 1988, began its account, "The present status of education for persons who are deaf in the United States is unsatisfactory. Unacceptably so. This is [our] primary and inescapable conclusion."

55 The explanation for these dreary findings, depending on who is carrying out the analysis, is either that deafness is so debilitating that poor results are inevitable or that something is wrong with current teaching methods. Total communication, its critics contend, is unworkable. No teacher can speak in English and simultaneously sign the same message in ASL, which has a completely different grammar and word order. "In practice," Harlan Lane writes, "'total communication' merely means that the teacher may accompany his spoken English with some signs from American Sign Language, if he knows a few. While the teacher is speaking, he occasionally 'shouts' a sign—that is, signs a prominent noun or verb if he knows it, in the wrong order and without using the complex grammar of ASL."

56 Lane and his allies support an approach called bilingual-bicultural. In this new and still rare program (so new that few measures of its success or failure are available) students are taught in ASL and eventually build on that knowledge to learn English as a second language. Since learning to speak is so difficult and time-consuming, the emphasis in English courses is on reading and writing rather than on speaking.

57 Neither this new approach nor any other single method may prove right for everyone. Take Cheryl Heppner, the director of the Northern Virginia Resource Center. She was deafened by meningitis as a second-grader, long after she had become expert in English. Today

Heppner is a great admirer of ASL, which she learned as an adult, but she says nonetheless that classes taught in ASL would not have been best for her. "Why should they have stripped English away from me?" she asks. "I already had to learn to cope with deafness."

58 The objections of many hearing parents to the bilingual scheme are far more strenuous. ASL is not simply a different language, they note, but a language without a written form. Partly as a consequence, deaf culture has a marked anti-book bias. (Lane himself confesses that he is "really frustrated" that so few deaf people have read his eloquent but lengthy accounts of deaf culture.) "If you give your child, as a first language, a language that has no written form," Oz Crosby says, "and if that language on average does not lead to good reading skills, then you're giving that child a life in which she reads at a third- to fifth-grade level. She will be in danger of being exploited, because low-end jobs are all that will be available to her."

59 Two deep and related fears lie at the heart of the resentment of the bilingual approach. First, many hearing parents suspect that bilingualism is a Trojan horse. Once ASL has been smuggled in, they fear, talk of English as a second language will dry up. Second, and more important, they resent the implication that deaf adults know better than a deaf child's own parents what is best for her. This is more than parental paranoia. Lane has written, for instance, that "most hearing parents make a botch of having a Deaf child."

60 Deaf leaders do their best to defuse such fears. "We don't say that hearing parents aren't qualified to make decisions about their deaf children," says Roslyn Rosen, of the National Association of the Deaf. "We say that they need to have contact with deaf people if they're going to make educated decisions. The way the system works now is that the first people the parents see are doctors and audiologists, who see deafness as a pathology. What we need are partnerships between hearing parents and the deaf community, so that parents can meet deaf people who are doing well."

61 Even deaf adults who don't identify with deaf culture often feel that they have important but untapped expertise on growing up deaf. "There is a strong feeling of community, and deaf people feel ownership of deaf children," Cheryl Heppner says. "I admit it. I feel it too. I really struggle in not wanting to interfere with a parent's right to parent and at the same time dealing with my own feelings and knowing that they have to accept that the child can never be one hundred percent theirs."

62 Such concessions rouse dark fears in hearing parents. Time and again their talk turns to laments about "giving up" or "losing" or "turning over" their child to the deaf community. Even Oz Crosby, who strives to be open-minded, observes that "sometimes Deaf Culture looks like the Moonies to me: 'Your child will be happy, just don't expect to see her anymore, she's too busy being happy.'"

63 These fears crystallize around the issue of residential schools for the deaf, which have far different associations for deaf and hearing families. Hearing parents think of residential schools and conjure up the bleakest scenes in Dickens or the angriest images in a Frederick Wiseman documentary, with their child stuck away in a human warehouse. But among the deaf, residential schools have tremendous support. Here deaf children will not "drown in the mainstream," as Lane puts it, but will instead flourish among their peers. The schools provide a lifesaving chance to escape from isolation into community.

64 Patrick Graybill, a prominent figure in the deaf community and a former member of the National Theatre of the Deaf, attended a residential school in Kansas starting at age five. His enthusiastic memories of those years are typical. "I was really happy at school," he says, through an interpreter. "I saw my first plays there, and I knew that's what I wanted to do when I grew up. There were deaf adults I looked up to, and a good support system."

65 The classes were by no means uniformly excellent. "The emphasis was on English, and we were hit if we were caught talking with our hands. The speech teacher couldn't sign, and I used to hate having to touch her throat and neck, to learn the sounds to make, and smelling her breath." But pedagogy wasn't the point. "ASL was allowed in the dormitories," Graybill says, "and that's where we learned Deaf culture. Now I see kids in public schools, and some accept themselves as Deaf people, but others have a problem with it. We knew who we were, but I'm afraid they'll be lost between two worlds, because they can't speak well enough to be understood by hearing people and they're ashamed to use ASL."

66 Residential schools play such an important role in deaf culture that when two deaf adults meet, they tell each other not only their names but also the names of the schools they attended. "These schools were the place where their culture was transmitted to them," Lane says. "If they had hearing parents, they weren't going to find out how to be deaf in their homes or in the local schools. This was where it happened,

and frequently it's where they found their spouses, too. The schools are what Israel is to the Jews, the land of a minority without a land."

67 The world of the deaf is heterogeneous, and the fault lines that run through it are twisted and tricky. Now politics has worsened the strains. Frances Parsons, for example, is a much honored Gallaudet professor who, though deaf herself, has denounced "the extremists fanatically hawking ASL and Deafism." Such views have brought her hate mail and denunciatory posters and, once, a punch in the neck. Parsons sees her attackers as cultists and propagandists; they call her and her allies traitors and Uncle Toms.

68 Much of the dispute has to do with who is authentically deaf. Parsons is suspect because she speaks and has hearing parents. To be the deaf child of deaf parents has cachet, because this is as deaf as one can be. (The four student leaders of the 1988 Gallaudet protest were all "deaf of deaf.") To use ASL is "better" than to use a manual language that mimics English grammar and arranges ASL signs in English word order. "Those born deaf deride those who become deaf at six years or twelve years or later," the Gallaudet psychologist Larry Stewart observed last year in a bitter essay titled "Debunking the Bilingual-Bicultural Snow Job in the American Deaf Community." "ASL-users who do not use lip movements scorn those who sign with mouthed English, or, the other way around. Residential school graduates turn up their nose at mainstream graduates, or the reverse. And so it goes; a once cohesive community now splintered apart by ideology."

69 Still, there is some common ground and even room for optimism. Captioning on television is universally welcomed; so are TTYs, keyboard devices that allow the deaf to use the telephone, provided the person called also has a TTY. In most states phone companies provide a free "relay" service, in which an operator with a TTY serves as a link between a deaf person with a TTY and a hearing person without one.

70 "Things are getting better," Roslyn Rosen says. "When I check into a hotel, because of the Americans With Disabilities Act, I expect the TV in the room will have captions, there'll be a TTY, the phone and the fire alarm will have flashing lights, and all that. And soon there will be TV-phones, which will be a wonderful boon for people who use sign language."

71 What's the difference between these technologies, which Rosen welcomes, and such a device as the cochlear implant, which she

denounces? "An implant," she says, "alters *me.* The critical point is, it changes me instead of changing the environment. Therefore the prob-
72 lem is seen as belonging to the deaf person, and *that's* a problem."

To an outsider, this sounds a bit forced. Do eyeglasses, say, belong to one moral category and eye surgery to another? A more useful distinction may be between approaches that allow deaf people to participate in the world and those that leave them stranded on the sidelines. "Part of the odyssey I've made," Cheryl Heppner says, "is in realizing that deafness is a disability, but it's a disability that is unique." It is unique in that a deaf person, unaided and independent, can travel wherever he wants, whenever he wants. The question is whether he will be able to communicate with anyone when he gets there.

Understanding Meaning

1. Dolnick opens his essay with a *narrative* outlining the historical view of deafness. What was the traditional definition of deafness?
2. What definition do many deaf advocates rebel against? If deafness is not a "disability" or a "handicap," what is it? Does a common language define a culture?
3. Dolnick *compares* blindness to deafness. Sighted people can wear a blindfold, he points out, and realize what obstacles the blind encounter. But why does wearing earmuffs and blocking out all sounds fail to approximate deafness in hearing people?
4. Dolnick states that "many deaf parents cheer on discovering that their baby is deaf." What does this reveal? Discuss whether it signifies a dramatic gulf between the hearing and deaf communities.
5. *Critical Thinking:* How do you respond to the idea that performing surgery to make a deaf child hear is akin to bleaching the skin of an African American child? Is this a rational comparison?

Evaluating Strategy

1. *Other Modes:* How does Dolnick use the *narrative* of the Crosby family to develop his essay?
2. *Other Modes:* How does Dolnick use *division* to explain the different methods of teaching deaf children to communicate? Where does he use *classification* to demonstrate the range of hearing impairment?
3. Dolnick uses quotes and interviews throughout the essay. Is this an effective technique in discussing a complex and controversial issue? Is it best to let people speak for themselves instead of paraphrasing their views? Does this help a writer maintain objectivity?

Appreciating Language

1. In discussing a controversial issue, Dolnick must choose words that are loaded with meaning. "Disability" and "culture" have clear connotations. Can one make an objective definition when forced to choose words that might contain subjective meanings to the reader?
2. How does Dolnick's word choice reflect his views on deafness? What words does he use to *describe* advocates who define deafness as a culture and not a handicap?
3. Why do people capitalize *deaf?* What is implied by the use of "the Deaf"?
4. How does Dolnick define the terms "total communication," "bicultural," and "cued speech"?

Connections across the Disciplines

1. Relate Dolnick's article to Richard Rodriguez's "The Tongue That Had to be Tied" (page 673). How does language, in any form, determine culture?
2. Consider Eileen Simpson's article about dyslexia (page 172). She describes coping skills dyslexics use to function. At what point do people who share a coping process become a "community" or a "culture"?

Writing Suggestions

1. Write an essay outlining your definition of *culture.* Include examples to support your view.
2. *Critical Writing:* Write an essay responding to this writing prompt: "If medical technology develops methods of curing deafness at birth, a valuable culture and unique language will be lost." Agree or disagree with this point of view.
3. *Collaborative Writing:* Ask other students about their own experience and knowledge of deaf people. Then write a brief *analysis* of how society has attempted to accommodate the needs of the deaf. Consider this point: Since many deaf people do not consider English their language, do closed-captioned television programs and related efforts really address the needs of the deaf?

WRITING BEYOND THE CLASSROOM

Two Definitions of Depression

THE ENCYCLOPEDIA OF PSYCHOLOGY

Definition is a critical feature of all professional writing. Professionals need common standards in order to communicate and operate efficiently. The way definitions are expressed depends on the writer's goal, the audience, and the discipline.

This definition is taken from a specialized encyclopedia designed for mental health professionals. As a standard reference, it seeks to establish a common understanding of terms for people who must diagnose and treat patients with psychological problems.

DEPRESSION

The Concept of Depression

1 *Depression* is a term used to describe a mood, a symptom, and syndromes of affective disorders. As a mood, it refers to a transient state of feeling sad, blue, forlorn, cheerless, unhappy, and/or down. As a symptom, it refers to a complaint that often accompanies a group of biopsychosocial problems. In contrast, the depressive syndromes include a wide spectrum of psychobiological dysfunctions that vary in frequency, severity, and duration. Normal depression is a transient period of sadness and fatigue that generally occurs in response to identifiable stressful life events. The moods associated with normal depression vary in length but generally do not exceed 7 to 10 days. If the problems continue for a longer period and if the symptoms grow in complexity and severity, clinical levels of depression may be present. Clinical depression generally involves sleep disorders, eating disorders, anergia, hopelessness, and despair. Sometimes problems assume psychotic proportions, and the depressed individual may attempt suicide and/or may experience hallucinations, delusions, and serious psychological and motor retardation.

DON D. ROSENBERG

This definition, written by a practicing psychologist, appeared in a brochure distributed in the waiting room of a Milwaukee mental health clinic. It is directed to the general public and seeks to explain the nature of depression to people seeking help from psychological problems they may have difficulty understanding.

WHAT IS DEPRESSION?

1 Depression is an internal state—a feeling of sadness, loss, "the blues," deep disappointment. *When it is more severe, you may have feelings of irritability, touchiness, guilt, self-reproach, loss of self-esteem, worthlessness, hopelessness, helplessness, and even thoughts of death and suicide.* It may include such other feelings as tearfulness, being sensitive and easily hurt, loss of interests, loss of sexual drive, loss of control in life, feeling drained and depleted, anger at yourself, and loss of the ability to feel pleasure.

2 It may be accompanied by *physical symptoms* similar to the sense of profound loss, including:

3
* *loss of appetite*, often with weight loss, but sometimes we find increased eating
* *insomnia or early morning waking*, often 2–4 times per night, nearly every day, but sometimes we see a need to sleep excessively
* moving and speaking slows down, but sometimes we see *agitation*
* *fatigue or loss of energy* nearly every day
* *loss of concentration*, foggy and indecisive
* sometimes it includes anxious and headachy feelings and also *frequent crying*

4 Besides the physical sensations and emotions of depression, depressed people may *withdraw, may brood or ruminate about problems*, have trouble remembering things, wonder if they would be better off dead, and become very concerned about bodily symptoms and pains. They may be grouchy, sulking, restless, and unwilling to interact with family and friends.

Understanding Meaning

1. *The Encyclopedia of Psychology* is a reference text for mental health students and professionals. What is the purpose of this definition? How does

it differ from the clinic's brochure's definition, aimed at the general public?
2. What role does definition play in the treatment of any disorder? How is addressing professionals different from addressing potential patients?
3. Which are the objective statements in both definitions? Do both definitions agree on the basic elements of depression?
4. How does the brochure address its readers differently from the encyclopedia? *Other Modes:* What *persuasive* elements are used in the brochure?

Evaluating Strategy

1. The brochure by Don Rosenberg uses italics, underlining, and asterisks for highlighting. What functions do these have? Discuss their suitability.
2. How does the brochure direct its message to the public and potential patients?

Appreciating Language

1. Does the purpose of the definition dictate the tone of the language in these two examples? Does the encyclopedia's *description* focus on objective, observable symptoms? Does the brochure seem to focus on feelings and emotions?
2. Would the language of the encyclopedia appear cold and unfeeling to a patient seeking help with depression?

Writing Suggestions

1. Take a definition from the glossary section of a textbook, and write a version for a general audience of clients, consumers, or students.
2. Using information from the encyclopedia and brochure, write a definition of depression targeted to college students. Describe symptoms in terms students will readily identify.
3. *Collaborative Writing:* Discuss a common problem or issue with fellow students: job insecurity, lack of sleep, stressful family relationships, child care, or the fear of crime. Select a term you often overhear, and provide a clear definition for it. Have each member of the group list features of this term. Try to incorporate objective elements. Write the definition in two versions: one designed for an "official" publication such as the college catalog or textbook, the other for an informal handout.

GUIDELINES FOR WRITING DEFINITIONS

1. **Determine your purpose.** Does your definition seek to provide a common language to prevent confusion, or does it seek to persuade readers by altering their perceptions?
2. **Define your role.** Your definition can be based on personal observation and opinion or standard principles and methods followed in a specific discipline or profession.
3. **Consider your audience.** What knowledge base do your readers have? Your definition should offer recognizable examples in language they will understand. Determine what uses your audience has for this definition. Will readers have to base decisions on your definition?
4. **Make extended definitions relevant.** Extended definitions depend on examples, illustrations, and narratives. The items you include to explain your topic should be relevant and understandable to your audience.
5. **Review special needs of the discipline or writing situation.** Each discipline can have a distinct history, research methodology, and set of concerns. Make sure your definition respects any special interests and addresses special needs.
6. **Use or refer to existing definitions.** Instead of attempting to create your own definition, you can adopt an existing one. If you accept the American Psychological Association's definition of *obsession*, you can simply restate the definition for readers. In using existing definitions, acknowledge their sources. If you disagree with an existing or official definition, restate it and then demonstrate how your interpretation differs.

SUGGESTED TOPICS FOR WRITING DEFINITIONS

General Assignments

Write a definition on any of the following topics. Your definition will probably contain other modes, such as description, comparison, and narration. Choose your terminology carefully, and avoid using words with misleading connotations. When defining complex and abstract concepts, consider using John Ciardi's method of defining extremes and then working toward the middle.

- A successful professional in your career. Define a good defense attorney, computer programmer, nurse, or teacher.
- A good relationship

- Pornography. Provide a personal definition including examples and social impact.
- Addiction
- The perfect career
- An educated person
- A healthy lifestyle
- The level of insanity at which a person should not be held criminally liable for his or her actions
- Racism
- Self-respect

Writing in Context

1. Imagine you have been asked to write a brief brochure about college life to be distributed to disadvantaged high school students. The principal stresses that she fears many of her students lack independent study skills and the discipline needed to succeed in college. Define the characteristics of a good college student, stressing hard work.
2. You have been asked to participate in a panel on sexual harassment. In preparation, provide two definitions of sexual harassment: one expressing attitudes, feelings, and statements you have observed and heard from males on campus, the other from females. Try to be as objective as possible, and state any differences fairly.

DEFINITION CHECKLIST

1. Is your purpose clear—to inform or to persuade?
2. Do you avoid defining a word with the same word, such as "a diffusion pump diffuses"?
3. Is your level of technical language appropriate for your audience?
4. Does your discipline require a specialized definition, such as a legal versus a medical definition of child abuse?
5. If intended for a professional audience, does your definition provide enough information for readers to make decisions or plan actions?
6. In writing an extended definition, do you avoid narratives, comparisons, and illustrations your audience may not understand or may misinterpret?

5

Comparison and Contrast

INDICATING SIMILARITIES AND DIFFERENCES

WHAT IS COMPARISON AND CONTRAST?

Comparison and contrast answers the question How are things alike or different? What distinguishes a gasoline engine from a diesel engine? Is it cheaper to buy or lease a car? What separates a misdemeanor from a felony? How does a bacterial infection differ from a viral one? What did Malcolm X and Martin Luther King Jr. have in common? Do men and women approach mathematics differently? All of these questions can be answered by comparing similarities and contrasting differences.

You have probably encountered essay questions that require comparison and contrast responses:

Compare the industrial output of the North and South at the outbreak of the Civil War. Which side was better equipped to prosecute a protracted conflict?

How do the rules of evidence differ in criminal and civil proceedings?

Which arrangement offers business owners greater protection of personal assets—full or limited partnerships?

Contrast Freud's dream theory with Jung's concept of the unconscious.

At the end of *The Great Gatsby* Nick Carraway decides to return to the West because he is too "squeamish" for the East. What differences did Fitzgerald see between the East and West?

Outline the principal differences between warm- and cold-blooded animals.

Comparison and contrast writing is commonly used to organize research papers. You might compare two short stories by Edgar Allan Poe in an English course, explain the differences among methods of depreciation in accounting, or contrast conflicting theories of childhood development for psychology. Comparison and contrast writing is also used by engineers to explain the fuel efficiency of different engines, by real estate developers to explore potential building sites, and by social workers to determine the best method of delivering medical services to the homeless.

The Purposes of Comparison and Contrast

Writers use comparison and contrast for two purposes:

1. **To draw distinctions among related subjects.** In many instances comparison is used to eliminate confusion. Many people, for instance, mistake an *optician,* who makes and sells eyeglasses, for an *optometrist,* who performs eye examinations and prescribes lenses. Comparison can pair extended definitions to show readers the difference, for example, between air-cooled and water-cooled engines, African and Indian elephants, or cross-country and downhill skiing. When drawing distinctions writers explain differences between similar subjects but do not choose one over the other. William Zinsser's essay "The Transaction" (page 247) contrasts the ways two writers work without endorsing either writer's method. The basic goal of drawing distinctions is to *inform readers of similarities and differences.*
2. **To recommend a choice between two things.** Television commercials compare competing products. Political campaign brochures urge voters to support a candidate over his or her rival. Articles in medical journals argue that one drug is more effective than another. Business proposals recommend one computer program or one security service over competitors. Government studies assert that one air-quality standard is preferable to another. In "Television and Reading" (page 287) Marie Winn argues that it is better for children to read rather than watch television. The basic purpose of stating recommendations is to *persuade readers to make a choice.*

Organizing Comparison and Contrast Papers

When developing a paper using comparison and contrast, you must be sure your subjects share enough common points for meaningful discussion. You can compare two sports cars, two action adventure films, or two diets. But comparing a sports car to a station wagon, an action film to a comedy, or a diet to plastic surgery is not likely to generate more than superficial observations. The entries in this chapter focus on related subjects, such as the ways two writers work or the backgrounds of two Civil War generals.

In addition, comparisons have to be carefully limited, especially when comparing broad or complex subjects. For contrasting the differences between American and Chinese cultures, Yi-Fu Tuan (page 244) limits the essay to demonstrating the different ways Americans and Chinese view space and place. By exploring this limited topic in depth, Yi-Fu Tuan reveals more about Chinese culture in a page or two than a twenty-page essay would that attempts to cover religion, politics, economics, history, and marriage customs. If you are comparing two presidents, you might focus your comparison on their relations with the press, the way they handled crises, or their trade policies.

Perhaps the most frustrating problem students face while writing comparison and contrast papers is organizing ideas. Without careful planning, you may find yourself awkwardly switching back and forth between subjects. Your reader may have difficulty following your train of thought and may confuse one subject with another. Whether drawing distinctions or making recommendations, writers use two methods of organizing comparison and contrast.

Subject by Subject

The *subject-by-subject* method divides the paper into two sections. Writers state all the information about topic A and then discuss topic B. Usually, the actual comparisons are drawn in the second part of the paper, where B is discussed in relation to A. In a short paper about two types of life insurance, the writer first explains "whole life" insurance and then discusses "term" insurance and draws distinctions between the two types. Since the purpose is to make distinctions, the conclusion does not offer a recommendation:

WHOLE LIFE AND TERM INSURANCE

Most life insurance companies offer a variety of life insurance products, investments, and financial services. Two of the most common policies provided are whole life and term insurance.

Whole life insurance is the oldest and most traditional form of life insurance. Life insurance became popular in the nineteenth century as a way of protecting the buyer's dependents in the event of premature death. A purchaser would select a policy amount to be paid to his or her beneficiaries after his or her death. Payments called premiums were made on a yearly, quarterly, or monthly basis. As the policyholder paid premiums, the policy gained cash value. Part of the payment earned interest like money in a bank account. Insurance served as an investment tool, allowing people to save for retirement and giving them access to guaranteed loans. For a low interest fee, insurance holders could borrow against the cash value of their policies.

Term insurance, introduced in the twentieth century, serves the same basic purpose as whole life insurance, protecting the insured's dependents. Unlike whole life, however, no cash value accrues. In a sense the policyholder is "renting" insurance, buying only a death benefit. The advantage of term insurance is its low cost. Because there is no money set aside for investment, the premiums are lower. This allows a person to afford a larger policy. A term policy for $100,000 could be cheaper than a whole life policy for $50,000.

The type of insurance a person needs depends on his or her income, family situation, investment goals, savings, and obligations. Most investment counselors agree, however, that anyone with a spouse or children should have some form of life insurance protection.

Advantages and Disadvantages The subject-by-subject method is best suited to short papers. A twenty-page report organized in this fashion would read much like two ten-page papers fastened together. It would be difficult for readers to remember enough of the first subject to appreciate how it differs from the second. This method, however, allows writers to compare abstract subjects with ease, especially when a subject has individual features the other does not share.

Point by Point

The *point-by-point* method organizes the comparison of A and B on a number of specific points. Following an introduction, A and B are discussed in a series of comparisons. Hotels, for example, have a number of common points: location, appearance, atmosphere, and room rates. In the following paper, the writer groups comments about the two hotels in each paragraph. For the recommendation, the writer states a clear preference in the opening and concluding paragraphs:

ST. GREGORY AND FITZPATRICK HOTELS

Campus organizations and academic conventions visiting the city hold special events in either the St. Gregory or Fitzpatrick. Both are large convention hotels, but for many reasons the St. Gregory is more desirable.

Opened in 1892, the St. Gregory is the oldest surviving hotel in the city. The Fitzpatrick is the newest, having opened just last spring. The St. Gregory has a commanding view of State Street. The Fitzpatrick is part of the $200 million Riverfront Centre.

The chief attraction of the St. Gregory is its famed domed lobby ornamented with carved mahogany and elaborate brass and marble fittings. Admiral Dewey was presented with the key to the city here following his victory in Manila Bay in 1898. In contrast, the sleek Fitzpatrick is noted for its sweeping thirty-story atrium. The open lobby is banked with massive video screens.

The main lounge of the St. Gregory is the Pump Room, a plush, turn-of-the-century Irish bar decorated with gilt-framed paintings of the Emerald Isle. The Fitzpatrick features two bars. Homerun, a sports bar, is popular with local students and young professionals. The Exchange is a smaller, quieter bar that is a favorite of visiting executives. Copies, fax machines, and computers are available in the nearby executive center.

Both hotels offer a range of room rates. The cheapest rooms at the St. Gregory are $95 a night. Though small, they are comfortable. The Fitzpatrick has only a dozen single traveler rooms for $125. Double rooms at the St. Gregory range from $175 to $250, depending on size and decor. All Fitzpatrick double rooms are identical and cost $195. In addition to convention rates, the St. Gregory offers 20 percent student discounts. The Fitzpatrick does not offer student discounts.

Both hotels provide excellent convention services. Since most professors and academic delegates have access to university computers and fax machines, they prefer the historic elegance of the St. Gregory. Students especially appreciate discount rates and the availability of public transport to the university.

Advantages and Disadvantages The point-by-point method is useful in organizing longer and more technical papers. The specific facts, statistics, and quotes about A and B appear side by side. Readers of a long report about two hotels organized in a subject-by-subject manner would be easily frustrated because instead of seeing room rates compared in the same paragraph, they might have to flip back a dozen pages. Point-by-point organization is helpful when addressing multiple readers who may be interested in only a portion of the paper. However, point-by-point papers about abstract subjects such as two films or two novels might be difficult to organize because many important details about one subject may have nothing in common with the other subject.

As you read the essays in this chapter, you may note that many writers blend both methods to develop their comparisons.

READING COMPARISON AND CONTRAST

When reading the comparison and contrast entries in this chapter, keep these questions in mind.

Meaning

1. What is the writer's goal—to draw distinctions or to recommend a choice?
2. What details does the writer present about each subject?
3. Who is the intended audience? Is the essay directed to a general or a specific reader?
4. Is the comparison valid? Is the writer comparing two subjects in a fair manner? Have any points been overlooked?
5. Does the author have an apparent bias?
6. If the comparison makes a recommendation, does the selection seem valid? What makes the chosen subject superior to the others? What evidence is offered?

Strategy

1. What is the basic pattern of the comparison—subject by subject or point by point? Do variations occur?
2. Does the author use a device to narrow the topic or to advance the comparison?
3. Does the writer make use of visual aids? Are they effective?

Language

1. Does the writer use connotations that ascribe positive or negative qualities to one or both of the items? How does the author describe the two subjects?

2. What does the diction, level of language, and use of technical terms reveal about the intended audience?
3. If suggesting a choice, how does the writer use language to highlight its desirability?

YI-FU TUAN

Yi-Fu Tuan (1930–) was born in China and later moved to the United States. Now a geography professor in Madison, Wisconsin, he has studied the cultural differences between America and his native country. He states that he writes "from a single perspective—namely that of experience." In this article published in Harper's, *he compares the way people in two cultures view their environments.*

Chinese Space, American Space

Cultures as diverse as America's and China's have many points of difference. In attempting to provide insight into their differences in a brief essay, Yi-Fu Tuan focuses on the concept of space and location. Americans, he asserts, are less rooted to place and are future oriented. The Chinese, savoring tradition, are deeply tied to specific locations.

1 Americans have a sense of space, not of place. Go to an American home in exurbia, and almost the first thing you do is drift toward the picture window. How curious that the first compliment you pay your host inside his house is to say how lovely it is outside his house! He is pleased that you should admire his vistas. The distant horizon is not merely a line separating earth from sky, it is a symbol of the future. The American is not rooted in his place, however lovely: his eyes are drawn by the expanding space to a point on the horizon, which is his future.

2 By contrast, consider the traditional Chinese home. Blank walls enclose it. Step behind the spirit wall and you are in a courtyard with perhaps a miniature garden around a corner. Once inside his private compound you are wrapped in an ambiance of calm beauty, an ordered world of buildings, pavement, rock, and decorative vegetation. But you have no distant view: nowhere does space open out before you. Raw nature in such a home is experienced only as weather, and the only open space is the sky above. The Chinese is rooted in his place. When he has to leave, it is not for the promised land on the terrestrial

horizon, but for another world altogether along the vertical, religious axis of his imagination.

3 The Chinese tie to place is deeply felt. Wanderlust is an alien sentiment. The Taoist classic *Tao Te Ching* captures the ideal of rootedness in place with these words: "Though there may be another country in the neighborhood so close that they are within sight of each other and the crowing of cocks and barking of dogs in one place can be heard in the other, yet there is no traffic between them; and throughout their lives the two peoples have nothing to do with each other." In theory if not in practice, farmers have ranked high in Chinese society. The reason is not only that they are engaged in a "root" industry of producing food but that, unlike pecuniary merchants, they are tied to the land and do not abandon their country when it is in danger.

4 Nostalgia is a recurrent theme in Chinese poetry. An American reader of translated Chinese poems may well be taken aback—even put off—by the frequency, as well as the sentimentality, of the lament for home. To understand the strength of this sentiment, we need to know that the Chinese desire for stability and rootedness in place is prompted by the constant threat of war, exile, and the natural disasters of flood and drought. Forcible removal makes the Chinese keenly aware of their loss. By contrast, Americans move, for the most part, voluntarily. Their nostalgia for home town is really longing for a childhood to which they cannot return: in the meantime the future beckons and the future is "out there," in open space. When we criticize American rootlessness, we tend to forget that it is a result of ideals we admire, namely, social mobility and optimism about the future. When we admire Chinese rootedness, we forget that the word "place" means both a location in space and position in society: to be tied to place is also to be bound to one's station in life, with little hope of betterment. Space symbolizes hope; place, achievement and stability.

Understanding Meaning

1. How does the author see a difference between "space" and "place"?
2. What do the traditional designs of American and Chinese homes reveal about cultural differences?
3. Why do the Chinese honor farmers?
4. What historical forces have shaped the Chinese desire for "rootedness"? How is American history different?

5. What negative aspects does Yi-Fu Tuan see in the Chinese sense of place?

Evaluating Strategy

1. The writer really only devotes a single paragraph to describing American concepts of space. Why? Is the essay out of balance? Discuss whether or not a comparison paper should devote half its space to each topic.
2. Is the author objective? Is it possible for a writer to discuss cultures without inserting a measure of bias?

Appreciating Language

1. What words does Yi-Fu Tuan use in describing the two cultures? Do they seem to differ in connotation?
2. Does the word *rootlessness* suggest something negative to most people? How does Yi-Fu Tuan define it?
3. Look up the word *wanderlust.* How does a German term fit in an essay comparing American and Chinese culture?

Connections across the Disciplines

1. Compare this article with those of Amy Tan (page 277) and William Ouchi (page 270). What do they reveal about the differences between Asian and Western culture?
2. Does Edward Abbey's "First Morning" (page 139) express what Yi-Fu Tuan would define as an American attitude toward space and place?

Writing Suggestions

1. If you have lived in or visited another country or region within the United States, write a brief essay outlining how it differs from your home. Just as Yi-Fu Tuan used the concept of space to focus a short article, you may wish to limit your comparison to discussing eating habits, dress, attitudes to work, music, or dating practices.
2. *Collaborative Writing:* Ask a group of students about their attitudes toward rootlessness and place. Determine how often students have moved in their lives. How many have spent their entire lives in a single house or apartment? Write a few paragraphs outlining the attitudes expressed by the group.

WILLIAM ZINSSER

William Zinsser (1922–) was born in New York City and graduated from Princeton in 1944. He was a feature writer, drama editor, and film critic for the New York Herald Tribune. *He wrote columns for* Life *and the* New York Times. *In the 1970s Zinsser taught English at Yale. For seven years he served as general editor for the Book-of-the-Month Club. Zinsser has written many books on a variety of subjects, including jazz and baseball. But he is best known by college students for his books and articles on writing and study skills. His book* On Writing Well: An Informal Guide to Writing Nonfiction *and an article "College Pressures" have become standard reading for a generation of freshmen.*

The Transaction

This article uses the point-by-point method to compare Zinsser's writing style with that of a popular writer. Zinsser organizes his article using interviewer questions as a device to contrast the responses of the two writers.

1 A school in Connecticut once held "a day devoted to the arts," and I was asked if I would come and talk about writing as a vocation. When I arrived I found that a second speaker had been invited—Dr. Brock (as I'll call him), a surgeon who had recently begun to write and had sold some stories to magazines. He was going to talk about writing as an avocation. That made us a panel, and we sat down to face a crowd of students, teachers and parents, all eager to learn the secrets of our glamorous work.

2 Dr. Brock was dressed in a bright red jacket, looking vaguely bohemian, as authors are supposed to look, and the first question went to him. What was it like to be a writer?

3 He said it was tremendous fun. Coming home from an arduous day at the hospital, he would go straight to his yellow pad and write his tensions away. The words just flowed. It was easy. I then said that writing wasn't easy and it wasn't fun. It was hard and lonely, and the words seldom just flowed.

4 Next Dr. Brock was asked if it was important to rewrite. Absolutely not, he said. "Let it all hang out," and whatever form the

sentences take will reflect the writer at his most natural. I then said that rewriting is the essence of writing. I pointed out that professional writers rewrite their sentences repeatedly and then rewrite what they have rewritten. I mentioned that E. B. White and James Thurber rewrote their pieces eight or nine times.

5 "What do you do on days when it isn't going well?" Dr. Brock was asked. He said he just stopped writing and put the work aside for a day when it would go better. I then said that the professional writer must establish a daily schedule and stick to it. I said that writing is a craft, not an art, and that the man who runs away from his craft because he lacks inspiration is fooling himself. He is also going broke.

6 "What if you're feeling depressed or unhappy?" a student asked. "Won't that affect your writing?"

7 Probably it will, Dr. Brock replied. Go fishing. Take a walk. Probably it won't, I said. If your job is to write every day, you learn to do it like any other job.

8 A student asked if we found it useful to circulate in the literary world. Dr. Brock said he was greatly enjoying his new life as a man of letters, and he told several stories of being taken to lunch by his publisher and his agent at Manhattan restaurants where writers and editors gather. I said that professional writers are solitary drudges who seldom see other writers.

9 "Do you put symbolism in your writing?" a student asked me.

10 "Not if I can help it," I replied. I have an unbroken record of missing the deeper meaning in any story, play or movie, and as for dance and mime, I have never had any idea of what is being conveyed.

11 "I *love* symbols!" Dr. Brock exclaimed, and he described with gusto the joys of weaving them through his work.

12 So the morning went, and it was a revelation to all of us. At the end Dr. Brock told me he was enormously interested in my answers—it had never occurred to him that writing could be hard. I told him I was just as interested in *his* answers—it had never occurred to me that writing could be easy. (Maybe I should take up surgery on the side.)

13 As for the students, anyone might think we left them bewildered. But in fact we probably gave them a broader glimpse of the writing process than if only one of us had talked. For there isn't any "right" way to do such intensely personal work. There are all kinds of writers and all kinds of methods, and any method that helps you to say what you want to say is the right method for you.

14 Some people write by day, others by night. Some people need silence, others turn on the radio. Some write by hand, some by typewriter or word processor, some by talking into a tape recorder. Some people write their first draft in one long burst and then revise; others can't write the second paragraph until they have fiddled endlessly with the first.

15 But all of them are vulnerable and all of them are tense. They are driven by a compulsion to put some part of themselves on paper, and yet they don't just write what comes naturally. They sit down to commit an act of literature, and the self who emerges on paper is far stiffer than the person who sat down to write. The problem is to find the real man or woman behind all the tension.

16 Ultimately the product that any writer has to sell is not the subject being written about, but who he or she is. I often find myself reading with interest about a topic I never thought would interest me—some scientific quest, perhaps. What holds me is the enthusiasm of the writer for his field. How was he drawn into it? What emotional baggage did he bring along? How did it change his life? It's not necessary to want to spend a year alone at Walden Pond to become deeply involved with a writer who did.

17 This is the personal transaction that's at the heart of good nonfiction writing. Out of it come two of the most important qualities that this book will go in search of: humanity and warmth. Good writing has an aliveness that keeps the reader reading from one paragraph to the next, and it's not a question of gimmicks to "personalize" the author. It's a question of using the English language in a way that will achieve the greatest strength and the least clutter.

18 Can such principles be taught? Maybe not. But most of them can be learned.

Understanding Meaning

1. What is the "transaction" suggested by the title?
2. What is the purpose of this comparison? What is Zinsser trying to say about the writing process?
3. Is Zinsser, who no doubt considers himself a "professional" writer, suggesting that his work is superior to the surgeon's? Is the surgeon an amateur?

4. Zinsser states that "ultimately the product that any writer has to sell is not his subject, but who he or she is." Do you agree with this assessment?
5. *Critical Thinking:* After reading this article, review your own writing habits. Can this article assist you to master techniques Zinsser admits cannot be "taught" but can be "learned"?

Evaluating Strategy

1. How effective is the device of using interviewer questions to organize the comparison? Does it put the professional writer and surgeon on an equal footing?
2. Zinsser describes the "Bohemian" dress of the doctor and his enthusiasm of entering literary circles. What does this suggest about Zinsser's attitude?
3. Is the comparison the heart of the essay or simply a device introducing Zinsser's comments about writing?

Appreciating Language

1. What language does Zinsser use to describe the surgeon? What impact does this have on the reader?
2. Zinsser calls writing "hard and lonely" and writers "solitary drudges." What was he attempting to express to the audience?

Connections across the Disciplines

1. Compare this essay with Peter Elbow's "Desperation Writing" (page 500). What do these writers suggest about the writing process?
2. Review Samuel Scudder's essay "Take This Fish and Look at It" (page 41). Is Zinsser, like Professor Agassiz, arguing that his profession demands hard work?

Writing Suggestions

1. Write a brief essay comparing two methods of accomplishing similar tasks: cooking, dieting, exercising, studying for exams, playing a sport, parenting, or managing employees.
2. *Collaborative Writing:* Have a number of students write a few paragraphs about their own writing practices. Remind the group to write honestly, to

describe how they really write. Have each member read his or her statement to the group, and then discuss how writing styles could be improved to overcome common problems. Have one member of the group record the suggestions.

BRUCE CATTON

Bruce Catton (1899–1978) grew up listening to stories of Civil War veterans. His own college career was interrupted by service in the First World War. Catton went to work as a reporter for the Cleveland Plain Dealer *and later served as information director for several government agencies. His interest in history, especially the Civil War, never flagged. In 1953 his book* A Stillness at Appomattox *became a best-seller, and Catton received a Pulitzer Prize. He wrote several other books about the Civil War and edited* American Heritage *magazine for two decades.*

Grant and Lee

Perhaps no other essay is as widely anthologized as a sample of comparison writing than Catton's "Grant and Lee," which first appeared in a collection, The American Story. *Directed to a general audience, the essay seeks to contrast the two most famous generals of the Civil War.*

1 When Ulysses S. Grant and Robert E. Lee met in the parlor of a modest house at Appomattox Court House, Virginia, on April 9, 1865, to work out the terms for the surrender of Lee's Army of Northern Virginia, a great chapter in American life came to a close, and a great new chapter began.

2 These men were bringing the Civil War to its virtual finish. To be sure, other armies had yet to surrender, and for a few days the fugitive Confederate government would struggle desperately and vainly, trying to find some way to go on living now that its chief support was gone. But in effect it was all over when Grant and Lee signed the papers. And the little room where they wrote out the terms was the scene of one of the poignant, dramatic contrasts in American history.

3 They were two strong men, these oddly different generals, and they represented the strengths of two conflicting currents that, through them, had come into final collision.

4 Back of Robert E. Lee was the notion that the old aristocratic concept might somehow survive and be dominant in American life.

5 Lee was tidewater Virginia, and in his background were family, culture, and tradition . . . the age of chivalry transplanted to a New World which was making its own legends and its own myths. He embodied a way of life that had come down through the age of knighthood and the English country squire. America was a land that was beginning all over again, dedicated to nothing much more complicated than the rather hazy belief that all men had equal rights and should have an equal chance in the world. In such a land Lee stood for the feeling that it was somehow of advantage to human society to have a pronounced inequality in the social structure. There should be a leisure class, backed by ownership of land; in turn, society itself should be keyed to the land as the chief source of wealth and influence. It would bring forth (according to this ideal) a class of men with a strong sense of obligation to the community; men who lived not to gain advantage for themselves, but to meet the solemn obligations which had been laid on them by the very fact that they were privileged. From them the country would get its leadership; to them it could look for the higher values—of thought, of conduct, of personal deportment—to give it strength and virtue.

6 Lee embodied the noblest elements of this aristocratic ideal. Through him, the landed nobility justified itself. For four years, the Southern states had fought a desperate war to uphold the ideals for which Lee stood. In the end, it almost seemed as if the Confederacy fought for Lee; as if he himself was the Confederacy . . . the best thing that the way of life for which the Confederacy stood could ever have to offer. He had passed into legend before Appomattox. Thousands of tired, underfed, poorly clothed Confederate soldiers, long since past the simple enthusiasm of the early days of the struggle, somehow considered Lee the symbol of everything for which they had been willing to die. But they could not quite put this feeling into words. If the Lost Cause, sanctified by so much heroism and so many deaths, had a living justification, its justification was General Lee.

7 Grant, the son of a tanner on the Western frontier, was everything Lee was not. He had come up the hard way and embodied nothing in particular except the eternal toughness and sinewy fiber of the men who grew up beyond the mountains. He was one of a body of men who owed reverence and obeisance to no one, who were self-reliant to a fault, who cared hardly anything for the past but who had a sharp eye for the future.

8 These frontier men were the precise opposite of the tidewater aristocrats. Back of them, in the great surge that had taken people over the Alleghenies and into the opening Western country, there was a deep, implicit dissatisfaction with a past that had settled into grooves. They stood for democracy, not from any reasoned conclusion about the proper ordering of human society, but simply because they had grown up in the middle of democracy and knew how it worked. Their society might have privileges, but they would be privileges each man had won for himself. Forms and patterns meant nothing. No man was born to anything, except perhaps to a chance to show how far he could rise. Life was competition.

9 Yet along with this feeling had come a deep sense of belonging to a national community. The Westerner who developed a farm, opened a shop, or set up in business as a trader, could hope to prosper only as his own community prospered—and his community ran from the Atlantic to the Pacific and from Canada down to Mexico. If the land was settled, with towns and highways and accessible markets, he could better himself. He saw his fate in terms of the nation's own destiny. As its horizons expanded, so did his. He had, in other words, an acute dollars-and-cents stake in the continued growth and development of his country.

10 And that, perhaps, is where the contrast between Grant and Lee becomes most striking. The Virginia aristocrat, inevitably, saw himself in relation to his own region. He lived in a static society which could endure almost anything except change. Instinctively, his first loyalty would go to the locality in which that society existed. He would fight to the limit of endurance to defend it, because in defending it he was defending everything that gave his own life its deepest meaning.

11 The Westerner, on the other hand, would fight with an equal tenacity for the broader concept of society. He fought so because everything he lived by was tied to growth, expansion, and a constantly widening horizon. What he lived by would survive or fall with the nation itself. He could not possibly stand by unmoved in the face of an attempt to destroy the Union. He would combat it with everything he had, because he could only see it as an effort to cut the ground out from under his feet.

12 So Grant and Lee were in complete contrast, representing two diametrically opposed elements in American life. Grant was the modern man emerging; beyond him, ready to come on the stage, was the great age of steel and machinery, of crowded cities and a restless burgeoning

vitality. Lee might have ridden down from the old age of chivalry, lance in hand, silken banner fluttering over his head. Each man was the perfect champion of his cause, drawing both his strengths and his weaknesses from the people he led.

13 Yet it was not all contrast, after all. Different as they were—in background, in personality, in underlying aspiration—these two great soldiers had much in common. Under everything else, they were marvelous fighters. Furthermore, their fighting qualities were really very much alike.

14 Each man had, to begin with, the great virtue of utter tenacity and fidelity. Grant fought his way down the Mississippi Valley in spite of acute personal discouragement and profound military handicaps. Lee hung on in the trenches at Petersburg after hope itself had died. In each man there was an indomitable quality . . . the born fighter's refusal to give up as long as he can still remain on his feet and lift his two fists.

15 Daring and resourcefulness they had, too; the ability to think faster and move faster than the enemy. These were the qualities which gave Lee the dazzling campaigns of Second Manassas and Chancellorsville and won Vicksburg for Grant.

16 Lastly, and perhaps greatest of all, there was the ability, at the end, to turn quickly from war to peace once the fighting was over. Out of the way these two men behaved at Appomattox came the possibility of a peace of reconciliation. It was a possibility not wholly realized, in the years to come, but which did, in the end, help the two sections to become one nation again . . . after a war whose bitterness might have seemed to make such a reunion wholly impossible. No part of either man's life became him more than the part he played in their brief meeting in the McLean house at Appomattox. Their behavior there put all succeeding generations of Americans in their debt. Two great Americans, Grant and Lee—very different, yet under everything very much alike. Their encounter at Appomattox was one of the great moments of American history.

Understanding Meaning

1. What does Catton see as the most striking differences between the two generals?
2. How did Grant and Lee differ in background and sense of allegiance?
3. What were the historical forces that shaped the two men?

4. What areas of similarity between the two does Catton detect?
5. *Critical Thinking:* Essentially Catton is telling the story of a confrontation between victor and vanquished, yet his account does not seem to depict the men as winner and loser. Catton does not dwell on what made Grant victorious or on the causes for Lee's defeat. What does this reveal about Catton's purpose?

Evaluating Strategy

1. How does Catton organize his comparison? Is this an effective method?
2. The Civil War was, in part, a battle over slavery. Catton does not mention this issue. Does his account appear to be ethically neutral, suggesting that neither the Union nor the Confederacy were morally superior in its war aims?

Appreciating Language

1. Does Catton appear to be neutral in his descriptions of the two men? What similes or metaphors does he use? Is the language balanced or biased?
2. What does the tone, level of language, and word choice suggest about Catton's intended audience?

Connections across the Disciplines

1. Catton uses words such as "nobility" and "virtue" to describe Robert E. Lee. How might an African American writer such as Cornel West or bell hooks respond to Catton's depiction of Lee's "daring" and "resourcefulness" as a defender of the Confederacy?
2. Compare Catton's discussion of two individuals with William Ouchi's comparison of two kinds of people (page 270). What are the similarities? Do comparisons risk simplification and stereotyping?

Writing Suggestions

1. Write an essay comparing two people in the same profession you have known. Compare two teachers, two bosses, two landlords, or two coworkers. Try to focus on their personalities rather than appearance. You may limit your discussion to a specific attitude, situation, or activity. For example, compare how two teachers dealt with troublesome students, how

two bosses motivated employees, or how two landlords maintained their properties.

2. *Collaborative Writing:* Work with a group of students to write a short dramatic scene based on Catton's essay. Use set descriptions to establish the locale, and invent dialogue. Discuss with members of the group how Lee and Grant might have sounded. What words would they have chosen? How would their vocabulary indicate their different backgrounds and personalities?

ANNIE DILLARD

Annie Dillard (1945–) was born in Pittsburgh and received degrees from Hollins College in Virginia. She now teaches writing at Wesleyan University. Dillard began her writing career as a columnist for The Living Wilderness *and as a contributing editor to* Harper's. *She has published several books, including* Pilgrim at Tinker Creek, *which received a Pulitzer Prize in 1975. Dillard is best known for her writing on natural science, based largely on her close observations of wildlife. In 1987 she published* An American Childhood, *an account of her upbringing in Pittsburgh. Her 1989 book* The Writing Life *analyzes the writing process.*

Living like Weasels

In this article from her book Teaching a Stone to Talk, *Dillard compares human beings to weasels. Like Samuel Scudder's essay "Take This Fish and Look at It," Dillard's comparison rests on close observation.*

1 A weasel is wild. Who knows what he thinks? He sleeps in his underground den, his tailed draped over his nose. Sometimes he lives in his den for two days without leaving. Outside, he stalks rabbits, mice, muskrats, and birds, killing more bodies than he can eat warm, and often dragging the carcasses home. Obedient to instinct, he bites his prey at the neck, either splitting the jugular vein at the throat or crunching the brain at the base of the skull, and he does not let go. One naturalist refused to kill a weasel who was socketed into his hand deeply as a rattlesnake. The man could in no way pry the tiny weasel off, and he had to walk half a mile to water, the weasel dangling from his palm, and soak him off like a stubborn label.

2 And once, says Ernest Thompson Seton—once, a man shot an eagle out of the sky. He examined the eagle and found the dry skull of a weasel fixed by the jaws to his throat. The supposition is that the eagle had pounced on the weasel and the weasel swiveled and bit as instinct taught him, tooth to neck, and nearly won. I would like to have seen that eagle from the air a few weeks or months before he was shot: was the whole weasel still attached to his feathered throat, a fur pendant? Or did the eagle eat what he could reach, gutting the living

weasel with his talons before his breast, bending his beak, cleaning the beautiful airborne bones?

3 I have been reading about weasels because I saw one last week. I startled a weasel who startled me, and we exchanged a long glance.

4 Twenty minutes from my house, through the woods by the quarry and across the highway, is Hollins Pond, a remarkable piece of shallowness, where I like to go at sunset and sit on a tree trunk. Hollins Pond is also called Murray's Pond; it covers two acres of bottomland near Tinker Creek with six inches of water and six thousand lily pads. In winter, brown-and-white steers stand in the middle of it, merely dampening their hooves; from the distant shore they look like miracle itself, complete with miracle's nonchalance. Now, in summer, the steers are gone. The water lilies have blossomed and spread to a green horizontal plane that is terra firma to plodding blackbirds, and tremulous ceiling to black leeches, crayfish, and carp.

5 This is, mind you, suburbia. It is a five-minute walk in three directions to rows of houses, though none is visible here. There's a 55 mph highway at one end of the pond, and a nesting pair of wood ducks at the other. Under every bush is a muskrat hole or a beer can. The far end is an alternating series of fields and woods, fields and woods, threaded everywhere with motorcycle tracks—in whose bare clay wild turtles lay eggs.

6 So. I had crossed the highway, stepped over two low barbed-wire fences, and traced the motorcycle path in all gratitude through the wild rose and poison ivy of the pond's shoreline up into high grassy fields. Then I cut down through the woods to the mossy fallen tree where I sit. This tree is excellent. It makes a dry, upholstered bench at the upper, marshy end of the pond, a plush jetty raised from the thorny shore between a shallow blue body of water and a deep blue body of sky.

7 The sun had just set. I was relaxed on the tree trunk, ensconced in the lap of lichen, watching the lily pads at my feet tremble and part dreamily over the thrusting path of a carp. A yellow bird appeared to my right and flew behind me. It caught my eye; I swiveled around—and the next instant, inexplicably, I was looking down at a weasel, who was looking up at me.

8 Weasel! I'd never seen one wild before. He was ten inches long, thin as a curve, a muscled ribbon, brown as fruitwood, soft-furred,

alert. His face was fierce, small and pointed as a lizard's; he would have made a good arrowhead. There was just a dot of chin, maybe two brown hairs' worth, and then the pure white fur began that spread down his underside. He had two black eyes I didn't see, any more than you see a window.

9 The weasel was stunned into stillness as he was emerging from beneath an enormous shaggy wild rose bush four feet away. I was stunned into stillness twisted backward on the tree trunk. Our eyes locked, and someone threw away the key.

10 Our look was as if two lovers, or deadly enemies, met unexpectedly on an overgrown path when each had been thinking of something else: a clearing blow to the gut. It was also a bright blow to the brain, or a sudden beating of brains, with all the charge and intimate grate of rubbed balloons. It emptied our lungs. It felled the forest, moved the fields, and drained the pond; the world dismantled and tumbled into that black hole of eyes. If you and I looked at each other that way, our skulls would split and drop to our shoulders. But we don't. We keep our skulls. So.

11 He disappeared. This was only last week, and already I don't remember what shattered the enchantment. I think I blinked, I think I retrieved my brain from the weasel's brain, and tried to memorize what I was seeing, and the weasel felt the yank of separation, the careening splash-down into real life and the urgent current of instinct. He vanished under the wild rose. I waited motionless, my mind suddenly full of data and my spirit with pleadings, but he didn't return.

12 Please do not tell me about "approach-avoidance conflicts." I tell you I've been in that weasel's brain for sixty seconds, and he was in mine. Brains are private places, muttering through unique and secret tapes—but the weasel and I both plugged into another tape simultaneously, for a sweet and shocking time. Can I help it if it was a blank?

13 What goes on in his brain the rest of the time? What does a weasel think about? He won't say. His journal is tracks in clay, a spray of feathers, mouse blood and bone: uncollected, unconnected, loose-leaf, and blown.

14 I would like to learn, or remember, how to live. I come to Hollins Pond not so much to learn how to live as, frankly, to forget about it. That is, I don't think I can learn from a wild animal how to live in particular—shall I suck warm blood, hold my tail high, walk with my footprints precisely over the prints of my hands?—but I might learn

something of mindlessness, something of the purity of living in the physical senses and the dignity of living without bias or motive. The weasel lives in necessity and we live in choice, hating necessity and dying at the last ignobly in its talons. I would like to live as I should, as the weasel lives as he should. And I suspect that for me the way is like the weasel's: open to time and death painlessly, noticing everything, remembering nothing, choosing the given with a fierce and pointed will.

15 I missed my chance. I should have gone for the throat. I should have lunged for that streak of white under the weasel's chin and held on, held on through mud and into the wild rose, held on for a dearer life. We could live under the wild rose wild as weasels, mute and uncomprehending. I could very calmly go wild. I could live two days in the den, curled, leaning on mouse fur, sniffing bird bones, blinking, licking, breathing musk, my hair tangled in the roots of grasses. Down is a good place to go, where the mind is single. Down is out, out of your ever-loving mind and back to your careless senses. I remember muteness as a prolonged and giddy fast, where every moment is a feast of utterance received. Time and events are merely poured, unremarked, and ingested directly, like blood pulsed into my gut through a jugular vein. Could two live that way? Could two live under the wild rose, and explore by the pond, so that the smooth mind of each is as everywhere present to the other, and as received and as unchallenged, as falling snow?

16 We could, you know. We can live any way we want. People take vows of poverty, chastity, and obedience—even of silence—by choice. The thing is to stalk your calling in a certain skilled and supple way, to locate the most tender and live spot and plug into that pulse. This is yielding, not fighting. A weasel doesn't "attack" anything; a weasel lives as he's meant to, yielding at every moment to the perfect freedom of single necessity.

17 I think it would be well, and proper, and obedient, and pure, to grasp your one necessity and not let it go, to dangle from it limp wherever it takes you. Then even death, where you're going no matter how you live, cannot you part. Seize it and let it seize you up aloft even, till your eyes burn out and drop; let your musky flesh fall off in shreds, and let your very bones unhinge and scatter, loosened over fields, over fields and woods, lightly, thoughtless, from any height at all, from as high as eagles.

Understanding Meaning

1. What characterizes the life of the weasel?
2. How does Dillard describe her encounter with a weasel?
3. What does Dillard mean by the statement, "I tell you I've been in that weasel's brain for sixty seconds, and he was in mine"? Does she mean this literally? Can a human ever determine how any animal thinks?
4. How does the weasel's life contrast with that of human beings? What does Dillard see as the principal differences?
5. What aspect of the weasel's life does Dillard appreciate most?
6. *Critical Thinking:* Does Dillard's desire to escape time, choice, and thought suggest a flight from responsibility? Is the weasel's "perfect freedom of single necessity" admirable? What kind of people give into the "freedom of single necessity"?

Evaluating Strategy

1. How does Dillard organize her comparison?
2. How does Dillard use comparisons to describe the weasel?
3. *Critical Thinking:* What impact does the title have? What is the common perception of weasels or people who are compared to weasels? Is this a difficult animal to get readers to contemplate seriously? Would "Living like Lions" or "Living like Eagles" stir different reactions?

Appreciating Language

1. How does Dillard seek to alter the popular reaction to the word *weasel?*
2. What similes and metaphors does Dillard use to describe the weasel she encountered?
3. What role does connotation play in this comparison?

Connections across the Disciplines

1. How does Dillard's article compare to Samuel Scudder's "Take This Fish and Look at It"(page 41)? How does her reaction to the weasel contrast with Scudder's view of the lab specimen?
2. Dillard states that she comes to Hollins Pond to "learn something of mindlessness." Does this compare to Edward Abbey's view of open spaces (p. 139)? How does contemplating nature alter people's sense of themselves and their world?

Writing Suggestions

1. Select an animal and compare how its life differs from yours in a few paragraphs. What aspects of this animal's life do you find beneficial? What can you learn from looking at the way this animal lives in its environment? How does it interact with other animals?
2. *Collaborative Writing:* Working with a group of students, select an animal and discuss what can be learned from its life. Ask if members believe people tend to romanticize wildlife and assume only humans damage the environment. Record the ideas your group develops. If members have different opinions, consider developing contrasting statements.

MARK MATHABANE

Mark Mathabane (1960–) was born in South Africa and grew up in a black township outside Johannesburg. He longed to escape the poverty and violence of apartheid. Through the efforts of tennis champion Stan Smith, Mathabane received an athletic scholarship to an American college. He began writing as an undergraduate and edited a student newspaper. After graduation from Dowling College, he studied journalism at Columbia University. Mathabane's autobiography Kaffir Boy, *published in 1986, recounted his South African childhood. Three years later he published* Kaffir Boy in America, *where this essay first appeared, about his first ten years living in the United States.*

At the Mercy of the Cure

In this essay Mathabane explores the differences between Western and traditional African medicine. When he examines the psychological impact of apartheid, he draws comparisons to Nazi concentration camps.

1 Upon returning to Dowling in the new year, 1982, I found a letter from home waiting for me with the miraculous news: my mother had finally been cured of her insanity. I was overwhelmed with joy. The contents of the letter related how Aunt Queen, the *isangoma,* had spent over a year treating my mother. She was said to have used *muti* (tribal medicine), consisting of special herbs, bark, and roots—and divination, a seeing into the past and future using bones.

2 Apparently my mother's kindness had done her in. While in South Africa she had, against my protestations and those of the family, taken in as boarders from the Giyani homeland in the Northern Transvaal a tall, raw-boned *nyanga* (medicine man) with bloodshot eyes, named Mathebula, and his family of five. They had nowhere else to go. The shack became home for about fifteen people; some slept under the tables, others curled up in corners and near the stove; there was no privacy. My mother had made it clear that their moving in with us was only a temporary measure, to provide them a roof over their heads while they hunted for their own shack. When months passed without the Mathebulas making any attempts at finding alternative housing,

my mother had politely requested them to leave. This angered the wizard, a proud and chauvinistic man. Nonetheless he speedily constructed a shack in one of the rat-infested alleyways. But he never forgave my mother.

3 From strands of my mother's hair and pieces of her clothing, which he had gathered while he lived in our house, he allegedly concocted his voodoo and drove my mother mad. It took Aunt Queen almost a year to piece together what she deemed a "dastardly plot." Daily, out in the yard, under the hot African sun, with my mother seated cross-legged across from her, my aunt shook bones and tossed them onto the ground. From interpreting their final positions she believed that she was able to name the sorcerer and the method he used to bewitch my mother. To a Western mind this of course sounds incredible and primitive. But witchcraft is a time-honored tradition among many African tribes, where convenient scapegoats are always blamed for events which, through limited knowledge and technology, seem inexplicable. Belief in witchcraft can be compared to a Westerner's belief in astrology holding answers to man's future and fate.

4 "Now you know the truth," Aunt Queen said to my mother at the end of her confinement, when she was finally cured. The two spoke in Tsonga. "What do you want me to do?"

5 "Protect my family from further mischief."

6 "Is that all?"

7 "That's all."

8 "Don't you want revenge? Are you simply going to let him go scot-free?"

9 "I'm not a witch. I'm a child of God. I harbor no malice toward him or his family. I seek no revenge." My mother, despite her belief in witchcraft, still considered the Christian God to be all-powerful. This position of course had its contradictions, and since this episode occurred I have pointed them out to her from time to time. She has modified her beliefs and is now more under the sway of Christianity.

10 "But your ancestors must be satisfied," Aunt Queen said. "And what about the pain he caused you? Do you know that he intended to kill you?"

11 "But Christ prevented that. He led me to you and gave you the power to cure me."

12 "You know, Mudjaji [my mother's maiden name], you're so loving that it's impossible for me to understand why anyone would want to harm you. The only thing left for me to do to complete the cure and

prevent a relapse is to send the mischief back to its perpetrator." It was believed that no cure of witchcraft was complete until the black magic had reverted to the sorcerer.

13 "Please don't do anything that would harm him or his family," my mother pleaded.

14 "The gods will decide," Aunt Queen said.

15 Two weeks after my mother returned to Alexandra, the sorcerer's favorite son was stabbed to death during an argument in a *shebeen.* Hardly had he been buried when another of his sons was stabbed to death by *tsotsis* (gangsters) during a robbery and dumped in a ditch. My mother felt remorse over the deaths and grieved for the sorcerer's family. Aunt Queen told her that there was nothing she could have done to prevent their fate.

16 Here I was in America, in the heart of Western civilization itself, having to grapple with the reality or unreality of witchcraft. I remember how my mother's incredible story tested my "civilized mentality," my Western education, my dependency on reason, my faith in science and philosophy. But in the end I realized that her insanity, of course, had rational causes, just as did Uncle Piet's gambling, matrimonial problems, my father's alcoholism, and the family's poverty—all of which they tended to blame on witchcraft. Either my mother's undiagnosed and untreated diabetes or the oppressive conditions under which she lived, or a combination of the two, had deranged her. Aunt Queen was the tribal equivalent of a shrink. Her "magical" treatments of diseases owed much to the power of suggestion and her keen knowledge of the medicinal effects of certain herbs, bark, leaves, and roots, from which, it has been discovered, a good deal of Western medicine has gained real remedies. As for the deaths of the Wizard's sons, this was, of course, pure coincidence, since Alexandra, especially the neighborhood in which my family lived, was an extremely violent place: on one weekend over a dozen murders were committed.

17 I realized all this from the knowledge I had gained since coming to America and discovering that there was a branch of medicine of which I had been completely ignorant while I lived in South Africa: psychoanalysis and psychiatry. The inhuman suffering experienced by blacks under apartheid had devastating effects on their mental and physical well-being. Given the primitive state of health care in the ghettos, endemic illiteracy, and the sway of tribal beliefs, my mother and most blacks were ignorant of causal relationships. They therefore blamed witchcraft for mental illnesses like schizophrenia and paranoia; dis-

eases like malnutrition and tuberculosis; problems like unemployment, alcoholism, and gambling; and unlucky coincidences, such as being arrested during a pass raid while neighbors escaped, or being fired from a job. Their lack of access to qualified medical doctors, psychotherapists, and social workers forced them to rely on the dubious and often dangerous "cures" of *isangomas,* especially since such "cures" at least offered the victim much-needed psychological relief.

18 Superstition is present in Western societies as well, astrology being one example. Some people also blame their misfortunes on the Devil. And many govern their lives through card-reading and palmistry, and rely on charlatans to cure them of cancer, AIDS, blindness, varicose veins, and other diseases. Until education dispelled my ignorance and fortified my reason I was to a degree superstitious and believed in witchcraft.

19 The psychological problems experienced by blacks in South African ghettos are somewhat similar to those experienced by inmates of concentration camps during the Second World War. *From Death-Camp to Existentialism,* by Viktor E. Frankl, explains how psychotic behavior can become a "normal" way of life, a means of survival, for helpless people whose sense of identity and self-worth are under constant attack by an all-powerful oppressor. Jews in concentration camps were at the mercy of their Nazi guards, just as blacks in the ghettos of South Africa are at the mercy of apartheid's Gestapo-like police. Some victims of oppression even come to identify with their oppressors and persecute with relish their own kind. There are cases of Jews, known as Capos, who, in return for special privileges like food and cigarettes doled out by SS guards, treated other Jews sadistically and even herded them into crematoriums and gas chambers. In South Africa black policemen, in return for special privileges such as better housing, residential permits, and passbooks for relatives, shoot and kill unarmed black protesters, torture them in jail, uproot black communities under the homeland policy, and launch brutal raids into the ghettos to enforce Kafkaesque apartheid laws. Such are the evil consequences of unbearable pressures.

Understanding Meaning

1. According to the relative's account, what caused Mathabane's mother to become disturbed?

2. How does the author respond to the concept of witchcraft?
3. How was Mathabane's mother cured? Since the cure required a year, what other explanations can be made for her recovery?
4. What does Mathabane believe led to her recovery?
5. What does this essay reveal about the differences between Western and traditional African medicine?
6. How does Mathabane's new knowledge of psychoanalysis lead him to view his mother's illness? How does it help him understand the effect of apartheid?
7. *Critical Thinking:* Discuss whether or not superstition such as witchcraft becomes a way for people to accept oppression, to perceive political problems in spiritual ways.

Evaluating Strategy

1. What method does Mathabane use to organize his comparison?
2. Mathabane points out that many people in the West believe in astrology and palmistry. How does this influence the way readers might view African witchcraft?
3. *Critical Thinking:* Mathabane makes comparisons between the plight of South Africans and concentration camp victims. Is this valid? How does he limit this comparison? Does he not address some differences?

Appreciating Language

1. What definitions does Mathabane offer for *muti*, *nyanga*, and *tsotsis?*
2. Mathabane uses the word *shebeen,* which is Irish for an illegal drinking establishment. What does this say about South Africa's history?
3. What connotation does *superstition* have? What does Mathabane's choice of words suggest about his attitudes toward traditional African beliefs?

Connections across the Disciplines

1. How do Mathabane's observations about superstition relate to one of the ways people confront oppression according to Martin Luther King Jr. (page 443)?
2. Mathabane's years in America led him to perceive his native country through Western eyes. How does this relate to the views of Jamaica Kincaid (page 147), who now views Antigua from an American perspective?

Writing Suggestions

1. Write a short essay about people who believe in astrology, numerology, crystal therapy, or palmistry. Even if you share in these beliefs, try to objectively examine why people accept ideas that many scientists discredit. Do these beliefs allow people to cope with problems? Does a belief in astrology help provide guidance to people faced with doubt and confusion? Can it lead people to deny the real cause of problems?
2. *Collaborative Writing:* Discuss Mathabane's essay with a small group of students. Ask members to share instances where their education has led them to question some of the beliefs they grew up with. How had education changed perceptions about race, gender, technology, careers, or college? Can mass education eradicate traditional beliefs and values? Have your group work together to draft a short statement on how college has affected student values.

WILLIAM OUCHI

William Ouchi (1943–) was born in Hawaii and educated at Williams College, Stanford, and the University of Chicago. A specialist in organizational behavior, he has written several books widely studied by executives and government administrators. In 1981 he published Theory Z: How American Business Can Meet the Japanese Challenge. *Appearing at a time when many American corporations felt threatened by Japanese imports, the book became a best-seller. Theory Z was developed in response to two contrasting views espoused by Douglas McGregor. According to Theory X, people hate work and need to be directed and motivated. Theory Y assumed people gain satisfaction from work and require the freedom to direct themselves. Ouchi's Theory Z, based on Japanese management practices, stresses the importance of involving workers in the process.*

Japanese and American Workers: Two States of Mind

In this essay from Theory Z, *Ouchi not only contrasts different business practices but different cultures. The incentives that work so well for American workers fail to motivate and in fact discourage Asian employees.*

1 Perhaps the most difficult aspect of the Japanese for Westerners to comprehend is the strong orientation to collective values, particularly a collective sense of responsibility. Let me illustrate with an anecdote about a visit to a new factory in Japan owned and operated by an American electronics company. The American company, a particularly creative firm, frequently attracts attention within the business community for its novel approaches to planning, organizational design, and management systems. As a consequence of this corporate style, the parent company determined to make a thorough study of Japanese workers and to design a plant that would combine the best of East and West. In their study they discovered that Japanese firms almost never make use of individual work incentives, such as piecework or even individual performance appraisal tied to salary increases. They concluded that rewarding individual achievement and individual ability is always a good thing.

2 In the final assembly area of their new plant long lines of young Japanese women wired together electronic products on a piece-rate system: The more you wired, the more you got paid. About two months after opening, the head foreladies approached the plant manager. "Honorable plant manager," they said humbly as they bowed, "we are embarrassed to be so forward, but we must speak to you because all of the girls have threatened to quit work this Friday." (To have this happen, of course, would be a great disaster for all concerned.) "Why," they wanted to know, "can't our plant have the same compensation system as other Japanese companies? When you hire a new girl, her starting wage should be fixed by her age. An eighteen-year-old should be paid more than a sixteen-year-old. Every year on her birthday, she should receive an automatic increase in pay. The idea that any one of us can be more productive than another must be wrong, because none of us in final assembly could make a thing unless all of the other people in the plant had done their jobs right first. To single one person out as being more productive is wrong and is also personally humiliating to us." The company changed its compensation system to the Japanese model.

3 Another American company in Japan had installed a suggestion system much as we have in the United States. Individual workers were encouraged to place suggestions to improve productivity into special boxes. For an accepted idea the individual received a bonus amounting to some fraction of the productivity savings realized from his or her suggestion. After a period of six months, not a single suggestion had been submitted. The American managers were puzzled. They had heard many stories of the inventiveness, the commitment, and the loyalty of Japanese workers, yet not one suggestion to improve productivity had appeared.

4 The managers approached some of the workers and asked why the suggestion system had not been used. The answer: "No one can come up with a work improvement idea alone. We work together, and any ideas that one of us may have are actually developed by watching others and talking to others. If one of us was singled out for being responsible for such an idea, it would embarrass all of us." The company changed to a group suggestion system, in which workers collectively submitted suggestions. Bonuses were paid to groups which would save bonus money until the end of the year for a party at a restaurant or, if there was enough money, for family vacations together. The suggestions and productivity improvements rained down on the plant.

5 One can interpret these examples in two quite different ways. Perhaps the Japanese commitment to collective values is an anachronism that does not fit with modern industrialism but brings economic success despite that collectivism. Collectivism seems to be inimical to the kind of maverick creativity exemplified in Benjamin Franklin, Thomas Edison, and John D. Rockefeller. Collectivism does not seem to provide the individual incentive to excel which has made a great success of American enterprise. Entirely apart from its economic effects, collectivism implies a loss of individuality, a loss of the freedom to be different, to hold fundamentally different values from others.

6 The second interpretation of the examples is that the Japanese collectivism is economically efficient. It causes people to work well together and to encourage one another to better efforts. Industrial life requires interdependence of one person on another. But a less obvious but far-reaching implication of the Japanese collectivism for economic performance has to do with accountability.

7 In the Japanese mind, collectivism is neither a corporate or individual goal to strive for nor a slogan to pursue. Rather, the nature of things operates so that nothing of consequence occurs as a result of individual effort. Everything important in life happens as a result of teamwork or collective effort. Therefore, to attempt to assign individual credit or blame to results is unfounded. A Japanese professor of accounting, a brilliant scholar trained at Carnegie-Mellon University who teaches now in Tokyo, remarked that the status of accounting systems in Japanese industry is primitive compared to those in the United States. Profit centers, transfer prices, and computerized information systems are barely known even in the largest Japanese companies, whereas they are a commonplace in even small United States organizations. Though not at all surprised at the difference in accounting systems, I was not at all sure that the Japanese were primitive. In fact, I thought their system a good deal more efficient than ours.

8 Most American companies have basically two accounting systems. One system summarizes the overall financial state to inform stockholders, bankers, and other outsiders. That system is not of interest here. The other system, called the managerial or cost accounting system, exists for an entirely different reason. It measures in detail all of the particulars of transactions between departments, divisions, and key individuals in the organization, for the purpose of untangling the interdependencies between people. When, for example, two departments

share one truck for deliveries, the cost accounting system charges each department for part of the cost of maintaining the truck and driver, so that at the end of the year, the performance of each department can be individually assessed, and the better department's manager can receive a larger raise. Of course, all of this information processing costs money, and furthermore may lead to arguments between the departments over whether the costs charged to each are fair.

9 In a Japanese company a short-run assessment of individual performance is not wanted, so the company can save the considerable expense of collecting and processing all of that information. Companies still keep track of which department uses a truck how often and for what purposes, but like-minded people can interpret some simple numbers for themselves and adjust their behavior accordingly. Those insisting upon clear and precise measurement for the purpose of advancing individual interests must have an elaborate information system. Industrial life, however, is essentially integrated and interdependent. No one builds an automobile alone, no one carries through a banking transaction alone. In a sense the Japanese value of collectivism fits naturally into an industrial setting, whereas the Western individualism provides constant conflicts. The image that comes to mind is of Chaplin's silent film *Modern Times* in which the apparently insignificant hero played by Chaplin successfully fights against the unfeeling machinery of industry. Modern industrial life can be aggravating, even hostile, or natural: All depends on the fit between our culture and our technology.

10 The *shinkansen* or "bullet train" speeds across the rural areas of Japan giving a quick view of cluster after cluster of farmhouses surrounded by rice paddies. This particular pattern did not develop purely by chance, but as a consequence of the technology peculiar to the growing of rice, the staple of the Japanese diet. The growing of rice requires construction and maintenance of an irrigation system, something that takes many hands to build. More importantly, the planting and the harvesting of rice can only be done efficiently with the cooperation of twenty or more people. The "bottom line" is that a single family working alone cannot produce enough rice to survive, but a dozen families working together can produce a surplus. Thus the Japanese have had to develop the capacity to work together in harmony, no matter what the forces of disagreement or social disintegration, in order to survive.

11 Japan is a nation built entirely on the tips of giant, suboceanic volcanoes. Little of the land is flat and suitable for agriculture. Terraced hillsides make use of every available square foot of arable land. Small homes built very close together further conserve the land. Japan also suffers from natural disasters such as earthquakes and hurricanes. Traditionally homes are made of light construction materials, so a house falling down during a disaster will not crush its occupants and also could be quickly and inexpensively rebuilt. During the feudal period until the Meiji restoration of 1868, each feudal lord sought to restrain his subjects from moving from one village to the next for fear that a neighboring lord might amass enough peasants with which to produce a large agricultural surplus, hire an army and pose a threat. Apparently bridges were not commonly built across rivers and streams until the late nineteenth century, since bridges increased mobility between villages.

12 Taken all together, this characteristic style of living paints the picture of a nation of people who are homogeneous with respect to race, history, language, religion, and culture. For centuries and generations these people have lived in the same village next door to the same neighbors. Living in close proximity and in dwellings which gave very little privacy, the Japanese survived through their capacity to work together in harmony. In this situation, it was inevitable that the one most central social value which emerged, the one value without which the society could not continue, was that an individual does not matter.

13 To the Western soul this is a chilling picture of society. Subordinating individual tastes to the harmony of the group and knowing that individual needs can never take precedence over the interests of all is repellent to the Western citizen. But a frequent theme of Western philosophers and sociologists is that individual freedom exists only when people willingly subordinate their self-interests to the social interest. A society composed entirely of self-interested individuals is a society in which each person is at war with the other, a society which has no freedom. This issue, constantly at the heart of understanding society, comes up in every century, and in every society, whether the writer be Plato, Hobbes, or B. F. Skinner. The question of understanding which contemporary institutions lie at the heart of the conflict between automatism and totalitarianism remains. In some ages, the kinship group, the central social institution, mediated between these opposing forces to preserve the balance in which freedom was realized; in other times the church or the government was most critical. Perhaps our present age puts the work organization as the central institution.

14 In order to complete the comparison of Japanese and American living situations, consider a flight over the United States. Looking out of the window high over the state of Kansas, we see a pattern of a single farmhouse surrounded by fields, followed by another single homestead surrounded by fields. In the early 1800s in the state of Kansas there were no automobiles. Your nearest neighbor was perhaps two miles distant; the winters were long, and the snow was deep. Inevitably, the central social values were self-reliance and independence. Those were the realities of that place and age that children had to learn to value.

15 The key to the industrial revolution was discovering that non-human forms of energy substituted for human forms could increase the wealth of a nation beyond anyone's wildest dreams. But there was a catch. To realize this great wealth, non-human energy needed huge complexes called factories with hundreds, even thousands of workers collected into one factory. Moreover, several factories in one central place made the generation of energy more efficient. Almost overnight, the Western world was transformed from a rural and agricultural country to an urban and industrial state. Our technological advance seems to no longer fit our social structure: In a sense, the Japanese can better cope with modern industrialism. While Americans still busily protect our rather extreme form of individualism, the Japanese hold their individualism in check and emphasize cooperation.

Understanding Meaning

1. What are the essential differences between American and Japanese workers according to Ouchi?
2. What historical forces have shaped the American and Japanese attitudes toward self-identity and community?
3. When you think of success, do you think of individuals or groups? Is it natural for most Americans to think of successful men and women rather than institutions or corporations? Explain your answer.
4. Why do the "primitive" accounting methods used by Japanese corporations seem to work so well?
5. *Critical Thinking:* Ouchi states that Western individualism creates many conflicts in an industrialized society. Discuss whether the American insistence on individuality and resistance to conformity causes needless social and psychological stress. Would Americans lose a sense of themselves if they identified with a corporation or institution?

Evaluating Strategy

1. How effective is Ouchi's analogy of Japanese and American farms in highlighting cultural differences?
2. How does Ouchi organize his comparison? What devices does he use?
3. *Other Modes:* Where does Ouchi use *narration* and *cause and effect* to develop his comparison?

Appreciating Language

1. What words does Ouchi use to describe Japanese and American cultures, values, and attitudes? Is his language neutral, or does it have an implied bias?
2. Ouchi holds a doctoral degree and is accustomed to addressing scholars and executives. What does his word choice and level of diction reveal about the readers he hoped to reach in this essay?

Connections across the Disciplines

1. Review Ellen Goodman's "The Company Man" (page 185). Does her essay reveal a typically American reaction against the Japanese dedication to collectivism? Does she suggest that working for a group causes a person to lose something in the process?
2. Compare this essay in the context of Yi-Fu Tuan's essay about Chinese space (page 244). Although Chinese and Japanese cultures are unique, do you see that they share similar differences between Asian and Western concepts of individual identity?

Writing Suggestions

1. Write a short essay about your own sense of individuality and your career goals. How much personal expression do you expect or desire in your work?
2. *Collaborative Writing:* After reading Ouchi's essay, discuss the issue of individual success with a group of students. Would Americans accept a more collective management system? Does the success of individual workers create conflict in the workplace? Have members reflect on their own job experiences. Have one member of the group take notes of the discussion and then draft a short paper outlining the views of the group.

AMY TAN

Amy Tan (1952–) was born in San Francisco to parents born in China. Visiting China at the age of thirty-five, she reported feeling an instant bond with the culture of her parents. A freelance writer, Tan has written several articles about the nature of immigrant cultures and the roles of women in Asian and Asian American society. Her novel The Joy Luck Club, *published in 1989, became a best-seller and later a motion picture. This novel, like her later* The Kitchen God's Wife, *explores the relationships between Chinese women and their Chinese American daughters.*

The Language of Discretion

In this essay, first published in The State of the Language, *edited by Christopher Ricks and Leonard Michaels, Tan compares two languages as well as two cultures. As you read this article, consider how languages do more than simply transmit different words or expressions. Consider how language differences complicate the process of translation.*

1 At a recent family dinner in San Francisco, my mother whispered to me: "Sau-sau [Brother's Wife] pretends too hard to be polite. Why bother? In the end, she always takes everything."

2 My mother thinks like a *waixiao*, an expatriate, temporarily away from China since 1949, no longer patient with ritual courtesies. As if to prove her point, she reached across the table to offer my elderly aunt from Beijing the last scallop from the Happy Family seafood dish.

3 Sau-sau scowled. "*B'yao, zhen b'yao!*" (I don't want it, really I don't!) she cried, patting her plump stomach.

4 "Take it! Take it!" scolded my mother in Chinese.

5 Full, I'm already full, Sau-sau protested weakly, eyeing the beloved scallop.

6 "Ai!" exclaimed my mother, completely exasperated. "Nobody else wants it. If you don't take it, it will only rot!"

7 At this point, Sau-sau sighed, acting as if she were doing my mother a big favor by taking the wretched scrap off her hands.

8 My mother turned to her brother, a high-ranking communist official who was visiting her in California for the first time: "In America a

Chinese person could starve to death. If you say you don't want it, they won't ask you again forever."

9 My uncle nodded and said he understood fully: Americans take things quickly because they have no time to be polite.

10 I thought about this misunderstanding again—of social contexts failing in translation—when a friend sent me an article from the *New York Times Magazine* (24 April 1988). The article, on changes in New York's Chinatown, made passing reference to the inherent ambivalence of the Chinese language.

11 Chinese people are so "discreet and modest," the article stated, there aren't even words for "yes" and "no."

12 That's not true, I thought, although I can see why an outsider might think that. I continued reading.

13 If one is Chinese, the article went on to say, "One compromises, one doesn't hazard a loss of face by an overemphatic response."

14 My throat seized. Why do people keep saying these things? As if we truly were those little dolls sold in Chinatown tourist shops, heads bobbing up and down in complacent agreement to anything said!

15 I worry about the effect of one-dimensional statements on the unwary and guileless. When they read about this so-called vocabulary deficit, do they also conclude that Chinese people evolved into a mild-mannered lot because the language only allowed them to hobble forth with minced words?

16 Something enormous is always lost in translation. Something insidious seeps into the gaps, especially when amateur linguists continue to compare, one-for-one, language differences and then put forth notions wide open to misinterpretation: that Chinese people have no direct linguistic means to make decisions, assert or deny, affirm or negate, just say no to drug dealers, or behave properly on the witness stand when told, "Please answer yes or no."

17 Yet one can argue, with the help of renowned linguists, that the Chinese are indeed up a creek without "yes" and "no." Take any number of variations on the old language-and-reality theory stated years ago by Edward Sapir: "Human beings are very much at the mercy of the particular language which has become the medium for their society. . . . The fact of the matter is that the 'real world' is to a large extent built upon the language habits of the group."[1]

[1] Edward Sapir, *Selected Writings*, ed. D. G. Mandelbaum (Berkeley and Los Angeles, 1949).

18 This notion was further bolstered by the famous Sapir-Whorf hypothesis, which roughly states that one's perception of the world and how one functions in it depend a great deal on the language used. As Sapir, Whorf, and new carriers of the banner would have us believe, language shapes our thinking, channels us along certain patterns embedded in words, syntactic structures, and intonation patterns. Language has become the peg and the shelf that enables us to sort out and categorize the world. In English, we see "cats" and "dogs"; what if the language had also specified *glatz,* meaning "animals that leave fur on the sofa," and *glotz,* meaning "animals that leave fur and drool on the sofa"? How would language, the enabler, have changed our perceptions with slight vocabulary variations?

19 And if this were the case—of language being the master of destined thought—think of the opportunities lost from failure to evolve two little words, *yes* and *no,* the simplest of opposites! Ghenghis Khan could have been sent back to Mongolia. Opium wars might have been averted. The Cultural Revolution could have been sidestepped.

20 There are still many, from serious linguists to pop psychology cultists, who view language and reality as inextricably tied, one being the consequence of the other. We have traversed the range from the Sapir-Whorf hypothesis to EST and neurolinguistic programming, which tell us "you are what you say."

21 I too have been intrigued by the theories. I can summarize, albeit badly, ages-old empirical evidence: of Eskimos and their infinite ways to say "snow," their ability to *see* the differences in snowflake configurations, thanks to the richness of their vocabulary, while non-Eskimo speakers like myself founder in "snow," "more snow," and "lots more where that came from."

22 I too have experienced dramatic cognitive awakenings via the word. Once I added "mauve" to my vocabulary I began to see it everywhere. When I learned how to pronounce *prix fixe,* I ate French food at prices better than the easier-to-say *á la carte* choices.

23 But just how seriously are we supposed to take this?

24 Sapir said something else about language and reality. It is the part that often gets left behind in the dot-dot-dots of quotes: ". . . No two languages are ever sufficiently similar to be considered as representing the same social reality. The worlds in which different societies live are distinct worlds, not merely the same world with different labels attached."

25 When I first read this, I thought, Here at last is validity for the dilemmas I felt growing up in a bicultural, bilingual family! As any

child of immigrant parents knows, there's a special kind of double bind attached to knowing two languages. My parents, for example, spoke to me in both Chinese and English; I spoke back to them in English.

26 "Amy-ah!" they'd call me.

27 "What?" I'd mumble back.

28 "Do not question us when we call," they scolded me in Chinese. "It is not respectful."

29 "What do you mean?"

30 "Ai! Didn't we just tell you not to question?"

31 To this day, I wonder which parts of my behavior were shaped by Chinese, which by English. I am tempted to think, for example, that if I am of two minds on some matter it is due to the richness of my linguistic experiences, not to any personal tendencies toward wishy-washiness. But which mind says what?

32 Was it perhaps patience—developed through years of deciphering my mother's fractured English—that had me listening politely while a woman announced over the phone that I had won one of five valuable prizes? Was it respect—pounded in by the Chinese imperative to accept convoluted explanations—that had me agreeing that I might find it worthwhile to drive seventy-five miles to view a time-share resort? Could I have been at a loss for words when asked, "Wouldn't you like to win a Hawaiian cruise or perhaps a fabulous Star of India designed exclusively by Carter and Van Arpels?"

33 And when this same woman called back a week later, this time complaining that I had missed my appointment, obviously it was my type A language that kicked into gear and interrupted her. Certainly, my blunt denial—"Frankly I'm not interested"—was as American as apple pie. And when she said, "But it's in Morgan Hill," and I shouted, "Read my lips. I don't care if it's Timbuktu," you can be sure I said it with the precise intonation expressing both cynicism and disgust.

34 It's dangerous business, this sorting out of language and behavior. Which one is English? Which is Chinese? The categories manifest themselves: passive and aggressive, tentative and assertive, indirect and direct. And I realize they are just variations of the same theme: that Chinese people are discreet and modest.

35 Reject them all!

36 If my reaction is overly strident, it is because I cannot come across as too emphatic. I grew up listening to the same lines over and over again, like so many rote expressions repeated in an English phrasebook. And I too almost came to believe them.

37 Yet if I consider my upbringing more carefully, I find there was nothing discreet about the Chinese language I grew up with. My parents made everything abundantly clear. Nothing wishy-washy in their demands, no compromises accepted: "Of course you will become a famous neurosurgeon," they told me. "And yes, a concert pianist on the side."

38 In fact, now that I remember, it seems that the more emphatic outbursts always spilled over into Chinese: "Not that way! You must wash rice so not a single grain spills out."

39 I do not believe that my parents—both immigrants from mainland China—are an exception to the modest-and-discreet rule. I have only to look at the number of Chinese engineering students skewing minority ratios at Berkeley, MIT, and Yale. Certainly they were not raised by passive mothers and fathers who said, "It is up to you, my daughter. Writer, welfare recipient, masseuse, or molecular engineer—you decide."

40 And my American mind says, See, those engineering students weren't able to say no to their parents' demands. But then my Chinese mind remembers: Ah, but those parents all wanted their sons and daughters to be *pre-med.*

41 Having listened to both Chinese and English, I also tend to be suspicious of any comparisons between the two languages. Typically, one language—that of the person doing the comparing—is often used as the standard, the benchmark for a logical form of expression. And so the language being compared is always in danger of being judged deficient or superfluous, simplistic or unnecessarily complex, melodious or cacophonous. English speakers point out that Chinese is extremely difficult because it relies on variations in tone barely discernible to the human ear. By the same token, Chinese speakers tell me English is extremely difficult because it is inconsistent, a language of too many broken rules, of Mickey Mice and Donald Ducks.

42 Even more dangerous to my mind is the temptation to compare both language and behavior *in translation.* To listen to my mother speak English, one might think she has no concept of past or future tense, that she doesn't see the difference between singular and plural, that she is gender blind because she calls my husband "she." If one were not careful, one might also generalize that, based on the way my mother talks, all Chinese people take a circumlocutory route to get to the point. It is, in fact, my mother's idiosyncratic behavior to ramble a bit.

43 Sapir was right about differences between two languages and their realities. I can illustrate why word-for-word translation is not enough to translate meaning and intent. I once received a letter from China which I read to non–Chinese speaking friends. The letter, originally written in Chinese, had been translated by my brother-in-law in Beijing. One portion described the time when my uncle at age ten discovered his widowed mother (my grandmother) had remarried—as a number three concubine, the ultimate disgrace for an honorable family. The translated version of my uncle's letter read in part:

> 44 In 1925, I met my mother in Shanghai. When she came to me, I didn't have greeting to her as if seeing nothing. She pull me to a corner secretly and asked me why didn't have greeting to her. I couldn't control myself and cried, "Ma! Why did you leave us? People told me: one day you ate a beancake yourself. Your sister-in-law found it and sweared at you, called your names. So . . . is it true?" She clasped my hand and answered immediately, "It's not true, don't say what like this." After this time, there was a few chance to meet her.

45 "What!" cried my friends. "Was eating a beancake so terrible?"

46 Of course not. The beancake was simply a euphemism; a ten-year-old boy did not dare question his mother on something as shocking as concubinage. Eating a beancake was his equivalent for committing this selfish act, something inconsiderate of all family members, hence, my grandmother's despairing response to what seemed like a ludicrous charge of gluttony. And sure enough, she was banished from the family, and my uncle saw her only a few times before her death.

47 While the above may fuel people's argument that Chinese is indeed a language of extreme discretion, it does not mean that Chinese people speak in secrets and riddles. The contexts are fully understood. It is only to those on the *outside* that the language seems cryptic, the behavior inscrutable.

48 I am, evidently, one of the outsiders. My nephew in Shanghai, who recently started taking English lessons, has been writing me letters in English. I had told him I was a fiction writer, and so in one letter he wrote, "Congratulate to you on your writing. Perhaps one day I should like to read it." I took it in the same vein as "Perhaps one day we can get together for lunch." I sent back a cheery note. A month went by and another letter arrived from Shanghai. "Last one perhaps I

hadn't writing distinctly," he said. "In the future, you'll send a copy of your works for me."

49 I try to explain to my English-speaking friends that Chinese language use is more *strategic* in manner, whereas English tends to be more direct; an American business executive may say, "Let's make a deal," and the Chinese manager may reply, "Is your son interested in learning about your widget business?" Each to his or her own purpose, each with his or her own linguistic path. But I hesitate to add more to the pile of generalizations, because no matter how many examples I provide and explain, I fear that it appears defensive and only reinforces the image: that Chinese people are "discreet and modest"—and it takes an American to explain what they really mean.

50 Why am I complaining? The description seems harmless enough (after all, the *New York Times Magazine* writer did not say "slippery and evasive"). It is precisely the bland, easy acceptability of the phrase that worries me.

51 I worry that the dominant society may see Chinese people from a limited—and limiting—perspective. I worry that seemingly benign stereotypes may be part of the reason there are few Chinese in top management positions, in mainstream political roles. I worry about the power of language: that if one says anything enough times—in *any* language—it might become true.

52 Could this be why Chinese friends of my parents' generation are willing to accept the generalization?

53 "Why are you complaining?" one of them said to me. "If people think we are modest and polite, let them think that. Wouldn't Americans be pleased to admit they are thought of as polite?"

54 And I do believe anyone would take the description as a compliment—at first. But after a while, it annoys, as if the only things that people heard one say were phatic remarks: "I'm so pleased to meet you. I've heard many wonderful things about you. For me? You shouldn't have!"

55 These remarks are not representative of new ideas, honest emotions, or considered thought. They are what is said from the polite distance of social contexts: of greetings, farewells, wedding thank-you notes, convenient excuses, and the like.

56 It makes me wonder, though. How many anthropologists, how many sociologists, how many travel journalists have documented so-called "natural interactions" in foreign lands, all observed with spiral

notebook in hand? How many other cases are there of the long-lost primitive tribe, people who turned out to be sophisticated enough to put on the stone-age show that ethnologists had come to see?

57 And how many tourists fresh off the bus have wandered into Chinatown expecting the self-effacing shopkeeper to admit under duress that the goods are not worth the price asked? I have witnessed it.

58 "I don't know," the tourist said to the shopkeeper, a Cantonese woman in her fifties. "It doesn't look genuine to me. I'll give you three dollars."

59 "You don't like my price, go somewhere else," said the shopkeeper.

60 "You are not a nice person," cried the shocked tourist, "not a nice person at all!"

61 "Who say I have to be nice," snapped the shopkeeper.

62 "So how does one say 'yes' and 'no' in Chinese?" ask my friends a bit warily.

63 And here I do agree in part with the *New York Times Magazine* article. There is no one word for "yes" or "no"—but not out of necessity to be discreet. If anything, I would say the Chinese equivalent of answering "yes" or "no" is dis*crete,* that is, specific to what is asked.

64 Ask a Chinese person if he or she has eaten, and he or she might say *chrle* (eaten already) or perhaps *meiyou* (have not).

65 Ask, "So you had insurance at the time of the accident?" and the response would be *dwei* (correct) or *meiyou* (did not have).

66 Ask, "Have you stopped beating your wife?" and the answer refers directly to the proposition being asserted or denied: stopped already, still have not, never beat, have no wife.

67 What could be clearer?

68 As for those who are still wondering how to translate the language of discretion, I offer this personal example.

69 My aunt and uncle were about to return to Beijing after a three-month visit to the United States. On their last night I announced I wanted to take them out to dinner.

70 "Are you hungry?" I asked in Chinese.

71 "Not hungry," said my uncle promptly, the same response he once gave me ten minutes before he suffered a low-blood-sugar attack.

72 "Not too hungry," said my aunt. "Perhaps you're hungry?"

73 "A little," I admitted.

74 "We can eat, we can eat," they both consented.

75 "What kind of food?" I asked.

76 "Oh, doesn't matter. Anything will do. Nothing fancy, just some simple food is fine."

77 "Do you like Japanese food? We haven't had that yet," I suggested.

78 They looked at each other.

79 "We can eat it," said my uncle bravely, this survivor of the Long March.

80 "We have eaten it before," added my aunt. "Raw fish."

81 "Oh, you don't like it"? I said. "Don't be polite. We can go somewhere else."

82 "We are not being polite. We can eat it," my aunt insisted.

83 So I drove them to Japantown and we walked past several restaurants featuring colorful plastic displays of sushi.

84 "Not this one, not this one either," I continued to say, as if searching for a Japanese restaurant similar to the last. "Here it is," I finally said, turning into a restaurant famous for its Chinese fish dishes from Shandong.

85 "Oh, Chinese food!" cried my aunt, obviously relieved.

86 My uncle patted my arm. "You think Chinese."

87 "It's your last night here in America," I said. "So don't be polite. Act like an American."

88 And that night we ate a banquet.

Understanding Meaning

1. What is Tan's thesis about language differences?
2. What does the opening narrative reveal about the nature of Chinese language and culture? How would a typical American family behave and speak differently?
3. Tan quotes a linguist named Sapir who states, "Human beings are very much at the mercy of the particular language which has become the medium for their society." Does Tan agree with this assumption?
4. *Critical Thinking:* Tan speaks two languages. Does she seem to reflect two distinct mindsets, two different ways of looking at and responding to the world around her? Do immigrants face making a choice, or can they continue maintaining a dual vision? Is this clash or blend of identity lost on succeeding generations?

Evaluating Strategy

1. How effective is the opening scene? Does Tan follow the standard writer's admonition to "show; don't tell"?
2. How successfully does Tan weave personal experience and observations with more scholarly commentary on linguistics?
3. Why is dialogue so important in this essay?
4. *Other Modes:* How does Tan use *description, narration,* and *cause and effect* in constructing her comparison?

Appreciating Language

1. Analyze Tan's use of Chinese words in the essay. How effective is it? Do you get a sense of how Chinese and English differ?
2. How much linguistic terminology does Tan use?

Connections across the Disciplines

1. Read Richard Rodriguez's "The Tongue That Had to Be Tied" (page 673). How does Tan's experience with a second language contrast with Rodriguez's? How much of the difference is driven by linguistic issues and how much by the impact of cultural identity? Does American society view Hispanics and Chinese Americans differently?
2. How does reading Yi-Fu Tuan's "Chinese Space, American Space" (page 244) assist you in understanding some of the issues raised by Tan's essay?

Writing Suggestions

1. Write a brief narrative or description of your own interactions with someone or some group of people who spoke a different language. Focus on word choices and behaviors you may have found mystifying, troubling, or humorous.
2. *Collaborative Writing:* Work with a group of students, and consider how Americans use English. What cultural features do you believe stand out? Consider Tan's closing statement: "So don't be polite. Act like an American." Do Americans live up to their stereotype of being brash, loud, impolite? Record remarks, and then write a short description detailing observations made by the group.

MARIE WINN

Marie Winn (1936–) was born in Czechoslovakia and grew up in New York. She was educated at Radcliffe College. She has written and edited ten children's books. This work led her to study the impact television has on childhood development. She has published articles in a number of popular magazines. Her books on television include the widely anthologized The Plug-in Drug: Television, Children and Family *and* Unplugging the Plug-in Drug.

Television and Reading

Television has been a dominant factor in American life since the early 1950s. In this essay from The Plug-in Drug, *Winn compares reading with television watching. As you read Winn's article, consider your own childhood experience with books and television.*

1 Until the television era a young child's access to symbolic representations of reality was limited. Unable to read, he entered the world of fantasy primarily by way of stories told to him or read to him from a book. But rarely did such "literary" experiences take up a significant proportion of a child's waking time; even when a willing reader or storyteller was available, an hour or so a day was more time than most children spent ensconced in the imagination of others. And when the pretelevision child *did* enter those imaginary worlds, he always had a grown-up escort along to interpret, explain, and comfort, if need be. Before he learned to read, it was difficult for the child to enter the fantasy world alone.

2 For this reason the impact of television was undoubtedly greater on preschoolers and pre-readers than on any other group. By means of television, very young children were able to enter and spend sizable portions of their waking time in a secondary world of incorporeal people and intangible things, unaccompanied, in too many cases, by an adult guide or comforter. School-age children fell into a different category. Because they could read, they had other opportunities to leave reality behind. For these children television was merely *another* imaginary world.

3 But since reading, once the school child's major imaginative experience, has now been virtually eclipsed by television, the television experience must be compared with the reading experience to try to discover whether they are, indeed, similar activities fulfilling similar needs in a child's life.

WHAT HAPPENS WHEN YOU READ

4 It is not enough to compare television watching and reading from the viewpoint of quality. Although the quality of the material available in each medium varies enormously, from junky books and shoddy programs to literary masterpieces and fine, thoughtful television shows, the *nature* of the two experiences is different and that difference significantly affects the impact of the material taken in.

5 Few people besides linguistics students and teachers of reading are aware of the complex mental manipulations involved in the reading process. Shortly after learning to read, a person assimilates the process into his life so completely that the words in books seem to acquire an existence almost equal to the objects or acts they represent. It requires a fresh look at a printed page to recognize that those symbols that we call letters of the alphabet are completely abstract shapes bearing no inherent "meaning" of their own. Look at an "o," for instance, or a "k." The "o" is a curved figure; the "k" is an intersection of three straight lines. Yet it is hard to divorce their familiar figures from their sounds, though there is nothing "o-ish" about an "o" or "k-ish" about a "k." A reader unfamiliar with the Russian alphabet will find it easy to look at the symbol "Щ" and see it as an abstract shape; a Russian reader will find it harder to detach that symbol from its sound, *shch.* And even when trying to consider "k" as an abstract symbol, we cannot see it without the feeling of a "k" sound somewhere between the throat and the ears, a silent pronunciation of "k" that occurs the instant we see the letter.

6 That is the beginning of reading: we learn to transform abstract figures into sounds, and groups of symbols into the combined sounds that make up the words of our language. As the mind transforms the abstract symbols into sounds and the sounds into words, it "hears" the words, as it were, and thereby invests them with meanings previously learned in the spoken language. Invariably, as the skill of reading de-

velops, the meaning of each word begins to seem to dwell within those symbols that make up the word. The word "dog," for instance, comes to bear some relationship with the real animal. Indeed, the word "dog" seems to *be* a dog in a certain sense, to possess some of the qualities of a dog. But it is only as a result of a swift and complex series of mental activities that the word "dog" is transformed from a series of meaningless squiggles into an idea of something real. This process goes on smoothly and continuously as we read, and yet it becomes no less complex. The brain must carry out all the steps of decoding and investing with meaning each time we read; but it becomes more adept at it as the skill develops, so that we lose the sense of struggling with symbols and meanings that children have when they first learn to read.

7 But not merely does the mind *hear* words in the process of reading; it is important to remember that reading involves images as well. For when the reader sees the word "dog" and understands the idea of "dog," an image representing a dog is conjured up as well. The precise nature of this "reading image" is little understood, nor is there agreement about what relation it bears to visual images taken in directly by the eyes. Nevertheless images necessarily color our reading, else we would perceive no meaning, merely empty words. The great difference between these "reading images" and the images we take in when viewing television is this: We *create* our own images when reading, based upon our own life experiences and reflecting our own individual needs, while we must accept what we receive when watching television images. This aspect of reading, which might be called "creative" in the narrow sense of the word, is present during all reading experiences, regardless of *what* is being read. The reader "creates" his own images as he reads, almost as if he were creating his own, small, inner television program. The result is a nourishing experience for the imagination. As Bruno Bettelheim notes, "Television captures the imagination but does not liberate it. A good book at once stimulates and frees the mind."

8 Television images do not go through a complex symbolic transformation. The mind does not have to decode and manipulate during the television experience. Perhaps this is a reason why the visual images received directly from a television set are strong, stronger, it appears, than the images conjured up mentally while reading. But ultimately they satisfy less. A ten-year-old child reports on the effects of seeing television dramatizations of books he has previously read: "The TV

people leave a stronger impression. Once you've seen a character on TV, he'll always look like that in your mind, even if you made a different picture of him in your mind before, when you read the book yourself." And yet, as the same child reports, "The thing about a book is that you have so much freedom. You can make each character look exactly the way you want him to look. You're more in control of things when you read a book than when you see something on TV."

9 It may be that television-bred children's reduced opportunities to indulge in this "inner picture-making" accounts for the curious inability of so many children today to adjust to nonvisual experiences. This is commonly reported by experienced teachers who bridge the gap between the pretelevision and the television eras.

10 "When I read them a story without showing them pictures, the children always complain—'I can't see.' Their attention flags," reports a first-grade teacher. "They'll begin to talk or wander off. I have to really work to develop their visualizing skills. I tell them that there's nothing to see, that the story is coming out of my mouth, and that they can make their own pictures in their 'mind's eye.' They get better at visualizing, with practice. But children never needed to learn how to visualize before television, it seems to me."

VIEWING VS. READING: CONCENTRATION

11 Because reading demands complex mental manipulations, a reader is required to concentrate far more than a television viewer. An audio expert notes that "with the electronic media it is openness [that counts]. Openness permits auditory and visual stimuli more direct access to the brain . . . someone who is taught to concentrate will fail to perceive many patterns of information conveyed by the electronic stimuli."

12 It may be that a predisposition toward concentration, acquired, perhaps, through one's reading experiences, makes one an inadequate television watcher. But it seems far more likely that the reverse situation obtains: that a predisposition toward "openness" (which may be understood to mean the opposite of focal concentration), acquired through years and years of television viewing, has influenced adversely viewers' ability to concentrate, to read, to write clearly—in short, to demonstrate any of the verbal skills a literate society requires.

PACE

13 A comparison between reading and viewing may be made in respect to the pace of each experience, and the relative control a person has over that pace, for the pace may influence the ways one uses the material received in each experience. In addition, the pace of each experience may determine how much it intrudes upon other aspects of one's life.

14 The pace of reading, clearly, depends entirely upon the reader. He may read as slowly or as rapidly as he can or wishes to read. If he does not understand something, he may stop and reread it, or go in search of elucidation before continuing. The reader can accelerate his pace when the material is easy or less than interesting, and slow down when it is difficult or enthralling. If what he reads is moving, he can put down the book for a few moments and cope with his emotions without fear of losing anything.

15 The pace of the television experience cannot be controlled by the viewer; only its beginning and end are within his control as he clicks the knob on and off. He cannot slow down a delightful program or speed up a dreary one. He cannot "turn back" if a word or phrase is not understood. The program moves inexorably forward, and what is lost or misunderstood remains so.

16 Nor can the television viewer readily transform the material he receives into a form that might suit his particular emotional needs, as he invariably does with material he reads. The images move too quickly. He cannot use his own imagination to invest the people and events portrayed on television with the personal meanings that would help him understand and resolve relationships and conflicts in his own life; he is under the power of the imagination of the show's creators. In the television experience the eyes and ears are overwhelmed with the immediacy of sights and sounds. They flash from the television set just fast enough for the eyes and ears to take them in before moving on quickly to the new pictures and sounds . . . so as *not to lose the thread.*

17 Not to lose the thread . . . it is this need, occasioned by the irreversible direction and relentless velocity of the television experience, that not only limits the workings of the viewer's imagination, but also causes television to intrude into human affairs far more than reading experiences can ever do. If someone enters the room while one is watching television—a friend, a relative, a child, someone, perhaps, one has not seen for some time—one must continue to watch or one

will lose the thread. The greetings must wait, for the television program will not. A book, of course, can be set aside, with a pang of regret, perhaps, but with no sense of permanent loss.

18 A grandparent describes a situation that is, by all reports, not uncommon:

19 "Sometimes when I come to visit the girls, I'll walk into their room and they're watching a TV program. Well, I know they love me, but it makes me feel *bad* when I tell them hello, and they say, without even looking up, 'Wait a minute . . . we have to see the end of this program.' It hurts me to have them care more about that machine and those little pictures than about being glad to see me. I know that they probably can't help it, but still. . . . "

20 Can they help it? Ultimately the power of a television viewer to release himself from his viewing in order to attend to human demands arising in the course of his viewing is not altogether a function of the pace of the program. After all, the viewer might *choose* to operate according to human priorities rather than electronic dictatorship. He might quickly decide "to hell with this program" and simply stop watching when a friend entered the room or a child needed attention.

21 He might . . . but the hypnotic power of television makes it difficult to shift one's attention away, makes one desperate not to lose the thread of the program. . . .

THE BASIC BUILDING BLOCKS

22 There is another difference between reading and television viewing that must affect the response to each experience. This is the relative acquaintance of readers and viewers with the fundamental elements of each medium. While the reader is familiar with the basic building blocks of the reading medium, the television viewer has little acquaintance with those of the television medium.

23 As a person reads, he has his own writing experience to fall back upon. His understanding of what he reads, and his feelings about it, are necessarily affected, and deepened, by his possession of writing as a means of communicating. As a child begins to learn reading, he begins to acquire the rudiments of writing. That these two skills are always acquired together is important and not coincidental. As the child learns to read words, he needs to understand that a word is some-

thing he can write himself, though his muscle control may temporarily prevent him from writing it clearly. That he wields such power over the words he is struggling to decipher makes the reading experience a satisfying one right from the start.

24 A young child watching television enters a realm of materials completely beyond his control—and understanding. Though the images that appear on the screen may be reflections of familiar people and things, they appear as if by magic. The child cannot create similar images, nor even begin to understand how those flickering, electronic shapes and forms come into being. He takes on a far more powerless and ignorant role in front of the television set than in front of a book.

25 There is no doubt that many young children have a confused relationship to the television medium. When a group of preschool children were asked, "How do kids get to be on your TV?" only 22 percent of them showed any real comprehension of the nature of the television images. When asked "Where do the people and kids and things go when your TV is turned off?" only 20 percent of the three-year-olds showed the smallest glimmer of understanding. Although there was an increase in comprehension among the four-year-olds, the authors of the study note that "even among the older children the vast majority still did not grasp the nature of television pictures."

26 The child's feelings of power and competence are nourished by another feature of the reading experience that does not obtain for television: the nonmechanical, easily accessible, and easily transportable nature of reading matter. The child can always count on a book for pleasure, though the television set may break down at a crucial moment. The child may take a book with him wherever he goes, to his room, to the park, to his friend's house, to school to read under his desk: He can *control* his use of books and reading materials. The television set is stuck in a certain place; it cannot be moved easily. It certainly cannot be casually transported from place to place by a child. The child must not only watch television wherever the set is located, but he must watch certain programs at certain times, and is powerless to change what comes out of the set and when it comes out.

27 In this comparison of reading and television experiences a picture begins to emerge that quite confirms the commonly held notion that reading is somehow "better" than television viewing. Reading involves a complex form of mental activity, trains the mind in concentration skills, develops the powers of imagination and inner visualization; the flexibility of its pace lends itself to a better and deeper comprehension

of the material communicated. Reading engrosses, but does not hypnotize or seduce the reader from his human responsibilities. Reading is a two-way process: the reader can also write; television viewing is a one-way street: The view cannot create television images. And books are ever available, ever controllable. Television controls.

Understanding Meaning

1. What are the principal differences Winn sees between reading and watching television?
2. Does she name any good qualities of television? Is she overlooking educational programming or the impact television can have for children who may have learning disabilities such as dyslexia?
3. What impact does television have on children? Does Winn suggest that television is a limiting influence?
4. *Critical Thinking:* Winn states that television can't be stopped or reversed, though a videotape, like a book, can be reviewed many times. She suggests television controls the viewer, yet now cable and video on demand provide access to hundreds of channels and thousands of titles. Will future technological developments lessen the differences between reading and television?

Evaluating Strategy

1. What method does Winn use to organize her essay?
2. Winn includes remarks made by children. Is this effective?
3. *Other Modes:* Where does Winn use *narrative* and *cause and effect* to develop her comparison?

Appreciating Language

1. Winn uses the term "openness" to discuss television viewing. Does Winn see "openness" in positive or negative terms?
2. Does Winn use words with negative connotations to describe television?

Connections across the Disciplines

1. Compare Winn's comments on childhood development with John Holt's article "Three Kinds of Discipline" (page 459). How does Winn's con-

cept of control relate to Holt's stress on developing discipline through experience?

2. Winn sees television as a controlling element. How does this compare to George Orwell's concerns about the effects of artificial environments (page 551)?

Writing Suggestions

1. People traditionally had favorite childhood books, books they often referred to into old age. Now people discuss with nostalgia the TV shows of their youth. Do you have favorite books you read as a child? If so, how was the experience of reading different from watching television? Write an essay about your own experiences as a reader.
2. *Collaborative Writing:* Discuss the role of reading and television in a child's life with a group of students. Ask how many had parents who read to them. Ask the parents in the group how they monitor their children's viewing habits. Have a member of the group note the issues raised and then write a brief analysis of the views emerging from your group.

SUNEEL RATAAN

Suneel Rataan wrote this article about the growing rift between young professionals entering the workforce and their middle-aged superiors. The "busters" in their twenties find themselves in conflict with the baby boomers now in their forties and fifties. Though the term "generation gap" faded from the popular press when the 1960s ended, Rataan suggests the current discord between the generations may have lasting impact on American society, politics, and social policies.

Why Busters Hate Boomers

In this article written for Fortune *magazine (1993), Rataan uses a number of modes within her comparison. As you read the article, pay attention to her use of* narration, description, *and* cause and effect. *Whatever your age, keep in mind the conflicts you may have witnessed or experienced between men and women in their twenties and those in their forties.*

1 Hate to break this to you, boomers, but among twentysomethings gathering in bars, coffee houses, and Lollapalooza festivals across America, bashing you folks has become the new national pastime. Some of it is playful—surely we've *all* heard enough about the Sixties—but much of it is deadly serious. The beef is that boomers seemed to get the best of everything, from free love to careers, while today's young people get AIDS and McJobs.

2 If the sound of young people whining sounds annoyingly familiar, as from time immemorial, listen closer. This time it's different. Unlike their boomer siblings, Generation X, as the new crop have taken to calling themselves, from the title of a Douglas Coupland novel, aren't rebelling against the government or the culture. Instead, today's kids (whose numbers include the author of this story) are up in arms over economic and career prospects that look particularly bleak—with boomers as the targets of their resentments. That makes the workplace center-stage of the twentysomethings' rebellion, with younger people referring privately to their boomer bosses as "knotheads and control freaks," in the phrase of Jeffrey McManus, a 26-year-old computer instructor.

3 To hear twentysomethings tell it, boomers spend too much office time politicking and not enough time working. Boomer managers claim to be seeking younger employees' input when in reality they couldn't care less what Xers think. Worst of all, boomers seem threatened by young, cheap-to-employ hotshots who come in brimming with energy and—note well—superior technological savvy, and thus are doing everything in their power to keep the young'uns down. And while we're at it, with downsizing taking a wicked toll on support staff, can't you boomers do your own faxing?

4 Boomers are more than willing to take on twentysomethings in what's shaping up as a generational grudge match. Xers, fortysomethings say, are too cocky and aren't willing to pay their dues. That complaint is as old as humanity, but other knocks are more particular to the Xers. They aren't loyal or committed to work, detractors say, changing jobs more casually than sex partners and refusing to go that extra mile to do things right. Unlike workaholic boomers, twentysomethings like to play, and they even expect work to be fun. Irony of ironies, the boomer generation that came of age rejecting authority charges the next generation with—*sacré bleu!*—being unwilling to, uh, show appropriate deference to *their* authority.

5 Interviews with more than 60 Xers and boomers in the business world, as well as with sociologists and management consultants, reveal that a combination of clashing workplace values and the sour economic scene is creating lasting tensions that managers will have to deal with long after hiring has picked up. Faced with working for boomer bosses they find oppressive, many twentysomethings have abandoned corporate America, retreating into slackerdom or striking out on their own as entrepreneurs. The challenge for managers is to figure out ways to capture twentysomethings' enthusiasm to enliven existing companies—many of which certainly could use an infusion of youthful energy.

6 To chart the generational fault line, throw out textbook definitions that identify boomers as the 78 million Americans born between 1946 and 1964 and baby-busters as the 38 million born from 1965 to 1975. Bill Strauss and Neil Howe, authors of two books on generational issues, *Generations* and *13th Gen*, correctly point out that people born after 1960 have difficulty identifying with the coming-of-age experiences of older boomers. They call the generation born from 1961 to 1981 "13ers," denoting their status as the 13th generation since the founding of the republic. Says Strauss: "Our shorthand is that boomers

are too young to remember Roosevelt dying, while 13ers are too young to remember Kennedy's assassination." Using Strauss and Howe's definition, 13ers—by subtracting from boomers' ranks the people born after 1960—*outnumber* boomers 79 million to 69 million. Of course, the still, small voice of the boomer skeptic intones, 32 million of the 13ers are under 21.

7 Just as the times in which they came of age are different, so too are the factors that provoked boomers' and Xers' rebellions. Against a backdrop of unparalleled U.S. economic strength, boomers rose up not only against the Vietnam war but also against a culture and social system they thought repressive. Twentysomethings see themselves as the children of America's economic and social decline. They aren't angry at the Silent and World War II generations that have steered the economy onto the rocks and whose Social Security and Medicare payments threaten to bankrupt the government. To young people, those older generations paid their dues in the Depression, World War II, and Korea.

8 Instead, twentysomethings train their resentments on boomers, whom the younger people see as having coasted through life—from their *Leave It to Beaver* childhoods in the 1950s to their current positions in management—without ever having built anything. Beyond that, twentysomethings identify boomers with the unraveling of American society that seemed to accompany the antiwar movement and the divorce wave that began sweeping across the country in the late 1960s.

9 For a taste of these sentiments, sit down on the banks of the Potomac River in Washington, D.C., for a drink with Dana Neilsen, 25, an account executive with *AAA World* magazine. "We're the generation of divorced families and latchkey homes, and that's a big dose of realism," says Neilsen, the child of divorced parents and of a working mother. "The boomers had elementary schools built for them and then secondary schools and then colleges, and then as they entered the work force, companies made room for them. Now we come along and it seems as if all the resources have been used. Now they've moved into management levels, and they're not going anywhere. Where does that leave us?"

10 Some Xers, forced into joblessness or underemployment, are downright bitter about the lousy cards they think they've been dealt. Says a disgruntled Xer, a 28-year-old temp for a *Fortune* 500 company in San Francisco who has a master's degree: "The boomer manager I

work for comes in and says, 'Wow, look at my shiny, new, red convertible.' And I'm like, 'Look at my battle-ax '76 Nova.' I mean, I'm a burb kid. My parents weren't big spenders, but they gave me a comfortable upbringing, and that's something I feel I could never give my children, if I have any. Baby-boomers drive themselves nutty talking about balancing work and family, but at least they have families."

11 Not all Xers blame the boomers entirely for their own frustrations; some instead cite their generation's inflated expectations. San Franciscan Paula Fujimoto, 24, says that paying $13,000 a year in tuition at Chicago's Northwestern University primed her to expect better than what she came to be in most of her first jobs: a glorified secretary. Even now, two years after graduation, she is settling for minimum wage—that's $4.25 an hour—trying to prove herself to a public relations firm. "I was frustrated because I grew up in a nice, upper-middle-class suburb, I studied hard, I did all the things you're supposed to do to get into a good school, and it was like people chose to ignore the fact I was intelligent," she says. Concludes Fujimoto, who still lives at her parents' home: "Our generation is way too cocky." Adds her friend 29-year-old My Tien Vo: "We've been significantly humbled."

12 Columnist Stanley Bing, the pseudonym of a 42-year-old executive too weak-kneed to let his real name be associated with his views, says Xers haven't been humbled nearly enough. "I didn't make more than $8,000 a year until I was 30," says Bing. "Instead of realizing that you eat dirt until you decide to get serious, you're whining. We didn't whine. We knew what it was to be young, poor, and striving."

13 The kids take remarks like these as emblematic of a smug boomer complacency about the difficulties young adults encounter today. Since 1968, when the Head Boomer, Bill Clinton, graduated from Georgetown, the annual cost of attending a four-year public university has risen 39 percent *after* inflation, to $6,500. Private university costs are up 94 percent, to $19,300. Despite the baby bust, universities are loosing 1.6 million newly minted bachelor's, professional, and doctoral degree recipients into the job market each year, 58 percent more than during the late 1960s. Yet employment in managerial and technical fields has grown only an average of 310,000 jobs annually over the past two years, compared with an average of 1.8 million jobs each year during the 1980s. Hiring may pick up again one day, but to people coming out of degree programs now, the outlook is bleak. Indeed, the Bureau of Labor Statistics forecasts that nearly one-third of college graduates

from the classes of 1990 through 2005 will take jobs whose content doesn't really require a degree, up sharply from 19 percent in 1980.

14 To hear twentysomethings tell it, boomer pinheadedness in the workplace runs far beyond lack of empathy to encompass a range of behaviors that can make working for people in their late 30s and 40s oppressive. To the over-50 set, some of the complaints will seem silly, such as boomer versus twentysomething clashes over dress and appearance. But such conflicts are serious to Xers, who brand them a symptom of boomer control-freakishness. Recounts an Xer employee of a Midwestern consultancy: "Last year I had my hair shaved on the sides so you could see my scalp. My 42-year-old boss went to see the human resources manager about whether she could send me home until it grew back. This woman says she's a flower child. She still goes to see the Rolling Stones, even though now she pays a broker $400 for tickets. And she's worried about my haircut?"

15 Far worse is young workers' perception that many boomers seem more caught up in maneuvering for status in an organization than in working. Towers Perrin consultant Margaret Regan and David Cannon, a doctoral student at London Business School who has conducted extensive research on Generation X in the workplace, report independently that in focus group after focus group, twentysomethings' biggest complaint about their boomer managers is the politicking in which they engage. Says Cannon: "Younger people want to make a contribution, and not a vague one, and they don't want to waste a lot of time. They see boomers, and not so much the senior people, as politicking and maneuvering and doing a lot of unnecessary make-work."

16 Xers *Fortune* interviewed aren't so naive as to think politics can be banished from the workplace. What amazes them is the degree to which scrapping for position and control can interfere with a company's work. A 29-year-old programmer for a Southern California software company described how a power struggle among the boomer managers overseeing development of a product delayed a planned 12-month project for a year.

17 The key villain, he says, was a middle-age vice president who insisted on making every decision—even if the staff had to wait weeks for her schedule to clear so she could weigh in. Says the programmer: "It's a bottom-line issue, but they ignore it and allow politics to drive decisions that could eventually cost them their jobs or their compa-

nies." That's what happened to the vice president, who was laid off when the company recently retrenched.

18 Twentysomethings see another aspect of their bosses' politicking in autocratic management that denies Xers a voice or the feeling that they have any ownership of their work. "For the young person, the attitude is, 'Just tell me what you want to do and leave me alone,'" says consultant Regan. "Obviously the boss above them wants more direction and control."

19 What really grates on Xers is when bosses publicly avow participatory management but then cling to their old hierarchical ways. Says Megan Wheeler, 31, who has started her own software company in San Diego: "At the other places I worked they would tell you that you could have input into all these choices about hardware and software, but when it came down to the final decision, it didn't matter at all."

20 This leaves a thick residue of cynicism among Xers that kicks in when their bosses seem to find God in nostrums such as Total Quality Management. The young employee of the Midwestern consulting firm recalls, "A couple of weeks ago we rolled out a group vision and mission statement. Then the partner asked us what we thought. I mean, what did she expect us to say? I was sitting there thinking, You know, it's a miracle you're getting paid for this."

21 Put it all together and you can get some pretty disaffected people. "In the Eighties there was a lot of this same silliness, but at least you could earn a lot of money," says Deroy Murdock, 29, who in 1991 was laid off from ad agency Ogilvy & Mather in New York and has since prospered as an independent marketing and media consultant. "Today, with wage stagnation the way it is, people's patience for nonsense has hit the floor."

22 What Xers don't see is that the same economic distress is often the source of what they perceive as doltish boomer behavior. Consultant Regan says that in a focus group of boomer managers, participants admitted that the advent of downsizing as the new corporate religion had made them so obsessed with keeping their jobs that career development for employees had gone out the window. "They weren't proud of it," Regan says. "From their perspective it has to do with the struggle for survival. They feel the pyramid was flattened and that they won't get the same opportunities as the people before them. At the same time, they don't feel the freedom that the twentysomethings have."

23 Margey Hillman, 44, director of multimedia programs for an educational software firm in San Diego, agrees that the fear among her boomer colleagues is palpable—and that much of it is focused on their twentysomething employees. "Middle management is middle-aged, and we're scared," Hillman says. "A lot of us have been sitting on our asses for ten years. We don't know how to do whatever it is we did to get where we are in the first place, and we've let our skills wither. Now, along come these young people who not only know how to do what middle managers do and are current on the technology, they have no respect for middle managers and they won't tolerate us not doing it."

24 But don't give Xers credit for too much insight. Hillman says their complaints about politics and what seem to be arbitrary, control-freak decisions by boomer managers are based on what she calls "smart innocence"—a nice way of saying twentysomethings are naive. "Say you've been on the job for a year or two, and there's an argument over the kind of software package you're going to use for something." Hillman explains. "The younger worker doesn't know that the reason you're using a particular program is because the president of the company is sleeping with the president of another company. You're not going to explain this to them, so they say, 'This other package will help me work two to three times faster,' and I end up saying, 'We're going to use this other one because I picked it.' "

25 The boomers also give voice to the age-old complaint heard every time a new crop of youngsters enters the workplace: that those whippersnappers aren't patiently learning how the game is played—or waiting their turn. Either they come into a company and expect that, in short order, they should be running it, or they always seem to be looking for something better to come along and are thus disloyal. Says Barry Horowitz, 46, director of international transportation at Nike in Portland, Oregon: "You have to be prepared to start at the bottom. People coming out of college today think they don't have to start at the bottom and work their way through the system."

26 What's different this time is that it appears to Xers—and pretty much everyone else—that lifetime employment is a thing of the past. Therefore, twentysomethings ask, where will loyalty and dues-paying get us?

27 Consider Jason James, 26, who has been temping for a year on a technical support desk at an IBM subsidiary in Raleigh, North Carolina. His father has spent his career at the computer giant, but James

has no similar expectation. "There are career IBMers in my area being laid off, and they're shocked," says James, who graduated from the University of North Carolina. "They thought they had a job for life, and I don't get it. IBM only would give me a one-year job, so it's hard to be sympathetic. Maybe it's because I'm young—I'm able to adapt. I'm current on new technology, and I'm willing to work harder for less. They can get me for $13 an hour, while the full-time people make a lot more than that and get benefits, and some of them don't work as hard."

28 Faced with that lack of security and the prospect of working for bosses they can't stand, many twentysomethings figure it's simply better to take advantage of their youth and risk going it alone. Look at Megan Wheeler, the aforementioned programmer, and Aaron Singer, 25, who last year founded Ad Hoc Technologies, an educational software firm in La Jolla, California. With no capital beyond Singer's stripped-down Apple Macintosh SE, they got a consulting job and invested the proceeds in new equipment. They've taken in over $100,000 over the past year consulting for other companies while they work on their first product, an interactive CD-ROM-based game.

29 Singer hooked up with Wheeler, whom he knew from his childhood in Enid, Oklahoma, after poking around New York for two years looking for a job and doing stints as a computer consultant. Wheeler, an experienced software developer, started off her 20s as a professional ballet dancer in New York and Austin, Texas, then got into programming as her knees began to give out. Her previous job was as a $34,000-a-year programmer for another San Diego software developer. "Here it's not just a feeling that we're going to work," Singer says. "We're creating something that means a lot to us."

30 In a seedy neighborhood on the northwest side of Chicago, another young entrepreneur, Vincent Cobb, 27, works out of a converted loft that's also his apartment. Cobb's product is a foam-rubber, plastic-topped deskpad for the "mice" that are now standard equipment on most computers. His innovation is to cover them with art images such as Da Vinci's *Mona Lisa* or Van Gogh's *Starry Night.* After graduating from Miami University in Ohio, Cobb worked for a year selling computers at Nynex Business Centers and then for an outfit that makes scheduling software.

31 "If Michael Dell hadn't started his business out of his dorm room in college, he would have shortly after he had gone to work and gotten

a taste of what corporate life is like," says Cobb of Dell Computer's wunderkind 28-year-old CEO and founder, the ultimate icon for Xer entrepreneurs. "It's frustrating trying to launch a business, but it's better than working for a big company that's boring, dry, dull, and conservative, or for a small company that's stifling."

32 Smart managers will see that taking what Xers say seriously not only will promote generational comity in the workplace but may also give companies a competitive edge. Consultant David Cannon says, "The fact is that Generation X is very well built for the organization of today. A company that gets into new products and does things differently is exhilarating to younger people."

33 One approach to harnessing twentysomethings' energy is to create an entrepreneurial environment in which they can thrive. At Hewlett-Packard in Sunnyvale, California, 30-year-old marketer Laura Demmons is a lead member of a so-called garage team that's developing a communications product to be launched in early 1994. Under the garage concept HP acts as a venture capitalist, in this case giving the team a $4 million budget—and virtually complete autonomy.

34 Demmons says her road hasn't been pothole-free. "The older managers look at us as these young whippersnappers. I was frustrated. I felt like I could run circles around the managers, and I was doing it for less than half the money. I was going to leave for a startup when the vice president of the group called me in. I told him, 'I don't fit in here.' And he said, 'But you do fit in here,' and I was offered this garage opportunity." After extensive focus-group research, Demmons and her teammates formulated a business plan for "a really hot communications software product."

35 Still, Demmons ran into trouble when the manager to whom she nominally reports, 38-year-old Kevin Schofield, tried to bring her back under his control. "Kevin was kind of stuck in the old hierarchy. But I can just see him. It's like, I was this creature. I didn't want to be mean to him, but I just wanted a field to run in," says Demmons, who counts horseback riding among her hobbies. The situation was fixed by restoring her autonomy, and Demmons says Schofield "in hindsight, has been one of my biggest supporters." For his part, Schofield says, "To the extent there are frustrations, I understand them. That's why we're doing things that are different." Demmons's conclusion: "This product is so good. It's more than just the money that's important—it's the ownership question. It's like, please let me do this job. There are so many young people who are so good at what they do."

36 The bottom line with twentysomethings is that they'll respond if boomer managers put meaning into the buzzwords they're prone to mouthing—empowerment, teamwork, communication. "You have to have two-way communication to be successful," says Cathy Sigismonti, a 28-year-old marketing analyst at IVAC, a San Diego division of Eli Lilly that makes medical devices. "If you're asking me to do something and you tell me why you need it and what you're going to use it for, maybe I can figure out a way to do it faster," Sigismonti says. "And if I tell you that what you're asking is going to take 100 hours, then maybe you'll decide you don't need it after all."

37 Feedback and recognition are other no-brainers that Xers say their boomer managers too often overlook. Says Sigismonti, her finger tapping on a table for emphasis: "Tell me that I did a good job. Let me know." Adds John Doyle, a 31-year-old San Diego programmer: "We want recognition because when we were growing up the family unit wasn't very strong. It can be financial or something else. At a company event, it could be just pointing someone out and saying their name."

38 Xers bring a different set of values to the workplace, values that in many ways are a reaction to the workaholism they associate with their older boomer brethren. Says Margaret Regan: "In my employee surveys, the factors that predict job satisfaction among people in their 20s is that it be a fun place to work." The peril of an un-fun workplace is that Xer employees will consider their jobs no more than a paycheck and will clock out regularly at 5 o'clock, when the real fun begins for them. Says Scott Hess, a 27-year-old Chicago marketing writer: "The god we're worshipping is not the bottom line—it's quality of life."

39 The moral of this tale is that feeling threatened by Generation X and tightening up is the worst possible reaction for a boomer manager to have toward younger employees. Yes, we kids are impetuous, naive, and just a tad arrogant—and that's why we need smart but sensitive boomer managers who can smooth our rough edges while channeling our enthusiasm. Ally yourself with us while you can—or don't be surprised if, one day, you're asking one of *us* for work.

Understanding Meaning

1. What does Rataan see as the principal differences between "busters" and "boomers"? Why do young people feel less animosity toward their grandparents' generation?
2. How do "busters" view the generation of the 1960s?

3. What role does technology play in the conflict?
4. *Critical Thinking:* How much of the conflict appears rooted in current political and economic conditions, and how much is caused by the age-old differences between young people coming into adulthood and those with decades of experience and greater responsibilities?

Evaluating Strategy

1. What is the impact of the title? Does using words like "buster" and "boomer" serve to attract attention? Does it risk trivializing the subject?
2. How does Rataan use brief *narratives* to advance the comparisons between young and old?
3. Where does Rataan employ *cause and effect* to provide reasons for differences between the generations?

Appreciating Language

1. What is the tone of the article? What role does word choice play in establishing the author's attitude?
2. Would you suggest revising and rewording this article if it were to be submitted to an academic journal? If so, what words would you alter?

Connections across the Disciplines

1. Compare this article to William Ouchi's (page 270). What do these essays reveal about the issues managers and employers face in supervising personnel?
2. Review Lisa Fried's article "A New Breed of Entrepreneur—Women" (page 368). Does the generation gap between "busters" and "boomers" have special significance for women?

Writing Suggestions

1. Write a brief essay about your own experiences with supervisors, professors, and bosses. How many conflicts or disagreements do you believe were caused by generational differences? Would a boss your own age or younger behave differently?
2. *Collaborative Writing:* Work with a group of students and discuss the "boomer"/"buster" conflict. If possible, try to get younger and older students included in your group. Discuss the issues raised by Rataan. Then draft a short analysis, comparing your group's observations to Rataan's.

WRITING BEYOND THE CLASSROOM

PEGGY KENNA
AND SONDRA LACY

Peggy Kenna and Sondra Lacy are communications specialists based in Arizona who work with foreign-born employees. In addition, they provide cross-cultural training to executives conducting international business. Kenna is a speech and language pathologist who specializes in accent modification. Kenna and Lacy have collaborated on a series of fifty-page booklets that compare American and foreign business organizations, habits, behaviors, and negotiating styles. Widely sold in airports, these booklets give Americans tips on doing business overseas.

Communication Styles: United States and Taiwan

This section from Business Taiwan *contrasts American and Taiwanese styles of communicating. In designing their booklets for quick skimming, Kenna and Lacy use charts to highlight cultural differences.*

1	UNITED STATES	TAIWAN
2	• ***Frank***	• ***Subtle***
3	Americans tend to be very straightforward and unreserved. The people of Taiwan often find them abrupt and not interested enough in human relationships.	Frankness is not appreciated by the people of Taiwan. They particularly dislike unqualified negative statements.
4	• ***Face saving less important***	• ***Face saving important***
5	To Americans accuracy is important but errors are tolerated. Admitting mistakes is seen as a sign of maturity. They believe you learn from failure and therefore encourage some risk taking.	The Chinese do not like to be put in the position of having to admit a mistake or failure. They also do not like to tell you when they don't understand your point.
6		You also should not admit too readily when you don't know something as it can cause you to lose face.
7	Americans believe criticism can be objective and not personal, however, all criticism should be done with tact.	

8	UNITED STATES	TAIWAN
9	• ***Direct eye contact***	• ***Avoid direct eye contact***
10	Direct eye contact is very important to Americans since they need to see the nonverbal cues the speaker is giving. Nonverbal cues are a very important part of the American English language. Americans use intermittent eye contact when they are speaking but fairly steady eye contact when they are listening.	Holding the gaze of another person is considered rude.
11	• ***Direct and to the point***	• ***Indirect and ambiguous***
12	Americans prefer people to say what they mean. Because of this they tend to sometimes miss subtle nonverbal cues. Americans are uncomfortable with ambiguousness and don't like to have to "fill in the blanks." They also tend to	People in Taiwan dislike saying "no." They may not tell you when they don't understand. They often hedge their answers if they know you won't like the answer. If they say something like, "We'll think about it," they may mean they aren't interested.
13	discuss problems directly.	They dislike discussing problems directly and will often go around the issue which can be frustrating for Americans.
14		The Chinese language (Mandarin) is so concise that the listener needs to use much imagination to "fill in the gaps."
15	• ***"Yes" means agreement***	• ***"Yes" means "I hear"***
16	Americans look for clues such as nodding of the head, a verbal "yes" or "uh huh" in order to determine if their arguments are succeeding.	People in Taiwan do not judge information given to them so they do not indicate agreement or disagreement; they only nod or say "yes" to indicate they are listening to you. The people of Taiwan believe politeness is more important than frankness so they will not directly tell you "no." The closest they will come to "no" is "maybe."

Understanding Meaning

1. What appear to be the major differences between American and Taiwanese methods of communicating?
2. Why is it important for Americans to be sensitive about making direct eye contact with Taiwanese?
3. How do Americans and Taiwanese accept failure?
4. *Critical Thinking:* Why would this booklet be valuable to Americans visiting Taiwan on business? Does such a brief, to-the-point guide risk relying on stereotypes?

Evaluating Strategy

1. How easy is this document to read and review? How accessible would the information be if it were written in standard paragraphs?
2. What does the directness of the document reveal about the intended audience? Would it be suitable for a college classroom?

Appreciating Language

1. What language do the writers use in describing the Taiwanese? Do they attempt to be neutral, or does their word choice favor one nationality over another?
2. Kenna and Lacy suggest that many Taiwanese find Americans to be "abrupt." Is this a good word choice? Does the guide express common prejudices?

Connections across the Disciplines

1. Compare Kenna and Lacy's observations with those stated in Yi-Fu Tuan's "Chinese Space, American Space" (page 244) and William Ouchi's "Japanese and American Workers" (page 270). Do these authors make similar observations about American attitudes and behaviors?
2. Review Amy Tan's article "The Language of Discretion" (page 277). How do her insights into the differences between English and Chinese explain differences in communication styles?

Writing Suggestions

1. Using William Ouchi's article about Japanese and American workers (page 270), write a similar chart to Kenna and Lacy's outlining national

differences in work habits and attitudes. Demonstrate how Japanese and American workers differ on issues of leadership, individuality, communications, and attitudes toward success.

2. Develop a chart outlining the differences between two groups of students, workers, professors, or employers you have known. Suggest to readers how to best communicate with each group.

GUIDELINES FOR WRITING COMPARISON AND CONTRAST

1. **Determine your purpose.** Is your goal to explain differences between two topics or to recommend one over the other? Do you want readers to be informed, or do you wish them to make a choice?
2. **Consider your audience.** Before you can compare two items, you may have to explain background information. Before comparing two treatments for arthritis, it may be necessary to explain the nature of the disease and to define basic terminology.
3. **Determine which method would best suit your topic.** A short, nontechnical paper might be best organized using the subject-by-subject method. Longer works with facts and statistics that should be placed side by side are better developed using the point-by-point method.
4. **Make use of transitional statements.** To prevent confusion in writing comparison, use transitional statements carefully. You may wish to invent labels or titles to clearly distinguish the different subjects you are examining.
5. **Use visual aids to guide your readers.** Careful paragraphing, page breaks, bold or italic headings, and charts can help readers follow your comparison and prevent confusion.

SUGGESTED TOPICS FOR COMPARISON AND CONTRAST WRITING

General Assignments

Write a comparative paper on one of the following topics. You may use either subject-by-subject or point-by-point methods of organization. Clearly determine your purpose. Is your goal to inform or recommend?

- High school versus college
- Your best and worst jobs
- Male and female student attitudes on dating/marriage/career/parenting
- The two most influential teachers you have known
- Two popular situation comedies
- Two computer programs you have worked with
- Your best and worst college courses
- Your parents' values and your own

- Two campus political organizations
- Two popular entertainers

Writing in Context

1. Imagine you have been asked by a British newsmagazine to write an article explaining the pro-and-con attitudes Americans have about a controversial topic such as gun control, capital punishment, or affirmative action. Your article should be balanced and objective and provide background information rather than express an opinion.
2. Write the text for a brief pamphlet directed to high school seniors comparing high school and college. You may wish to use a chartlike format.
3. Write a letter to a friend comparing the best and worst aspects of your college, dorm room, community, or job.
4. Examine a magazine on cars, computers, or entertainment. Write a letter to the editor comparing the magazine's best and worst features.
5. Compare two popular student clubs or restaurants for a review in the campus newspaper. Direct your comments to students interested in inexpensive entertainment.

COMPARISON AND CONTRAST CHECKLIST

1. Are your subjects closely related enough to make a valid comparison?
2. Have you identified the key points of both subjects?
3. Have you selected the best method of organizing your paper?
4. Is the comparison easy to follow? Are transitions clear and consistent?
5. Does the comparison meet reader needs and expectations?
6. Have you defined terms or provided background information needed by readers to understand the comparison?

6

Analysis

MAKING EVALUATIONS

WHAT IS ANALYSIS?

Analysis moves beyond description and narration to make judgments or evaluations about persons, places, objects, ideas, or situations. A movie reviewer *describes* a new film and then *analyzes* it—critiquing the plot, acting, special effects, and social message. A historian *narrates* an event and then *evaluates* its lasting significance. Marketing executives *summarize* sales reports to *judge* the results of their advertising campaign. A psychiatrist *examines* a patient and then *diagnoses* the individual's mental condition.

Analysis often seeks to answer questions. Does aspirin prevent heart attacks? What are Vicki Shimi's chances for being elected governor? Is General Motor's new minivan fuel efficient? Does America have too many lawyers? Is addiction a disease? How effective were the poverty programs launched in the 1960s? What is the best way to remove asbestos from a public school? Is a defendant mentally competent to stand trial? Is the central figure of *Death of a Salesman*, Willy Loman, a victim of society or of his own delusions? The answers to all these questions require a careful gathering of information, critical thinking, and a clear presentation of the writer's thesis.

Analysis entails more than expressing an opinion or creating an impression. In an analytical paper, you cannot simply write, "I hated *Streetcar Named Desire* because it was stupid," or "Welfare programs waste taxpayers' money." You must base your positions on observations and evidence. Why is the play stupid? What facts demonstrate that welfare programs are wasteful? When asked to write analytical papers, students often supply description and narration, summarizing a short story or describing a social problem. To keep your paper analytical, you can use the journalists' "five W's"—*Who? What? When? Where? Why?*—to develop your thesis. By answering questions, you are forced to find evidence and provide answers instead of simply retelling a story or describing a situation.

Subjective and Objective Analysis

The way writers develop analytical writing depends greatly on context. In many situations, writers rely wholly on personal observation and experience. Film critics, political columnists, book reviewers, fashion consultants, and social commentators tend to write subjective analysis. *Subjective analysis* is based on close observation and careful interpretation. The writer's points are supported by examples and illustrations he or she has chosen rather than by research. Subjective analysis is informed opinion. In a newspaper column, "The Handicap of Definition" (page 320), William Raspberry analyzes the negative impact of the popular definition of "blackness" accepted by many African American children:

> What we have here is a tragically limited definition of blackness, and it isn't only white people who buy it.
>
> Think of all the ways black children can put one another down with charges of "whiteness." For many of these children, hard study and hard work are "white." Trying to please a teacher might be criticized as acting "white." Speaking correct English is "white." Scrimping today in the interest of tomorrow's goals is "white." Educational toys and games are "white."
>
> An incredible array of habits and attitudes that are conducive to success in business, in academia, in the nonentertainment professions are likely to be thought of as somehow "white." Even economic success, unless it involves such "black" undertakings as numbers banking, is defined as "white."
>
> And the results are devastating.

After analyzing how children label activities as being "black" or "white," Raspberry explains how limited definitions lead to limited opportunities. Raspberry's article, written for a general audience, makes conclusions, although it provides no independent research such as surveys or interviews.

Objective analysis begins with close observations but seeks to answer questions through factual research. In objective analysis, the writer needs more than personal experience and anecdotal examples to support a position. In writing about female entrepreneurs, Lisa Fried cites government studies documenting the growth of female-owned enterprises:

> From 1980 to 1986, the number of women owning small-business sole proprietorships—those with 500 employees or less—increased by almost 63 percent to more than 4 million. During the same period, the growth rate for male owners was 35 percent. And with women owning 30 percent of all small-business sole proprietorships by 1986, women have clearly become a driving force in the economy.

The methods writers use in collecting information is important in objective analysis. After presenting statistics about the increase of female-owned businesses, Lisa Fried explains the research methods used for her magazine article:

> *Management Review* set out to get a closer look at this new breed of entrepreneurs. We interviewed women who head up businesses in the broadcasting, wine making, advertising, computer consulting and photography industries. Their visions for their companies, career motivations and management styles may surprise you.

The blending of statistics and personal interviews strengthens her analysis because her conclusions are drawn from more than one source of information.

The way writers develop their analytical writing is often influenced by their readers and their discipline. A widely respected restaurant critic will review a new cafe in wholly personal and subjective terms. But an engineer analyzing the structure of a hurricane-damaged bridge will use standard tests and procedures and will only provide conclusions clearly supported by scientific findings and observable detail. Kimberly Crawford, an attorney, analyzes the admissibility of surreptitious recordings of suspects by strictly studying Supreme Court rulings. Suppose the police arrest a man suspected of a bank robbery and place him in a cell with an officer posing as a fellow criminal. The officer engages the suspect in conversation, leading him to boast of his robbery. Could a recording of this admission be admitted as evidence in court, even though the fifth amendment of the Constitution protects citizens from self-incrimination? Crawford provides this analysis of the Constitution's guarantee against self-incrimination:

> To be successful, a challenge to the admissibility of surreptitiously recorded conversations based on the fifth amendment self-incrimination clause would have to establish that the conversations in question were the product of unlawful custodial interrogation. Because statements made to individuals not known to the defendant as government actors do not normally amount to interrogation for purposes of the fifth amendment, this challenge is destined to fail.

Crawford is writing strictly as a legal analyst of the Constitution. A defense attorney concerned with defendant rights or an ethicist might analyze this issue in moral rather than legal terms.

Detailed Observation

Analysis requires close observation, critical thinking, and in some instances outside research. If you have not read Samuel Scudder's "Take This Fish and Look at It" (page 41), you might wish to review it. This essay demonstrates the value of close observation. Good analysis cannot rely on first impressions. Before you can analyze a short story or a poem, you will have to read the work several times. If you are thinking of evaluating how women are depicted in television commercials, you may wish to videotape two or three evenings' worth of commercials and watch them several times rather than relying on memory. The more you observe about your subject, the more likely you will move from superficial observation to detecting details you may have previously overlooked.

CRITICAL THINKING FOR WRITING ANALYSIS

Analytical writing can be challenging. Even the best writers often fall into common traps called *logical fallacies* and make errors in judgment.

Following these guidelines can help you improve your analytical writing skills:

1. **Ask questions to avoid summarizing.** The most common error students make is mistaking summary or description for analysis. Asking questions such as *why?* or *who?* can help you avoid simply retelling the plot of a story rather than analyzing it. For example, before starting to write an analysis of Hemingway's short story "Hills Like White Elephants," you might develop questions. Answering a question such as "Who is the stronger character, the man or the girl?" will guide you toward evaluating the story rather than supplying a two-page summary.
2. **Limit the scope of your analysis.** Unless you are willing to devote months to research, it would be difficult to gather sufficient material to fully analyze a subject such as day-care centers. You might restrict your topic to day-care centers in one neighborhood or focus commentary on a single issue such as licensing requirements.
3. **Evaluate sources for bias.** If you were analyzing the use of animals in medical research, you would not want to base your judgments solely on information from an animal rights group. When evaluating controversial subjects, you may be unable to obtain objective information, but you can achieve a measure of balance by examining data provided by organizations with opposing viewpoints.
4. **Apply common standards.** Analyzing data from different sources will be accurate only if all the sources have the same standards and definitions. If you were analyzing juvenile delinquency, you might face a problem of examining studies if each has a different definition of just who is a delinquent.
5. **Distinguish between opinion and fact.** Opinions are judgments or inferences, not facts. Facts are reliable pieces of information that can be verified by studying other sources:

   OPINION: John Smith is an alcoholic.
   FACT: John Smith drinks two martinis at lunch and frequents nightclubs on weekends.

   The factual statement relies on observation. The judgment of alcoholism is based on limited evidence and probably requires more support.
6. **Avoid hasty generalizations.** Generalizations should be based on adequate information, not a few instances that you may find dramatic or interesting. The fact that two friends had purses stolen in the Student Union last week and that your car was broken into this morning does not mean the college is in the grip of a crime wave. You would have to examine several months of police reports to determine if an actual increase in campus crime has occurred.

7. **Consider alternative interpretations.** Facts do not always indicate what they imply at first glance. A rise in reported cases of child abuse may not indicate increasing violence against children but instead better reporting. If a school has a low retention rate, does that indicate it is failing to address the needs of students or that it instead maintains such rigorous standards that only the best students graduate?
8. **Avoid "filtering" data.** If you begin with a preconceived thesis, you may consciously or unconsciously select evidence that supports your view and omit evidence that contradicts it. Good analysis is objective; it does not consist of simply collecting facts to support a previously held conviction.
9. **Do not assume parts represent the whole.** Just because one or more patients respond favorably to a new drug does not mean that it will cure all people suffering from the same disease. In the extreme, because individual men and women die does not mean the human race will eventually become extinct.
10. **Do not assume the whole represents each part.** If 50 percent of students on campus receive financial aid, it does not mean you can assume that half the English majors receive aid. The student population in any given department may be less or more than the college average.
11. **Avoid reasoning on false analogies.** Analogy or comparison essays often provide weak evidence because they overlook that no two situations are exactly alike. Avoid assuming, for example, that results from a study conducted in Japan provide valid evidence for researchers in the United States. Because airbags have been proven to save lives in car accidents does not mean they should be installed in airplanes.

READING ANALYSIS

As you read the analysis entries in this chapter, keep the following questions in mind.

Meaning

1. What is the author's purpose—to provide a personal opinion or an evaluation based on standard research methods?
2. What discipline is the writer operating in? What kinds of evidence and what analytical methods are presented?
3. Does the writer present sources for his or her information?
4. What does the original source of the entry indicate about the intended audience and discipline?
5. What is the most significant conclusion the author draws?

Strategy

1. Does the writer rely on close observation, surveys, statistics, or expert testimony?
2. How were the data collected? Does the writer cite sources and supply footnotes?
3. Did the writer consider alternative interpretations?
4. Does the entry appear to be biased? Does the writer present facts to support a preconceived theory?
5. Does the writer avoid the logical fallacies?

Language

1. Do the author's choice of words and use of connotations indicate bias?
2. What language does the writer use in discussing people or organizations that hold different beliefs?
3. Are standard terms defined?

WILLIAM RASPBERRY

William Raspberry was born in Mississippi and began his journalism career as a photographer and reporter for the Indianapolis Recorder *in 1956. In 1962 he began working for the* Washington Post. *He received the Capital Press Club's Journalist of the Year Award in 1965 for his coverage of the Watts riot in Los Angeles. In 1971 Raspberry began an urban affairs column for the* Washington Post *that has been nationally syndicated since 1977. William Raspberry was awarded the Pulitzer Prize for Distinguished Commentary in 1994.*

The Handicap of Definition

In this Washington Post *article Raspberry analyzes the effect the definition of "blackness" has on African American children. Typically, stereotypes are viewed as limiting definitions imposed on people. Raspberry suggests that in many instances young African Americans accept negative stereotypes that limit their opportunities.*

1 I know all about bad schools, mean politicians, economic deprivation and racism. Still, it occurs to me that one of the heaviest burdens black Americans—and black children in particular—have to bear is the handicap of definition: the question of what it means to be black.

2 Let me explain quickly what I mean. If a basketball fan says that the Boston Celtics' Larry Bird plays "black," the fan intends it—and Bird probably accepts it—as a compliment. Tell pop singer Tom Jones he moves "black" and he might grin in appreciation. Say to Teena Marie or the Average White Band that they sound "black" and they'll thank you.

3 But name one pursuit, aside from athletics, entertainment or sexual performance, in which a white practitioner will feel complimented to be told he does it "black." Tell a white broadcaster he talks "black" and he'll sign up for diction lessons. Tell a white reporter he writes "black" and he'll take a writing course. Tell a white lawyer he reasons "black" and he might sue you for slander.

4 What we have here is a tragically limited definition of blackness, and it isn't only white people who buy it.

5 Think of all the ways black children can put one another down with charges of "whiteness." For many of these children, hard study and hard work are "white." Trying to please a teacher might be criticized as acting "white." Speaking correct English is "white." Scrimping today in the interest of tomorrow's goals is "white." Educational toys and games are "white."

6 An incredible array of habits and attitudes that are conducive to success in business, in academia, in the nonentertainment professions are likely to be thought of as somehow "white." Even economic success, unless it involves such "black" undertakings as numbers banking, is defined as "white."

7 And the results are devastating. I wouldn't deny that blacks often are better entertainers and athletes. My point is the harm that comes from too narrow a definition of what is black.

8 One reason black youngsters tend to do better at basketball, for instance, is that they assume they can learn to do it well, and so they practice constantly to prove themselves right.

9 Wouldn't it be wonderful if we could infect black children with the notion that excellence in math is "black" rather than white, or possibly Chinese? Wouldn't it be of enormous value if we could create the myth that morality, strong families, determination, courage and love of learning are traits brought by slaves from Mother Africa and therefore quintessentially black?

10 There is no doubt in my mind that most black youngsters could develop their mathematical reasoning, their elocution and their attitudes the way they develop their jump shots and their dance steps: by the combination of sustained, enthusiastic practice and the unquestioned belief that they can do it.

11 In one sense, what I am talking about is the importance of developing positive ethnic traditions. Maybe Jews have an innate talent for communication; maybe the Chinese are born with a gift for mathematical reasoning; maybe blacks are naturally blessed with athletic grace. I doubt it. What is at work, I suspect, is assumption, inculcated early in their lives, that this is a thing our people do well.

12 Unfortunately, many of the things about which blacks make this assumption are things that do not contribute to their career success—except for that handful of the truly gifted who can make it as entertainers and athletes. And many of the things we concede to whites are the things that are essential to economic security.

13 So it is with a number of assumptions black youngsters make about what it is to be a "man": physical aggressiveness, sexual prowess, the refusal to submit to authority. The prisons are full of people who, by this perverted definition, are unmistakably men.

14 But the real problem is not so much that the things defined as "black" are negative. The problem is that the definition is much too narrow.

15 Somehow, we have to make our children understand that they are intelligent, competent people, capable of doing whatever they put their minds to and making it in the American mainstream, not just in a black subculture.

16 What we seem to be doing, instead, is raising up yet another generation of young blacks who will be failures—by definition.

Understanding Meaning

1. What kind of analysis does Raspberry provide?
2. What do readers expect in a personal column? What standards for gathering and studying data do they require?
3. According to the author, how does the definition of "blackness," internalized by many young African Americans, affect the development of many children?
4. *Critical Thinking:* Does Raspberry ignore other definitions of "blackness" encountered by African American children, such as black literature they read in school and black politicians they see on television? If so, does it affect his thesis?

Evaluating Strategy

1. Raspberry opens his essay by briefly referring to other burdens hampering the success of African American children. Why is this important?
2. What evidence does Raspberry provide readers to support his views?
3. *Other Modes:* How does Raspberry *define* popular concepts of "blackness"? How does he use *comparison* to other ethnic groups to illustrate how definitions shape people's self-concept?

Appreciating Language

1. How does Raspberry use connotations to shape his analysis?

2. Raspberry talks of an idea to "infect" black children and create a "myth" that morality is a "black" value. What is the impact of this language?

Connections across the Disciplines

1. How did Miss Bessie, Carl Rowan's teacher, help African American children overcome negative stereotypes (page 122)?
2. Review Edward Dolnick's article about deafness as culture (page 214). Should deaf children define themselves as members of a cultural minority or as victims of a disease?

Writing Suggestions

1. Look back on your own childhood, and write a brief essay describing how you came to define yourself. Then analyze how it helped or hindered your development.
2. Write an essay analyzing how stereotyped attitudes have led women, the elderly, the disabled, or others to define themselves.
3. *Collaborative Writing:* Working in a group of students, write your own lists of behaviors defined as "black," "white," "Asian," "male," or "female." Discuss these definitions, and then draft a short analysis of your views and experiences.

BETSY HILBERT

Betsy Hilbert (1941–) grew up in Miami and earned degrees from the University of Miami. In 1976 she received a doctorate from the Union Graduate School. She began her teaching career at Miami-Dade Community College in the 1960s, where she now serves as chair of the Independent Studies Department. A specialist in women's nature writing, she has advocated that environmental studies be included in college humanities programs. In 1990 she published a bibliography of women nature writers that brought attention to many previously neglected authors. In addition to scholarly research, Hilbert has written several nature articles for magazines such as North American Review.

Disturbing the Universe

In this essay Hilbert questions whether human beings can intervene in nature without causing harm. Can even the most well-intentioned actions by environmentalists have negative consequences?

1 Five thirty A.M.; the parking lot of Crandon Park is deserted. An empty plastic drinking cup crunches under the tires as we pull in. Nothing seems worth doing in the world this early. Ute and I climb groggily out of the car. Then the dawn blazes up out over the ocean, rose and gold across the sky. Everything has its compensations.

2 The beach is still in shadow under the brightening sky, and the dim figures of the morning cleanup crew make a clatter among the trash bins. The two of us are on a cleanup of a different kind this morning, amid the beachwrack and the crumpled potato-chip bags.

3 "Seen anything?" my partner calls to one of the crew further down the beach, who is slamming a trash can with particular vengeance.

4 "*No, Señora,*" a voice drifts back, in the soft, mixed-ethnic accents of Miami. "*No tortugas* today."

5 Actually, we don't want the turtles themselves; it is turtle eggs we're looking for, in their night-laid nests along this populous beach. Our job is to find and rescue the eggs of endangered loggerhead turtles, and to move them to a fenced area nearby maintained by the local Audubon Society, where the hatchlings can be safe from the picnick-

ers and the beach-cleaning machines, and other dangers inherent on a public beach.

6 We begin our long walk south, where miles ahead the condominiums of Key Biscayne loom in the pale light. Pity the sea turtle who tries to climb their seawalls, or dig her nest in a carefully landscaped patch of St. Augustine grass. A series of grunts and swishes erupts behind us, as an early-morning beach jogger huffs past.

7 Ute's practiced strides take her up the beach almost faster than I can follow, distracted as I am by the pelican practicing hang-gliding in the morning air and the rippled sand in the tidal shallows. She stops suddenly, taking a soft breath, and I rush up to look. Leading upward from the high-water mark is a long, two-ridged scrape, balanced on either side by the zig-zag series of close, rounded alternating prints. Turtle crawl. Has she nested? Like all good predators, we sniff around a bit before deciding where to dig.

8 Just below the high dunes, in a circular patch about six feet across, the sand has been conspicuously flailed around. She has tried to discourage nest-robbers not by camouflage or hiding, but by leaving too much notice; the disturbed area is so big, and digging in the packed sand so difficult, that the attempt would discourage hunters with less sense of mission than we have. We could poke a sharp stick into the sand until it came up sticky with egg white, as is the traditional technique throughout the Caribbean, but that would damage eggs we are trying to protect. Nothing to do but start digging.

9 Beneath the turbulence of the dry top sand, the rough, damp subsurface scrapes against the skin of our hands. We run our fingers across the hard sand, hoping to find a soft spot. When no depression becomes apparent—this time it isn't going to be easy—we hand-dig trenches at intervals across the area. Sometimes it takes an hour or more of digging before the nest is found; sometimes there are no eggs at all.

10 In my third trench, about four inches down, there is a lump that doesn't feel like rock or shell. A smooth white surface appears, and another next to it and slightly lower. The eggs look exactly like ping-pong balls, little white spheres, but the shell is soft and flexible. With infinite care, I lift the little balls out as Ute counts them, then place them in a plastic container, trying always to keep them in the same position they were laid. Turtle embryos bond to the shells, and turning the eggs as we rebury them might put the infants in the wrong position, with catastrophic results.

11 One hundred fourteen little worlds come out of their flask-shaped, smooth-sided nest. The eggs are spattered lightly with sand, and my probing fingers hit patches of sticky wetness among them, apparently some kind of lubricating fluid from the mother. The surprising softness of the shells make sense to me as I dig deeper; hard shells might have cracked as the eggs dropped onto one another.

12 Carrying the egg container to the reburying place, I am glowing like the sunrise with self-satisfaction. Savior of sea turtles, that's me. Defender of the endangered. Momma turtle would be very pleased that her babies were receiving such good care.

13 Or would she? I look down at the eggs in their plastic box, and realize that she'd regard me as just another predator, if she regarded me at all. That turtle, if we ever met, would be much more concerned about my species' taste for turtle meat than about my professed interest in her offspring. What would I be to her except another kind of nuisance? Perhaps the Mother of Turtles might respond as the Pigeon in *Alice in Wonderland* does when Alice tries to explain that she's not a snake, but a little girl: "No, no! You're a serpent; and there's no use denying it. I suppose you'll be telling me next that you never tasted an egg!"

14 What was I to these eggs but just another nest-robber? Did I really know the impact of my actions, the extended chain of events I was setting in motion? With present scientific knowledge, no human alive could chart the course of that one loggerhead as she found her way across the seas. Where she bred and slept, where her food came from, are still mysteries. Not only are there too few scientists searching for the answers, too little money for research, but ultimately there are "answers" we can probably never have. Our ways of knowing are species-locked, our understandings limited by human perceptual processes. I was a shadow on a dusky beach, groping in the dark for more than turtle eggs, digging, shoulder-deep, in holes not of my making.

15 Suppose we save these eggs, and the turtles that hatch return years later as hoped, to nest on this beach? This land will never be wild any more; the skyscrapers that rise across Biscayne Bay bear megalithic testimony that the future of South Florida is written in concrete. The beach, if preserved, will continue public, and pressured, one of a small number of recreation areas for an ever-growing number of people. So there will never be a time when these animals can live out their lives without the intervention of people like Ute and me. Like so much

else of nature now, the turtles of Crandon Park will be forever dependent on human action. Thanks to us, they are surviving; but thanks to us, they are also less than self-sufficient.

16 And why am I so convinced I'm actually doing good, anyway? Suppose more babies survive than can be supported by their environment, and next year there is a crash in their food supply, or that something we do, entirely unknowing, weakens the hatchlings so that their survival rate is actually lowered? Maybe we should just leave them alone. Maybe they would be better off taking their chances where their mothers first laid them, risking the raccoons and the beach parties.

17 None of us knows the final outcome of any action, the endless chain of ripples that we start with every movement. We walk in the world blindly, crashing into unidentified objects and tripping over rough edges. We human beings are too big for our spaces, too powerful for our understanding. What I do today will wash up somewhere far beyond my ability to know about it.

18 And yet, last year, five thousand new turtles were released from the Audubon compound, five thousand members of a threatened species, which would almost certainly not have been hatched otherwise. A friend who urged me to join the turtle project said that on a recent trip to Cape Sable in the Everglades he found at least fifteen nests on a short walk, every one of them dug up and destroyed by raccoons. Whatever chance these hundred fourteen embryos have, nestled inside their shells in the styrofoam cradle, is what we give them.

19 In *The Encantadas*, his description of what are now called the Galápagos Islands, Herman Melville depicted the sea tortoises of "dateless, indefinite endurance" which the crew of the whaling ship takes aboard. Melville pointed out that those who see only the bright undersides of the tortoises might swear the animal has no dark side, while those who have never turned the tortoise over would swear it is entirely "one total inky blot." "The tortoise is both black and bright," Melville cautioned. So, too, my morning beach walk has two sides, one purposeful, the other full of doubt.

20 Whatever my ambivalences may be, the eggs are still in my hands. Ute and I reach the hatchery enclosure and unlock the chain-link fence. We dig another hole as close in size and shape to the original as we can imitate, and then rebury our babies, brushing our doubts back into the hole with the sand. As we mark the location of the new nest with a circle of wire fencing, I am reminded that in the world today

there is no way, any more, not to do something. Even if despite our best efforts there will never again be any loggerhead turtles, even if the numbers of the people concerned are few and our knowledge pitifully limited, even if we sometimes do unconscious harm in trying to do good, we no longer have the option of inaction. The universe is already disturbed, disturbed by more than my presence on an early-morning beach, with the sunlight glinting off the blue-tiled hotel swimming pools. While the choice is mine, I choose to walk.

Understanding Meaning

1. How did Hilbert seek to rescue the turtle eggs? What endangered them?
2. How does Hilbert view her role? Why does she become ambivalent about her actions?
3. What care do Hilbert and her companion exert in rescuing the eggs? What does this reveal about their knowledge of the turtles?
4. Do humans endanger the turtle eggs any more than ravenous raccoons?
5. What does Hilbert mean when she states, "We human beings are too big for our spaces, too powerful for our understanding"?
6. *Critical Thinking:* Does Hilbert seem to view humans as being alien to nature, apart from other animals who affect the environment? Can beachfront construction be compared to the destructive actions of wildlife?

Evaluating Strategy

1. Does the title "Disturbing the Universe" suit Hilbert's actions? How does it dramatize her point?
2. *Other Modes:* Where does Hilbert use *comparison* to develop her analysis?

Appreciating Language

1. What do words like "predator" and "savior" suggest about how Hilbert views her role?
2. Underline the words Hilbert uses to describe animal and human behaviors. Do you detect a bias?

Writing Suggestions

1. Analyze an environmental program you are familiar with for negative side effects. Recycling paper, for example, requires the use of dangerous

chemicals and produces tons of toxic waste. Write a brief essay outlining the harmful effects of well-intentioned programs. Can any human activity be free of harm?

2. *Collaborative Writing:* Discuss Hilbert's comment that "even if we sometimes do unconscious harm in trying to do good, we no longer have the option of inaction" with a group of students. Can this comment apply to all acts to improve living conditions? Does legislation seeking to curb fraud, discrimination, pollution, or crime injure innocent parties? Does the notion of "the greater good" justify penalizing a few individuals? Record comments from the members, and write a short analysis of their views. If members disagree, consider writing several short statements clearly stating their views.

JOEL CONNELLY

Joel Connelly is the national correspondent for the Seattle Post Intelligencer. *In 1990 he wrote this essay for a special nature issue of* Aperture, *a photography magazine. Connelly analyzes the way environmentalists came to understand the power of visual images and use the media to project their concerns to the American public through photographs and videotapes.*

A Growing Awareness: Environmental Groups and the Media

In this essay Connelly provides several examples of how environmentalists have used dramatic images to influence the public and conduct what he calls "visual lobbying."

1 A half century ago, Mao Zedong taught his followers that political power grows out of the barrel of a gun. In the world of the 1990s, however, political and societal change flow through the lens of a camera. Environmentalists learned this lesson long ago. These days the "green lobby" packs political clout in many countries. In its infancy, however, the movement found that the only way to save species and preserve wild places was to arouse the public with visual images. Some of these images, both the brutal and the beautiful, will remain in our memories for a long time.

2 A pioneer in the use of visual images to alert the public to environmental threats was Dr. Fred Darvill, a Mt. Vernon, Washington, family doctor. Darvill was among the first to display images of sublime places followed by the horrors that awaited them. Over twenty years ago, Darvill flew to New York armed only with a painting of Image Lake, a 10,000-foot-high tarn in Washington's Glacier Peak Wilderness Area, some slides, and three shares in the Kennecott Copper Company. He was bound for the annual meeting of the multinational mining company, which proposed to build a half-mile-wide open-pit copper mine in the wilderness area. Kennecott had the legal right to do so, in the form of a mining claim that predated the Wilderness Act.

Darvill set out to test the company's will. "The Sierra Club had alerted the wire services," he recalls. "I showed the painting of Image Lake, and explained what a mine would do in the area. I mentioned that it would be so big it could be seen through a telescope from the moon."

3 The presentation received nationwide publicity. It also attracted the eye of David Brower, then executive director of the Sierra Club and a man who pioneered the use of visual images in conservation battles. A full-page ad appeared in the *New York Times* under the heading: "AN OPEN PIT LARGE ENOUGH THAT IT CAN BE SEEN FROM THE MOON." Readers were presented with a picture of alpine glory beside one of a gouged-out open-pit mine in Utah.

4 In the end Kennecott never touched the wilderness. Brower would later deploy the same sorts of imagery—in a style described by John McPhee as "Early Paul Revere"—to stop two planned dams in the Grand Canyon. Above a canyon sunset picture was the classic headline: "WOULD YOU FLOOD THE SISTINE CHAPEL SO TOURISTS COULD GET CLOSER TO THE CEILING?" The Sierra Club lost its tax-exempt status, but the Grand Canyon was saved. Congressman Morris Udall of Arizona later paid grudging tribute to Brower's genius for capturing public attention, and for stopping an unwise project that Udall at the time had supported.

5 A prime goal of conservationists, according to Brock Evans of the National Audubon Society, has been to nationalize and even internationalize key battles. "Visual images are the key for us," says Evans. "They've kept ancient forests standing and oil rigs out of the Arctic Refuge." Cameras connect the global village. Viewers thousands of miles away can watch pictures of thousand-year-old Sitka spruce trees falling under a logger's chain saw. They can see oil-covered otters being lifted from Prince William Sound. They can feel the fear of those on a Greenpeace Zodiac boat as Soviet whalers fire a harpoon over its bow to mortally wound one of the world's largest marine mammals. Such pictures can generate thousands of words in citizen anger, enough to sway Congress or force the new president of Brazil to name an environmentalist to his cabinet.

6 When the Exxon *Valdez* fouled Prince William Sound, it disrupted a slick campaign aimed at persuading Congress to allow oil drilling in Alaska's Arctic National Wildlife Refuge. Oil lobbyists had effectively argued the necessity of reducing dependence on foreign petroleum. Environmentalists had been unable to sway the public with pretty

pictures of caribou. But images of oil-soaked beaches, birds, and seals triggered outrage. Alaska Senator Ted Stevens put it best: The Exxon *Valdez* spill had set drilling back at least two years. Asked when it would resurface, he replied: "When the oil spill is no longer news."

7 Direct action has proven a potent way to focus the camera on environmental events. "The Fox" was its prophet. This anonymous ecological saboteur stalked Chicago in the late 1960s. He never showed his face, but publicized his deeds with calls to TV stations and explained his outrage to columnist Mike Royko. Refineries found their outfalls plugged. Banners were hung from smokestacks. The Fox even invaded the executive offices of a steel company to dump smelly effluent on its carpets.

8 Over twenty years later, the Fox is frequently copied. Greenpeace protestors recently decorated a stack at the Longview Fiber Company pulp mill in Washington, on the Columbia River. When the press arrived, the activists were ready with documentation of dioxin dumping into one of North America's great rivers.

9 Direct action is sometimes condemned by mainstream environmentalists who stress action through Congress and the courts. But confrontations can purchase time. In rain forests along the Northwest coast, the radical environmental group Earth First has plunked down protesters in ancient trees marked for logging. When hauled down and arrested, they've given such names as "Doug Fir" and "Bobcat." These tree-ins have generated nationwide attention and slowed the pace of logging.

10 A daring, filmed protest can focus attention on activities that some might wish to remain unnoticed. The Greenpeace Foundation was formed in Vancouver, British Columbia, in 1971, an outgrowth of protests aimed at planned U.S. nuclear tests in Alaska's Aleutian Islands. In 1973 Greenpeace began stalking bigger game—atmospheric nuclear tests being conducted by the French. Greenpeace vessels were boarded by the French navy, and crew members beaten. But the protesters kept sailing into test zones, and kept arguing that radiation posed a danger to peoples of the South Pacific. In 1986 French commandos sank a Greenpeace ship as it prepared to sail from a New Zealand harbor. One crew member was killed. The resulting uproar strained French relations with New Zealand, drove the French defense minister to resign, and cast France in the role of international outlaw.

11 Greenpeace has chosen the camera lens as its weapon for a variety of environmental crusades. "We go to the scene of a crime and bring

back images of what's going on," says Alan Reichman, ocean ecology director for Greenpeace International. "In that way we mobilize public concern and pressure. We're not talking abstractions and descriptions. We're showing a factory ship which cuts up whales. We're showing marine mammals trapped in nets. We're showing what comes out of pulp mills." Reichman has helped create memorable images. He was part of a flotilla of Zodiac boats that tried to stop a supertanker test run up the Strait of Juan de Fuca between British Columbia and Washington. Airborne photographers had a field day as the tiny craft buzzed around the 185,000-ton oil ship. A maneuverability test by the U.S. Coast Guard was turned into a political confrontation over whether to permit supertankers in sensitive West Coast estuaries.

12 A Greenpeace photo service makes pictures available to news sources, and engages in visual lobbying on Capitol Hill. Members of Congress, aides, and press gathered in a Longworth Building office last year to watch films of dolphins and birds entangled in the thick mesh of driftnet fishing lines. The seventy-mile-long driftnets are set on the North Pacific by Japanese and Taiwanese fishermen, supposedly to catch tuna and squid. In real life, they snare thousands of birds, marine mammals, and salmon. Congress has since pressed a reluctant Bush administration to support a worldwide ban on driftnet fishing.

13 The media savvy of such groups as Greenpeace has reached the environmental mainstream. The Natural Resources Defense Council has generally stayed far removed from visual imagery: Its battles have been fought in court, notably with suits that have forced the U.S. Department of Energy to abide by the nation's environmental laws in operating its nuclear weapons plants. On February 26, 1989, though, NRDC entered the court of public opinion. It gave CBS's *60 Minutes* a study entitled "Intolerable Risk: Pesticides in Our Children's Food." One of the pesticides in the report was daminozide (trade name Alar), a chemical sprayed on apples to improve their color, crispness, and shelf life. In its study, NRDC predicted that Alar might cause one case of cancer for every 4,200 preschool children—a rate of risk 240 times the standard considered acceptable by the Environmental Protection Agency.

14 Although written by scientists, "Intolerable Risk" translated well to the TV screen. *60 Minutes* focused on Alar. Americans saw apples being sprayed in fields. They watched those apples going into baby food. And a day later, Oscar-winning actress (and parent) Meryl Streep went before a Senate hearing to argue the case for a ban on Alar. During the week following the *60 Minutes* report, apple sales fell 14 percent,

and industry losses were estimated at over $100 million. A few months later, Uniroyal Chemical, Inc., announced it was taking the product off the market.

15 The media determines what is seen, and often what is saved. Photographs taken in a remote corner of northwest Wyoming helped create Yellowstone National Park over a century ago. Pictures can also lift politicians' sights up from ledger sheets. The U.S. Forest Service urged a veto of 1976 legislation creating a 393,000-acre Alpine Lakes Wilderness Area in Washington, arguing that it would cost too much to acquire private lands. Washington Governor Dan Evans, an avid backpacker, carried a picture book into an Oval Office meeting with President Gerald Ford. Evans turned to photos of the Enchantment Lakes region and told of guiding his three young sons over rugged, 7,800-foot Aasgard Pass during a violent storm. "Dan, we've got to save it," said Ford. He signed the bill.

16 As a writer I hate to admit it, but the camera's lens can be more powerful than the writer's pen. A physical confrontation convinced me. The state had let a logging contract on one of the few stands of old-growth trees left on Whidbey Island in Washington's scenic Puget Sound. Island environmentalists vowed to block the logging. I stood at the end of a narrow logging track with Mark Anderson, a young photographer with KING-TV in Seattle. A logging rig rumbled into view; protesters sat down in its path, and Anderson began filming. The truck stopped. After much waving of arms, the loggers retreated. A few hours later, KING carried an unforgettable film of trucks and bodies. It followed up with a film of the undisturbed forest. Birds chirped and sunlight wafted through 500-year-old trees. Anderson grew up in a logging town and knew the difference between a natural scene and a "working forest." Logging plans were promptly suspended.

17 The lawyering over Whidbey's forest was long and tedious. Not long ago, however, I enjoyed a walk among those same ancient trees, now—thanks at least in part to the powerful images presented by KING-TV and others—part of South Whidbey State Park.

Understanding Meaning

1. Why does Connelly assert that power now comes not from the barrel of a gun but from the lens of a camera?
2. How have environmentalists used visual images to achieve their goals?

3. What gives visual images their power, according to Connelly? How does a picture or video create a "global village"?
4. How do scenes of oil spills, dying whales, and ravaged forests affect the public?
5. What does Connelly mean by "direct action"? What examples does he provide?
6. *Critical Thinking:* Would your reaction to the use of images to influence public opinion be different if the subject were not the environment but abortion, busing, or gun control? Would you view the selected presentation of media images as something sinister if used to promote a cause you opposed? Is Connelly after all simply writing about *propaganda?*

Evaluating Strategy

1. What is Connelly's method of analysis? What standards does he use? Does he supply enough evidence?
2. *Other Modes:* What role does *narration* play in Connelly's essay?

Appreciating Language

1. What does Connelly mean by "global village"?
2. What meaning does "working forest" suggest?
3. *Critical Thinking:* Underline the words Connelly uses to describe "direct action" taken by environmentalists. What do the connotations of his words suggest? Do you detect a bias?

Connections across the Disciplines

1. What similarities do you see between the workings of the environmentalists and the "color Mafia" described by Helen Mundell (page 487)? Can a small group make selections that affect the lives of all Americans? Do we appreciate the influence of these small, unofficial groups?
2. Does Connelly's article suggest a lack of critical thinking on the part of politicians, corporate executives, and the public? Are people too easily influenced by images? Examine the examples cited by Darrell Huff in "How to Lie with Statistics" (page 337). Is a similar article needed titled "How to Lie with Pictures"?

Writing Suggestions

1. Select a photo or image that greatly affected you. Perhaps it was a television commercial, a news report about a famine, or an illustration in one of your textbooks. Describe the image in a short essay, and then analyze why you found it so powerful.
2. *Collaborative Writing:* Discuss this essay with a group of students. Ask members of the group to provide examples of photographs or films they found moving or disturbing. Consider if pictures can lie through distortion or omission. Work together and develop a list of questions people should ask themselves before being moved to action by a photograph.

DARRELL HUFF

Darrell Huff was born in 1913 and received his B.A. and M.A. at the State University of Iowa in the 1930s. He published hundreds of articles in popular magazines and served as editor of Better Homes and Gardens *for several years. "How to Lie with Statistics" appeared in* Harper's *in 1950. His analysis of how statistics are misused remains a useful primer on what he calls "the secret language of statistics," which is used to "sensationalize, inflate, confuse, and oversimplify."*

How to Lie with Statistics

Perhaps no other evidence is more misinterpreted or misunderstood than statistics. People often hear and repeat statistics without knowing their source or their true meaning. As you read Huff's article, consider why appreciating statistics is an important element of critical thinking.

1 "The average Yaleman, Class of '24," *Time* magazine reported last year after reading something in the New York *Sun*, a newspaper published in those days, "makes $25,111 a year."

2 Well, good for him!

3 But, come to think of it, what does this improbably precise and salubrious figure mean? Is it, as it appears to be, evidence that if you send your boy to Yale you won't have to work in your old age and neither will he? Is this average a mean or is it a median? What kind of sample is it based on? You could lump one Texas oilman with two hundred hungry freelance writers and report *their* average income as $25,000-odd a year. The arithmetic is impeccable, the figure is convincingly precise, and the amount of meaning there is in it you could put in your eye.

4 In just such ways is the secret language of statistics, so appealing in a fact-minded culture, being used to sensationalize, inflate, confuse, and oversimplify. Statistical terms are necessary in reporting the mass data of social and economic trends, business conditions, "opinion" polls, this year's census. But without writers who use the words with honesty and understanding and readers who know what they mean, the result can only be semantic nonsense.

5 In popular writing on scientific research, the abused statistic is almost crowding out the picture of the white-jacketed hero laboring

overtime without time-and-a-half in an ill-lit laboratory. Like the "little dash of powder, little pot of paint," statistics are making many an important fact "look like what she ain't." Here are some of the ways it is done.

6 *The sample with the built-in bias.* Our Yale men—or Yalemen, as they say in the Time-Life building—belong to this flourishing group. The exaggerated estimate of their income is not based on all members of the class nor on a random or representative sample of them. At least two interesting categories of 1924-model Yale men have been excluded.

7 First there are those whose present addresses are unknown to their classmates. Wouldn't you bet that these lost sheep are earning less than the boys from prominent families and the others who can be handily reached from a Wall Street office?

8 There are those who chucked the questionnaire into the nearest wastebasket. Maybe they didn't answer because they were not making enough money to brag about. Like the fellow who found a note clipped to his first pay check suggesting that he consider the amount of his salary confidential: "Don't worry," he told the boss. "I'm just as ashamed of it as you are."

9 Omitted from our sample then are just the two groups most likely to depress the average. The $25,111 figure is beginning to account for itself. It may indeed be a true figure for those of the Class of '24 whose addresses are known and who are willing to stand up and tell how much they earn. But even that requires a possibly dangerous assumption that the gentlemen are telling the truth.

10 To be dependable to any useful degree at all, a sampling study must use a representative sample (which can lead to trouble too) or a truly random one. If *all* the Class of '24 is included, that's all right. If every tenth name on a complete list is used, that is all right too, and so is drawing an adequate number of names out of a hat. The test is this: Does every name in the group have an equal chance to be in the sample?

11 You'll recall that ignoring this requirement was what produced the *Literary Digest's* famed fiasco. When names for polling were taken only from telephone books and subscription lists, people who did not have telephones or *Literary Digest* subscriptions had no chance to be in the sample. They possibly did not mind this underprivilege a bit, but their absence was in the end very hard on the magazine that relied on the figures.

12 This leads to a moral: You can prove about anything you want to by letting your sample bias itself. As a consumer of statistical data—a

reader, for example, of a news magazine—remember that no statistical conclusion can rise above the quality of the sample it is based upon. In the absence of information about the procedures behind it, you are not warranted in giving any credence at all to the result.

13 *The truncated, or gee-whiz, graph.* If you want to show some statistical information quickly and clearly, draw a picture of it. Graphic presentation is the thing today. If you don't mind misleading the hasty looker, or if you quite clearly *want* to deceive him, you can save some space by chopping the bottom off many kinds of graphs.

14 Suppose you are showing the upward trend of national income month by month for a year. The total rise, as in one recent year, is 7 per cent. It looks like this:

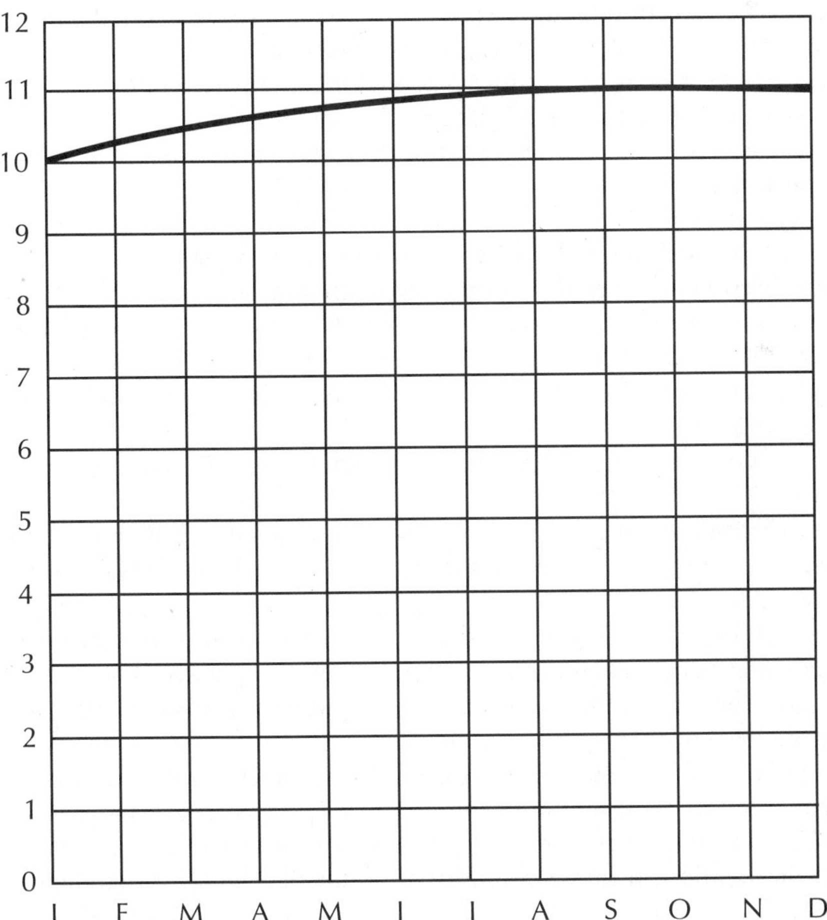

15 That is clear enough. Anybody can see that the trend is slightly upward. You are showing a 7 per cent increase and that is exactly what it looks like.

16 But it lacks schmaltz. So you chop off the bottom, this way:

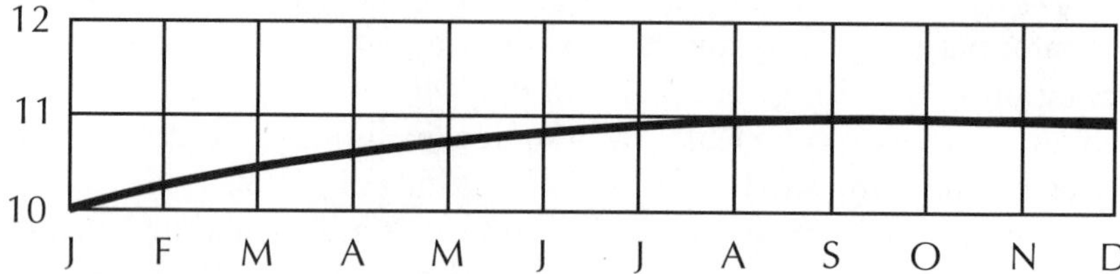

17 The figures are the same. It is the same graph and nothing has been falsified—except the impression that it gives. Anyone looking at it can just feel prosperity throbbing in the arteries of the country. It is a subtler equivalent of editing "National income rose 7 per cent" into ". . . climbed a whopping 7 per cent."

18 It is vastly more effective, however, because of that illusion of objectivity.

19 *The souped-up graph.* Sometimes truncating is not enough. The trifling rise in something or other still looks almost as insignificant as it is. You can make that 7 per cent look livelier than 100 per cent ordinarily does. Simply change the proportion between the ordinate and the abscissa. There's no rule against it, and it does give your graph a prettier shape.

20 But it exaggerates, to say the least, something awful [see page 341].

21 *The well-chosen average.* I live near a country neighborhood for which I can report an average income of $15,000. I could also report it as $3,500.

22 If I should want to sell real estate hereabouts to people having a high snobbery content, the first figure would be handy. The second figure, however, is the one to use in an argument against raising taxes, or the local bus fare.

23 Both are legitimate averages, legally arrived at. Yet it is obvious that at least one of them must be as misleading as an out-and-out lie. The $15,000-figure is a mean, the arithmetic average of the incomes of all the families in the community. The smaller figure is a median; it

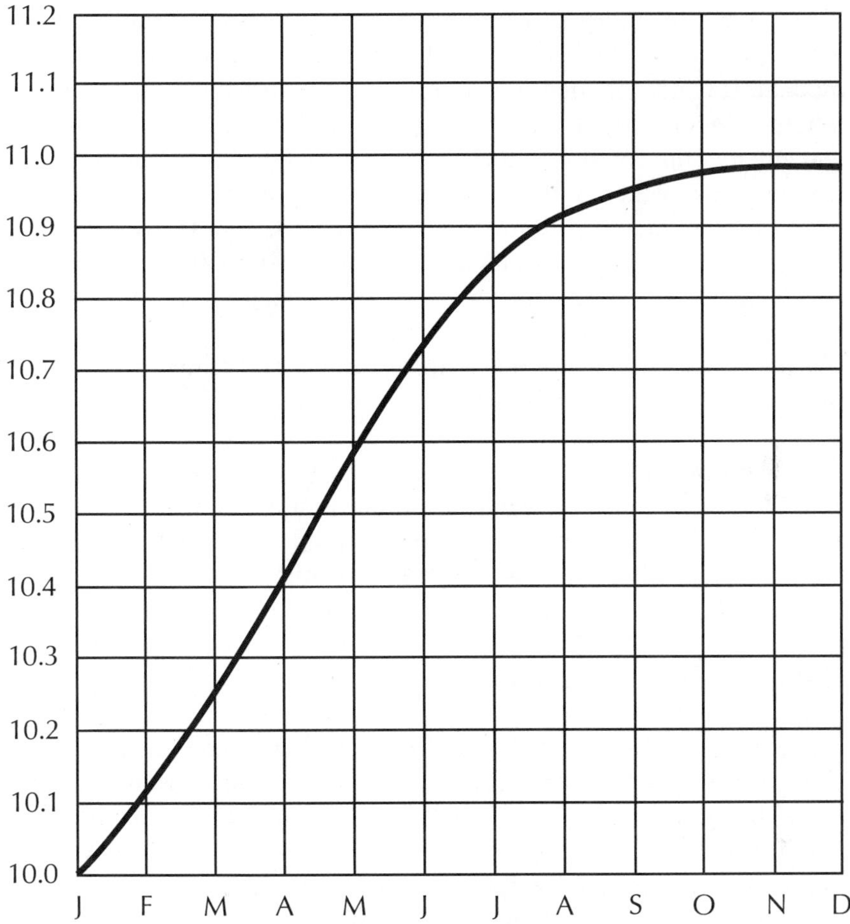

might be called the income of the average family in the group. It indicates that half the families have less than $3,500 a year and half have more.

24 Here is where some of the confusion about averages comes from. Many human characteristics have the grace to fall into what is called the "normal" distribution. If you draw a picture of it, you get a curve that is shaped like a bell. Mean and median fall at about the same point, so it doesn't make very much difference which you use.

25 But some things refuse to follow this neat curve. Income is one of them. Incomes for most large areas will range from under $1,000 a year to upward of $50,000. Almost everybody will be under $10,000, way over on the left-hand side of that curve.

26 One of the things that made the income figure for the "average Yaleman" meaningless is that we are not told whether it is a mean or a median. It is not that one type of average is invariably better than the other; it depends upon what you are talking about. But neither gives you any real information—and either may be highly misleading—unless you know which of those two kinds of average it is.

27 In the country neighborhood I mentioned, almost everyone has less than the average—the mean, that is—of $10,500. These people are all small farmers, except for a trio of millionaire week-enders who bring up the mean enormously.

28 You can be pretty sure that when an income average is given in the form of a mean nearly everybody has less than that.

29 *The insignificant difference or the elusive error.* Your two children Peter and Linda (we might as well give them modish names while we're about it) take intelligence tests. Peter's IQ, you learn, is 98 and Linda's is 101. Aha! Linda is your brighter child.

30 Is she? An intelligence test is, or purports to be, a sampling of intellect. An IQ, like other products of sampling, is a figure with a statistical error, which expresses the precision or reliability of the figure. The size of this probable error can be calculated. For their test the makers of the much-used Revised Stanford-Binet have found it to be about 3 per cent. So Peter's indicated IQ of 98 really means only that there is an even chance that it falls between 95 and 101. There is an equal probability that it falls somewhere else—below 95 or above 101. Similarly, Linda's has no better than a fifty-fifty chance of being within the fairly sizeable range of 98 to 104.

31 You can work out some comparisons from that. One is that there is rather better than one chance in four that Peter, with his lower IQ rating, is really at least three points smarter than Linda. A statistician doesn't like to consider a difference significant unless you can hand him odds a lot longer than that.

32 Ignoring the error in a sampling study leads to all kinds of silly conclusions. There are magazine editors to whom readership surveys are gospel; with a 40 per cent readership reported for one article and a 35 per cent for another, they demand more like the first. I've seen even smaller differences given tremendous weight, because statistics are a mystery and numbers are impressive. The same thing goes for market surveys and so-called public-opinion polls. The rule is that you cannot make a valid comparison between two such figures unless you know the deviations. And unless the difference between the figures is

many times greater than the probable error of each, you have only a guess that the one appearing greater really is.

33 Otherwise you are like the man choosing a camp site from a report of mean temperature alone. One place in California with a mean annual temperature of 61 is San Nicolas Island on the south coast, where it always stays in the comfortable range between 47 and 87. Another with a mean of 61 is in the inland desert, where the thermometer hops around from 15 to 104. The deviation from the mean marks the difference, and you can freeze or roast if you ignore it.

34 *The one-dimensional picture.* Suppose you have just two or three figures to compare—say the average weekly wage of carpenters in the United States and another country. The sums might be \$60 and \$30. An ordinary bar chart makes the difference graphic.

35 That is an honest picture. It looks good for American carpenters, but perhaps it does not have quite the oomph you are after. Can't you make that difference appear overwhelming and at the same time give it what I am afraid is known as eye-appeal? Of course you can. Following tradition, you represent these sums by pictures of money bags. If the \$30 bag is one inch high, you draw the \$60 bag two inches high. That's in proportion, isn't it? The catch is, of course, that the American's money bag, being twice as tall as that of the \$30 man, covers an area on your page four times as great. And since your two-dimensional picture represents an object that would in fact have three dimensions, the money bags actually would differ much more than that. The

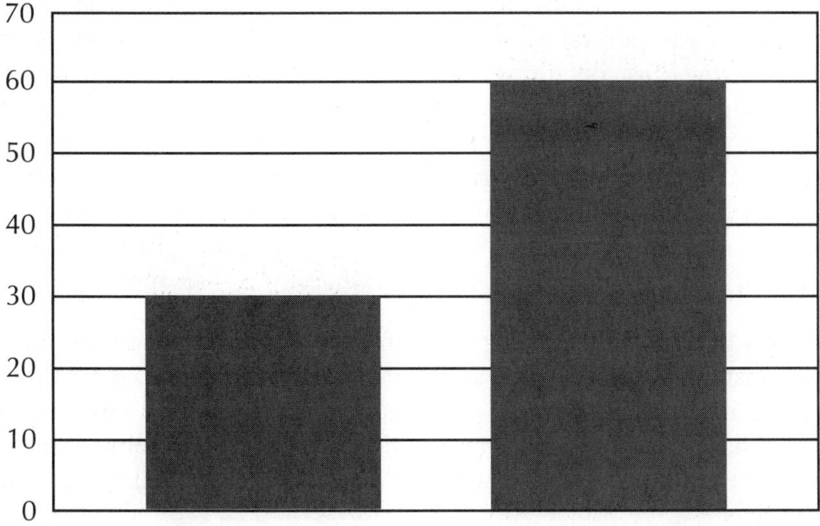

volumes of any two similar solids vary as the cubes of their heights. If the unfortunate foreigner's bag holds $30 worth of dimes, the American's would hold not $60 but a neat $240.

36 You didn't say that, though, did you? And you can't be blamed, you're only doing it the way practically everybody else does.

37 *The ever-impressive decimal.* For a spurious air of precision that will lend all kinds of weight to the most disreputable statistics, consider the decimal.

38 Ask a hundred citizens how many hours they slept last night. Come out with a total of, say, 781.3. Your data are far from precise to begin with. Most people will miss their guess by fifteen minutes or more and some will recall five sleepless minutes as half a night of tossing insomnia.

39 But go ahead, do your arithmetic, announce that people sleep an average of 7.813 hours a night. You will sound as if you knew precisely what you are talking about. If you were foolish enough to say 7.8 (or "almost 8") hours it would sound like what it was—an approximation.

40 *The semi-attached figure.* If you can't prove what you want to prove, demonstrate something else and pretend that they are the same thing. In the daze that follows the collision of statistics with the human mind, hardly anybody will notice the difference. The semi-attached figure is a durable device guaranteed to stand you in good stead. It always has.

41 If you can't prove that your nostrum cures colds, publish a sworn laboratory report that the stuff killed 31,108 germs in a test tube in eleven seconds. There may be no connection at all between assorted germs in a test tube and the whatever-it-is that produces colds, but people aren't going to reason that sharply, especially while sniffling.

42 Maybe that one is too obvious and people are beginning to catch on. Here is a trickier version.

43 Let us say that in a period when race prejudice is growing it is to your advantage to "prove" otherwise. You will not find it a difficult assignment.

44 Ask that usual cross section of the population if they think Negroes have as good a chance as white people to get jobs. Ask again a few months later. As Princeton's Office of Public Opinion Research has found out, people who are most unsympathetic to Negroes are the ones most likely to answer yes to this question.

45 As prejudice increases in a country, the percentage of affirmative answers you will get to this question will become larger. What looks on the face of it like growing opportunity for Negroes actually is mounting prejudice and nothing else. You have achieved something rather remarkable: the worse things get, the better your survey makes them look.

46 *The unwarranted assumption, or* post hoc *rides again.* The interrelation of cause and effect, so often obscure anyway, can be most neatly hidden in statistical data.

47 Somebody once went to a good deal of trouble to find out if cigarette smokers make lower college grades than non-smokers. They did. This naturally pleased many people, and they made much of it.

48 The unwarranted assumption, of course, was that smoking had produced dull minds. It seemed vaguely reasonable on the face of it, so it was quite widely accepted. But it really proved nothing of the sort, any more than it proved that poor grades drive students to the solace of tobacco. Maybe the relationship worked in one direction, maybe in the other. And maybe all this is only an indication that the sociable sort of fellow who is likely to take his books less than seriously is also likely to sit around and smoke many cigarettes.

49 Permitting statistical treatment to befog causal relationships is little better than superstition. It is like the conviction among the people of the Hebrides that body lice produce good health. Observation over the centuries had taught them that people in good health had lice and sick people often did not. *Ergo,* lice made a man healthy. Everybody should have them.

50 Scantier evidence, treated statistically at the expense of common sense, has made many a medical fortune and many a medical article in magazines, including professional ones. More sophisticated observers finally got things straightened out in the Hebrides. As it turned out, almost everybody in those circles had lice most of the time. But when a man took a fever (quite possibly carried to him by those same lice) and his body became hot, the lice left.

51 Here you have cause and effect not only reversed, but intermingled.

52 There you have a primer in some ways to use statistics to deceive. A well-wrapped statistic is better than Hitler's "big lie": it misleads, yet it can't be pinned onto you.

53 Is this little list altogether too much like a manual for swindlers? Perhaps I can justify it in the manner of the retired burglar whose published reminiscences amounted to a graduate course in how to pick a lock and muffle a footfall: The crooks already know these tricks. Honest men must learn them in self-defense.

Understanding Meaning

1. Why do statistics impress people? What is their appeal in advertising?
2. What are the principal methods used to create misleading statistics?
3. Is Huff suggesting that advertisers deliberately lie, or is he suggesting that advertisers often do not understand the meaning of their own numbers?
4. Armed with computers, many people love to construct elaborate graphs to include in their reports. What does Huff's article reveal about the reliability of many visual aids?
5. *Critical Thinking:* What are the implications of Huff's observation that "A well-wrapped statistic is better than Hitler's 'big lie': it misleads, yet it can't be pinned onto you"? Can you think of examples of falsely stated statistics that have been used to influence the public?

Evaluating Strategy

1. What impact does the title have?
2. How effective are Huff's examples in communicating complex ideas to a general audience?
3. How does Huff try to maintain reader interest while explaining a topic many readers find abstract, boring, or intimidating?

Appreciating Language

1. What does Huff's choice of words suggest about the tone he was trying to establish?
2. What changes in language would you suggest making if the article were to be rewritten for inclusion in a textbook?

Connections across the Disciplines

1. How does the tone of Huff's article differ from Lisa Fried's essay on female entrepreneurs (page 368)? What does this reveal about each of their purposes and audiences?
2. Refer to John Allen Paulos's article on innumeracy (page 178). How does so many people having a limited grasp of math affect the use of statistics?
3. How does Christina Hoff Sommers's article "Figuring Out Feminism" (page 348) illustrate Huff's thesis?

Writing Suggestions

1. Select a statistic you have heard people cite. Write a brief essay analyzing why the statistic is popular. Do statistics that support a cause serve the same purpose as a slogan on a bumper sticker by providing a shorthand argument?
2. Imagine you plan to publish this article as a brochure for distribution. Write a brief analysis of the audience that would benefit most from its contents.
3. *Collaborative Writing:* Working with a group of students, use this writing exercise to learn more about statistics:

> Imagine that a school district has 1,000 teachers earning an average of $30,000 a year. After a bitter dispute, the school board agrees to provide teachers with a 5 percent raise. Discuss the impact of the following newspaper headlines:
>
> Teachers Get 5% Pay Hike
> Teachers Get $1,500 Raise
> Teachers Get $31.5 Million

Write a short analysis of how presenting numbers in different forms can influence readers. Which statistic do members of the group feel to be the most accurate?

CHRISTINA HOFF SOMMERS

Christina Hoff Sommers teaches philosophy at Clark University and is the author of Who Stole Feminism?, *a book that is highly critical of many aspects of the current feminist movement. This article, taken from her book, was published in the conservative magazine* National Review (1994). *Sommers analyzes the way statistics are used by some feminists to shape and distort public opinion.*

Figuring Out Feminism

If you have not read Darrell Huff's article, "How to Lie with Statistics" (page 337), you may wish to refer to it before reading this article. Whatever your views of feminism, focus on how Sommers constructs her analysis by applying critical thinking.

1 In *Revolution from Within*, Gloria Steinem informs her readers that "in this country alone . . . about 150,000 females die of anorexia each year." That is more than three times the annual number of fatalities from car accidents for the total population. Miss Steinem refers readers to Naomi Wolf's *The Beauty Myth*, where one again finds the statistic, along with the author's outrage. "How," she asks, "would America react to the mass self-immolation by hunger of its favorite sons?" Although "nothing justifies comparison with the Holocaust," she cannot refrain from making one anyway. "When confronted with a vast number of emaciated bodies starved not by nature but by men, one must notice a certain resemblance."

2 Where did Miss Wolf get her figures? Her source is *Fasting Girls: The Emergence of Anorexia Nervosa as a Modern Disease* by Joan Brumberg, a historian and former director of women's studies at Cornell University. She, too, is fully aware of the political significance of the startling statistic. She points out that the women who study eating problems "seek to demonstrate that these disorders are an inevitable consequence of a misogynistic society that demeans women . . . by objectifying their bodies." Professor Brumberg, in turn, attributes the figure to the American Anorexia and Bulimia Association.

3 I called the American Anorexia and Bulimia Association and spoke to Dr. Diane Mickley, its president. "We were misquoted," she said. In a 1985 newsletter the association had referred to 150,000 to 200,000

4 *sufferers* (not *fatalities*) of anorexia nervosa. What is the correct morbidity rate? Most experts are reluctant to give exact figures. One clinician told me that of 1,400 patients she had treated in ten years, 4 had died—all through suicide. The National Center for Health Statistics reported 101 deaths from anorexia nervosa in 1983 and 67 deaths in 1988. Thomas Dunn of the Division of Vital Statistics at the National Center for Health Statistics reports that in 1991 there were 54 deaths from anorexia nervosa and no deaths from bulimia. The deaths of these young women are a tragedy, certainly, but in a country of 100 million adult females, such numbers are hardly evidence of a "holocaust."

5 Yet now the false figure, supporting the view that our "sexist society" demeans women by objectifying their bodies, is widely accepted as true. Ann Landers repeated it in her syndicated column in April 1992: "Every year, 150,000 American women die from complications associated with anorexia and bulimia."

6 Will Miss Steinem advise her readers of the egregious statistical error? Will Mrs. Landers? Will it even matter? By now, the 150,000 figure has made it into college textbooks. A recent women's studies text, aptly titled *The Knowledge Explosion*, contains the erroneous figure in its preface.

NEXT CRISIS, PLEASE

7 The anorexia "crisis" is only one example of the kind of provocative but inaccurate information being purveyed by women about "women's issues" these days. On November 4, 1992, Deborah Louis, president of the National Women's Studies Association, sent a message to the Women's Studies Electronic Bulletin Board: "According to [the] last March of Dimes report, domestic violence (versus pregnant women) is now responsible for more birth defects than all other causes combined. Personally [this] strikes me as the most disgusting piece of data I've seen in a long while." This was, indeed, unsettling news. But it seemed implausible. I asked my neighbor, a pediatric neurologist at Boston's Children's Hospital, about the report. He told me that although severe battery may occasionally cause miscarriage, he had never heard of battery as a significant cause of birth defects.

8 I called the March of Dimes to get a copy of the report. Maureen Corry, director of the March's Education and Health Promotion Program, denied any knowledge of it. "We have never seen this research

before," she said. I did a search and found that—study or no study—journalists around the country were citing it.

9 "Domestic violence is the leading cause of birth defects, more than all other medical causes combined, according to a March of Dimes study." (*Boston Globe,* September 2, 1991.)

10 "Especially grotesque is the brutality reserved for pregnant women: the March of Dimes has concluded that the battering of women during pregnancy causes more birth defects than all the diseases put together for which children are usually immunized." (*Time* magazine, January 18, 1993.)

11 "The March of Dimes has concluded that the battering of women during pregnancy causes more birth defects than all the diseases put together for which children are usually immunized." (*Dallas Morning News,* February 7, 1993.)

12 I called the March of Dimes again. Andrea Ziltzer of their media-relations department told me that the rumor was spinning out of control. Governors' offices, state health departments, and Washington politicians had flooded the office with phone calls. Even the office of Senator Edward Kennedy had requested a copy of the "report."

13 When I finally reached Jeanne McDowell, who had written the *Time* article, the first thing she said was, "That was an error." She sounded genuinely sorry and embarrassed. She explained that she is always careful about checking sources, but this time, for some reason, she had not. *Time* has since called the March of Dimes to apologize. An official retraction finally appeared in the magazine on December 6, 1993, under the heading "Inaccurate Information."

14 I asked Miss McDowell about her source. She had relied on information given her by the San Francisco Family Violence Prevention Fund, which had obtained it from Sarah Buel, a founder of the domestic-violence advocacy project at Harvard Law School. She in turn had obtained it from Caroline Whitehead, a maternal nurse and child-care specialist in Raleigh, North Carolina. I called Miss Whitehead.

15 "It blows my mind. *It is not true,*" she said. The whole mixup began, she explained, when she introduced Sarah Buel as a speaker at a 1989 conference for nurses and social workers. In presenting her, Miss Whitehead mentioned that according to some March of Dimes research she had seen, more women are screened for birth defects than are ever screened for domestic battery. Miss Whitehead had said nothing at all about battery *causing* birth defects. "Sarah misunderstood me," she said. Miss Buel went on to put the erroneous information

into a manuscript which was then circulated among family-violence professionals. They saw no reason to doubt its authority.

16 I called Sarah Buel and told her that it seemed she had misheard Caroline Whitehead. She was surprised. "Oh, I must have misunderstood her. I'll have to give her a call. She is my source." She thanked me for having informed her of the error, pointing out that she had been about to repeat it yet again in a new article.

WHERE WERE THE SKEPTICS?

17 Why was everybody so credulous? Battery responsible for more birth defects than *all* other causes combined? More than genetic disorders such as spina bifida, Down syndrome, Tay-Sachs, sickle-cell anemia? More than congenital heart disorders? More than alcohol, crack, or AIDS—more than all these things *combined?* Where were the fact-checkers, the editors, the skeptical journalists?

18 To that question we must add another: Why are certain feminists so eager to put men in a bad light? I shall try to answer both these questions.

19 American feminism is currently dominated by a group of women who seek to persuade the public that American women are not the free creatures we think we are. The leaders and theorists of the women's movement believe that our society is best described as a patriarchy, a "male hegemony," a "sex/gender system" in which the dominant gender works to keep women cowering and submissive. The feminists who hold this divisive view of our social and political reality believe that all our institutions, from the state to the family to the grade schools, perpetuate male dominance. Believing that women are virtually under siege, the "gender feminists" naturally seek recruits to their side of the gender war. They seek support. They seek vindication. They seek ammunition.

20 Not everyone, including many women who consider themselves feminists, is convinced that contemporary American women live in an oppressive "male hegemony." To confound the skeptics and persuade the undecided, the gender feminists are constantly on the lookout for the smoking gun, the telling fact that will drive home how profoundly the system is rigged against women. It is not enough to remind us that many brutal and selfish men harm women. They must

persuade us that the system itself sanctions male brutality. They must convince us that the oppression of women, sustained from generation to generation, is a structural feature of our society.

21 Thus gender-feminist ideology holds that physical menace toward women is the norm. Gloria Steinem's portrait of male-female intimacy under patriarchy is typical: "Patriarchy *requires* violence or the subliminal threat of violence in order to maintain itself. . . . The most dangerous situation for a woman is not an unknown man in the street, or even the enemy in wartime, but a husband or lover in the isolation of their own home."

22 Miss Steinem's description of the dangers women face in their own home is reminiscent of the Super Bowl hoax of January 1993. Here is the chronology:

23 *Thursday, January 27.* A news conference was called in Pasadena, California, the site of the forthcoming Super Bowl game, by a coalition of women's groups. At the news conference, reporters were informed that Super Bowl Sunday is "the biggest day of the year for violence against women." Forty per cent more women would be battered on that day. In support of the 40 per cent figure, Sheila Kuehl of the California Women's Law Center cited a study done at Virginia's Old Dominion University three years before. The presence of Linda Mitchell, a representative of a media "watchdog" group called Fairness and Accuracy in Reporting (FAIR), lent credibility to the claim.

24 At about the same time a very large media mailing was sent by Dobisky Associates, FAIR's publicists, warning at-risk women: "Don't remain at home with him during the game." The idea that sports fans are prone to attack their wives or girlfriends on that climactic day persuaded many men as well: Robert Lipsyte of the *New York Times* would soon be referring to the "Abuse Bowl."

25 *Friday, January 28.* Lenore Walker, a Denver psychologist and author of *The Battered Woman,* appeared on *Good Morning America* claiming to have compiled a ten-year record showing a sharp increase in violent incidents against women on Super Bowl Sundays.

26 Here, again, a representative from FAIR, Laura Flanders, was present to lend credibility to the claim.

27 *Saturday, January 29.* A story in the *Boston Globe* written by Lynda Gorov reported that women's shelters and hot lines are "flooded with more calls from victims [on Super Bowl Sunday] than on any other day of the year." Miss Gorov cited "one study of women's shelters out

West" that "showed a 40 per cent climb in calls, a pattern advocates said is repeated nationwide, including in Massachusetts."

28 In this roiling sea of media credulity was a lone island of professional integrity. Ken Ringle, a *Washington Post* staff writer, took the time to call around. When he asked Janet Katz—professor of sociology and criminal justice at Old Dominion, and one of the principal authors of the study cited by Miss Kuehl—about the connection between violence and football games, she said: "That's not what we found at all." Instead, she told him, they had found that an increase in emergency-room admissions "was not associated with the occurrence of football games in general."

29 Mr. Ringle checked with Lynda Gorov, who told him she had never seen the study she cited but had been told of it by FAIR. Linda Mitchell of FAIR told Mr. Ringle that the authority for the 40 per cent figure was Lenore Walker. Miss Walker's office, in turn, referred calls on the subject to Michael Lindsey, a Denver psychologist and an authority on battered women. Pressed by Mr. Ringle, Mr. Lindsey admitted he could find no basis for the report. "I haven't been any more successful than you in tracking down any of this," he said. "You think maybe we have one of these myth things here?"

30 Later, other reporters pressed Miss Walker to detail her findings. She said they were not available. "We don't use them for public consumption," she explained, "we used them to guide us in advocacy projects."

31 It would have been more honest for the feminists who initiated the campaign to admit that there was no basis for saying that football fans are more brutal to women than are chess players or Democrats nor any basis for saying that there was a significant rise in domestic violence on Super Bowl Sunday.

32 Ken Ringle's unraveling of the "myth thing" was published on the front page of the *Washington Post* on January 31. On February 2, *Boston Globe* staff writer Bob Hohler published what amounted to a retraction of Miss Gorov's story. Mr. Hohler had done some more digging and had gotten FAIR's Steven Rendell to back off from the organization's earlier support of the claim. "It should not have gone out in FAIR materials," said Mr. Rendell.

33 Linda Mitchell would later acknowledge that she was aware during the original news conference that Miss Kuehl was misrepresenting the Old Dominion study. Mr. Ringle asked her whether she did not

feel obligated to challenge her colleague. "I wouldn't do that in front of the media," Miss Mitchell said. "She has a right to report it as she wants."

34 The shelters and hot lines, which monitored the Sunday of the 27th Super Bowl with special care, reported no variation in the number of calls for help that day, not even in Buffalo, whose team (and fans) had suffered a crushing defeat.

35 But despite Ken Ringle's exposé, the Super Bowl "statistic" will be with us for a while, doing its divisive work of generating fear and resentment. In the book *How to Make the World a Better Place for Women in Five Minutes a Day,* a comment under the heading "Did You Know?" informs readers that "Super Bowl Sunday is the most violent day of the year, with the highest reported number of domestic battering cases." How a belief in that misandrist canard can make the world a better place for women is not explained.

FEMALE GAINS OR MALE BACKLASH?

36 How a feminist reacts to data about gender gaps in salaries and economic opportunities is an excellent indication of the kind of feminist she is. In general, the equity feminist points with pride to the many gains women have made toward achieving parity in the workplace. By contrast, the gender feminist makes it a point to disparage these gains and to speak of backlash. It disturbs her that the public may be lulled into thinking that women are doing well and that men are allowing it. The gender feminist insists that any so-called progress is illusory.

37 By most measures, the Eighties were a time of rather spectacular gains by American women—in education, in wages, and in such traditionally male professions as business, law, and medicine. The gender feminist will have none of this. According to Susan Faludi, in her much ballyhooed book, the Eighties were the backlash decade, in which men successfully retracted many of the gains wrested from them in preceding decades. And since any criticism of Miss Faludi's claim is apt to be construed as just more backlashing, one must be grateful to the editors of the *New York Times* business section for braving the wrath of feminist ideologues by presenting an objective account of the economic picture as it affects women.

38 Surveying several reports by women economists on women's gains in the 1980s, *New York Times* business writer Sylvia Nasar rejected Susan Faludi's thesis. She pointed to masses of empirical data showing that "Far from losing ground, women gained more in the 1980s than in the entire postwar era before that. And almost as much as between 1890 and 1980."

39 The *Times* reports that the proportion women earn of each dollar of men's wages rose to a record 72 cents by 1990. But the *Times* points out that even this figure is misleadingly pessimistic, because it includes older women who are only marginally in the work force, such as "the mother who graduated from high school, left the work force at twenty, and returned to a minimum wage at a local store." Younger women, says the *Times,* "now earn 80 cents for every dollar earned by men of the same age, up from 69 cents in 1980."

40 None of these facts has made the slightest impression on the backlash mongers. For years, feminist activists have been wearing buttons claiming women earn "59 cents to a man's dollar." Some journalists have questioned this figure. Miss Faludi calls them "spokesmen" for the backlash and says: "By 1988, women with a college diploma could still wear the famous 59-cent buttons. They were still making 59 cents to their male counterparts' dollar. In fact, the pay gap for them was now a bit worse than five years earlier."

41 The sources Miss Faludi cites do not sustain her figure. The actual figure for 1988 is 68 cents, both for all women and for women with a college diploma. This is substantially higher, not lower, than it was five years earlier. The most recent figures, for 1992, are considerably higher yet: 71 cents for all women and 73 cents for women with a college diploma.

42 What of the remaining gap between male and female earnings? For the gender feminists, the answer is simple: the wage gap is the result of discrimination against women. But in fact, serious economic scholars who are trained to interpret these data (including many eminent female economists) point out that most of the differences in earnings reflect such prosaic matters as shorter work weeks. For example, the average work week for full-time, year-round female workers is shorter than for comparable male workers. When economists compare men's and women's *hourly* earnings instead of their *yearly* earnings, the wage gap narrows even more.

43 Economists differ on exactly how much, if any, of the remaining gap is discrimination. Most economists agree that much of it simply

represents the fact that, on average, women have accrued less workplace experience than men of the same age. One recent scholarly estimate shows that as of 1987, females who were currently working full-time and year-round had, on average, one-quarter year less of work experience than comparable males.

44 These data are important in understanding the oft-cited claim of a "glass ceiling" for women. Promotion in high-powered professional jobs often goes to those who have put in long hours in evenings and on weekends. Husbands may be more likely to do so than wives, for a variety of reasons, including unequal division of responsibilities at home, in which case the source of the difficulty is at home, not in the marketplace.

45 Obviously, the experience gap also reflects the fact that many women choose to move into and out of the work force during child-bearing and child-rearing years. This reduces the amount of experience they acquire in the workplace and naturally results in lower earnings, quite apart from any possible discrimination. Some evidence of this is provided by data on childless workers, for whom the experience gap should be much narrower, resulting in a narrower earnings gap. This, in fact, is the case: as of 1987, among childless white workers aged 20 to 44, females' hourly earnings were between 86 to 91 per cent of males' hourly earnings.

46 Robert Reich, the U.S. secretary of labor, wrote a blurb for *Backlash* describing it as "spellbinding and frightening . . . a wake-up call to the men as well as the women who are struggling to build a gender-respectful society." One can only hope that Mr. Reich was too spell-bound to have read *Backlash* with a discriminating mind. What is more alarming than anything Miss Faludi has to say about an undeclared war against American women is the credulity it has met in high public officials on whose judgment we ought to be able to rely.

Understanding Meaning

1. What is Sommers's purpose—to analyze the way feminists misuse statistics or to criticize feminism?
2. How does Sommers explain the wage differences between men and women?
3. Why did the press not question the statistics presented by feminists? Does Sommers suggest that the media is biased toward feminism? Does the press evaluate statistics presented by other special interests?

4. Why does Sommers believe that feminists have a vested interest in presenting distorted statistics to the press and public?
5. *Critical Thinking:* Although Sommers focuses on feminists misusing figures, she presents examples of mainstream publications such as *Time* quoting erroneous statistics. Does this suggest that "innumeracy" (see John Allen Paulos, page 178) is widespread? Are feminists any more prone to misunderstanding statistics than environmentalists, labor unions, corporations, or government agencies?

Evaluating Strategy

1. Compare Sommers's essay about statistics with Darrell Huff's (page 337). Both begin with anecdotes. Why do the authors feel compelled to use dramatic attention-getters to arouse interest in a subject many readers may find abstract?
2. Sommers includes several narratives, detailing how she tracked down the original sources cited for many widely quoted figures. What does this reveal about her methods?

Appreciating Language

1. Sommers refers to Gloria Steinem as "Miss" Steinem rather than "Ms." Steinem. What does this choice suggest? Why does Sommers point out that Susan Faludi, a feminist, uses the term "spokesmen" to refer to critics of feminism?
2. This article appeared in a leading conservative journal. How does Sommers's vocabulary appeal to her audience's values?

Connections across the Disciplines

1. Lisa Fried's article (page 368) describes the growth in female-owned and -operated businesses in the United States. Do her findings support Sommers's view that women have made measurable gains in our society? Does the success of female entrepreneurs dispute or support feminist arguments about women's social status?
2. In "The Handicap of Definition" (page 320), William Raspberry argues that many African American young people have adopted negative stereotypes about themselves that limit their opportunities. Do the ideas of some feminists lead women to see their options as being limited? In arousing awareness about issues such as the "glass ceiling" and sexual

harassment, do feminists create a view of the marketplace as being hostile and therefore intimidating to women?

Writing Suggestions

1. Select any group or movement you are familiar with, and write a brief analysis of how data are gathered, studied, and presented. Do these people latch onto facts and figures they have heard and quote them without question?
2. *Collaborative Writing:* Work with a group of students, and briefly discuss Sommers's article. Try to avoid arguing about the subject of feminism, and debate her use of critical thinking skills. Write a brief list of guidelines suggesting how students should approach statistics they encounter.

SLAVENKA DRAKULIĆ

Slavenka Drakulić is a Croatian journalist and novelist. Her first articles about life in Eastern Europe appeared in Danas, *a magazine published in the former Yugoslavia. She now contributes to American publications such as* The New York Times Magazine, The New Republic, *and* The Nation. *She has published several books, including* How We Survived Communism and Even Laughed (1991) *and* The Balkan Express (1993), *an account of the war in Bosnia.*

Pizza in Warsaw, Torte in Prague

This essay from her book How We Survived Communism and Even Laughed *analyzes life in Eastern Europe by focusing on items people in the West take for granted—fresh fruit and pizza.*

1 We were hungry, so I said "Let's have a pizza!" in the way you would think of it in, say, New York, or any West European city—meaning "Let's go to a fast-food place and grab something to eat." Jolanta, a small, blond, Polish translator of English, looked at me thoughtfully, as if I were confronting her with quite a serious task. "There are only two such places," she said in an apologetic tone of voice. Instantly, I was overwhelmed by the guilt of taking pizza in Poland for granted. "Drop it," I said. But she insisted on this pizza place. "You must see it," she said. "It's so different from the other restaurants in Warsaw."

2 We were lucky because we were admitted without reservations. This is a privately owned restaurant, one of the very few. We were also lucky because we could afford a pizza and beer here, which cost as much as dinner in a fancy hotel. The restaurant was a small, cozy place, with just two wooden tables and a few high stools at the bar—you couldn't squeeze more than twenty people in, even if you wanted to.

3 It was raining outside, a cold winter afternoon in Warsaw. Once inside, everything was different: two waiters dressed in impeccable white shirts, with bow ties and red aprons, a bowl of fresh tropical fruit

on the bar, linen napkins and the smell of pizza baked in a real charcoal-fired oven. Jolanta and I were listening to disco music, eating pizza, and drinking Tuborg beer from long, elegant glasses. Perhaps this is what you pay for, the feeling that you are somewhere else, in a different Warsaw, in a dreamland where there is everything—pizza, fruit juice, thick grilled steaks, salads—and the everyday life of shortages and poverty can't seep in, at least, for the moment.

4 Yet to understand just how different this place is, one has to see a "normal" coffee shop, such as the one in the modernistic building of concrete and glass that we visited the same day. Inside neon lights flicker, casting a ghostly light on the aluminum tables and chairs covered with plastic. This place looks more like a bus terminal than like a *kawiarnia.* It's almost empty and the air is thick with cigarette smoke. A bleached blond waitress slowly approaches us with a very limited menu: tea, some alcoholic beverages, Coke, coffee. "With milk?" I ask.

5 "No milk," she shakes her head.

6 "Then, can I get a fruit juice perhaps?" I say, in the hopes of drinking just one in a Polish state-owned restaurant.

7 "No juice." She shakes her head impatiently (at this point, of course, there is no "sophisticated" question about the kind of juice one would perhaps prefer). I give up and get a cup of coffee. It's too sweet. Jolanta is drinking Coke, because there is Coke everywhere—in the middle of Warsaw as, I believe, in the middle of the desert. There may be neither milk nor water, but there is sure to be a bottle of Coke around. Nobody seems to mind the paradox that even though fruit grows throughout Poland, there is no fruit juice yet Coke is everywhere. But here Coke, like everything coming from America, is more of a symbol than a beverage.

8 To be reduced to having Coke and pizza offered not only as fancy food, but, what's more, as the idea of choice, strikes me as a form of imperialism, possibly only where there is really very little choice. Just across the street from the private restaurant, where Jolanta parked her tiny Polski Fiat, is a grocery store. It is closed in the afternoon, so says a handwritten note on the door. Through the dusty shop window we can see the half-empty shelves, with a few cans of beans, pasta, rice, cabbage, vinegar. A friend, a Yugoslav living in Warsaw, told me that some years ago vinegar and mustard were almost all you could find in the stores. At another point, my friend noticed that shelves were stocked with prune compote. One might easily conclude that this is what Poles probably liked the best or why else would it be in stores in

such quantities? But the reason was just the opposite: Prune compote was what they had, not what they liked. However, the word "like" is not the best way to explain the food situation (or any situation) in Poland. Looking at a shop window where onions and garlic are two of the very few items on display, what meaning could the word "like" possibly have?

9 Slowly, one realizes that not only is this a different reality, but that words have a different meaning here, too. It makes you understand that the word "like" implies not only choice but refinement, even indulgence, *savoir-vivre*—in fact, a whole different attitude toward food. It certainly doesn't imply that you stuff yourself with whatever you find at the farmer's market or in a grocery that day. Instead, it suggests a certain experience, a knowledge, a possibility of comparing quality and taste. Right after the overthrow of the Ceausescu government in Romania in December 1989, I read a report in the newspaper about life in Bucharest. There was a story about a man who ate the first banana in his life. He was an older man, a worker, and he said to a reporter shyly that he ate a whole banana, together with the skin, because he didn't know that he had to peel it. At first, I was moved by the isolation this man was forced to live in, by the fact that he never read or even heard what to do with a banana. But then something else caught my attention: "*It tasted good,*" he said. I can imagine this man, holding a sweet-smelling, ripe banana in his hand, curious and excited by it, as by a forbidden fruit. He holds it for a moment, then bites. It tastes strange but "good." It must have been good, even together with a bitter, tough skin, because it was something unachievable, an object of desire. It was not a banana that he was eating, but the promise, the hope of the future. So, he liked it no matter what its taste.

10 One of the things one is constantly reminded of in these parts is not to be thoughtless with food. I remember my mother telling me that I had to eat everything in front of me, because to throw away food would be a sin. Perhaps she had God on her mind, perhaps not. She experienced World War II and ever since, like most of the people in Eastern Europe, she behaves as if it never ended. Maybe this is why they are never really surprised that even forty years afterwards there is a lack of sugar, oil, coffee, or flour. To be heedless—to behave as if you are somewhere else, where everything is easy to get—is a sin not against God, but against people. Here you have to think of food, because it has entirely diverse social meanings. To bring a cake for dessert when you are invited for a dinner—a common gesture in

another, more affluent country—means you invested a great deal of energy to find it if you didn't make it yourself. And even if you did, finding eggs, milk, sugar, and butter took time and energy. That makes it precious in a very different way from if you had bought it in the pastry shop next door.

11 When Jaroslav picked me up at Prague airport, I wanted to buy a torte before we went to his house for dinner. It was seven o'clock in the evening and shops were already closed. Czechs work until five or six, which doesn't leave much time to shop. "The old government didn't like people walking in the streets. It might cause them trouble," said Jaroslav, half joking. "Besides, there isn't much to buy anyway." My desire to buy a torte after six o'clock appeared to be quite an extravagance, and it was clear that one couldn't make a habit of bringing a cake for dessert. In the Slavia Café there were no pastries at all, not to mention a torte. The best confectioner in Prague was closed, and in the Hotel Zlatá Husa restaurant a waitress repeated "Torte?" after us as if we were in the wrong place. Then she shook her head. With every new place, my desire to buy a torte diminished. Perhaps it is not that there are no tortes—it's just hard to find them at that hour. At the end, we went to the only shop open until eight-thirty and bought ice cream. There were three kinds and Jaroslav picked vanilla, which is what his boys like the best.

12 On another occasion, in the Bulgarian capital Sofia, Evelina is preparing a party. I am helping her in the small kitchen of the decaying apartment that she shares with a student friend, because as an assistant professor at the university, she cannot afford to rent an apartment alone. I peel potatoes, perhaps six pounds of them. She will make a potato salad with onions. Then she will bake the rest of them in the oven and serve them with . . . actually nothing. She calls it "a hundred-ways potato party"—sometimes humor is the only way to overcome depression. There are also four eggs for an omelet and two cans of sardines (imported from Yugoslavia), plus vodka and wine, and that's it, for the eight people she has invited.

13 We sit around her table: a Bulgarian theater director who lives in exile in Germany, three of Evelina's colleagues from the university, a historian friend and her husband, and the two of us. We eat potatoes with potatoes, drink vodka, discuss the first issue of the opposition paper *Demokratia,* the round-table talks between the Union of Democratic Forces and the communist government, and calculate how many

votes the opposition will get in the forthcoming free elections—the first. Nobody seems to mind that there is no more food on the table—at least not as long as a passionate political discussion is going on. "*This* is our food," says Evelina. "We are used to swallowing politics with our meals. For breakfast you eat elections, a parliament discussion comes for lunch, and at dinner you laugh at the evening news or get mad at the lies that the Communist Party is trying to sell, in spite of everything." Perhaps these people can live almost without food—either because it's too expensive or because there is nothing to buy, or both—without books and information, but not without politics.

14 One might think that this is happening only now, when they have the first real chance to change something. Not so. This intimacy with political issues was a part of everyday life whether on the level of hatred, or mistrust, or gossip, or just plain resignation during Todor Živkov's communist government. In a totalitarian society, one *has* to relate to the power directly; there is no escape. Therefore, politics never becomes abstract. It remains a palpable, brutal force directing every aspect of our lives, from what we eat to how we live and where we work. Like a disease, a plague, an epidemic, it doesn't spare anybody. Paradoxically, this is precisely how a totalitarian state produces its enemies: politicized citizens. The "velvet revolution" is the product not only of high politics, but of the consciousness of ordinary citizens, infected by politics.

15 Before you get here, you tend to forget newspaper pictures of people standing in line in front of shops. You think they serve as proof in the ideological battle, the proof that communism is failing. Or you take them as mere pictures, not reality. But once here, you cannot escape the *feeling* of shortages, even if you are not standing in line, even if you don't see them. In Prague, where people line up only for fruit, there was enough of all necessities, except for oranges or lemons, which were considered a "luxury." It is hard to predict what will be considered a luxury item because this depends on planning, production, and shortages. One time it might be fruit, as in Prague, or milk, as in Sofia. People get used to less and less of everything. In Albania, the monthly ration for a whole family is two pounds of meat, two pounds of cheese, ten pounds of flour, less than half a pound each of coffee and butter. Everywhere, the bottom line is bread. It means safety—because the lack of bread is where real fear begins. Whenever I read a headline "No Bread" in the newspaper, I see a small, dark,

almost empty bakery on Vladimir Zaimov Boulevard in Sofia, and I myself, even without reason, experience a genuine fear. It makes my bread unreal, too, and I feel as if I should grab it and eat it while it lasts.

16 Every mother in Bulgaria can point to where communism failed, from the failures of the planned economy (and the consequent lack of food, milk), to the lack of apartments, child-care facilities, clothes, disposable diapers, or toilet paper. The banality of everyday life is where it has really failed, rather than on the level of ideology. In another kitchen in Sofia, Ana, Katarine and I sit. Her one-year-old daughter is trying to grab our cups from the table. She looks healthy. "She is fine now," says Ana, "but you should have seen her six months ago. There was no formula to buy and normal milk you can hardly get as it is. At one point our shops started to sell Humana, imported powdered milk from the dollar shops, because its shelf life was over. I didn't have a choice. I had to feed my baby with that milk, and she got very, very sick. By allowing this milk to be sold, our own government poisoned babies. It was even on TV; they had to put it on because so many babies in Sofia got sick. We are the Third World here."

17 If communism didn't fail on bread or milk, it certainly failed on strawberries. When I flew to Warsaw from West Berlin, I bought cosmetics, oranges, chocolates, Nescafé, as a present for my friend Zofia—as if I were going home. I also bought a small basket of strawberries. I knew that by now she could buy oranges or even Nescafé from the street vendors at a good price—but not strawberries. I bought them also because I remembered when we were together in New York for the first time, back in the eighties, and we went shopping. In a downtown Manhattan supermarket, we stood in front of a fruit counter and just stared. It was full of fruits we didn't know the names of—or if we did, like the man with the banana in Bucharest, we didn't know how they would taste. But this sight was not a miracle; we somehow expected it. What came as a real surprise was fresh strawberries, even though it was December and decorated Christmas trees were in the windows already. In Poland or Yugoslavia, you could see strawberries only in spring. We would buy them for children or when we were visiting a sick relative, so expensive were they. And here, all of a sudden—strawberries. At that moment, they represented all the difference between the world we lived in and this one, so strange and uncomfortably rich. It was not so much that you could see them in the middle of the winter, but because you could afford them. When I

handed her the strawberries in Warsaw, Zofia said: "How wonderful! I'll save them for my son." The fact that she used the word "save" told me everything: that almost ten years after we saw each other in New York, after the victory of Solidarity, and private initiatives in the economy, there are still no strawberries and perhaps there won't be for another ten years. She was closer to me then, that evening, in the apartment where she lives with her sick, elderly, mother (because there is nobody else to take care of her and to put your parent in a state-run institution would be more than cruelty, it would be a crime). Both of them took just one strawberry each, then put the rest in the refrigerator "for Grzegorz." This is how we tell our kids we love them, because food is love, if you don't have it, or if you have to wait in lines, get what you can, and then prepare a decent meal. Maybe this is why the chicken soup, cabbage stew, and mashed potatoes that evening tasted so good.

18 All this stays with me forever. When I come to New York and go shopping at Grace Balducci's Marketplace on Third Avenue and 71st Street, I think of Zofia, my mother, my friend Jasmina who loves Swiss chocolates, my daughter's desire for Brooklyn chewing gum, and my own hungry self, still confused by the thirty kinds of cheese displayed in front of me. In an article in *Literaturnaya Gazeta* May 1989 the Soviet poet Yevgenii Yevtushenko tells of a *kolkhoz* woman who fainted in an East Berlin shop, just because she saw twenty kinds of sausages. When she came back to her senses, she repeated in despair: "Why, but why?" How well I understand her question—but knowing the answer doesn't really help.

Understanding Meaning

1. What does a simple suggestion of getting a pizza reveal to the author about life in Poland?
2. What does the Warsaw restaurant offer in addition to food? What are the patrons really paying for?
3. What makes Coca-Cola more of a "symbol" than a soft drink in Eastern Europe?
4. How did the author's experiences in Warsaw alter her attitudes about food?
5. What makes politics in Eastern Europe different from the West?
6. Why did communism fail in the eyes of Eastern Europeans?

7. *Critical Thinking:* What does Drakulić's article reveal about American life? What do Americans expect? Is American life based on the precept that what other people view as luxuries Americans must consider necessities?

Evaluating Strategy

1. Is food a good device to highlight the differences between Eastern Europe and the West? Why?
2. How effective is the opening? Does the story about ordering a pizza suggest Drakulić intended this article for an American audience? Would opening with a description of an election or press censorship better highlight the political realities of life in Eastern Europe?
3. *Other Modes:* What role do *narration* and *comparison* play in Drakulić's essay?

Appreciating Language

1. How does your dictionary define the word *luxury?* What makes something a luxury in Eastern Europe, according to Drakulić?
2. What does *kolkholz* mean? Should a term like this be defined for American readers?
3. What words does Drakulić use to describe common foods like strawberries to demonstrate how scarce they are in Eastern Europe? How does she move readers to see as rare commodities what they take for granted?

Connections across the Disciplines

1. How would John Ciardi's definition of happiness (page 194) apply to the attitudes of Eastern Europeans? Would they measure happiness in terms of consumption?
2. Drakulić describes the soul-crushing effects of shortages, struggle, and deprivation. George Orwell's "Pleasure Spots" (page 551) argues that comfort and effortless consumption also can rob people of their humanity. Does a happy medium exist? How much material wealth is necessary for people to live full, human lives? How much is too much?

Writing Suggestions

1. Write a short essay about something you take for granted, and analyze why it would be a luxury for others. How would a homeless person view

your dorm room or apartment? Why would the simple act of walking across the street be a triumph for a disabled person? Consider how the people Drakulić describes respond to foods Americans eat every day. Do people appreciate things only when they are rare and difficult to obtain?

2. *Collaborative Writing:* Discuss this essay with a group of students. Does Drakulić's commentary suggest that political systems should be judged by the amount of goods and services they deliver? Is a prosperous dictatorship more "successful" than an impoverished democracy where all citizens are free but equally poor? Do the conditions Drakulić describes indicate why people often follow dictators who promise a better standard of living? How should governments be judged? Take notes on the comments made by the group, and develop a list of agreed points. Work together and draft a short statement expressing the opinions of your group.

LISA FRIED

Lisa Fried is a business writer and editor. She has analyzed the development of industrial consortiums in which competitive enterprises cooperate to conduct research. In addition, she published a study of corporate involvement in public education. While managing editor of Management Review, *Fried wrote this article, analyzing the growth of female entrepreneurship.*

A New Breed of Entrepreneur—Women

In this article published in 1984, Fried uses both personal interviews and government statistics to study women-owned businesses. Before reading Fried's essay, you may wish to see how your dictionary defines entrepreneur.

1 After 21 years of service at a leading photography and graphic arts firm, Judie Eakins, the president of the company's Dallas subsidiary, found herself out of a job. Five months earlier, a stockholders' dispute over management philosophies prompted the termination of Sidney Gayle, the chairman of the board and president. Eakins' pink slip came when the new management team at The Alderman Co. converted the Dallas operation from a wholly owned subsidiary to a division, eliminating her position.

2 At that point in April 1987, Eakins had two choices: go work for someone else or work for herself. Eakins had worked for Gayle in a number of capacities at The Alderman Co. So three months after losing her job, she teamed up with him to start two design and photography studios. Eakins, who had managed the turnaround of Alderman-Dallas from a loser into a $6 million company in three years, now heads up Omega Studios Inc. Southwest in Irving, Texas. Gayle heads up a twin studio in North Carolina, Omega Studios Inc. Southeast, and is chairman of the board of the Texas studio. (Postscript: Alderman-Dallas closed its doors one year after Eakins' position was eliminated.)

3 In an era marked by widespread mergers, acquisitions and downsizing, the circumstances leading to Eakins' departure from Alderman

are not that surprising. However, it may surprise some that she jumped into her own business less than three months after losing her job. But Eakins' decision probably wouldn't shock analysts at the Small Business Administration (SBA), who have been watching the escalation of female entrepreneurs for some time now. From 1980 to 1986, the number of women owning small-business sole proprietorships—those with 500 employees or less—increased by almost 63 percent to more than 4 million. During the same period, the growth rate for male owners was 35 percent. And with women owning 30 percent of all small-business sole proprietorships by 1986, women have clearly become a driving force in the economy.

4 With that in mind, *Management Review* set out to get a closer look at this new breed of entrepreneurs. We interviewed women who head up businesses in the broadcasting, wine making, advertising, computer consulting and photography industries. Their visions for their companies, career motivations and management styles may surprise you.

A LOOK AT PAST JOBS

5 When executives leave the corporate life to start their own ventures, their past employment experiences weigh heavily on their management and leadership styles. For these women, the lessons of how *not* to manage have sometimes been the strongest. "I knew that I wanted to do things differently than Alderman had done," explains Eakins, referring to her former employer. "We had four stockholders all involved in the company, all in upper management . . . who wanted to run things their way. Decisions were typically made by committee, and in many cases, the necessary sense of urgency was not there."

6 While Eakins recognizes the value in having a lot of people participate in management, ultimately one person needs to make the final decision, she says. "You need one person willing to take responsibility and make the decision—right or wrong."

7 As a result, Eakins has set up her studio with thin layers of management. In addition, her organizational chart is an inverted one; she is on the bottom, responsible to everyone above her. The next positions up the organizational chart are filled by the operations manager (her husband), the controller and leaders. Leaders "are supervisors but not in the traditional sense," explains Eakins, who is a member of

AMA's General Management Council for Growing Organizations. "We are not stressing the supervisory aspect as much as leadership. We want them to lead other people and to get them to buy into what they want them to do—not create a dictatorial situation."

8 Elaine Lyerly, who started her own marketing/advertising/public relations firm in Charlotte, North Carolina, in 1977, was familiar with many management styles before her startup. Her six years at Group C, another Charlotte public relations agency, exposed her to many types of clients and, as a result, many different management styles. "When you're servicing an account, you learn the inner workings of a company," she says. "There were a number of different companies and management styles that I liked, that motivated employees and that produced the greatest results. I guess I'm sort of a smorgasbord of management styles."

9 Lyerly refers to Group C, which went out of business in the late '70s, as a creative-driven agency with lots of room for expression. This philosophy seems to have carried over into her firm, Lyerly Agency, as well. Elaine and her sister, Melia, the firm's executive vice president, hold meetings regularly for employees to complain, acknowledge accomplishments, discuss problems and, in general, air their views. "Employees are going to complain," Elaine contends. "And if these complaints are not dealt with, managers are really out of touch with a big pull on the company's effectiveness. Our approach is that we welcome complaints. We view them as an opportunity to interact with employees."

10 For example, if an employee complains about the copy machine, in many companies that person is labeled as a complainer, she says. But if, instead, managers realize that employees don't complain about things unless they are committed to them, they will deal with the incidents differently. One approach is to recognize that the employee may be interested in having an operation run in a more efficient way. "Look at how employees can impact the growth, direction and results of the company," Lyerly advises.

11 Barbara Lamont, president and CEO of WCCL-TV and the New Orleans Teleport, a satellite facility, has certainly heeded that advice. "In broadcasting, there are the 'them's' and the 'us's.' The them's are the unskilled who panic at the slightest thing, and there's always one of them in charge. I try to avoid those types in my business," explains Lamont, whose broadcast career included stints at ABC, CBS, Metromedia in New York and several stations outside of the United States

before she started her own television station. "If something happens here, no one looks for whom to blame. Everyone just jumps in to help.

12 "We have a very high ratio of women and blacks and, in general, very highly skilled people. . . . It's most important to me that this be a healthy place for people to work—a place where freedom and creativity is encouraged, where people don't lay blame or [play] politics, one of racial and sexual equality—and, eventually, healthy financially. It shows up on the screen . . . and in our relationships with the community, our viewers and advertisers. Lamont believes that the work environments at WCCL-TV and the teleport are the "most supportive" ones she and her staff have ever worked in.

FOSTERING A POSITIVE ENVIRONMENT

13 Several female presidents cite the importance of fostering a positive environment for employees. Some measure their success by it, while others consider their emphasis on it a typically "female" management response. "If you're having fun, the people that work for you are having fun, and if you are satisfying your customer base, that spells success," explains Eakins, whose firm employs 67. "The people working with me are the whole company. It's not the building or the equipment that makes our company. It's our people's talent, and that is what makes us what we are and better than our competitor down the street. Seeing these people develop . . . into superior talent, good managers and good leaders is exciting to me.

14 "I would probably never make it in a *Fortune* 500 company," she admits. "They're probably more bottom-line oriented. You have to be bottom-line oriented, but you also have to have all those people working toward the same goal, and you have to pay attention to them. I consider it a challenge to take someone who's been a problem for others to deal with and figure out how to make that person a star," she says.

15 Eakins' outlook is common among women business owners. In fact, the need for self-fulfillment, the desire to achieve and an interest in helping others motivate women owners *more* than the quest for profits, according to the 1989 Avon Report, a national survey of successful women entrepreneurs. Only 12 percent of 319 women entrepreneurs surveyed regard profits as the primary hallmark of success. More than one-third say it is self-fulfillment; 30 percent equate

success with achievement, and almost 20 percent say success is in helping others.

16 Nevertheless, women entrepreneurs who focus on these nonmonetary factors can make just as much money as those who concentrate on sales growth and profit, according to the study. "Women entrepreneurs may choose different paths to success, yet each path can lead to a profitable enterprise," explains Marilyn Frasier Pollack, Ph.D., an expert on women entrepreneurship and co-owner of New World Decisions, the research firm that conducted the Avon Report. "In fact, successful women entrepreneurs who pursue goals other than sales or profit are found slightly more often at the highest level of annual gross sales [indicated by respondents]—$500,000 and above," she adds.

17 All the female entrepreneurs *MR* interviewed have staffs of fewer than 100 people. Thus, it's not surprising that many thrive on their personal involvement with employees. Deborah Aguiar-Velez, president and owner of Sistemas Corp., a Princeton, N.J.-based computer consulting and training firm, exemplifies this approach. This past year she took a leave of absence from her firm to run New Jersey's Office for the Development of Small Businesses and Women and Minority Businesses, which assists entrepreneurs throughout the Garden State.

18 Of the 33 employees in the division, she replies, "I love these people dearly. . . . They're like my children. I try to nurture them." At the same time, Aguiar-Velez has surprised some staff members by saying "I love you and respect you and that's why I'm being very tough with you." For example, consider a conversation she had with the secretaries. "I told [them] that they should dress for the future. One asked if that meant a dress code was being established. I said, 'No, if you want to acquire power you have to dress in a different way. You dress for the position you want in the future.' Everyone changed their dress," she reports.

19 Other female entrepreneurs point out that their management style is a people-oriented one, which requires skills that may come more naturally to women than to men.

20 For example, Carolyn Martini, who became president of her family's winery after a more than 50-year patriarchy, comments on the impact of gender in international business deals: "American males are pretty straightforward in how they do business," explains Martini, who is also a member of AMA's General Management Council for Growing Organizations. "If they want something or want to sell something, they find someone who wants to buy it. They work out a deal

and it's done. They're considerably less concerned with getting to know someone or feeling they trust someone.

21 "There has been the suggestion that the Japanese think more like women. They, of course, don't feel that way. But they definitely take a different approach than an American male manager would normally take. Women go into business trusting their intuition and men can't understand what that is. The person feels good, you get to know them a bit. For women, it's the way they operate."

EMPLOYEE RELATIONSHIPS ARE CRUCIAL

22 Lyerly, who started her agency with a sister, runs her firm with what she terms a "transformational" or "New Age" management style. Dictatorial management is becoming extinct, she explains, noting that some may label it a "male" style because companies have been traditionally run by men. "What my agency is about—and I think women bring this to the table—is a transformational type of management. It's not motivation by fear. It's empowerment and team building. It eliminates some things from the old style, such as jockeying for position, power and authority," and encourages employee input.

23 She credits women for taking this approach since "they're the ones who are really good at listening and interacting and [don't tend to say] 'this is the way it is.'" Lyerly says her agency's employee discussion meetings signify this approach. Departments meet weekly and the entire staff—12 employees—meets monthly. "There's an opportunity to discuss the agency, complain and acknowledge. The acknowledgement is really important. When someone in the art department acknowledges the media buyer for the great job that was done for a particular client on a tight deadline, it's great."

24 She is quick to point out, however, that employees are free to comment both positively and negatively. "Melia and I know we're accountable for the results we produce and accountable for our employees. We have to create the right environment for that, so we can't judge them by what they say. And, we stress that it is safe [for them] to say anything." Lyerly says that employees feel free to have frank discussions. "It's usually what's *not* said in companies that is devastating," she continues. "Sometimes Melia and I are there to moderate and keep things going in a positive direction; other times we're not. People usually leave feeling great about themselves. . . . "

25 If one gets the impression that these women take their relationships with employees seriously, it's because they do. At the same time, these managers have learned that, despite their efforts, some skills just can't be taught and some employees just don't work out. And, in small companies like these, the responsibility for firing someone often falls on their shoulders. "This has always been a real difficult thing for me to do," explains Eakins, who had to fire a large number of employees during the turnaround of Alderman-Dallas. "I go over things again and again to be sure that when I do fire someone, I'm doing the right thing.

26 "You don't just walk in and fire people. You work with them and give them time to make changes. . . . To some degree you feel as if you've failed if you can't bring those people around. But if they don't work out, you do fire them."

27 These decisions can be particularly difficult when another manager disagrees with the president's decision. It can be especially troublesome when that other manager is a spouse. Sistemas' Deborah Aguiar-Velez experienced that recently. A programmer who made client presentations was not bringing in new business. Debbie's husband, German Velez, who joined the firm as vice president and senior consultant two years after its startup, thought the employee needed more time to develop. Both German and Deborah agreed to wait it out for three months.

28 "After three months, he still wasn't getting contracts," Deborah says, "and my husband didn't want to let him go. He thought that long term he was the best programmer we'd ever find. I kept thinking, 'he's not costing us any money but he's not making us any either.'" Hoping he would improve, she allowed him to stay for two more months to finish his computer science training, which would help his career outside of Sistemas. At the end of that time, she and her husband agreed he had to go.

Understanding Meaning

1. How does the growth of female-owned businesses compare with that of male-owned enterprises?
2. Why are more women becoming entrepreneurs?
3. What lessons in management have aided women in operating their own businesses?

4. What factors do women entrepreneurs see as critical to their success?
5. What rewards do women seek from owning businesses? Do they have more than financial considerations?
6. What does Carolyn Martini's statement that "Japanese think more like women" imply?
7. *Critical Thinking:* Do gender differences create different management styles? Do women bosses behave differently from male bosses? Do traditionally male institutions such as banks or the military change as women enter leadership roles, or do women adopt prevailing attitudes?

Evaluating Strategy

1. How much outside research does Fried offer readers?
2. Would this article be different if statistics were omitted in favor of adding more interviews?
3. How important are quotations in this article? Is it effective to have the subjects of an analysis speak for themselves?
4. *Other Modes:* Where does Fried use *narration* and *comparison* in her article?

Appreciating Language

1. How do you define *entrepreneur?* Has it become a buzz word? Is it often an inflated term? Can a shopkeeper or barber be called an *entrepreneur?*
2. Fried refers to a "female" style of business management. How would you define it? How does it compare to "male" patterns of leadership?

Connections across the Disciplines

1. Do the new female entrepreneurs risk becoming a generation of "company women"? Refer to Ellen Goodman's "The Company Man" (page 185).
2. Do the rewards of working for themselves prevent female entrepreneurs from suffering the stresses described by Juliet Schor in "The Overworked American" (page 377)?
3. How does the view that "Japanese think like women" reflect the findings of William Ouchi about American and Japanese workers (page 270)?

Writing Suggestions

1. Write a short essay analyzing the differences you have detected between male and female bosses. Did you see differences between your male and female teachers? Have you been treated differently by bosses of different genders? Do women, in your opinion, practice a distinctly different management style?
2. *Collaborative Writing:* Discuss Fried's article with a group of students, and ask members to respond to this question: How will the emergence of female-owned businesses change the marketplace and American society? Record the ideas members raise, and draft a brief essay highlighting those the group feels are most significant.

JULIET B. SCHOR

Juliet B. Schor is an economist who has served as an associate professor at Harvard University. She has edited several books, including Financial Openness and National Autonomy: Opportunities and Constraints *and* Golden Age of Capitalism: Reinterpreting the Postwar Experience. *In 1991 she published* The Overworked American: The Unexpected Decline of Leisure. *The introduction of computers and new industrial methods that have made Americans more productive workers, Schor discovered, has not led to an increase in leisure time.*

The Overworked American

As you read Schor's analysis of American workers, pay attention to her presentation and interpretation of statistics. Consider if the stresses of work and the joys of leisure are best measured in hours.

1 In the last twenty years the amount of time Americans have spent at their jobs has risen steadily. Each year the change is small, amounting to about nine hours, or slightly more than one additional day of work. In any given year, such a small increment has probably been imperceptible. But the accumulated increase over two decades is substantial. When surveyed, Americans report that they have only sixteen and a half hours of leisure a week, after the obligations of job and household are taken care of. Working hours are already longer than they were forty years ago. If present trends continue, by the end of the century Americans will be spending as much time at their jobs as they did back in the nineteen twenties.

2 The rise of worktime was unexpected. For nearly a hundred years, hours had been declining. When this decline abruptly ended in the late 1940s, it marked the beginning of a new era in worktime. But the change was barely noticed. Equally surprising, but also hardly recognized, has been the deviation from Western Europe. After progressing in tandem for nearly a century, the United States veered off into a trajectory of declining leisure, while in Europe work has been disappearing. Forty years later, the differences are large. U.S. manufacturing

employees currently work 320 more hours—the equivalent of over two months—than their counterparts in West Germany or France.

3 The decline in Americans' leisure time is in sharp contrast to the potential provided by the growth of productivity. Productivity measures the goods and services that result from each hour worked. When productivity rises, a worker can either produce the current output in less time, or remain at work the same number of hours and produce more. Every time productivity increases, we are presented with the possibility of either more free time or more money. That's the productivity dividend.

4 Since 1948, productivity has failed to rise in only five years. The level of productivity of the U.S. worker has more than doubled. In other words, we could now produce our 1948 standard of living (measured in terms of marketed goods and services) in less than half the time it took in that year. We actually could have chosen the four-hour day. Or a working year of six months. Or, *every worker in the United States could now be taking every other year off from work—with pay.* Incredible as it may sound, this is just the simple arithmetic of productivity growth in operation.

5 But between 1948 and the present we did not use any of the productivity dividend to reduce hours. In the first two decades after 1948, productivity grew rapidly, at about 3 percent a year. During that period, worktime did not fall appreciably. Annual hours per labor force participant fell only slightly. And on a per-capita (rather than a labor force) basis, they even rose a bit. Since then, productivity growth has been lower, but still positive, averaging just over 1 percent a year. Yet hours have risen steadily for two decades. In 1990, the average American owns and consumes more than twice as much as he or she did in 1948, but also has less free time.

6 How did this happen? Why has leisure been such a conspicuous casualty of prosperity? In part, the answer lies in the difference between the markets for consumer products and free time. Consider the former, the legendary American market. It is a veritable consumer's paradise, offering a dazzling array of products varying in style, design, quality, price, and country of origin. The consumer is treated to GM versus Toyota, Kenmore versus GE, Sony, or Magnavox, the Apple versus the IBM. We've got Calvin Klein, Anne Klein, Liz Claiborne, and Levi-Strauss; McDonald's, Burger King, and Colonel Sanders. Marketing experts and advertisers spend vast sums of money to make these choices appealing—even irresistible. And they have been suc-

cessful. In cross-country comparisons, Americans have been found to spend more time shopping than anyone else. They also spend a higher fraction of the money they earn. And with the explosion of consumer debt, many are now spending what they haven't earned.

7 After four decades of this shopping spree, the American standard of living embodies a level of material comfort unprecedented in human history. The American home is more spacious and luxurious than the dwellings of any other nation. Food is cheap and abundant. The typical family owns a fantastic array of household and consumer appliances: we have machines to wash our clothes and dishes, mow our lawns, and blow away our snow. On a per-person basis, yearly income is nearly $22,000 a year—or sixty-five times the average income of half the world's population.

8 On the other hand, the "market" for free time hardly even exists in America. With few exceptions, employers (the sellers) don't offer the chance to trade off income gains for a shorter work day or the occasional sabbatical. They just pass on income, in the form of annual pay raises or bonuses, or, if granting increased vacation or personal days, usually do so unilaterally. Employees rarely have the chance to exercise an actual choice about how they will spend their productivity dividend. The closest substitute for a "market in leisure" is the travel and other leisure industries that advertise products to occupy our free time. But this indirect effect has been weak, as consumers crowd increasingly expensive leisure spending into smaller periods of time.

9 Nor has society provided a forum for deliberate choice. The growth of worktime did not occur as a result of public debate. There has been little attention from government, academia, or civic organizations. For the most part, the issue has been off the agenda, a non-choice, a hidden trade off. It was not always so. As early as 1791, when Philadelphia carpenters went on strike for the ten-hour day, there was public awareness about hours of work. Throughout the nineteenth century, and well into the twentieth, the reduction of worktime was one of the nation's most pressing social issues. Employers and workers fought about the length of the working day, social activists delivered lectures, academics wrote treatises, courts handed down decisions, and government legislated hours of work. Through the Depression, hours remained a major social preoccupation. Today these debates and conflicts are long forgotten. Since the 1930s, the choice between work and leisure has hardly been a choice at all, at least in any conscious sense.

10 In its starkest terms, my argument is this: Key incentive structures of capitalist economies contain biases toward long working hours. As a result of these incentives, the development of capitalism led to the growth of what I call "long hour jobs." The eventual recovery of leisure came about because trade unions and social reformers waged a protracted struggle for shorter hours. Some time between the Depression and the end of the Second World War, that struggle collapsed. As the inevitable pressures toward long hours reasserted themselves, U.S. workers experienced a new decline that now, at the century's end, has created a crisis of leisure time. I am aware that these are strong claims which overturn most of what we have been taught to believe about the way our economy works. . . .

11 Ironically, the tendency of capitalism to expand work is often associated with a growth in joblessness. In recent years, as a majority have taken on the extra month of work, nearly one-fifth of all participants in the labor force are unable to secure as many hours as they want or need to make ends meet. While many employees are subjected to mandatory overtime and are suffering from overwork, their co-workers are put on involuntary part-time. In the context of my story, these irrationalities seem to make sense. The rational, and humane, solution—reducing hours to spread the work—has practically been ruled out of court.

12 In speaking of "long hour jobs" exclusively in terms of the capitalist marketplace, I do not mean to overlook those women who perform their labor in the privacy of their own homes. Until the late nineteenth century, large numbers of single and married women did participate in the market economy, either in farm labor or through various entrepreneurial activities (taking in boarders, sewing at home, and so on). By the twentieth century, however, a significant percentage of married women, particularly white women, spent all their time outside the market nexus, as full-time "domestic laborers," providing goods and, increasingly, services for their families. And they, too, have worked at "long hour jobs."

13 Studies of household labor beginning in the 1910s and continuing through to the 1970s show that the amount of time a full-time housewife devoted to her work remained virtually unchanged for over fifty years—despite dramatic changes in household technology. As homes, like factories, were "industrialized," refrigerators, laundry machines, vacuum cleaners, and microwaves took up residence in the American

domicile. Ready-made clothes and processed food supplanted the home-produced variety. Yet with all these labor-saving innovations, no labor has been saved. Instead, housework expanded to fill the available time. Norms of cleanliness rose. Standards of mothering grew more rigorous. Cooking and baking became more complicated. At the same time, a variety of cheaper and more efficient ways of providing household services failed in the market, and housewives continued to do their own.

14 The stability of housewives' hours was due to a particular bias in the incentives of what we may term the "labor market for housewives." Just as the capitalist labor market contains structural biases toward long hours, so too has the housewife's situation. . . . And in neither case has technology automatically saved labor. It has taken women's exodus from the home itself to reduce their household labor. As women entered paid employment, they cut back their hours of domestic work significantly—but not by enough to keep their total working time unchanged. According to my estimates, when a woman takes a paying job, her schedule expands by at least twenty hours a week. The overwork that plagues many Americans, especially married women, springs from a combination of full-time male jobs, the expansion of housework to fill the available hours, and the growth of employment among married women.

15 However scarce academic research on the rising workload may be, what we do know suggests it has contributed to a variety of social problems. For example, work is implicated in the dramatic rise of "stress." Thirty percent of adults say that they experience high stress nearly every day; even higher numbers report high stress once or twice a week. A third of the population says that they are rushed to do the things they have to do—up from a quarter in 1965. Stress-related diseases have exploded, especially among women, and jobs are a major factor. Workers' compensation claims related to stress tripled during just the first half of the 1980s. Other evidence also suggests a rise in the demands placed on employees on the job. According to a recent review of existing findings, Americans are literally working themselves to death—as jobs contribute to heart disease, hypertension, gastric problems, depression, exhaustion, and a variety of other ailments. Surprisingly, the high-powered jobs are not the most dangerous. The most stressful workplaces are the "electronic sweatshops"

and assembly lines where a demanding pace is coupled with virtually no individual discretion.

16 Sleep has become another casualty of modern life. According to sleep researchers, studies point to a "sleep deficit" among Americans, a majority of whom are currently getting between 60 and 90 minutes less a night than they should for optimum health and performance. The number of people showing up at sleep disorder clinics with serious problems has skyrocketed in the last decade. Shiftwork, long working hours, the growth of a global economy (with its attendant continent-hopping and twenty-four-hour business culture), and the accelerating pace of life have all contributed to sleep deprivation. If you need an alarm clock, the experts warn, you're probably sleeping too little.

17 The juggling act between job and family is another problem area. Half the population now says they have too little time for their families. The problem is particularly acute for women: In one study, half of all employed mothers reported it caused either "a lot" or an "extreme" level of stress. The same proportion feel that "when I'm at home I try to make up to my family for being away at work, and as a result I rarely have any time for myself." This stress has placed tremendous burdens on marriages. Two-earner couples have less time together, which researchers have found reduces the happiness and satisfaction of a marriage. These couples often just don't have enough time to talk to each other. And growing numbers of husbands and wives are like ships passing in the night, working sequential schedules to manage their child care. Among young parents, the prevalence of at least one partner working outside regular daytime hours is now close to one half. But this "solution" is hardly a happy one. According to one parent: "I work 11–7 to accommodate my family—to eliminate the need for babysitters. However, the stress on myself is tremendous."

18 A decade of research by Berkeley sociologist Arlie Hochschild suggests that many marriages where women are doing the "second shift" are close to the breaking point. When job, children, and marriage have to be attended to, it's often the marriage that is neglected. The failure of many men to do their share at home creates further problems. A twenty-six-year-old legal secretary in California reports that her husband "does no cooking, no washing, no anything else. How do I feel? Furious. If our marriage ends, it will be on this issue. And it just might."

19 Serious as these problems are, the most alarming development may be the effect of the work explosion on the care of children. According to economist Sylvia Hewlett, "child neglect has become endemic to our society." A major problem is that children are increasingly left alone, to fend for themselves while their parents are at work. Nationwide, estimates of children in "self"—or, more accurately, "no"—care range up to seven million. Local studies have found figures of up to one-third of children caring for themselves. At least half a million preschoolers are thought to be left at home part of each day. One 911 operator reports large numbers of frightened callers: "It's not uncommon to hear from a child of six or seven who has been left in charge of even younger siblings."

20 Even when parents are at home, overwork may leave them with limited time, attention, or energy for their children. One working parent noted, "My child has severe emotional problems because I am too tired to listen to him. It is not quality time; it's bad quantity time that's destroying my family." Economist Victor Fuchs has found that between 1960 and 1986, the time parents actually had available to be with children fell ten hours a week for whites and twelve for blacks. Hewlett links the "parenting deficit" to a variety of problems plaguing the country's youth: poor performance in school, mental problems, drug and alcohol use, and teen suicide. According to another expert, kids are being "cheated out of childhood. . . . There is a sense that adults don't care about them."

21 Of course, there's more going on here than lack of time. Child neglect, marital distress, sleep deprivation and stress-related illnesses all have other causes. But the growth of work has exacerbated each of these social ailments. Only by understanding why we work as much as we do, and how the demands of work affect family life, can we hope to solve these problems.

22 The past forty years should provide a warning. They have brought us nothing in the way of leisure time and a saner pace of life. The bias of the system is strongly toward the status quo. But time poverty is straining the social fabric. Continued growth threatens environmental balance, and gender equality requires new work patterns. Despite these obstacles, I am hopeful. By understanding how we came to be caught up in the cycle of work-and-spend, perhaps we can regain a reasonable balance between work and leisure.

Understanding Meaning

1. How does Schor explain the loss of leisure time? Was it expected?
2. Are Americans willing to trade free time for material goods? Is it truly our nature to measure success in terms of houses and cars rather than leisure time?
3. What effects do longer working hours have on employees and their families?
4. Can smaller families and laborsaving appliances offset the loss of leisure time? How much "leisure" time was previously spent washing dishes and ironing clothes?
5. If Americans are working longer hours and have less leisure time, how does one explain the continued growth of the travel industry and sales of ski equipment, boats, and expensive home entertainment centers?
6. *Critical Thinking:* Do most people work out of choice or necessity? For many Americans has the office become their true home? Do the relationships with like-minded colleagues and clearly established reward systems of work provide some people with more support than they receive from their families? Do some people feel more secure and more happy behind their desks than in their living rooms? Why or why not?

Evaluating Strategy

1. What kinds of evidence does Schor present?
2. Schor places her thesis statement, "In its starkest terms, my argument is this: Key incentive structures of capitalist economies contain biases toward long working hours," in the middle of her essay. Would this be better situated at the opening or close of the article?
3. Do statements such as "Americans are literally working themselves to death" require more support to be credible?

Appreciating Language

1. How does Schor define "productivity"?
2. What does Schor mean by the term "long hour jobs"?
3. Circle words that indicate a bias toward or against long working hours. Does Schor use connotations to express her views?

Connections across the Disciplines

1. Is Schor describing America as a nation of Ellen Goodman's "company" men (page 185)?

2. Review Darrell Huff's article about statistics (page 337). Does Schor avoid the errors in interpretation he describes?
3. Consider Lisa Fried's analysis of female entrepreneurs (page 368). Does working long hours for your own business bring greater rewards and cause less stress than working for someone else? Does a difference in satisfaction exist between being the boss and being an employee?

Writing Suggestions

1. Keep a journal for a week, and record the number of hours you spend at school or work. How much leisure time do you have? Write an analysis of your schedule. What effects is it having on your health, family, relationships, and self-esteem?
2. *Collaborative Writing:* Discuss Schor's article with a group of students, and ask them to consider how their parents' and their own work has affected their lives. How many grew up in a two-career family? How many members of the group have working partners? What barriers, if any, has work imposed on personal fulfillment, family, and friends? Take notes of the comments developed by the group, and work together to draft a short analysis of your observations. What general conclusions can be drawn from the experiences of the group?

FRANK PILIPP
AND CHARLES SHULL

Frank Pilipp is an assistant professor of German at Lynchburg College in Virginia. He has conducted research in modern European literature and film and is the author of The Novels of Martin Walser: A Critical Introduction. *Charles Shull is an associate professor of sociology at Lynchburg College, where he teaches courses about AIDS. He served as president of an AIDS support group and assisted people with HIV. Pilipp and Shull collaborated to write an analysis of how movies made for television have treated the epidemic and its victims.*

TV Movies of the First Decade of AIDS

First published in the Journal of Popular Film and Television *in 1993, Pilipp and Shull's article analyzes the messages about AIDS contained in four television movies that appeared between 1985 and 1991.*

1 Among the media of popular culture, television, over the past decade, has hesitantly become a mouthpiece for reporting and responding to the AIDS epidemic.[1] In addition to documentary and news-related coverage, a small array of fictional accounts, that is full-length feature films spawned by the disease, have constituted a general, albeit basic, chronicle of the multi-faceted dimensions of the epidemic. As a set, these movies both challenge *and* reinforce a number of basic values and stereotypes linked to nurturing, caretaking, parenting, and sexuality. Consequently, these movies generate an imagery of the first AIDS decade as multifarious and, perhaps, as confusing as the epidemic itself. Contrasting the presentations of the gay male AIDS protagonists and their families in the films *An Early Frost* (1985), *As Is* (1986), *Andre's Mother* (1990), and *Our Sons* (1991) should not only show the degree to which the AIDS epidemic has been a cultural catalyst and influenced American society but also how cultural values predetermine public and personal perceptions of such an issue as AIDS.

2 These films present the views of the AIDS issue[2] through images of those who are either "inside" or "outside" the social worlds of gay

men and/or of AIDS. This division reflects the parallel worlds of the "gay"/"straight" and AIDS involved/non-involved experiential worlds of contemporary American society. The films illustrate the tensions generated when a terminal illness forces strangers to acknowledge the experiences of the other; to confront, accept, and interact with a social (or medical) world alien to them. The walls that divide these worlds have been built by the dynamics of fear: families fearing and rejecting those who are gay and/or AIDS infected and gay men fearing rejection by their families. That insider/outsider dichotomy has also been identified as the worlds of the *immune* and the *implicated*.[3] In a compelling manner, Goldstein illustrates how popular culture and the arts have reacted differently to the AIDS epidemic. He indicates that although the treatment or representation of AIDS in the arts reflects the insider perspective of the implicated, often the traumatized view of the artist himself, popular culture represents the unassailable refuge of the immune, the unaffected, and presumably non-infected, outside platform of the broad masses. Unquestionably this premise is well argued, though we must disagree with Goldstein's view that "TV movies about AIDS shy away from gay male protagonists" and that "the typical protagonist is a young, virtuous, and vulnerable woman" (28–29). Although this holds true for most of those films of the '80s that deal with terminal diseases in general[4] (which are generically indebted to the AIDS epidemic), the films to be discussed here all introduce single, white, professionally successful, gay, male protagonists experiencing AIDS.

3 On the other hand, Goldstein aptly comments:

> 4 In television, where demography is destiny, the person with AIDS is rarely an innocent everyman. . . . Adult males are usually represented as transgressors whose behavior places others in jeopardy; infected women are usually exempt from blame, but rendered nearly as helpless as their children. In these prime-time masques, it is not the person with AIDS who is victimized but those threatened or affected by the disease. Family and community occupy center stage, and the issue is not survival but cohesion: how to deal with a breach in the safety net. (21)

5 He suggests that in order to appeal to rather than appall the populace, television must resort to cautious and sensible treatment of the AIDS threat for, as one critic comments, "the social stigma surrounding homosexuality and intravenous drug use create a distance that precludes

automatic sympathy."[5] Therefore TV movies redirect primary emphasis away from the anxieties, self-reproaches, and fears of the HIV-infected (or the world of homosexuals) and toward the reactions of those around him. Only secondarily do these movies focus on the AIDS epidemic as experienced by gay men—in fact, modes of contraction (or prevention for that matter) are mostly silenced and sex and drug use are not discussed.[6]

6 Unlike the independent theatrical releases *Parting Glances* (1986) and *Longtime Companion* (1990), the movies made for commercial television lack any direct presentation of the linkage of their protagonists, usually gay couples, with other members of the gay community.[7] *Parting Glances* and *Longtime Companion,* however, are documentary-style investigations of the impact of the AIDS epidemic *specifically* upon the gay male community. Set in New York City, these two movies examine the issue through distinctly different approaches. Both these movies must be seen from the point of view of the respective temporal context (i.e., knowledge about and impact of the AIDS crisis in 1986 vs. 1990). Both are rich with interwoven subtle and complex motifs presenting issues of the lives of gay men and of gay men dealing with AIDS during the 1980s.

7 *Parting Glances* uses a micro-level lens, limiting the action to a period of twenty-four hours. Within that time, the impact of the epidemic is presented as a force that is a presence, a given that pervades and invades reality in the lives of the characters. Good-byes must be said; caretaking must be carried out; relationships must be resolved. Each must deal with the possibility of the death of friends and relationships. *Longtime Companion* reverses the view and, using a macro-level approach, scans across the first decade of the crisis, presenting the multi-faceted AIDS experiences and responses of gay men during those years. The viewer is shown how the disease reorganizes the lives of a network of friends. Friends die alone; partners take care of partners; some become AIDS activists; and each must deal with personal feelings about dying and death. Although the two movies apply a direct and exclusive approach in their focus on the gay community, their intentions do not seem notably different from that of those films made for television. Both force the viewer to confront (1) the social world of gay men; (2) the multiple dimensions of the destructiveness of AIDS; and (3) the complications of unresolved relationships.

8 *An Early Frost* is the first of the AIDS films made for TV, starring Aidan Quinn as the infected Michael, Gena Rowlands as his caring

mother, and Ben Gazzara as the prejudiced father. An eminently successful Ivy League law school graduate, Michael inhabits a luxurious house in Chicago with his lover, Peter. Diagnosed as having AIDS, Michael ejects Peter when Peter confesses infidelity during their two-year relationship and resorts to the support of his (Michael's) family in suburbia. His return forces his parents to deal with a double-barrelled issue: their son's sexuality and his terminal disease. They are facing a diseased stranger. Additionally, the son now must break down the false image of himself that he has worked to maintain for his parents and that has helped the denial pattern of his parents to continue. Michael is the only "closeted" gay man in these films. Contrary to him, his lover, Peter, is said to be open to his parents/family. Michael's fear of disclosing himself is validated by his father's reaction of pure repulsion and hatred, perceiving it as a family shame having to call "a homosexual [with] this disease" his son and he relegates Michael to "his own kind." The father asks "How can a son of mine become a stranger?" This is a hollow question since it is unclear whether he is saying that his son is a stranger because he (Michael) is gay or because he (Michael) had not been honest with his parents. It is not entirely clear whether he is questioning Michael's sexuality, his own lack of perception, or his son's not telling him the truth.

9 Michael's revelations force both father and mother to realize that they do not know their son as an adult; they merely remember him as a child/teenager playing Chopin and running track. They have allowed him privacy as an adult but that choice means not having to ask too many questions about his life in the city.[8] After Michael's disclosures the film illustrates how the protagonist's "otherness" shatters the harmony of this representative middle-class family and meticulously traces the path as one by one family members and friends accept his strangeness. The film's strategy is such that it repeatedly pits two characters against each other in all possible (relevant) constellations in order to expound the views on the AIDS/gay-issue from various outsider perspectives. These views are shown both by the reactions of family members who know nothing about the disease, and even by the rescue squad who refuse to transport Michael to the hospital. The mother's fear and confusion is balanced by her unflagging understanding and love and her resolute demand for information from his doctor and for her husband's acceptance of Michael. Her reaction forms a sharp contrast with his pregnant sister's fear of possible transmission to her small son and unborn child and his father's fear when Michael

moves to kiss his mother. Within the family only Michael's totally reasonable grandmother offers nothing but love and support pronouncing the film's message: "It's a disease, not a disgrace."

10 Two scenes reflect that Michael as a gay man knew about AIDS but was able to stand outside until his own illness transformed him into an insider. When Michael's doctor explains to him that someone can be a "carrier of the disease without actually showing the symptoms himself," Michael responds "You mean you can pass it on without actually getting it?"[9] Michael's anger at Peter's infidelity is an all too understandable reaction to the breaking of the safety bond that protected them from what was happening to others.

11 As an insider Michael comes into contact with the larger world of AIDS when he joins a hospital AIDS support group: mostly young—by inference, gay—white men, but also including a heterosexual male infected through a prostitute, and a black male. There he is exposed to their fears and the humiliating reactions of others to their illness. Only the blackest of humors displayed by a fellow-patient, Victor (John Glover in a superb performance), grants the viewer temporary comic relief. Representing the popular stereotype of the effeminate, flamboyant homosexual man, this character is easy to laugh at, and to discount without taking him seriously as a man or acknowledging his sexuality. Yet the viewer is forced to acknowledge the humanness of Victor as he is seen dictating his will to Michael. When Michael sees Victor's belongings in a trash can after Victor's death, both Michael and the viewer are shown the deadly physical and social power of the disease as well as a forecast of Michael's future. The insider gay male messages also focus on the problem of accepting one's sexual orientation as part of one's individual identity and being accepted by others. Peter, who is open to his family, has criticized Michael for never admitting his homosexuality to his parents: "When are they going to find out who you really are? After you're dead?" Michael's difficulty becomes evident in a hospital conversation with his mother about his being gay. His statement "I haven't been unhappy" certainly is not a very strong self-affirmation.

12 The fear of the outsiders' reaction to Michael's "coming out" is one dynamic that drives this movie. Faced with the panicky reactions of those around him, most notably his father's, and in order to rid the latter of the burden of society's disapproval, while at the same time not wanting to burden Peter with his sickness, Michael attempts suicide. After Michael is rescued by his father, the ensuing, violently ver-

bose altercation between father and son allows the father to break through his own fears and to demand that Michael fight, because the father does not want to see his life's work destroyed. Although this patriarchal reasoning is probably based on material values (the life-long struggle of the hard-working petit bourgeois may serve as an explanation for the prejudices rampant in this social class), the film's ending celebrates reconciliations all around. Sister and father have fully accepted Michael's fate. Yet Michael, the "contaminated stranger," has to leave the restored family order (reinforced by the final image of the parents in an endearing embrace) and return to "his own kind," to the world of gay men and AIDS where his family does not belong. Although he has gained acceptance within the social microcosm of his familial circle, he has to "win that case" alone. He is still the "other," the outcast who represents a threat, but an outsider who enjoys universal familial sympathy.

13 In *As Is,* Robert Carradine plays Rich, a gay man in New York City newly diagnosed as having AIDS. Structurally far less complex than *An Early Frost,* this film, adapted from the play of the same title, shows Rich returning to Saul (Jonathan Hadary), his lover of many years. Rich's new lover has left him; his catering business is gone; his health insurance company is trying to get out of covering his illness; he is nearly broke. In this film the viewer is shown the double insider experience from the narrow focus of two gay men struggling against the onslaught of the disease. Together the two recall friends who are sick or have already died of AIDS; remember their life together; and, ultimately, move apprehensively to face the future. Assuring Rich of his unconditional acceptance ("as is"), Saul finally succeeds in dissuading Rich from his intentions to commit suicide. The film ends on a didactic note when a hospice worker (Colleen Dewhurst), whose function as a narrative framing device has been adopted from the play, states that she is "angry with God" and that for the HIV infected "(i)t's a long way to finding acceptance."

14 This second film, like the first, "reads" much like a popular introduction to AIDS, presenting again the typical symptoms (persistent cough, weight-loss, night sweats, seizures, recurrent flu, swollen glands) and admitting medicine's ignorance and inability to cope with the problem. Like Peter in *An Early Frost,* Saul also has to face the possibility of being infected and getting sick. Contrary to the first film, *As Is* dispels popular misconceptions such as that the disease can be contracted through mere physical contact or by air. *As Is* also draws more attention

to the diversity of AIDS victims. For example, among the patients of an AIDS crisis center we hear the story of a pregnant woman who contracted AIDS from her husband who "shot up." Nevertheless, the film seems to suggest that the disease originated in the gay male, thus reaffirming the social stigma imposed on homosexuality. Indeed homosexuality is shown to be accepted only by homosexuals, first and foremost by the loyal Saul or by minorities, such as Saul's Jewish father, whom we never meet, and Rich's actress friend, Lilly.

15 Outsider responses are minimal in this film as the parents of the two protagonists remain off-stage or are assumed to be dead. However, the open-minded approval of Saul's family is contrasted with the conservative and fearful attitude of Rich's brother (whose name is never used). Aware of but not entirely accepting Rich's life (he can never remember Saul's name), the brother is the only immediate family member to visit Rich in the hospital. He enters the room appearing frightened and ridiculous in gown and mask. Rich has become the doubly threatening "other" who represents a threat to his brother's outside, untainted rural—south Jersey—environment. Yet, in the end, brotherly love overrides fear and, breaking through his reservations—"Richie, you're my brother!"—the two characters finally embrace.

16 *Andre's Mother*, a film adapted from a play by Terrence McNally, displays an unmistakable staginess with its monologues and its oftentimes too brisk dialogues. The two central figures are Cal (Richard Thomas), the lover of the deceased Andre, and Andre's mother (Sada Thompson) who still has not accepted her late son's social-sexual identity.[10] The tension of the film is created by Cal's fight for that acceptance from Andre's mother. The events portrayed center on Andre's memorial service. There, for one last time, the characters attest to their attachment to the admired, beloved, almost worshipped friend. The outsider AIDS dimension in this film is illustrated by Andre's mother, who does not understand the releasing of the memorial balloons in Central Park as a symbol of a final "letting go," a ceremony that has become part of many AIDS memorials. Cal's behavior toward her shows the inside perspective of someone who has lived through months of caretaking of a loved one during the illness. His own need for resolution and closure of his anger and pain may explain his demands upon the mother who has remained an outsider to her son's being gay and to his disease.

17 Cal introduces the final scene when he attempts resolution of that tension by forcing acknowledgement of what caused Andre's death:

"Andre died of AIDS." When he cries "I didn't kill him!" and reveals that he is HIV-negative, he hopes to get the mother to accept and share his love for the deceased Andre. In a vehement tirade of anger and tears about the walls of denial—"how many of us . . . don't want to disappoint our mothers?"—he demands her approval. Indeed, her aversion surprisingly turns to hesitant affection (she returns Cal's embrace) and Cal earns her acceptance. In this scene the musical score, "L'amero, Saro Costante" from Mozart's "Il Re Pastore" underscores the theme of loyalty and commitment but also contributes to the stylized ambiance of this film that never manages to convincingly develop the motivation for the title character's change or Cal's obsessive behavior. In sum, this short film deals with the two main characters resolving tensions: coming to terms with the "other" and making peace with themselves. Again, attitudes about gay men are reflected in the clashing views of two families. Cal's sister and father are shown as accepting Cal's sexuality, although the latter indicates minimal understanding, "a lack of imagination on my part"; Cal's mother and Andre's father are shown as rejecting it. Andre's mother is moving towards acceptance only as the film ends.

18 Although the stage of physical deterioration of the AIDS victim was intimated in *As Is* and briefly illustrated in *Early Frost,* the TV movie *Our Sons* is more graphic in revealing the suffering of the AIDS victim. Here the central protagonist, twenty-eight-year-old Donald (Zeljko Ivanek), previously a successful architect in San Diego, is near death. In a fairly simple plot, his lover, James (Hugh Grant), enlists his own mother, Audrey (Julie Andrews), to help in reuniting Donald and his mother, Lou-Anne (Ann-Margaret), before death occurs. Audrey, a successful, liberal and open-minded, upper-class executive business woman, has to travel to Fayetteville, Arkansas, to confront the waitress Lou-Anne, who is presented as typifying the prejudices and ignorance of the lower-middle class in small-town America. Her frighteningly immature view that "homosexuality is an offense against God, man, and nature" seems like a learned prejudice. She is embittered that her son is "one of them," "a queer," and it takes all of Audrey's persuasive powers to induce her to return with her to visit the dying Donald. When she (all too quickly and quite predictably) overcomes her reluctance and visits Donald, she is controlled and unemotional, still blaming her son. The movie suggests that Lou-Anne's anger and denial begins to break only when Audrey makes the central statement, "Our sons are two of us" (as opposed to two of *them*). Those words seem to

work wonders. Lou-Anne hastens to cleanse herself of the past by swimming nude in Audrey's pool; seeks reconciliation with Donald at his bedside in a touching, albeit somewhat pathetic scene; and stays with James and Donald until the end. The movie ends with Donald's coffin being carried onto the plane on which Lou-Anne takes off—into a cliché-glorious California sunset. Dedicated to all the United States AIDS victims, the movie, similar to *As Is*, pleads for emancipation from "centuries of rules and revulsions." [11]

19 This film, too, centers on the issue of overcoming prejudices about homosexuality by presenting the conflicting perspectives of the two single parents. Both mothers have already confronted the issues of their sons' homosexuality, which led to two distinctly different reactions. Lou-Anne drove Donald away so that she would not have to know anything about him and his life while Audrey accepted James's gay life-style. But that acceptance is revealed as having been superficial and non-confrontational. Audrey has always refrained from prying into her son's personal life and has chosen to ignore his homosexuality because, as James says, "(w)e know what we want to know." In parallel fashion, Donald has created a life without any family connection while James has never breached the wall of privacy and non-interference that he and his mother maintain. Just as both mothers have chosen not to know their sons as adult men, the sons have not forced their mothers to know. The crisis of the disease forces the walls to be broken.

20 This film minimally deals with the AIDS insider-outsider dichotomy. Here the mothers represent only slightly different AIDS knowledge patterns, probably reflecting education levels more than anything else. Lou-Anne is fearful of even touching Donald and Audrey is surprised when James says that he and Donald have "been to twenty different funerals in the past eighteen months"; the sons are insiders, the mothers outsiders. Audrey's contact with Donald and James forces her to deal with her son as a gay man and with the possibility that he might also become sick and die. Part of this mother-son dynamic is her belated questioning about his HIV status and urging him to be tested. The fact that James has not been tested reflects an insider AIDS issue that troubles many gay men. That choice requires a personal confrontation with the possibility of being anti-body positive, of having to deal with the probability of impending disease and death. James must break through his own very honest fear. He is able to face this when he and his mother begin to deal with each other as concerned adults.

21 Throughout these four films certain messages, images, and stereotypes are presented about AIDS and gay men. As for demographics, two images of the city are presented: one as a refuge for gay men where they can be free, anonymous, and create their lives as gay men, and another as a location of the AIDS infected.[12] On the other hand, in the rural, suburban settings where there are few gay men, the disease is perceived as an alien phenomenon. Naturally, this reinforces the classic American "city" myth. In reality, gay men do live in rural-suburban America and, even when the earliest of these films was released, most rural-suburban areas had their own indigenous AIDS populations. Bigotry, prejudice, and fear of gay men and AIDS have no geographical boundaries. On a medical level, mixed images of medical professionals illustrate the experiences of many AIDS patients. Some doctors (although not portrayed in these films) are still AIDS-phobic, although most others are both concerned and overworked. And, as these films indicate, some rescue squads, nurses, and other staff members have refused to treat AIDS patients, whereas most others have proven to be deeply compassionate in working with their patients.

22 As to the familial issues of acceptance, we can discern interesting generational and gender combination patterns. The two grandmothers presented in these films (both played by Sylvia Sidney) are accepting characters. In *An Early Frost* she reacts more to the disease issue than to the fact of having a gay grandson. In *Andre's Mother*, it is—ironically—the grandmother who accepts her grandson as he is. She is also a catalyst pushing her daughter to break through the wall of denial. Similarly, the two sisters presented in the movies both know about and accept their brothers being gay, although Michael's pregnant sister (*An Early Frost*) withdraws in fear because of AIDS. The mothers in the films have difficulties accepting their sons as men bonding with other men. Four mothers, two of them on camera, have known about and rejected their sons. However, the stereotypical female gender roles of nurturing and defending ultimately help all of them to overcome their fears. We only *hear* of cases in which this does not happen, e.g., the family that disowned its son who had AIDS (Victor in *An Early Frost*). That, on the other hand, is used by Michael's mother to reaffirm that this "is not going to happen to *our* son."

23 Men tend to have greater difficulties with acceptance than women. Grandfathers and brothers are absent in these films—with one nameless exception in *As Is*. Even Michael's brother-in-law (*An Early Frost*), who knows Michael is gay, is absent after Michael's return to his family

and Cal's future brother-in-law (*Andre's Mother*), who is said to be supportive, is off camera. Like their wives, the fathers of the HIV-infected protagonists, as far as they are introduced, reflect minimal variation of the male parent struggling to accept his gay son. Michael's father in *An Early Frost* rejects but shifts towards more acceptance when his son agrees to fight the disease—like a man. In *Andre's Mother*, Cal's father accepts his son although Andre's father turns his back on his son completely. The absence of the other five fathers, for whatever reason, seems to emphasize the difficulties in presenting male parent acceptance of the gay son to viewers. Overall, the parental generation is shown struggling (presumably because of their own unfulfilled wishes for their sons) with acceptance.

24 Three variations of gay male interaction with the "straight world" occur in these films: There is the son who is open and accepted by his family (Peter, Saul, Cal, James, the lovers of the HIV-infected protagonists); the son who is open but not accepted or discussed (Rich, Andre, and Donald); and the son who lives in hiding from his family (Michael). An interesting pattern is that those gay men who are neither open to nor accepted by their families are the men stricken with AIDS. Those who are open to their families are uninfected[13] and are shown as supportive, nurturing, caretaking, and constant companions who are willing to sacrifice their energies and emotions for their partners. They choose, even insist on remaining with their partners, reaffirming the positive force of parental acceptance overcoming all stereotypes and fears. These caring characters present an interesting variation on the stereotype of gay men. Their model of personal and social responsibility may be the beginning of a new gay male image in film. On the other hand, however, all of the other characters who are shown as nurturers are women, which may one more time reinforce the general stereotype of gay men not really being "men."

25 In all the films a certain blame seems to be imputed to the biased parent, who perhaps did not provide sufficient understanding, openness, warmth, and security for the son to breed the right "virtues." Because of this, the parent becomes partly responsible for the son's exodus to a life in an environment harboring "sin" and disease, away and separate from the mainstream, conservative middle-class values. The flight of the sons can be perceived as an escape from these values, from a world in which they are strangers. Their homosexuality and infection contaminates their identities and they become, much like

Kafka's Gregor Samsa, estranged, almost metamorphosized (physically in some films) into a socially unacceptable "other." Usually, the family is unable to provide that much needed ultimate support for its sons; this can only be rendered by the respective lover, their "own kind." And, as in Samsa's case, sometimes only their deaths can restore the former identities as respectable sons and citizens.

26 Although scattered comments in these films mark the HIV virus as blind to gender, race, or sexual orientation, this does not necessarily neutralize the false image of AIDS as a purely homosexual disease. In these films the virus is often seen as a punishment inflicted on the protagonists and their families for their breach with middle-class norms and values. By contrast, it is most striking that if the son's openness is reciprocated by the family's approval, he does not experience HIV infection. The conclusion lies at hand: Unflagging adherence to the solid values of parental or companion love and honesty, constancy and exclusiveness in love relationships, or simply, "doing the right thing" precludes contraction. Although this exhortation to middle-class conformism would weaken the otherwise socio-critical and emancipatory impact with regard to the implicated, these values are presented as larger than the issues that make the characters strangers to each other. These values and behaviors are shown to heal the wounds caused by that strangeness. Throughout these movies the terror of the destruction of AIDS leads most of the characters of both worlds to be involved with each other, to resolve tensions about sexuality or fear of rejection, to break the walls between them. Ultimately, however, and despite parental and sibling love overriding stereotypes and fears, the movies seem to suggest that these walls should have never been built.

NOTES

1. For a detailed synopsis see Timothy E. Cook and David Colby, "The Mass-Mediated Epidemic: The Politics of AIDS on the Nightly Network News," in *AIDS: The Making of a Chronic Disease*, ed. Elizabeth Fee, and Daniel M. Fox (Berkeley and Los Angeles: University of California Press, 1992) 84–122.
2. The term AIDS will be used here to refer both to the condition of infection with the human immunosuppressive virus (HIV infection) and to the condition of anyone experiencing the multiple disease pattern referred to as acquired immune depressive syndrome (AIDS).

3. Richard Goldstein, "The Implicated and the Immune: Responses to AIDS in the Arts and Popular Culture," in *A Disease of Society: Cultural and Institutional Responses to AIDS*, ed. Dorothy Nelkin, et. al. (Cambridge: Cambridge UP, 1991) 17–42. Goldstein's dichotomy is somewhat simplified because it does not deal with the complexities that this epidemic has engendered, i.e., what happens when the disease process forces the two groups into a confrontation, which is precisely the central conflict of the films discussed here.
4. Unlike the independent, and mostly made-for-television "AIDS movies," the films in this category are all star-studded, major Hollywood productions and have been enormous box office hits—for example *Terms of Endearment* (1983), *Beaches* (1988), *Steel Magnolias* (1989), *Silence Like Glass* (1990), *Dying Young* (1991; the only film with a male victim), or *The Doctor* (1991). These films usually appeal to the whole gamut of emotions in the spectator, ranging from flighty and frivolous comedy to the tear-jerking drama of the young and innocent protagonist's slow decease. The audience strongly identifies with the "heroines" of these films, whereas in the "AIDS movies" the HIV-infected protagonist does not necessarily serve as a figure of identification.
5. Don Shewey, "In Memory of My Feelings," *Film Comment*, vol. 24, May/June 1990: 12.
6. Contrary to this squeamish treatment indigenous to American culture, the German film *A Virus Knows No Morals* (1986), a cynical black comedy by Rosa von Praunheim (Holger Mischwitzki), employs a casual directness and explicitness in its depiction of the world of gays.
7. Vice-versa, in *Parting Glances* the parents are all "off stage" and there is no indication of their acceptance or rejection, and *Longtime Companion* makes no mention of parents of any of the gay male protagonists.
8. In an earlier bantering table conversation, the parents question Michael about relationships to which Michael ambiguously jokes about not being celibate and the conversation is dropped. The parents are satisfied and Michael has successfully fended off any probing into his personal life.
9. This is a reflection of the lack of medical knowledge in 1985 about the incubation period of the virus. Justifiably scared that he may have been the transmitter, Peter refuses to be checked himself. In fact, any further discussion of the disquieting issue of "finding out" is strictly avoided.
10. Her somewhat dubious rationale is that approving of her son would mean "too terrible a criticism" of herself.
11. These words are uttered by James. Incidentally, it is somewhat surprising that when Audrey hears about Donald she does not immediately ask her son James about his own health, but rather the issue of finding out is saved for the end.
12. However, as Cal in *Andre's Mother* indicates, the choice of many gays to live in the "dreadful, anonymous city" is simply to spare their family the disappointment.
13. What is not mentioned, however, is that they may have to face infection in the future, depending on what transmission-risk behaviors they shared with their partners. Another issue glossed over is that Cal's negative HIV result does not guarantee that he will not later test positive. And finally, throughout these films no mention is made of transmission prevention or of safe sex techniques.

Understanding Meaning

1. What general impressions do the authors have about the films they describe?
2. How have commercial television movies about AIDS dealt with homosexuality? How have they differed from independently produced, theatrical releases?
3. Do Pilipp and Shull see these films educating the public or reinforcing common stereotypes about people with AIDS?
4. According to Pilipp and Shull's analysis, do television films present scientifically accurate information about the disease?
5. How are images of the city and the suburb presented in these films? What do they suggest about American values?
6. What seems to be the common message apparent in most of these television dramas about AIDS?
7. *Critical Thinking:* Commercial television is after all an entertainment medium. Can a movie made for television seriously address complex and controversial topics? Does the need to present characters people can identify with lead to a "good guys" and "bad guys" formula? Are stereotypes bound to emerge?

Evaluating Strategy

1. How do the authors provide readers with enough information about four films without turning the article into a series of plot summaries?
2. What analytical methods do the authors use? How important is detailed observation in their analysis?
3. How do the authors use direct quotes from characters in the films to dramatize their points? Is this an effective device?

Appreciating Language

1. This article appeared in a journal dedicated to film and television. Does it have technical terms that many readers would find confusing or unfamiliar?
2. How do the authors describe the attitudes expressed by characters in the films? Does their choice of words reveal a bias?
3. What do the authors mean by "the worlds of the *immune* and the *implicated*"?

Connections across the Disciplines

1. Joel Connelly (page 330) asserts that visual images have tremendous power to influence people's attitudes and social policy. Do Pilipp and Shull sense that the values implied in television movies will have lasting influence on the American public?
2. Edward Dolnick's "Deafness as Culture" (page 214) reveals that many deaf people resent being viewed as disabled. How might gay advocates respond to the way homosexuals are defined in the films Pilipp and Shull discuss?

Writing Suggestions

1. Select a recent made-for-television film, and write a short analysis of the social messages it seems to advocate. Do television films seek to reinforce widely held values or to challenge them?
2. *Collaborative Writing:* Discuss Pilipp and Shull's conclusions with a group of students. What opinions do members of the group have about the way television has treated people with AIDS? Has the media responded with intelligence and compassion or simply exploited the public's fears? Write a brief paper outlining the views of the group.

BELL HOOKS

bell hooks is the pen name of Gloria Watkins (1952–). An English teacher at Oberlin College, hooks has become widely known as a theorist and commentator on issues facing women and African Americans. She is a poet and a social activist whose column "Sisters of the Yam" appears in Z Magazine. *Her recent books include* Yearnings *and* Black Looks: Race and Representation.

Straightening Our Hair

In analyzing her decision to stop straightening her hair in the 1960s, bell hooks uses comparison, narration, description, *and* cause and effect *to develop her essay.*

1 On Saturday mornings we would gather in the kitchen to get our hair fixed, that is straightened. Smells of burning grease and hair, mingled with the scent of our freshly washed bodies, with collard greens cooking on the stove, with fried fish. We did not go to the hairdresser. Mama fixed our hair. Six daughters—there was no way we could have afforded hairdressers. In those days, this process of straightening black women's hair with a hot comb (invented by Madame C.J. Walker) was not connected in my mind with the effort to look white, to live out standards of beauty set by white supremacy. It was connected solely with rites of initiation into womanhood. To arrive at that point where one's hair could be straightened was to move from being perceived as child (whose hair could be neatly combed and braided) to being almost a woman. It was this moment of transition my sisters and I longed for.

2 Hair pressing was a ritual of black women's culture—of intimacy. It was an exclusive moment when black women (even those who did not know one another well) might meet at home or in the beauty parlor to talk with one another, to listen to the talk. It was as important a world as that of the male barber shop—mysterious, secret. It was a world where the images constructed as barriers between one's self and the world were briefly let go, before they were made again. It was a moment of creativity, a moment of change.

3 I wanted this change even though I had been told all my life that I was one of the "lucky" ones because I had been born with "good

hair"—hair that was fine, almost straight—not good enough but still good. Hair that had no nappy edges, no "kitchen," that area close to the neck that the hot comb could not reach. This "good hair" meant nothing to me when it stood as a barrier to my entering this secret black woman world. I was overjoyed when mama finally agreed that I could join the Saturday ritual, no longer looking on but patiently waiting my turn. I have written of this ritual: "For each of us getting our hair pressed is an important ritual. It is not a sign of our longing to be white. There are no white people in our intimate world. It is a sign of our desire to be women. It is a gesture that says we are approaching womanhood . . . Before we reach the appropriate age we wear braids, plaits that are symbols of our innocence, our youth, our childhood. Then, we are comforted by the parting hands that comb and braid, comforted by the intimacy and bliss. There is a deeper intimacy in the kitchen on Saturdays when hair is pressed, when fish is fried, when sodas are passed around, when soul music drifts over the talk. It is a time without men. It is a time when we work as women to meet each other's needs, to make each other feel good inside, a time of laughter and outrageous talk."

4 Since the world we lived in was racially segregated, it was easy to overlook the relationship between white supremacy and our obsession with hair. Even though black women with straight hair were perceived to be more beautiful than those with thick, frizzy hair, it was not overtly related to a notion that white women were a more appealing female group or that their straight hair set a beauty standard black women were struggling to live out. While this is probably the ideological framework from which the process of straightening black women's hair emerged, it was expanded so that it became a real space of black woman bonding through ritualized, shared experience. The beauty parlor was a space of consciousness raising, a space where black women shared life stories—hardship, trials, gossip; a place where one could be comforted and one's spirit renewed. It was for some women a place of rest where one did not need to meet the demands of children or men. It was the one hour some folk would spend "off their feet," a soothing, restful time of meditation and silence. These positive empowering implications of the ritual of hair pressing mediate but do not change negative implications. They exist alongside all that is negative.

5 Within white supremacist capitalist patriarchy, the social and political context in which the custom of black folks straightening our hair emerges, it represents an imitation of the dominant white group's ap-

pearance and often indicates internalized racism, self-hatred, and/or low self-esteem. During the 1960s black people who actively worked to critique, challenge, and change white racism pointed to the way in which black people's obsession with straight hair reflected a colonized mentality. It was at this time that the natural hairdo, the "afro," became fashionable as a sign of cultural resistance to racist oppression and as a celebration of blackness. Naturals were equated with political militancy. Many young black folks found just how much political value was placed on straightened hair as a sign of respectability and conformity to societal expectations when they ceased to straighten their hair. When black liberation struggles did not lead to revolutionary change in society the focus on the political relationship between appearance and complicity with white racism ceased and folks who had once sported afros began to straighten their hair.

6 In keeping with the move to suppress black consciousness and efforts to be self-defining, white corporations began to acknowledge black people and most especially black women as potential consumers of products they could provide, including hair-care products. Permanents specially designed for black women eliminated the need for hair pressing and the hot comb. They not only cost more but they also took much of the economy and profit out of black communities, out of the pockets of black women who had previously reaped the material benefits (see Manning Marable's *How Capitalism Underdeveloped Black America*, South End Press). Gone was the context of ritual, of black woman bonding. Seated under noisy hair dryers, black women lost a space for dialogue, for creative talk.

7 Stripped of the positive binding rituals that traditionally surrounded the experience, black women straightening our hair seemed more and more to be exclusively a signifier of white supremacist oppression and exploitation. It was clearly a process that was about black women changing their appearance to imitate white people's looks. This need to look as much like white people as possible, to look safe, is related to a desire to succeed in the white world. Before desegregation black people could worry less about what white folks thought about their hair. In a discussion with black women about beauty at Spelman College, students talked about the importance of wearing straight hair when seeking jobs. They were convinced and probably rightly so that their chances of finding good jobs would be enhanced if they had straight hair. When asked to elaborate they focused on the connection between radical politics and natural hairdos, whether

natural or braided. One woman wearing a short natural told of purchasing a straight wig for her job search. No one in the discussion felt black women were free to wear our hair in natural styles without reflecting on the possible negative consequences. Often older black adults, especially parents, respond quite negatively to natural hairdos. I shared with the group that when I arrived home with my hair in braids shortly after accepting my job at Yale my parents told me I looked disgusting.

8 Despite many changes in racial politics, black women continue to obsess about their hair, and straightening hair continues to be serious business. It continues to tap into the insecurity black women feel about our value in this white supremacist society. Talking with groups of women at various college campuses and with black women in our communities there seems to be general consensus that our obsession with hair in general reflects continued struggles with self-esteem and self-actualization. We talk about the extent to which black women perceive our hair as the enemy, as a problem we must solve, a territory we must conquer. Above all it is a part of our black female body that must be controlled. Most of us were not raised in environments where we learned to regard our hair as sensual or beautiful in an unprocessed state. Many of us talk about situations where white people ask to touch our hair when it is unprocessed then show surprise that the texture is soft or feels good. In the eyes of many white folks and other non-black folks, the natural afro looks like steel wool or a helmet. Responses to natural hairstyles worn by black women usually reveal the extent to which our natural hair is perceived in white supremacist culture as not only ugly but frightening. We also internalize that fear. The extent to which we are comfortable with our hair usually reflects on our overall feelings about our bodies. In our black women's support group, *Sisters of the Yam*, we talk about the ways we don't like our bodies, especially our hair. I suggested to the group that we regard our hair as though it is not part of our body but something quite separate—again a territory to be controlled. To me it was important for us to link this need to control with sexuality, with sexual repression. Curious about what black women who had hot-combed or had permanents felt about the relationship between straightened hair and sexual practice I asked whether people worried about their hairdo, whether they feared partners touching their hair. Straightened hair has always seemed to me to call attention to the desire for hair to stay in place. Not surprisingly many black women responded that they felt uncomfortable if too much attention was focused on their hair, if it seemed to be too

messy. Those of us who have liberated our hair and let it go in whatever direction it seems fit often receive negative comments.

9 Looking at photographs of myself and my sisters when we had straightened hair in high school I noticed how much older we looked than when our hair was not processed. It is ironic that we live in a culture that places so much emphasis on women looking young, yet black women are encouraged to change our hair in ways that make us appear older. This past semester we read Toni Morrison's *The Bluest Eye* in a black women's fiction class. I ask students to write autobiographical statements which reflect their thoughts about the connection between race and physical beauty. A vast majority of black women wrote about their hair. When I asked individual women outside class why they continued to straighten their hair, many asserted that naturals don't look good on them, or that they required too much work. Emily, a favorite student with very short hair, always straightened it and I would tease and challenge her. She explained to me convincingly that a natural hairdo would look horrible with her face, that she did not have the appropriate forehead or bone structure. Later she shared that during spring break she had gone to the beauty parlor to have her perm and as she sat there waiting, thinking about class reading and discussion, it came to her that she was really frightened that no one else would think she was attractive if she did not straighten her hair. She acknowledged that this fear was rooted in feelings of low self-esteem. She decided to make a change. Her new look surprised her because it was so appealing. We talked afterwards about her earlier denial and justification for wearing straightened hair. We talked about the way it hurts to realize connection between racist oppression and the arguments we use to convince ourselves and others that we are not beautiful or acceptable as we are.

10 In numerous discussions with black women about hair one of the strongest factors that prevent black women from wearing unprocessed hairstyles is the fear of losing other people's approval and regard. Heterosexual black women talked about the extent to which black men respond more favorably to women with straight or straightened hair. Lesbian women point to the fact that many of them do not straighten their hair, raising the question of whether or not this gesture is fundamentally linked to heterosexism and a longing for male approval. I recall visiting a woman friend and her black male companion in New York years ago and having an intense discussion about hair. He took it

upon himself to share with me that I could be a fine sister if I would do something about my hair (secretly I thought mama must have hired him). What I remember is his shock when I calmly and happily asserted that I like the touch and feel of unprocessed hair.

11 When students read about race and physical beauty, several black women describe periods of childhood when they were overcome with longing for straight hair as it was so associated with desirability, with being loved. Few women had received affirmation from family, friends, or lovers when choosing not to straighten their hair and we have many stories to tell about advice we receive from everyone, including total strangers, urging to understand how much more attractive we would be if we would fix (straighten) our hair. When I interviewed for my job at Yale, white female advisers who had never before commented on my hair encouraged me not to wear braids or a large natural to the interview. Although they did not say straighten your hair, they were suggesting that I change my hairstyle so that it would most resemble theirs, so that it would indicate a certain conformity. I wore braids and no one seemed to notice. When I was offered the job I did not ask if it mattered whether or not I wore braids. I tell this story to my students so that they will know by this one experience that we do not always need to surrender our power to be self-defining to succeed in an endeavor. Yet I have found the issue of hairstyle comes up again and again with students when I give lectures. At one conference on black women and leadership I walked into a packed auditorium, my hair unprocessed wild and all over the place. The vast majority of black women seated there had straightened hair. Many of them looked at me with hostile contemptuous stares. I felt as though I was being judged on the spot as someone out on the fringe, an undesirable. Such judgments are made particularly about black women in the United States who choose to wear dreadlocks. They are seen and rightly so as the total antithesis of straightening one's hair, as a political statement. Often black women express contempt for those of us who choose this look.

12 Ironically, just as the natural unprocessed hair of black women is the subject of disregard and disdain we are witnessing return of the long dyed, blonde look. In their writing my black women students described wearing yellow mops on their heads as children to pretend they had long blonde hair. Recently black women singers who are working to appeal to white audiences, to be seen as crossovers, use

hair implanting and hair weaving to have long straight hair. There seems to be a definite connection between a black female entertainer's popularity with white audiences and the degree to which she works to appear white, or to embody aspects of white style. Tina Turner and Aretha Franklin were trend setters; both dyed their hair blonde. In everyday life we see more and more black women using chemicals to be blonde. At one of my talks focusing on the social construction of black female identity within a sexist and racist society, a black woman came to me at the end of the discussion and shared that her seven-year-old daughter was obsessed with blonde hair, so much so that she had made a wig to imitate long blonde curls. This mother wanted to know what she was doing wrong in her parenting. She asserted that their home was a place where blackness was affirmed and celebrated. Yet she had not considered that her processed straightened hair was a message to her daughter that black women are not acceptable unless we alter our appearance or hair texture. Recently I talked with one of my younger sisters about her hair. She uses bright colored dyes, various shades of red. Her skin is very dark. She has a broad nose and short hair. For her these choices of straightened dyed hair were directly related to feelings of low self-esteem. She does not like her features and feels that the hairstyle transforms her. My perception was that her choice of red straightened hair actually called attention to the features she was trying to mask. When she commented that this look receives more attention and compliments, I suggested that the positive feedback might be a direct response to her own projection of a higher level of self-satisfaction. Folk may be responding to that and not her altered looks. We talked about the messages she is sending her dark-skinned daughters—that they will be most attractive if they straighten their hair.

13 A number of black women have argued that straightened hair is not necessarily a signifier of low self-esteem. They argue that it is a survival strategy; it is easier to function in this society with straightened hair. There are fewer hassles. Or as some folk stated, straightened hair is easier to manage, takes less time. When I responded to this argument in our discussion at Spelman by suggesting that perhaps the unwillingness to spend time on ourselves, caring for our bodies, is also a reflection of a sense that this is not important or that we do not deserve such care. In this group and others, black women talked about being raised in households where spending too much time on appearance was ridiculed or considered vanity. Irrespective of the way

individual black women choose to do their hair, it is evident that the extent to which we suffer from racist and sexist oppression and exploitation affects the degree to which we feel capable of both self-love and asserting an autonomous presence that is acceptable and pleasing to ourselves. Individual preferences (whether rooted in self-hate or not) cannot negate the reality that our collective obsession with straightening black hair reflects the psychology of oppression and the impact of racist colonization. Together racism and sexism daily reinforce to all black females via the media, advertising, etc. that we will not be considered beautiful or desirable if we do not change ourselves, especially our hair. We cannot resist this socialization if we deny that white supremacy informs our efforts to construct self and identity.

14 Without organized struggles like the ones that happened in the 1960s and early 1970s, individual black women must struggle alone to acquire the critical consciousness that would enable us to examine issues of race and beauty, our personal choices, from a political standpoint. There are times when I think of straightening my hair just to change my style, just for fun. Then I remind myself that even though such a gesture could be simply playful on my part, an individual expression of desire, I know that such a gesture would carry other implications beyond my control. The reality is: straightened hair is linked historically and currently to a system of racial domination that impresses upon black people, and especially black women, that we are not acceptable as we are, that we are not beautiful. To make such a gesture as an expression of individual freedom and choice would make me complicit with a politic of domination that hurts us. It is easy to surrender this freedom. It is more important that black women resist racism and sexism in every way; that every aspect of our self-representation be a fierce resistance, a radical celebration of our care and respect for ourselves.

15 Even though I have not had straightened hair for a long time, this did not mean that I am able to really enjoy or appreciate my hair in its natural state. For years I still considered it a problem. (It wasn't naturally nappy enough to make a decent interesting afro. It was too thin.) These complaints expressed my continued dissatisfaction. True liberation of my hair came when I stopped trying to control it in any state and just accepted it as it is. It has been only in recent years that I have ceased to worry about what other people would say about my hair. It has been only in recent years that I could feel consistent pleasure

washing, combing, and caring for my hair. These feelings remind me of the pleasure and comfort I felt as a child sitting between my mother's legs feeling the warmth of her body and being as she combed and braided my hair. In a culture of domination, one that is essentially anti-intimacy, we must struggle daily to remain in touch with ourselves and our bodies, with one another. Especially black women and men, as it is our bodies that have been so often devalued, burdened, wounded in alienated labor. Celebrating our bodies, we participate in a liberatory struggle that frees mind and heart.

Understanding Meaning

1. What did straight hair represent to hooks as a young girl? Did she associate it with race?
2. What did the process of straightening hair mean to African American women?
3. Why does hooks reject the notion that straightening hair simply reflected a desire to imitate white concepts of beauty?
4. What are hooks's views of her own hair?
5. How did the Civil Rights movement alter African American hairstyles? Was this change significant or superficial in hooks's view?
6. *Critical Thinking:* hooks argues that African American women feel insecure about their bodies, especially their hair. She states that they see their hair as the "enemy" and "a territory we must conquer." Are these insecurities exclusively African American or female? Don't numerous television commercials promise to liberate white women from "bad hair" days and extoll the virtues of being blonde? Do men of all races fear hair loss and view baldness as a sign of age and undesirability?

Evaluating Strategy

1. hooks refers to "this white supremacist society." Do assertions like this require qualification or proof? Is hooks begging the question?
2. How does hooks *compare* white and African American women? How are their lives different? Does hooks see similar forces shaping the experiences of all women?
3. What role does *narration* play in hooks's essay? Why are stories important to establish her point?

Appreciating Language

1. Underline the words such as "self-esteem" hooks associates with hair. What do these words suggest about the significance of hairstyle and identity?
2. What connotations do words such as "process," "straighten," and "press" suggest?
3. hooks repeatedly uses the term "domination" to refer to American society. How does your dictionary define the term? Does hooks's use imply a different meaning?

Connections across the Disciplines

1. How does hooks's article about cultural identity, self-esteem, and conformity compare with Armando Rendón's "Kiss of Death" (page 667)?
2. hooks comments primarily about hair and not complexion. Do her observations about hairstyles associated with blackness mirror those in Mary Mebane's "Black Wasn't Beautiful" (page 434)?

Writing Suggestions

1. Write a brief essay analyzing your own hairstyle or dress. Does your outer image make a political statement? Do you seek to conform with others or stand out? How much of your self-esteem is derived from getting approving looks from others?
2. *Collaborative Writing:* Discuss hooks's comments about hair with a group of students. Do they share her analysis of society's view of African American hairstyles? Comment on the hairstyles you see on campus. Work together to draft a short analysis of the comments made by your group.

KIMBERLY A. CRAWFORD, J.D.

Kimberly A. Crawford is an attorney specializing in criminal law. In this article written for law enforcement officers, she analyzes the constitutionality of secretly recording suspects' conversations to gather evidence. Her article appeared in the FBI Law Enforcement Bulletin *in 1993.*

Surreptitious Recording of Suspects' Conversations

Crawford's analysis focuses on the legality, not the morality or political implications, of using secret recordings to gather evidence about suspects. She addresses the needs of her audience, law enforcement professionals seeking direction on which investigative techniques they can legally use.

1 Whether in a prison cell, interrogation room, or the back seat of a police car, suspects left seemingly unattended with a co-conspirator, friend, or total stranger often seize the opportunity to discuss or lament their current predicament. Very often, incriminating statements are made. Law enforcement officers who put themselves in a position to hear and record suspects' conversations, either by planting a listening device or by posing as a co-conspirator, friend, or stranger, are apt to obtain very valuable incriminating evidence.

2 Of course, in any subsequent prosecution, the government is likely to be confronted with a vehement constitutional and statutory attack to the admissibility of such damaging evidence. Specifically, the defense is likely to argue that the surreptitious recording of the suspects' conversations violated rights guaranteed by the fourth, fifth, and sixth amendments to the U.S. Constitution, as well as certain protections afforded individuals under Title III of the Omnibus Crime Control and Safe Streets Act[1] (hereinafter title III).

3 This article discusses the validity of these constitutional and statutory challenges. It then provides a review of court decisions that have dealt with the admissibility of such surreptitiously recorded conversations and related issues.

FIFTH AMENDMENT— SELF-INCRIMINATION CLAUSE CHALLENGE

4 To be successful, a challenge to the admissibility of surreptitiously recorded conversations based on the fifth amendment self-incrimination clause would have to establish that the conversations in question were the product of unlawful custodial interrogation. Because statements made to individuals not known to the defendant as government actors do not normally amount to interrogation for purposes of the fifth amendment, this challenge is destined to fail.

5 The fifth amendment to the U.S. Constitution provides in part that "no person . . . shall be compelled in any criminal case to be a witness against himself. . . . "[2] Over two decades ago, the U.S. Supreme Court in *Miranda* v. *Arizona*[3] held that custodial interrogation of an individual creates a psychologically compelling atmosphere that works against this fifth amendment protection.[4] In other words, the Court in *Miranda* believed that an individual in custody undergoing police interrogation would feel compelled to respond to police questioning. This compulsion, which is a byproduct of most custodial interrogation, directly conflicts with every individual's fifth amendment protection against self-incrimination.

6 Accordingly, the Court developed the now-familiar *Miranda* warnings as a means to reduce the compulsion attendant in custodial interrogation. The *Miranda* rule requires that these warnings be given to individuals in custody prior to the initiation of interrogation. This rule, however, is not absolute.[5]

7 *Stanley* v. *Wainwright*[6] is one of the original cases to deal with a fifth amendment challenge to the admissibility of surreptitiously recorded suspect conversations. In *Stanley*, two robbery suspects were arrested and placed in the back seat of a police car. Unbeknownst to the suspects, one of the arresting officers had activated a tape recorder on the front seat of the car before leaving the suspects unattended for a short period of time. During that time, the suspects engaged in a conversation that later proved to be extremely incriminating.

8 On appeal, the defense argued that the recording violated the rule in *Miranda*, because the suspects were in custody at the time the recording was made and placing of the suspects alone in the vehicle with the activated recorder was interrogation for purposes of *Miranda*. The Court of Appeals for the Fifth Circuit, however, summarily dis-

missed this argument and found that the statements were spontaneously made and not the product of interrogation.

9 The Supreme Court later validated the rationale in *Stanley* with its decision in *Illinois* v. *Perkins.*[7] Although *Perkins* did not deal specifically with the issue of surreptitious recordings, the Court's analysis of *Miranda* is applicable to situations in which suspects' conversations with either private individuals or undercover government actors are recorded.

10 In *Perkins,* police placed an informant and an undercover officer in a cell block with Lloyd Perkins, a suspected murderer incarcerated on an unrelated charge of aggravated assault. While planning a prison break, the undercover officer asked Perkins whether he had ever "done" anyone. In response, Perkins described at length the details of a murder-for-hire he had committed.

11 When Perkins was subsequently charged with the murder, he argued successfully to have the statements that he made in prison suppressed, because no *Miranda* warnings had been given prior to his conversation with the informant and undercover officer. On review, however, the Supreme Court reversed the order of suppression.

12 Rejecting Perkins' argument, the Supreme Court recognized that there are limitations to the rule announced in *Miranda.* The Court expressly declined to accept the notion that "*Miranda* warnings are required whenever a suspect is in custody in a technical sense and converses with someone who happens to be a government agent."[8] Rather, the Court concluded that not every custodial interrogation creates the psychologically compelling atmosphere that *Miranda* was designed to protect against. When the compulsion is lacking, so is the need for *Miranda* warnings.

13 The Court in *Perkins* found the facts at issue to be a clear example of a custodial interrogation that created no compulsion. Pointing out that compulsion is "determined from the perspective of the suspect,"[9] the Court noted that Perkins had no reason to believe that either the informant or the undercover officer had any official power over him, and therefore, he had no reason to feel any compulsion. On the contrary, Perkins bragged about his role in the murder in an effort to impress those he believed to be his fellow inmates. *Miranda* was not designed to protect individuals from themselves.

14 Applying this rationale to the surreptitious recording of suspects' conversations while they are in the back seat of a police car, a prison

cell, or an interrogation room, it is clear that *Miranda* warnings are unnecessary if the suspect is conversing with someone who either is, or is presumed by the suspect to be, a private individual. Because suspects in this situation would have no reason to believe that the person to whom they are speaking has any official power over them, they have no reason to feel the compulsion that *Miranda* was designed to protect against.

SIXTH AMENDMENT—RIGHT-TO-COUNSEL CHALLENGE

15 Because of its limited application, a successful challenge to the admissibility of surreptitiously recorded suspect conversations based on the sixth amendment right to counsel will require the convergence of certain factors. Specifically, the defense must be able to establish that the suspect's right to counsel had attached and that the government took deliberate steps to elicit information from the suspect about a crime with which the suspect had been previously charged.

Right to Counsel Attaches at Critical Stage

16 The sixth amendment to the U.S. Constitution guarantees that "[i]n all criminal prosecutions, the accused shall . . . have the Assistance of Counsel for his defense."[10] The U.S. Supreme Court has interpreted the sixth amendment as guaranteeing not merely the right to counsel but, more importantly, the right to the *effective assistance* of counsel.[11] To be effective, an attorney must be permitted to form a relationship with the accused some time prior to trial,[12] and the government cannot needlessly interfere with that relationship.[13]

17 Although the right to counsel would be meaningless if the suspect and attorney were not permitted to form a relationship some time prior to trial, the Supreme Court has held that it is not necessary to allow this relationship to form simply because the individual becomes a suspect in a case.[14] Instead, the Court has found that the sixth amendment guarantee of the effective assistance of counsel is satisfied if the attorney and suspect are permitted to form their relationship once the prosecution has reached a critical stage.[15] The Court has defined

the critical stage as the filing of formal charges (i.e., an indictment or information) or the initiation of adversarial judicial proceedings.[16]

18 Thus, a necessary first step in a successful sixth amendment challenge to the admissibility of a surreptitiously recorded conversation is to establish that the right to counsel had attached at the time of the recording. If the suspect was neither formally charged nor subjected to adversarial judicial proceedings at the time the recorded conversation took place, the sixth amendment challenge will fail.

Deliberate Elicitation by the Government

19 If successful in establishing that the suspect's right to counsel had attached at the time a surreptitious recording took place, the defense will also have to prove that the conversation in question was the result of deliberate elicitation on the part of the government. The Supreme Court has determined that simply placing suspects in situations where they are likely to incriminate themselves does not, in and of itself, constitute a sixth amendment violation.[17] Rather, there must be some deliberate attempt on the part of the government to elicit information from the suspect.[18] It is the act of deliberate elicitation that creates the sixth amendment violation.

20 In *Kuhlmann* v. *Wilson*,[19] the Supreme Court held that placing an informant in a cell with a formally charged suspect in an effort to gain incriminating statements did not amount to deliberate elicitation on the part of the government. In doing so, the Court made the following statement:

> 21 'Since the Sixth Amendment is not violated whenever—by luck or happenstance—the State obtains incriminating statements from the accused after the right to counsel has attached,' a defendant does not make out a violation of that right simply by showing that an informant, either through prior arrangement or voluntarily, reported his incriminating statements to the police. Rather, the defendant must demonstrate that the police and their informant took some action, *beyond merely listening*, that was designed deliberately to elicit incriminating remarks.[20] (emphasis added)

22 As a result of the Supreme Court's decision in *Kuhlmann,* the mere placing of a recorder in a prison cell, interrogation room, or police

vehicle will not constitute deliberate elicitation by the government. Instead, to raise a successful sixth amendment challenge, the defense has to show that someone acting on behalf of the government went beyond the role of a mere passive listener (often referred to by the courts as a "listening post") and actively pursued incriminating statements from the suspect.

Right to Counsel Is Crime-Specific

23 Even if it can be established that the government deliberately elicited and recorded incriminating conversations from a suspect after the right to counsel had attached, a sixth amendment challenge to the admissibility of those recordings will not succeed if the conversations in question pertained to crimes with which the suspect had not yet been charged at the time of the recording. Because the sixth amendment is crime-specific, a suspect only has the right to the assistance of counsel with respect to the crimes formally charged against him.[21] Consequently, the surreptitious recording of a conversation with a formally charged suspect that pertains to some unrelated, uncharged offense, will not violate the sixth amendment, regardless of whether there is deliberate elicitation on the part of the government.

FOURTH AMENDMENT— RIGHT-TO-PRIVACY CHALLENGE

24 Another constitutional attack waged against the admissibility of surreptitiously recorded conversations is the claim that monitoring and recording these conversations violates the suspects' fourth amendment right of privacy. However, if the recorded conversations take place in government space, whether it be a prison cell, interrogation room, or back seat of a police car, the fourth amendment challenge is bound to fail unless law enforcement officers give suspects specific assurances that their conversations will be private.

25 The fourth amendment to the U.S. Constitution guarantees the right of the people to be secure from unreasonable searches and seizures.[22] As it is used in the fourth amendment, the term "search" includes any governmental action that intrudes into an area where

there is an expectation of privacy that is both subjectively and objectively reasonable.[23] To be objectively reasonable, an expectation of privacy must be one that society as a whole is willing to recognize and protect.[24]

26 Thus, to be successful, a fourth amendment challenge to the surreptitious recording of suspects' conversations would have to establish that the suspects expected their conversations to be private and that society as a whole recognizes those expectations as reasonable. Although sometimes willing to accept suspects' assertions that they believed their conversations were private,[25] courts generally reject the notion that the suspects' beliefs were objectively reasonable.

27 For example, in *Ahmad A.* v. *Superior Court*,[26] the California Court of Appeals confronted a fourth amendment challenge to the admissibility of a surreptitiously recorded conversation between the defendant and his mother. The defendant, a juvenile arrested for murder, asked to speak with his mother when advised of his constitutional rights. The defendant and his mother were thereafter permitted to converse in an interrogation room with the door closed. During the surreptitiously recorded conversation that ensued, the defendant admitted his part in the murder.

28 Reviewing the defendant's subsequent fourth amendment challenge, the California court noted that at the time the mother and her son were permitted to meet in the interrogation room, "no representations or inquiries were made as to privacy or confidentiality."[27] Finding the age-old truism "Walls have ears" to be applicable, the court held that any subjective expectation that the defendant had regarding the privacy of his conversation was not objectively reasonable.

29 Several Federal and State courts have adhered to the rationale announced in *Ahmad A.* and have concluded that any expectation of privacy a suspect may foster in a conversation occurring in government space is objectively unreasonable.[28] While some courts predicate their conclusion on an arrest having taken place, thereby reducing the suspects' expectations of privacy,[29] other courts have taken the position that the lack of an expectation of privacy in government space is not dependent on an arrest.[30]

30 This latter position is demonstrated by the holding of the U.S. Court of Appeals for the 11th Circuit in *United States* v. *McKinnon*.[31] In *McKinnon*, law enforcement officers stopped the vehicle in which the defendant was riding for failing to abide traffic laws. Once stopped,

the driver of the vehicle was asked to submit to a sobriety test. After successfully completing the test, officers asked the driver whether they could search his vehicle for drugs. Upon receiving consent, the officers invited the driver and defendant to sit in the back seat of the police car until the search was completed.

31 Accepting the officers' invitation, defendant and the driver sat in the police car and engaged in an incriminating conversation that was surreptitiously recorded. Cocaine was found during the search of the vehicle, and both the defendant and driver were subsequently arrested. Following their arrest, the defendant and driver were again placed, seemingly unattended, in the back seat of the police car, where they once again engaged in an incriminating conversation.

32 Conceding the admissibility of the post-arrest statements, the defendant argued that prior to arrest, he had an expectation of privacy in his conversation that was violated by the surreptitious recording. The court, however, found "no persuasive distinction between pre-arrest and post-arrest situation"[32] and refused to suppress the recordings. In support of its decision, the court in *McKinnon* cited several cases in which surreptitious recordings of conversations were found to be admissible against visitors and guests of arrestees and other individuals not under formal arrest at the time of the recorded conversations.[33]

Specific Assurances

33 Although courts generally find no reasonable expectation of privacy in suspects' conversations occurring in government space, specific assurances offered by officers that such conversations will be private may generate a valid fourth amendment claim. As previously noted, in the case of *Ahmad A.*, the court was particularly impressed by the fact that "no representations or inquiries were made as to privacy or confidentiality."[34]

34 A reasonable inference to be drawn from this case is that the resulting expectations would have been reasonable, had there been some representations or inquiries regarding privacy that were met with assurances. This inference is supported by the case of *People* v. *Hammons*,[35] in which a California court found that law enforcement officers' actions had fostered the suspects' expectations of privacy, and therefore, the expectations were reasonable.[36]

35 Consequently, when placing suspects together with co-conspirators, friends, or strangers for the purpose of surreptitiously recording a conversation, law enforcement officers should be careful not to give the suspects any specific assurances that their conversations will be private. To do so would likely create a reasonable expectation of privacy in their subsequent conversations that would be protected by the fourth amendment.

TITLE III—STATUTORY CHALLENGE

36 The only statutory attack based on Federal law likely to be raised regarding the surreptitious recording of suspects' conversations is that the recording violates Title III of the Omnibus Crime Control and Safe Streets Act.[37] Because title III protects only oral conversations in which there is a reasonable expectation of privacy, such challenges are resolved by reference to fourth amendment analysis.

37 To be protected under title III, oral communications must be "uttered by a person exhibiting an expectation that such communication is not subject to interception under circumstances justifying such expectation."[38] In other words, the statute only affords protection to oral conversations uttered under conditions indicating that there was a reasonable expectation of privacy. Consequently, the warrantless surreptitious recording of suspects' oral conversations does not violate title III where the suspects lack a fourth amendment expectation of privacy in those conversations.[39]

CONCLUSION

38 The surreptitious recording of suspects' conversations is an effective investigative technique that, if done properly, can withstand both constitutional and statutory challenges. Law enforcement officers contemplating the use of this technique should keep the following points in mind:

39 1. Because the technique does not amount to "interrogation" for purposes of *Miranda*, it is not necessary to advise suspects of their constitutional rights and obtain a waiver prior to using this technique.

40 2. To avoid a sixth amendment problem, this technique should not be used following the filing of formal charges or the initial appearance in court, unless the conversation does not involve a government actor, the conversation involves a government actor who has assumed the role of a "listening post," or the conversation pertains to a crime other than the one with which the suspect has been charged.

41 3. To avoid both fourth amendment and title III concerns, suspects should not be given any specific assurances that their conversations are private.

42 In addition, State and local law enforcement officers should consult with their legal advisors prior to using this investigative technique. This will ensure compliance with State statutes or local policies that may be more restrictive than the Federal law discussed in this article.

ENDNOTES

1. 18 U.S.C. §§ 2510 *et seq.* Defendants may also claim that the surreptitious recording of their conversations violated State eavesdropping statutes. Although many State eavesdropping statutes closely follow title III, law enforcement officers should consult their State statute before using this technique, because some State laws are more restrictive than title III.
2. U.S. Const. amend. V.
3. 394 U.S. 436 (1966).
4. *Id.* at 467.
5. *See, e.g., Berkemer* v. *McCarty,* 468 U.S. 420 (1984), wherein the Supreme Court held *Miranda* inapplicable to traffic stops. *See also, New York* v. *Quarles,* 467 U.S. 649 (1984), which recognizes a public safety exception to *Miranda.*
6. 604 F.2d 379 (5th Cir. 1979), *cert. denied,* 100 S.Ct. 3019.
7. 110 S.Ct. 2394 (1990).
8. *Id.* at 2397.
9. *Id.* in *Perkins,* the Supreme Court used the words coercion and compulsion interchangeably.
10. U.S. Const. amend. VI.
11. *Cuyler* v. *Sullivan,* 100 S.Ct. 1708 (1980).
12. *United States* v. *Wade,* 338 U.S. 218 (1967).
13. In *Weatherford* v. *Bursey,* 429 U.S. 545 (1977), the Supreme Court held that some interference with the right to counsel may be justified.
14. *United States* v. *Gouveia,* 104 S.Ct. 2292 (1984).
15. *Massiah* v. *United States,* 377 U.S. 201 (1964).
16. *Id.*
17. *Kuhlmann* v. *Wilson,* 106 S.Ct. 2616 (1986).
18. *Id.*
19. *Id.*

20. *Id.* at 2630.
21. *Hoffa* v. *United States,* 377 U.S. 201 (1964).
22. U.S. Const. amend. IV.
23. *Katz* v. *United States,* 389 U.S. 347 (1967).
24. *Oliver* v. *United States,* 104 S.Ct. 1735 (1984).
25. Most courts reject this notion as well. In *United States* v. *Harrelson,* 754 F.2d 1153 (5th Cir. 1985), *cert. denied,* 106 S.Ct. 277 (1985), the Court found that "one who expects privacy under the circumstances of a prison visit is, if not actually foolish, exceptionally naive." *Id.* at 1169.
26. 263 Cal. Rptr. 747 (Cal.App. 2 Dist. 1989), *cert. denied,* 11 S.Ct. 102 (1991).
27. *Id.* at 751.
28. *See, e.g., United States* v. *McKinnon,* 985 F.2d 525 (11th Cir. 1993) *cert. pending* (filed 1/7/93 No. 92-8963); *United States* v. *Harrelson,* 754 F.2d 1153 (5th Cir. 1985), *cert. denied,* 106 S.Ct. 277 (1985); *United States* v. *Sallee,* (unreported; 1991 WL 352613 N.D. Ill. 1991); *State* v. *McAdams,* 559 So.2d 601 (Fla.App. 5th Dist. 1990); *People* v. *Marland,* 355 N.W. 2d 378 (Mich.App. 1984).
29. *See, e.g., Brown* v. *State,* 349 So.2d 1196 (Fla.App. 4th Dist. 1977), *cert. denied,* 98 S.Ct. 1271 (1978).
30. *See, e.g., United States* v. *McKinnon,* 985 F.2d 525 (11th Cir. 1993), *cert. pending* (filed 1/7/93 No. 92-8963); and *State* v. *Hussey,* 469 So.2d 346 (La. Ct. App. 2d Cir. 1985), reconsideration denied, 477 So.2d 700 (La. 1985).
31. 985 F.2d 525 (11th Cir. 1993).
32. *Id.* at 528.
33. *Id.*
34. 263 Cal Rptr. 747 (Cal.App. 2 Dist. 1989), *cert. denied,* 111 S.Ct. 102 (1991).
35. 5 Cal. Rptr.2d 317 (Cal.App. 1st Dist. 1991).
36. *See also, State* v. *Calhoun,* 479 So.2d 241 (Fla.App. 4th Dist. 1985).
37. U.S.C. §§ 2510 *et seq.*
38. 18 U.S.C. § 2510(2).
39. *See, e.g., United States* v. *Harrelson,* 754 F.2d 1153 (1985), *cert. denied,* 106 S.Ct. 277 (1986).

Understanding Meaning

1. What is the purpose of Crawford's analysis? Why does her audience need this information?
2. How does she analyze the Fourth, Fifth, and Sixth Amendments?
3. What rights do criminals have in custody? Do they surrender all pretense of privacy when they are arrested?
4. *Critical Thinking:* Does the surreptitious recording of suspects' conversations threaten privacy and democracy or protect it? Would you approve of using this techniques to gather evidence that would establish the guilt of a child molester or a terrorist? Should the technique be used to secure evidence against people accused of "victimless" crimes?

Evaluating Strategy

1. Does citing specific cases help readers understand what is constitutional and what is not?
2. How is Crawford's analysis organized?
3. Crawford concludes the article with a list of suggestions. What does this imply about the needs of her readers?

Appreciating Language

1. How much legal terminology does the writer use? What does this reveal about her audience?
2. What language does Crawford use to describe suspects? What does this suggest about suspects?

Connections across the Disciplines

1. How does Crawford's professional role as attorney shape her writing? Compare her article to the one written by physician Oliver Sacks (page 75). What similarities do you see?
2. Compare this article with the FBI report on Lee Harvey Oswald (page 87). What do these entries reveal about writing in law enforcement?

Writing Suggestions

1. Write a short essay analyzing your view of secretly recording suspects' conversations. Should police officers advise suspects that anything they say in private may be held against them? Is surreptitious recording a violation of people's rights? How would you feel if the person who admitted killing a friend of yours was acquitted because his or her statements could not be entered into evidence?
2. *Collaborative Writing:* Working with a group of students, consider the following scenario. A student suspects his or her lover of being unfaithful and installs a recording device in the lover's apartment that transmits clear evidence that this person is engaging in unsafe practices with multiple partners. Discuss the ethics of this situation. Have a member of the group record responses, and as a group review the list and each write a brief analysis. Does a consensus exist? Do the responses indicate gender differences?

GUIDELINES FOR WRITING ANALYSIS

1. **Determine your purpose.** Does your analysis seek to explain the parts of a complex object, issue, condition, or situation, or does it seek to identify a reason, a cause, or a solution to a problem? Persuasive analysis requires greater attention to context.
2. **Define your role.** Are you expressing personal opinion supported by facts and examples of your own choosing, or are you following the dictates of a specific discipline? When writing in a professional role, use standard methods and tools of analysis. If you use unconventional methods, explain your rationale, and be prepared for criticism.
3. **Consider your audience.** In addition to evaluating your readers' knowledge base, you should consider their perceptual world. Are your readers likely to be receptive or hostile to your conclusions? What kind of evidence will most impress them?
4. **Limit your subject.** Analysis requires close study, and an ill-defined topic likely will lead to confusion.
5. **Gather appropriate sources, data, and information.** The strength of your analysis will depend on the quantity and quality of the information you examine. Avoid making judgments on limited data. Evaluate the sources of your data for possible flaws, oversights, or bias.
6. **Be open to alternative interpretations.** Do not make general statements based on data without entertaining alternative interpretations. Consider possible data you may have overlooked.
7. **Apply the rules of critical thinking, and avoid the logical fallacies (review page 317).**

SUGGESTED TOPICS FOR WRITING ANALYSIS

General Assignments

Write an analysis on any of the following topics. Your analysis will require careful thinking, observation, and possibly outside research. Remember to avoid the logical fallacies and to qualify your remarks.

- Affordable student housing (Define "affordable" in your area.)
- Current movies (Use the newspaper listings as a source.)
- Status of women in your college's faculty and administration
- The principal problem facing fellow students

- The political climate on your campus
- The popularity of a current fad or celebrity
- Your generation's attitude toward the Vietnam War, the Civil Rights movement, or any other historical event
- Gender differences
- The effect of divorce on children
- America's role in international affairs

Writing in Context

1. Assume you have been asked by the campus newspaper to analyze how students feel about abortion, gun control, or another controversial issue. Design a method to gather and analyze data. Indicate what methods you would use, such as focus groups, surveys, or personal interviews.
2. Analyze the image of women, the elderly, black males, businessmen, or any other group presented in popular television shows. Include as many examples as possible in your analysis.
3. Analyze editions of the largest newspaper in your area to determine the amount of attention given to international events versus domestic news. Explain your research methods—the number of editions reviewed and the methods of measurement (number of articles or amount of space).

ANALYSIS CHECKLIST

1. Is your topic clearly limited?
2. Is your approach appropriate for your context?
3. Have you amassed enough evidence?
4. Have you evaluated your evidence for inaccuracy or bias?
5. Have you avoided the logical fallacies?
6. Are your research methods clearly explained?
7. Are your results clearly presented?

Division and Classification

SEPARATING INTO PARTS AND RATING CATEGORIES

WHAT ARE DIVISION AND CLASSIFICATION?

Division helps readers understand complex subjects by separating them into parts. *Classification,* often used to aid decision making, rates subjects by placing them on a scale of different categories.

Division

If you enter a hospital, you will probably see signs directing you to different departments: cardiology, radiology, psychiatry, and pediatrics. Hospitals are divided into specific services. Universities consist of separate colleges, such as business and liberal arts. American literature can be divided into courses by historical era (nineteenth- and twentieth-century American writers), by genre (American poetry and American drama), or by special interest (women's literature and science fiction). Corporations place personnel into different departments: design, production, maintenance, marketing, sales, and accounting.

Division makes complicated subjects easier to comprehend and work with. For example, the human body is overwhelmingly intricate. In order to understand how it functions, medical disciplines divide it into systems: digestive, respiratory, nervous, muscular-skeletal, reproductive, and others. By studying individual systems, medical students come to a fuller understanding of how the whole body operates. Crime is such a vast social problem that writers discuss it in terms of traditional divisions—robbery, car theft, homicide, and fraud—or invent their own categories, dividing crime by causes: power, greed, identity, and revenge. People use the term *depression* to express everything from minor disappointment to suicidal despair. In order to inform patients about the variety of depressive illnesses, a mental health brochure divides the disorder into specific types:

> **Bereavement**—a 2–8 week process of grieving with sad and empty feelings after the death of someone important to you. May linger for much longer after loss of parent, child, or partner, but tends to gradually improve over time. You should observe steady readjustment to your changed world and resumption of social activities and pleasures.
>
> **Adjustment Reaction**—a period of up to 6 months after a major stressful event during which depressed mood, or hopeless feelings are more intense than normal and interfere with daily social and school or work activities. Like BEREAVEMENT, it is often helped by brief crisis therapy or family therapy.
>
> **Major Depression**—depressed mood or loss of interests with a variety of the symptoms and feelings of depression discussed earlier, lasting at least 2 weeks. Major depression ranges from mild cases with few symptoms to severe cases (known as "*clinical depression*") marked by a persistent bleak outlook which may lead to thoughts of escape through suicide. Depression may begin to lift after several weeks or may become chronic, lasting 2 years or more.

In this case division presents readers with a series of definitions. Division writing can also organize a set of narratives, descriptions, processes, or persuasive arguments.

Critical Thinking for Writing Division

Dividing any subject can be challenging. Would it make more sense to explain American politics to a foreign visitor in terms of political parties or specific issues? Would you group used cars by year, by price, or by model? When division writing, follow these guidelines:

1. **Avoid oversimplifying your subject.** You have no doubt seen magazine articles announcing three kinds of bosses, four types of marriages, or five methods of childrearing. Writers often invent descriptive or humorous labels, warning you to avoid "the toxic controller" or advising you how to

negotiate with the "whiny wimp." Although these divisions can be amusing and insightful, they can trivialize or oversimplify a subject. Not all people or situations can neatly fit into three or four types. *When discussing complex topics, inform readers of possible exceptions to your categories.*

2. **Select a method of division that includes all parts of the whole.** If you divide college students into four types, for example, make sure everyone on campus is included in one group. Eliminate potential gaps. You cannot simply divide students into Protestants, Catholics, and Jews if some are agnostics or Muslims. Every member or part of the whole must be accounted for.
3. **Make sure individual parts fit only one category.** If you were to divide businesses by geographical region—North, South, East, and West—how would you handle a company with operations on both coasts? If items can fit in more than one category, your method of division is not suited to your subject. It might be better to discuss businesses in terms of their gross sales, products, or size rather than location.
4. **Avoid categories that include too many differences.** If you were examining people of different ages, it could make sense to write about people in groups from age thirty to forty or fifty to sixty. But a category of age sixty to seventy would include both working and retired people, both those still paying into Social Security and those receiving benefits. It might be more accurate to break this group into people who are age sixty to sixty-five and those who are older than sixty-five.

Classification

Like division, classification breaks a complex subject into parts. But for classification, the categories are ranked or rated according to a single standard. In medicine, for example, burns are classified first-, second-, and third-degree based on the amount of tissue damage. Teachers grade tests according to the number of correct answers. Insurance companies set rates based on their clients' history of loss. Motion pictures are judged G, PG, PG13, R, and X based on depictions of sex and violence.

Perhaps no more serious an incident occurs in society than when an individual causes the death of another. In addressing this issue, the law identifies a range of situations in which a fatality occurs and ranks them from the most to least objectionable:

> *Felonious homicide.* The wrongful killing of a human being, of any age or either sex, without justification or excuse in law; of which offense there are two degrees, manslaughter and murder.

Homicide by misadventure. The accidental killing of another, where the slayer is doing a lawful act, unaccompanied by any criminally careless or reckless conduct. . . .

Homicide by necessity. A species of justifiable homicide, because it arises from some unavoidable necessity, without any will, intention, or desire, and without any inadvertence or negligence in the party killing, and therefore without any shadow of blame.

Classification assists people to make decisions and to direct actions. Classifications can set prices, establish salaries, and in some cases save lives. The importance of classification is demonstrated by the use of triage in emergency medicine. When a hospital is flooded with accident victims, doctors place patients into three categories: those who will die with or without immediate medical attention, those who will survive without emergency care, and those who will survive only if treated without delay. The last group is given priority to ensure that doctors do not waste time on the dying or those with minor injuries.

Critical Thinking for Writing Classification

As with division writing, classification requires careful planning. To avoid common problems, follow these guidelines:

1. **Avoid confusing division with classification.** Perhaps the most frequent mistake students make in classification writing papers is simply dividing a subject into parts. *Classification not only divides a subject into parts but also rates the parts on a scale.*
2. **Establish a clearly defined standard of measurement.** To successfully teach writing, for example, an English professor must provide students with a clear understanding of what distinguishes an A paper from a B paper. Even if you are making up your own categories, each one should be clearly defined so readers understand what distinguishes one from the other.
3. **Do not mix standards.** You can classify automobiles, for instance, from the cheapest to the most expensive, from the safest to the most dangerous, or from the most fuel efficient to the least fuel efficient. But you cannot write a classification essay that rates cars as being safe, fuel efficient, or expensive since many cars could be both expensive and fuel efficient.
4. **Arrange categories in order.** Organize the categories so they follow a ladderlike pattern, such as judging items from the best to the worst, the cheapest to the most expensive, or the newest to the oldest.

5. **Provide enough categories to include all parts of the whole.** If you were to classify cars as being either American or foreign, how would you account for Toyotas produced in the United States or Chryslers assembled in Mexico?

READING DIVISION AND CLASSIFICATION

As you read the division and classification entries in this chapter, keep the following questions in mind.

Meaning

1. What is the writer trying to explain by dividing or classifying his or her topic? Does the division or classification help you understand the subject better than a simple description would?
2. Do the divisions risk oversimplifying the subject?
3. Do the classification essays have a clearly defined standard?
4. Do the standards seem fair? Do they adequately measure what they claim to evaluate?

Strategy

1. How does the writer introduce or set up the division or classification?
2. How does the author use definitions and examples to create distinct categories?
3. Does the writer use standard divisions and classifications accepted by a particular discipline or profession, or does he or she invent new ones?
4. Does the writer use division or classification to explain a topic, or is it used as a device to recommend one item over another?

Language

1. What does the level of language reveal about the writer's discipline and intended audience?
2. What words does the author use to describe or define standards of classification? Do you detect a bias?

E. B. WHITE

Elwyn Brooks White (1899–1985) attended Cornell University, where he studied under William Strunk Jr. Years later, White revised Strunk's textbook on writing, renaming it The Elements of Style. *First published in 1952, the book remains one of the most popular guides for writers. White began working for the* New Yorker *magazine in 1927 and later wrote columns for* Harper's. *Although best known as an essayist, White is also remembered for his best-selling children's books,* Charlotte's Web *and* Stuart Little.

Three New Yorks

New York City is a maze of buildings, boroughs, literary associations, and contrasts between rich and poor. An international center, it is home to neighborhoods as intimate as small villages. For approaching a topic this large, White divides New York into three cities, as defined by the experiences and attitudes of the native, the settler, and the commuter. This excerpt is from White's book Here Is New York *(1949).*

1 There are roughly three New Yorks. There is, first, the New York of the man or woman who was born here, who takes the city for granted and accepts its size and its turbulence as natural and inevitable. Second, there is the New York of the commuter—the city that is devoured by locusts each day and spat out each night. Third, there is the New York of the person who was born somewhere else and came to New York in quest of something. Of these three trembling cities the greatest is the last—the city of final destination, the city that is a goal. It is this third city that accounts for New York's high-strung disposition, its poetical deportment, its dedication to the arts, and its incomparable achievements. Commuters give the city its tidal restlessness; natives give it solidity and continuity; but the settlers give it passion. And whether it is a farmer arriving from Italy to set up a small grocery store in a slum, or a young girl arriving from a small town in Mississippi to escape the indignity of being observed by her neighbors, or a boy arriving from the Corn Belt with a manuscript in his suitcase and a pain in his heart, it makes no difference; each embraces New York with the intense excitement of first love, each absorbs New York with

the fresh eyes of an adventurer, each generates heat and light to dwarf the Consolidated Edison Company.

2 The commuter is the queerest bird of all. The suburb he inhabits has no essential vitality of its own and is a mere roost where he comes at day's end to go to sleep. Except in rare cases, the man who lives in Mamaroneck or Little Neck or Teaneck, and works in New York, discovers nothing much about the city except the time of arrival and departure of trains and buses, and the path to a quick lunch. He is desk-bound, and has never, idly roaming in the gloaming, stumbled suddenly on Belvedere Tower in the Park, seen the ramparts rise sheer from the water of the pond, and the boys along the shore fishing for minnows, girls stretched out negligently on the shelves of the rocks; he has never come suddenly on anything at all in New York as a loiterer, because he has had no time between trains. He has fished in Manhattan's wallet and dug out coins, but has never listened to Manhattan's breathing, never awakened to its morning, never dropped off to sleep in its night. About 400,000 men and women come charging onto the Island each week-day morning, out of the mouths of tubes and tunnels. Not many among them have ever spent a drowsy afternoon in the great rustling oaken silence of the reading room of the Public Library, with the book elevator (like an old water wheel) spewing out books onto the trays. They tend their furnaces in Westchester and in Jersey, but have never seen the furnaces of the Bowery, the fires that burn in oil drums on zero winter nights. They may work in the financial district downtown and never see the extravagant plantings of Rockefeller Center—the daffodils and grape hyacinths and birches of the flags trimmed to the wind on a fine morning in spring. Or they may work in a midtown office and may let a whole year swing round without sighting Governor's Island from the sea wall. The commuter dies with tremendous mileage to his credit, but he is no rover. His entrances and exits are more devious than those in a prairie-dog village; and he calmly plays bridge while his train is buried in the mud at the bottom of the East River. The Long Island Rail Road alone carried 40 million commuters last year; but many of them were the same fellow retracing his steps.

3 The terrain of New York is such that a resident sometimes travels farther, in the end, than a commuter. The journey of the composer Irving Berlin from Cherry Street in the lower East Side to an apartment uptown was through an alley and was only three or four miles in length; but it was like going three times around the world.

Understanding Meaning

1. How is New York seen differently by a native and by a settler?
2. What makes, in White's opinion, the commuter "the queerest bird of all"?
3. Can a commuter, even one who has worked in the city for decades, really understand New York?

Evaluating Strategy

1. *Critical Thinking:* The title might lead you to believe that White is going to describe the city, but in fact he focuses on people's reactions to it. Is this an effective way of limiting a short essay? Is White suggesting that New York, like any city, is ultimately a state of mind?
2. *Other Modes:* Where does White use *description* and *comparison* to develop his essay?

Appreciating Language

1. What connotations does White use to describe the various types? How does he depict commuters?
2. What impressions does White's descriptive language give about the city itself?

Connections across the Disciplines

1. Compare White's essay to Truman Capote's description of Holcomb, Kansas (page 105). Could White's classification work as well in writing about such a small town?
2. White is writing about a complex city. Mary Mebane (page 434) comments about racial attitudes. By separating their subjects into parts, do White and Mebane give readers a greater concept of the whole?

Writing Suggestions

1. If you are familiar with New York City, write a few paragraphs analyzing the validity of White's observations. Do you see the "three New Yorks" he does? You may suggest alternative ways of seeing the city.

2. Write a brief essay about your own city or town. Do people see it differently? Can you distinguish between natives and visitors, rich and poor, or those who work for the town's largest employer and those who do not?
3. *Collaborative Writing:* Working with a group of students, expand White's discussion to include the entire United States. Do differences exist between native-born Americans, people who have immigrated to America, and those who "commute," such as tourists and foreign students? Take notes on the discussion, and write a description of each type. You may wish to collaborate on a brief essay that classifies people's attitudes—based on their origin—toward patriotism, crime, social values, or success.

MARY MEBANE

Mary Mebane (1933–) received a doctorate in English from the University of North Carolina. She teaches English at the University of South Carolina at Columbia. Mebane is the author of a play, Take a Sad Song, *and two autobiographical books,* Mary *and* Mary Wayfarer. *In 1982 she received a National Endowment of the Arts Creative Writing Fellowship. Much of her work has focused on the experience of African Americans in the South.*

Black Wasn't Beautiful

This section from Mebane's autobiography Mary *(1981) details the four options that dark-complexioned African American women faced in the segregated South. Attending a black college in the 1950s, Mebane encountered a rigid system of discrimination in which lighter-skinned African Americans considered themselves superior to those with darker skin.*

1 In the fall of 1951 during my first week at North Carolina College, a black school in Durham, the chairman's wife, who was indistinguishable from a white woman, stopped me one day in the hall. She wanted to see me, she said.

2 When I went to her office, she greeted me with a big smile. "You know," she said, "you made the highest mark on the verbal part of the examination." She was referring to the examination that the entire freshman class took upon entering the college. In spite of her smile, her eyes and tone of voice were saying, "How could this black-skinned girl score higher on the verbal than some of the students who've had more advantages than she? It must be some sort of fluke." I felt it, but I managed to smile my thanks and back off. For here at North Carolina College, social class and color were the primary criteria used in deciding status. The faculty assumed light-skinned students were more intelligent, and they were always a bit nonplussed when a dark-skinned student did well, especially if she was a girl.

3 I don't know whether African men recently transported to the New World considered themselves handsome or, more important, whether they considered African women beautiful in comparison with native

American Indian women or immigrant European women. But one thing I know for sure: By the twentieth century, really black skin on a woman was considered ugly in this country. In the 1950s this was particularly true among those who were exposed to college. Black skin was to be disguised at all costs. Since a black face is rather hard to disguise, many women took refuge in ludicrous makeup.

4 I observed all through elementary and high school, in various entertainments, the girls were placed on the stage in order of color. And very black ones didn't get into the front row. If they were past caramel-brown, to the back row they would go. Nobody questioned the justice of this—neither the students nor the teachers.

5 Oddly enough, the lighter-skinned black male did not seem to feel so much prejudice toward the black black woman. It was no accident, I felt, that Mr. Harrison, the eighth-grade teacher, who was reddish-yellow himself, once protested to the science and math teacher about the fact that he always assigned sweeping duties to Doris and Ruby, two black black girls. Mr. Harrison said to them one day in the other teacher's presence, "You must be some bad girls. Every day I come down here you all are sweeping." The science and math teacher got the point and didn't ask them to sweep any more. Uneducated black males, too, sometimes related very well to the black black woman. They had been less indoctrinated by the white society around them.

6 Because of the stigma attached to having dark skin, a black black woman had to do many things to find a place for herself. One possibility was to attach herself to a light-skinned woman, hoping that some of the magic would rub off on her. A second was to make herself sexually available, hoping thereby to attract a mate. Third, she could resign herself to a more chaste life-style—either (for the professional woman) teaching and work in established churches or (for the uneducated woman) domestic work and zealous service in "holy and sanctified" churches.

7 Lucy had chosen the first route. Lucy was short, skinny, short-haired and black black, and thus unacceptable. So she made her choice. She selected Patricia, the lightest-skinned girl in the school, as her friend and followed her around. Patricia and her friends barely tolerated Lucy, but Lucy smiled and doggedly hung on, hoping that those who noticed Patricia might notice her also. Though I felt shame for her behavior, even then I understood.

8 A fourth avenue open to the black black woman is excellence in a career. Since in the South the field most accessible to such women is

education, a great many of them prepared to become teachers. But here, too, the black black woman had problems. Grades weren't given to her lightly in school, nor were promotions on the job. She had to pass examinations with flying colors or be left behind. She had to be overqualified for a job because otherwise she didn't stand a chance of getting it—and she was competing only with other blacks.

9 The black woman's training would pay off in the 1970s. With the arrival of integration, the black black woman would find, paradoxically enough, that her skin color in an integrated situation was not the handicap it had been in an all-black situation. But it wasn't until the middle and late 1960s, when the post-1945 generation of black males arrived in college that I noticed any change in the situation at all. *He* wore an Afro and *she* wore an Afro, and sometimes the only way you could tell them apart was when his Afro was taller than hers. Black had become beautiful. It was then that the dread I felt at dealing with the college-educated black male began to ease. Even now, though, when I have occasion to engage in any transaction with a college-educated black man, I gauge his age. If I guess he was born after 1945, I feel confident that the transaction will turn out all right. If he probably was born before 1945, my stomach tightens, I find myself taking shallow breaths, and I try to state my business and escape as soon as possible.

10 When the grades from the first quarter at North Carolina College came out, I had the highest average in the freshman class. The chairman's wife called me into her office again. We did a replay of the same scene we had played during the first week of the term. She complimented me on my grades. Then she reached into a drawer and pulled out a copy of the freshman English final examination. She asked me to take the exam over again.

11 At first I couldn't believe what she was saying. I had taken the course under another teacher; and it was so incredible to her that I should have made the highest score in the class that she was trying to test me again personally. For a few moments I knew rage so intense that I wanted to take my fists and start punching her. I have seldom hated anyone so deeply. I handed the examination back to her and walked out.

Understanding Meaning

1. What caused the African American community to discriminate against those with dark skin?

2. What evidence of discrimination does Mebane offer?
3. Briefly describe the four options dark-skinned women faced.
4. How did gender affect people's attitudes toward dark-skinned women?
5. What changes occurred in the 1970s?
6. *Critical Thinking:* What other examples of discrimination *within* a group can you think of? Have some members of ethnic groups attempted to distance themselves from those seen as less desirable by mainstream society, hence the conflict, for example, between "lace curtain Irish" and "shanty Irish"? Do women discriminate against other women they see as less attractive, less respectable, too traditional, or too radical?

Evaluating Strategy

1. Mebane begins and ends the piece with a narrative. How effective is this device?
2. *Other Modes:* Where does Mebane use *comparison* and *contrast* within her essay?

Appreciating Language

1. How does Mebane describe the differences among African Americans?
2. What does her word choice reveal about her attitudes toward those who discriminated against her?

Connections across the Disciplines

1. Compare Mebane's account of discrimination *within* the black community with Nathan McCall's essay (page 47), which discusses black-white racial conflict. How did these experiences shape the writers' attitudes? How did they respond to discrimination?
2. Martin Luther King Jr.'s essay (page 443) suggests three ways oppressed people respond to their condition. Does this essay suggest a fourth way? Do oppressed people often build a separate society mirroring the values of their oppressors?

Writing Suggestions

1. Write an essay describing a situation in which you were unfairly classified because of your race, age, appearance, or occupation.

2. *Collaborative Writing:* Discuss Mebane's essay with a small group of students. How often is discrimination internalized? Have members of the group offer examples they have witnessed or experienced. After taking notes, work together to write a brief division or classification paper stating the reasons for this behavior.

KESAYA E. NODA

Although born in the United States, Kesaya Noda has always been viewed as an alien. "A third-generation German-American," she notes, "is an American. A third-generation Japanese-American is a Japanese-American." Seen as being Japanese, Japanese American, or simply Asian, Noda came to question the ways she is perceived by other Americans.

Growing Up Asian in America

In this essay from 1989, Kesaya Noda uses division to answer the question "How is one to know and define oneself?" In this instance, Noda employs division to help her select one of several possible identities.

1 Sometimes when I was growing up, my identity seemed to hurtle toward me and paste itself right to my face. I felt that way, encountering the stereotypes of my race perpetuated by non-Japanese people (primarily white) who may or may not have had contact with other Japanese in America. "You don't like cheese, do you?" someone would ask. "I know your people don't like cheese." Sometimes questions came making allusions to history. That was another aspect of the identity. Events that had happened quite apart from the me who stood silent in that moment connected my face with an incomprehensible past. "Your parents were in California? Were they in those camps during the war?" And sometimes there were phrases or nicknames: "Lotus Blossom." I was sometimes addressed or referred to as racially Japanese, sometimes as Japanese-American, and sometimes as an Asian woman. Confusions and distortions abounded.

2 How is one to know and define oneself? From the inside—within a context that is self-defined, from a grounding in community and a connection with culture and history that are comfortably accepted? Or from the outside—in terms of messages received from the media and people who are often ignorant? Even as an adult I can still see two sides of my face and past. I can see from the inside out, in freedom. And I can see from the outside in, driven by the old voices of childhood and lost in anger and fear.

I AM RACIALLY JAPANESE

3 A voice from my childhood says: "You are other. You are less than. You are unalterably alien." This voice has its own history. We have indeed been seen as other and alien since the early years of our arrival in the United States. The very first immigrants were welcomed and sought as laborers to replace the dwindling numbers of Chinese, whose influx has been cut off by the Chinese Exclusion Act of 1882. The Japanese fell natural heir to the same anti-Asian prejudice that had arisen against the Chinese. As soon as they began striking for better wages, they were no longer welcomed.

4 I can see myself today as a person historically defined by law and custom as being forever alien. Being neither "free white," nor "African," our people in California were deemed "aliens, ineligible for citizenship," no matter how long they intended to stay here. Aliens ineligible for citizenship were prohibited from owning, buying, or leasing land. They did not and could not belong here. The voice in me remembers that I am always a *Japanese*-American in the eyes of many. A third-generation German-American is an American. A third-generation Japanese-American is a Japanese-American. Being Japanese means being a danger to the country during the war and knowing how to use chopsticks. I wear this history on my face.

5 I move to the other side. I see a different light and claim a different context. My race is a line that stretches across ocean and time to link me to the shrine where my grandmother was raised. Two high, white banners lift in the wind at the top of the stone steps leading to the shrine. It is time for the summer festival. Black characters are written against the sky as boldly as the clouds, as lightly as kites, as sharply as the big black crows I used to see above the fields in New Hampshire. At festival time there is liquor and food, rituals, discipline, and abandonment. There is music and drunkenness and invocation. There is hope. Another season has come. Another season has gone.

6 I am racially Japanese. I have a certain claim to this crazy place where the prayers intoned by a neighboring Shinto priest (standing in for my grandmother's nephew who is sick) are drowned out by the rehearsals for the pop singing contest in which most of the villagers will compete later that night. The village elders, the priest, and I stand respectfully upon the immaculate, shining wooden floor of the outer shrine, bowing our heads before the hidden powers. During the patchy intervals when I can hear him, I notice the priest has a stutter. His

voice flutters up to my ears only occasionally because two men and a woman are singing gustily into a microphone in the compound, testing the sound system. A prerecorded tape of guitars, samisens, and drums accompanies them. Rock music and Shinto prayers. That night, to loud applause and cheers, a young man is given the award for the most *netsuretsu*—passionate, burning—rendition of a song. We roar our approval of the reward. Never mind that his voice had wandered and slid, now slightly above, now slightly below the given line of the melody. Netsuretsu. Netsuretsu.

7 In the morning, my grandmother's sister kneels at the foot of the stone stairs to offer her morning prayers. She is too crippled to climb the stairs, so each morning she kneels here upon the path. She shuts her eyes for a few seconds, her motions as matter of fact as when she washes rice. I linger longer than she does, so reluctant to leave, savoring the connection I feel with my grandmother in America, the past, and the power that lives and shines in the morning sun.

Understanding Meaning

1. What confusion did Noda encounter as a child?
2. Are the comments about cheese, her parents' possible internment during World War II, or being nicknamed "Lotus Blossom" intentionally hostile? Would people of other ethnic groups have more troubling, more wounding experiences to relate?
3. Why does her childhood voice tell her "You are other. You are less than" and not "You are other. You are different from"? What does this reveal about her self-esteem?
4. *Critical Thinking:* At what point do people become "Americans"? Teddy Roosevelt once declared that "no hyphenated Americans" must exist—no Irish-Americans, German-Americans, or Italian-Americans. Can this apply to Asian Americans and African Americans (with or without hyphens)?

Evaluating Strategy

1. How does Noda separate the different identities she has confronted?
2. *Other Modes:* Where does Noda use *description* and *comparison* to develop her essay?
3. *Critical Thinking:* Is division an effective method of making a decision? By separating and identifying different options, does a danger of overlooking possible alternatives arise?

Appreciating Language

1. Noda uses the Japanese word *netsuretsu*. What does this add to the essay? What does it demonstrate?
2. What language does Noda use to describe Japanese traditions and festivals? What images stand out?

Connections across the Disciplines

1. How does Noda's sense of alternative identities contrast with the choices Mary Mebane describes African American women faced in the 1950s (page 434)?
2. How does Noda's perception of being Japanese contrast to the views of ethnic identity expressed by Armando Rendón (page 667) and Richard Rodriguez (page 673)?

Writing Suggestions

1. Write a short essay about the way people identified you as you were growing up. Were you seen as black or Jewish, the minister's daughter, a rich kid, or fat? How did these perceptions affect your self-awareness and self-esteem?
2. *Collaborative Writing:* Discuss Noda's essay with a group of students. Does every ethnic group have negative associations to some people? Can any ethnic group be viewed as being totally free of prejudice? Record the views of your group, and write a brief division paper, outlining the principal observations raised in the discussion.

MARTIN LUTHER KING JR.

Martin Luther King Jr. (1929–1968) was a leading figure in the Civil Rights movement in the 1950s and 1960s. A noted minister, King blended his deeply felt religious values and his sense of political and social justice. He created the Southern Christian Leadership Conference, organized many demonstrations, and lobbied for voting rights. In 1964 he received the Nobel Peace Prize. He was assassinated in 1968.

The Ways of Meeting Oppression

In this section from his 1958 book Stride toward Freedom, *King classifies three ways oppressed people have responded to oppression. King uses classification to rate which response is the most effective and concludes his comments persuading readers to accept his choice.*

1 Oppressed people deal with their oppression in three characteristic ways. One way is acquiescence: The oppressed resign themselves to their doom. They tacitly adjust themselves to oppression, and thereby become conditioned to it. In every movement toward freedom some of the oppressed prefer to remain oppressed. Almost 2,800 years ago Moses set out to lead the children of Israel from the slavery of Egypt to the freedom of the promised land. He soon discovered that slaves do not always welcome their deliverers. They become accustomed to being slaves. They would rather bear those ills they have, as Shakespeare pointed out, than flee to others that they know not of. They prefer the "fleshpots of Egypt" to the ordeals of emancipation.

2 There is such a thing as the freedom of exhaustion. Some people are so worn down by the yoke of oppression that they give up. A few years ago in the slum areas of Atlanta, a Negro guitarist used to sing almost daily: "Been down so long that down don't bother me." This is the type of negative freedom and resignation that often engulfs the life of the oppressed.

3 But this is not the way out. To accept passively an unjust system is to cooperate with that system; thereby the oppressed become as evil

as the oppressor. Noncooperation with evil is as much a moral obligation as is cooperation with good. The oppressed must never allow the conscience of the oppressor to slumber. Religion reminds every man that he is his brother's keeper. To accept injustice or segregation passively is to say to the oppressor that his actions are morally right. It is a way of allowing his conscience to fall asleep. At this moment the oppressed fails to be his brother's keeper. So acquiescence—while often the easier way—is not the moral way. It is the way of the coward. The Negro cannot win the respect of his oppressor by acquiescing; he merely increases the oppressor's arrogance and contempt. Acquiescence is interpreted as proof of the Negro's inferiority. The Negro cannot win the respect of the white people of the South or the peoples of the world if he is willing to sell the future of his children for his personal and immediate comfort and safety.

4 A second way that oppressed people sometimes deal with oppression is to resort to physical violence and corroding hatred. Violence often brings about momentary results. Nations have frequently won their independence in battle. But in spite of temporary victories, violence never brings permanent peace. It solves no social problem; it merely creates new and more complicated ones.

5 Violence as a way of achieving racial injustice is both impractical and immoral. It is impractical because it is a descending spiral ending in destruction for all. The old law of an eye for an eye leaves everybody blind. It is immoral because it seeks to humiliate the opponent rather than win his understanding; it seeks to annihilate rather than to convert. Violence is immoral because it thrives on hatred rather than love. It destroys community and makes brotherhood impossible. It leaves society in monologue rather than dialogue. Violence ends by defeating itself. It creates bitterness in the survivors and brutality in the destroyers. A voice echoes through time saying to every potential Peter, "Put up your sword."* History is cluttered with the wreckage of nations that failed to follow this command.

6 If the American Negro and other victims of oppression succumb to the temptation of using violence in the struggle for freedom, future generations will be the recipients of a desolate night of bitterness, and our chief legacy to them will be an endless reign of meaningless chaos. Violence is not the way.

*The apostle Peter had drawn his sword to defend Christ from arrest. The voice was Christ's, who surrendered himself for trial and crucifixion (John 18:11).

7 The third way open to oppressed people in their quest for freedom is the way of nonviolent resistance. Like the synthesis in Hegelian philosophy, the principle of nonviolent resistance seeks to reconcile the truths of two opposites—the acquiescence and violence—while avoiding the extremes and immoralities of both. The nonviolent resister agrees with the person who acquiesces that one should not be physically aggressive toward his opponent; but he balances the equation by agreeing with the person of violence that evil must be resisted. He avoids the nonresistance of the former and the violent resistance of the latter. With nonviolent resistance, no individual or group need submit to any wrong, nor need anyone resort to violence in order to right a wrong.

8 It seems to me that this is the method that must guide the actions of the Negro in the present crisis in race relations. Through nonviolent resistance the Negro will be able to rise to the noble height of opposing the unjust system while loving the perpetrators of the system. The Negro must work passionately and unrelentingly for full stature as a citizen, but he must not use inferior methods to gain it. He must never come to terms with falsehood, malice, hate, or destruction.

9 Nonviolent resistance makes it possible for the Negro to remain in the South and struggle for his rights. The Negro's problem will not be solved by running away. He cannot listen to the glib suggestion of those who would urge him to migrate en masse to other sections of the country. By grasping his great opportunity in the South he can make a lasting contribution to the moral strength of the nation and set a sublime example of courage for generations yet unborn.

10 By nonviolent resistance, the Negro can also enlist all men of good will in his struggle for equality. The problem is not a purely racial one, with Negroes set against whites. In the end, it is not a struggle between people at all, but a tension between justice and injustice. Nonviolent resistance is not aimed against oppressors but against oppression. Under its banner consciences, not racial groups, are enlisted.

Understanding Meaning

1. Briefly describe the three ways people respond to oppression, according to King. Do you know of a fourth or fifth way? Do people, for instance, respond to oppression by blaming each other?
2. Humility is a Christian value. How does King, a minister, argue that humble acceptance of injustice is immoral?

3. King admits that nations have won freedom through violence, but why does he reject it for African Americans?
4. *Critical Thinking:* King defines the third way as a blend or synthesis of the first two. Why does he argue that this last manner is the most successful? What are its advantages?

Evaluating Strategy

1. Why does King use classification to suggest a solution instead of writing a direct persuasive argument?
2. How does King use his religious values as a way of arguing the desirability of his choice?
3. What transition statements does King use to direct his readers?

Appreciating Language

1. How does King define the difference between "acquiescence" and "nonviolent resistance"?
2. What do King's use of biblical analogies and reference to Hegelian philosophy reveal about his intended audience?

Connections across the Disciplines

1. In attempting to define happiness, John Ciardi (page 194) suggests the best way is to define the outer boundaries and work toward the center. Does King use this device in classifying or ranking responses to oppression?
2. Read Leonce Gaiter's "The Revolt of the Black Bourgeoisie" (page 636). Does this article suggest the situation of African Americans has changed since King wrote *Stride toward Freedom?*

Writing Suggestions

1. Use King's essay as a model to write your own classification paper revealing the way people generally respond to a common issue or problem—the death of a loved one, the loss of a job, the discovery that a partner has been unfaithful, or being victimized. Rank the responses from the least effective to most effective.

2. *Collaborative Writing:* Discuss King's classification with a group of students. How many people suffering oppression appear to be following his "third way"? Have a member of the group take notes, then work together to draft a short paper dividing or classifying, if possible, your group's responses.

MEG GREENFIELD

Meg Greenfield (1930–) was born in Seattle, began working for the Reporter *in 1957, and served as the magazine's Washington editor for three years. In 1968 she joined the* Washington Post *as editorial writer, becoming editor of the newspaper's editorial page in 1979. She has also written a column for* Newsweek. *In 1978 Meg Greenfield received a Pulitzer Prize for her editorial writing.*

Why Nothing Is "Wrong" Anymore

In this essay from a 1996 Newsweek, *Greenfield comments on the fact that few people seem willing to condemn antisocial behavior as morally wrong. To illustrate her point, Greenfield creates various categories to catalog people's responses to "negative" behavior.*

1 There has been an awful lot of talk about sin, crime, and plain old antisocial behavior this summer—drugs and pornography at home, terror and brutality abroad. Maybe it's just the heat; or maybe these categories of conduct (sin, crime, etc.) are really on the rise. What strikes me is our curiously deficient, not to say defective, way of talking about them. We don't seem to have a word anymore for "wrong" in the moral sense, as in, for example, "theft is wrong."

2 Let me quickly qualify. There is surely no shortage of people condemning other people on such grounds, especially their political opponents or characters they just don't care for. Name-calling is still very much in vogue. But where the concept of wrong is really important—as a guide to one's own behavior or that of one's own side in some dispute—it is missing; and this is as true of those on the religious right who are going around pronouncing great masses of us sinners as it is of their principal antagonists, those on the secular left who can forgive or "understand" just about anything so long as it has not been perpetrated by a right-winger.

3 There is a fairly awesome literature that attempts to explain how we have changed as a people with the advent of psychiatry, the weakening of religious institutions and so forth, but you don't need to address these matters to take note of a simple fact. As a guide and a standard to

live by, you don't hear so much about "right and wrong" these days. The very notion is considered politically, not to say personally, embarrassing, since it has such a repressive, Neanderthal ring to it. So we have developed a broad range of alternatives to "right and wrong." I'll name a few.

4 **Right and stupid:** This is the one you use when your candidate gets caught stealing, or, for that matter, when anyone on your side does something reprehensible. "It was really so dumb of him"—head must shake here—"I just can't understand it." Bad is dumb, breathtakingly dumb and therefore unfathomable; so, conveniently enough, the effort to fathom it might just as well be called off. This one had a big play during Watergate and has had mini-revivals ever since whenever congressmen and senators investigating administration crimes turn out to be guilty of something similar themselves.

5 **Right and not necessarily unconstitutional:** I don't know at quite what point along the way we came to this one, the avoidance of admitting that something is wrong by pointing out that it is not specifically or even inferentially prohibited by the Constitution or, for that matter, mentioned by name in the criminal code or the Ten Commandments. The various parties that prevail in civil-liberty and civil-rights disputes before the Supreme Court have gotten quite good at making this spurious connection: It is legally permissible, therefore it is morally acceptable, possibly even good. But both as individuals and as a society we do things every day that we know to be wrong even though they may not fall within the class of legally punishable acts or tickets to eternal damnation.

6 **Right and sick:** Crime or lesser wrongdoing defined as physical and/or psychological disorder—this one has been around for ages now and as long ago as 1957 was made the butt of a great joke in the "Gee Officer Krupke!" song in "West Side Story." Still, I think no one could have foreseen the degree to which an originally reasonable and humane assumption (that some of what once was regarded as wrongdoing is committed by people acting out of ailment rather than moral choice) would be seized upon and exploited to exonerate every kind of misfeasance. This route is a particular favorite of caught-out officeholders who, when there is at last no other recourse, hold a press conference, announce that they are "sick" in some wise and throw themselves

and their generally stunned families on our mercy. At which point it becomes gross to pick on them; instead we are exhorted to admire them for their "courage."

7 **Right and only to be expected:** You could call this the tit-for-tat school; it is related to the argument that holds moral wrongdoing to be evidence of sickness, but it is much more pervasive and insidious these days. In fact it is probably the most popular dodge, being used to justify, or at least avoid owning up to, every kind of lapse: The other guy, or sometimes just plain circumstance, "asked for it." For instance, I think most of us could agree that setting fire to live people, no matter what their political offense, is—dare I say it?—wrong. Yet if it is done by those for whom we have sympathy in a conflict, there is a tendency to extenuate or disbelieve it, receiving it less as evidence of wrongdoing on our side than as evidence of the severity of the provocation or as enemy-supplied disinformation. Thus the hesitation of many in the antiapartheid movement to confront the brutality of so-called "necklacing," and thus the immediate leap of Sen. Jesse Helms to the defense of the Chilean government after the horrifying incineration of protesters there.

8 **Right and complex:** This one hardly takes a moment to describe; you know it well. "Complex" is the new "controversial," a word used as "controversial" was for so long to flag trouble of some unspecified, dismaying sort that the speaker doesn't want to have to step up to. "Well, you know, it's very complex. . . ." I still can't get this one out of my own vocabulary.

9 In addition to these various sophistries, we also have created a rash of "ethics committees" in our government, of course, whose function seems to be to dither around writing rules that allow people who have clearly done wrong—and should have known it and probably did—to get away because the rules don't cover their offense (see Right and not necessarily unconstitutional). But we don't need any more committees or artful dodges for that matter. As I listen to the moral arguments swirling about us this summer I become ever more persuaded that our real problem is this: The "still, small voice" of conscience has become far too small—and utterly still.

Understanding Meaning

1. What does Greenfield see as "defective" about the way people now describe antisocial behavior?
2. Why do people seem unwilling to use terms like "right" and "wrong"?
3. What do the alternatives to right and wrong Greenfield describes have in common?
4. When do people dismiss or excuse activities they would normally condemn as immoral or illegal?
5. How common is it for people to blame their behavior on an illness or personality disorder? Have we become a nation of victims?
6. *Critical Thinking:* Consider the adage "To understand all is to forgive all." In seeking to understand criminals, for instance, do we find ourselves excusing their behavior? Can you think of recent instances in which people accused of terrible crimes have been presented as victims themselves?

Evaluating Strategy

1. Greenfield opens her essay with a general description of the societal condition. Would a specific example or narrative dramatize her point more clearly?
2. What method does Greenfield use to divide her subject?

Appreciating Language

1. How does your dictionary define *wrong?* What does the term imply?
2. What are the connotations of the words people use in place of "wrong"?
3. What does "necklacing" mean? Does use of this euphemism make a horrible practice acceptable to contemplate?

Connections across the Disciplines

1. William Raspberry (page 320) suggests that accepting limited definitions can cripple people's options. Does defining antisocial behavior as less than immoral or as wrong make society less humane, less safe, and less livable?
2. Gloria Steinem's essay (page 557) reveals how the women's movement has changed our language. What social forces have led us to abandon the word *wrong?*

Writing Suggestions

1. Write an essay classifying your own views of antisocial behavior. Your classification may include brief definitions, descriptions, and narratives.
2. *Collaborative Writing:* Work with a group of students, and discuss Greenfield's essay. Do members of your group share her concern? In a diverse culture are all citizens expected to follow common standards of behavior? Take notes on comments made by the group, and write a few paragraphs classifying or dividing the group's opinions.

JAMES AUSTIN

Dr. James Austin (1925–) graduated from Harvard Medical School and is a specialist in neurology. He devoted more than twenty years to research on the brain. While serving as professor and chairman of the Department of Neurology at the University of Colorado Medical School, he received the American Association of Neuropathologists Prize. Austin has also earned a reputation as a writer with an ability to make complicated scientific issues understandable to general readers.

Four Kinds of Chance

James Austin has written widely on the role of chance or luck in scientific discovery. In this article, written for the Saturday Review *(1974), he classifies the four kinds of chance that occur in scientific research. Luck, he explains, is not as simple as drawing a winning hand in poker. As you read the article, consider how many of the varieties of chance you have experienced.*

1 What is chance? Dictionaries define it as something fortuitous that happens unpredictably without discernable human intention. Chance is unintentional and capricious, but we needn't conclude that chance is immune from human intervention. Indeed, chance plays several distinct roles when humans react creatively with one another and with their environment.

2 We can readily distinguish four varieties of chance if we consider that they each involve a different kind of motor activity and a special kind of sensory receptivity. The varieties of chance also involve distinctive personality traits and differ in the way one particular individual influences them.

3 Chance I is the pure blind luck that comes with no effort on our part. If, for example, you are sitting at a bridge table of four, it's "in the cards" for you to receive a hand of all 13 spades, but it will come up only once in every 6.3 trillion deals. You will ultimately draw this lucky hand—with no intervention on your part—but it does involve a longer wait than most of us have time for.

4 Chance II evokes the kind of luck Charles Kettering had in mind when he said: "Keep on going and the chances are you will stumble on

something, perhaps when you are least expecting it. I have never heard of anyone stumbling on something sitting down."

5 In the sense referred to here, Chance II is not passive, but springs from an energetic, generalized motor activity. A certain basal level of action "stirs up the pot," brings in random ideas that will collide and stick together in fresh combinations, lets chance operate. When someone, *anyone,* does swing into motion and keeps on going, he will increase the number of collisions between events. When a few events are linked together, they can then be exploited to have a fortuitous outcome, but many others, of course, cannot. Kettering was right. Press on. Something will turn up. We may term this the Kettering Principle.

6 In the two previous examples, a unique role of the individual person was either lacking or minimal. Accordingly, as we move on to Chance III, we see blind luck, but in camouflage. Chance presents the clue, the opportunity exists, but it would be missed except by that one person uniquely equipped to observe it, visualize it conceptually, and fully grasp its significance. Chance III involves a special receptivity and discernment unique to the recipient. Louis Pasteur characterized it for all time when he said: "Chance favors only the prepared mind."

7 Pasteur himself had it in full measure. But the classic example of his principle occurred in 1928, when Alexander Fleming's mind instantly fused at least five elements into a conceptually unified nexus. His mental sequences went something like this: (1) I see that a mold has fallen by accident into my culture dish; (2) the staphylococcal colonies residing near it failed to grow; (3) the mold must have secreted something that killed the bacteria; (4) I recall a similar experience once before; (5) if I could separate this new "something" from the mold, it could be used to kill staphylococci that cause human infections.

8 Actually, Fleming's mind was exceptionally well prepared for the penicillin mold. Six years earlier, while he was suffering from a cold, his own nasal drippings had found their way into a culture dish, for reasons not made entirely clear. He noted that nearby bacteria were killed, and astutely followed up the lead. His observations led him to discover a bactericidal enzyme present in nasal mucus and tears, called lysozyme. Lysozyme proved too weak to be of medical use, but imagine how receptive Fleming's mind was to the penicillin mold when it later happened on the scene!

9 One word evokes the quality of the operations involved in the first three kinds of chance. It is *serendipity.* The term describes the facility for encountering unexpected good luck, as the result of: accident

(Chance I), general exploratory behavior (Chance II), or sagacity (Chance III). The word itself was coined by the Englishman-of-letters Horace Walpole, in 1754. He used it with reference to the legendary tales of the Three Princes of Serendip (Ceylon), who quite unexpectedly encountered many instances of good fortune on their travels. In today's parlance, we have usually watered down *serendipity* to mean the good luck that comes solely by accident. We think of it as a result, not an ability. We have tended to lose sight of the element of sagacity, by which term Walpole wished to emphasize that some distinctive personal receptivity is involved.

10 There remains a fourth element in good luck, an unintentional but subtle personal prompting of it. The English Prime Minister Benjamin Disraeli summed up the principle underlying Chance IV when he noted that "we make our fortunes and we call them fate." Disraeli, a politician of considerable practical experience, appreciated that we each shape our own destiny, at least to some degree. One might restate the principle as follows: *Chance favors the individualized action.*

11 In Chance IV the kind of luck is peculiar to one person, and like a personal hobby, it takes on a distinctive individual flavor. This form of chance is one-man-made, and it is as personal as a signature. . . . Chance IV has an elusive, almost miragelike, quality. Like a mirage, it is difficult to get a firm grip on, for it tends to recede as we pursue it and advance as we step back. But we still accept a mirage when we see it, because we vaguely understand the basis for the phenomenon. A strongly heated layer of air, less dense than usual, lies next to the earth, and it bends the light rays as they pass through. The resulting image may be magnified as if by a telescopic lens in the atmosphere, and real objects, ordinarily hidden far out of sight over the horizon, are brought forward and revealed to the eye. What happens in a mirage then, and in this form of chance, not only appears farfetched but indeed is farfetched.

12 About a century ago, a striking example of Chance IV took place in the Spanish cave of Altamira.[1] There, one day in 1879, Don Marcelino de Sautuola was engaged in his hobby of archaeology, searching Altamira for bones and stones. With him was his daughter, Maria, who had asked him if she could come along to the cave that day. The

[1] The cave had first been discovered some years before by an enterprising hunting dog in search of game. Curiously, in 1932 the French cave of Lascaux was discovered by still another dog.

indulgent father had said she could. Naturally enough, he first looked where he had always found heavy objects before, on the *floor* of the cave. But Maria, unhampered by any such preconceptions, looked not only at the floor but also all around the cave with the open-eyed wonder of a child! She looked up, exclaimed, and then he looked up, to see incredible works of art on the cave ceiling! The magnificent colored bison and other animals they saw at Altamira, painted more than 15,000 years ago, might lead one to call it "the Sistine Chapel of Prehistory." Passionately pursuing his interest in archaeology, de Sautuola, to his surprise, discovered man's first paintings. In quest of science, he happened upon Art.

13 Yes, a dog did "discover" the cave, and the initial receptivity was his daughter's, but the pivotal reason for the cave paintings' discovery hinged on a long sequence of prior events originating in de Sautuola himself. For when we dig into the background of this amateur excavator, we find he was an exceptional person. Few Spaniards were out probing into caves 100 years ago. The fact that he—not someone else—decided to dig that day in the cave of Altamira was the culmination of his passionate interest in his hobby. Here was a rare man whose avocation had been to educate himself from scratch, as it were, in the science of archaeology and cave exploration. This was no simple passive recognizer of blind luck when it came his way, but a man whose unique interests served as an active creative thrust—someone whose own actions and personality would focus the events that led circuitously but inexorably to the discovery of man's first paintings.

14 Then, too, there is a more subtle manner. How do you give full weight to the personal interests that imbue your child with your own curiosity, that inspire her to ask to join you in your own musty hobby, and that then lead you to agree to her request at the critical moment? For many reasons, at Altamira, more than the special receptivity of Chance III was required—this was a different domain, that of the personality and its actions.

15 A century ago no one had the remotest idea our caveman ancestors were highly creative artists. Weren't their talents rather minor and limited to crude flint chippings? But the paintings at Altamira, like a mirage, would quickly magnify this diminutive view, bring up into full focus a distant, hidden era of man's prehistory, reveal sentient minds and well-developed aesthetic sensibilities to which men of any age might aspire. And like a mirage, the events at Altamira grew out of de Sautuola's heated personal quest and out of the invisible forces of chance we know exist yet cannot touch. Accordingly, one may intro-

duce the term *altamirage* to identify the quality underlying Chance IV. Let us define it as the facility for encountering unexpected good luck as the result of highly individualized action. Altamirage goes well beyond the boundaries of serendipity in its emphasis on the role of personal action in chance.

16 Chance IV is favored by distinctive, if not eccentric, hobbies, personal life-styles, and modes of behavior peculiar to one individual, usually invested with some passion. The farther apart these personal activities are from the area under investigation, the more novel and unexpected will be the creative product of the encounter.

Understanding Meaning

1. What are the four categories of chance?
2. What is meant by "blind" or "dumb" luck? Give some examples from your own life.
3. What is the Kettering Principle? Would Edison's famous trial-and-error experiments to discover a filament for the incandescent lightbulb fit this kind of chance?
4. How does the Pasteur principle differ from the Kettering Principle?
5. How did the dog's discovery of a cave differ from "blind luck" or Chance I?
6. *Critical Thinking:* How often have you discovered things by chance? What role has chance played in your career and education? Does understanding Austin's four kinds of chance enhance your ability to be "lucky" in the future? Can you "make your own kind of luck"?

Evaluating Strategy

1. What principle does Austin use to divide chance into four categories?
2. What examples does Austin use to illustrate each type? Are they accessible by a general audience?
3. Would a chart aid in explaining the four types of chance?
4. *Other Modes:* How does Austin make use of *definition* and *narration* in developing his classification essay?

Appreciating Language

1. How much technical language does Austin include?
2. *Critical Thinking:* Is part of Austin's task in this article to invent new terms to create categories of chance? Do most of our words for chance—"luck," "fortune," "lot"—all suggest the same meaning?

Connections across the Disciplines

1. Relate this article to Carl Sagan's "Why We Need to Understand Science" (page 642) and John Allen Paulos's "Innumeracy" (page 178). Do all these articles suggest that most of us lack critical thinking skills?
2. Did any of Austin's varieties of chance play a role in Jane Goodall's discoveries about chimpanzee behavior (page 68)?

Writing Suggestions

1. List a number of instances in your life you considered lucky. Using Austin's four categories, write a paper categorizing your experiences. Have you ever gotten past Chance I?
2. *Collaborative Writing:* Discuss the role of chance with a group of students. Do many people use the idea of chance to dismiss the accomplishments of others? Do people use luck as an excuse for not trying? Talk about these issues, and then collaborate on a short paper suggesting how Austin's concept of chance should be taught to children.

JOHN HOLT

John Holt (1923–1985) was the author of several books about children and education, including How Children Fail *and* How Children Learn. *Having taught in grade and high schools for fourteen years, Holt became a critic of the American educational system. He created and edited* Growing Without Schooling, *a magazine dedicated to home schooling.*

Three Kinds of Discipline

In this section from his book Freedom and Beyond *(1972), Holt classifies three types of discipline that occur in children's lives. Most people assume discipline only comes from authority figures, such as parents and teachers. Holt reveals that discipline also comes from a child's environment.*

1 A child, in growing up, may meet and learn from three different kinds of disciplines. The first and most important is what we might call the Discipline of Nature or of Reality. When he is trying to do something real, if he does the wrong thing or doesn't do the right one, he doesn't get the result he wants. If he doesn't pile one block right on top of another, or tries to build on a slanting surface, his tower falls down. If he hits the wrong key, he hears the wrong note. If he doesn't hit the nail squarely on the head, it bends, and he has to pull it out and start with another. If he doesn't measure properly what he is trying to build, it won't open, close, fit, stand up, fly, float, whistle, or do whatever he wants it to do. If he closes his eyes when he swings, he doesn't hit the ball. A child meets this kind of discipline every time he tries to *do* something, which is why it is so important in school to give children more chances to do things, instead of just reading or listening to someone talk (or pretending to). This discipline is a good teacher. The learner never has to wait long for his answer; it usually comes quickly, often instantly. Also it is clear, and very often points toward the needed correction; from what happened he can not only see that what he did was wrong, but also why, and what he needs to do instead. Finally, and most important, the giver of the answer, call it Nature, is impersonal, impartial, and indifferent. She does not give opinions, or make judgments; she cannot be wheedled, bullied, or fooled; she does not get

angry or disappointed; she does not praise or blame; she does not remember past failures or hold grudges; with her one always gets a fresh start, this time is the one that counts.

2 The next discipline we might call the Discipline of Culture, of Society, of What People Really Do. Man is a social, a cultural animal. Children sense around them this culture, this network of agreements, customs, habits, and rules binding the adults together. They want to understand it and be a part of it. They watch very carefully what people around them are doing and want to do the same. They want to do right, unless they become convinced they can't do right. Thus children rarely misbehave seriously in church, but sit as quietly as they can. The example of all those grownups is contagious. Some mysterious ritual is going on, and children, who like rituals, want to be part of it. In the same way, the little children that I see at concerts or operas, though they may fidget a little, or perhaps take a nap now and then, rarely make any disturbance. With all those grownups sitting there, neither moving nor talking, it is the most natural thing in the world to imitate them. Children who live among adults who are habitually courteous to each other, and to them, will soon learn to be courteous. Children who live surrounded by people who speak a certain way will speak that way, however much we may try to tell them that speaking that way is bad or wrong.

3 The third discipline is the one most people mean when they speak of discipline—the Discipline of Superior Force, of sergeant to private, of "you do what I tell you or I'll make you wish you had." There is bound to be some of this in a child's life. Living as we do surrounded by things that can hurt children, or that children can hurt, we cannot avoid it. We can't afford to let a small child find out from experience the danger of playing in a busy street, or of fooling with the pots on the top of a stove, or of eating up the pills in the medicine cabinet. So, along with other precautions, we say to him, "Don't play in the street, or touch things on the stove, or go into the medicine cabinet, or I'll punish you." Between him and the danger too great for him to imagine we put a lesser danger, but one he can imagine and maybe therefore wants to avoid. He can have no idea of what it would be like to be hit by a car, but he can imagine being shouted at, or spanked, or sent to his room. He avoids these substitutes for the greater danger until he can understand it and avoid it for its own sake. But we ought to use this discipline only when it is necessary to protect the life, health, safety, or well-being of people or other living creatures, or to prevent

destruction of things that people care about. We ought not to assume too long, as we usually do, that a child cannot understand the real nature of the danger from which we want to protect him. The sooner he avoids the danger, not to escape our punishment, but as a matter of good sense, the better. He can learn that faster than we think. In Mexico, for example, where people drive their cars with a good deal of spirit, I saw many children no older than five or four walking unattended on the streets. They understood about cars, they knew what to do. A child whose life is full of the threat and fear of punishment is locked into babyhood. There is no way for him to grow up, to learn to take responsibility for his life and acts. Most important of all, we should not assume that having to yield to the threat of our superior force is good for the child's character. It is never good for *anyone's* character. To bow to superior force makes us feel impotent and cowardly for not having had the strength or courage to resist. Worse, it makes us resentful and vengeful. We can hardly wait to make someone pay for our humiliation, yield to us as we were once made to yield. No, if we cannot always avoid using the discipline of Superior Force, we should at least use it as seldom as we can.

4 There are places where all three disciplines overlap. Any very demanding human activity combines in it the disciplines of Superior Force, of Culture, and of Nature. The novice will be told, "Do it this way, never mind asking why, just do it that way, that is the way we always do it." But it probably *is* just the way they always do it, and usually for the very good reason that it is a way that has been found to work. Think, for example, of ballet training. The student in a class is told to do this exercise, or that; to stand so; to do this or that with his head, arms, shoulders, abdomen, hips, legs, feet. He is constantly corrected. There is no argument. But behind these seemingly autocratic demands by the teacher lie many decades of custom and tradition, and behind that, the necessities of dancing itself. You cannot make the moves of classical ballet unless over many years you have acquired, and renewed every day, the needed strength and suppleness in scores of muscles and joints. Nor can you do the difficult motions, making them look easy, unless you have learned hundreds of easier ones first. Dance teachers may not always agree on all the details of teaching these strengths and skills. But no novice could learn them all by himself. You could not go for a night or two to watch the ballet and then, without any other knowledge at all, teach yourself how to do it. In the same way, you would be unlikely to learn any complicated and difficult

human activity without drawing heavily on the experience of those who know it better. But the point is that the authority of these experts or teachers stems from, grows out of their greater competence and experience, the fact that what they do *works*, not the fact that they happen to be the teacher and as such have the power to kick a student out of the class. And the further point is that children are always and everywhere attracted to that competence, and ready and eager to submit themselves to a discipline that grows out of it. We hear constantly that children will never do anything unless compelled to by bribes or threats. But in their private lives, or in extracurricular activities in school, in sports, music, drama, art, running a newspaper, and so on, they often submit themselves willingly and wholeheartedly to very intense disciplines, simply because they want to learn to do a given thing well. Our Little-Napoleon football coaches, of whom we have too many and hear far too much, blind us to the fact that millions of children work hard every year getting better at sports and games without coaches barking and yelling at them.

Understanding Meaning

1. What lessons in discipline do children learn from experience?
2. How does Holt *define* discipline? Is learning about limits of experience in the physical world, such as the effect of gravity, a kind of discipline?
3. Does Holt's Discipline of Culture indicate that parents should make sure their children participate in adult activities, such as attending concerts and religious services?
4. What is Holt's opinion of parental authority and direction? When does he feel that strict discipline is justified?
5. *Critical Thinking:* What does Holt's view of discipline reveal about his attitude toward children? How much discipline can children learn on their own? Is strict discipline from parents and teachers effective? Would some people view Holt as being permissive?

Evaluating Strategy

1. How does Holt organize his classification?
2. How effective are the titles, which he capitalizes, for defining each type of discipline?
3. *Other Modes:* Where does Holt include *definition* and *narration* in his essay?

Appreciating Language

1. What connotations does the word *discipline* have?
2. How does Holt's word choice reveal his bias toward and against the different types of discipline?

Connections across the Disciplines

1. How does the structure of Holt's essay compare to that of Martin Luther King Jr.'s (page 443)? Are both writers really using classification as a means to persuade readers?
2. Review Mary Mebane's essay (page 434), and analyze the kinds of discipline she faced in childhood.

Writing Suggestions

1. Holt wrote this essay before the tide of school violence and teenage homicide dominated the media. In an era when many public schools require students to wear uniforms and parents are concerned about teenage pregnancy and gangs, would many reject Holt's views? Write an essay expressing your views.
2. *Collaborative Writing:* Working with a group of students, discuss the issue of raising and disciplining children. Consider your own childhood. If any of the members are parents, ask their honest opinion of Holt's essay. Take notes on the comments, and work together to write a *definition* of good childhood discipline.

S. I. HAYAKAWA

Samuel Ichiye Hayakawa (1906–1992) was born in Vancouver, British Columbia. He attended the University of Manitoba and McGill University before earning a doctorate at the University of Wisconsin in 1935. A noted linguist and educator, he published a pioneering book on semantics, Language in Action, *in 1941 that became a best-seller. His later books include* Language, Meaning and Maturity *and* Our Language and Our World. *In 1968 he received national attention as the law-and-order president of San Francisco State College during a five-month student strike. Hayakawa, who led the movement to make English the official language of the United States, served in the U.S. Senate from 1977 to 1983.*

Reports, Inferences, Judgments

In this essay from Language in Thought and Action *(1964), Hayakawa dissects the way we speak and separates statements into three distinct groups: reports, which are precise and readily proven; inferences, which are assumptions based on reports; and judgments, which express approval or disapproval for a subject. Reading Hayakawa's essay can help make you a critical reader as you evaluate when writers are expressing themselves through reports, inferences, and judgments. Note where Hayakawa uses definition, narration, description, and persuasion.*

1 For the purposes of interchange of information, the basic symbolic act is the *report* of what we have seen, heard, or felt: "There is a ditch on each side of the road." "You can get those at Smith's hardware store for $2.75." "There aren't any fish on that side of the lake, but there are on this side." Then there are reports of reports: "The longest waterfall in the world is Victoria Falls in Rhodesia." "The Battle of Hastings took place in 1066." "The papers say that there was a smash-up on Highway 41 near Evansville." Reports adhere to the following rules: First, they are *capable of verification;* second, they *exclude,* as far as possible, *inferences* and *judgments.* (These terms will be defined later.)

2 Reports are verifiable. We may not always be able to verify them ourselves, since we cannot track down the evidence for every piece of history we know, nor can we all go to Evansville to see the remains of the smash-up before they are cleared away. But if we are roughly agreed on the names of things, on what constitutes a "foot," "yard,"

"bushel," and so on, and on how to measure time, there is relatively little danger of our misunderstanding each other. Even in a world such as we have today, in which everybody seems to be quarreling with everybody else, *we still to a surprising degree trust each other's reports.* We ask directions of total strangers when we are traveling. We follow directions on road signs without being suspicious of the people who put them up. We read books of information about science, mathematics, automotive engineering, travel, geography, the history of costume, and other such factual matters, and we usually assume that the author is doing his best to tell us as truly as he can what he knows. And we are safe in so assuming most of the time. With the interest given today to the discussion of biased newspapers, propagandists, and the general untrustworthiness of many of the communications we receive, we are likely to forget that we still have an enormous amount of reliable information available and that deliberate misinformation, except in warfare, is still more the exception than the rule. The desire for self-preservation that compelled men to evolve means for the exchange of information also compels them to regard the giving of false information as profoundly reprehensible.

3 At its highest development, the language of reports is the language of science. By "highest development" we mean greatest general usefulness. Presbyterian and Catholic, workingman and capitalist, East German and West German, *agree* on the meanings of such symbols as $2 \times 2 = 4$, *100°C*, HNO_3, *3:35* A.M., A.D. 1940, *1000 kilowatts*, *Quercus agrifolia*, and so on. But how, it may be asked, can there be agreement about even this much among people who disagree about political philosophies, ethical ideas, religious beliefs, and the survival of my business *versus* the survival of yours? The answer is that circumstances *compel men to agree*, whether they wish to or not. If, for example, there were a dozen different religious sects in the United States, each insisting on its own way of naming the time of the day and the days of the year, the mere necessity of having a dozen different calendars, a dozen different kinds of watches, and a dozen sets of schedules for business hours, trains, and television programs to say nothing of the effort that would be required for translating terms from one nomenclature to another, would make life as we know it impossible.[1]

[1] According to information supplied by the Association of American Railroads, "Before 1883 there were nearly 100 different time zones in the United States. It wasn't until November 18 of that year that . . . a system of standard time was adopted here and in Canada. Before then there

4 The language of reports, then, including the more accurate reports of science, is "map" language, and because it gives us reasonably accurate representations of the "territory," it enables us to get work done. Such language may often be dull or uninteresting reading: One does not usually read logarithmic tables or telephone directories for entertainment. But we could not get along without it. There are numberless occasions in the talking and writing we do in everyday life that *require that we state things in such a way that everybody will be able to understand and agree with our formulation.*

INFERENCES

5 The reader will find that practice in writing reports is a quick means of increasing his linguistic awareness. It is an exercise which will constantly provide him with his own examples of the principles of language and interpretation under discussion. The reports should be about first-hand experience—scenes the reader has witnessed himself, meetings and social events he has taken part in, people he knows well. They should be of such a nature that they can be verified and agreed upon. For the purpose of this exercise, inferences will be excluded.

6 Not that inferences are not important—we rely in everyday life and in science as much on *inferences* as on reports—in some areas of thought, for example, geology, paleontology, and nuclear physics, reports are the foundations, but inferences (and inferences upon inferences) are the main body of the science. An inference, as we shall use the term, is *a statement about the unknown made on the basis of the known.* We may *infer* from the material and cut of a woman's clothes her wealth

was nothing but local or 'solar' time. . . . The Pennsylvania Railroad in the East used Philadelphia time, which was five minutes slower than New York time and five minutes faster than Baltimore time. The Baltimore & Ohio used Baltimore time for trains running out of Baltimore, Columbus time for Ohio, Vincennes (Indiana) time for those going out of Cincinnati. . . . When it was noon in Chicago, it was 12:31 in Pittsburgh; 12:24 in Cleveland; 12:17 in Toledo; 12:13 in Cincinnati; 12:09 in Louisville; 12:07 in Indianapolis; 11:50 in St. Louis; 11:48 in Dubuque; 11:39 in St. Paul, and 11:27 in Omaha. There were 27 local time zones in Michigan alone. . . . A person traveling from Eastport, Maine, to San Francisco, if he wanted always to have the right railroad time and get off at the right place, had to twist the hands of his watch 20 times en route." Chicago *Daily News* (September 29, 1948).

or social position; we may *infer* from the character of the ruins the origin of the fire that destroyed the building; we may *infer* from a man's calloused hands the nature of his occupation; we may *infer* from a senator's vote on an armaments bill his attitude toward Russia; we may *infer* from the structure of the land the path of a prehistoric glacier; we may *infer* from a halo on an unexposed photographic plate that it has been in the vicinity of radioactive materials; we may *infer* from the sound of an engine the condition of its connecting rods. Inferences may be carelessly or carefully made. They may be made on the basis of a broad background of previous experience with the subject matter, or no experience at all. For example, the inferences a good mechanic can make about the internal condition of a motor by listening to it are often startlingly accurate, while the inferences made by an amateur (if he tries to make any) may be entirely wrong. But the common characteristic of inferences is that they are statements about matters which are not directly known, statements made on the basis of what has been observed.

7 The avoidance of inferences in our suggested practice in report-writing requires that we make no guesses as to what is going on in other people's minds. When we say, "He was angry," we are not reporting; we are making an inference from such observable facts as the following: "He pounded his fist on the table; he swore; he threw the telephone directory at his stenographer." In this particular example, the inference appears to be fairly safe; nevertheless, it is important to remember, especially for the purposes of training oneself, that it is an inference. Such expressions as "He thought a lot of himself," "He was scared of girls," "He has an inferiority complex," made on the basis of casual social observation, and "What Russia really wants to do is to establish a world communist dictatorship," made on the basis of casual newspaper reading, are highly inferential. We should keep in mind their inferential character and, in our suggested exercises, should substitute for them such statements as "He rarely spoke to subordinates in the plant," "I saw him at a party, and he never danced except when one of the girls asked him to," "He wouldn't apply for the scholarship although I believe he could have won it easily," and "The Russian delegation to the United Nations has asked for *A*, *B*, and *C*. Last year they voted against *M* and *N*, and voted for *X* and *Y*. On the basis of facts such as these, the newspaper I read makes the inference that what Russia really wants is to establish a world communist dictatorship. I agree."

8 In spite of the exercise of every caution in avoiding inferences and reporting only what is seen and experienced, we all remain prone to error, since the making of inferences is a quick, almost automatic process. We may watch a car weaving as it goes down the road and say, "Look at that *drunken driver*," although what we *see* is only *the irregular motion of the car*. The writer once saw a man leave a one-dollar tip at a lunch counter and hurry out. Just as the writer was wondering why anyone should leave so generous a tip in so modest an establishment, the waitress came, picked up the dollar, put it in the cash register as she punched up ninety cents, and put a dime in her pocket. In other words, the writer's description to himself of the event, "a one-dollar tip," turned out to be not a report but an inference.

9 All this is not to say that we should never make inferences. The inability to make inferences is itself a sign of mental disorder. For example, the speech therapist Laura L. Lee writes, "The aphasic [brain-damaged] adult with whom I worked had great difficulty in making inferences about a picture I showed her. She could tell me what was happening at the moment in the picture, but could not tell me what might have happened just before the picture or just afterward."[2] Hence the question is not whether or not we make inferences; the question is whether or not we are aware of the inferences we make.

JUDGMENTS

10 In our suggested writing exercise, judgments are also to be excluded. By judgments, we shall mean *all expressions of the writer's approval or disapproval of the occurrences, persons, or objects he is describing*. For example, a report cannot say, "It was a wonderful car," but must say something like this: "It has been driven 50,000 miles and has never required any repairs." Again statements such as "Jack lied to us" must be suppressed in favor of the more verifiable statement, "Jack told us he didn't have the keys to his car with him. However, when he pulled a handkerchief out of his pocket a few minutes later, a bunch of car keys fell out." Also a report may not say, "The senator was stubborn, defiant, and uncooperative," or "The senator courageously stood by his

[2] "Brain Damage and the Process of Abstracting: A Problem in Language Learning," *ETC.: A Review of General Semantics*, XVI (1959), 154–62.

principles"; it must say instead, "The senator's vote was the only one against the bill."

11 Many people regard statements such as the following as statements of "fact": "Jack *lied* to us," "Jerry is a *thief*," "Tommy is *clever*." As ordinarily employed, however, the word "lied" involves first an inference (that Jack knew otherwise and deliberately misstated the facts) and second a judgment (that the speaker disapproves of what he has inferred that Jack did). In the other two instances, we may substitute such expressions as, "Jerry was convicted of theft and served two years at Waupun," and "Tommy plays the violin, leads his class in school, and is captain of the debating team." After all, to say of a man that he is a "thief" is to say in effect, "He has stolen *and will steal again*"—which is more of a prediction than a report. Even to say, "He has stolen," is to make an inference (and simultaneously to pass a judgment) on an act about which there may be difference of opinion among those who have examined the evidence upon which the conviction was obtained. But to say that he was "convicted of theft" is to make a statement capable of being agreed upon through verification in court and prison records.

12 Scientific verifiability rests upon the external observation of facts, not upon the heaping up of judgments. If one person says, "Peter is a deadbeat," and another says, "I think so too," the statement has not been verified. In court cases, considerable trouble is sometimes caused by witnesses who cannot distinguish their judgments from the facts upon which those judgments are based. Cross-examinations under these circumstances go something like this:

13 **Witness:** That dirty double-crosser Jacobs ratted on me.

Defense attorney: Your honor, I object.

Judge: Objection sustained. (Witness's remark is stricken from the record.) Now, try to tell the court exactly what happened.

Witness: He double-crossed me, the dirty, lying rat!

Defense attorney: Your honor, I object!

Judge: Objection sustained. (Witness's remark is again stricken from the record.) Will the witness try to stick to the facts.

Witness: But I'm telling you the facts, your honor. He did double-cross me.

14 This can continue indefinitely unless the cross-examiner exercises some ingenuity in order to get at the facts behind the judgment. To the witness it is a "fact" that he was "double-crossed." Often patient questioning is required before the factual bases of the judgment are revealed.

15 Many words, of course, simultaneously convey a report and a judgment on the fact reported, as will be discussed more fully in a later chapter. For the purposes of a report as here defined, these should be avoided. Instead of "sneaked in," one might say "entered quietly"; instead of "politicians," "congressmen" or "aldermen" or "candidates for office"; instead of "bureaucrat," "public official"; instead of "tramp," "homeless unemployed"; instead of "dictatorial set-up," "centralized authority"; instead of "crackpots," "holders of nonconformist views." A newspaper reporter, for example, is not permitted to write, "A crowd of suckers came to listen to Senator Smith last evening in that rickety firetrap and ex-dive that disfigures the south edge of town." Instead he says, "Between seventy-five and a hundred people heard an address last evening by Senator Smith at the Evergreen Gardens near the South Side city limits."

Understanding Meaning

1. *Define* what Hayakawa means by "report," "inference," and "judgment."
2. Why is it important to distinguish between a report and an inference?
3. How often do we make decisions based on inferences rather than reports?
4. Why does Hayakawa value reports over statements that are inferences or judgments?
5. *Critical Thinking:* Hayakawa clearly values precision in writing. But can any writer be free of bias? Are writers bound to be influenced by their culture, personal experience, and education?

Evaluating Strategy

1. How important are examples in developing this essay?
2. What standard does the essay use to evaluate statements?
3. *Other Modes:* Why is *definition* important in this essay? Why are sections put in italics? Where does Hayakawa use *narration*, *description*, and *persuasion?*

Appreciating Language

1. What does the tone, style, and vocabulary suggest about Hayakawa's intended audience?
2. How does Hayakawa make use of connotations to demonstrate judgments?

Connections across the Disciplines

1. Read one of the shorter articles from the "Argument and Persuasion" chapter, and label where the author presents reports, inferences, and judgments. Does being aware of these three kinds of statements aid you in evaluating the merit of someone's argument?
2. How does Hayakawa's discussion of language relate to Meg Greenfield's observations about the word "wrong" (page 448)?

Writing Suggestions

1. Write a brief narrative about a recent occurrence in as many "report" statements as possible. How difficult is it to attempt total objectivity? Do inferences and judgments naturally creep into your writing?
2. *Collaborative Writing:* Working with a group of students, read over Suneel Rataan's "Why Busters Hate Boomers" or Mary Mebane's "Black Wasn't Beautiful." Have members of the group spot examples of inference and judgments. Have each member of the group rewrite a section of the essay, attempting a totally objective approach. Have each member read his or her work to the group. Identify where students inadvertently make inferences and judgments.

WRITING BEYOND THE CLASSROOM

BLACK'S LAW DICTIONARY

Black's Law Dictionary *is a standard reference used by attorneys, paralegals, administrators, and law enforcement personnel. Like any dictionary, it serves to define terms.*

Homicide

When reading this entry, which includes a classification, pay attention to the specialized use of language. Note that the authors stress that the word "homicide" is neutral and does not even imply that a crime has been committed. Notice how television and movies have distorted the complexities of this legal issue.

1 **Homicide.** The killing of one human being by the act, procurement, or omission of another. A person is guilty of criminal homicide if he purposely, knowingly, recklessly or negligently causes the death of another human being. Criminal homicide is murder, manslaughter or negligent homicide. Model Penal Code, §210.1; 18 U.S.C.A. §1111 et seq. *See* Manslaughter; Murder.

2 Homicide is not necessarily a crime. It is a necessary ingredient of the crimes of murder and manslaughter, but there are other cases in which homicide may be committed without criminal intent and without criminal consequences, as, where it is done in the lawful execution of a judicial sentence, in self-defense, or as the only possible means of arresting an escaping felon. The term "homicide" is neutral; while it describes the act, it pronounces no judgment on its moral or legal quality. People v. Mahon, 77 Ill.App.3d 413, 395 N.E.2d 950, 958. *See Excusable homicide; Justifiable homicide, below.*

CLASSIFICATION

3 Homicide is ordinarily classified as "justifiable," "excusable," and "felonious." For the definitions of these terms, and of some other compound terms, see *below.*

4 *Culpable homicide.* Described as a crime varying from the very lowest culpability, up to the very verge of murder.

5 *Excusable homicide.* The killing of a human being, either by misadventure or in self-defense. Such homicide consists of a perpetrator's acting in a manner which the law does not prohibit, such as self-defense or accidental homicide. Law v. State, 21 Md.App. 13, 318 A.2d 859, 869. The name itself imports some fault, error, or omission, so trivial, however, that the law excuses it from guilt of felony, though in strictness it judges it deserving of some little degree of punishment. It is of two sorts,—either *per infortunium,* by misadventure, or *se defendendo,* upon a sudden affray. Homicide *per infortunium* is where a man, doing a lawful act, without any intention of hurt, unfortunately kills another; but, if death ensues from any unlawful act, the offense is manslaughter, and not misadventure. Homicide *se defendendo* is where a man kills another upon a sudden affray, merely in his own defense, or in defense of his wife, child, parent, or servant, and not from any vindictive feeling. *See* Self-defense; also *Justifiable homicide, below.*

6 *Felonious homicide.* The wrongful killing of a human being, of any age or either sex, without justification or excuse in law; of which offense there are two degrees, manslaughter and murder.

7 *Homicide by misadventure.* The accidental killing of another, where the slayer is doing a lawful act, unaccompanied by any criminally careless or reckless conduct. The same as "homicide *per infortunium.*" *See* Manslaughter.

8 *Homicide by necessity.* A species of justifiable homicide, because it arises from some unavoidable necessity, without any will, intention, or desire, and without any inadvertence or negligence in the party killing, and therefore without any shadow of blame. *See* Self-defense.

9 *Homicide per infortunium.* Homicide by misfortune, or accidental homicide; as where a man doing a lawful act without any intention of hurt, accidentally kills another; a species of excusable homicide. *See* Negligent homicide.

10 *Homicide se defendendo.* Homicide in self-defense; the killing of a person in self-defense upon a sudden affray, where the slayer had no other possible (or, at least, probable) means of escaping from his assailant. A species of excusable homicide. *See* Self-defense.

11 *Justifiable homicide.* Such as is committed intentionally, but without any evil design, and under such circumstances of necessity or duty as render the act proper, and relieve the party from any shadow of blame; as where a

12 sheriff lawfully executes a sentence of death upon a malefactor, or where the killing takes place in the endeavor to prevent the commission of felony which could not be otherwise avoided, or, as a matter of right, such as self-defense or other causes provided for by statute. *See* Self-defense; also *Excusable homicide, above.*

13 *Negligent homicide.* Criminal homicide constitutes negligent homicide when it is committed negligently. Model Penal Code, §210.4. *See* Negligent homicide; also *Vehicular homicide, below.*

14 *Reckless homicide.* See that title.

15 *Vehicular homicide.* The killing of a human being by the operation of an automobile, airplane, motorboat or other motor vehicle in a manner which creates an unreasonable risk of injury to the person or property of another and which constitutes a material deviation from the standard of care which a reasonable person would observe under the same circumstances.

Understanding Meaning

1. Does it surprise you to learn that homicide may not be a crime? Do most people equate that term with "murder"?
2. What does the law regard as the most serious, most criminal forms of homicide?
3. Provide your own examples of felonious homicide, homicide by misadventure, and homicide by necessity.
4. *Critical Thinking:* What values seem to play a role in determining what is excusable and what is criminal homicide?

Evaluating Strategy

1. How well organized is this entry? Is it easy to follow?
2. How important are the examples used to support the definitions?

Appreciating Language

1. What does the tone, style, and word choice reveal about the intended audience?
2. How might you reword this entry for a general audience?

Connections across the Disciplines

1. How does the writing style of this entry compare to Kimberly Crawford's article written for the *FBI Law Enforcement Journal* (page 441)?
2. How does the style differ from the chart developed for *Communication Styles: Taiwan* (page 307)?

Writing Suggestions

1. Select one of the types of homicide listed in the entry, and provide a fictional example in a brief narrative.
2. *Collaborative Writing:* Discuss the types of homicide listed in the entry with fellow students, and ask members to provide their own version of justifiable homicide. Work together to create a definition.

RINEHART GUIDE TO GRAMMAR AND USAGE

Textbooks and reference works often use division and classification to explain concepts, processes, objects, or conditions.

Kinds of Sentences

This section from a grammar handbook explains four types of sentences by classifying them according to number of and type of clauses. Independent clauses contain a subject and verb and make a complete statement: I drive to school. *Dependent clauses contain a subject and verb but do not make a complete statement and are not a sentence:* Because I drive to school.

7E KINDS OF SENTENCES

1 Independent clauses appear alone or in combinations—with other independent clauses or with dependent clauses. One method of classifying sentences is based on the number and kinds of clauses in a single construction. According to this classification system, there are four categories of sentences: simple, compound, complex, and compound-complex.

(1) Simple sentence

2 A **simple sentence** is made up of only one independent clause. The sentence may contain modifiers and compound elements (for example, compound subjects and verbs); but it may not contain more than one subject-predicate structure.

3 Cigarette smoke contains carbon monoxide.

4 For most college students, computers and calculators have become essential.

5 The Rhone flows south through France and then empties into the Mediterranean.

(2) Compound sentence

6 A **compound sentence** is made up of two or more independent clauses. The primary ways to coordinate independent clauses are with commas and coordinating conjunctions *(and, but, or, for, nor, so, yet)* and with semicolons.

7 For centuries, Brittany was an independent state, but now the area is part of France.

8 The restaurant was dark, the air was filled with smoke, and the music was deafening.

9 Socrates wrote nothing; his thoughts are known only through the works of Plato and Xenophon.

(3) Complex sentence

10 A **complex sentence** is made up of one independent clause and one or more dependent clauses—adverb, adjective, or noun.

11 Although most rifle experts have 20/20 vision, pistol experts are often very nearsighted.

12 The game involves three contestants who spin a roulette wheel.

13 Whoever could solve the riddle of the Sphinx would be spared her wrath.

(4) Compound-complex sentence

14 A **compound-complex sentence** is made up of two or more independent clauses and one or more dependent clauses.

15 London's Great Exhibition, which opened in 1851, was designed to show human progress; it brought together in the "Crystal Palace" industrial displays remarkable for their day.

16 Alchemists believed that they could change lesser metals into gold, and although they failed, they helped establish the science of chemistry.

17 The fathom once was the distance that a Viking could encompass in a hug; a gauge was the distance that lay between the wheels of a Roman chariot; an acre was an area that could be plowed in one day by a team of two oxen.

Understanding Meaning

1. Provide an example of each sentence type.
2. How does understanding the four types of sentences help with writing?

Evaluating Strategy

1. How effective is the method of organizing this information?
2. Do the visual effects such as bold print, underscores, numerals, and italics assist readers?
3. *Other Modes:* How are the different sentence types *defined?*

Appreciating Language

1. What does the level of language assume about the readers, who are mostly college students?
2. Are these terms initially misleading? Does "simple" suggest a short or easily read sentence? Would the term "complex sentence" lead you to expect a long, complicated statement?

Connections across the Disciplines

1. Compare this entry to that from *Black's Law Dictionary* (page 472). How important are visual effects in reference books?
2. Compare this explanation with one available in your own grammar book. What are the differences? Is one easier to read than the other?

Writing Suggestions

1. Rewrite this entry for a junior high school audience.
2. Analyze your own use of sentences by reviewing one of your previous papers. How often do you use each type?

GUIDELINES FOR DIVISION AND CLASSIFICATION WRITING

1. **Determine which mode you will use.** Which method will best suit your purpose: dividing your subject into subtopics or measuring subtopics against a common standard?
2. **Select an effective method of division.** If you were writing about improving the public schools, for example, it might be more effective to divide the paper by discipline, discussing how to improve math skills, writing ability, and knowledge of geography rather than improving elementary schools, junior high schools, and high schools.
3. **Avoid divisions that oversimplify or distort meaning.** Your paper should aid in helping readers grasp a complex subject without trivializing or misstating the issues. You may wish to qualify your division and explain to readers that exceptions and situations may exist where the division may not apply.
4. **Avoid overlapping categories.** When writing both division and classification make sure the categories are distinct. Do not separate cars into "domestic, foreign, and antique models" because antique cars would clearly have to belong to the first two groups.
5. **Use a single, clearly defined standard to classify subjects.** Classification relies on a clearly stated standard that is used to measure all the items you discuss. Avoid mixing standards. In some instances you may have to explain or justify why you are using a particular standard.
6. **In classification writing, make sure all topics fit into *one* category.** In a properly written classification paper, every unit should fit only one category. For example, a term paper is either an A− or a B+. In addition, make sure no items are left over that cannot be logically placed.

SUGGESTED TOPICS FOR DIVISION AND CLASSIFICATION WRITING

General Assignments

Write a division essay on any of the following topics. Your division may make use of standard categories or ones you invent. Remember to clearly state the way you are dividing your subject. Each subject or example should be supported with definitions, brief narratives, or descriptions.

- Dates you have had
- Student housing on campus and off
- Baseball, basketball, or football teams
- Popular music
- Careers for women

Write a classification essay on any of the following topics. Make sure to use a single method of rating the subtopics, from best to worst, easiest to hardest, or least desirable to most desirable, for example.

- Jobs you have had
- Student services, including health, police, food, etc.
- Vacation destinations
- Bosses or professors you have known
- Talk shows or news programs

Writing in Context

1. Assume you have been asked by a national magazine to write about students' political attitudes. You may develop your essay by division or classification. You can discuss politics in general terms of liberal and conservative or restrict your comments on students' attitudes toward a particular issue, such as abortion, capital punishment, or health care.
2. Write a humorous paper about campus fashion by dividing students into types. Invent titles or labels for each group, and supply enough details so readers can readily fit the people they meet into one of your categories.

DIVISION AND CLASSIFICATION CHECKLIST

1. Are your categories clearly defined?
2. Do you avoid overlapping categories?
3. Do you classify all items with a single standard?
4. Does your standard truly measure what you want to measure?
5. Do your categories oversimplify a complex issue?
6. Do all the items in your paper clearly fit into a single category? Are any items left over?

8

PROCESS

EXPLAINING HOW THINGS WORK AND GIVING DIRECTIONS

WHAT IS PROCESS?

Process writing shows how things work or how specific tasks are accomplished. The first type of process writing is used to demonstrate how a complex procedure takes place. Biology textbooks describe how the heart operates by separating its actions into a series of steps. This chain-of-events explanation also can illustrate how an engine works, how inflation affects the economy, how the IRS audits an account, or how police respond to a 911 call. Process writing is a directed form of narration that explains how a procedure or event occurs.

The second type of process writing instructs readers how to complete a specific task. Recipes, owners' manuals, textbooks, and home repair articles provide readers with step-by-step directions to bake a cake, rotate tires, set up a stereo system, write a research paper, lose weight, or fix a leaking roof. These instructions are challenging to create because writers may be unable to determine how much background information to provide and may easily forget a critical piece of information.

Explaining How Things Work

Just as division writing seeks to explain an abstract or complex subject by separating it into smaller categories, process writing separates the workings of complicated operations into distinct steps. In her essay "Why Leaves Turn Color in the Fall" (page 490), Diane Ackerman explains the chain of events that causes leaves to change color in autumn:

> A turning leaf stays partly green at first, then reveals splotches of yellow and red as the chlorophyll gradually breaks down. Dark green seems to stay longest in the veins, outlining and defining them. During the summer, chlorophyll dissolves in the heat and light, but it is also being steadily replaced. In the fall, on the other hand, no new pigment is produced, and so we notice the other colors that were always there, right in the leaf, although chlorophyll's shocking green hid them from view. With their camouflage gone, we see these colors for the first time all year, and marvel, but they were always there, hidden like a vivid secret beneath the hot glowing greens of summer.

In writing explanations such as this, it is important to consider the knowledge base of your readers. You may have to define technical terms; make use of illustrative analogies, such as comparing the heart to a pump; and tell brief narratives so readers will understand the process. Some writers will use an extended analogy, comparing a nuclear power plant to a tea kettle or a computer virus to a brush fire. One of the challenges of explanatory writing can be deciding which details to leave out and where to make separations.

Critical Thinking for Writing Explanations

1. **Study the process carefully.** Note principal features that need emphasis. Identify areas that are commonly confused or might be difficult for readers to understand.
2. **Determine how much background information is needed.** Your readers may require, for example, a basic knowledge of how normal cells divide before being able to comprehend the way cancer cells develop. In some instances, you may have to address common misconceptions. If you were to explain criminal investigation methods, you first might have to point out how actual police operations differ from those depicted on television.
3. **Determine the beginning and end of the process.** In some cases the process may have an obvious beginning and end. Leaves emerge from buds, flower, grow, turn color, and fall off. But the process of a recession may have no clear-cut beginning and no defined end. If you were to write a paper about the process of getting a divorce, would you stop when the

final papers are signed or continue to discuss alimony and child visitation rights? When does a divorce end?

4. **Separate the process into logical stages.** Readers will naturally assume all the stages are equally significant unless you indicate their value or importance. Minor points should not be overemphasized by being isolated in separate steps.
5. **Alert readers to possible variations.** If the process is subject to change or alternative forms, present readers with the most common type. Indicate, either in the introduction or in each stage, that exceptions or variations to the pattern of events exist.
6. **Use transitional phrases to link the stages.** Statements such as *at the same time*, *two hours later*, and *if additional bleeding occurs* help readers follow explanations.
7. **Stress the importance of time relationships.** Process writing creates a slow-motion effect that can be misleading if the chain of events naturally occurs within a short period. You can avoid this confusion by opening with a "real time" description of the process:

 > The test car collided with the barrier at thirty-five miles an hour. In less than a tenth of a second the bumper crumpled, sending shock waves through the length of the vehicle as the fenders folded back like a crushed beer can. At the same instant sensors triggered the air bag to deploy with a rapid explosion so that it inflated before the test dummy struck the steering wheel.

 The rest of the paper might repeat this process for four or five pages, slowly relating each stage in great detail.
8. **Use images, details, narratives, and examples to enrich the description of each stage.** Give readers a full appreciation of each stage by describing it in details they can grasp. Avoid long strings of nonessential, technical language. Use comparisons and narratives to provide readers with clear pictures of events and situations.
9. **Review the final draft for undefined technical terms.** Use a level of language your readers understand. Include technical terms only when necessary, and define ones your readers may not know or may find confusing.

Giving Directions

Directions are step-by-step instructions guiding readers to accomplish a specific goal or task. Process writing can include advice such as how to buy a house or negotiate a loan. In "Desperation Writing" (page 500), Peter Elbow offers students this initial advice about writing under stress:

> Just write and keep writing. . . . Just write and keep writing. It will probably come in waves. After a flurry, stop and take a brief rest. But don't stop too long. Don't think about what you are writing or what you have written or else you will overload the circuit again. Keep writing as though you are drugged or drunk. Keep doing this till you feel you have a lot of material that might be useful; or, if necessary, till you can't stand it any more—even if you doubt that there's anything useful there.

Some writers find it more effective to tell people what *not* to do. Negative instructions work best when you are trying to get readers to change their habits or to avoid common mistakes. Fran Martin (page 505), a nurse with extensive experience in medical malpractice trials, offers tips on avoiding four common errors made in charting:

> 1. **Not charting the correct time when events occurred.** Suppose a procedure is charted in several different places, but each entry indicates that it was done at a different time. Lawyers use these times to reconstruct the sequence of events, and inconsistencies like this can make their case—they can easily raise questions about the accuracy of the entire record.

Martin employs numbered steps and italicized topic sentences to highlight major points. She also dramatizes the importance of her advice by citing a case in which a nurse's documentation errors cost a hospital $450,000.

When giving instructions, you may find it helpful to add visual aids such as bold type, capital letters, and underlining, as well as pictures, graphs, and charts. Visual aids are commonly used in documents that must be read quickly or referred to while working. A recipe printed in standard paragraphs instead of lists and numbered steps would be extremely difficult to follow while one is cooking. The description of the Heimlich maneuver on page 536, taken from the *American Red Cross First Aid and Safety Handbook*, illustrates how directions can be arranged for quick, accurate reading.

Critical Thinking for Writing Directions

1. **Consider your readers carefully.** Determine your readers' current knowledge. They may need background information to understand the process. Readers may also have misconceptions that must be cleared up.
2. **Make sure the directions are self-contained.** A recipe, for example, should list *all* the ingredients, appliances, and instructions needed. *Readers should not be directed to another source for information to complete the process.*

3. **Consider using numbered steps.** Readers find it easier to follow numbered steps and can mark their places if interrupted.
4. **Provide complete instructions.** Do not tell readers to "put the cake in the oven for thirty minutes or until done." Someone baking the cake for the first time has no idea what the cake is supposed to look like at that point—should it be evenly browned, or can the center remain soft? When is it "done"?
5. **Warn readers of possible events they may misinterpret as mistakes.** If, at some point in the process, the mixture readers are working with suddenly changes color or a machine they are operating makes excess noise, they may assume they have made a mistake and stop. If a person assembling a desk discovers the legs are wobbly, he or she may assume the product is defective. If this is normal, if the legs tighten up when the drawers are installed, let readers know what to expect.
6. **Give negative instructions.** Tell readers what not to do, especially if you know people have a tendency to misuse materials, skip difficult steps, or substitute cheaper materials.
7. **Warn readers of any hazards to their safety, health, property, or the environment.** Warnings about dangerous chemicals, fire hazards, and electrical shocks should be clearly stated and placed in large print. *In giving instructions to customers and employees, you are assuming a legal liability.*

READING PROCESS

As you read the process entries in this chapter, keep these questions in mind.

Meaning

1. What is the writer's goal, to explain or instruct?
2. Is the goal clearly stated?
3. What are the critical steps in the process?
4. What errors should readers avoid?

Strategy

1. What is the nature of the intended audience?
2. How much existing knowledge does the writer assume readers have? Are terms explained?
3. What is the beginning and ending point of the process? Are these clearly defined?

4. How are steps or stages separated? Are the transitions clear?
5. Does the writer use paragraph breaks, numbers, bold type, and other visual prompts? Are these skillfully used?
6. Are instructions easy to follow?
7. Does the writer demonstrate the significance of the process or the value of his or her advice?

Language

1. Are technical terms clearly defined and illustrated?
2. Does the writer use language that creates clear images of what is being explained?

HELEN MUNDELL

Helen Mundell is a contributing writer to American Demographics, *a magazine that follows business trends, population shifts, and economic indicators to help marketers and others plan for the future. By studying changing patterns, corporations can determine future needs for products and services. This brief review explains how a small group of nameless people determines the color of everything from clothes to automobiles.*

How the Color Mafia Chooses Your Clothes

As you read this article from American Demographics *(1993), pay attention to Mundell's word choice and sentence structure. This article was written to entertain as well as inform.*

1 Why did American kitchens spend the 1970s draped in avocado and harvest gold? "The Color Mafia," explains Leatrice Eiseman, a member of the Color Mafia (also called the Color Marketing Group). In September 1993, the 1,300-member group met to set the palette for 1996.

2 "It's not ten people sitting in an ivory tower decreeing what will be," says Eiseman. Members reach a consensus on colors based on socioeconomic and other trends, she says. The result limits consumer choices, but consumers may benefit from the limits. When manufacturers coordinate their efforts, towels and accessories automatically match wallpaper, paint, and flooring.

3 Now the Color Marketing Group has more than intuition to guide its choices. Last year, the Pantone Color Institute of Carlstadt, New Jersey, asked 5,000 adults about their color preferences. Respondents indicated what colors of clothing, home products, and automobiles they own, and what colors they are likely to choose the next time they buy those products. The results: blue, red, and black are the favorite colors for clothing, with red-violets and blue-greens likely to gain in popularity. Beige is the favorite for big-ticket home products like carpets, upholstered furniture, and paint, with blue gaining in popularity.

4 Economic insecurity may motivate people to choose safe, neutral colors like beige for big-ticket items because they aren't sure when they might be able to replace them, says Eiseman. But beige victims might choose accent pieces in bright colors. For automobiles, blue, gray, red, white, and black are the most popular colors, with blue-green gaining fast.

5 Age affects color preferences. Older adults lean toward beiges, browns, and white, while young adults surveyed for Pantone prefer black. The affluent prefer subtle grays for clothing and automobiles, but choose beige for home furnishings.

6 The survey found no strong regional color preferences. The reason is the mass media, says Eiseman. Fashion magazines and catalogs, home shopping shows, and big clothing chains all present the same options. Eiseman even sees the same clothing and colors in North Carolina and Taiwan.

7 Not all manufacturers follow the Color Mafia's rules. Victoria McKenzie-Childs owns a pottery studio in upstate New York. When the studio began more than a decade ago, its trademark was pastel colors while others were using earth tones. More recently, the studio has added deeper, richer colors while keeping its trademark pastels. McKenzie-Childs says she tries to stay unaware of trends in the marketplace and to follow her own tendencies.

8 Conservative businesses shy away from the Color Mafia, too. Talbots, an upscale women's clothing chain based in Hingham, Massachusetts, ignores color trends. For decades, the catalog has stuck to navy, red, white, charcoal, and hunter green. The clothier does add some new colors and designs each season, but "we're careful about going out on a limb," says vice president Kathy Staab.

Understanding Meaning

1. How does the Color Marketing Group operate?
2. Who actually chooses the colors?
3. Why would manufacturers of everything from towels and blouses to wallpaper and flooring be interested in this group's results?
4. *Critical Thinking:* What does this brief article reveal about consumer research? What does it suggest about the influence of color in our lives?

Evaluating Strategy

1. What impact does the title have? Would it be appropriate for a scholarly journal?
2. What role do direct quotes have in the review?

Appreciating Language

1. What do the tone, style, and word choice suggest about the readers of *American Demographics?* What do they expect?
2. How do you respond to Mundell's use of the word "Mafia"? Is it appropriate?

Connections across the Disciplines

1. Compare this process essay with Diane Ackerman's (page 490). What does this reveal about their goals and intended audiences?
2. How does Mundell's information about attitudes toward color explain some of the racial views held by people described by Mary Mebane in "Black Wasn't Beautiful" (page 434)?

Writing Suggestions

1. Write a brief analysis of your favorite color. What do you think it says about your personality?
2. *Collaborative Writing:* Experiment with the process Mundell describes. Have members of your group rate a variety of colors for a product or article of clothing. Take notes and then work together to draft a paper describing your group's actions in terms of a process. Briefly analyze your group's recommendations.

DIANE ACKERMAN

Diane Ackerman (1948–) was born in Waukegan, Illinois, and began publishing poems while working on her masters degree and doctorate at Cornell University. She has published several volumes of poetry as well as nonfiction books that often blend her scientific knowledge and artistic sensibilities. This section appeared in her best-selling book A Natural History of the Senses *(1990).*

Why Leaves Turn Color in the Fall

As you read this process entry, consider how Ackerman's language differs from that found in a college botany textbook.

1 The stealth of autumn catches one unaware. Was that a goldfinch perching in the early September woods, or just the first turning leaf? A red-winged blackbird or a sugar maple closing up shop for the winter? Keen-eyed as leopards, we stand still and squint hard, looking for signs of movement. Early-morning frost sits heavily on the grass, and turns barbed wire into a string of stars. On a distant hill, a small square of yellow appears to be a lighted stage. At last the truth dawns on us: Fall is staggering in, right on schedule, with its baggage of chilly nights, macabre holidays, and spectacular, heart-stoppingly beautiful leaves. Soon the leaves will start cringing on the trees, and roll up in clenched fists before they actually fall off. Dry seedpods will rattle like tiny gourds. But first there will be weeks of gushing color so bright, so pastel, so confettilike, that people will travel up and down the East Coast just to stare at it—a whole season of leaves.

2 Where do the colors come from? Sunlight rules most living things with its golden edicts. When the days begin to shorten, soon after the summer solstice on June 21, a tree reconsiders its leaves. All summer it feeds them so they can process sunlight, but in the dog days of summer the tree begins pulling nutrients back into its trunk and roots, pares down, and gradually chokes off its leaves. A corky layer of cells forms at the leaves' slender petioles, then scars over. Undernourished, the leaves stop producing the pigment chlorophyll, and photosynthesis

ceases. Animals can migrate, hibernate, or store food to prepare for winter. But where can a tree go? It survives by dropping its leaves, and by the end of autumn only a few fragile threads of fluid-carrying xylem hold leaves to their stems.

3 A turning leaf stays partly green at first, then reveals splotches of yellow and red as the chlorophyll gradually breaks down. Dark green seems to stay longest in the veins, outlining and defining them. During the summer, chlorophyll dissolves in the heat and light, but it is also being steadily replaced. In the fall, on the other hand, no new pigment is produced, and so we notice the other colors that were always there, right in the leaf, although chlorophyll's shocking green hid them from view. With their camouflage gone, we see these colors for the first time all year, and marvel, but they were always there, hidden like a vivid secret beneath the hot glowing greens of summer.

4 The most spectacular range of fall foliage occurs in the northeastern United States and in eastern China, where the leaves are robustly colored, thanks in part to a rich climate. European maples don't achieve the same flaming reds as their American relatives, which thrive on cold nights and sunny days. In Europe, the warm, humid weather turns the leaves brown or mildly yellow. Anthocyanin, the pigment that gives apples their red and turns leaves red or red-violet, is produced by sugars that remain in the leaf after the supply of nutrients dwindles. Unlike the carotenoids, which color carrots, squash, and corn, and turn leaves orange and yellow, anthocyanin varies from year to year, depending on the temperature and amount of sunlight. The fiercest colors occur in years when the fall sunlight is strongest and the nights are cool and dry (a state of grace scientists find vexing to forecast). This is also why leaves appear dizzyingly bright and clear on a sunny fall day: The anthocyanin flashes like a marquee.

5 Not all leaves turn the same colors. Elms, weeping willows, and the ancient ginkgo all grow radiant yellow, along with hickories, aspens, bottlebrush buckeyes, cottonweeds, and tall, keening poplars. Basswood turns bronze, birches bright gold. Water-loving maples put on a symphonic display of scarlets. Sumacs turn red, too, as do flowering dogwoods, black gums, and sweet gums. Though some oaks yellow, most turn a pinkish brown. The farmlands also change color, as tepees of cornstalks and bales of shredded-wheat-textured hay stand drying in the fields. In some spots, one slope of a hill may be green and the other already in bright color, because the hillside facing south gets more sun and heat than the northern one.

6 An odd feature of the colors is that they don't seem to have any special purpose. We are predisposed to respond to their beauty, of course. They shimmer with the colors of sunset, spring flowers, the tawny buff of a colt's pretty rump, the shuddering pink of a blush. Animals and flowers color for a reason—adaptation to their environment—but there is no adaptive reason for leaves to color so beautifully in the fall any more than there is for the sky or ocean to be blue. It's just one of the haphazard marvels the planet bestows every year. We find the sizzling colors thrilling, and in a sense they dupe us. Colored like living things, they signal death and disintegration. In time, they will become fragile and, like the body, return to dust. They are as we hope our own fate will be when we die: Not to vanish, just to sublime from one beautiful state into another. Though leaves lose their green life, they bloom with urgent colors, as the woods grow mummified day by day, and Nature becomes more carnal, mute, and radiant.

7 We call the season "fall," from the Old English *feallan,* to fall, which leads back through time to the Indo-European *phol,* which also means to fall. So the word and the idea are both extremely ancient, and haven't really changed since the first of our kind needed a name for fall's leafy abundance. As we say the word, we're reminded of that other Fall, in the garden of Eden, when fig leaves never withered and scales fell from our eyes. Fall is the time when leaves fall from the trees, just as spring is when flowers spring up, summer is when we simmer, and winter is when we whine from the cold.

8 Children love to play in piles of leaves, hurling them into the air like confetti, leaping into soft unruly mattresses of them. For children, leaf fall is just one of the odder figments of Nature, like hailstones or snowflakes. Walk down a lane overhung with trees in the never-never land of autumn, and you will forget about time and death, lost in the sheer delicious spill of color. Adam and Eve concealed their nakedness with leaves, remember? Leaves have always hidden our awkward secrets.

9 But how do the colored leaves fall? As a leaf ages, the growth hormone, auxin, fades, and cells at the base of the petiole divide. Two or three rows of small cells, lying at right angles to the axis of the petiole, react with water, then come apart, leaving the petioles hanging on by only a few threads of xylem. A light breeze, and the leaves are airborne. They glide and swoop, rocking in invisible cradles. They are all wing and may flutter from yard to yard on small whirlwinds or up-

drafts, swiveling as they go. Firmly tethered to earth, we love to see things rise up and fly—soap bubbles, balloons, birds, fall leaves. They remind us that the end of a season is capricious, as is the end of life. We especially like the way leaves rock, careen, and swoop as they fall. Everyone knows the motion. Pilots sometimes do a maneuver called a "falling leaf," in which the plane loses altitude quickly and on purpose, by slipping first to the right, then to the left. The machine weighs a ton or more, but in one pilot's mind it is a weightless thing, a falling leaf. She has seen the motion before, in the Vermont woods where she played as a child. Below her the trees radiate gold, copper, and red. Leaves are falling, although she can't see them fall, as she falls, swooping down for a closer view.

10 At last the leaves leave. But first they turn color and thrill us for weeks on end. Then they crunch and crackle underfoot. They *shush*, as children drag their small feet through leaves heaped along the curb. Dark, slimy mats of leaves cling to one's heels after a rain. A damp, stuccolike mortar of semidecayed leaves protects the tender shoots with a roof until spring, and makes a rich humus. An occasional bulge or ripple in the leafy mounds signals a shrew or a field mouse tunneling out of sight. Sometimes one finds in fossil stones the imprint of a leaf, long since disintegrated, whose outlines remind us how detailed, vibrant, and alive are the things of this earth that perish.

Understanding Meaning

1. What background information does Ackerman provide readers?
2. What are the principal forces that explain the change of color?
3. Why are the colors of leaves brighter in the United States than in Europe?
4. *Critical Thinking:* What impact does the change of color have on human beings? How do they react to the sight of falling leaves?

Evaluating Strategy

1. What do the opening and closing of the essay have in common? How are they different from the body?
2. How does Ackerman blend her poetic descriptions of nature with scientific detail?

Appreciating Language

1. What comments does Ackerman make on the word "fall"?
2. How does Ackerman define terms such as "carotenoids"?

Connections across the Disciplines

1. Compare Ackerman's essay with Edward Abbey's "The First Morning" (page 139). What similarities do they share in tone, style, and imagery?
2. How do Ackerman's comments on people's reactions to nature relate to Jamaica Kincaid's observations (page 147) that people impress their culture on nature through landscaping?

Writing Suggestions

1. In a few paragraphs describe a scientific process you are familiar with in terms designed for a general reader. Use everyday language, and try to use as many images as possible.
2. *Collaborative Writing:* Discuss autumn and the change of leaf colors with a group of students. Note what reactions they have experienced, and draft a brief essay explaining how the change in season affects people's moods, thoughts, and attitudes. You may also write about people who live in regions with few seasonal changes. How does the sense of constancy in weather and climate affect their lives? Are they denied contact with an element that leads people to important insights?

MARVIN HARRIS

Marvin Harris (1927–) was born in Brooklyn and received degrees from Columbia University. After teaching at Columbia for many years, Harris moved to the University of Florida where he now is a graduate research professor in anthropology. Harris has conducted research in Harlem, Africa, South America, and Asia. He has published several scholarly works but is best known for books written to general readers such as Cows, Pigs, Wars, and Witches: The Riddles of Culture *and* Cannibals and Kings: The Origins of Cultures. *Much of Harris's work focuses on how people's basic needs for food and shelter influence their culture.*

How Our Skins Got Their Color

In this essay from Our Kind: Who We Are, Where We Came From, Where We Are Going *(1988), Harris explains how human beings developed different skin colors. In reading this account, determine how he addresses a topic laden with controversy.*

1 Most human beings are neither very fair nor very dark, but brown. The extremely fair skin of northern Europeans and their descendants, and the very black skins of central Africans and their descendants, are probably special adaptations. Brown-skinned ancestors may have been shared by modern-day blacks and whites as recently as ten thousand years ago.

2 Human skin owes it color to the presence of particles known as melanin. The primary function of melanin is to protect the upper levels of the skin from being damaged by the sun's ultraviolet rays. This radiation poses a critical problem for our kind because we lack the dense coat of hair that acts as a sunscreen for most mammals. Hairlessness exposes us to two kinds of radiation hazards: ordinary sunburn, with its blisters, rashes, and risk of infection; and skin cancers, including malignant melanoma, one of the deadliest diseases known. Melanin is the body's first line of defense against these afflictions. The more melanin particles, the darker the skin, and the lower the risk of sunburn and all forms of skin cancer. This explains why the highest rates

for skin cancer are found in sun-drenched lands such as Australia, where light-skinned people of European descent spend a good part of their lives outdoors wearing scanty attire. Very dark-skinned people such as heavily pigmented Africans of Zaire seldom get skin cancer, but when they do, they get it on depigmented parts of their bodies—palms and lips.

3 If exposure to solar radiation had nothing but harmful effects, natural selection would have favored inky black as the color for all human populations. But the sun's rays do not present an unmitigated threat. As it falls on the skin, sunshine converts a fatty substance in the epidermis into vitamin D. The blood carries vitamin D from the skin to the intestines (technically making it a hormone rather than a vitamin), where it plays a vital role in the absorption of calcium. In turn, calcium is vital for strong bones. Without it, people fall victim to the crippling diseases rickets and osteomalacia. In women, calcium deficiencies can result in a deformed birth canal, which makes childbirth lethal for both mother and fetus.

4 Vitamin D can be obtained from a few foods, primarily the oils and livers of marine fish. But inland populations must rely on the sun's rays and their own skins for the supply of this crucial substance. The particular color of a human population's skin, therefore, represents in large degree a trade-off between the hazards of too much versus too little solar radiation: acute sunburn and skin cancer on the one hand, and rickets and osteomalacia on the other. It is this trade-off that largely accounts for the preponderance of brown people in the world and for the general tendency for skin color to be darkest among equatorial populations and lightest among populations dwelling at higher latitudes.

5 At middle latitudes, the skin follows a strategy of changing colors with the seasons. Around the Mediterranean basin, for example, exposure to the summer sun brings high risk of cancer but low risk for rickets; the body produces more melanin and people grow darker (i.e., they get suntans). Winter reduces the risk of sunburn and cancer; the body produces less melanin, and the tan wears off.

6 The correlation between skin color and latitude is not perfect because other factors—such as the availability of foods containing vitamin D and calcium, regional cloud cover during the winter, amount of clothing worn, and cultural preferences—may work for or against the predicted relationship. Arctic-dwelling Eskimos, for example, are not as light-skinned as expected, but their habitat and economy afford them a diet that is exceptionally rich in both vitamin D and calcium.

7 Northern Europeans, obliged to wear heavy garments for protection against the long, cold, cloudy winters, were always at risk for rickets and osteomalacia from too little vitamin D and calcium. This risk increased sometime after 6000 B.C., when pioneer cattle herders who did not exploit marine resources began to appear in northern Europe. The risk would have been especially great for the brown-skinned Mediterranean peoples who migrated northward along with the crops and farm animals. Samples of Caucasian skin (infant penile foreskin obtained at the time of circumcision) exposed to sunlight on cloudless days in Boston (42°N) from November through February produced no vitamin D. In Edmonton (52°N) this period extended from October to March. But further south (34°N) sunlight was effective in producing vitamin D in the middle of the winter. Almost all of Europe lies north of 42°N. Fair-skinned, nontanning individuals who could utilize the weakest and briefest doses of sunlight to synthesize vitamin D were strongly favored by natural selection. During the frigid winters, only a small circle of a child's face could be left to peek out at the sun through the heavy clothing, thereby favoring the survival of individuals with translucent patches of pink on their cheeks characteristic of many northern Europeans. . . .

8 If light-skinned individuals on the average had only 2 percent more children survive per generation, the changeover in their skin color could have begun five thousand years ago and reached present levels well before the beginning of the Christian era. But natural selection need not have acted alone. Cultural selection may also have played a role. It seems likely that whenever people consciously or unconsciously had to decide which infants to nourish and which to neglect, the advantage would go to those with lighter skin, experience having shown that such individuals tended to grow up to be taller, stronger, and healthier than their darker siblings. White was beautiful because white was healthy.

9 To account for the evolution of black skin in equatorial latitudes, one has merely to reverse the combined effects of natural and cultural selection. With the sun directly overhead most of the year, and clothing a hindrance to work and survival, vitamin D was never in short supply (and calcium was easily obtained from vegetables). Rickets and osteomalacia were rare. Skin cancer was the main problem, and what nature started, culture amplified. Darker infants were favored by parents because experience showed that they grew up to be freer of disfiguring and lethal malignancies. Black was beautiful because black was healthy.

Understanding Meaning

1. What is Harris's thesis?
2. What is the "natural" color for human skin?
3. What caused people to develop different complexions?
4. What role did sunlight play in human evolution?
5. *Critical Thinking:* What impact could this scientific explanation of skin color have on debates about race and discrimination? Can biological aspects of humanity be separated from social, cultural, political, or psychological attitudes?

Evaluating Strategy

1. How does Harris organize his essay?
2. What research does Harris use to support his views?
3. *Other Modes:* Where does Harris use *narration*, *comparison*, and *definition* in his explanation?

Appreciating Language

1. How does Harris define *melanin?*
2. Does Harris's selection of words describing color contain connotations that suggest a bias? Is his essay wholly objective? How often does he use words such as *white* and *black?*
3. Would the average newspaper reader be able to understand this essay? What does the level of language suggest about the intended audience?

Connections across the Disciplines

1. Does Harris's essay differ from Diane Ackerman's "Why Leaves Turn Color in the Fall" (page 490)? Why does writing about skin color pose more problems than describing plant life?
2. Would this essay make a good preface for an essay such as Nathan McCall's "The Lesson" (page 47)? Why?

Writing Suggestions

1. Using this essay for background information, draft a brief explanation about skin color for an elementary school brochure on race relations. Use

easily understood language, and employ comparisons and short narratives to explain scientific principles. Avoid words that may have negative connotations.

2. *Critical Writing:* Write an essay analyzing the effect reading this essay had on you. Did it affect your attitudes toward people of different races? Does the knowledge that all humans probably once shared the same complexion change the way you view yourself?
3. *Collaborative Writing:* Discuss Harris's essay with a group of students. What value does a scientific explanation of skin color have in addressing racial problems? Would it be beneficial to share this information with children? Record members' reactions, and create a short statement about the importance of understanding the origins of skin color. If members disagree, consider developing pro and con responses.

PETER ELBOW

Peter Elbow (1935–) was educated at Williams College, Brandeis, Harvard, and Oxford. A noted director of college writing programs, Elbow started a highly acclaimed "Workshop in Language and Thinking" at Bard College. He has published numerous articles about writing and several books including Writing without Teachers *and* Writing with Power.

Desperation Writing

In this section from Writing without Teachers *(1973), Peter Elbow offers advice to students writing under stress. Facing deadlines, many students feel almost paralyzed, unable to even start an assignment. Elbow presents his recommendations in the form of a process.*

1 I know I am not alone in my recurring twinges of panic that I won't be able to write something when I need to, I won't be able to produce coherent speech or thought. And that lingering doubt is a great hindrance to writing. It's a constant fog or static that clouds the mind. I never got out of its clutches till I discovered that it was possible to write something—not something great or pleasing but at least something usable, workable—when my mind is out of commission. The trick is that you have to do all your cooking out on the table: Your mind is incapable of doing any inside. It means using symbols and pieces of paper not as a crutch but as a wheelchair.

2 The first thing is to admit your condition: Because of some mood or event or whatever, your mind is incapable of anything that could be called thought. It can put out a babbling kind of speech utterance, it can put a simple feeling, perception or sort-of-thought into understandable (though terrible) words. But it is incapable of considering anything in relation to anything else. The moment you try to hold that thought or feeling up against some other to see the relationship, you simply lose the picture—you get nothing but buzzing lines or waving colors.

3 So admit this. Avoid anything more than one feeling, perception, or thought. Simply write as much as possible. Try simply to steer your

mind in the direction or general vicinity of the thing you are trying to write about and start writing and keep writing.

4 Just write and keep writing. (Probably best to write on only one side of the paper in case you should want to cut parts out with scissors—but you probably won't.) Just write and keep writing. It will probably come in waves. After a flurry, stop and take a brief rest. But don't stop too long. Don't think about what you are writing or what you have written or else you will overload the circuit again. Keep writing as though you are drugged or drunk. Keep doing this till you feel you have a lot of material that might be useful; or, if necessary, till you can't stand it any more—even if you doubt that there's anything useful there.

5 Then take a pad of little pieces of paper—or perhaps 3 × 5 cards—and simply start at the beginning of what you were writing, and as you read over what you wrote, every time you come to any thought, feeling, perception, or image that could be gathered up into one sentence or one assertion, do so and write it by itself on a little sheet of paper. In short, you are trying to turn, say, ten or twenty pages of wandering mush into twenty or thirty hard little crab apples. Sometimes there won't be many on a page. But if it seems to you that there are none on a page, you are making a serious error—the same serious error that put you in this comatose state to start with. You are mistaking lousy, stupid, second-rate, wrong, childish, foolish, worthless ideas for no ideas at all. Your job is not to pick out *good* ideas but to pick out ideas. As long as you were conscious, your words will be full of things that could be called feelings, utterances, ideas—things that can be squeezed into one simple sentence. This is your job. Don't ask for too much.

6 After you have done this, take those little slips or cards, read through them a number of times—not struggling with them, simply wandering and mulling through them; perhaps shifting them around and looking through in various sequences. In a sense these are cards you are playing solitaire with, and the rules of this particular game permit shuffling the unused pile.

7 The goal of this procedure with the cards is to get them to distribute themselves in two or three or ten or fifteen different piles on your desk. You can get them to do this almost by themselves if you simply keep reading through them in different orders; certain cards will begin to feel like they go with other cards. I emphasize this passive, thoughtless mode because I want to talk about desperation writing in its pure

state. In practice, almost invariably at some point in the procedure, your sanity begins to return. It is often at this point. You actually are moved to have thoughts or—and the difference between active and passive is crucial here—to *exert* thought; to hold two cards together and *build* or *assert* a relationship. It is a matter of bringing energy to bear.

8 So you may start to be able to do something active with these cards, and begin actually to think. But if not, just allow the cards to find their own piles with each other by feel, by drift, by intuition, by mindlessness.

9 You have now engaged in the two main activities that will permit you to get something cooked out on the table rather than in your brain: writing out into messy words, summing up into single assertions, and even sensing relationships between assertions. You can simply continue to deploy these two activities.

10 If, for example, after the first round of writing, assertion-making, and pile-making, your piles feel as though they are useful and satisfactory for what you are writing—paragraphs or sections or trains of thought—then you can carry on from there. See if you can gather each pile up into a single assertion. When you can, then put the subsidiary assertions of that pile into their best order to fit with that single unifying one. If you *can't* get the pile into one assertion, then take the pile as the basis for doing some more writing out into words. In the course of this writing, you may produce for yourself the single unifying assertion you were looking for; or you may have to go through the cycle of turning the writing into assertions and piles and so forth. Perhaps more than once. The pile may turn out to want to be two or more piles itself; or it may want to become part of a pile you already have. This is natural. This kind of meshing into one configuration, then coming apart, then coming together and meshing into a different configuration—this is growing and cooking. It makes a terrible mess, but if you can't do it in your head, you have to put up with a cluttered desk and a lot of confusion.

11 If, on the other hand, all that writing *didn't* have useful material in it, it means that your writing wasn't loose, drifting, quirky, jerky, associative enough. This time try especially to let things simply remind you of things that are seemingly crazy or unrelated. Follow these odd associations. Make as many metaphors as you can—be as nutty as possible—and explore the metaphors themselves—open them out. You may have all your energy tied up in some area of your experience that

you are leaving out. Don't refrain from writing about whatever else is on your mind: how you feel at the moment, what you are losing your mind over, randomness that intrudes itself on your consciousness, the pattern on the wallpaper, what those people you see out the window have on their minds—though keep coming back to the whateveritis you are supposed to be writing about. Treat it, in short, like ten-minute writing exercises. Your best perceptions and thoughts are always going to be tied up in whatever is really occupying you, and that is also where your energy is. You may end up writing a love poem—or a hate poem—in one of those little piles while the other piles will finally turn into a lab report on data processing or whatever you have to write about. But you couldn't, in your present state of having your head shot off, have written that report without also writing the poem. And the report will have some of the juice of the poem in it and vice versa.

Understanding Meaning

1. What is Elbow's purpose?
2. What problems does Elbow want students to overcome?
3. Do you find this advice helpful? Would you use it?
4. *Critical Thinking:* What does Elbow's essay reveal to you about the writing process? Why is it important to see writing as a process and not merely a product?

Evaluating Strategy

1. Does the opening adequately demonstrate the need for this process?
2. Are the stages or steps clearly defined?
3. How does Elbow signal transitions?

Appreciating Language

1. Elbow writes of ideas that are "lousy" and "stupid" but still have value. What is he trying to indicate to students with these word choices?
2. Judging by the language, what audience, what type of student, is this essay targeted to?

Connections across the Disciplines

1. How do Elbow's comments about writing compare to William Zinsser's (page 247)?
2. How does Elbow's advice differ from S. I. Hayakawa's (page 464)?

Writing Suggestions

1. Experiment with the freewriting process Elbow describes. Select a topic and write nonstop for at least ten minutes. Afterward underline the ideas you came up with while writing.
2. *Collaborative Writing:* Talk about writing with other students. Discuss working methods. Take notes on the tips you feel helpful. Work with others to craft these into a process essay.

FRAN MARTIN

Fran Martin earned a nursing degree at Wheaton College and completed a doctorate at Florida State University. Martin is the Assistant Professor of maternal-child nursing at the University of Southern Mississippi in Hattiesburg. In addition to her teaching career, Martin often appears in court as an expert witness in medical malpractice cases. In this article, first published in Nursing *in 1994, Martin explains how properly documented charts can protect nurses from litigation.*

Documentation Tips

This article is directed to nurses, though it applies to nearly every professional who must document his or her actions: law enforcement officers, counselors, therapists, maintenance supervisors, and school administrators. As you read the article, notice that Martin stresses what might be called "defensive writing."

1 A nursing student who was reviewing charts for a senior honors class commented to me, "It's amazing how much is left undocumented or unexplained in the record. I had so many questions."

2 Exactly.

3 I often have the same reaction when I read the charts for the cases I consult on. And I think, *If only these nurses had taken the time to completely document the care they claim they'd given, they could have avoided liability.* But, unfortunately, lack of documentation suggests nursing malpractice.

4 Here's what you can do to avoid ending up in the same situation.

TIPS FOR AVOIDING TROUBLE

5 • ***Make sure your charting is complete.*** Documentation is a pivotal part of a lawsuit—it can be the best way for you to refute charges of malpractice. I've seen four common problem areas.

6 1. *Not charting the correct time when events occurred.* Suppose a procedure is charted in several different places, but each entry indicates that it was

done at a different time. Lawyers use these times to reconstruct the sequence of events, and inconsistencies like this can make their case—they can easily raise questions about the accuracy of the entire record.

7 2. *Failing to record verbal orders or to have them signed.* In an emergency or during a particularly hectic shift, you could overlook this important step. But if you don't record the order and have it signed according to policy and something happens to the patient, the doctor could deny that he gave the order. And without documentation, the jury would wonder whether to believe your word or the doctor's.

8 3. *Charting your actions in advance to save time.* You may be particularly tempted to do this with standing orders for medications, but nothing should be charted until after it's done or administered. You wouldn't want to have to explain how you administered a drug when you were participating in a code at the same time.

9 4. *Charting incorrect data.* You communicate with other health care providers through the chart and, obviously, incorrect data doesn't give an accurate picture of your patient's condition. That could lead to life-threatening errors. It also raises the specter of fraud, which could make your actions appear not just negligent, but also criminal.

10 • ***Collect and analyze data from the patient's history and physical, and from laboratory reports.*** The doctor may point out pertinent facts, but you're responsible for using your experience to interpret the information you've obtained. In one case I consulted on, a pregnant patient with poor weight gain and uterine growth was 3 weeks overdue. Yet none of her nurses recognized the increased risk of fetal distress.

11 • ***Use your data to identify patients at increased risk for complications.*** Even if you don't initially think the patient is at risk for complications, you're responsible for monitoring the patient as ordered, watching for trends that signal a developing problem, and calling the doctor if a change occurs. For example, monitoring and recording vital signs shouldn't become meaningless routine. You need to look at what the numbers tell you and act accordingly.

12 • ***Don't get into a diagnostic rut.*** If you're too focused on the diagnosis, you could be distracted from accurately analyzing your data. I consulted on the case of a woman who died of beta-hemolytic streptococci peritonitis from endometritis after giving birth to her second child. Uninterested in caring for the child, she'd been diagnosed with "poor maternal bonding." Her nurses did an excellent job of documenting this problem. However, they'd overlooked her persistently high heart rate and complaints of pain, with disastrous results.

13 • ***Periodically review and revise the policy and procedure manuals.*** Lawyers scrutinize hospital and unit policy and procedure manuals to spot

inconsistencies between a nurse's actions and written policy. They also ask experts like me to determine whether these manuals conform to national standards of care. Some of these manuals are frightening—they devote pages to routine things (such as gowning and gloving the doctor for delivery) but ignore serious situations (such as nursing actions for fetal distress). My advice is to ensure that your policy and procedure manuals are complete, current (that is, they reflect changes in nursing practice and technology), and clear to the reader (including any nurses who might float to the unit). If the manuals haven't been updated in years, talk with your nurse-manager—you've got a disaster waiting to happen.

14 Now that I've given you my advice, I'd like to share a case I recently consulted on. It illustrates why these tips are so important.

A CASE IN POINT

15 Patti Bailey was admitted to deliver her third child. During her pregnancy, she'd gained 63 pounds, her blood pressure had risen from 100/70 in her first trimester to 140/80 at term, and an ultrasound done at 22 weeks showed possible placenta previa.

16 Over the next 4 hours, she received 10 units of oxytocin (Pitocin) in 500 ml of 5 percent dextrose in lactated Ringer's solution. Charting during this period was scant—her blood pressure was never recorded, and there were only single notations of the fetal heart rate and how labor was progressing. The nurses failed to record either the baby's reaction to the drug or the nature of Mrs. Bailey's contractions.

17 Suddenly, after complaining of nausea and epigastric pain, Mrs. Bailey suffered a generalized tonic-clonic seizure. Because her condition was so unstable, she couldn't undergo a cesarean section. So her baby girl was delivered by low forceps. Mrs. Bailey developed disseminated intravascular coagulation and required 20 units of whole blood, platelets, and packed red blood cells within 8 hours of delivery.

18 Incredibly, Mrs. Bailey's nurse had essentially documented nothing on the labor or delivery records or the progress notes. And when I reviewed the unit's policy and procedure manuals, I couldn't find a protocol for administering oxytocin and assessing the patient. At the very least, there should have been an oxytocin flow sheet to record vital signs, labor progress, fetal status, and changes in the drug administration rate.

19 Although Mrs. Bailey recovered, her daughter has seizures and is developmentally disabled. Now 15, the daughter can't walk or talk and she has a gastrostomy tube for nutrition. The case was settled out of court for $450,000, with the nurse and hospital responsible for one-third of the amount; the doctor paid the rest.

PRACTICING SAFELY

20 Being named in a lawsuit is unnerving, at the very least. So you need to do your best to practice safely—and to accurately document as proof of your care. If you do, there's a good chance you'll stay out of court.

Understanding Meaning

1. Why is it important for nurses to carefully document their actions?
2. What common mistakes do nurses make?
3. What can happen when nurses fail to report their actions?
4. *Critical Thinking:* What does Martin's article reveal about how people write outside the classroom? How is this writing different from that taught in most English courses?

Evaluating Strategy

1. Why does Martin give negative instructions at the opening?
2. *Other Modes:* How does Martin use *narration* and *analysis* to support her advice?

Appreciating Language

1. Martin does not define "beta-hemolytic streptococci peritonitis" or "epigastric pain." What does this say about her intended reader?
2. How much technical language does she use to describe the legal or writing process?

Connections across the Disciplines

1. Why should nurses consider S. I. Hayakawa's admonition (page 464) to write in "report" statements, avoiding "inferences" and "judgments"?
2. How does Martin's advice differ from Peter Elbow's (page 500)? Why?

Writing Suggestions

1. Experiment with charting. Write a chart of your activities throughout a single school day. You might refer to the logbook of the *Titanic* (page 92) as a model. At the end of the day, review your writing. How difficult is it to keep a running journal? Did you forget to record any activities?
2. *Collaborative Writing:* Discuss writing on the job with a group of students. What reports, letters, and memos have they had to write? Discuss whether schools and colleges adequately prepare students for writing "in the real world." Record suggestions and comments, and then collaborate on writing a process paper explaining how English classes could be made more practical.

ANNE WEISBORD

Anne Weisbord has a masters in education and served as director of Career Services at Hahnemann University in Philadelphia before beginning a career as a private career counselor. Widely published, she has appeared on radio and television providing advice on careers, job search strategies, and interviewing. In this article, written for Nurse Extra, *Weisbord tells nurses how to write effective résumés.*

Resumes That Rate a Second Look

Although directed to nurses, Weisbord's advice applies to most professionals. As you read the article, notice how her terse, to-the-point phrases mirror the kind of writing found on most résumés.

1 In today's business and professional environment—in which health-care positions can be eliminated STAT—every nurse should have a resume ready to send to potential employers.

2 The purpose of the resume is to get you a job interview. Employers use resumes to screen out undesirable, or less desirable, candidates. Your resume should summarize your skills and experience, and convince employers of the value they will gain in hiring you. It's an advertisement for yourself, and as with all ads, it should generate interest and motivate the reader.

3 Before you prepare your resume, take a few moments to consider your marketable skills. Identify the strengths and accomplishments that are relevant to the position you are seeking, and present them as succinctly and as clearly as possible. You'll need to organize all of this information in no more than two pages, in an easy-to-read, attractive format. Beyond this, there are really no hard-and-fast rules about writing resumes.

4 Let's look at the standard components of the traditional resume that presents your relevant nursing background in reverse chronological order.

5 1. **Personal identification.** You need include only your name, degree, and your professional certification, address, and phone number. Omit date of birth, marital status, and health; these can be discriminatory factors in hiring.

6 2. **Career objective.** This is optional. If you know *exactly* what you want to do, you can use a phrase that describes the type and level of position you are seeking. An objective might be "Nurse Coordinator in Pediatrics," or "Nurse Manager, ICU." However, if you would consider a variety of positions, skip the objective and use only a summary.

7 3. **Summary.** Describe your background in a few punchy sentences. This is the "hook" that will pique the reader's interest in the rest of the resume.

8 4. **Professional experience.** List names, places, job titles, and dates of employment. Link your experience to your summary or objective. Stress accomplishments, and emphasize responsibilities that will impress the potential employer. Use brief phrases with vivid verbs and nouns to describe the skills essential to each position. Omit obvious duties. Emphasize accomplishments with bullets.

9 As you go back into your work history, present fewer details. When you first became a nurse, you naturally had fewer responsibilities. Devote more space to higher-level, more professional duties.

10 5. **Education.** If you are a recent graduate with little nursing experience, put education before professional experience. Always list the most recent school, degree or certificate program and work backward. Do include honors or academic awards. Don't list high school. If you have a college degree, the employer will assume you earned a high-school diploma.

11 6. **Professional certification(s).** List certifications in reverse chronological order, or organize them according to specialty areas.

12 7. **License(s).** List only the state and title of each professional license. Don't give your license number(s). You will be asked to provide them later in the interview process.

13 8. **Activities.** No one will hire you for a healthcare position based on your interest in golf or coin collecting, but volunteer community involvement shows positive personal characteristics. Be careful about listing political or religious activities. Your reader may have biases against your persuasions.

14 Remember that your resume serves as a first impression of you. To a potential employer, your coffee-stained copy or your misspellings say something about your attention (or lack of attention) to detail, your neatness, and even your attitude. Also, modesty is not an asset in a resume. Toot your own horn!

Understanding Meaning

1. Summarize Weisbord's key points on résumés.
2. What is the purpose of a résumé? Why does this seemingly obvious fact need to be explained? Do many people have misconceptions about résumés?
3. What information does Weisbord suggest omitting? Why?
4. *Critical Thinking:* What is the context of a résumé? How does this document reflect the roles of writer, audience, and discipline?

Evaluating Strategy

1. How effective is the format of Weisbord's article?
2. Weisbord tells readers "there are really no hard-and-fast rules about writing resumes." Why is this important?
3. How does her article mirror the document she is training readers to write?

Appreciating Language

1. How effective is Weisbord's style and choice of words? Is the article readable?
2. How does Weisbord's emphasis on verbs, "*Describe* your background . . ." and "*List* names, places . . ." (italics added) reflect the kind of language found on most résumés?

Connections across the Disciplines

1. Review Monica Ramos's résumé (page 160). Does it follow Weisbord's advice?
2. How does her advice to nurses on writing a résumé differ from Martin's advice on charting (page 505)? Why?

Writing Suggestions

1. If you have not written a résumé already, draft one adopting Weisbord's advice.
2. *Collaborative Writing:* Meet with a group of students, and review each other's résumés. Select the best features you discover, and then write a brief process essay explaining step by step how to create an effective résumé.

EUGENE RAUDSEPP

Eugene Raudsepp is president of Princeton Creative Research Inc., based in New Jersey. An expert on job interviewing techniques, Raudsepp created this article for Machine Design *(1993), a magazine read widely by engineers and industrial managers.*

Seeing Your Way Past Interview Jitters

This article, directed toward engineers, instructs candidates to use a psychological technique called visualization to improve their performance during job interviews.

1 It is not unusual to experience a mild attack of nerves before a job interview. But there are engineers whose interview jitters are intense enough to be harmful. They have such overwhelming apprehension and fear that they either become tongue-tied or proceed to talk themselves out of the job. Even many capable and articulate engineers act stiff and awkward in interviews, often fidgeting or sitting on the edge of the chair.

2 When we're anxious, we frequently become self-conscious spectators of our own behavior during interviews, observing and judging our every utterance and movement. This makes us not only more anxious and less convincing, but also divides our attention.

3 Excessive self-consciousness is particularly true among engineers who go to interviews with a do-or-die attitude. Trying too hard to succeed increases tension and reduces effectiveness. "The self-imposed pressure of trying to ace an interview can make some people focus too much on how they look and act," says Steven Berglas, a psychiatry instructor at Harvard Medical School. He feels that those who are overly conscious of their grooming, speech, body language, and other interviewing behavior frequently "suppress those elements of their personality that won them the interview in the first place."

4 Perfectionist engineers particularly experience high anxiety during job interviews. Because they have a strong need to do well and

have such inflated expectations of their own performance, any real or imaginary deviation from their self-imposed high, and often unrealistic, standards triggers excessive nervousness and self-critical ruminations. From one slight, innocuous mistake they automatically assume the entire interview will turn out badly.

5 This anticipation often drives them to behaviors and statements that would seem self-sabotage to an innocent bystander.

REDUCING TENSION

6 Although you may feel your blood pressure rise, palms moisten, and stomach tighten before an important interview, you can control these reactions.

7 According to H. Anthony Medley, author of *Sweaty Palms: The Neglected Art of Being Interviewed*, there are four sound reasons why you have nothing to fear but fear itself, and they can help you keep an interview in perspective:

8
1. The interview centers on the subject you know best: yourself.
2. If you've done your homework, you have a decided advantage: You know more about the interviewer's company than it knows about you.
3. Interviewers expect job candidates to be a bit nervous.
4. You have nothing to lose. You didn't have the job offer before the interview, so if you don't have it afterward, you're no worse off.

9 Some interview failures may be inevitable. Most engineers have experienced at least one. The important point is to refrain from exaggerating the importance of an interview situation. Also, if possible, generate several interviews; don't pin your hopes on just one. A winning-at-all-costs attitude seldom wins a job offer.

10 It is detrimental to adopt a confrontational stance with the interviewer. If you feel overly tense or belligerent, it is helpful to pretend that the interviewer is a good friend. A little make-believe can go a long way toward calming hostile feelings.

11 One interesting method of lessening interview stress is suggested by Lawrence Darius, president of Corporate Communication Skills Inc., New York. He is convinced that one of the more effective ways to overcome interview jitters is to separate yourself from your performance. "Just as an actor or actress creates the character in a script, you

must try to create a character for the position you're seeking," he explains. "You probably have an image of the ideal engineer or, better yet, of the perfect candidates for the job. How do they differ from you? How do they walk, talk, and act?"

12 Daralee Schulman, a New York City–based career counselor, teaches her clients to relax before an interview by doing this exercise: "Visualize a serene and beautiful scene, perhaps a moonlit beach, while becoming aware of the rhythm of your breathing. On each breath in, think 'I am' and on each breath out, think 'calm.' Ten repetitions of 'I am calm' breathing done in the reception area before an interview can ease your tension." A "reliving" of a past interview in which you did well boosts your self-confidence, too.

13 A more advanced and exceedingly effective breathing technique is offered by Dan Lang, who conducts stress-reducing workshops in New York. First, exhale totally, imagining that you are relaxing all your tension. Next, close your mouth and place your right thumb on your right nostril so that it is completely closed. Then slowly and deeply inhale and exhale through your left nostril a couple of minutes, or 25 to 30 times. This enables you to tap into the right hemisphere of your brain, particularly the limbic part that governs emotions. You will experience an immediate reduction of fear and anxiety resulting in a more relaxed, in-charge feeling.

THE POWER OF VISUALIZATION

14 Many top athletes experience almost overwhelming stress before important events. However, most of them have learned—through the new sports psychology of visualization—how to manage performance anxiety, improve concentration, and enhance athletic performance.

15 Tennis champion Chris Evert, for example, used to carefully and repeatedly visualize every detail of an upcoming championship match in her mind's eye. She pictured her opponent's style and form, and then visualized how she would counter and respond to every possible maneuver or tactic.

16 Golf great Jack Nicklaus programs his "bio-computer" for success this way: "I never hit a shot, even in practice, without having a sharp, in-focus picture of it in my head. It's like a color movie. First, I 'see' the ball where I want it to finish. I 'see' the ball going there: its path,

trajectory, and shape. The next scene shows me making the kind of swing that will turn the previous image into reality."

17 There are significant emotional parallels between sports and job interviews. Through visualizing your ideal interview performance, you can build confidence and reduce anxiety to manageable levels.

18 Visualization of a successful interview is impressed upon the memory. When the actual event happens, there is complete confidence of success, as if one had done it before with a positive outcome.

Understanding Meaning

1. Does Raudsepp suggest engineers suffer from more anxiety at interviews than other professionals?
2. Describe the process of visualization in your own words. Why does it work?
3. Why does "trying too hard" often defeat a candidate interviewing for a job?
4. What does Raudsepp tell engineers not to do?
5. *Critical Thinking:* Could these techniques aid students facing an oral exam or essay test? Could visualizing your completed paper help in the writing process?

Evaluating Strategy

1. How effective are the examples Raudsepp uses for support?
2. How does Raudsepp reinforce his views with quotes from other authorities? Why is this important in giving advice?

Appreciating Language

1. What kind of language does Raudsepp use in explaining psychological techniques to engineers? How might this article be stated if written for a psychological journal?
2. Does the tone and style of the article help ease a reader's anxiety about facing a job interview? Explain.

Connections across the Disciplines

1. Refer to Anne Weisbord's article about résumé writing (page 510). Would visualization assist a job applicant in highlighting his or her key strengths?

Could reviewing a well-stated résumé help prepare an applicant for an interview by reinforcing his or her accomplishments?

2. Consider Lisa Fried's study of female entrepreneurs (page 368). Is visualization a critical skill for women to master?

Writing Suggestions

1. Write a narrative essay about a job interview you have had. At the end provide a brief analysis of your performance. Could it have been better?
2. *Collaborative Writing:* Discuss job interview experiences with a group of students. Ask the members what were the toughest questions they were asked. Have the members suggest possible answers. Collect the comments, and collaborate on a process paper: "How to Handle Tough Questions in a Job Interview."

LIZ GRINSLADE

Liz Grinslade is vice president of MSI Healthcare, a national executive search firm that specializes in locating professionals for health care providers. In this 1993 article published in Healthcare Financial Management, *she tells executives how to evaluate a job opportunity.*

Evaluating a Job Opportunity

Grinslade's advice is directed toward health care professionals but applies to almost anyone considering a job offer. Her article is important because for some people taking the wrong job can do more damage to their careers than not being hired.

1 For financial managers, as well as other job candidates, the decision to accept or reject a position offered during the job hunting process can be a difficult one. However, if eight basic areas are investigated and considered, the decision to accept or reject an offer can be made more easily. During the job interview, the job candidate should try and obtain information that will help answer the following questions:

2

1. Will the work be fulfilling and challenging?
2. What skills are necessary to be successful at the job? If the skills are not already possessed, can they readily be developed?
3. Is the facility stable? Is the position stable?
4. Is the management philosophy acceptable?
5. Is there good chemistry between the job candidate and the hiring manager and prospective coworkers?
6. Is the location satisfying?
7. Will there be opportunities for continuing growth and new challenges?
8. Is the compensation fair and equitable?

3 The answers to these questions can lead a job candidate to the right decision.

4 *What skills are necessary to be successful at the job? If the skills are not already possessed, can they readily be developed?* The candidate should consider the scope of responsibilities of the position, as well as the expectations of others, including the facility's administrator, board of

directors, and hiring manager. The candidate should try and determine if these expectations are realistic. One way to gather relevant information is to ask what was liked and what was disliked about the performance of the employee previously in the position.

5 Lynn Boltuch, business office director at Mount Sinai Medical Center of Greater Miami, Miami, Florida, suggests that job applicants try to ascertain whether a company is genuinely anxious to hire someone who can make changes to improve operations. Has the company identified specific problems in a department that need to be solved? If the company is seeking a turnaround specialist, will the person hired be given the autonomy, resources, and support needed to make necessary changes? How many layers of management will be involved in making decisions? What are the administrator's overall goals for the position? Are schedules established for implementation of change and does meeting the schedule seem feasible? Are staffing levels adequate?

6 *Is the facility stable? Is the position stable?* Employers expect a job applicant to inquire about a facility's current financial condition. (For independent verification, a Medicare cost report on U.S. healthcare facilities is available for $75 through the Center for Healthcare Industry Performance Studies—CHIPS—in Columbus, Ohio.) If recent financial reports have not been positive, consider the trend. Is the facility's financial position cyclical and approaching an upswing or does an ongoing downslide seem probable? While asking about the financial picture, the job candidate should note not only what the hiring manager says but also the confidence level of his or her response.

7 There are other aspects of stability that should be explored. For instance, the candidate should try to ascertain why the position is open. Has someone been promoted within the system or has there been a "revolving door" of CFOs who could not work with the administrator or the board? What are the market conditions? Are there two other competing hospitals of similar or larger size in the immediate service area? And how tough is the managed care environment?

8 *Is the management philosophy acceptable? Is there good chemistry between the job candidate and the hiring manager and prospective coworkers?* Overall job satisfaction may rest with the answers to these questions. To assess the management philosophy, the candidate should inquire about the priorities for the position and how they should be accomplished. Job candidates should be able to adapt to new ways of doing things and, just as important, organizations should be open to employees' suggestions for change.

9 The job candidate also should ask other staff members, such as the chief operating officer or director of personnel, about the administrator's management style. How does the administrator react in different situations? Is he or she emotional and erratic? Does he or she avoid confrontations at all costs? Boltuch says one factor that determines how well a job candidate will enjoy working with a hiring manager is noting how the manager makes the candidate feel upon entering the office for the first interview. Did the manager make the candidate feel at ease or "on display?"

10 When it comes to evaluating the chemistry between the candidate and the management team and other coworkers, the candidate should make a point of meeting as many people he or she would come in contact with in a position as soon as possible. Meeting off-site is preferable. A lot more can be learned over a casual lunch than in a potential coworker's office. "Gut" feelings should be given strong consideration when evaluating the position.

11 *Is the location satisfying?* If accepting the position means moving to another city, the job candidate should make a list of important considerations, including climate, affordability, quality of school systems, proximity to family and friends, potential cultural and recreational activities, and educational opportunities. The needs of the candidate's spouse should not be forgotten.

12 Cost of living also can be a significant factor to weigh in making a decision. Using the cost-of-living index, produced by the American Chamber of Commerce Researchers Association, the candidate can compare the relative cost of living in a city. The index is updated quarterly and is available at most libraries.

13 *Will there be opportunities for continuing growth and new challenges?* By asking about the organizational structure of a facility, a potential career path can be outlined. Are there higher positions within the company that can be pursued in the future? Have specific situations been mentioned where individuals have been promoted internally? Does the organization provide tuition reimbursement for advanced degrees? Does the organization support/pay for membership in professional associations? In addition to paying for membership, does the organization also allow for time off to attend meetings or serve as a volunteer on committees? All of these factors can indicate the potential for future advancement.

14 *Is the compensation fair and equitable?* The candidate should gather information about competitive salary structures from mentors, human

resource departments, executive recruiters, and professional associations. HFMA periodically surveys and publishes salary data for CFOs and patient accounts managers. But money is only one of many factors to consider.

The old "rule of thumb" requiring a certain percentage of increase in compensation to change jobs is no longer valid. Many healthcare financial professionals accept lateral salary moves or even lower salaries to gain valuable experience from a particular position. Opting for a higher salary at the expense of quality of life or job satisfaction can be a poor tradeoff.

Understanding Meaning

1. What key issues should people consider before accepting a job?
2. In their eagerness to accept jobs, what problems can people create for themselves?
3. What questions should an applicant ask about the employer?
4. Why does Grinslade suggest that a high salary is sometimes worth passing over?
5. *Critical Thinking:* Does Grinslade's article suggest that many people, including skilled professionals, are too passive in the job process? Do people fail to interview their potential employers? Are they too trusting? Do you think many people feel they will be perceived as being rude or ungrateful if they seem critical of an organization offering them a job?

Evaluating Strategy

1. How effectively is the article organized? Are points easy to follow?
2. How does Grinslade use transitions?
3. Grinslade offers sources for gaining further information. Do many other writers fail to do this?

Appreciating Language

1. This article is directed to financial managers in the health care industry. Would it require much rewriting to be reprinted in a sales, engineering, or computer magazine?
2. Grinslade uses clichés such as "rule of thumb" and "'gut' feelings." Are these appropriate phrases in this context?

Connections across the Disciplines

1. Review the 3M want ad (page 158) and Monika Ramos's résumé (page 160). What questions should Ramos consider before accepting a job with 3M?
2. Review Ellen Goodman's "The Company Man" (page 185). How does her workaholic figure compare with the kind of professional Grinslade describes in her article? What makes one person a drone and another a critical consumer of job opportunities?

Writing Suggestions

1. Have you ever been burned by a job that did not work out? Were you hired only to find the company was facing bankruptcy or that you would not receive the equipment or resources needed to do the job? Write a narrative essay about your experience.
2. *Collaborative Writing:* Meet with a group of students and discuss experiences, both good and bad, with job opportunities. Take notes and write a process essay similar to Grinslade's offering advice on evaluating job offers. You may wish to target your essay to college students seeking part-time or summer jobs.

CHARLES N. JAMISON JR.

Charles N. Jamison Jr. became the first African American vice president at Ted Bates Advertising. With ten years' experience in advertising and a doctorate in psychology, Jamison was well-equipped to launch his own ad agency. He teamed up with Kathryn Leary, who also worked at Bates, to create Jamison and Leary. Backed by their former employer and armed with powerful contacts, the team did well. Jamison and Leary landed major accounts such as Bacardi, NYNEX, and the Alvin Ailey dance company. Employing a dozen people, the firm was generating $5 million in billings when it began to fail.

Why My Business Failed

In this "reverse success" story, a talented entrepreneur provides advice to people hoping to achieve success. This article appeared in Black Enterprise *(1994), a magazine aimed at African American executives and business owners. Notice how Jamison uses* narrative, description, cause and effect, *and* analysis *to develop his guidelines.*

1 For nearly five years I ran an advertising agency, Jamison & Associates Advertising Inc. (originally Jamison & Leary Advertising).

2 Starting out, I believed that I knew a lot about making advertising work. I proved to myself that I was right.

3 During our glory years, we did work for such large clients as Bacardi, General Foods, PepsiCo, TIAA-CREF, NYNEX, Dow Jones & Co. Inc., and M&M/MARS, as well as for black clients like *Emerge* magazine, Yaska Shoes Ltd. and the Alvin Ailey American Dance Theater. We did video, television, radio and print. We sold a lot of goods, services and tickets. We even won a CEBA (Communication Excellence in Black Advertising) our second year out.

4 The agency is closed now. A victim of the most recent recession. Bankrupt. Chapter 7. History. Past tense.

5 What I learned, somewhat painfully, was that knowing how to create effective advertising doesn't necessarily mean that you're going to know how to run an advertising business. During a recession, which is what we ran into, it's easy to say that the economic climate is the cause

of a business' demise. But there is usually more to the story than the most obvious answer. Along the way, I learned some things that I wish I had known before I got started. If you're thinking about running a business, I've got 10 tips to consider that may prove helpful to you along the way.

6 1. Be sure to have more than one major backer. When we started the agency, we put all our chips in the same basket. We launched the business as an arm of Bates, our employer at the time.

7 We capitalized on Bates' entry into strategically focused market research. Bates already had a Hispanic ad agency. So, it seemed natural to build a business that offered psychosocial data on African Americans. This information would give Bates clear-cut ways to predict how cultural differences among blacks affect the buying habits of different segments of the market.

8 Ironically, just as our agency was about to turn profitable, Bates dissolved the relationship. The reason was no one's fault and had nothing to do with either side's respect for the other. I still do business with Bates (now Backer Spielvogel & Bates). It was simply that Saatchi and Saatchi, which had purchased Bates, had a different set of business priorities.

9 Despite all this, our agency survived for four more years. But the loss of that early backing definitely affected our ability to weather the financial storms to come.

10 The motto of all this? Never assume that all the business givens will stay that way, and be sure to line up a diverse set of backers early on in starting your firm.

11 2. Sell something people want to buy. When I went into business, I believed that my agency would provide a necessary and potentially profitable service in the marketplace.

12 I spent nearly a decade in large general-market advertising agencies learning how to develop award-winning strategic advertising. I also have a Ph.D. in psychology, where my primary research had been on black culture. Furthermore, I had sole access to a large database on black consumer preferences, attitudes and media behavior.

13 I was convinced that if I had an opportunity to present a story to a client about their product or service, then they would have to give us the business. I had been on enough new-business pitches to know how this works. How could we miss?

14 It didn't work. We made pitch after pitch presenting data to marketing managers about the black consumer presence within their

brand products. Instead of giving me the business, they would (a) praise me for giving them better insight into and a more sophisticated understanding of the black consumer market, and (b) tell me that despite this compelling story, they didn't feel the need to target this consumer base.

15 For instance, one packaged-goods marketing manager told us our presentation made a lot of sense. But when we tried to follow up, we were told that the company had "other priorities."

16 After a while, I realized that I was trying to sell a very good product that, for whatever reason, few people wanted. Sure, I got some business, but nowhere near the amount I had expected.

17 My advice to you is to realize the real potential for what it is you have to offer and adjust your actions and perceptions accordingly. In other words, do the same kind of in-depth research on your marketplace and industry as you would on the clients you want to land.

18 We looked at the tremendous growth in targeted black advertising and assumed we could expand the marketplace even further. What we failed to see was that most of the African-American ad agencies were not growing much. There was a ceiling on the amount of total business out there. Rather than relying solely on breaking new ground with companies that did not yet have carefully targeted black ad campaigns, we should have been trying to take existing business away from other black ad agencies.

19 3. Pick your partner carefully, and be sure you both have a similar approach to doing business. This one should come as no surprise given that my agency changed from a two-person firm into a one-person operation. But what I have to say may be a surprise.

20 Business isn't about making money. Oh yes, that's part of it, but not even the most important part. No, business is about power, decision-making power, control-over-your-destiny power.

21 If you take on a partner or are invited to be one, make sure that you have a clear understanding of the power relationship between you.

22 Those businesses where the power definitions are clear between the partners have a better chance of maximizing those partners' efforts to ensure the survival of the business, instead of continually putting the business through internecine bouts.

23 What happened to me and my partner? We had the same *goals* for the agency, but two radically different *approaches* to running an agency.

24 For example, we had different philosophies about landing new business. My partner believed that to get business one had to socialize and make contacts. It was something she did very well. In contrast, I

believed, during the formal presentation process, you had to create a legitimate reason for the company to need your services. This was something I did very well.

25 What we encountered in working together was simply a clash in styles. Plus, we both believed strongly that our individual approach to landing clients was the *right* way.

26 Of course, successful agencies have been built on both approaches to landing new business. But because we had a new business with limited resources, it was difficult to try to take the agency in two different directions at the same time.

27 The problem here is that it's not easy to discover beforehand what control your potential partner really wants over the direction of the business. Ordinary conversation may give you some clues about how each of you views the process of doing business and a feel for one another's goals and values. But coming to a clear understanding of the issues of power and control requires straightforward discussion. You need to be direct with each other *before* you form a partnership.

28 To understand what someone wants out of a business you must really get to know a potential partner. Details about his or her upbringing, family life, social style, fears, expectations, business philosophy and priorities are all key.

29 The success of your venture will require a productive balance of powers—and way of doing things—between the two of you.

30 4. Never stop marketing your business. The breakup in our partnership happened during 1990 and 1991, just before the recession and the really tough times hit. Nonetheless, my partner and I were so distracted dealing with interpersonal issues that we had no time for marketing to new clients.

31 The result was that during the year the partnership was splitting up, I managed to pitch only two pieces of major business, instead of the 12 pitches I had been making before. Needless to say, this had a big impact on total billings.

32 My advice to you: Market, market, market. No matter how well you've done before or how well you're doing now, keep that new business coming in the door.

33 5. Don't hire your friends to work for you. Boy, that sounds cold. But does it sound less cold to lay off, or even worse, fire a friend?

34 When you hire a friend, you are less likely to make strictly business decisions about that person, and any time this happens, you've put yourself in a compromising situation.

35 Objectivity helps an effective boss get his employees to produce great work, but there is nothing objective about friendship. For instance, I should have laid people off at the first stroke of losing business. But because I had personal ties with some friends I had hired, I kept them on payroll even during tough times.

36 And speaking about being a boss . . .

37 6. Don't be a manager. Be a boss. I was a very good people person when I worked in corporate America. I helped a lot of coworkers get through problems and issues in their lives and they liked working with me. So, naturally, I thought those skills were necessary when I started doing my own thing.

38 Yes. And no.

39 Being a good capitalist means keeping your eyes on the prize. How is what I am doing today going to help the business be more profitable tomorrow than it was yesterday?

40 In any business dealings, there will be distractions that can keep you from focusing on that prize.

41 As a boss with a small business to run, you have no one to fall back on if someone has problems, plus you can't afford the time to support someone emotionally. Trying to be a "good guy" also breaks down your authority, and it wastes energy you could be putting into running your company better.

42 If someone has a personal problem, don't make it your problem. If the problem is affecting productivity and there is a work-related solution to it, implement it. If someone's problems interfere with his or her getting the job done and there is no way that the job can be restructured to provide a solution, replace that person as quickly as possible.

43 7. Charge what you are worth. This primarily concerns those in the service industry where pricing can be somewhat variable.

44 Calculate what your contribution is to your client's bottom line and then charge accordingly. Many people will want your services at reduced fee because they perceive you as hungry or as offering a service that can be derived from other sources. This perception may also be influenced negatively if you are black.

45 If our agency had charged our clients what the value of our services were really worth, we would have been profitable before the tough times hit. You also need to charge a rate that takes into consideration what it costs you to service a particular client. Some accounts required so many agency man hours that we wound up not getting paid for the actual amount of overhead we were investing.

46 In other words, set your fees high enough to reflect what those services really cost you to provide. Be prepared to make a case for why your charges are what they are, and stick to it. Obviously, I am not suggesting inflexibility. You should make adjustments in what you would charge a *Fortune* 500 company, compared with a mom-and-pop store. But keep in mind, all clients will demand your best work, no matter what price you agree on.

47 8. Turn down bad clients. You won't know whether someone is going to be a good or bad client until you start working with them. However, as soon as you recognize that you've landed a bad client, get rid of them—no matter how much cash you are letting walk out the door.

48 Recognizing them is a lot easier when you're supplying goods and products as opposed to services. In the product industries, a bad client is someone who doesn't pay within 30 days.

49 In the service industry, someone who's paying within 30 days could still create havoc in your business. How? By placing demands on the business that, in the process of fulfilling the work requirements, end up poisoning your work environment.

50 This position can take a variety of forms, but let me mention one example so you get the flavor. We had a packaged-goods client with top executives who had a need for control. Every time we would work on this client's account, these executives would pit one of our staffers against another. Each person who was working on the account would end up getting criticized to another staffer working on the account. The result was that they were demoralizing my people.

51 Everyone in your company can get tangled up in it when there is a client who is consciously trying to manipulate egos.

52 All the usual ways of stopping any intentional miscommunications are done routinely in large companies through written reports. In a small business, few have the time to write "CYA" memos.

53 Why would any client try to undermine your business in this way? The worst clients create trouble so that they either can get more services for free or can justify not paying for services already rendered.

54 If you want to learn from my experience, save yourself the mental anguish. Resign the account and keep your sanity.

55 9. Make sure you save for a rainy day. The advice here is tricky. Once you start a business, you must realize that the business is not you, and that as soon as you bring other people into the venture, it takes on a life all its own. Like any newborn, it has an insatiable appetite and will take all the nurturing you have to offer. That nurturance comes in two forms: capital and psychic energy.

56 You run a significant risk of losing your shirt when you start a business, and it's essential never to forget that. However, as I learned the hard way, taking all of your personal cash and pouring it into your business is ill-advised, no matter how much you are on the verge of making it. Just as ill-advised is pouring so much of yourself into the enterprise that you have no life outside the office.

57 Therefore, prepare for every contingency, even failure. That's not a defeatist attitude; it's a realistic strategy. Even generals preparing for battle leave themselves a way out so that they can fight again another day. Making sure that you can play the game another day—by having some money put away as well as by keeping your emotional options open—means that a failed business can be thought of as a single chapter in your life, rather than your entire story.

58 10. Know what you want to do with your life the day after. The day after what?

59 The day after you realize that your business is either a success or a failure. If the business is a true success, then for all intents and purposes, it can run without you, which means you'll need something else to do next. If it's a failure, then you don't have to worry about it anymore, which could leave a big hole in your day-to-day life.

60 Either way, you'll have time on your hands. I know because I had prepared no contingency plans in case something happened to my business. As a result of my lack of personal disaster planning, despite all the setbacks, I kept automatically looking for more business for our agency to do, rather than heading out to hunt for a marketing job on someone else's payroll.

61 The moral of this story is: If you know what you want to do the day after, you're giving yourself an alternative that will have meaning over and above what you derive from being associated with your business.

62 Trust me. That's a good idea.

63 These 10 confessions represent the personal knowledge I gained from being an entrepreneur. Now that I know them, I am ready to write a happier ending to the book of my business life. Hopefully, you can learn something from them, too.

Understanding Meaning

1. What appear to have been the chief *causes* for the demise of Jamison & Associates?
2. What lessons did Jamison feel he learned about running a business versus creating advertising?

3. What advice does Jamison offer about selecting partners and employees?
4. Jamison tells readers to "be a boss." What are the elements of a good boss?
5. *Critical Thinking:* Many of Jamison's statements are negative, telling readers what not to do. Does this emphasis on avoiding mistakes suggest that he feels many people who dream of opening their own businesses are naive? What does it take to start and maintain a business? What do people often overlook?

Evaluating Strategy

1. What impact does the title have in a magazine dedicated to success and achievement?
2. How effective is the opening *narration?*
3. How does Jamison use *analysis* to diagnose the forces that caused his business to fail?
4. What would make this article easier to read?

Appreciating Language

1. Jamison uses tips like "save for a rainy day." Does this homey language work in this article?
2. What tone comes across in this essay? Does it convey any sense of bitterness or blame seeking?

Connections across the Disciplines

1. Leadership is a critical aspect of running a business. How does Jamison's concept of "being a boss" compare to the views of leadership presented in Michael Korda's "What Makes a Leader?" (page 189)? Do they define leadership differently?
2. Do you see a difference between Jamison and Ellen Goodman's "company man" (page 185)?

Writing Suggestions

1. Write a similar essay in which you offer advice to readers based on a failure you have experienced. Tell readers, for example, how to avoid paying

too much for a car, renting the wrong apartment, losing a lawsuit, or failing a college course.

2. *Collaborative Writing:* Discuss with a number of students the pros and cons of owning a business. Take notes and then work together to write a set of instructions making use of comparison to demonstrate the advantages and disadvantages of working for yourself instead of someone else.

WRITING BEYOND THE CLASSROOM

PRESIDENT WILLIAM J. CLINTON

Bill Clinton (1946–) was elected the forty-second president of the United States in 1992. Like all presidents, his signature is applied to numerous documents each day, many of which he and his predecessors have not read. Though many documents produced by the chief executive are controversial or historical, the majority concern routine matters of policy and bureaucracy. This memo directs heads of federal departments and agencies to follow specific directions for landscaping government property.

Memorandum on Environmentally Beneficial Landscaping

1 *As you read this document, note the tone, style, and wording. You may wish to refer to the FBI report (page 87) for another sample of government writing.*

2 *April 26, 1994*

3 *Memorandum for the Heads of Executive Departments and Agencies*

4 *Subject:* Environmentally and Economically Beneficial Practices on Federal Landscaped Grounds

5 The Report of the National Performance Review contains recommendations for a series of environmental actions, including one to increase environmentally and economically beneficial landscaping practices at Federal facilities and federally funded projects. Environmentally beneficial landscaping entails utilizing techniques that complement and enhance the local environment and seek to minimize the adverse affects that the landscaping will have on it. In particular, this means using regionally native plants and employing landscaping practices and technologies that conserve water and prevent pollution.

6 These landscaping practices should benefit the environment, as well as generate long-term costs savings for the Federal Government.

For example, the use of native plants not only protects our natural heritage and provides wildlife habitat, but also can reduce fertilizer, pesticide, and irrigation demands and their associated costs because native plants are suited to the local environment and climate.

7 Because the Federal Government owns and landscapes large areas of land, our stewardship presents a unique opportunity to provide leadership in this area and to develop practical and cost-effective methods to preserve and protect that which has been entrusted to us. Therefore, for Federal grounds, Federal projects, and federally funded projects, I direct that agencies shall, where cost-effective and to the extent practicable:

8 (a) use regionally native plants for landscaping;

9 (b) design, use, or promote construction practices that minimize adverse effects on the natural habitat;

10 (c) seek to prevent pollution by, among other things, reducing fertilizer and pesticide use, using integrated pest management techniques, recycling green waste, and minimizing runoff. Landscaping practices that reduce the use of toxic chemicals provide one approach for agencies to reach reduction goals established in Executive Order No. 12856, "Federal Compliance with Right-To-Know Laws and Pollution Prevention Requirements;"

11 (d) implement water-efficient practices, such as the use of mulches, efficient irrigation systems, audits to determine exact landscaping water-use needs, and recycled or reclaimed water and the selecting and siting of plants in a manner that conserves water and controls soil erosion. Landscaping practices, such as planting regionally native shade trees around buildings to reduce air conditioning demands, can also provide innovative measures to meet the energy consumption reduction goal established in Executive Order No. 12902, "Energy Efficiency and Water Conservation at Federal Facilities"; and

12 (e) create outdoor demonstrations incorporating native plants, as well as pollution prevention and water conservation techniques, to promote awareness of the environmental and economic benefits of implementing this directive. Agencies are encouraged to develop other methods for sharing information on landscaping advances with interested nonfederal parties.

13 In order to assist agencies in implementing this directive, the Federal Environmental Executive shall:

14 (a) establish an interagency working group to develop recommendations for guidance, including compliance with the requirements of the National Environmental Policy Act, 42 U.S.C. 4321, 4331–4335, and 4341–4347, and training needs to implement this directive. The recommendations are to be developed by November 1994; and

15 (b) issue the guidance by April 1995. To the extent practicable, agencies shall incorporate this guidance into their landscaping programs and practices by February 1996.

16 In addition, the Federal Environmental Executive shall establish annual awards to recognize outstanding landscaping efforts of agencies and individual employees. Agencies are encouraged to recognize exceptional performance in the implementation of this directive through their awards programs.

17 Agencies shall advise the Federal Environmental Executive by April 1996 on their progress in implementing this directive.

18 To enhance landscaping options and awareness, the Department of Agriculture shall conduct research on the suitability, propagation, and use of native plants for landscaping. The Department shall make available to agencies and the public the results of this research.

William J. Clinton

Understanding Meaning

1. What is the underlying policy or philosophy behind these directives?
2. What message is the administration hoping to send to the public and private sector?
3. What specific steps are agencies ordered to follow?
4. *Critical Thinking:* What does this document reveal about the way the government shapes the society we live in? What other subtle messages does the government send?

Evaluating Strategy

1. What do you notice about the format of this memorandum?
2. How does the writer address readers? What assumptions are being made?

Appreciating Language

1. What do you notice about the tone, style, and word choice of the memorandum?

2. Is this stated in what S. I. Hayakawa (page 464) would call "report" statements?

Connections across the Disciplines

1. How is the reader addressed differently in this set of instructions than in Charles N. Jamison Jr.'s article (page 523)?
2. Review Jamaica Kincaid's article "Alien Soil" (page 147). How is the American government attempting to impose its will and philosophy on the landscape in a manner different from the British? Do they share similarities? Do governments see the land as a slate to write on?

Writing Suggestions

1. Practice writing a government directive by drafting a short memo to fellow students instructing them to recycle papers and soft-drink cans.
2. *Collaborative Writing:* Using this memorandum as a prompt, discuss the role of government with a group of students. Should federal policy dictate to the public on matters such as the environment? Is this an acceptable use of resources? Does it help stimulate change, or can it lead to wasteful projects? Take notes of your group's comments, and then work together on wording a memo outlining your views. Make sure conflicting ideas are stated in neutral terms.

THE AMERICAN RED CROSS

The American Red Cross First Aid and Safety Handbook *includes these instructions on how to perform the Heimlich maneuver, a lifesaving technique used to unblock the airways of choking victims.*

The Heimlich Maneuver

As you read these instructions, imagine how readers would use them in the case of an actual emergency. Consider how quickly you could read and follow these steps to save a life.

CONSCIOUS ADULT OR CHILD (OVER 1 YEAR OF AGE)

1 • Ask the victim if he or she is choking. If the victim can't answer, the obstruction is life-threatening. Call EMS.

2 • Tell the victim you are going to try to help and ask for permission to proceed.

3 DO NOT interfere if the victim is coughing forcefully and has good air exchange (is able to breathe in and out). However, be ready to act instantly if the victim's air exchange worsens.

4 DO NOT pinch or poke an object that is lodged in the victim's throat. This might force it farther down the airway.

5 1. Perform abdominal thrusts as described below. (If you cannot get your arms around a large victim to give abdominal thrusts, or if the victim is noticeably pregnant, use chest thrusts. . . .)
2. Stand behind the victim.
3. Wrap your arms around the victim's waist.

4. Make a fist. Place the thumb side of your fist in the middle of the victim's abdomen, just above the navel and well below the lower tip of the breastbone. . . .
5. Grasp your fist with your other hand.
6. Keeping your elbows out, press your fist with a quick, upward thrust into the victim's abdomen. . . . Each thrust is a separate attempt to clear the victim's airway by forcing air out the windpipe.
7. Continue performing this maneuver until the obstruction is cleared or the victim loses consciousness.

   If the victim loses consciousness, give first aid for an unconscious victim. . . .
8. If the victim starts having seizures, see **Seizures**. . . .

MORE ON THE SUBJECT

6 Keep the victim still and get medical help. All choking victims should have a medical examination, since complications can arise not only from the incident but also from the first aid measures that were taken.

Understanding Meaning

1. What is the very first step you should follow?
2. Why should you ask permission to proceed?
3. What should you not do if someone is choking?
4. Why should a choking victim receive medical attention even if the foreign object is dislodged?

Evaluating Strategy

1. How effectively organized is this page? Can it be understood quickly?
2. How do numbered points, illustrations, and typeface variations assist rapid reading?

Appreciating Language

1. What does the level of diction and word choice reveal about the intended audience?
2. Why does the author refrain from using medical terminology?

Connections across the Disciplines

1. Write a set of instructions on first aid, car or home repair, or campus security to be read in an emergency. Use visual aids and short, direct sentences to communicate in as few words as possible.
2. *Collaborative Writing:* Analyze the effectiveness of these instructions with a group of students. Have members read the instructions and then close their books. One person should refer to the instructions and quiz the group on the steps. Note how much people remembered, and identify areas that more than one person forgot. Based on your group's experiences, work collaboratively to write a short analysis, suggesting changes for greater readability if needed.

GUIDELINES FOR PROCESS WRITING

1. **Define your goal—to explain or to instruct.** Is your purpose to explain how something takes place, or do you seek to instruct readers how to accomplish a specific task?
2. **Evaluate your audience's existing knowledge.** How much does your audience know about the subject? Do any common misconceptions need to be clarified? What terms should be defined?
3. **Define clear starting and ending points.** When does this process begin? What is the end? Readers must have a clear concept of the beginning and end, especially in instructions.
4. **Separate the process into understandable stages or steps.** To explain a process, it is important to break it down into a chain of separate events that makes the process understandable without distorting it. When giving instructions, do not include too many operations in a single step.
5. **Number steps for clarity in the instructions.** Instructions are easier to follow if organized in numbered steps. If interrupted, readers can easily mark their places and later resume the process without confusion.
6. **Consider using visual aids.** Large print, capital letters, bold or italic type, and underlining can highlight text. Graphs, drawings, diagrams, and other visual aids can be beneficial to reinforce both explanatory writing and instructions.
7. **Measure readability of instructions.** Instructions, especially directions people will have to refer to while working, should communicate at a glance. Short sentences and wide spacing between steps are used in cookbooks and repair manuals so a person working in a kitchen or garage can read the text at a distance.
8. **Test your writing.** Because it is easy to skip steps when explaining a process you are familiar with, it is important to have other people read your writing. Other readers can be objective and easily detect missing information.

SUGGESTED TOPICS FOR PROCESS WRITING

General Assignments

Write a process paper on any of the following topics. Assume you are writing for a general, college-educated audience. You may develop your explanation using narratives, comparisons, and definitions. Explain the process as a clearly stated chain of events. Draw from your own experiences.

- How the university processes student applications
- The operation of an appliance such as a microwave, refrigerator, or washing machine
- The process of a disease or disability
- The way small children learn to talk
- The method your employer used in training
- The stages of childbirth
- How a computer virus "infects" a computer
- The way corporations market a new product
- The way the body loses fat through diet or exercise
- How networks select television programs

Write a process paper giving directions to complete a specific task. You may wish to place your instructions in numbered steps rather than standard paragraphs. Remember to highlight any safety hazards.

- How to protect your computer against viruses
- How to purchase a new or used car at the best price
- How to deter a mugger or attacker
- How to quit smoking
- How to find a job
- How to handle sexual harassment on campus or in a job
- How to prepare for an IRS audit
- How to operate a drill press, microscope, or other piece of industrial or scientific equipment
- How to treat a second-degree burn
- How to teach children the importance of saving money

Writing in Context

1. Imagine you have been selected to write a section for a student handbook instructing freshmen how to register for classes. Write a step-by-step paper giving complete instructions. Give exact room numbers, times, and locations. You may wish to refer to a campus map. When you complete a draft of your paper, review it carefully to see if you have left out any pieces of essential information.
2. Select a process you learned on a job, and write instructions suitable for training a new employee. Consider how your job may have changed. Give trainees the benefit of your experience, and add tips that might not be included in the standard job descriptions. Warn readers, for instance, of common problems that arise.

3. Select a process from one of your textbooks, and rewrite it for a sixth-grade class. Simplify the language, and use analogies sixth graders would understand.

PROCESS CHECKLIST

1. Is the process clearly defined?
2. Do you supply background information readers need?
3. Is the information easy to follow? Is the chain of events or are the steps logically arranged?
4. Could the text be enhanced by large print, bold or italic type, diagrams, or charts?
5. Are your instructions complete? Do readers know when one step is over and another begins?
6. Do your instructions alert readers to normal changes they might mistake for errors?
7. *Are hazards clearly stated?*
8. Did you test your instructions with readers?

9

Cause and Effect

Determining Reasons and Predicting Results

WHAT IS CAUSE AND EFFECT?

What led to the stock market crash of 1929? Why did the *Hindenburg* explode? What caused the Soviet Union to collapse? How did Microsoft corner the software market? How will budget cuts affect education? Would a handgun ban lower street crime? Can a Supreme Court ruling prevent frivolous law suits? The answers to these questions call for the use of *cause and effect,* writing that either seeks to establish reasons why something occurred or to predict future results.

Historians devote much of their time determining the causes of events. Did Lenin cause the Russian Revolution or did the revolution create Lenin? Why did Hitler rise to power? What led to the women's movement of the 1970s? Historians also consider the ramifications of current events and speculate about the future. Will another oil crisis occur? How will a change in American foreign policy affect chances for peace in the Middle East?

Nearly all professions and disciplines engage in cause-and-effect reasoning. Marketers try to determine why a product succeeded. Engineers work to discover why a test engine failed. Medical researchers measure the results of a new drug. City planners predict the effect a major earthquake would have on emergency services. Educators consider if curriculum changes will improve Scholastic Aptitude Test scores. Federal Aviation Administration (FAA) investigators examine wreckage to establish why a plane crashed.

Many of the research papers you will be assigned in college and the letters and reports you write in your future career will be developed using cause and effect. Identifying the reasons why something occurred can be formidable. Determining future outcomes, no matter how much data are examined or how many experiments are conducted, can remain largely guesswork.

Deduction and Induction

Writers often formulate cause-and-effect papers using deduction and induction. *Deduction* is a form of logic in which a *major premise* or general rule is applied to a *minor premise* or specific instance in order to reach a *conclusion.* You may be familiar with this classic example of deduction:

Major Premise: All cows are mammals.
Minor Premise: Bessie is a cow.
Conclusion: Bessie is a mammal.

This illustration, though famous, fails to show the practical value of deduction. Other examples should give you an idea of how often we use deduction:

Major Premise: All full-time students are eligible for financial aid.
Minor Premise: Sandra Lopez is a full-time student.
Conclusion: Sandra Lopez is eligible for financial aid.

Major Premise: The student health plan is only available to California residents.
Minor Premise: Amy Kwan is a resident of New York.
Conclusion: Amy Kwan cannot join the student health plan.

Deduction can be used to solve problems and answer questions: Are dental exams deductible on my income tax? Can I sublet my apartment? Will the college give me a refund if I drop a class in the fourth week? All of these questions form a minor premise. The IRS rules, apartment leases, and college policies you consult for answers serve as major premises.

Deduction can be used to help determine both causes and effects. Was a plane crash caused by a defective part?

Major Premise: FAA regulations consider this part defective if three bolts are missing.
Minor Premise: One bolt was missing from this part.
Conclusion: This part was not defective.

How will an increase in bus fares affect ridership?

MAJOR PREMISE: Bus ridership declines with fare increases.
MINOR PREMISE: The city authorized a fifty-cent fare increase.
CONCLUSION: Bus ridership will decline.

Problems occur with deductive reasoning if the major and minor premises are not precisely stated. The statement that "All full-time students are eligible for financial aid" might be clearer if it included a definition of who is considered a full-time student: "All students taking twelve credits are eligible for financial aid." Other problems arise if the major premise is subject to interpretation. A warranty for snow tires might refuse to cover "improper use." Is off-road driving considered "improper"? How much damage can be considered "normal wear and tear"? Some major premises may prove to be false or require qualification:

MAJOR PREMISE: Democrats are antibusiness.

Are *all* Democrats antibusiness? What is meant by *antibusiness?*

MAJOR PREMISE: Gun control reduces crime.

Can this be proven? Could a drop in crime in a city that passed gun control be caused by other factors—a decrease in unemployment, a shift in population, or more effective policing?

Induction, unlike deduction, does not open with a major premise. Instead it presents and interprets data and then makes a conclusion:

X X X X X
X X X X
X X X X X
X X X X
X X X

X = Data
Inductive Leap → Conclusion

The *X*'s in the diagram could represent stolen cars, the number of computers sold last month, blood tests of patients taking a new fertility drug, satellite photographs, interviews with consumers, or evidence collected at a crime scene. Based on a review of the evidence, a conclusion is drawn: Car thefts are increasing in the suburbs, the new fertility drug damages red blood cells, coastline erosion is worse than last year, the consumers' major complaint is poor service, or the murder suspect is a Caucasian female with O-positive blood and dyed hair.

As these examples illustrate, effective induction requires a large body of valid evidence to achieve reasonable conclusions. Ford Motor Company would have to interview more than a handful of Taurus owners to determine customer satisfaction. Medical researchers must rule out other reasons for damaged red-blood cells. As the diagram notes, the movement from specific details to conclusion requires an *inductive leap*. No matter how much evidence is discovered and examined, no absolute assurance can be made that the conclusion is totally true.

The best demonstration of inductive reasoning takes place in a courtroom. In a criminal case the prosecutor tells members of the jury that if they examine all the evidence they will conclude that the defendant is guilty *beyond a reasonable doubt.* The defense attorney will attempt to raise doubt by providing alternative interpretations and by introducing conflicting evidence. He or she will tell the jury that *reasonable doubt* exists and that not enough evidence has been found to reach a conclusion of guilt.

Establishing Causes

By the 1920s surgeons and physicians began noticing that many of their patients with lung cancer were heavy smokers. An observable association was discovered but not clear proof of a cause-and-effect relationship. Not all lung cancer patients smoked, and millions of smokers were free of the disease. Though scientists were concerned, they had no evidence that smoking *caused* cancer. In fact, throughout the 1930s and 1940s cigarette ads featured endorsements by doctors who claimed the calming effect of nicotine reduced stress and prevented stomach ulcers. It was not until 1964 that researchers assembled enough data to convince the surgeon general of the United States to proclaim cigarette smoking a health hazard.

In some instances causes can be established through investigation and research. Doctors can diagnose an infection as the cause of a fever. Accountants can study financial records to discover why a company lost money. But many controversial issues remain subject to debate for decades. Why are men and women different? James Dobson (page 592) argues that biology causes gender differences and cites current research to support his conclusion:

> Careful research is revealing that the basic differences between the sexes are neurological in origin, rather than being purely cultural as ordinarily presumed. As Dr. Richard Restak stated in his book, *The Brain: The Last Frontier:*
>
> > . . . Recent psychological research indicates that many of the differences in brain function between the sexes are innate, biologically determined, and relatively resistant to change through the influences of culture.

Other experts, such as John Archer and Barbara Lloyd, disagree, stating that biology is not responsible for causing gender differences. They even question the possibility of isolating biological factors from cultural influences:

> Even if early gender differences did occur regularly and consistently, this would not necessarily indicate that they were of biological origin. Adults differentiate between baby boys and girls from birth onward, so that we cannot tell whether a particular behavioral gender difference observed during infancy is produced by different parental reactions or by different biological maturation.

When evaluating a writer attempting to establish a cause, consider the amount of evidence, the degree of objective analysis, and the willingness to qualify assertions.

Predicting Results

In 1936 the *Literary Digest* predicted that Alf Landon would defeat Franklin Roosevelt in his bid for a second term as president. The editors based their prediction on a detailed telephone survey. By randomly selecting names from phone books and asking people whom they planned to vote for, the surveyors assumed they would get an accurate prediction. Their responses from men and women, government employees and business executives, Italians and Jews, farmers and factory workers, and young and old strongly indicated a preference for Landon. But their research failed to accurately predict the outcome of the election because the survey method did not measure a significant population. In 1936 many Americans could not afford telephones, and these economically deprived voters tended to favor Roosevelt.

Predicting future outcomes can be challenging because evidence may be difficult to collect or may be subject to various interpretations. In addition, numerous unforeseen factors can take place to alter expected events. A school board that determines to close schools because of a declining birth rate may fail to account for an influx of immigrants or the closure of private schools that would place more students into the public system.

In "Swept Away" (page 574), Jodi Jacobson asserts that global warming will dramatically affect the climate in the next century:

> Most scientists now agree that a global warming has begun. Its causes are by now depressingly familiar: Greenhouse gases generated by human activity are accumulating in the atmosphere and trapping the sun's radiant heat. These gases include carbon dioxide and nitrous oxides from the combustion of wood and fossil fuels, chlorofluorocarbons (used as a refrigerant and in industrial applications), and methane (from ruminant animals and rice paddies). Meanwhile, population pressures in the Third World are forcing wholesale forest clearing for fuel, farmland and living space. The result is fewer trees left to recapture the chief greenhouse gas, carbon dioxide.

Jacobson continues to predict that global warming will cause the polar ice caps to melt. The rising oceans will flood cities, consume islands, and devastate low-lying deltas.

Jocelyn Tomkin, on the other hand, dismisses these grim predictions. Tomkin's article "Hot Air" (page 585) cautions that the effects of global warming may not be severe. In fact, no global warming may be happening at all:

> The observational evidence that global warming is actually increasing is very shaky. Some researchers claim to see an increase in global warming of about 0.8 degree since 1860. Although average temperatures since then have increased by this much, it's doubtful that the rise reflects carbon-dioxide-induced global warming.

> The large year-to-year fluctuations of average temperature . . . mean that the behavior of average global temperature is somewhat like that of a stock market index. Spotting a "real" temperature trend is like deciding if one is in a bull or a bear market. . . .
>
> Moreover, natural causes, rather than the increase in carbon dioxide, are a more likely explanation of the temperature increase. Most of the rise took place prior to 1940, *before* the main increase in the carbon-dioxide level.

When examining writing that predicts future effects, consider the amount of evidence presented, the recognition of other factors that may affect results, and the use of critical thinking.

CRITICAL THINKING FOR CAUSE-AND-EFFECT WRITING

When writing cause-and-effect essays, avoid these common traps, many of which are known as logical fallacies.

1. **Avoid mistaking a time relationship for a cause** (post hoc ergo propter hoc). If your brakes fail after taking your car into the dealer for an oil change, does that mean the mechanics are to blame? Can the president take credit for a drop in unemployment six months after signing a labor bill? Because events occur in time, it can be easy to assume an action that precedes another is a cause. The mechanics may have not touched your brakes, which were bound to wear out with or without an oil change. A drop in unemployment could be caused by a decline in interest rates or an upsurge in exports and may have nothing to do with a labor bill. *Do not assume events were caused by preceding events.*
2. **Do not mistake an effect for a cause.** Early physicians saw fever as a cause of disease rather than as an effect or symptom. If you observe that children with poor reading skills watch a lot of television, you might easily assume that television interferes with their reading. In fact excessive viewing could be a symptom. Because they have trouble reading, they watch television.
3. **Do not confuse associations with causes.** For years researchers argued that marijuana use led to heroin addiction. The evidence was clear. Nearly every heroin addict interviewed admitted to starting with marijuana. But since most addicts also drank beer, smoked cigarettes, chewed gum, and attended high school, this association could not alone be con-

sidered proof. Associations can be compelling and command attention, but they are not proof of a cause-and-effect relationship.

4. **Anticipate unexpected changes.** Many researchers qualify their predictions with the statement "all things being equal, we can anticipate . . ." But conditions never remain frozen. An increase in sales following a major ad campaign could be caused by a competitor going out of business or a drop in unemployment rather than by television commercials.
5. **Avoid "slippery slope" interpretations.** Do not assume that changes will start a trend that will snowball without restraint. If the government allows euthanasia for the terminally ill, you cannot argue that eventually all the elderly and handicapped will be put to death.
6. **Realize that past performance, though an important factor, cannot predict future results.** During the oil crisis of the 1970s, the price of oil soared from $10 to $40 a barrel. Alarmists predicted financial disaster when Americans would have to pay $50–$100 a barrel for oil to run cars and to fuel industry. But the dramatic price escalation was short-lived. Price increases spurred exploration for new oil fields and launched conservation efforts. Soon the world was awash in surplus oil, and prices dropped to precrisis levels. *Past trends cannot be assumed to continue into the future.*

READING CAUSE AND EFFECT

When reading the cause-and-effect entries in this chapter, keep these questions in mind.

Meaning

1. Is the writer seeking to establish a cause or to predict results?
2. What is the source of the evidence? A writer opposed to atomic power citing only studies commissioned by an antinuclear group is not as credible as one who presents data collected by neutral organizations.
3. Are alternative interpretations possible? Does a rise in the number of people receiving food stamps mean an increase in poverty, or does it reflect better government assistance?

Strategy

1. Does the writer mistake a symptom for a cause? A survey revealing that 90 percent of batterers in domestic violence cases are abusing alcohol

might lead to a call for more treatment centers. In fact alcohol abuse and domestic violence may both result from unemployment.
2. Does the writer assume past trends will continue into the future?
3. Does the essay rest on unproven assumptions?
4. Does the writer demonstrate skills in critical thinking?
5. Does the author use narratives or comparisons to demonstrate his or her conclusions?

Language

1. Does the author's choice of words indicate bias?
2. How does the writer introduce technical terms? Are definitions supplied?
3. What does the tone and style of the entry suggest about the intended audience?

GEORGE ORWELL

George Orwell (1903–1950) was born Eric Blair in India where his father served as a British civil servant. After attending Eton, he chose to join the Indian Imperial Police rather than attend university. He resigned after five years to become a writer, adopting his famous pseudonym in the process. His first book Down and Out in Paris and London *described his experiences living with the homeless. A series of novels followed, including* Burmese Days, *based on his years in Asia. An early environmentalist, Orwell questioned the value of technological "progress." His last two books* Animal Farm *and* Nineteen Eighty-Four *earned him an international reputation.*

Pleasure Spots

In this 1946 Tribune *review, Orwell pondered how pleasure resorts envisioned by postwar planners would affect human beings. An air-conditioned resort with indoor pools and buffets, Orwell argues, can have the same deadening effects as a brutal dictatorship. This review reflects some of the issues Orwell would discuss in a much bleaker way in* Nineteen Eighty-Four.

1 Some months ago I cut out of a shiny magazine some paragraphs written by a female journalist and describing the pleasure resort of the future. She had recently been spending some time at Honolulu, where the rigours of war do not seem to have been very noticeable. However, "a transport pilot . . . told me that with all the inventiveness packed into this war, it was a pity someone hadn't found out how a tired and life-hungry man could relax, rest, play poker, drink, and make love, all at once, and round the clock, and come out of it feeling good and fresh and ready for the job again." This reminded her of an entrepreneur she had met recently who was planning a "pleasure spot which he thinks will catch on tomorrow as dog racing and dance halls did yesterday." The entrepreneur's dream is described in some detail:

> 2 His blue-prints pictured a space covering several acres, under a series of sliding roofs—for the British weather is unreliable—and with a central space spread over with an immense dance floor made of translucent

> plastic which can be illuminated from beneath. Around it are grouped other functional spaces, at different levels. Balcony bars and restaurants commanding high views of the city roofs, and ground-level replicas. A battery of skittle alleys. Two blue lagoons: one, periodically agitated by waves, for strong swimmers, and another, a smooth and summery pool, for playtime bathers. Sunlight lamps over the pools to simulate high summer on days when the roofs don't slide back to disclose a hot sun in a cloudless sky. Rows of bunks on which people wearing sun-glasses and slips can lie and start a tan or deepen an existing one under a sun-ray lamp.
>
> 3 Music seeping through hundreds of grills connected with a central distributing stage, where dance or symphonic orchestras play or the radio programme can be caught, amplified, and disseminated. Outside, two 1,000-car parks. One, free. The other, an open-air cinema drive-in, cars queueing to move through turnstiles, and the film thrown on a giant screen facing a row of assembled cars. Uniformed male attendants check the cars, provide free aid and water, sell petrol and oil. Girls in white satin slacks take orders for buffet dishes and drinks, and bring them on trays.

4 Whenever one hears such phrases as "pleasure spot," "pleasure resort," "pleasure city," it is difficult not to remember the often-quoted opening of Coleridge's "Kubla Khan."

5 In Xanadu did Kubla Khan
A stately pleasure-dome decree:
Where Alph, the sacred river, ran
Through caverns measureless to man
Down to a sunless sea.
So twice five miles of fertile ground
With walls and towers were girdled round:
And there were gardens bright with sinuous rills
Where blossomed many an incense-bearing tree;
And here were forests ancient as the hills,
Enfolding sunny spots of greenery.

6 But it will be seen that Coleridge has got it all wrong. He strikes a false note straight off with that talk about "sacred" rivers and "measureless" caverns. In the hands of the above-mentioned entrepreneur, Kubla Khan's project would have become something quite different.

The caverns, air-conditioned, discreetly lighted and with their original rocky interior buried under layers of tastefully-coloured plastics, would be turned into a series of tea-grottoes in the Moorish, Caucasian or Hawaiian styles. Alph, the sacred river, would be dammed up to make an artificially-warmed bathing pool, while the sunless sea would be illuminated from below with pink electric lights, and one would cruise over it in real Venetian gondolas each equipped with its own radio set. The forests and "spots of greenery" referred to by Coleridge would be cleaned up to make way for glass-covered tennis courts, a bandstand, a roller-skating rink and perhaps a nine-hole golf course. In short, there would be everything that a "life-hungry" many could desire.

7 I have no doubt that, all over the world, hundreds of pleasure resorts similar to the one described above are now being planned, and perhaps are even being built. It is unlikely that they will be finished—world events will see to that—but they represent faithfully enough the modern civilised man's idea of pleasure. Something of the kind is already partially attained in the more magnificent dance halls, movie palaces, hotels, restaurants and luxury liners. On a pleasure cruise or in a Lyons Corner House one already gets something more than a glimpse of this future paradise. Analysed, its main characteristics are these:

8
1. One is never alone.
2. One never does anything for oneself.
3. One is never within sight of wild vegetation or natural objects of any kind.
4. Light and temperature are always artificially regulated.
5. One is never out of the sound of music.

9 The music—and if possible it should be the same music for everybody—is the most important ingredient. Its function is to prevent thought and conversation, and to shut out any natural sound, such as the song of birds or the whistling of the wind, that might otherwise intrude. The radio is already consciously used for this purpose by innumerable people. In very many English homes the radio is literally never turned off, though it is manipulated from time to time so as to make sure that only light music will come out of it. I know people who will keep the radio playing all through a meal and at the same time continue talking just loudly enough for the voices and the music to cancel out. This is done with a definite purpose. The music prevents the conversation from becoming serious or even coherent, while the

chatter of voices stops one from listening attentively to the music and thus prevents the onset of that dreaded thing, thought. For

10 The lights must never go out.
The music must always play,
Lest we should see where we are;
Lost in a haunted wood,
Children afraid of the dark
Who have never been happy or good.

11 It is difficult not to feel that the unconscious aim in the most typical modern pleasure resorts is a return to the womb. For there, too, one was never alone, one never saw daylight, the temperature was always regulated, one did not have to worry about work or food, and one's thoughts, if any, were drowned by a continuous rhythmic throbbing.

12 When one looks at Coleridge's very different conception of a "pleasure dome," one sees that it revolves partly round gardens and partly round caverns, rivers, forests and mountains with "deep romantic chasms"—in short, round what is called Nature. But the whole notion of admiring Nature, and feeling a sort of religious awe in the presence of glaciers, deserts or waterfalls, is bound up with the sense of man's littleness and weakness against the power of the universe. The moon is beautiful partly because we cannot reach it, the sea is impressive because one can never be sure of crossing it safely. Even the pleasure one takes in a flower—and this is true even of a botanist who knows all there is to be known about the flower—is dependent partly on the sense of mystery. But meanwhile man's power over Nature is steadily increasing. With the aid of the atomic bomb we could literally move mountains: We could even, so it is said, alter the climate of the earth by melting the polar ice-caps and irrigating the Sahara. Isn't there, therefore, something sentimental and obscurantist in preferring bird-song to swing music and in wanting to leave a few patches of wildness here and there instead of covering the whole surface of the earth with a network of *Autobahnen* flooded by artificial sunlight?

13 The question only arises because in exploring the physical universe man has made no attempt to explore himself. Much of what goes by the name of pleasure is simply an effort to destroy consciousness. If

one started by asking, what is man? what are his needs? how can he best express himself? one would discover that merely having the power to avoid work and live one's life from birth to death in electric light and to the tune of tinned music is not a reason for doing so. Man needs warmth, society, leisure, comfort and security: He also needs solitude, creative work and the sense of wonder. If he recognised this he could use the products of science and industrialism eclectically, applying always the same test: Does this make me more human or less human? He would then learn that the highest happiness does *not* lie in relaxing, resting, playing poker, drinking and making love simultaneously. And the instinctive horror which all sensitive people feel at the progressive mechanisation of life would be seen not to be a mere sentimental archaism, but to be fully justified. For man only stays human by preserving large patches of simplicity in his life, while the tendency of many modern inventions—in particular the film, the radio and the aeroplane—is to weaken his consciousness, dull his curiosity, and, in general, drive him nearer to the animals.

Understanding Meaning

1. What is Orwell's attitude toward the glowing description of a pleasure resort?
2. What does Orwell see as the principal effects of these artificial environments?
3. What observations does Orwell make about the radio and music?
4. Why is nature important to Orwell? What do people lose when nature is managed by human designers?
5. *Critical Thinking:* Consider the shopping malls, convention complexes, and resorts you have visited. Have these had the effect Orwell described? Do malls turn us into pleasure-seeking zombies?

Evaluating Strategy

1. Orwell devotes much of his short article to lengthy quotes. How effective is this?
2. What impact does Orwell's numbered list make?
3. *Other Modes:* Where does Orwell use *comparison* to develop his article? What parts can be considered *persuasion?*

Appreciating Language

1. What connotations does Orwell employ to suggest something negative about an environment designed to enhance pleasure and comfort?
2. Review the language used to describe the entrepreneur's dream. What is Orwell reacting against?

Connections across the Disciplines

1. Consider John Ciardi's article on happiness (page 194). How might he react to the pleasure resort designed to create happiness?
2. How does the desire to manage the environment recall many of the issues raised by Jamaica Kincaid's article "Alien Soil" (page 147)?

Writing Suggestions

1. Consider your own reactions to artificial environments. Write a brief essay outlining how malls or resorts affect your behavior. Does an afternoon in a shopping mall deaden your senses? Do you leave relaxed or disoriented?
2. *Collaborative Writing:* Discuss this essay with a group of students. Has concern about the environment changed attitudes toward nature in the past fifty years? Note the comments students make, and work together to draft a short response to Orwell's review.

GLORIA STEINEM

Gloria Steinem (1934–) was born in Toledo, Ohio, and graduated from Smith College. In 1968 she helped found New York *magazine. Three years later she played a major role in creating* Ms. *magazine, which she edited until 1987. A contributor to* Vogue, Cosmopolitan, Time, *and* Esquire, *Steinem has published several books, including* Outrageous Acts and Everyday Rebellions.

Words and Change

In this article, taken from the 1995 edition of Outrageous Acts and Everyday Rebellions, *Steinem reveals how feminism has changed the English language.*

1 Think for a minute. Who were you before this wave of feminism began?

2 Trying to remember our way back into past realities, past rooms, past beliefs, is a first step toward measuring the depth of change. New words and phrases are one organic measure of change. They capture transformations of perception and sometimes of reality itself.

3 Now, we have terms like *sexual harassment* and *battered women.* A few years ago, they were just called *life.*

4 Now, we are becoming the men we wanted to marry. Once, women were trained to marry a doctor, not be one.

5 Now, placing *women's* in front of words like *center* or *newspaper, network* or *rock band,* indicates a positive choice. Before feminism, it was a put-down.

6 Now, we've made the revolutionary discovery that children have two parents. Once, even the kindly Dr. Spock held mothers solely responsible for children.

7 In 1972, a NASA official's view of women's function in space was "sexual diversion [on] long-term flights such as Mars." Now, women are simply *astronauts.*

8 *Art* used to be definable as what men created. *Crafts* were made by women and "natives." Only recently have we discovered they are the same, thus bringing craft techniques into art, and art into everyday life.

9 In the seventies, policemen were protesting against the very idea of working with women. Now, females serve in every major city, and the *policeman* has become the *police officer.*

10 Now, some lesbians have kept their jobs and custody of their children, and have even been elected to public office—all without having to lie or hide. A decade ago, *lesbian* was a secret word, and *lesbian mother* was thought to be a contradiction in terms.

11 Much of this newness in putting accuracy into existing language—for instance, changing *congressmen* to *congresspeople,* or MEN WORKING to PEOPLE WORKING—though even those changes spell major differences in power. But new coinage is also needed to capture new perceptions.

12 Before the current wave of feminism, for instance, we were still discussing *population control,* the enlightened answer to the *population explosion.* Both were negative phrases, the first implying the necessity of an outside force, and the second suggesting endless impersonal breeding. Though feminists were expected to come down on the side of *population control,* one of its underlying assumptions was that women themselves could not possibly be given the power to achieve it. Liberal men who were the population "experts" assumed that women were fulfilled only through motherhood, and so would bear too many babies if given the power to make the choice (unless, of course, they could achieve a higher degree of literacy and education, thus becoming more rational: more like men). On the other hand, very religious or conservative males—who often seemed intent on increasing the numbers of the faithful—treated women as potentially sex-obsessed creatures who would use contraception to avoid childbirth totally, behave sinfully, and thus weaken the patriarchal family and civilization itself.

13 In the seventies, however, feminism transformed the terms of discussion by popularizing *reproductive freedom.* This umbrella term includes safe contraception and abortion, as well as freedom from coerced sterilization (of women or of men) and decent health care during pregnancy and birth. In other words, *reproductive freedom* stated the right of the individual to decide to have or not to have a child. It also allowed the building of new trust and coalitions between white women and women of color, who had rightly suspected that the power implied by *population control* would be directed at some groups more than others.

14 *Reproductive freedom* is simply a way of stating what feminism has been advancing for thousands of years. Witches were freedom fighters for women because they taught contraception and abortion. The mod-

ern contribution is to elevate *reproductive freedom* to a universal human right, at least as basic as freedom of speech. Men who want children must find women willing to bear them; that seems little enough to ask. And governments that want increased rates of population growth must resort to such humane measures as reducing infant mortality, improving health care during pregnancy, sharing the work of child-rearing through child care and equal parenthood, and lengthening people's lives.

15 This reproductive veto power on the part of women is exactly what male supremacists fear most. That's why their authoritarian impulse is so clearly against any sexuality not directed toward childbirth within the patriarchal family. This understanding helped feminists to see why the adversaries of such apparently disparate concerns as contraception and homosexuality are almost always the same. It also helped us to stand together on the side of any consenting, freely chosen sexuality as a rightful form of human expression.

16 In recent years, words like *lover* (whether referring to someone of the same or different gender), *sexual preference,* and *gay rights* have begun to be commonly used. *Homophobia* was invented to describe the irrational fear of sexual expression between people of the same gender, a fear so common in the past that it needed no name. There was also a challenge of such rote phrases as *man-hating lesbian.* As Rita Mae Brown pointed out, it's not lesbians who hate men, but women who depend on men and are thus more likely to be hurt and angry.

17 The feminist spirit has also reclaimed some words with defiance and humor. *Witch, bitch, dyke,* and other formerly pejorative epithets started to turn up in the brave names of feminist groups. A few women artists dubbed their new female imagery *cunt art* in celebration of the discovery that not all sexual symbols were phallic. Humor encouraged the invention of *jockocracy* to describe a certain male obsession with athletics and victory; also *loserism* as a rueful recognition of women's cultural discomfort with anything as "unfeminine" as success. *Supermom* and *Superwoman* were words that relieved us all by identifying the Perfect Wife and Mother, plus the Perfect Career Woman, as humanly impossible goals.

18 The nature of work has been a major area of new understanding, beginning with the word itself. Before feminism, *work* was largely defined as what men did or would do. Thus, a *working woman* was someone who labored outside the home for money, masculine-style. Though still alarmingly common, the term is being protested, especially by

homemakers, who work harder than any other class of workers and are still called people who "don't work." Feminists tend to speak of *work inside the home* or *outside the home,* of *salaried* or *unsalaried workers.* Attributing a financial value to work in the home would go a long way toward making marriage an equal partnership and ending the semantic slavery inherent in the phrase *women who don't work.* It would also begin to untangle the *double-role problem* of millions of women who work both inside and outside the home. Defining human maintenance and home care as a job in itself clarifies that men can and should do it as well as women.

19 In order to reach each other across barriers, feminists have tried to be sensitive to our own linguistically divisive habits: for instance, the racist habit of using images of darkness or blackness as negative (*the dark side of human nature, a black heart, blackmail*) and whiteness as positive (*a white lie, white magic, fair-haired boy*).

20 The difficult efforts to make language more accurate often include the invention of such alternatives as *chairperson* or *spokesperson.* Clearly, only a single-sex organization can have a position of *chairman* or *chairwoman.* An integrated organization needs to have a position that can be occupied by any of its members—thus, *chairperson* or better yet, just *chair.* Given the imbalance of power, however, these gender-free words are sometimes used to neuter women and leave men as the status quo. Thus, a woman might be a *spokesperson,* but a man is still a *spokesman.* Females might become *people,* but men remain *men.*

21 Women sometimes collaborated with our own exclusion by trying to skip to gender-free words too soon. *Humanism* was a special temptation (as in, "Don't be threatened, feminists are really just talking about humanism"). *Androgyny* also raised the hope that female and male cultures could be perfectly blended; but because the female side of the equation has yet to be affirmed, *androgyny* usually tilted toward the male. As a concept, it also raised anxiety levels by conjuring up a unisex or desexed vision, the very opposite of the individuality and freedom that feminism has in mind.

22 *Battered women* is a phrase that named major, long-hidden violence. It helped us to face the fact that the most dangerous place for a woman is in her own home, not in the streets. *Sexual harassment* on the job also exposed a form of intimidation that about a third of all women workers suffer. Naming it allowed women to come forward and legal remedies to be created. By identifying *pornography* (literally, "writing about female slavery") as the preaching of woman hatred and thus

quite different from *erotica,* with its connotation of love and mutuality, there was also the beginning of an understanding that pornography is a major way in which violence and dominance are taught and legitimized.

23 Even *female sexual slavery* (once known by the nineteenth-century racist term *white slavery* because it was the only form of slavery to which whites were also subjected) has been exposed by this wave of feminism. We now know it flourishes in many cities where prostitution and pornography are big business and facts of international life.

24 In response to such realizations of injustice, it's no wonder that *radicalism* began to lose some of its equation with excess or unreasonableness. By exposing the injustice of the sexual caste system and its role as a root of other injustices based on race and class, *radical feminism* laid the groundwork for a common cause among diverse women. And by challenging this masculine-feminine, dominant-passive structure as the chief cause and justification of violence, it also proved that *radicalism* can not only take nonviolent forms, but is the only way to challenge the origins of violence itself.

25 In this wave, words and consciousness have forged ahead, so reality can follow. Measuring the distance between the new and the old evokes the unique part of history that lives in each of us.

UPDATE

26 There are many readers who cannot answer the question, "Who were you before this wave of feminism began?" They were simply born into some degree of feminist consciousness, and their higher expectations, their lack of the female cultural problem of *terminal gratitude,* are necessary for the long path ahead.

27 More women are becoming the men they wanted to marry, but too few men are becoming the women they wanted to marry. That leaves most women with two jobs, one outside the home and one in it, a problem that poor women always had but that is now shared by middle-class women—which means that together, we ought to be able to solve it.

28 In many areas, there is now more recognition of ways that polarized, *either/or* choices, modeled on dividing human nature into "feminine" and "masculine," are disappearing or uniting into *and,* a nonhierarchical, full-circle paradigm. In science, the *new physics* and *chaos theory* have blown apart our old linear, mechanistic, and hierarchical

assumptions. They have helped us think about *linking,* not *ranking.* Feminist scientists offer us *field dependency:* the understanding that nothing can be studied out of its context. In sexuality, the assumption that a person must be either heterosexual or homosexual has begun to loosen up enough to honor both the ancient tradition of *bisexuality* and the new one of individuals who themselves are *transgender* and cross what once seemed an immutable line. Many groups within the lesbian and gay movement now add these two words to their descriptions. People in couples are more likely to speak of each other as *partner* or *life partner,* a relationship that goes beyond the limited connotation of *lover. Homophobic* has been joined by *heterosexist,* a way of describing a person or entity that places heterosexuality at the center, or assumes that all other sexualities are peripheral or nonexistent. *Sexual preference* is frequently replaced by the term *sexual identity,* a way of including both those who feel they were born with a particular sexuality and those who feel they chose it.

29 We're also looking at the way language has allowed the victim to be identified, but not the victimizer. In addition to talking about *how many women have been raped,* for instance, we've begun to talk about *how many men rape.* In addition to talking about *why women don't or can't leave a violent situation,* we're beginning to question *why men are violent.* The term *domestic violence* itself has begun to seem trivializing and inadequate, as if it were a lesser kind of violence. Since violence in the home is actually the training ground for and origin of most other violence, *original violence* is one suggested alternative. In these dozen years, *hate crimes* have finally begun to include crimes against women as well as those directed at people of a particular race, religion, ethnicity, or sexuality. *Terrorism* is now also applied to the bombing of abortion clinics, not just to acts that are perceived as political by a masculine definition.

30 Feminist academics have brought into feminism an imitative group of words. *Deconstruction* is the act of divorcing something from its original context and meaning. Phrases like *the production of women's agency* are substituted for *empowerment; problematize* instead of simply talking about problems and what creates them; and even *feminist praxis* when *feminist practice* would do just as well. Academic and other generalized language often obfuscates, distances, and removes insight and information from readers who need them most—but perhaps this is all necessary to get taken seriously and tenured in an academic world.

31 If there was any doubt about the importance of language, it has been put to rest by an anti-equality right wing that is insisting again on using *unwed mother* and *illegitimate children* instead of *single mother* and *children*. As the representative of the only world religion to have permanent observer status in the United Nations, the Vatican has set out to oppose *reproductive rights* and *reproductive health* as phrases, and even to challenge the use of the word *gender* in the U.N. documents. Clearly, the choice of what words we may use determines what dreams we are able to express.

32 Consider the changes already made or still to come in your own language. They are a good indication of where we are and where we need to go.

Understanding Meaning

1. What change in attitude is Steinem referring to when she states that in the past "*sexual harassment*" and "*battered women*" were just called "*life*"?
2. Was the word "women's" traditionally a "put-down"?
3. What does Steinem mean when she states, "More women are becoming the men they wanted to marry, but too few men are becoming the women they wanted to marry"?
4. How have feminist scientists changed traditional views of the universe? Can this change be attributed to gender or prevailing theories?
5. *Critical Thinking:* Steinem asserts "the choice of what words we may use determines what dreams we are able to express." Do you agree? Does a change in language alter consciousness? Without words to describe issues like sexual harassment, does the problem remain undefined and accepted as just "*life*"?

Evaluating Strategy

1. How important are examples in Steinem's essay? Does she provide enough to convince readers that feminism has affected our language?
2. Do newly termed words and phrases that demean women counter Steinem's thesis? For example, movie reviewers now use the term "chick flick" to describe romantic films that appeal to women. Can you give other examples?
3. How important is the study of connotations in Steinem's essay?

Appreciating Language

1. Consider Steinem's use of the word "feminist." Is this a term that requires definition? Since this article first appeared in *Ms.*, does she seem to feel her readers share her understanding of the term?
2. Steinem defines pornography as "writing about female slavery." Would most people share this view? Is the use of the word "slavery" appropriate?
3. *Critical Thinking:* In focusing on vocabulary, did Steinem miss perhaps the most significant change in our language—the shift from using "he" as a universal pronoun for words like "everyone" or "student"? Does the shift to saying "his or her" suggest a more profound change than the addition of words such as *sexual harassment* and *battered women?*

Connections across the Disciplines

1. Refer to Joel Connelly's article, "A Growing Awareness: Environmental Groups and the Media" (page 330). Do groups influence public opinion through words as well as images?
2. In "The Handicap of Definition" (page 320), William Raspberry argues that numerous African American children accept many positive values as being "white" and therefore alien to them. Have women been socialized to see many attributes or behaviors as being "male"? Can defining endeavors as male or female limit people's options?

Writing Suggestions

1. Write an essay about how words have changed our consciousness of women, ethnic groups, the environment, government, and technology. For instance, how has the connotation of "computer" changed since it now refers to a household appliance and not a mammoth, mysterious machine operated by only corporations and governments?
2. *Collaborative Writing:* Discuss Steinem's article with a group of students. How has the women's movement changed society? Have one student record comments and list the effects of feminism. Develop a short essay highlighting the changes your group considers the most significant.

BLENDING THE MODES

ALICE WALKER

Alice Walker (1944–) was born to a poor family in Georgia. By the time she graduated from college in 1965, she was already writing and participating in the Civil Rights movement. Walker has taught at Jackson State College, the University of Massachusetts, and Wellesley. Much of her writing concerns the problems of African American women. She has published several novels, including The Color Purple, *which was made into a motion picture.*

The Civil Rights Movement: What Good Was It?

In this 1967 article first published in The American Scholar, *Alice Walker comments on the Civil Rights movement of the 1960s, which many critics and media experts declared dead before the decade was over. As you read the article, consider the often-stated observation that Americans have short attention spans and expect immediate gratification. What did people expect the Civil Rights movement to deliver? Notice how Walker blends* narration, comparison, *and* definition *in developing her essay.*

1 Someone said recently to an old black lady from Mississippi, whose legs had been badly mangled by local police who arrested her for "disturbing the peace," that the Civil Rights Movement was dead, and asked, since it was dead, what she thought about it. The old lady replied, hobbling out of his presence on her cane, that the Civil Rights Movement was like herself, "if it's dead, it shore ain't ready to lay down!"

2 This old lady is a legendary freedom fighter in her small town in the Delta. She has been severely mistreated for insisting on her rights as an American citizen. She has been beaten for singing Movement songs, placed in solitary confinement in prisons for talking about freedom, and placed on bread and water for praying aloud to God for her jailers' deliverance. For such a woman the Civil Rights Movement will never be over as long as her skin is black. It also will never be over for twenty million others with the same "affliction," for whom the Movement can never "lay down," no matter how it is killed by the press and made dead and buried by the white American public. As long as one

black American survives, the struggle for equality with other Americans must also survive. This is a debt we owe to those blameless hostages we leave to the future, our children.

3 Still, white liberals and deserting Civil Rights sponsors are quick to justify their disaffection from the Movement by claiming that it is all over. "And since it is over," they will ask, "would someone kindly tell me what has been gained by it?" They then list statistics supposedly showing how much more advanced segregation is now than ten years ago—in schools, housing, jobs. They point to a gain in conservative politicians during the last few years. They speak of ghetto riots and of the survey that shows that most policemen are admittedly too anti-Negro to do their jobs in ghetto areas fairly and effectively. They speak of every area that has been touched by the Civil Rights Movement as somehow or other going to pieces.

4 They rarely talk, however, about human attitudes among Negroes that have undergone terrific changes just during the past seven to ten years (not to mention all those years when there was a Movement and only the Negroes knew about it). They seldom speak of changes in personal lives because of the influence of people in the Movement. They see general failure and few, if any, individual gains.

5 They do not understand what it is that keeps the Movement from "laying down" and Negroes from reverting to their former *silent* second-class status. They have apparently never stopped to wonder why it is always the white man—on his radio and in his newspaper and on his television—who says that the Movement is dead. If a Negro were audacious enough to make such a claim, his fellows might hanker to see him shot. The Movement is dead to the white man because it no longer interests him. And it no longer interests him because he can afford to be uninterested: he does not have to live by it, with it, or for it, as Negroes must. He can take a rest from the news of beatings, killings, and arrests that reach him from North and South—if his skin is white. Negroes cannot now and will never be able to take a rest from the injustices that plague them, for they—not the white man—are the target.

6 Perhaps it is naive to be thankful that the Movement "saved" a large number of individuals and gave them something to live for, even if it did not provide them with everything they wanted. (Materially, it provided them with precious little that they wanted.) When a movement awakens people to the possibilities of life, it seems unfair to frustrate them by then denying what they had thought was offered. But what was offered? What was promised? What was it all about? What

good did it do? Would it have been better, as some have suggested, to leave the Negro people as they were, unawakened, unallied with one another, unhopeful about what to expect for their children in some future world?

7 I do not think so. If knowledge of my condition is all the freedom I get from a "freedom movement," it is better than unawareness, forgottenness, and hopelessness, the existence that is like the existence of a beast. Man only truly lives by knowing; otherwise he simply performs, copying the daily habits of others, but conceiving nothing of his creative possibilities as a man, and accepting someone else's superiority and his own misery.

8 When we are children, growing up in our parents' care, we await the spark from the outside world. Sometimes our parents provide it—if we are lucky—sometimes it comes from another source far from home. We sit, paralyzed, surrounded by our anxiety and dread, hoping we will not have to grow up into the narrow world and ways we see about us. We are hungry for a life that turns us on; we yearn for a knowledge of living that will save us from our innocuous lives that resemble death. We look for signs in every strange event; we search for heroes in every unknown face.

9 It was just six years ago that I began to be alive. I had, of course, been living before—for I am now twenty-three—but I did not really know it. And I did not know it because nobody told me that I—a pensive, yearning, typical high-school senior, but Negro—existed in the minds of others as I existed in my own. Until that time my mind was locked apart from the outer contours and complexion of my body as if it and the body were strangers. The mind possessed both thought and spirit—I wanted to be an author or a scientist—which the color of the body denied. I had never seen myself and existed as a statistic exists, or as a phantom. In the white world I walked, less real to them than a shadow; and being young and well hidden among the slums, among people who also did not exist—either in books or in films or in the government of their own lives—I waited to be called to life. And, by a miracle, I was called.

10 There was a commotion in our house that night in 1960. We had managed to buy our first television set. It was battered and overpriced, but my mother had gotten used to watching the afternoon soap operas at the house where she worked as maid, and nothing could satisfy her on days when she did not work but a continuation of her "stories." So she pinched pennies and bought a set.

11 I remained listless throughout her "stories," tales of pregnancy, abortion, hypocrisy, infidelity, and alcoholism. All these men and women were white and lived in houses with servants, long staircases that they floated down, patios where liquor was served four times a day to "relax" them. But my mother, with her swollen feet eased out of her shoes, her heavy body relaxed in our only comfortable chair, watched each movement of the smartly coiffed women, heard each word, pounced upon each innuendo and inflection, and for the duration of these "stories" she saw herself as one of them. She placed herself in every scene she saw, with her braided hair turned blond, her two hundred pounds compressed into a sleek size-seven dress, her rough dark skin smooth and *white.* Her husband became "dark and handsome," talented, witty, urbane, charming. And when she turned to look at my father sitting near her in his sweat shirt with his smelly feet raised on the bed to "air," there was always a tragic look of surprise on her face. Then she would sigh and go out to the kitchen looking lost and unsure of herself. My mother, a truly great woman who raised eight children of her own and half a dozen of the neighbors' without a single complaint, was convinced that she did not exist compared to "them." She subordinated her soul to theirs and became a faithful and timid supporter of the "Beautiful White People." Once she asked me, in a moment of vicarious pride and despair, if I didn't think that "they" were "jest naturally smarter, prettier, better." My mother asked this: a woman who never got rid of any of her children, never cheated on my father, was never a hypocrite if she could help it, and never even tasted liquor. She could not even bring herself to blame "them" for making her believe what they wanted her to believe: that if she did not look like them, think like them, be sophisticated and corrupt-for-comfort's-sake like them, she was a nobody. Black was not a color on my mother; it was a shield that made her invisible.

12 Of course, the people who wrote the soap-opera scripts always made the Negro maids in them steadfast, trusty, and wise in a home-remedial sort of way; but my mother, a maid for nearly forty years, never once identified herself with the scarcely glimpsed black servant's face beneath the ruffled cap. Like everyone else, in her daydreams at least, she thought she was free.

13 Six years ago, after half-heartedly watching my mother's soap operas and wondering whether there wasn't something more to be asked of life, the Civil Rights Movement came into my life. Like a good omen for the future, the face of Dr. Martin Luther King, Jr., was the

first black face I saw on our new television screen. And, as in a fairy tale, my soul was stirred by the meaning for me of his mission—at the time he was being rather ignominiously dumped into a police van for having led a protest march in Alabama—and I fell in love with the sober and determined face of the Movement. The singing of "We Shall Overcome"—that song betrayed by nonbelievers in it—rang for the first time in my ears. The influence that my mother's soap operas might have had on me became impossible. The life of Dr. King, seeming bigger and more miraculous than the man himself, because of all he had done and suffered, offered a pattern of strength and sincerity I felt I could trust. He had suffered much because of his simple belief in nonviolence, love, and brotherhood. Perhaps the majority of men could not be reached through these beliefs, but because Dr. King kept trying to reach them in spite of danger to himself and his family, I saw in him the hero for whom I had waited so long.

14 What Dr. King promised was not a ranch-style house and an acre of manicured lawn for every black man, but jail and finally freedom. He did not promise two cars for every family, but the courage one day for all families everywhere to walk without shame and unafraid on their own feet. He did not say that one day it will be us chasing prospective buyers out of our prosperous well-kept neighborhoods, or in other ways exhibiting our snobbery and ignorance as all other ethnic groups before us have done; what he said was that we had a right to live anywhere in this country we chose, and a right to a meaningful well-paying job to provide us with the upkeep of our homes. He did not say we had to become carbon copies of the white American middle class; but he did say we had the right to become whatever we wanted to become.

15 Because of the Movement, because of an awakened faith in the newness and imagination of the human spirit, because of "black and white together"—for the first time in our history in some human relationship on and off TV—because of the beatings, the arrests, the hell of battle during the past years, I have fought harder for my life and for a chance to be myself, to be something more than a shadow or a number, than I had ever done before in my life. Before, there had seemed to be no real reason for struggling beyond the effort for daily bread. Now there was a chance at that other that Jesus meant when He said we could not live by bread alone.

16 I have fought and kicked and fasted and prayed and cursed and cried myself to the point of existing. It has been like being born again,

literally. Just "knowing" has meant everything to me. Knowing has pushed me out into the world, into college, into places, into people.

17 Part of what existence means to me is knowing the difference between what I am now and what I was then. It is being capable of looking after myself intellectually as well as financially. It is being able to tell when I am being wronged and by whom. It means being awake to protect myself and the ones I love. It means being a part of the world community, and being *alert* to which part it is that I have joined, and knowing how to change to another part if that part does not suit me. To know is to exist: to exist is to be involved, to move about, to see the world with my own eyes. This, at least, the Movement has given me.

18 The hippies and other nihilists would have me believe that it is all the same whether the people in Mississippi have a movement behind them or not. Once they have their rights, they say, they will run all over themselves trying to be just like everybody else. They will be well fed, complacent about things of the spirit, emotionless, and without the marvelous humanity and "soul" that the Movement has seen them practice time and time again. "What has the Movement done," they ask, "with the few people it has supposedly helped?" "Got them white-collar jobs, moved them into standardized ranch houses in white neighborhoods, given them nondescript gray flannel suits?" "What are these people now?" they ask. And then they answer themselves, "Nothings!"

19 I would find this reasoning—which I have heard many, many times from hippies and nonhippies alike—amusing if I did not also consider it serious. For I think it is a delusion, a cop-out, an excuse to disassociate themselves from a world in which they feel too little has been changed or gained. The real question, however, it appears to me, is not whether poor people will adopt the middle-class mentality once they are well fed; rather, it is whether they will ever be well fed enough to be able to choose whatever mentality they think will suit them. The lack of a movement did not keep my mother from *wishing* herself bourgeois in her daydreams.

20 There is widespread starvation in Mississippi. In my own state of Georgia there are more hungry families than Lester Maddox* would like to admit—or even see fed. I went to school with children who ate

*Editors' note—Governor of Georgia between 1967 and 1971, Maddox was widely known for his segregationist views.

red dirt. The Movement has prodded and pushed some liberal senators into pressuring the government for food so that the hungry may eat. Food stamps that were two dollars and out of the reach of many families not long ago have been reduced to fifty cents. The price is still out of the reach of some families, and the government, it seems to a lot of people, could spare enough free food to feed its own people. It angers people in the Movement that it does not; they point to the billions in wheat we send free each year to countries abroad. Their government's slowness while people are hungry, its unwillingness to believe that there are Americans starving, its stingy cutting of the price of food stamps, make many Civil Rights workers throw up their hands in disgust. But they do not give up. They do not withdraw into the world of psychedelia. They apply what pressure they can to make the government give away food to hungry people. They do not plan so far ahead in their disillusionment with society that they can see these starving families buying identical ranch-style houses and sending their snobbish children to Bryn Mawr and Yale. They take first things first and try to get them fed.

21 They do not consider it their business, in any case, to say what kind of life the people they help must lead. How one lives is, after all, one of the rights left to the individual—when and if he has opportunity to choose. It is not the prerogative of the middle class to determine what is worthy of aspiration. There is also every possibility that the middle-class people of tomorrow will turn out ever so much better than those of today. I even know some middle-class people of today who are not *all* bad.

22 I think there are so few Negro hippies because middle-class Negroes, although well fed, are not careless. They are required by the treacherous world they live in to be clearly aware of whoever or whatever might be trying to do them in. They are middle class in money and position, but they cannot afford to be middle class in complacency. They distrust the hippie movement because they know that it can do nothing for Negroes as a group but "love" them, which is what all paternalists claim to do. And since the only way Negroes can survive (which they cannot do, unfortunately, on love alone) is with the support of the group, they are wisely wary and stay away.

23 A white writer tried recently to explain that the reason for the relatively few Negro hippies is that Negroes have built up a "supercool" that cracks under LSD and makes them have a "bad trip." What this writer doesn't guess at is that Negroes are needing drugs less than ever

these days for any kind of trip. While the hippies are "tripping," Negroes are going after power, which is so much more important to their survival and their children's survival than LSD and pot.

24 Everyone would be surprised if the Israelis ignored the Arabs and took up "tripping" and pot smoking. In this country we are the Israelis. Everybody who can do so would like to forget this, of course. But for us to forget it for a minute would be fatal. "We Shall Overcome" is just a song to most Americans, *but we must do it.* Or die.

25 What good was the Civil Rights Movement? If it had just given this country Dr. King, a leader of conscience, for once in our lifetime, it would have been enough. If it had just taken black eyes off white television stories, it would have been enough. If it had fed one starving child, it would have been enough.

26 If the Civil Rights Movement is "dead," and if it gave us nothing else, it gave us each other forever. It gave some of us bread, some of us shelter, some of us knowledge and pride, all of us comfort. It gave us our children, our husbands, our brothers, our fathers, as men reborn and with a purpose for living. It broke the pattern of black servitude in this country. It shattered the phony "promise" of white soap operas that sucked away so many pitiful lives. It gave us history and men far greater than Presidents. It gave us heroes, selfless men of courage and strength, for our little boys and girls to follow. It gave us hope for tomorrow. It called us to life.

27 Because we live, it can never die.

Understanding Meaning

1. When did the Civil Rights movement end for Alice Walker?
2. When did Alice Walker become "alive"? What altered her views of life?
3. What did her mother's television viewing habits reveal to Walker about the status of African Americans?
4. What attracted Walker to the Civil Rights movement?
5. What does Walker see as the lasting effects of the Civil Rights movement? How does she define the goals of the movement?
6. *Critical Thinking:* What does Alice Walker mean with the statement that Martin Luther King Jr. did not promise "a ranch-style house and an acre of manicured lawn for every black man, but jail and finally freedom"? Do most people measure progress in material terms? Do people equate justice with prosperity?

Evaluating Strategy

1. How does Walker blend her comments about the Civil Rights movement and her personal development?
2. *Other Modes:* How does Walker use *narration* and *comparison* to develop her essay?

Appreciating Language

1. How does Walker describe white, middle-class life? What attitude does she seem to have?
2. What language does Walker use to describe her mother? What does this reveal about her feelings toward her?

Connections across the Disciplines

1. Review Martin Luther King Jr.'s essay, "The Ways of Meeting Oppression" (page 443). Does Walker's commitment suggest she was following his vision of nonviolent protest?
2. How did Alice Walker's growing self-awareness compare with that experienced by bell hooks (page 401) and Mary Mebane (page 434)?

Writing Suggestions

1. This essay was written thirty years ago. What do you consider the lasting effects of the Civil Rights movement? Write a short essay outlining your opinion. Try to support your ideas with details.
2. *Collaborative Writing:* Working with a group of students, consider why so many people were willing to write off the Civil Rights movement. Do Americans expect immediate change? Are they easily distracted by other issues? Make notes of the members' comments, and then collaborate to write a brief essay expressing the major views of the group. If significant differences of opinion occur, consider writing pro and con statements.

JODI JACOBSON

Jodi Jacobson is a senior researcher at the World Watch Institute, an environmental organization that monitors the impact human activity has on the planet. She is also the author of Environmental Refugees: A Yardstick of Habitability.

Swept Away

In this World Watch *(1989) article, Jodi Jacobson describes the effects global warming will have in the future. Theorists claim that pollution is causing atmospheric changes that will trap heat and slowly cause the earth to become warmer. Climate changes will alter weather patterns and plant growth and raise ocean levels as the polar ice caps melt. Read Jacobson's account of the effects of global warming, and then read Jocelyn Tomkin's opposing piece.*

1 "Don't buy land in New Orleans," warns John Milliman of the Woods Hole Oceanographic Institution in Massachusetts. The scientist's comment stems from his knowledge of how sea level rise—an expected consequence of global warming—will affect the habitability of low-lying coastal regions around the world. In the 21st century, waves now breaking on the shores of Louisiana's coast could be lapping at the doors of homes in the Big Easy. Miami is another case in point. The first settlements in this city were built on what little high ground could be found, but today most of greater Miami lies at or just above sea level on swampland reclaimed from the Everglades. Water for its three million residents is drawn from the Biscayne aquifer that flows only feet below the city streets. That the city exists and prospers is due to what engineers call a "hydrologic masterwork" of natural and artificial systems that hold back swamp and sea.

2 Against a three-foot rise in ocean levels, which is expected by the year 2050, the city's only defense would be a costly system of sea walls and dikes. But that might not be enough to spare the city from insidious assault. Fresh water floats atop salt water, so as sea levels rise the water table would be pushed three feet closer to the surface. The elaborate pumping and drainage system that currently maintains the integrity of the highly porous aquifer could be overwhelmed. Roads would buckle, bridge abutments sink, and land revert back to swamp.

3 Miami's experience would not be unique. Large cities around the world—New Orleans, New York, Venice, Bangkok and Taipei, to name a few—would face the prospect of inundation by invading seas. For each, the choice would be fight or flight.

4 Protecting infrastructure and water supplies of coastal cities, not to mention saving shorelines and wetlands, will require many billions of dollars, perhaps even more than most well-off nations could afford. Sea levels have only gone up several inches over the past century, but their rise is sure to accelerate in the coming decades as global warming sets in motion an expansion of ocean volume and a melting of mountain glaciers and polar icecaps. While some universal increase in sea level is now inevitable, the rate and extent of change depends on preemptive action adopted by society today.

THE EXPANDING OCEAN

5 Most scientists now agree that a global warming has begun. Its causes are by now depressingly familiar: greenhouse gases generated by human activity are accumulating in the atmosphere and trapping the sun's radiant heat. These gases include carbon dioxide and nitrous oxides from the combustion of wood and fossil fuels, chlorofluorocarbons (used as a refrigerant and in industrial applications), and methane (from ruminant animals and rice paddies). Meanwhile, population pressures in the Third World are forcing wholesale forest clearing for fuel, farmland and living space. The result is fewer trees left to recapture the chief greenhouse gas, carbon dioxide.

6 It is now all but certain that the delicate balance between incoming sunlight and reflected heat that keeps the earth at a relatively constant average temperature has been upset. What is not certain is just how much higher the temperature will go, and how quickly the increase will take place. Estimates based on current trends project that an average global rise of between three and eight degrees Fahrenheit can be expected within the next 40 years.

7 As temperatures rise the waters of the earth will expand. Glaciers and icecaps will melt. Still higher sea levels may occur if the warming breaks loose such large frozen ice masses as the West Antarctic sheet. If correct, the predicted temperature changes would escalate sea level by five to seven feet over the next century. Some climatologists now estimate that the rate of increase will accelerate after 2050, reaching about an inch per year.

8 The heat and dryness of the summer of 1988 drew attention to the withering effects global warming could have on agricultural productivity, but its most lasting legacy could well be the displacement of peoples, the abandonment of entire delta regions, and the destruction of vital coastal ecosystems caused by inundation.

AN UNAFFORDABLE BILL

9 China's 1,500-mile-long Great Wall is considered the largest construction project ever carried out, but it may soon be superseded in several countries by modern-day analogues: the "Great Seawalls." If nothing is done to slow global warming, then building structures to hold back the sea will become essential, but their multi-billion dollar price tags may be higher than even some well-to-do countries can afford.

10 Nowhere is the battle against the sea more actively engaged than in the Netherlands. The Dutch are perhaps best known for their achievements in building a nation on the deltas of the Meuse, Rhine and Schedule rivers. And well they should be: Without the carefully maintained stretches of dikes (250 miles long) and sand dunes (120 miles) built by Holland's engineers to hold back the sea, more than half the country would be under water.

11 As the engineers know, the ocean doesn't relinquish land easily. In early 1953, a storm surge that hit the delta region caused an unprecedented disaster. More than 100 miles of dikes were breached, leading to the inundation of 600 square miles of land and the deaths of more than 1,800 people. In response, the Dutch government put together the Delta Plan, a massive public works project that took two decades and the equivalent of 6 percent of the country's gross national product each year to complete.

12 The Dutch continue to spend heavily to keep their extensive system of dikes and pumps in shape, and are now protected against storms up to those with a probability of occurring once in 10,000 years. But, due to sea level rise, maintaining this level of safety may require additional investments of up to $10 billion by 2040.

13 Large though these expenditures are, they are trivial compared with what the United States, with more than 19,000 miles of coastline, will have to spend to protect Cape Cod, Long Island, the Maryland, Massachusetts and New Jersey shores, North Carolina's Outer Banks,

most of Florida, the bayous of Louisiana, the Texas Gulf Coast and the San Francisco Bay Area.

14 Even so, industrial countries are in a far better financial position to protect their coastal regions than are developing nations. Bangladesh, for instance, can ill afford to match the Dutch mile for mile in seawalls. But its danger is no less real. The cyclones originating in the Bay of Bengal before and after the monsoon season already devastate the southern part of Bangladesh on a regular basis. Storm surges 18 feet higher than normal can reach as far as 125 miles inland and cover a third of the country.

15 In addition to lifting the ocean's level, global warming is likely to increase the frequency of these tropical storms. When added to the ongoing alteration of the Bengal Delta's natural processes by human activity, these conditions may wreak so much damage that Bangladesh as it is known today may virtually cease to exist.

SUBSIDING AWAY

16 Low-lying delta regions, vulnerable even to slight increases in sea level, will be among the first land areas lost to inundation. Residents of these regions are joined in activities that amount to a lowering of defenses. By overpumping groundwater and interfering with the natural ground-building that rivers achieve through sedimentation, they are causing the land to sink. In a vicious circle, the more populated these regions become, the more likely this subsidence—and the more devastating and immediate the hike in the level of the sea.

17 Under natural conditions, deltas are in a state of dynamic equilibrium, forming and breaking down in a continuous pattern of accretion and subsidence. Over time, these sediments accumulate to form marshes and swamps. But regional and local tectonic effects, along with compaction, cause the land to subside by as much as 4 inches a year if additional sediments are not laid down.

18 Channeling, diverting or damming rivers can greatly reduce the amount of sediment that reaches a delta. Where humans interfere with river systems, sediment either shoots past lowlands and is borne out to sea, as with the Mississippi River, or it is blocked upriver, as with the Nile. When this happens, sediment accumulation does not offset subsidence. The result is more severe shoreline erosion and a relative

increase in sea water levels. Subsidence also occurs where subterranean stores of water or oil are drained. In Bangkok, Thailand, net subsidence has reached 5 inches per year due to a drop in the water table caused by excessive withdrawals of groundwater over the past three decades.

19 In Louisiana, reduced sedimentation along with extensive tapping of groundwater and underground stores of oil and gas have accelerated the disintegration of the Mississippi Delta. That state now loses more land to subsidence and sea level rise on an annual basis—50 square miles per year—than any other state or country in the world.

20 According to Woods Hole's Milliman, the combined effects of sea level rise and subsidence in Bangladesh and Egypt, whose populations are concentrated on deltas, threaten the homes and livelihoods of some 46 million people.

21 To arrive at that figure Milliman's research team started with two estimates of sea level rise: a minimum of 5 inches by 2050 and 11 inches by 2100, and a maximum of 31 inches by 2050 and 85 inches by 2100. They then calculated the effects under three scenarios.

22 Under the "best case" scenario, the researchers assume the minimum rise in sea level and a delta region in equilibrium. The second scenario, called the "worst case," assumes the maximum rate of sea level rise and the complete damming or diversion of the river system draining into the delta. As mentioned, the resulting subsidence must then be added to the absolute rise in sea level. The third scenario is referred to as the "really worst case." It assumes that excessive groundwater pumping from irrigation and other uses accelerates subsidence.

23 To calculate the economic implications of these three cases on both Egypt and Bangladesh, Milliman and his colleagues assumed present-day conditions, such as the estimated share of total population now living in areas that would be inundated and the share of economic activity that is derived from them. Continued settlement and population growth in these areas will only make for more environmental refugees.

SEVEN FEET FROM DISASTER

24 Milliman's calculations bode poorly for Bangladesh, which is nothing more than the world's largest deltaic plain. The Bengal Delta, built at

the confluence of the Ganges, Brahmaputra and Meghna rivers, occupies about 80 percent of Bangladesh's total area. Much of the remainder is water. As a result, the nation's inhabitants are subject to annual floods from the rivers and from ocean storm surges.

25 Just how severely sea level rise will affect Bangladesh depends in part on the pace at which damming and channeling proceeds on the three giant rivers and their tributaries. Although annual flooding is severe and can damage crops grown on the flood plains, large areas of the delta region suffer drought for the rest of the year. The diversion of river water to parched fields leaves Bangladesh in its present predicament: sedimentation is decreasing and subsidence is increasing.

26 The Woods Hole researchers have also concluded that the increasing withdrawal of groundwater in Bangladesh is exacerbating subsidence. Between 1978 and 1985, there was at least a sixfold increase in the number of wells drilled in the country. Sediment samples suggest that the withdrawal of well water may have doubled the natural rate of subsidence.

27 Taking these factors into account, Milliman and his colleagues estimate Bangladesh is going to experience the "really worst case" scenario. The effect of sea level rise will be as much as 82 inches along the coast by 2050, in which event it's likely 18 percent of the habitable land will be under water. More than 17 million people would become environmental refugees. The 57-inch rise in the worst case wouldn't spare the nation: 16 percent of its land would be lost.

28 By the year 2100, the really worst case scenario would have progressed to the point that 38 million Bangladeshis will be forced to relocate. The social and economic effects will be jarring. Because nearly a third of the country's gross national product is generated within the land area that will be lost, an already poor country will have to accommodate its people on a far smaller economic base. Coastal mangrove forests, upon which 30 percent of the country's population depends to some extent for its livelihood, will be the first victims of advancing seas and extensive river diversion.

29 Where will those displaced by rising seas go? Moving further inland, millions of refugees will have to compete with the local populace for scarce food, water and land, perhaps spurring regional clashes. Moreover, existing tensions between Bangladesh and its large neighbor to the west, India, are likely to heighten as the trickle of environmental refugees from the former becomes a torrent.

UP THE NILE

30 Egypt's habitable area is even more densely populated than that of Bangladesh. By and large, Egypt is desert except for the thin ribbon of productive land along the Nile River and its delta. Egypt's millions crowd onto less than 4 percent of the country's land, leading to a population density there of 700 people per square mile.

31 Milliman's study points out that because the Nile has already been dammed—which means most of the sediment that would offset subsidence of the delta is trapped upstream—only the "worst" and "really worst" cases are relevant for Egypt. Consequently, local sea level rise would range between 16 and 22 inches by 2050, rendering up to 19 percent of Egypt's good land uninhabitable.

32 If the increase is 22 inches, more than 8.5 million people would be forced to relinquish their homes to the sea, and Egypt would lose 16 percent of its gross national product. By 2100, local sea level rise will range between 101 and 131 inches, submerging up to 26 percent of habitable land and affecting an equal portion—24 percent—of both population and domestic economic output.

33 While neither Bangladesh nor Egypt is likely to influence the global emission of greenhouse gases or sea level rise, they do wield considerable control over local sea levels. The development policies they choose in the near future will have a significant effect on the future of their deltas and the people who live on them.

ECOSYSTEMS AT RISK

34 Coastal swamps and marshes are areas of prodigious biological productivity. The ecological and economic benefits derived from areas such as Louisiana's wetlands are inestimable. Nearly two-thirds of the migratory birds using the Mississippi flyway make a pitstop in those wetlands, while existing marshlands and barrier islands buffer inland areas against devastating hurricane surges. Marshes not only hold back the intrusion of the Gulf of Mexico's salt water into local rivers but are a major source of fresh water for coastal communities, agriculture and industry. Louisiana's wetlands supply 25 percent of the U.S. seafood catch and support a $500-million-a-year recreational industry devoted to fishing, hunting and birding.

35 What was laid down over millions of years by the slow deposit of silt washed off of land from the Rockies to the Appalachians could be jeopardized in a little over a century. Louisiana's famous bayous and marshland may be overrun by the year 2040, when the Gulf of Mexico surges up to 33 miles inland. With the delicate coastal marsh ecology upset, fish and wildlife harvests would decline precipitously and a ripple effect would flatten the coastal economy. Communities, water supplies and infrastructure will all be threatened.

36 According to U.S. Environmental Protection Agency estimates, erosion, inundation and salt water intrusion could reduce the area of coastal wetlands in the United States by 30 to 80 percent if today's projections of sea level rise are realized. Vital wetlands such as the Mississippi Delta and Chesapeake Bay regions would be irreparably damaged. No one has yet calculated the immense economic and ecological costs of such a loss for the United States, much less extrapolated it to the global level.

37 Were it not for the enormous pressure human encroachment puts on them, coastal swamps and marshes might have a chance to handle rising seas by reestablishing upland. But heavy development of beach resorts and other coastal areas throughout the United States means that few wetlands have the leeway to "migrate."

38 Highly productive mangrove forests throughout the world will also be lost to the rising tide. Mangroves are the predominant type of vegetation on the deltas along the Atlantic coast of South America. On the north coast of Brazil active shoreline retreat is possible because there is little human settlement; the mangroves can possibly adapt. In the south, however, once-extensive mangroves have been depleted or hemmed in by urban growth, especially near Rio de Janeiro in Brazil. No more than 40 square miles of mangroves remain where once thousands of square miles stood. As sea level rises, these remaining areas will disappear.

MODERN-DAY ATLANTIS

39 In 2100, cartographers will likely be redrawing the coastlines of many countries. They may also make an important deletion: By that year, if current projections are borne out, the Maldives will have been washed from the earth. The small nation, made up of a series of 1,190 islands

in atolls, is nowhere higher in elevation than six feet. A mean sea level rise of equal height would submerge the entire country. With a three-foot rise, well within the expected increase of the next century, a storm surge would, in the words of President Maumoon Abdul Gayoom, be "catastrophic and possibly fatal." Other such endangered places include the Pacific islands of Kiribati, Tuvalu and the Marshalls.

40 By 2050, the Florida Keys "will no longer exist," according to Elton J. Gissendanner, past executive director of the Florida Department of Natural Resources. Loss of the Keys will displace thousands of permanent residents and wipe out a tourist industry that brings 100,000 people to the area each year. Approximately 70 percent of Florida's residents live right on the mainland coast, but no study has been done to determine how many will become environmental refugees.

41 Although increases in sea level will occur gradually over the next several decades—accelerating in 2030, when the greenhouse effect is expected to really kick in—the issue has already sparked a number of current debates.

42 For one, should society continue on its current path and accept sea level rise as inevitable, or should it change consumption patterns for fossil fuels and chemicals to mitigate a global warming? How long should local and national governments wait before investing heavily to defend their shores against a future threat, especially when other needs are pressing? When will it be too late? Conversely, should they seek to protect these areas at all? How can coastal residential and resort development be allowed to continue if the land is projected to disappear within a few decades? And who should provide insurance against catastrophe to those living in high-risk areas? Perhaps most important, who will help the Third World cope with the massive dislocations envisioned?

43 The industrial nations, heavily reliant on the burning of fossil fuels over the past century, are primarily responsible for initiating global warming. But, today virtually every citizen of every nation engages in activities that make the problem worse. Meanwhile, development strategies currently being adopted by many poorer countries—water projects that lead to subsidence, policies that encourage deforestation, and development programs based on fossil-fuel-intensive technologies—are likely to exacerbate, rather than abate, the warming and its effects.

44 If current trends persist, global warming and the subsequent rise in sea level will accelerate. If, on the other hand, concerted action is taken now—to raise energy efficiency and curtail overall fossil fuel use, to find substitutes for chlorofluorocarbons and other industrial chemicals that aggravate the greenhouse effect, to stem the tide of deforestation that destroys carbon-fixing trees—then sea level rise can be kept to a minimum.

45 President Gayoom of the Maldives frames the situation in blunt terms: "The predicted effects of the change are unnerving. . . . Reconstruction, rehabilitation and strengthening of coastal defense systems could turn out to be crippling for most affected countries." When the economic and environmental consequences are added in, no citizen of the planet is likely to remain unaffected.

Understanding Meaning

1. What is global warming?
2. What causes these changes, according to Jacobson?
3. How will global warming affect the planet? When will these changes occur?
4. How will governments be forced to respond to changes wrought by global warming?
5. *Critical Thinking:* What proof does Jacobson offer that these changes are likely to take place? How difficult is it to predict the future? What changes could alter the impact of global warming?

Evaluating Strategy

1. Jacobson begins the essay with a quote warning against buying land in New Orleans. Is this an effective attention getter, or does it risk being too sensational?
2. How does Jacobson explain complex scientific theories to a general audience?

Appreciating Language

1. How much technical language does Jacobson use? What does this reveal about her intended audience?

2. How does Jacobson use language to dramatize her view of the effects of global warming?

Connections across the Disciplines

1. How does this article support the argument made by Carl Sagan's "Why We Need to Understand Science" (page 642)?
2. *Critical Thinking:* Read Jocelyn Tomkin's refuting article (page 585). How does this article change your way of viewing Jacobson's assertions?

Writing Suggestions

1. Consider Jacobson's worst-case scenario. In your opinion, could the nations of the world cope with the slow rise of the oceans? Would the expenditure be much more than that spent on armaments? Write a short essay explaining how governments could respond to the crisis Jacobson describes.
2. *Collaborative Writing:* Discuss this essay with a group of students. Are they accustomed to reading articles full of gloom, predicting dire events in the future? Do writers overstate their cases to capture attention? Discuss instances where past predictions have been proven wrong. Work together to write a short paper outlining the issues raised in your group. You can develop the paper using comparison or cause and effect.

JOCELYN TOMKIN

Jocelyn Tomkin is an astronomer at the University of Texas at Austin. He wrote this article for Reason *(1993), a publication of the Reason Foundation based in Los Angeles. Tomkin argues that the effects of a rise in carbon dioxide are overstated. Instead of seeing global warming as an environmental threat, Tomkin asserts it "has been an essential ingredient in the evolution of life on earth."*

Hot Air

Read Tomkin's article after studying the preceding essay by Jodi Jacobson. As you read Tomkin's piece, refer to Jacobson's. Which writer seems better at applying critical thinking skills?

1 In his best-selling book, *Earth in the Balance,* Vice President Al Gore speculates that global warming caused by the greenhouse effect will throw "the whole global climate system . . . out of whack," dramatically reducing rainfall in parts of the world already troubled by drought, melting the polar icecaps, raising ocean levels, and devastating low-lying countries such as Bangladesh, India, Pakistan, Egypt, Indonesia, Thailand, and China. "In the lifetimes of people now living, we may experience a 'year without winter,'" Gore writes. "We are carelessly initiating climate changes that could well last for hundreds or even thousands of years."

2 Do such predictions have a basis in reality? Central to this question is the greenhouse effect. Contrary to the impression given by the mainstream media, the greenhouse effect is not of recent origin; it has been around for billions of years. But the link between this indisputable phenomenon and Gore's doomsday scenarios is tenuous at best. To understand why, you have to know something about the mechanics of the greenhouse effect.

3 The sun bathes the earth in sunshine. Some of the sunshine is reflected straight back into space, either by clouds or by the earth's surface. The remainder is absorbed by the earth's surface and thus heats it. Predictions about global warming hinge on the question of where this heat goes. Answering this question requires a brief trip into

4 the world of electromagnetic radiation—light in all its forms, both visible and invisible.

5 All bodies radiate heat. A simple physical law says that the cooler a body is, the longer the wavelength at which it radiates its heat. The hot plate of a stove, for example, glows an orange-red when it's running at full blast. But turn it down, and as it cools it radiates its heat at longer and longer wavelengths, until it cools to the point where it's radiating exclusively in the infrared. To the eye it now appears to be off, although it is still too hot to touch.

6 Even everyday objects at everyday temperatures are busy radiators of heat in the infrared. A block of ice at melting point, for instance, has a temperature of 273 degrees Kelvin and is a raging furnace compared to a block of ice at absolute zero. (The Kelvin temperature scale is the same as the Celsius scale, except its zero is absolute zero, instead of the freezing point of water.) The earth itself continually radiates heat from both its dayside and its nightside. The balance between sunshine's heating effect and the cooling effect of the radiation the earth pours back into space allows the planet's surface to maintain a roughly constant temperature (apart from diurnal and seasonal variations).

7 But the earth's surface, with an average temperature of 288 degrees Kelvin, is much cooler than the sun's, with a temperature of 5,800 degrees Kelvin. So while the sun pumps most of its heat into space in the form of user-friendly visible light, the earth returns this heat to space in the form of much-longer-wavelength, invisible, infrared radiation. A greenhouse gas is a gas that is transparent at visible wavelengths but opaque at infrared wavelengths. It thus admits sunshine but blocks the escape of the earth's infrared radiation, thereby warming the planet's surface. As a rule, gases whose molecules have three or more atoms, such as carbon dioxide, are greenhouse gases, while gases whose molecules have only two atoms, such as oxygen, are not.

8 Among the greenhouse gases, carbon dioxide gets the lion's share of attention because its concentration is increasing, largely due to industrial activity. But it is actually a minor player. If the concentration of carbon dioxide in the atmosphere doubled, the blocking of the earth's infrared radiation would rise from 150 to 154 watts per square meter, an increase of roughly 3 percent. This means that the increasing level of carbon dioxide in the atmosphere is not matched by a corresponding increase in the greenhouse effect.

9 Over the last 100 years, for example, the level of carbon dioxide has increased by 25 percent, while the greenhouse effect has increased

by around 1 percent. (This 1-percent figure assumes that other things have stayed equal in the meantime, but in the real world "other things" are usually not so obliging, so the actual behavior of the greenhouse effect during this time is unknown. Nonetheless, its variation has been much closer to 1 percent than to 25 percent.)

10 Ordinary water vapor is actually the main contributor to the greenhouse effect. The balance between the natural processes of evaporation, which pumps water vapor into the atmosphere, and condensation into clouds, which squeezes it out, sets the level of water vapor in the atmosphere.

11 This means that the greenhouse effect and global warming are an integral part of the biosphere. They have been around at least since the formation of the first oceans and must therefore have preceded mankind's appearance by a few billion years. Indeed, if there were no global warming, if the earth's atmosphere were perfectly transparent at infrared wavelengths, the planet's average surface temperature would be a brisk zero degrees Fahrenheit, instead of the pleasant 59 degrees that we enjoy. Global warming has been an essential ingredient in the evolution of life on the earth.

12 Yet the illusion that carbon dioxide is the dominant greenhouse gas is extremely widespread. In an impromptu, totally nonscientific survey, I asked 10 of my fellow astronomers, "What is the major greenhouse gas?" Six said carbon dioxide. One added, "But isn't water vapor in there?" Two said water vapor. And one said, "Don't know."

13 Evidently a surprisingly large number of astronomers think that carbon dioxide is the major greenhouse gas, despite the fact that astronomers need to know how the earth's atmosphere stamps its spectral imprint on the radiation from heavenly bodies and what gases are responsible. In scientific disciplines that do not deal with the earth's atmosphere on a professional basis, the illusion that carbon dioxide is the major greenhouse gas is probably even more prevalent. Among the general public it must be well-nigh universal.

14 But even if carbon dioxide is a minor greenhouse gas, its level is increasing. Doesn't this mean global warming is increasing? Yes. But the real question is at what level, and is it significant compared to the changes in global warming that take place independent of mankind's activities? Will it cause an 8-degree increase during the next century, as predicted in the most alarming scenarios, or will there be a much more gradual, and mostly beneficial, increase of 1 degree or so?

15 We cannot answer this question by means of mere calculation, because our theoretical understanding of the biosphere is too incomplete. The *immediate* result of increased carbon dioxide is, indeed, an increase of global warming. The slightly higher average temperature leads to increased evaporation from the oceans, which leads to a further increase in global warming because water vapor is also a greenhouse gas. But this is far from the end of the story.

16 More water vapor in the atmosphere leads to increased cloudiness over the earth as a whole. This means more sunshine is reflected straight back into space and so never reaches the earth's surface. This, in turn, means less heating of the earth's surface and hence lower temperatures.

17 We don't know which one of these opposing mechanisms wins, so we don't know if the increase in the greenhouse effect is amplified or dampened by the time it feeds through to global warming. The availability of faster computers promises that during the next decade we will be able to get a better grip on these factors and many other, more complicated ones that are currently neglected.

18 In the meantime, the observational evidence that global warming is actually increasing is very shaky. Some researchers claim to see an increase in global warming of about 0.8 degree since 1860. Although average temperatures since then have increased by this much, it's doubtful that the rise reflects carbon-dioxide-induced global warming.

19 The large year-to-year fluctuations of average temperature—which are in the neighborhood of 1 degree—mean that the behavior of average global temperature is somewhat like that of a stock market index. Spotting a "real" temperature trend is like deciding if one is in a bull or a bear market. It's not impossible, but no bell rings when one trend ends and a new one begins.

20 Moreover, natural causes, rather than the increase in carbon dioxide, are a more likely explanation of the temperature increase. Most of the rise took place prior to 1940, *before* the main increase in the carbon-dioxide level.

21 Some climatologists interpret this pre-1940 temperature increase as an after-effect of the so-called Little Ice Age, a period of unusual worldwide cold that prevailed from 1600 to 1850. If we look at the 50 years or so from 1940 to the present, which have seen the major part of the increase in carbon-dioxide concentration, the increase in average global temperatures has been only 0.2 degree. This small increment is within the noise of natural variation. Although the level of carbon

dioxide in the atmosphere is increasing, it does not seem to be affecting global temperatures much.

22 In examining the historical record, we also have to consider the urban heat island effect. The buildings and pavement of a city give it a microclimate slightly warmer than that of the surrounding countryside. As cities have grown, their heat islands have grown with them, so their weather stations, which tend to be in downtown locations, have been more and more prejudiced in favor of higher temperatures.

23 Phoenix is a dramatic example. Between 1960 and 1990, as its population grew from 650,000 to 2.1 million, its mean annual temperature heated up by 5 degrees, almost in lockstep with the population increase.

24 Climatologists who have tried to quantify the urban heat island's influence on the global temperature record estimate that it accounts for somewhere in the neighborhood of 0.2 degree of the 0.8-degree increase seen since 1860. And when Kirby Hanson, Thomas Karl, and George Maul of the National Oceanic and Atmospheric Administration conducted a study of the U.S. temperature record that took into account the urban heat island effect, they found no long-term warming. They confirmed the temperature rise prior to 1940 but found that temperatures have fallen since then.

25 Another consideration is that most of the earth's surface is covered with water. Temperature data over the oceans is extremely sparse, so the record of the earth's historic average temperature over both land and water is much vaguer than the land record. The recent advent of satellites with the capability to measure global temperatures accurately over both land and sea may solve the problem, but so far their time base is limited to a few years. However, global measurements by satellite of atmospheric (as distinct from surface) temperatures over the last decade show no sign of increasing temperatures.

26 Far more than historical evidence, the hullabaloo about global warming is based on predictions by computer models. The global climate modeler gives his computer some basic facts, plus a program that recognizes the relevant physical processes and principles insofar as we know them and insofar as they can be calculated. With luck, the computer arrives at a climate not unlike that of the earth. Then the model gets a retroactive "tuning," so that its average global temperature is right.

27 A calculation of the greenhouse effect and associated global warming is one step in the procedure. Assuming a doubling of atmospheric carbon dioxide, these models predict an increase in global warming of somewhere between 3 degrees and 8 degrees during the next century.

28 When they are judged by their verifiable accomplishments, however, these computer models are not very impressive. They predict that the temperatures at the poles are lower than those at the equator, and they predict that it's hotter in summer than in winter. But they are weak on specifics. One model predicts an annual rainfall in the central Sahara that is the same as Ireland's.

29 Clearly, these global climate models are still in a primitive stage of development. They neglect many important factors—both known, such as the poleward transport of heat from the equatorial regions by ocean currents and the atmosphere, and unknown. When it comes to telling us things we don't know already, such as trends in global warming during the next century, they are not far removed from the crystal-ball school of climatology.

30 Alarmists such as the vice president are impatient with people who point this out. Gore writes: "If, when the remaining unknowns about the environmental challenge enter the public debate, they are presented as signs that the crisis may not be real after all, it undermines the effort to build a solid base of support for the difficult actions we must soon take. . . . The insistence on complete certainty about the full details of global warming—the most serious threat that we have ever faced—is actually an effort to avoid facing the awful, uncomfortable truth: that we must act boldly, decisively, comprehensively, and quickly, even before we know every last detail of the crisis."

31 But one of the "details" we still don't know is whether we are in fact facing a crisis requiring drastic action. The burden of proof is on the alarmists. They have failed to meet it.

Understanding Meaning

1. How does Tomkin define global warming?
2. When did the process of global warming begin, according to Tomkin?
3. What is the principal element causing the greenhouse effect?
4. What are the opposing effects of the greenhouse effect? Does Tomkin suggest outcomes?

5. *Critical Thinking:* What problems does Tomkin cite in making accurate predictions about global warming? In Tomkin's view, does enough evidence exist to make a prediction?

Evaluating Strategy

1. What impact does the article's opening have? Does Tomkin's questioning of Al Gore directly suggest that Jacobson's views lack credibility?
2. Tomkin is writing to a general audience about complex issues. Does his analogy of measuring climatic changes to making judgments about the stock market serve to enlighten or confuse readers?

Appreciating Language

1. What level of scientific language does Tomkin use? What does this reveal about his readers?
2. How does Tomkin refer to those he calls "alarmists"? Does he see them as fellow scientists making honest errors in judgment or as determined ideologues?

Connections across the Disciplines

1. Does Tomkin's article suggest that some environmentalists are motivated by political rather than scientific considerations? Does Joel Connelly's article (page 330) indicate that some environmentalists are more interested in making an impression than advocating sound science?
2. Compare Tomkin's and Jacobson's articles. Is one writer more interested in making a political point than a scientific one?

Writing Suggestions

1. Consider the pro and con arguments by Jacobson and Tomkin. Which author's article in your opinion is more persuasive? Write an essay that defends your point of view.
2. *Collaborative Writing:* Discuss the two articles with a group of students, and decide which author is correct. If you feel you do not know enough about the topic to decide, make a list of information you would need before making a judgment. Work together to draft a brief analysis of your group's views on the subject.

PRO AND CON VIEWS:
BIOLOGY AND GENDER DIFFERENCES

JAMES C. DOBSON

James Dobson, a television evangelist and Christian family counselor, is the author of Straight Talk to Men and Their Wives. *Dobson believes that biological factors cause men and women to think and behave differently. The menstrual cycle, Dobson asserts, causes women to have different emotional natures than men.*

Biology Determines Gender Differences

As you read this article taken from Straight Talk to Men and Their Wives *(1980), consider the amount of proof Dobson provides to support his view. Try to be open-minded and to reserve judgment until you have read both Dobson's article and the opposing article that follows. Men and women are different, but what are the implications if these differences are determined to be biological or cultural in origin?*

1 I would like to offer some evidence to show that men and women are biologically unique. The women's movement, in its assault on traditional sex roles, has repeatedly asserted that males and females are identical except for the ability to bear children. Nothing could be farther from the truth.

THE HUMAN BRAIN

2 Let's begin by discussing the human brain, where maleness and femaleness are rooted. Careful research is revealing that the basic differences between the sexes are neurological in origin, rather than being purely cultural as ordinarily presumed. As Dr. Richard Restak stated in his book, *The Brain: The Last Frontier:*

3 Certainly, anyone who has spent time with children in a playground or school setting is aware of the differences in the way boys and girls respond to similar situations. Think of the last time you supervised a

> birthday party attended by five-year-olds. It's not usually the girls who pull hair, throw punches, or smear each other with food. Usually such differences are explained on a cultural basis. Boys are expected to more aggressive and play rough games, while girls are presumably encouraged to be more gentle, nonassertive, and passive. After several years of exposure to such expectations, so the theory goes, men and women wind up with widely varying behavioral and intellectual repertoires. As a corollary to this, many people believe that if child-rearing practices could be equalized and sexual-role stereotypes eliminated, most of these differences would eventually disappear. As often happens, however, the true state of affairs is not that simple.
>
> 4 Recent psychological research indicates that many of the differences in brain function between the sexes are innate, biologically determined, and relatively resistant to change through the influences of culture.

5 Dr. Restak presents numerous studies that document this statement, and then concludes this chapter by quoting Dr. David Wechsler, creator of the most popular intelligence test for use with adults.

> 6 Our findings do confirm what poets and novelists have often asserted, and the average layman long believed, namely, that men not only behave but 'think' differently from women.

7 Both Drs. Restak and Wechsler are right. Males and females differ anatomically, sexually, emotionally, psychologically, and biochemically. We differ in literally every cell of our bodies, for each sex carries a unique chromosomal pattern. Much is written today about so-called sex-change operations, whereby males are transformed into females or vice versa. Admittedly, it is possible to alter the external genitalia by surgery, and silicone can be used to pad the breasts or round out a bony frame. Hormones can then be injected to feminize or masculinize the convert. But nothing can be done to change the assignment of sex made by God at the instant of conception. That determination is carried in each cell, and it will read "male" or "female" from the earliest moment of life to the point of death. The Bible says emphatically, "Male *and* female created he them." Not one sex, but *two!*

8 Furthermore, it is my deep conviction that each sex displays unique emotional characteristics that are genetically endowed. Cultural influences cannot account for these novelties. Few psychologists have had the courage to express this view in recent years, because the

women's movement has perceived it as insulting. But to be *different* from men does not make women *inferior* to men. Males and females are original creations of God, each bearing strengths and weaknesses that counterbalance and interface with one another. It is a beautiful design that must not be disassembled.

THE MENSTRUAL CYCLE

9 Just how do female emotions differ from those of males? Let's consider first the importance of the menstrual cycle. I'm reminded of the late 1960s when hairy young men and women became almost undistinguishable from each other. Two of these hippies, a male and female, were involved in a minor traffic accident and were taken to a local hospital for treatment. The nurse who was completing the intake forms could not determine from their clothing and appearance which sex they represented. After considering the dilemma for a moment she asked, "Okay, which one of you has a menstrual cycle?"

10 The hippie with the bass voice looked at her through his bangs and said, "Not me, man. I gots a Honda."

11 The question was more significant then merely determining the sex of the patients. Included in this matter of menstruation are many implications for the way females feel about life during the course of the month. It has been said, quite accurately, that the four weeks of the menstrual cycle are characteristic of the four seasons of the year. The first week after a period can be termed the springtime of the physiological calendar. New estrogens (female hormones) are released each day and a woman's body begins to rebound from the recent winter.

12 The second week represents the summertime of the cycle, when the living is easy. A woman during this phase has more self-confidence than during any other phase of the month. It is a time of maximum energy, enthusiasm, amiability, and self-esteem. Estrogen levels account for much of this optimism, reaching a peak during mid-cycle when ovulation occurs. The relationship between husband and wife is typically at its best during these days of summer, when sexual desire (and the potential for pregnancy) are paramount.

13 But alas, the fall must surely follow summer. Estrogen levels steadily dwindle as the woman's body prepares itself for another period of menstruation. A second hormone, called progesterone, is

released, which reduces the effect of estrogen and initiates the symptoms of premenstrual tension. It is a bleak phase of the month. Self-esteem deteriorates day by day, bringing depression and pessimism with it. A bloated and sluggish feeling often produces not only discomfort but also the belief that "I am ugly." Irritability and aggression become increasingly evident as the week progresses, reaching a climax immediately prior to menstruation.

PSYCHOLOGICAL DIFFERENCES

14 Then come the winter and the period of the menstrual flow. Women differ remarkably in intensity of these symptoms, but most experience some discomfort. Those most vulnerable even find it necessary to spend a day or two in bed during the winter season, suffering from cramping and generalized misery. Gradually, the siege passes and the refreshing newness of springtime returns.

15 How can anyone who understands this cyclical pattern contend that there are no genetically determined psychological differences between males and females? No such system operates in men. The effect of the menstrual cycle is not only observable clinically, but it can be documented statistically.

16 The incidences of suicides, homicides, and infanticides perpetrated by women are significantly higher during the period of premenstrual tension than any other phase of the month. Consider also the findings of Alec Coppen and Neil Kessel, who studied 465 women and observed that they were more irritable and depressed during the premenstrual phase than during midcycle. "This was true for neurotic, psychotic and normal women alike. Similarly Natalie Sharness found the premenstrual phase associated with feelings of helplessness, anxiety, hostility, and yearning for love. At menstruation, this tension and irritability eased, but depression often accompanied the relief, and lingered until estrogen increased."

17 I doubt that these facts will come as a great revelation to men or women. Both sexes know that behavior and attitudes are related to the monthly pattern. I receive interesting letters from men who ask, "How can I cope with my wife's irritability during this phase?" Their question reminds me of an incident shared with me by my friend Dr. David Hernandez, who is an obstetrician and gynecologist in private practice.

The true story involves Latin men whose wives were given birth control pills by a pharmaceutical company. The Food and Drug Administration in America would not permit hormonal research to be conducted, so the company selected a small fishing village in South America which agreed to cooperate. All the women in the town were given the pill on the same date, and after three weeks the prescription was terminated to permit menstruation. That meant, of course, that every adult female in the community was experiencing premenstrual tension at the same time. The men couldn't take it. They all headed for their boats each month and remained at sea until the crisis passed at home. They knew, even if militant liberationists don't, that females are different from males . . . especially every twenty-eight days.

18 But there are other ways women are unique. Female emotions are also influenced by two other exclusively feminine functions, lactation and pregnancy. Furthermore, the hypothalamus, which is located at the base of the brain and has been called the "seat of the emotions," is apparently wired very differently for males than females. For example, a severe emotional shock or trauma can be interpreted by the hypothalamus, which then sends messages to the pituitary by way of neurons and hormones. The pituitary often responds by changing the body chemistry of the woman, perhaps interrupting the normal menstrual cycle for six months or longer. Female physiology is a finely tuned instrument, being more vulnerable and complex than the masculine counterpart. Why some women find that fact insulting is still a mystery to me.

19 How do these differences translate into observable behavior? Medical science has not begun to identify all the ramifications of sexual uniqueness. Some of the implications are extremely subtle. For example, when researchers quietly walked on high school and college campuses to study behavior of the sexes, they observed that males and females even transported their books in different ways. The young men tended to carry them at their sides with their arms looped over the top. Women and girls, by contrast, usually cradled their books at their breasts, in much the same way they would a baby. Who can estimate how many other sex-related influences lie below the level of consciousness?

20 Admittedly, some of the observed differences between the sexes *are* culturally produced. I don't know how to sort out those which are exclusively genetic from those which represent learned responses. Frankly, it doesn't seem to matter a great deal. The differences exist,

for whatever reason, and the current cultural revolution will not alter most of them significantly. At the risk of being called a sexist, or a propagator of sexual stereotypes, or a male chauvinistic pig (or worse), let me delineate a few of the emotional patterns typical of women as compared with men.

EMOTIONAL PATTERNS

21 The reproductive capacity of women results in a greater appreciation for stability, security, and enduring human relationships. In other words, females are more *future*-oriented because of their concern for children.

22 Related to the first item is a woman's emotional investment in her home, which usually exceeds that of her husband. She typically cares more than he about the minor details of the house, family functioning, and such concerns. To cite a personal example, my wife and I decided to install a new gas barbecue unit in our backyard. When the plumber completed the assignment and departed, Shirley and I both recognized that he had placed the appliance approximately six inches too high. I looked at the device and said, "Hmmm, yes sir, he sure made a mistake. That post is a bit too high. By the way, what are we having for dinner tonight?" Shirley's reaction was dramatically different. She said, "The plumber has that thing sticking up in the air and I don't think I can stand it!" Our contrasting views represented a classic difference of emotional intensity relating to the home.

23 Anyone who doubts that males and females are unique should observe how they approach a game of Ping Pong or Monopoly or dominoes or horseshoes or volleyball or tennis. Women often use the event as an excuse for fellowship and pleasant conversation. For men, the name of the game is *conquest.* Even if the setting is a friendly social gathering in the host's backyard, the beads of sweat on each man's forehead reveal his passion to win. This aggressive competitiveness has been attributed to cultural influences. I don't believe it. As Richard Restak said, "At a birthday party for five-year-olds, it's not usually the girls who pull hair, throw punches, or smear each other with food."

24 Males and females apparently differ in the manner by which they develop self-esteem. Men draw the necessary evidence of their worthiness primarily from their jobs—from being respected in business,

profession or craft. Women, however, *especially those who are homemakers,* depend primarily on the romantic relationship with their husbands for ego support. This explains why the emotional content of a marriage is often of greater significance to women than men and why tokens of affection are appreciated more by wives, who obtain esteem from these expressions of love and generosity.

INSTINCT AND PREFERENCES

25 A maternal instinct apparently operates in most women, although its force is stronger in some than others. This desire to procreate is certainly evident in those who are unable to conceive. I receive a steady influx of letters from women who express great frustration from their inability to become mothers. Although culture plays a major role in these longings, I believe they are rooted in female anatomy and physiology.

26 Perhaps the most dramatic differences between males and females are evident in their contrasting sexual preferences. He is more visually oriented, caring less about the romantic component. She is attracted not to a photograph of an unknown model or by a handsome stranger, but to a *particular* man with whom she has entered into an emotional relationship. This differing orientation is merely the tip of the iceberg in delineating the sexual uniqueness of males and females.

27 These items are illustrative and are not intended to represent a scientific delineation of sexual differences. The reader is invited to add his own observations to the list and to make his own interpretations.

Understanding Meaning

1. Does the women's movement suggest that men and women are identical except in childbearing?
2. How much of Dobson's argument rests on science and how much on his religious faith?
3. How does biology, in Dobson's view, shape gender roles?
4. According to Dobson, what role does the menstrual cycle play in causing women to behave differently from men?
5. *Critical Thinking:* In stating that gender differences are caused by innate, biological factors, is Dobson stating that the sexes are unequal? Does he argue that men are superior or merely different?

Evaluating Strategy

1. How much of Dobson's support rests on scientific results and how much on expert testimony?
2. Dobson admits that culture plays a role in determining gender differences. Does this weaken his argument or demonstrate his understanding of the complexity of the issue?

Appreciating Language

1. How does Dobson refer to feminists? Is his language neutral or biased?
2. Dobson is a minister. How much of his language reflects his religious training? What does this say about the audience he is trying to reach?

Connections across the Disciplines

1. Discussing gender differences is bound to be controversial. Review S. I. Hayakawa's article (page 464). Where does Dobson use "report" statements, and where does he make "inferences" and "judgments"?
2. Refer to Lisa Fried's article about female entrepreneurs (page 368). Does their different management style reflect different values caused by genetics or by socialization?

Writing Suggestions

1. Think about your own attitudes, feelings, and views of the opposite sex. Are you like others of your own sex? What common male or female traits do you possess? Were they caused by biology or by the way adults treated you as you grew up? Write a brief essay expressing your views on biology and gender differences.
2. *Collaborative Writing:* Discuss Dobson's article with a group of students, preferably a group combining both males and females. What views about biology and gender do members of the group express? Take notes and work together to draft either a short statement listing the effects of biology or a comparison paper contrasting conflicting theories within the group.

GERDA LERNER

Gerda Lerner is a history professor at the University of Wisconsin. She argues that many studies of gender differences are biased. Social customs and historical forces, which can be changed, she insists are the reasons for gender differences, not biology. The following essay comes from her book The Creation of Patriarchy *(1986).*

Biology Does Not Determine Gender Differences

Read Lerner's article after reviewing the preceding essay by Dobson. As you compare the articles, consider that you are reading the views of a family counselor and a history professor and not two scientists. Consider how they evaluate evidence taken from a discipline in which they have no formal training.

1 Traditionalists, whether working within a religious or a "scientific" framework, have regarded women's subordination as universal, God-given, or natural, hence immutable. Thus, it need not be questioned. What has survived, survived because it was best; it follows that it should stay that way.

2 Scholars critical of androcentric assumptions and those seeing the need for social change in the present have challenged the concept of the universality of female subordination. They reason that if the system of patriarchal dominance had a historic origin, it could be ended under altered historical conditions. Therefore, the question of the universality of female subordination has, for over 150 years, been central to the debate between traditionalists and feminist thinkers.

3 For those critical of patriarchal explanations, the next important question is: If female subordination was not universal, then was there ever an alternative model of society? This question has most often taken the form of the search for a matriarchal society in the past. Since much of the evidence in this search derives from myth, religion, and symbol, there has been little attention given to historical evidence.

FEMALE SUBORDINATION

4 For the historian, the more important and significant question is this: How, when, and why did female subordination come into existence?

5 Therefore, before we can undertake a discussion of the historical development of patriarchy, we need to review the major positions in the debate on these three questions.

6 The traditionalist answer to the first question is, of course, that male dominance is universal and natural. The argument may be offered in religious terms: Woman is subordinate to man because she was so created by God. Traditionalists accept the phenomenon of "sexual asymmetry," the assignment of different tasks and roles to men and women, which has been observed in all known human societies, as proof of their position and as evidence of its "naturalness." Since woman was, by divine design, assigned a different biological function than man was, they argue, she should also be assigned different social tasks. If God or nature created sex differences, which in turn determined the sexual division of labor, no one is to blame for sexual inequality and male dominance.

7 The traditionalist explanation focuses on woman's reproductive capacity and sees in motherhood woman's chief goal in life, by implication defining as deviant women who do not become mothers. Woman's maternal function is seen as a species necessity, since societies could not have survived into modernity without the majority of women devoting most of their adult lives to child-bearing and child-rearing. Thus the sexual division of labor based on biological differences is seen as functional and just.

BIOLOGICAL FACTORS

8 A corollary explanation of sexual asymmetry locates the causes of female subordination in biological factors affecting males. Men's greater physical strength, their ability to run faster and lift heavier weights, and their greater aggressiveness cause them to become hunters. As such they become the providers of food for their tribes and are more highly valued and honored than women. The skills deriving from their hunting experience in turn equip them to become warriors. Man-the-hunter, superior in strength, ability, and the experience derived from

using tools and weapons, "naturally" protects and defends the more vulnerable female, whose biological equipment destines her for motherhood and nurturance. Finally, this biological deterministic explanation is extended from the Stone Age into the present by the assertion that the sexual division of labor based on man's natural "superiority" is a given and therefore as valid today as it was in the primitive beginnings of human society.

9 This theory, in various forms, is currently by far the most popular version of the traditionalist argument and has had a powerful explanatory and reinforcing effect on contemporary ideas of male supremacy. This is probably due to its "scientific" trappings based on selected ethnographic evidence and on the fact that it seems to account for male dominance in such a way as to relieve contemporary men of all responsibility for it. The profound way in which this explanation has affected even feminist theoreticians is evident in its partial acceptance by Simone de Beauvoir, who takes as a given that man's "transcendence" derives from hunting and warfare and the use of the tools necessary for these pursuits.

10 Quite apart from its dubious biological claims of male physical superiority, the man-the-hunter explanation has been disproven by anthropological evidence concerning hunting and gathering societies. In most of these societies, big-game hunting is an auxiliary pursuit, while the main food supply is provided by gathering activities and small-game hunting, which women and children do. Also, it is precisely in hunting and gathering societies that we find many examples of complementarity between the sexes and societies in which women have relatively high status, which is in direct contradiction to the claims of the man-the-hunter school of thought.

CHALLENGING MALE DOMINANCE

11 Feminist anthropologists have challenged many of the earlier generalizations, which found male dominance virtually universal in all known societies, as being patriarchal assumptions on the part of ethnographers and investigators of those cultures. When feminist anthropologists have reviewed the data or done their own field work, they have found male dominance to be far from universal. They have found societies in which sexual asymmetry carries no connotation of dominance

or subordination. Rather, the tasks performed by both sexes are indispensable to group survival, and both sexes are regarded as equal in status in most aspects. In such societies the sexes are considered "complementary"; their roles and status are different, but equal.

12 Another way in which man-the-hunter theories have been disproven is by showing the essential, culturally innovative contributions women made to the creation of civilization by their invention of basketry and pottery and their knowledge and development of horticulture. Elise Boulding, in particular, has shown that the man-the-hunter myth and its perpetuation are social-cultural creations which serve the interest of maintaining male supremacy and hegemony.

13 Traditionalist defenses of male supremacy based on biological-deterministic reasoning have changed over time and proven remarkably adaptive and resilient. When the force of the religious argument was weakened in the nineteenth century the traditionalist explanation of women's inferiority became "scientific." Darwinian theories reinforced beliefs that species survival was more important than individual self-fulfillment. Much as the Social Gospel used the Darwinian idea of the survival of the fittest to justify the unequal distribution of wealth and privilege in American society, scientific defenders of patriarchy justified the definition of women through their maternal role and their exclusion from economic and educational opportunities as serving the best interest of species survival. It was because of their biological constitution and their maternal function that women were considered unsuited for higher education and for many vocational pursuits. Menstruation and menopause, even pregnancy, were regarded as debilitating, as diseased or abnormal states which incapacitated women and rendered them actually inferior.

14 Similarly, modern psychology observed existing sex differences with the unquestioned assumption that they were natural, and constructed a psychological female who was as biologically determined as had been her forebears. Viewing sex roles ahistorically, psychologists had to arrive at conclusions from observed clinical data which reinforced predominant gender roles.

15 Sigmund Freud's theories further reinforced the traditionalist explanation. Freud's normal human was male; the female was by his definition a deviant human being lacking a penis, whose entire psychological structure supposedly centered on the struggle to compensate for this deficiency. Even though many aspects of Freudian theory would prove helpful in constructing feminist theory, it was Freud's

dictum that for the female "anatomy is destiny" which gave new life and strength to the male supremacist argument.

16 The often vulgarized applications of Freudian theory to child-rearing and to popular advice literature lent new prestige to the old argument that woman's primary role is as child-bearer and child-rearer. It was popularized Freudian doctrine which became the prescriptive text for educators, social workers, and the general audiences of the mass media.

SOCIOBIOLOGY

17 E. O. Wilson's sociobiology has offered the traditionalist view on gender in an argument which applies Darwinian ideas of natural selection to human behavior. Wilson and his followers reason that human behaviors which are "adaptive" for group survival become encoded in the genes, and they include in these behaviors such complex traits as altruism, loyalty, and maternalism. They not only reason that groups practicing a sex-based division of labor in which women function as child-rearers and nurturers have an evolutionary advantage, but they claim such behavior somehow becomes part of our genetic heritage, in that the necessary psychological and physical propensities for such societal arrangements are selectively developed and genetically selected. Mothering is not only a socially assigned role but one fitting women's physical and psychological needs. Here, once again, biological determinism becomes prescriptive, in fact a political defense of the status quo in scientific language.

CIRCULAR REASONING

18 Feminist critics have revealed the circular reasoning, absence of evidence and unscientific assumptions of Wilsonian sociobiology. From the point of view of the nonscientist, the most obvious fallacy of sociobiologists is their ahistoricity in disregarding the fact that modern men and women do not live in a state of nature. The history of civilization describes the process by which humans have distanced themselves from nature by inventing and perfecting culture. Traditionalists ignore technological changes, which have made it possible to bottle-feed in-

fants safely and raise them to adulthood with care-takers other than their own mothers. They ignore the implications of changing life spans and changing life cycles. Until communal hygiene and modern medical knowledge cut infant mortality to a level where parents could reasonably expect each child born to them to live to adulthood, women did indeed have to bear many children in order for a few of them to survive. Similarly, longer life expectancy and lower infant mortality altered the life cycles of both men and women. These developments were connected with industrialization and occurred in Western civilization (for whites) toward the end of the nineteenth century, occurring later for the poor and for minorities due to the uneven distribution of health and social services. Whereas up to 1870 child-rearing and marriage were co-terminus—that is, one or both parents could expect to die before the youngest child reached adulthood—in modern American society husbands and wives can expect to live together for twelve years after their youngest child has reached adulthood, and women can expect to outlive their husbands by seven years.

OUTDATED ROLES

19 Traditionalists expect women to follow the same roles and occupations that were functional and species-essential in the Neolithic. They accept cultural changes by which men have freed themselves from biological necessity. The supplanting of hard physical labor by the labor of machines is considered progress; only women, in their view, are doomed forever to species-service through their biology. To claim that of all human activities only female nurturance is unchanging and eternal is indeed to consign half the human race to a lower state of existence, to nature rather than to culture.

20 The qualities which may have fostered human survival in the Neolithic are no longer required of modern people. Regardless of whether qualities such as aggressiveness or nurturance are genetically or culturally transmitted, it should be obvious that the aggressiveness of males, which may have been highly functional in the Stone Age, is threatening human survival in the nuclear age. At a time when overpopulation and exhaustion of natural resources represent a real danger for human survival, to curb women's procreative capacities may be more "adaptive" than to foster them.

21 Further, in opposition to any argument based on biological determinism, feminists challenge the hidden androcentric assumptions in the sciences dealing with humans. They have charged that in biology, anthropology, zoology, and psychology such assumptions have led to a reading of scientific evidence that distorts its meaning. Thus, for example, animal behavior is invested with anthropomorphic significance, which makes patriarchs of male chimpanzees. Many feminists argue that the limited number of proven biological differences among the sexes has been vastly exaggerated by cultural interpretations and that the value put on sex differences is in itself a cultural product. Sexual attributes are a biological given, but gender is a product of historical process. The fact that women bear children is due to sex; that women nurture children is due to gender, a cultural construct. It is gender which has been chiefly responsible for fixing women's place in society.

Understanding Meaning

1. What evidence does Lerner provide to refute the view that biological factors cause gender differences?
2. What assumptions does Lerner feel have invalidated much of the research that has asserted the primacy of biology as the determining factor in shaping human behavior?
3. Lerner states that women have children from "sex" but raise them because of "gender." What differences does Lerner see between sex and gender?
4. *Critical Thinking:* Does Lerner refute Dobson's assertion or the concept of male supremacy? Does Dobson argue that men are naturally superior? Can men and women be biologically different but equal?

Evaluating Strategy

1. How does Lerner refute the idea that biology determines gender differences?
2. At several points Lerner states that feminists have challenged or questioned ideas. Does she provide proof of the validity of their arguments?

Appreciating Language

1. Lerner does not define words such as "androcentric" and "anthropomorphic." What does this suggest about her intended audience?
2. How does her language reflect her training as a historian?

Connections across the Disciplines

1. Consider the articles written by Amy Tan (page 277), bell hooks (page 401), and Kesaya Noda (page 439). Do these women see their lives and attitudes as caused more by their culture or by their gender?
2. Examine the role that culture has on African American women as stated by bell hooks (page 401). Will it ever be possible to determine which factor, biology or culture, affects people more?

Writing Suggestions

1. Write a comparison and contrast essay summarizing the views of Dobson and Lerner. You may simply discuss the different views or recommend one over the other.
2. *Collaborative Writing:* Discuss Lerner and Dobson with a group of students. Determine what research would be needed to evaluate the role of biology in gender differences. Take notes and then write a brief paper outlining the process needed to collect and analyze evidence.

THOMAS JEFFERSON ET AL.

During the hot summer of 1776, the Second Continental Congress met in Philadelphia. Following a call for a resolution of independence from Britain, John Adams, Thomas Jefferson, Benjamin Franklin, Robert Livingston, and Roger Sherman were charged with drafting a declaration. Jefferson wrote the original draft, which was revised by Adams and Franklin before being presented to the entire Congress. After further changes, the Declaration of Independence was adopted and signed.

The Declaration of Independence

The Declaration of Independence presents a theory of government greatly influenced by the concept of natural rights espoused by Locke and Rousseau and then provides evidence that the British have failed to respect these rights. Notice that most of the declaration is a list of grievances or causes for the colonies to seek independence.

1 *In Congress, July 4, 1776. The unanimous Declaration of the thirteen united States of America,*

2 When in the Course of human events, it becomes necessary for one people to dissolve the political bands which have connected them with another, and to assume among the powers of the earth, the separate and equal station to which the Laws of Nature and of Nature's God entitle them, a decent respect to the opinions of mankind requires that they should declare the causes which impel them to the separation.

3 We hold these truths to be self-evident, that all men are created equal, that they are endowed by their Creator with certain unalienable Rights, that among these are Life, Liberty and the pursuit of Happiness.

4 That to secure these rights, Governments are instituted among Men, deriving their just powers from the consent of the governed,

5 That whenever any Form of Government becomes destructive of these ends, it is the Right of the People to alter or to abolish it, and to institute new Government, laying its foundation on such principles and organizing its powers in such form, as to them shall seem most likely to effect their Safety and Happiness. Prudence, indeed, will dictate that Governments long established should not be changed for

light and transient causes; and accordingly all experience hath shown, that mankind are more disposed to suffer, while evils are sufferable, than to right themselves by abolishing the forms to which they are accustomed. But when a long train of abuses and usurpations, pursuing invariably the same Object evinces a design to reduce them under absolute Despotism, it is their right, it is their duty, to throw off such Government, and to provide new Guards for their future security.

6 Such has been the patient sufferance of these Colonies; and such is now the necessity which constrains them to alter their former Systems of Government. The history of the present King of Great Britain is a history of repeated injuries and usurpations, all having in direct object the establishment of an absolute Tyranny over these States. To prove this, let Facts be submitted to a candid world.

7 He has refused his Assent to Laws, the most wholesome and necessary for the public good.

8 He has forbidden his Governors to pass Laws of immediate and pressing importance, unless suspended in their operation till his Assent should be obtained; and when so suspended, he has utterly neglected to attend to them.

9 He has refused to pass other Laws for the accommodation of large districts of people, unless those people would relinquish the right of Representation in the Legislature, a right inestimable to them and formidable to tyrants only.

10 He has called together legislative bodies at places unusual, uncomfortable, and distant from the depository of their public Records, for the sole purpose of fatiguing them into compliance with his measures.

11 He has dissolved Representative Houses repeatedly, for opposing with manly firmness his invasions on the rights of the people.

12 He has refused for a long time, after such dissolutions, to cause others to be elected; whereby the Legislative powers, incapable of Annihilation, have returned to the People at large for their exercise; the State remaining in the mean time exposed to all the dangers of invasion from without, and convulsions within.

13 He has endeavoured to prevent the population of these States; for that purpose obstructing the Laws for Naturalization of Foreigners; refusing to pass others to encourage their migrations hither, and raising the conditions of new Appropriations of Lands.

14 He has obstructed the Administration of Justice, by refusing his Assent to Laws for establishing Judiciary powers.

15 He has made Judges dependent on his Will alone, for the tenure of their offices, and the amount and payment of their salaries.

16 He has erected a multitude of New Offices, and sent hither swarms of Officers to harrass our people, and eat out their substance.

17 He has kept among us in times of peace, Standing Armies without the Consent of our legislatures.

18 He has affected to render the Military independent of and superior to the Civil power.

19 He has combined with others to subject us to a jurisdiction foreign to our constitution, and unacknowledged by our laws; giving his Assent to their Acts of pretended Legislation:

20 For quartering large bodies of armed troops among us:

21 For protecting them, by a mock Trial, from punishment for any Murders which they should commit on the Inhabitants of these States:

22 For cutting off our Trade with all parts of the world:

23 For imposing Taxes on us without our Consent:

24 For depriving us in many cases, of the benefits of Trial by Jury:

25 For transporting us beyond Seas to be tried for pretended offences:

26 For abolishing the free System of English Laws in a neighbouring Province, establishing therein an Arbitrary government, and enlarging its Boundaries so as to render it at once an example and fit instrument for introducing the same absolute rule in these Colonies:

27 For taking away our Charters, abolishing our most valuable Laws, and altering fundamentally the Forms of our Governments:

28 For suspending our own Legislatures, and declaring themselves invested with power to legislate for us in all cases whatsoever.

29 He has abdicated Government here, by declaring us out of his Protection and waging War against us.

30 He has plundered our seas, ravaged our Coasts, burnt our towns, and destroyed the lives of our people.

31 He is at this time transporting large Armies of foreign Mercenaries to compleat the works of death, desolation and tyranny, already begun with circumstances of Cruelty & perfidy scarcely paralleled in the most barbarous ages, and totally unworthy the Head of a civilized nation.

32 He has constrained our fellow Citizens taken Captive on high Seas to bear Arms against their Country, to become the executioners of their friends and Brethren, or to fall themselves by their Hands.

33 He has excited domestic insurrections amongst us, and has endeavoured to bring on the inhabitants of our frontiers, the merciless Indian Savages, whose known rule of warfare, is an undistinguished destruction of all ages, sexes and conditions.

34 In every stage of these Oppressions We have Petitioned for Redress in the most humble terms: Our repeated Petitions have been answered only by repeated injury. A Prince, whose character is thus marked by every act which may define a Tyrant, is unfit to be the ruler of a free people.

35 Nor have We been wanting in attentions to our Brittish brethren. We have warned them from time to time of attempts by their legislature to extend an unwarrantable jurisdiction over us. We have reminded them of the circumstances of our emigration and settlement here. We have appealed to their native justice and magnanimity, and we have conjured them by the ties of our common kindred to disavow these usurpations, which, would inevitably interrupt our connections and correspondence. They too have been deaf to the voice of justice and consanguinity. We must, therefore, acquiesce in the necessity, which denounces our Separation, and hold them, as we hold the rest of mankind, Enemies in War, in Peace Friends.

36 We, therefore, the Representatives of the united States of America, in General Congress, Assembled, appealing to the Supreme Judge of the world for the rectitude of our intentions, do, in the Name, and by Authority of the good People of these Colonies, solemnly publish and declare, That these United Colonies are, and of Right ought to be, Free and Independent States; that they are Absolved from all Allegiance to the British Crown, and that all political connection between them and the State of Great Britain, is and ought to be totally dissolved; and that as Free and Independent States, they have full Power to levy War, conclude Peace, contract Alliances, establish Commerce, and to do all other Acts and Things which Independent States may of right do.

37 And for the support of this Declaration, with a firm reliance on the protection of divine Providence, we mutually pledge to each other our Lives, our Fortunes and our sacred Honor.

Understanding Meaning

1. What are the principal causes for the Congress to declare independence?
2. Why do Jefferson and the other authors argue that these grievances cannot be resolved in any other fashion?
3. *Critical Thinking:* When was the last time you read the Declaration of Independence? Do some items strike you as relevant to current conditions?

Should Americans be more familiar with a document that helped create their own country and establish its values?

Evaluating Strategy

1. How does the Declaration of Independence use induction and deduction?
2. How much space is devoted to the list of causes? Is enough evidence provided to support severing ties with Britain?
3. The causes are placed in separate paragraphs rather than combined. What impact does this have?

Appreciating Language

1. How does the document refer to the king?
2. This document was drafted in 1776. How readable is it today? How has language changed in two hundred years?

Connections across the Disciplines

1. Compare the Declaration of Independence which severed relations with Britain and led to war to President Clinton's memorandum on landscaping (page 532). What does this say about modern bureaucracy? Would current politicians be able to communicate with as much force and poetry as the Continental Congress?
2. Compare the Declaration of Independence to Albert Einstein's letter to President Roosevelt (page 676). What characteristics do many of the world's most important writings seem to have?

Writing Suggestions

1. Write a personal analysis of the Declaration of Independence. What do you think is the most significant feature of the document? What does the phrase "Life, Liberty and the pursuit of Happiness" mean to you?
2. *Collaborative Writing:* Discuss the declaration with a group of students. Does the current government reflect the ideals of Jefferson? How has America changed since 1776? For further discussion, look up the original draft, which contained a passage denouncing slavery, a passage Jefferson had to delete to pacify southern delegates. Develop a statement with other students reflecting your opinion of the Declaration of Independence's importance in the twenty-first century.

HEWLETT-PACKARD

Cause-and-effect writing is often used in manuals, textbooks, training guides, and consumer information packets. Hewlett-Packard includes this troubleshooting guide in the owner manual of a laser printer.

Solving Printer Operation Problems

As you examine the cause-and-effect guide, consider the intended audience and the use of a chart. How easy would this information be to follow if written in standard paragraphs?

1 Use the following steps to help solve problems you experience with your printer. If you need more help, refer to the service and support information. . . . That chapter will guide you in getting help from your dealer or, if necessary, contacting Hewlett-Packard for help.

	SYMPTOM	POSSIBLE CAUSE	SOLUTION
2	***The printer does not respond when you send a print job from software.***	The printer's parallel cable is loose.	Check the connections on the printer and on the computer. Make sure the cable on the printer is not attached upside-down (some cables have a flexible plastic sleeve that allows an improper connection).
3			Secure the cable to the computer with screws and to the printer with the wire clips.

4	***The printer does not respond when you send a print job from software, continued.***	The parallel cable is defective.	Try your cable on another system with a print job that you know works.
5		The printer is malfunctioning.	If the printer is in Intelligent Off mode, press the front panel button to turn on the Ready light. Then press it again to print a self test page. If the self test page prints, the printer is working correctly.
6			If all the lights are on, there is a hardware error. Disconnect the printer from its power source and wait 15 minutes. Then reconnect it. If all four lights come back on, contact your HP authorized service representative. . . .
7		You did not select the correct printer through your software.	Check your software's printer selection menu to see if you selected the HP LaserJet 4L printer.
8		Your software or your printer is not yet configured for the correct printer port.	Check your software's configuration menu to make sure it is accessing the correct printer port.
9			If your computer has more than one parallel port, make sure you are connected to the correct one.

10	***The printer does not respond when you send a print job from software, continued.***	The printer is not connected to power, or the power source is not active.	Check your power cord, switches, and fuses.
11		You did not reset the printer after clearing a paper jam.	Press the front panel button, or open and close the top printer door to reset the printer after a jam.
12		The printer's top door or rear door is open.	Make sure both doors are closed securely.
13		The printer is connected to a switch box, and the switch box is not set up to receive data from your printer.	Check the switch box setting.
14	***The Error light is on steadily.***	The printer's top door is open, or the toner cartridge is not installed completely.	Open the door, reinstall the toner cartridge, then close the door firmly.
15	***The Error light is blinking.***	There was a memory error in your print job.	Press the front panel button to resume printing. (There may be some data loss.)
16			Change your page to make it less complex, or add optional printer memory.
17	***The Paper light is on steadily.***	The paper cassette is empty.	Load more paper into the paper cassette.
18	***The Paper light is blinking.***	There is a paper jam.	See . . . instructions on how to clear paper jams.
19	***Both the Data light and the Ready light are on steadily.***	There is unprinted data in the printer. (Your software did not send an "end of job" command.)	Briefly press the front panel button to print the rest of the data.

20	***The Data light is blinking.***	The printer is in Manual Feed mode and the manual feed slot is waiting for paper.	Insert a piece of paper into the manual feed slot.
21	***All the printer's lights are off.***	The printer is in Inteligent Off mode.	Briefly press the front panel button to activate the Ready light. If the Ready light does not come on, check the power cord and your power source. If the printer still does not respond, contact your local HP authorized service representative. . . .
22	***All the printer's lights are on.***	The printer has a hardware error.	Disconnect the printer from its power source and wait 15 minutes. Then reconnect it. If all four lights come back on, contact your HP authorized service representative. . . .
23	***The printer is feeding multiple sheets or jams frequently.***	The paper does not meet HP's specifications for print media (embossed, damaged, too slick or too rough, too much moisture, wrong weight).	Try another kind of paper. See the paper specifications. . . .
24		The paper is sticking together.	Take the paper out of the cassette and fan it to separate the sheets.
25		The paper cassette is too full.	Remove some of the paper.
26		The printer may need service.	Contact your HP authorized service representative. . . .

27	***The printer jams when you attempt a manual feed.***	You removed and reinserted your paper while trying to do a manual feed.	Once the printer senses that the paper is in the manual feed slot (you feel it grab the corner), do not remove it and reinsert it. This causes the printer to pull the paper through the paper path too late, and results in a paper jam. Let the printer automatically realign the paper to straighten it in the paper path.

Understanding Meaning

1. What causes the "Paper light" to blink?
2. When should you call a service representative?
3. What should you try when the printer jams or feeds multiple sheets?

Evaluating Strategy

1. How readable is this guide? Is it clearly stated?
2. What impact does the format have?
3. *Critical Thinking:* What would be the best way for technical writers to test their owner's manual before printing it and shipping to hundreds of thousands of consumers worldwide?

Appreciating Language

1. Does any of the wording seem confusing to you? Could this set of instructions be read by nontechnical consumers?
2. Why do all the solution statements open with verbs?

Connections across the Disciplines

1. Compare these instructions with "The Heimlich Maneuver" (page 536). Do they share common features?

2. Compare these instructions with "Communications Styles Taiwan" (page 307). When are chartlike presentations of text acceptable?

Writing Suggestions

1. Write a similar cause-and-effect chart about a product you are familiar with.
2. *Collaborative Writing:* Discuss manuals you have encountered as students or consumers with a small group. What problems and frustrations do people report having? Work together to write a list of causes of reader confusion. You may place these in a chart.

GUIDELINES FOR CAUSE-AND-EFFECT WRITING

1. **Determine your goal.** Are you attempting to explain a cause or to predict future outcomes?
2. **Evaluate your readers' needs.** What evidence does your reader require to accept your conclusions? Are government statistics more impressive than the testimony of experts? Does any background information or do any definitions need to be presented?
3. **Offer logical, acceptable evidence.** Present support that comes from reliable sources readers will accept. Present evidence in a clearly organized manner. Use brief narratives or analogies to dramatize data.
4. **Review your use of deduction or induction.** Does your major premise contain unproven assumptions? Is it clearly stated, or is it subject to different interpretations? Does your inductive leap move beyond reasonable doubt? Do you provide enough evidence to support your inductive conclusion?
5. **Qualify assertions and conclusions.** A writer who admits that alternative interpretations or conflicting evidence exist can appear more credible to readers than one who narrowly insists he or she has the only possible conclusion.
6. **Evaluate sources.** Do not allow yourself to automatically assume everything you read is valid. Experts have made errors of judgment. Read books, articles, and studies carefully. Look for signs of bias, unproven assumptions, or mistakes in logic. Look for what is missing.
7. **Use other modes to organize information.** It may be beneficial to use a narrative, comparison, extended definition, or division and classification to present your cause-and-effect thesis.

SUGGESTED TOPICS FOR CAUSE-AND-EFFECT WRITING

General Assignments

Write a cause-and-effect paper on any of the following topics. Your paper may use other modes to organize and present evidence. Cause-and-effect papers usually require research. It is possible to use cause and effect in less formal papers, in which you offer personal experience and observations as examples. However, the more objective facts you can cite, the stronger your writing will be.

Write a paper explaining the cause(s) of the following topics:

- Teenage pregnancy
- Sexual harassment
- Divorce
- The success or failure of a local business
- The victory or defeat of a political candidate

Write a paper predicting the effects of the following topics:

- The information superhighway
- Immigration
- Harsher drunk-driving laws
- An aging population
- The death of a spouse or loved one

Writing in Context

1. Analyze in a short essay a recent event on campus, in your community, or at your place of work. Examine what caused this event to take place. If several causes exist, you may use division to explain them or classification to rank them from the most important to the least important.
2. Write a letter to the editor of the campus newspaper predicting the effects of a current policy change, incident, or trend in student behavior.
3. Imagine a job application asks you to write a 250-word essay presenting your reasons for choosing your career. Write a one-page essay that lists your most important reasons. As you write, consider how an employer would evaluate your response.

CAUSE AND EFFECT CHECKLIST

1. Is your thesis clearly defined?
2. Are causes clearly stated, logically organized, and supported by details?
3. Are conflicting interpretations disproven or discredited?
4. Are effects supported by evidence? Do you avoid overdramatizing results?
5. Do you anticipate future changes that will alter effects?
6. Do you avoid making logical fallacies, especially hasty generalizations and mistaking a time relationship for cause and effect?

10

Argument and Persuasion

INFLUENCING READERS

WHAT IS ARGUMENT AND PERSUASION?

We are bombarded by argument and persuasion every day. Newspaper editorials encourage us to change our opinions about abortion, gun control, or public financing of religious schools. Sales brochures convince us to invest in stocks or buy life insurance. Fundraising letters ask us to contribute to homeless shelters or the local symphony. Billboards, magazine ads, and television commercials urge us to buy automobiles and soft drinks. Political candidates solicit our votes. Public service announcements warn us against smoking and drunk driving.

As a student you have to develop persuasive arguments in essays and research papers to demonstrate your skills and knowledge. After graduation you will need a persuasive résumé and cover letter to secure job interviews. In your career you will have to impress clients, motivate employees, justify decisions, and propose new ideas to superiors with well-stated arguments and persuasive appeals.

Arguments are assertions designed to convince readers to accept an idea, adopt a solution, or change their way of thinking. Writers use reason and facts to support their arguments, often disproving or disputing conflicting theories or alternative proposals in the process. Attorneys prepare written arguments stating why a client has a valid claim or deserves a new trial. Scientists present the results of experiments to argue for new medical treatments or to disprove current assumptions. Economists assemble data to support arguments to raise or lower interest rates. Addressing trial attorneys, Senator Joseph Biden argues that domestic violence should be seen as a social issue and not a personal problem. In stating his case, Biden uses statistics to demonstrate the seriousness of the problem:

> One million women a year seek medical assistance for injuries caused by violence at the hands of a male partner. That is a public health menace, not a private malady. Children in homes with domestic violence are 15 times more likely to be abused or neglected than children in peaceful homes. That is a public tragedy for future generations, not a private failure of communication. We spend $5 billion to $10 billion a year on health care, criminal justice, and other social costs of domestic violence. That is a public budget crisis, not a minor shortfall.

The way writers present evidence depends on their discipline or profession. Each field has specific methods and standards of presenting evidence and stating arguments.

The audience plays a critical role in the way writers shape an argument, especially when they suspect readers may hold alternative viewpoints or be prejudiced against them or the ideas they advocate. In his article "Why Prisons Don't Work" (page 628), Wilbert Rideau, a convicted murderer, understands that few readers have sympathy for convicts. He begins by agreeing with those who advocate punishing criminals but then presents his own views:

> Prison has a role in public safety, but it is not a cure-all. Its value is limited, and its use should also be limited to what it does best: isolating young criminals long enough to give them a chance to grow up and get a grip on their impulses. It is a traumatic experience, certainly, but it should be only a temporary one, not a way of life.

In directing an argument to readers, writers often use *persuasion,* making emotional or dramatic statements that stir people's passions and beliefs. Advertisers use sex appeal to sell everything from toothpaste to cars. Commercials for charities flash 800-numbers over images of starving children to motivate people to make donations. In creating persuasive arguments, you should consider the perceptual world of your readers (page 10).

Persuasive Appeals

Writers traditionally use three basic appeals to convince readers to accept their ideas or take action: logic, emotion, and ethics. Because each appeal has advantages and disadvantages, writers generally use more than one.

LOGIC supports a point of view or proposed action through reasoned arguments and a presentation of evidence:

Test results Findings established by experiments or standard research methods.
Statistics Data represented by numbers and percentages.
Expert testimony Opinions or statements made by respected authorities.
Eyewitness testimony Statements by those who experienced or witnessed events and situations.
Surveys Measurements of public opinion or sample audiences.

Logic is widely used in academic, business, and government reports.

Advantages: Provides evidence needed for major decisions, especially group decisions.
Disadvantages: Can demand a high degree of reader attention and specialized knowledge.

EMOTION uses images, sensations, or shock appeals to lead people to react in a desired manner. Emotional appeals call on people's deeply felt needs and desires:

Creativity The desire for recognition by self-expression.
Achievement The need to attain money, fame, or fulfillment.
Independence The drive to be unique, to stand out, and to be individual.
Conformity The desire to be part of a group, to be included, and to be *in*.
Endurance To achieve satisfaction by bearing burdens others could not or feeling successful by simply surviving.
Fear To resist, avoid, or defeat threats to the self or society, such as cancer, crime, or terrorism.

Emotional appeals are found most frequently in public relations, marketing, and advertising.

Advantages: Produces immediate results.
Disadvantages: Has limited impact, can backfire, and provides limited factual support for readers to share with others.

ETHICS use shared values to influence people. Ethics may call on reasoning but do not rest wholly on logical analysis of data. Like emotional appeals, ethics reflect deeply held convictions rather than personal motivations.

Religion The desire to follow the rules and behavior espoused by one's faith, such as to be a good Christian or practicing Jew.
Patriotism The urge to place one's country before personal needs: "Ask not what your country can do for you; ask what you can do for your country."
Standards The desire to be a good citizen, a good lawyer, or a good parent, to express the higher ideals of a community, profession, or family role.
Humanitarianism A secular appeal to help others, save the environment, protect the weak, or to be a "citizen of the world."

Ethical appeals form the basis of many sermons, editorials, and political speeches.

Advantages: Can be very powerful, especially if the writer is addressing an audience with the same value system.
Disadvantages: Depends on readers who accept the principles espoused by the writer. A Muslim cleric's appeal, for example, may have little impact on Catholics or atheists.

To be effective, writers frequently mix factual detail with emotionally charged human interest. An article on homeless children might use the story of a single child to arouse sympathy, then provide statistics to illustrate the severity of the problem, and, finally, outline possible solutions.

Appealing to Hostile Readers

Perhaps most challenging is attempting to persuade a hostile audience, readers you anticipate having negative attitudes toward you, the organization you represent, or the ideas you advocate. Although no technique will magically convert opponents into supporters, you can overcome a measure of hostility and influence those who may still be undecided with a few approaches:

1. **Openly admit differences.** Instead of attempting to pretend no conflict exists, openly state that your view may differ from your readers. This honest admission can win a measure of respect.
2. **Responsibly summarize opposing viewpoints.** By fairly restating your opponents' views, you force readers to agree with you and demonstrate impartiality.
3. **Avoid making judgmental statements.** Do not label your opponents' ideas with negative language. Use neutral terms to make distinctions. If you call your ideas intelligent and your readers' naive, you will have difficulty getting people to accept your points because in the process they will have to accept your insults as being valid.
4. **Point to shared values, experiences, and problems.** Build common bridges with your readers by demonstrating past cooperation and common goals.
5. **Ask your readers to keep an open mind.** Don't demand or expect to convert readers. But almost everyone will agree to try to be open-minded and receptive to new ideas.
6. **Work to overcome negative stereotypes.** Play the devil's advocate, and determine what negative stereotypes your readers might have about you and your ideas. Then work to include examples, references, and evidence in your paper to counter negative assumptions.

CRITICAL THINKING FOR WRITING ARGUMENT AND PERSUASION

Perhaps no other form of writing demands more critical thinking than argument and persuasion. When using logical, emotional, and ethical appeals, avoid the common traps or fallacies writers often fall into:

- **Absolute statements** Although it is important to convince readers by making a strong impression, avoid making absolute claims that can be dismissed with a single exception. If you state "all lawyers are honest," a reader has only to think of a single dishonest attorney to repudiate your argument. A qualified claim can make a strong impression and leave room for exceptions: "The legal profession is known for its high standards of ethical conduct."

- ***Non sequitur* (it does not follow)** Avoid making assertions based on irrelevant evidence: "Bill Smith was a great football coach—he'll make a great mayor." Although a coach may possess leadership and skills in strategy, he may lack the political knowledge and diplomatic skills needed in government.
- **Begging the question** Do not assume what has to be proved: "Nancy is lying because she never tells the truth." Asserting that Nancy never tells the truth offers no evidence that she is lying.
- **False dilemma** Do not offer or accept only two alternatives to a problem: "Either employees must take a wage cut, or the company will go bankrupt." This statement ignores other possible solutions such as raising prices, lowering production costs, or increasing sales.
- **False analogy** Comparisons make very weak arguments: "Crack cocaine should be legalized since Prohibition did not work." Alcohol and crack cocaine are not like substances. Alcohol has been consumed by humans for thousands of years. Crack cocaine has never been socially acceptable to most Americans.
- **Red herring** Resist the temptation to dodge the real issue by drawing attention to something controversial: "How can you endorse the budget proposal of a congressman indicted for soliciting bribes?" Corruption charges alone do not invalidate a politician's policies.
- **Borrowed authority** Avoid assuming that an expert in one field can be accepted as an authority in another: "Senator Johnson is convinced Dallas will win by ten points." A respected senator may have no more insight into the National Football League than a cab driver or a hairdresser. Celebrity endorsements are common examples of borrowed authority.
- ***Ad hominem* (attacking the person)** Attack ideas, not the people who advocate them: "The only people who oppose gun control are paranoid Nazis and Uzi-toting drug dealers." The merits of the issue and not the personalities have to be discussed to create a convincing argument.

READING ARGUMENT AND PERSUASION

When reading the argument and persuasion entries in this chapter, keep these questions in mind:

Meaning

1. What is the author's thesis? What does he or she want readers to accept?
2. How credible is the thesis? Does it make sense? Are alternatives discussed?
3. How does the writer characterize those who advocate differing views? Does the writer appear to have an unfair bias?

Strategy

1. Which appeals are used—logic, emotion, or ethics?
2. Do the appeals seem to work with the intended audience?
3. Are the factual details interesting, believable, and effective?
4. Are emotional appeals suitable, or do they risk backfiring or distorting the issue?
5. Are the logical fallacies avoided?
6. Does the writer appear to anticipate rejection or approval?

Language

1. What role does connotation play in shaping arguments using logical, emotional, or ethical appeals?
2. What does the author's choice of words suggest about the intended audience?
3. Does word choice indicate a bias?

WILBERT RIDEAU

Wilbert Rideau is a convicted murderer serving a life sentence at Algoma prison in Louisiana. He has been incarcerated since 1962. Rideau is the editor of the Louisiana State Penitentiary newsmagazine The Angolite *and co-editor of* Life Sentences.

Why Prisons Don't Work

This essay appeared in Time *magazine (1994). As you read the article, consider Rideau's situation as an inmate denouncing prison policies. Notice how the essay weaves emotional appeals based on personal experience and observation with factual support.*

1 I was among 31 murderers sent to the Louisiana State Penitentiary in 1962 to be executed or imprisoned for life. We weren't much different from those we found here, or those who had preceded us. We were unskilled, impulsive and uneducated misfits, mostly black, who had done dumb, impulsive things—failures, rejects from the larger society. Now a generation has come of age and gone since I've been here, and everything is much the same as I found it. The faces of the prisoners are different, but behind them are the same impulsive, uneducated, unskilled minds that made dumb, impulsive choices that got them into more trouble than they ever thought existed. The vast majority of us are consigned to suffer and die here so politicians can sell the illusion that permanently exiling people to prison will make society safe.

2 Getting tough has always been a "silver bullet," a quick fix for the crime and violence that society fears. Each year in Louisiana—where excess is a way of life—lawmakers have tried to outdo each other in legislating harsher mandatory penalties and in reducing avenues of release. The only thing to do with criminals, they say, is get tougher. They have. In the process, the purpose of prison began to change. The state boasts one of the highest lockup rates in the country, imposes the most severe penalties in the nation and vies to execute more criminals per capita than anywhere else. This state is so tough that last

year, when prison authorities here wanted to punish an inmate in solitary confinement for an infraction, the most they could inflict on him was to deprive him of his underwear. It was all he had left.

3 If getting tough resulted in public safety, Louisiana citizens would be the safest in the nation. They're not. Louisiana has the highest murder rate among states. Prison, like the police and the courts, has a minimal impact on crime because it is a response after the fact, a mop-up operation. It doesn't work. The idea of punishing the few to deter the many is counterfeit because potential criminals either think they're not going to get caught or they're so emotionally desperate or psychologically distressed that they don't care about the consequences of their actions. The threatened punishment, regardless of its severity, is never a factor in the equation. But society, like the incorrigible criminal it abhors, is unable to learn from its mistakes.

4 Prison has a role in public safety, but it is not a cure-all. Its value is limited, and its use should also be limited to what it does best: isolating young criminals long enough to give them a chance to grow up and get a grip on their impulses. It is a traumatic experience, certainly, but it should be only a temporary one, not a way of life. Prisoners kept too long tend to embrace the criminal culture, its distorted values and beliefs; they have little choice—prison is their life. There are some prisoners who cannot be returned to society—serial killers, serial rapists, professional hit men and the like—but the monsters who need to die in prison are rare exceptions in the criminal landscape.

5 Crime is a young man's game. Most of the nation's random violence is committed by young urban terrorists. But because of long, mandatory sentences, most prisoners here are much older, having spent 15, 20, 30 or more years behind bars, long past necessity. Rather than pay for new prisons, society would be well served by releasing some of its older prisoners who pose no threat and using the money to catch young street thugs. Warden John Whitley agrees that many older prisoners here could be freed tomorrow with little or no danger to society. Release, however, is governed by law or by politicians, not by penal professionals. Even murderers, those most feared by society, pose little risk. Historically, for example, the domestic staff at Louisiana's Governor's mansion has been made up of murderers, hand-picked to work among the chief-of-state and his family. Penologists have long known that murder is almost always a once-in-a-lifetime act. The most dangerous criminal is the one who has not yet killed but has a history of escalating offenses. He's the one to watch.

6 Rehabilitation can work. Everyone changes in time. The trick is to influence the direction that change takes. The problem with prisons is that they don't do more to rehabilitate those confined in them. The convict who enters prison illiterate will probably leave the same way. Most convicts want to be better than they are, but education is not a priority. This prison houses 4,600 men and offers academic training to 240, vocational training to a like number. Perhaps it doesn't matter. About 90 percent of the men here may never leave this prison alive.

7 The only effective way to curb crime is for society to work to prevent the criminal act in the first place, to come between the perpetrator and crime. Our youngsters must be taught to respect the humanity of others and to handle disputes without violence. It is essential to educate and equip them with the skills to pursue their life ambitions in a meaningful way. As a community, we must address the adverse life circumstances that spawn criminality. These things are not quick, and they're not easy, but they're effective. Politicians think that's too hard a sell. They want to be on record for doing something now, something they can point to at re-election time. So the drumbeat goes on for more police, more prisons, more of the same failed policies.

8 Ever see a dog chase its tail?

Understanding Meaning

1. Why does Rideau consider "getting tough" a "'silver bullet,' a quick fix?"
2. Why, in Rideau's opinion, do prisons fail to make society safer?
3. How does Rideau argue that murderers are less dangerous to society than other inmates?
4. What effect does prison have on inmates? Do prisons deter crime?
5. *Critical Thinking:* Rideau argues that older prisoners should be released. He also argues that murderers pose little danger to society. Rideau is a murderer who has been in prison for more than thirty years. How much of this article is really a personal appeal?

Evaluating Strategy

1. How effective is the opening?
2. How does Rideau use statistics to support his point of view? Are they convincing?
3. *Other Modes:* Where does Rideau use *cause and effect* and *narrative?*

Appreciating Language

1. What is the general style and tone of the essay? Is it suited for the readers of *Time?*
2. How does Rideau's language reveal his attitude toward politicians?

Connections across the Disciplines

1. How does Rideau's appeal compare or conflict with Joseph Biden's "get tough" policy on domestic violence (page 651)?
2. Could John Holt's theories of self-discipline (page 459) be applied to prison rehabilitation?

Writing Suggestions

1. Write a letter to *Time* magazine supporting or criticizing Rideau's argument. What should prisons do—rehabilitate or warehouse?
2. *Collaborative Writing:* Discuss Rideau's essay with a group of students. Do you want to know more about the murder he was convicted of committing? Does focusing on the inmates obscure the plight of victims? How would family members feel if the man or woman who took the life of their loved one was released because he or she was deemed no longer a threat to the community? Should prisons punish? Work together on writing a letter to *Time* reflecting your opinions. Your group may divide and compose two letters in a point/counterpoint pair of arguments.

BARBARA EHRENREICH

Barbara Ehrenreich (1941–) was born in Butte, Montana, and attended Reed College in Oregon, where she received a bachelor's degree in chemical physics. In 1968 she completed a doctorate in cell biology at Rockefeller University in New York. While in graduate school, she became actively involved in political and social issues such as education, low-income housing, and the war in Vietnam. She has published numerous articles in Time, Ms., Mother Jones, New Republic, *and the* Nation. *Many of these essays appeared in her collection* The Worst Years of Our Lives: Irreverent Notes from a Decade of Greed. *Her first novel,* Kipper's Game, *was published in 1993.*

. . . Or Is It Creative Freedom?

In this essay first published in Time *in 1992, Ehrenreich responds to the outcry against Ice-T's song* Cop Killer, *which spearheaded a general attack on rap music for being racist, sexist, and violent. While Ehrenreich agrees with basic observations made by the detractors of rap music, she draws different conclusions about its message.*

1 Ice-T's song *Cop Killer* is as bad as they come. This is black anger—raw, rude and cruel—and one reason the song's so shocking is that in postliberal America, black anger is virtually taboo. You won't find it on TV, not on the *McLaughlin Group* or *Crossfire*, and certainly not in the placid features of Arsenio Hall or Bernard Shaw. It's been beaten back into the outlaw subcultures of rap and rock, where, precisely because it is taboo, it sells. And the nastier it is, the faster it moves off the shelves. As Ice-T asks in another song on the same album, "Goddamn what a brotha gotta do/To get a message through/To the red, white and blue?"

2 But there's a gross overreaction going on, building to a veritable paroxysm of white denial. A national boycott has been called, not just of the song or Ice-T, but of all Time Warner products. The President himself has denounced Time Warner as "wrong" and Ice-T as "sick." Ollie North's Freedom Alliance has started a petition drive aimed at bringing Time Warner executives to trial for "sedition and anarchy."

3 Much of this is posturing and requires no more courage than it takes to stand up in a VFW hall and condemn communism or crack. Yes, *Cop Killer* is irresponsible and vile. But Ice-T is as right about some things as he is righteous about the rest. And ultimately, he's not even dangerous—least of all to the white power structure his songs condemn.

4 The "danger" implicit in all the uproar is of empty-headed, suggestible black kids, crouching by their boom boxes, waiting for the word. But what Ice-T's fans know and his detractors obviously don't is that *Cop Killer* is just one more entry in pop music's long history of macho hyperbole and violent boast. Flip to the classic-rock station, and you might catch the Rolling Stones announcing "the time is right for violent revolooshun!" from their 1968 hit *Street Fighting Man*. And where were the defenders of our law-enforcement officers when a white British group, the Clash, taunted its fans with the lyrics: "When they kick open your front door/How you gonna come?/With your hands on your head/Or on the trigger of your gun?"

5 "Die, Die, Die Pig" is strong speech, but the Constitution protects strong speech, and it's doing so this year more aggressively than ever. The Supreme Court has just downgraded cross burnings to the level of bonfires and ruled that it's no crime to throw around verbal grenades like "nigger" and "kike." Where are the defenders of decorum and social stability when prime-time demagogues like Howard Stern deride African Americans as "spear chuckers"?

6 More to the point, young African Americans are not so naive and suggestible that they have to depend on a compact disc for their sociology lessons. To paraphrase another song from another era, you don't need a rap song to tell which way the wind is blowing. Black youths know that the police are likely to see them through a filter of stereotypes as miscreants and potential "cop killers." They are aware that a black youth is seven times as likely to be charged with a felony as a white youth who has committed the same offense, and is much more likely to be imprisoned.

7 They know, too, that in a shameful number of cases, it is the police themselves who indulge in "anarchy" and violence. The U.S. Justice Department has received 47,000 complaints of police brutality in the past six years, and Amnesty International has just issued a report on police brutality in Los Angeles, documenting 40 cases of "torture or cruel, inhuman or degrading treatment."

8 Menacing as it sounds, the fantasy in *Cop Killer* is the fantasy of the powerless and beaten down—the black man who's been hassled once too often ("A pig stopped me for nothin'!"), spread-eagled against a police car, pushed around. It's not even a "responsible" fantasy (fantasies seldom are). It's not even a very creative one. In fact, the sad thing about *Cop Killer* is that it falls for the cheapest, most conventional image of rebellion that our culture offers: the lone gunman spraying fire from his AK-47. This is not "sedition"; it's the familiar, all-American, Hollywood-style pornography of violence.

9 Which is why Ice-T is right to say he's no more dangerous than George Bush's pal Arnold Schwarzenegger, who wasted an army of cops in *Terminator 2*. Images of extraordinary cruelty and violence are marketed every day, many of far less artistic merit than *Cop Killer*. This is our free market of ideas and images, and it shouldn't be any less free for a black man than for other purveyors of "irresponsible" sentiments, from David Duke to Andrew Dice Clay.

10 Just, please, don't dignify Ice-T's contribution with the word sedition. The past masters of sedition—men like George Washington, Toussaint-Louverture, Fidel Castro or Mao Ze-dong, all of whom led and won armed insurrections—would be unimpressed by *Cop Killer* and probably saddened. They would shake their heads and mutter words like "infantile" and "adventurism." They might point out that the cops are hardly a noble target, being, for the most part, honest working stiffs who've got stuck with the job of patrolling ghettos ravaged by economic decline and official neglect.

11 There is a difference, the true seditionist would argue, between a revolution and a gesture of macho defiance. Gestures are cheap. They feel good, they blow off some rage. But revolutions, violent or otherwise, are made by people who have learned how to count very slowly to 10.

Understanding Meaning

1. Is black anger "taboo"? Is it only found in rap music?
2. What fuels the reaction against rap music, according to Ehrenreich? What does she mean by "white denial"?
3. What is Ehrenreich persuading people to see about the protest against rap music?
4. Why does Ehrenreich see Ice-T as not a true revolutionary?

5. *Critical Thinking:* Does society overreact to depictions of black men defying authority or engaging in crime? Are people less shocked by gangsters when they are portrayed by Jimmy Cagney or Robert De Niro? Do country-western songs about shooting lawmen evoke the same outrage as "gangsta" rap?

Evaluating Strategy

1. How important is Ehrenreich's opening statement? Is it important for her not to appear as an admirer of Ice-T?
2. How important is *comparison* in her argument? Can offensive statements made with anger be equated with offensive jokes? Is one more troubling or threatening?

Appreciating Language

1. What does Ehrenreich mean by the term "postliberal America"? When was America liberal?
2. What words does Ehrenreich use to describe rap music? What attitude do her connotations reflect?

Connections across the Disciplines

1. How do Ehrenreich's comments about Ice-T compare to observations made by Nat Hentoff in "Should This Student Have Been Expelled?" (page 660)?
2. How would Leonce Gaiter (page 636) likely respond to Ehrenreich's comments about rap music?

Writing Suggestions

1. Write a short essay analyzing reactions to a current movie, book, speaker, song, or demonstration many people found controversial. Briefly describe—in neutral terms—the subject, and then analyze the response. Why are people upset? Is their concern justified? Is the reaction purely political? You may include your own opinions if you wish.
2. *Collaborative Writing:* Discuss Ehrenreich's article with a group of students. What attitudes do they have toward her views and toward rap music itself? Have a member record the group's responses, and then work together to write a brief statement outlining your group's opinion. If members disagree, consider drafting pro and con statements.

LEONCE GAITER

Leonce Gaiter is an African American writer living in Los Angeles who has commented frequently on social issues. A graduate of Harvard, Gaiter has worked in media, including network television. He has been long concerned with the media depiction of African Americans. Gaiter argues that well-intentioned whites maintain a sense of black inferiority, an attitude embraced by many African American young people.

The Revolt of the Black Bourgeoisie

This article, written for The New York Times *in 1994, argues that young African Americans are presented crippling stereotypes by both mainstream and black media. Gaiter blends personal observation and experience with factual support.*

1 At a television network where I once worked, one of my bosses told me I almost didn't get hired because his superior had "reservations" about me. The job had been offered under the network's Minority Advancement Program. I applied for the position because I knew I was exceptionally qualified. I would have applied for the position regardless of how it was advertised.

2 After my interview, the head of the department told my boss I wasn't really what he had in mind for a Minority Advancement Program job. To the department head, hiring a minority applicant meant hiring someone unqualified. He wanted to hire some semiliterate, hoop-shooting former prison inmate. That, in his view, was a "real" black person. That was someone worthy of the program.

3 I had previously been confronted by questions of black authenticity. At Harvard, where I graduated in 1980, a white classmate once said to me, "Oh, you're not really a black person." I asked her to explain. She could not. She had known few black people before college, but a lifetime of seeing black people depicted in the American media had taught her that real black people talked a certain way and were raised in certain places. In her world, black people did not attend elite colleges. They could not stand as her intellectual equals or superiors. Any African-American who shared her knowledge of Austen and Balzac—

while having to explain to her who Douglass and Du Bois were—had to be *willed* away for her to salvage her sense of superiority as a white person. Hence the accusation that I was "not really black."

4 But worse than the white majority harboring a one-dimensional vision of blackness are the many blacks who embrace this stereotype as our true nature. At the junior high school I attended in the mostly white Washington suburb of Silver Spring, Md., a black girl once stopped me in the hallway and asked belligerently, "How come you talk so proper?" Astonished, I could only reply, "It's proper*ly*," and walk on. This girl was asking why I spoke without the so-called black accent pervasive in the lower socioeconomic strata of black society, where exposure to mainstream society is limited. This girl was asking, Why wasn't I impoverished and alienated? In her world view, a black male like me couldn't exist.

5 Within the past year, however, there have been signs that blacks are openly beginning to acknowledge the complex nature of our culture. Cornel West, a professor of religion and the director of Afro-American Studies at Princeton University, discusses the growing gulf between the black underclass and the rest of black society in his book "Race Matters"; black voices have finally been raised against the violence, misogyny, and vulgarity marketed to black youth in the form of gangsta rap; Ellis Cose's book "The Rage of a Privileged Class," which concentrates on the problems of middle- and upper-income blacks, was excerpted as part of a *Newsweek* magazine cover story; Bill Cosby has become a vocal crusader against the insulting depiction of African-Americans in "hip-hop generation" TV shows.

6 Yes, there are the beginnings of a new candor about our culture, but the question remains, How did one segment of the African-American community come to represent the whole? First, black society itself placed emphasis on that lower caste. This made sense because historically that's where the vast majority of us were placed; it's where American society and its laws were designed to keep us. Yet although doors have opened to us over the past 20 years, it is still commonplace for black leaders to insist on our community's uniform need for social welfare programs, inner-city services, job skills training, etc. Through such calls, what has passed for a black political agenda has been furthered only superficially; while affirmative action measures have forced an otherwise unwilling majority to open some doors for the black middle class, social welfare and Great Society-style programs aimed at the black lower class have shown few positive results.

7 According to 1990 census figures, between 1970 and 1990 the number of black families with incomes under $15,000 rose from 34.6 percent of the black population to 37 percent, while the number of black families with incomes of $35,000 to $50,000 rose from 13.9 percent to 15 percent of the population and those with incomes of more than $50,000 rose from 9.9 percent to 14.5 percent of the black population.

8 Another reason the myth of an all-encompassing black underclass survives—despite the higher number of upper-income black families—is that it fits with a prevalent form of white liberalism, which is just as informed by racism as white conservatism. Since the early 70's, good guilt-liberal journalists and others warmed to the picture of black downtrodden masses in need of their help. Through the agency of good white people, blacks would rise. This image of African-Americans maintained the lifeline of white superiority that whites in this culture cling to, and therefore this image of blacks stuck. A strange tango was begun. Blacks seeking advancement opportunities allied themselves with whites eager to "help" them. However, those whites continued to see blacks as inferiors, victims, cases, and not as equals, individuals or, heaven forbid, competitors.

9 It was hammered into the African-American psyche by media-appointed black leaders and the white media that it was essential to our political progress to stay or seem to stay economically and socially deprived. To be recognized and recognize oneself as middle or upper class was to threaten the political progress of black people. That girl who asked why I spoke so "proper" was accusing me of political sins—of thwarting the progress of our race.

10 Despite progress toward a more balanced picture of black America, the image of black society as an underclass remains strong. Look at local news coverage of the trial of Damian Williams and Henry Watson, charged with beating the white truck driver Reginald Denny during the 1992 South-Central L.A. riots. The press showed us an African-print-wearing cadre of Williams and Watson supporters trailing Edi M. O. Faal, William's defense attorney, like a Greek chorus. This chorus made a point of standing in the camera's range. They presented themselves as the voice of South-Central L.A., the voice of the oppressed, the voice of the downtrodden, the voice of the city's black people.

11 To anyone watching TV coverage of the trial, all blacks agreed with Faal's contention that his clients were prosecuted so aggressively because they are black. Period. Reporters made no effort to show op-

posing black viewpoints. (In fact, the media portrait of the Los Angeles riot as blacks vs. whites and Koreans was a misrepresentation. According to the Rand Corporation, a research institute in Santa Monica, blacks made up 36 percent of those arrested during the riot; Latinos made up 51 percent.) The black bourgeoisie and intelligentsia remained largely silent. We had too long believed that to express disagreement with the "official line" was to be a traitor.

12 TV networks and cable companies gain media raves for programs like "Laurel Avenue," an HBO melodrama about a working-class black family lauded for its realism, a real black family complete with drug dealers, drug users, gun toters and basketball players. It is akin to the media presenting "Valley of the Dolls" as a realistic portrayal of the ways of white women.

13 The Fox network offers a differing but equally misleading portrait of black Americans, with "Martin." While blue humor has long been a staple of black audiences, it was relegated to clubs and records for *mature* black audiences. It was not peddled to kids or to the masses.

14 Now the blue humor tradition is piped to principally white audiences. If TV was as black as it is white—if there was a fair share of black love stories, black dramas, black detective heroes—these blue humor images would not be a problem. Right now, however, they stand as images to which whites can condescend.

15 Imagine being told by your peers, the records you hear, the programs you watch, the "leaders" you see on TV, classmates, prospective employers—imagine being told by virtually everyone that in order to be your true self you must be ignorant and poor, or at least seem so.

16 Blacks must now see to it that our children face no such burden. We must see to it that the white majority, along with vocal minorities within the black community (generally those with a self-serving political agenda), do not perpetuate the notion that African-Americans are invariably doomed to the underclass.

17 African-Americans are moving toward seeing ourselves—and demanding that others see us—as individuals, not as shards of a degraded monolith. The American ideal places primacy on the rights of the individual, yet historically African-Americans have been denied those rights. We blacks can effectively demand those rights, effectively demand justice only when each of us sees him or herself as an individual with the right to any of the opinions, idiosyncracies and talents accorded any other American.

Understanding Meaning

1. What is the "black bourgeoisie"?
2. Why does Gaiter argue that the definition of a "'real' black" is crippling to young African Americans?
3. Why does Gaiter believe that negative stereotypes of blacks are more destructive when embraced by African Americans rather than whites?
4. Why does Gaiter argue for individual rather than group rights?
5. *Critical Thinking:* Gaiter argues that many liberals have a vested interest in keeping a black underclass. Do people gain political power by using the disadvantaged as a power base, a voting bloc? At some point do reformers realize that if they are successful they will be out of a job?

Evaluating Strategy

1. What kinds of appeals does Gaiter use in his argument?
2. *Other Modes:* How does Gaiter use *narration* and *definition* in his essay?
3. How much factual support does Gaiter offer?

Appreciating Language

1. What is the tone of this essay? What words and phrases help shape it?
2. Is Gaiter angry or disillusioned with anyone or any institution? What do his connotations suggest?

Connections across the Disciplines

1. Would Gaiter likely see Charles Jamison's article "Why My Business Failed" (page 523) as a kind of positive example for young African Americans?
2. How do Gaiter's observations compare to William Raspberry's (page 320)?

Writing Suggestions

1. Write an essay reflecting your views of how your ethnic group is depicted in the media. How are Jews, Koreans, the Irish, Italians, or Poles portrayed? Is your group ignored? Are the representations accurate or stereotyped? Argue for a more balanced approach, or approve of fair reporting.

2. *Collaborative Writing:* Discuss with a group of students the way African Americans are portrayed in the media. Are middle-class African Americans eclipsed by images of an underclass? Are black success stories missing in black history? Write an open letter to television networks advocating your group's position. If members have different opinions, draft additional letters. Read all member's versions to the group. Ask members to comment on the clarity of each thesis and the quality of supporting detail.

CARL SAGAN

Carl Sagan (1934–) was born in New York City and educated at the University of Chicago, where he received his doctorate in 1960. A widely published astronomer, Sagan became widely known to American television audiences through a popular series called Cosmos. *An expert on the atmospheres of Venus, Mars, and Titan, he is also noted for his ability to explain scientific issues for a general audience.*

Why We Need to Understand Science

This article originally appeared in the popular magazine Parade *(1993). As you read the article, notice how Sagan moves from humorous narrative to a serious argument, supported by facts, that Americans are woefully lacking in their knowledge of science.*

1 As I got off the plane, he was waiting for me, holding up a sign with my name on it. I was on my way to a conference of scientists and TV broadcasters, and the organizers had kindly sent a driver.

2 "Do you mind if I ask you a question?" He said as we waited for my bag. "Isn't it confusing to have the same name as that science guy?"

3 It took me a moment to understand. Was he pulling my leg? "I *am* that science guy," I said. He smiled. "Sorry. That's my problem. I thought it was yours too." He put out his hand. "My name is William F. Buckley." (Well, his name wasn't *exactly* William F. Buckley, but he did have the name of a contentious TV interviewer, for which he doubtless took a lot of good-natured ribbing.)

4 As we settled into the car for the long drive, he told me he was glad I was "that science guy"—he had so many questions to ask about science. Would I mind? And so we got to talking. But not about science. He wanted to discuss UFOs, "channeling" (a way to hear what's on the minds of dead people—not much it turns out), crystals, astrology. . . . He introduced each subject with real enthusiasm, and each time I had to disappoint him: "The evidence is crummy," I kept saying. "There's a much simpler explanation." As we drove on through

the rain, I could see him getting glummer. I was attacking not just pseudoscience but also a facet of his inner life.

5 And yet there is so much in real science that's equally exciting, more mysterious, a greater intellectual challenge—as well as being a lot closer to the truth. Did he know about the molecular building blocks of life sitting out there in the cold tenuous gas between the stars? Had he heard of the footprints of our ancestors found in 4-million-year-old volcanic ash? What about the raising of the Himalayas when India went crashing into Asia? Or how viruses subvert cells, or the radio search for extraterrestrial intelligence or the ancient civilization of Ebla? Mr. "Buckley"—well-spoken, intelligent, curious—had heard virtually nothing of modern science. He *wanted* to know about science. It's just that all the science got filtered out before it reached him. What the society permitted to trickle through was mainly pretense and confusion. And it had never taught him how to distinguish real science from the cheap imitation.

6 All over America there are smart, even gifted, people who have a built-in passion for science. But that passion is unrequited. A recent survey suggests that 94 percent of Americans are "scientifically illiterate."

A PRESCRIPTION FOR DISASTER

7 We live in a society exquisitely dependent on science and technology, in which hardly anyone knows anything about science and technology. This is a clear prescription for disaster. It's dangerous and stupid for us to remain ignorant about global warming, say, or ozone depletion, toxic and radioactive wastes, acid rain. Jobs and wages depend on science and technology. If the United States can't manufacture, at high quality and low price, products people want to buy, then industries will drift out of the United States and transfer a little prosperity to another part of the world. Because of the low birthrate in the '60s and '70s, the National Science Foundation projects a shortage of nearly a million professional scientists and engineers by 2010. Where will they come from? What about fusion, supercomputers, abortion, massive reductions in strategic weapons, addiction, high-resolution TV, airline and airport safety, food additives, animal rights, superconductivity, Midgetman versus rail-garrison MX missiles, going to Mars, finding cures for

AIDS and cancer? How can we decide national policy if we don't understand the underlying issues?

8 I know that science and technology are not just cornucopias pouring good deeds out into the world. Scientists not only conceived nuclear weapons; they also took political leaders by the lapels, arguing that *their* nation—whichever it happened to be—had to have one first. Then they arranged to manufacture 60,000 of them. Our technology has produced thalidomide, CFCs, Agent Orange, nerve gas, and industries so powerful they can ruin the climate of the planet. There's a *reason* people are nervous about science and technology.

9 And so the image of the mad scientist haunts our world—from Dr. Faust to Dr. Frankenstein to Dr. Strangelove to the white-coated loonies of Saturday morning children's TV. (All of this doesn't inspire budding scientists.) But there's no way back. We can't just conclude that science puts too much power into the hands of morally feeble technologists or corrupt, power-crazed politicians and decide to get rid of it. Advances in medicine and agriculture have saved more lives than have been lost in all the wars in history. Advances in transportation, communication, and entertainment have transformed the world. The sword of science is double-edged. Rather, its awesome power forces on all of us, including politicians, a new responsibility—more attention to the long-term consequences of technology, a global and transgenerational perspective, an incentive to avoid easy appeals to nationalism and chauvinism. Mistakes are becoming too expensive.

10 Science is much more than a body of knowledge. It is a way of thinking. This is central to its success. Science invites us to let the facts in, even when they don't conform to our preconceptions. It counsels us to carry alternative hypotheses in our heads and see which best match the facts. It urges on us a fine balance between no-holds-barred openness to new ideas, however heretical, and the most rigorous skeptical scrutiny of everything—new ideas *and* established wisdom. We need wide appreciation of this kind of thinking. It works. It's an essential tool for a democracy in an age of change. Our task is not just to train more scientists but also to deepen public understanding of science.

HOW BAD IS IT?

11 Very bad. "It's Official," reads one newspaper headline: "We Stink in Science." Less than half of all Americans know that the Earth moves

around the Sun and takes a year to do it—a fact established a few centuries ago. In tests of average 17-year-olds in many world regions, the U.S. ranked dead last in algebra. On identical tests, the U.S. kids averaged 43 percent and their Japanese counterparts 78 percent. In my book, 78 percent is pretty good—it corresponds to a C+, or maybe even a B−; 43 percent is an F. In a chemistry test, students in only two of 13 nations did worse than the U.S. Compared to us, Britain, Singapore, and Hong Kong were so high they were almost off-scale, and 25 percent of Canadian 18-year-olds knew just as much chemistry as a select 1 percent of American high school seniors (in their second chemistry course, and most of them in "advanced" programs). The best of 20 fifth-grade classrooms in Minneapolis was outpaced by every one of the 20 classrooms in Sendai, Japan, and 19 out of 20 in Taipei, Taiwan. South Korean students were far ahead of American students in all aspects of mathematics and science, and 13-year-olds in British Columbia (in Western Canada) outpaced their U.S. counterparts across the boards (in some areas they did better than the Koreans). Of the U.S. kids, 22 percent say they dislike school; only 8 percent of the Koreans do. Yet two-thirds of Americans, but only a quarter of the Koreans, say they are "good at mathematics."

WHY WE'RE FLUNKING

12 How do British Columbia, Japan, Britain, and Korea manage so much better than we do? During the Great Depression, teachers enjoyed job security, good salaries, respectability. Teaching was an admired profession, partly because learning was widely recognized as the road out of poverty. Little of that is true today. And, so, science (and other) teaching is too often incompetently or uninspiringly done, its practitioners, astonishingly, having little or no training in their subjects—sometimes themselves unable to distinguish science from pseudoscience. Those who do have the training often get higher-paying jobs elsewhere.

13 We need more money for teachers' training and salaries, and for laboratories—so kids will get hands-on experience rather than just reading what's in the book. But all across America, school-bond issues on the ballot are regularly defeated. U.S. parents are much more satisfied with what their children are learning in science and math than are, say, Japanese and Taiwanese parents—whose children are

doing so much better. No one suggests that property taxes be used to provide for the military budget, or for agriculture, or for cleaning up toxic wastes. Why just education? Why not support it from general taxes on the local and state levels? What about a special education tax for those industries with special needs for technically trained workers?

14 American kids don't do enough schoolwork. The average high school student spends 3.5 hours a week on homework. The total time devoted to studies, in and out of the classroom, is about 20 hours a week. Japanese *fifth*-graders average 33 hours a week.

15 But most American kids aren't stupid. Part of the reason they don't study hard is that they've received few tangible benefits when they do. Competency (that is, actually knowing the stuff) in verbal skills, mathematics, and science these days doesn't increase earnings for average young men in their first eight years out of high school—many of whom take service rather than industrial jobs.

16 In the productive sectors of the economy, though, the story is different. There are furniture factories, for example, in danger of going out of business—not because there are no customers but because few entry-level workers can do simple arithmetic. A major electronics company reports that 80 percent of its job applicants can't pass a *fifth*-grade math text—and that's an American, not a Korean, fifth-grade test. The United States is already losing some $25 billion a year (mainly in lost productivity and the cost of remedial education) because workers, to too great a degree, can't read, write, count, or think. Parents should know that their children's livelihoods may depend on how much math and science they know. Now, while the kids are in school, is the time for them to learn. Parents might encourage their schools to offer—and their kids to take—comprehensible, well-taught advanced science courses. They might also limit the amount of mind-numbing TV their children watch.

WHAT WE CAN DO

17 Those in America with the most favorable view of science tend to be young, well-to-do, college-educated white males. But three-quarters of new American workers between now and 2001 will be women, nonwhites, and immigrants. Discriminating against them isn't only unjust, it's also self-defeating. It deprives the American economy of desperately needed skilled workers.

18 Black and Hispanic students are doing better in standardized science tests now than in the late 1960s, but they're the only ones who are. The average math gap between white and black U.S. high school graduates is still huge—two to three grade levels; but the gap between white U.S. high school graduates and those in, say, Japan, Canada, Great Britain or Finland is more than *twice* as big. If you're poorly motivated and poorly educated, you won't know much—no mystery here. Suburban blacks with college-educated parents do just as well in college as suburban whites with college-educated parents. Enrolling a poor child in a Head Start program doubles his or her chances to be employed later in life; one who completes an Upward Bound program is four times as likely to get a college education. If we're serious, we know what to do.

19 What about college and university? There are obvious steps similar to what should be done in high schools; salaries for teachers that approach what they could get in industry; more scholarships, fellowships, and laboratory equipment; laboratory science courses required of everyone to graduate; and special attention paid to those traditionally steered away from science. We should also provide the financial and moral encouragement for academic scientists to spend more time on public education—lectures, newspaper and magazine articles, TV appearances. This requires scientists to make themselves understandable and fun to listen to. To me, it seems strange that some scientists, who depend on public funding for their research, are reluctant to explain to the public what it is that they do. Fortunately, the number of scientists willing to speak to the public—and capably—has been increasing each year. But there are not yet nearly enough.

20 Virtually every newspaper in America has a daily astrology column. How many have a daily science column? When I was growing up, my father would bring home a daily paper and consume (often with great gusto) the baseball box scores. There they were, to me dry as dust, with obscure abbreviations (W, SS, SO, W-L, AB, RBI), but they spoke to him. Newspapers everywhere printed them. I figured maybe they weren't too hard for me. Eventually I too got caught up in the world of baseball statistics. (I know it helped me in learning decimals, and I still cringe a little when I hear that someone is "batting a thousand." But 1.000 is not 1,000. The lucky player is batting one.)

21 Or take a look at the financial page. Any introductory material? Explanatory footnotes? Definitions of abbreviations? None. It's sink or swim. Look at those acres of statistics! Yet people voluntarily read the

stuff. It's not beyond their ability. It's only a matter of motivation. Why can't we do the same with math, science, and technology?

22 By far the most effective means of raising interest in science is television. There's lots of pseudoscience on TV, a fair amount of medicine and technology, but hardly any science—especially on the three big commercial networks, whose executives think science programming means ratings declines and lost profits, and nothing else matters. Why in all America is there no TV drama that has as its hero someone devoted to figuring out how the universe works?

23 Stirring projects in science and technology attract and inspire youngsters. The number of science Ph.D.s peaked around the time of the Apollo program and declined thereafter. This is an important potential side-effect of such projects as sending humans to Mars, or the Superconducting Supercollider to explore the fine structure of matter, or the program to map all human genes.

24 Every now and then, I'm lucky enough to teach a class in kindergarten or the first grade. Many of these children are curious, intellectually vigorous, ask provocative and insightful questions, and exhibit great enthusiasm for science. When I talk to high school students, I find something different. They memorize "facts." But, by and large, the joy of discovery, the life behind those facts, has gone out of them. They're worried about asking "dumb" questions; they're willing to accept inadequate answers; they don't pose follow-up questions; the room is awash with sidelong glances to judge, second-by-second, the approval of their peers. Something has happened between first and 12th grade, and it's not just puberty. I'd guess that its partly peer pressure *not* to excel (except in sports); partly that the society teaches short-term gratification; partly the impression that science or math won't buy you a sports car; partly that so little is expected of students; and partly that there are so few role models for intelligent discussion of science and technology or for learning for its own sake.

25 But there's something else. Many adults are put off when youngsters pose scientific questions. Children ask why the Sun is yellow, or what a dream is, or how deep you can dig a hole, or when is the world's birthday or why we have toes. Too many teachers and parents answer with irritation or ridicule, or quickly move on to something else. Why adults should pretend to omniscience before a 5-year-old, I can't for the life of me understand. What's wrong with admitting that you don't know? Children soon recognize that somehow this kind of question

annoys many adults. A few more experiences like this, and another child has been lost to science.

26 There are many better responses. If we have an idea of the answer, we could try to explain. If we don't, we could go to the encyclopedia or library. Or we might say to the child: "I don't know the answer. Maybe no one knows. Maybe when you grow up, you'll be the first to find out."

27 But mere encouragement isn't enough. We must also give children the tools to winnow the wheat from the chaff. I'm haunted by the vision of a generation of Americans unable to distinguish reality from fantasy, hopefully clutching their crystals for comfort, unequipped even to frame the right questions or to recognize the answers. I want us to rescue Mr. "Buckley" and the millions like him. I also want us to stop turning out leaden, incurious, unimaginative high school seniors. I think America needs, and deserves, a citizenry with minds wide awake and a basic understanding of how the world works.

28 Public understanding of science is more central to our national security than half a dozen strategic weapons systems. The sub-mediocre performance of American youngsters in science and math, and the widespread adult ignorance and apathy about science and math, should sound an urgent alarm.

Understanding Meaning

1. What is the difference between pseudoscience and science?
2. Why is American "scientific illiteracy" dangerous?
3. Why are people, in Sagan's view, disinterested in science?
4. What does Sagan persuade readers to accept? What must be done to improve our nation's understanding of science?
5. What does Sagan mean when he says that science is more than "knowledge" but "a way of thinking"? What is the difference?
6. *Critical Thinking:* Sagan argues that the media has portrayed science in a way children find unappealing. What image of scientists did you develop as a child? Were scientists depicted as less glamorous than police officers or lawyers?

Evaluating Strategy

1. How important is the opening narrative? What does it suggest about Sagan's intended readers?

2. What factual appeals does Sagan make?
3. How does he attempt to make his concerns about science relevant to general readers?
4. How does he present statistics? Are they understandable?

Appreciating Language

1. What level of language does Sagan use? How does it differ from that expected in a scientific paper or textbook?
2. How does Sagan use language to arouse reader concern about scientific illiteracy?

Connections across the Disciplines

1. How does Sagan's appeal about "scientific illiteracy" match John Allen Paulos's concern about "innumeracy" (page 178)?
2. Sagan argues that science is driven by facts and truth. How does Sagan's argument relate to Samuel Scudder's nineteenth-century article (page 41)?

Writing Suggestions

1. Write a short essay arguing that Americans lack a general knowledge of an important topic—science, mathematics, the Constitution, the environment, or their own bodies.
2. *Collaborative Writing:* Discuss Sagan's article with a group of students. What impressions of science and scientists did the group have in childhood? Write a brief, persuasive, open letter to parents encouraging them to invest more in their children's knowledge of science. You may use facts from Sagan's article for support.

JOSEPH R. BIDEN

Joseph R. Biden (1942–) was born in Scranton, Pennsylvania, and received a bachelor degree at the University of Delaware in 1965. Three years later Biden completed his law degree at Syracuse University. After practicing criminal law in Wilmington, Delaware, he began his own law firm and became active in politics. First elected to the U.S. Senate in 1972, Biden became an influential Democrat, serving on both the Foreign Relations and Judiciary Committees. As chair of the Senate Judiciary Committee, Biden has commented widely on crime legislation.

Domestic Violence: A Crime, Not a Quarrel

This article appeared in Trial *(1993), a journal widely read by trial attorneys. Notice that although the essay is written in a readable style accessible to nonlawyers, Biden includes the notes that his readers expect in a professional article.*

1 Imagine a world in which 3 to 4 million people are suddenly struck by a serious, recurring illness. There is chronic pain, trauma, and injury. Authorities fail to draw any connection between individual bouts with the disease and the greater public threat. Many suffer in silence.

2 This is the United States of America in 1993: The disease is violence, and the victims are predominantly women who are beaten in their own homes.

3 For too long, we as a nation have failed to grasp either the scope or the seriousness of domestic violence. If the leading newspapers were to announce tomorrow the discovery of a new disease affecting 3 to 4 million women every year, few would fail to appreciate the seriousness of the illness. Yet, when it comes to the 3 to 4 million women who are victimized by violence in their own homes,[1] the alarms sound faintly.

4 For the past four years, the U.S. surgeons general have warned that domestic violence—not heart attacks or cancer or strokes—poses the single largest threat of injury to adult women in this country.[2] But no matter how often this has been repeated, we still hear those who deny and distance this violence by calling it a family problem, a private matter, or a question of miscommunication.

5 Until the 20th century, this nation actually condoned domestic violence, following a common law rule known as the "rule of thumb." This barred a husband from "restrain[ing] a wife of her liberty" by "chastisement" with a stick any thicker than a man's thumb.[3] The rule, originally intended to protect women from excessive violence, ironically institutionalized domestic violence.

6 Unfortunately, this common law principle has left a legacy of legal blindness toward violence against women. Decades after the "rule of thumb" disappeared, many jurisdictions in the United States still refused to arrest and prosecute spouse abusers, even in cases where a comparable assault by a stranger on the street would have led to a lengthy jail term. For example, a 1989 study in the nation's capital found that in over 85 percent of the domestic violence cases where a woman was found bleeding from wounds, police did not arrest her abuser.[4]

7 History and language have conspired to convince us that domestic violence is somehow "domesticated"—tame. Every time we use the words "domestic violence," we invoke this history and suggest that this violence is somehow less serious than an assault on the street. The reality is far different than our language suggests. For example, family violence accounts for a significant number of murders in this country. Every day four women are killed by their male partners, and at least one-third of all women who are murdered die at the hands of a husband or boyfriend.[5]

8 Indeed, *most* domestic violence is far removed from a "push and shove." According to the U.S. Department of Justice, one-third of these attacks, if reported, would be classified as felony rapes, robberies, or aggravated assaults. The remaining two-thirds would be classified as simple assaults, though up to half of them involved "bodily injury at least as serious as the injury inflicted in 90 percent of all robberies and aggravated assaults."[6]

SCOPE OF BATTERING PROBLEM

9 In 1990, the U.S. Senate Judiciary Committee began to investigate violence against women. As chairman of the committee, I held hearings and then drafted legislation—the Violence Against Women Act.[7] During the preliminary investigation it became clear to me that this nation has, for decades, operated under a false idea of violence against women.

What the public was calling a private affair turns out to be a very public tragedy.

10 One million women a year seek medical assistance for injuries caused by violence at the hands of a male partner.[8] That is a public health menace, not a private malady. Children in homes with domestic violence are 15 times more likely to be abused or neglected than children in peaceful homes.[9] That is a public tragedy for future generations, not a private failure of communication. We spend $5 billion to $10 billion a year on health care, criminal justice, and other social costs of domestic violence.[10] That is a public budget crisis, not a minor shortfall.

11 Our false idea of this violence has in turn left us in the dark about some of the most important basic questions about domestic violence. For example, until recently we have had little reliable data on the scope of the problem. Independent estimates range from 2 million to 12 million victims a year, with the most often cited numbers showing that between 3 million and 4 million women are severely battered annually.[11] Official government agencies charged with collecting crime data, like the FBI, do not specifically include domestic violence in their yearly national crime statistics.[12]

12 To fill this gap, the majority staff of the Senate Judiciary Committee conducted an extensive survey of authorities across the nation. Last October the committee released *Violence Against Women: A Week in the Life of America*,[13] which for the first time provided a national estimate of domestic crimes reported to the police each year. The report included the following findings:

13 • In 1991 alone, 21,000 domestic crimes against women were reported each week to the police.

14 • One-fifth of all the aggravated assaults in the country occurred in the home.

15 • That year 11 million assaults, rapes, and murders were committed in homes and reported to the police. The total for unreported attacks is estimated to be as much as three times this figure.[14]

A WEEK IN THE LIFE

16 Unfortunately, statistics like these do not always speak loudly enough about the human tragedy that they reflect. To help us better understand the problem, the committee collected and included accounts of

individual acts of violence that occurred during a single week in September 1992. Compiled from a random survey of rape crisis centers, domestic violence shelters, and other service providers across the country, these accounts revealed the tragic human face of domestic abuse. What emerged was a gruesome portrait of violence—a violence that destroys individual lives, rips apart families, and condemns children to repeat the violent acts of their parents in an unending chain of harm.

17 Here are a few of the 200 incidents compiled in the committee's report:

18 • September 1, 5 P.M., suburban Connecticut—A 26-year-old woman is attacked by her boyfriend of five years. He breaks her right arm with a hammer.

19 • September 2, 11:17 P.M., rural West Virginia—A woman calls a local hotline because her husband has broken the window of her car and threatened her life. He has been harassing her at work, and she fears losing her job.

20 • September 3, time unknown, Florida—A 21-year-old woman is beaten in the head by her father with a 3-inch-diameter pipe. He is arrested after neighbors call the police.

21 • September 4, morning, Kansas—A 39-year-old woman is taken to a shelter. Her ex-husband has custody of their children. When she went to pick up the children for visitation, he took her into the bathroom and raped her. The children were in the house and called the police when they heard her screaming.

22 • September 5, night, New Hampshire—A 23-year-old woman with two children is held at gunpoint and raped twice by her live-in boyfriend. Her injuries require her to be hospitalized for six days. She is then transferred to a local domestic violence shelter.

23 • September 6, 9 A.M., a city in Colorado—A 15-year-old girl is hit in the face and thrown against a wall by her boyfriend; police escort her out of the apartment. The boyfriend is arrested because of outstanding abuse charges by two other women.

24 • September 7, 2 P.M., New Mexico—A 20-year-old woman, six months pregnant, is beaten and abandoned by her boyfriend of one year.

25 This sad chronicle represents only a tiny fraction of the violence suffered by U.S. women every week of every year. The committee's report took 20 pages of typewritten text to describe 200 violent incidents, yet it covered less than 1 percent of the violent attacks against women reported to the police in that week alone. If we had included every incident, our time line would have been 2,000 pages long—just for a single week in the life of U.S. women.

26 What do these stories tell us about domestic violence? As the report put it: "At the most basic level, they tell us that *no one is immune.* Violence happens to young women and old women, to rich women and poor women, to homeless women and working women." [15]

27 At another level, these stories help to remind us of the ripple effects of violence in the home, which "affects everyday lives, imperils jobs, infects the workplace, ruins leisure time and educational opportunities." [16]

28 Finally, the stories warn us of a future generational transfer of violence. It is sad but true that in many of these incidents, we found children who saw their mothers raped, children who saw their mothers beaten, children who were forced to call 911. Unless something is done, these child victims of domestic violence may go on to repeat the very same violent patterns they have witnessed.

THE VIOLENCE AGAINST WOMEN ACT

29 During the past 20 years, many sincere efforts have been launched to assist victims of crime, particularly victims of rape and domestic violence. Rape laws now focus on the defendant's conduct, not the victim's previous behavior or life-style. Sex crimes units and domestic crimes units have sprouted up in major metropolitan areas. On the federal level, Congress has provided aid, albeit modest, to domestic violence shelters and instituted a fund to help the victims of rape and domestic violence.

30 Unfortunately, the promise of these efforts has not always been realized. Despite our growing awareness of the depth and extent of violence against women, our society's response remains inadequate. It is still easier to convict a car thief than a rapist or a spouse abuser. It is possible to find cities that spend more on their zoos than the entire state spends on helping the victims of domestic violence.[17] Indeed, the United States has three times as many shelters to care for unwanted pets than it has shelters to harbor battered women.[18]

31 To help respond to these needs, I have re-introduced the Violence Against Women Act.[19] The purpose of the legislation is not only to implement important legal reforms but also to attack the subtle prejudices that have helped mask the problem from public view. National leadership on this issue is sorely needed. To put it in the words of one

witness who testified at hearings on the bill, "We have to make a . . . clear[er], a louder statement that this is criminal, that in this country this is not accepted, nor will it be tolerated."[20]

32 The bill includes a number of important reforms targeting *all* crimes against women, including rapes and beatings. With respect to domestic violence, specifically, the bill emphasizes both safety for survivors and accountability for abusers. The act—

33 • authorizes $300 million in new funding to provide training for police, prosecutors, and victim advocates; to create special police and prosecution units devoted to crimes against women (including rape and domestic violence); and to increase computerized communications between criminal and family law agencies and courts;

34 • creates the first federal penalties for crime committed by abusers who cross state lines to continue their abuse;

35 • requires that protection orders issued by the courts of one state be accorded "full faith and credit" by other states;

36 • provides significant incentives to encourage states to treat domestic violence as a serious crime;

37 • authorizes the U.S. Department of Education to disseminate model programs to educate young people about domestic violence, with programs for primary, middle, and secondary schools;

38 • triples existing federal funding for battered women's shelters; and

39 • creates training programs for state and federal judges to raise awareness and increase sensitivity about rape, sexual assault, and domestic violence.

40 Finally, and perhaps most important, the bill recognizes that violence against women raises issues of equality as well as issues of safety and accountability. Every woman has a right to be free from violent attacks motivated solely by the fact that she is a woman. The Violence Against Women Act could help to guarantee that right. It recognizes, for the first time, a civil rights remedy for victims of crimes "motivated by gender."

41 Long ago we recognized that hate beatings of African-Americans or Asian-Americans violate their right to be free and equal. We should guarantee the same protection for victims who are assaulted only because they are women. Whether an attack is motivated by racial bias or ethnic bias or gender bias, the results are the same. The violence not only wounds physically, it degrades and terrorizes, instilling fear and inhibiting the lives of all those similarly situated.

42 As Illinois Attorney General Roland Burris testified before the Senate Judiciary Committee: "Until women, as a class, have the same protection offered others who are the object of irrational hate-motivated abuse and assault, we as a society should be humiliated and ashamed."[21]

43 I realize that this legislation will not eradicate violence against women, but I believe that it is a step in the right direction in the direction of changing this nation's false idea that domestic violence is second-class crime. We like to believe that home is a place of safety, tranquility, and comfort, but for millions of women, it is a place of danger and fear. Until we recognize that fact and brand these attacks as brutal and wrong, we can never hope to change the course of domestic violence.

NOTES

1. Nancy K. Sugg & Thomas Inui, *Primary Care Physicians Response to Domestic Violence,* 267 JAMA 3157 (1992) (adopting the 3 to 4 million estimate); *Women and Violence: Hearings Before the Senate Comm. on the Judiciary on Legislation to Reduce the Growing Problem of Violent Crime Against Women,* 101st Cong., 2d Sess. 111 (1990) (hereafter *Women and Violence*) (testimony of Dr. Angela Browne) (estimating 4 million women are severely beaten each year).
2. Surgeon General Antonia Novelio has echoed former Surgeon General C. Everett Koop's concerns. *See From the Surgeon General, U.S. Public Health Service,* 267 JAMA 3132 (1992).
3. Sir William Blackstone, *Commentaries on the Laws of England, quoted in* WOMEN, THE FAMILY, AND FREEDOM: THE DEBATE IN DOCUMENTS 34 (Susan G. Bell & Karen M. Offen, eds., 1983).
4. Karen Baker et al., joint project, D.C. Coalition Against Domestic Violence & Women's Law & Public Policy Fellowship Prog. at Georgetown U Law Center, Report on District of Columbia Police Response to Domestic Violence, Nov. 3, 1989, at 44 (on file with Sen. Comm. on Judiciary).
5. U.S. DEP'T OF JUSTICE, FED. BUREAU OF INVESTIGATIONS, CRIME IN THE U.S. 1991, UNIFORM CRIME REPORTS 19 (1992).
6. NATIONAL INST. OF JUSTICE, U.S. DEP'T OF JUSTICE, CIVIL PROTECTION ORDERS: LEGISLATION, CURRENT COURT PRACTICE, AND ENFORCEMENT 4 (1990).
7. S. 2754, 101st Cong., 2d Sess. (1990); *reintroduced at* S. 15, 102d Cong., 1st Sess. (1991); *now pending as* S. 11, 103d Cong., 1st Sess. (1993).
8. Congressional Caucus for Women's Issues, Violence Against Women 5 (Oct. 1992 fact sheet).

9. National Woman Abuse Prevention Project, Effects of Domestic Violence on Children (undated fact sheet) (on file with Sen. Comm. on Judiciary).
10. *See* Harris Meyer, *The Billion-Dollar Epidemic* AM. MED. NEWS, Jan. 6, 1992, at 7.
11. *See* H. J. Cummins, *Domestic Violence Crosses Over into the Workplace,* NEWSDAY, July 12, 1992, at 94 (U.S. Centers for Disease Control and Prevention in Atlanta estimate that 2 million to 12 million women are battered, depending on definition of "battering" used); MILDRED D. PAGELOW, FAMILY VIOLENCE 45–46 (1984) (adopting the 12 million estimate), *see also* Sugg & Inui, *supra* note 1, at 3157; *Women and Violence, supra* note 1.
12. CRIME IN THE U.S. 1991, *supra* note 6.
13. SENATE COMM. ON JUDICIARY, VIOLENCE AGAINST WOMEN: A WEEK IN THE LIFE OF AMERICA, S. DOC. NO. 118, 102D CONG., 2D SESS. (Oct. 1992).
14. *Id.* at 4.
15. *Id.* at 5.
16. *Id.* at 6.
17. *See* Nancy Gibbs, *'Til Death Do Us Part,* TIME, Jan. 18, 1993, at 42.
18. *Women and Violence, supra* note 1, at 128 (testimony of Sarah Bach).
19. S. H., *supra* note 7.
20. *Women and Violence, supra* note 1, at 171 (testimony of Dr. Angela Browne).
21. *Violence Against Women: Victims of the System: Hearings on S.1.5 Before the Sen. Comm. of the Judiciary,* 102d Cong., 1st Sess. 76 (1991) (testimony of Ill. Atty. Gen. Roland Burris).

Understanding Meaning

1. How does Biden define "domestic violence"?
2. How common is domestic violence?
3. What solutions does Biden advocate? What must be done?
4. How does he support his argument in favor of the Violence Against Women Act?
5. *Critical Thinking:* How much of Biden's argument concerns changing reader perceptions? Is it hard for many people to see a conflict between spouses in the same light as an altercation between strangers in public?

Evaluating Strategy

1. How effective is Biden's opening? Does it seem targeted to lawyers or to a general audience?
2. What factual support does Biden provide?
3. Is it effective to compare domestic violence to a disease?
4. How does Biden present statistics? Are they made understandable?
5. *Critical Thinking:* What role does *definition* play in his argument?

Appreciating Language

1. What troubles Biden about the term *domestic violence?*
2. How does Biden use language to try to alter perceptions?

Connections across the Disciplines

1. Consider the articles about gender differences (pages 592 and 600). Does violence against women suggest cultural or biological causes to you?
2. How might Wilbert Rideau (page 628) view Biden's "get tough" policy? Would prison deter men from abusing women?

Writing Suggestions

1. Write a letter to the editor of a local publication supporting or opposing legislation such as the Violence Against Women Act. Provide reasons and support for your views.
2. *Collaborative Writing:* Discuss the issue of domestic violence with a group of students. Is it serious or overstated? Do men and women view this issue differently? Do cultures differ in the way people define what behavior is abusive? Work together to draft a brief statement outlining how domestic violence could be prevented. If differences of opinion arise within the group, consider drafting two documents.

NAT HENTOFF

Nat Hentoff (1925–) was born in Boston. The author of more than twenty-five books, Hentoff is also known for his numerous articles in the Village Voice, New Yorker, *and* The Washington Post. *A committed liberal, he has been outspoken on issues ranging from drug testing and the draft to racism and abortion. Although considered a leftist, Hentoff has criticized those on the Left who have advocated suppressing what they call "hate speech."*

Should This Student Have Been Expelled?

In this 1991 article from the Village Voice, *Hentoff persuades readers to accept "hate speech," no matter how offensive it is, as "speech" and therefore protected by the Constitution. As you read Hentoff's essay, notice how he uses* definition, narration, *and* comparison *to build his argument.*

The day that Brown denies any student freedom of speech is the day I give up my presidency of the university.
—Vartan Gregorian, president of Brown University,
February 20, 1991

1 Doug Hann, a varsity football player at Brown, was also concentrating on organizational behavior and management and business economics. On the night of October 18, 1990, Hann, a junior, was celebrating his twenty-first birthday, and in the process had imbibed a considerable amount of spirits.

2 At one point, Hann shouted into the air, "Fuck you, niggers!" It was aimed at no one in particular but apparently at all black students at Brown. Or in the world. A freshman leaned out a dormitory window and asked him to stop being so loud and offensive.

3 Hann, according to reporters on the *Brown Daily Herald*, looked up and yelled, "What are you, a faggot?" Hann then noticed an Israeli flag in the dorm. "What are you, a Jew?" he shouted. "Fucking Jew!"

4 Hann had achieved the hat trick of bigotry. (In hockey, the hat trick is scoring three goals in a game.) In less than a minute, Hann had engaged in racist, anti-Semitic, and homophobic insults.

5 He wasn't through. As reported by Smita Nerula in the *Brown Daily Herald,* the freshman who had asked Hann to cool it recruited a few people from his dorm "and followed Hann and his friends.

6 "This resulted in a verbal confrontation outside of Wayland Arch. At this time, [Hann] was said to have turned to one of the freshman's friends, a black woman, and shouted, 'My parents own your people.'"

7 To the Jewish student, or the student he thought was Jewish, Hann said, "Happy Hanukkah."

8 There are reports that at this juncture Hann tried to fight some of the students who had been following him. But, the *Brown Daily Herald* reports, he "was held back by one of his friends, while [another] friend stretched his arm across the Wayland Gates to keep the students from following Hann."

9 John Howard Crouch—a student and Brown chapter secretary of the American Civil Liberties Union there—tells me that because Hann had friends restraining him, "nobody seriously expected fighting, regardless of anyone's words."

10 Anyway, there was no physical combat. Just words. Awful words, but nothing more than speech. (Nor were there any threats.)

11 This was not the first time Hann's graceful drunken language had surfaced at Brown. Two years before, in an argument with a black student at a fraternity bar, Hann had called the student a "nigger." Thereupon he had been ordered to attend a race relations workshop and to get counseling for possible alcohol abuse. Obviously, he has not been rehabilitated.

12 Months went by after Hann's notorious birthday celebration as Brown's internal disciplinary procedures cranked away. (To steal a phrase from Robert Sherrill, Brown's way of reaching decisions in these matters is to due process as military music is to music. But that's true of any college or university I know anything about.)

13 At last, the Undergraduate Disciplinary Council (five faculty or administration members and five students) ruled that Doug Hann was to leave the university forevermore. Until two years ago, it was possible for a Brown student to be dismissed, which meant that he or she could reapply after a decent period of penance. But now, Brown has enshrined the sentence of expulsion. You may go on to assist Mother

Teresa in caring for the dying or you may teach a course in feminism to 2 Live Crew, but no accomplishments, no matter how noble, will get you back into Brown once you have been expelled.

14 Doug Hann will wander the earth without a Brown degree for the rest of his days.

15 The president of Brown, Vartan Gregorian—formerly the genial head of the New York Public Library—had the power to commute or even reverse the sentence. But the speech code under which Hann was thrown out had been proposed by Gregorian himself shortly after he was inaugurated in 1989, so he was hardly a detached magistrate.

16 On January 25, 1991, Vartan Gregorian affirmed, with vigor, the expulsion decision by the Undergraduate Disciplinary Council.

17 Hann became a historic figure. Under all the "hate speech" codes enacted around the country in recent years, he is the first student to actually be expelled for violating one of the codes.

18 The *New York Times* (February 12) reported that "Howard Ehrlich, the research director of the National Institute Against Prejudice and Violence, said that he did not know of any other such expulsions, but that he was familiar with cases in which students who had harassed others were moved to other dormitories or ordered to undergo counseling."

19 But that takes place in *educational* institutions, whose presidents recognize that there are students who need help, not exile.

20 At first, there didn't seem to be much protest among the student body at Brown on free speech grounds—except for members of the Brown chapter of the ACLU and some free thinkers on the student paper, as well as some unaffiliated objectors to expelling students for what they say, not for what they do. The number of these dissenters is increasing, as we shall see.

21 At the student paper, however, the official tone has changed from the libertarian approach of Vernon Silver, who was editor-in-chief last semester. A February 13 *Brown Daily Herald* editorial was headed: "*Good Riddance.*"

22 It began: "Doug Hann is gone, and the university is well to be rid of him."

23 But President Gregorian has been getting a certain amount of flack and so, smiting his critics hip and thigh, he wrote a letter to the *New York Times*. Well, that letter (printed on February 21) was actually a press release, distributed by the Brown University News Bureau to all sorts of people, including me, on February 12. There were a few

changes—and that *Brown Daily Herald* editorial was attached to it—but Gregorian's declaration was clearly not written exclusively for the *Times.*

24 Is this a new policy at the *Times*—taking public relations handouts for the letters page?

25 Next week I shall include a relentlessly accurate analysis of President Gregorian's letter by the executive director of the Rhode Island ACLU. But first, an account of what Gregorian said in that letter to the *Times.*

26 President Gregorian indignantly denies that Brown has ever expelled "anyone for the exercise of free speech, nor will it ever do so." Cross his heart.

27 He then goes into self-celebration: "My commitment to free speech and condemnation of racism and homophobia are well known. . . .

28 "The university's code of conduct does not prohibit speech; it prohibits *actions.*"

29 Now watch this pitiable curve ball:

30 "Offence III [of the Brown code]—which deals with harassment—prohibits inappropriate, abusive, threatening, or demeaning actions based on race, religion, gender, handicap, ethnicity, national origin, or sexual orientation."

31 In the original press release, Gregorian underlined the word *actions.* There, and in the letter to the *Times*—lest a dozing reader miss the point—Gregorian emphasizes that "The rules do not proscribe words, epithets, or slanders, they proscribe behavior." Behavior that "shows flagrant disrespect for the well-being of others or is unreasonably disruptive of the University community."

32 Consider the overbreadth and vagueness of these penalty-bearing provisions. What are the definitions of "harassment," "inappropriate," "demeaning," "flagrant," "disrespect," "well-being," "unreasonably"?

33 Furthermore, with regard to Brown's termination of Doug Hann with extreme prejudice, Gregorian is engaging in the crudest form of Orwellian newspeak. Hann was kicked out for *speech,* and only speech—not for *actions,* as Gregorian huffily insists. As for behavior, the prickly folks whose burning of the American flag was upheld by the Supreme Court were indeed engaged in behavior, but that behavior was based entirely on symbolic speech. So was Hann's. He didn't punch anybody or vandalize any property. He brayed.

34 Art Spitzer, legal director of the ACLU's National Capital Area affiliate, wrote a personal letter to Gregorian:

35 "There is a very simple test for determining whether a person is being punished for his actions or his speech. You just ask whether he would have received the same punishment if he had spoken different words while engaging in the same conduct.

36 "Thus, would your student have been expelled if he had gotten drunk and stood in the same courtyard at the same hour of the night, shouting at the same decibel level, 'Black is Beautiful!' 'Gay is Good!' or 'Go Brown! Beat Yale!' or even 'Nuke Baghdad! Kill Saddam!'?

37 "I am confident," Spitzer said, that "he would not have been expelled for such 'actions.' If that is correct, it follows that *he was expelled for the unsavory content of his speech,* and not for his actions. I have no doubt that you can understand this distinction. (Emphasis added.)

38 "Now, you are certainly entitled to believe that it is appropriate to expel a student for the content of his speech when that content is sufficiently offensive to the 'university community.' . . .

39 "If that is your position, why can't you deliver it forthrightly? Then the university community can have an open debate about which opinions it finds offensive, and ban them. Perhaps this can be done once a year, so that the university's rules can keep pace with the tenor of the times—after all, it wouldn't do to have outmoded rules banning procommunist or blasphemous speech still on the books, now that it's 1991. Then students and teachers applying for admission or employment at Brown will know what they are getting into.

40 "Your recent statements, denying the obvious, are just hypocritical. . . ."

41 And what did the *New York Times*—in a stunningly fatuous February 21 editorial—say of Vartan Gregorian's sending Doug Hann into permanent exile? "A noble attempt both to govern and teach."

42 The *Times* editorials should really be signed, so that the rest of the editorial board isn't blamed for such embarrassments.

Understanding Meaning

1. What events led to Hann's expulsion? Why does Hentoff call him "a historic figure"?
2. Can one make both a "commitment to free speech" and a "condemnation of racism"?
3. What are "hate speech" codes? Does it strike you odd that no one seemed offended by Hann's use of the infamous "f-word"? Is obscenity less disturbing than racial slurs?

4. Would comments about Irish drunks or Italian gangsters be considered "hate speech"?
5. *Critical Thinking:* How do you separate "speech" from "action"? Does the concept of free speech, for instance, allow us to insult a person without facing the legal consequences that would arise from a physical assault?

Evaluating Strategy

1. Hentoff opens his article with a quote from the president of Brown University. How does this set up the rest of his argument?
2. Label where Hentoff uses logical, emotional, and ethical appeals.
3. Do you find Hentoff's inclusion of the press release effective?
4. *Other Modes:* Where does Hentoff use *narration, comparison,* and *definition?*

Appreciating Language

1. Hentoff refers to Hann's activity as a "hat trick of bigotry"—scoring racist, anti-Semitic, and homophobic insults in one outburst. Does the use of this hockey term suggest mockery? Would "triple threat" have different connotations?
2. What tone does Hentoff create with comments about military music and statements such as "Doug Hann will wander the earth without a Brown degree for the rest of his days"? How serious does he take the issue of "hate speech" and those who condemn it?

Connections across the Disciplines

1. Does Hentoff suggest that colleges overreact to "hate speech" the way Barbara Ehrenreich (page 632) feels the public exaggerates the dangers of rap music? If Hann's comments had been put to music like Ice-T's, would they be protected as art?
2. *Critical Thinking:* Consider the impact the word "nigger" had on Nathan McCall (page 47). When speech has a devastating effect on people, does it become an "action" as opposed to speech or "expression"?

Writing Suggestions

1. Assume you were a student at Brown University during the Hann controversy. Write a letter to the editor of the college paper arguing whether or

not Hann should be expelled. Support your argument with more than one persuasive appeal.

2. *Collaborative Writing:* Discuss the concept of "hate speech" with a group of students. Ask members to consider the fate of Doug Hann. Should he have been expelled? Is "hate speech" protected by the Bill of Rights? Record comments and write a brief argument for or against disciplining students for expressing racist comments.

PRO AND CON VIEWS: LANGUAGE AND IDENTITY

ARMANDO RENDÓN

Armando Rendón (1939–) was raised in San Antonio, Texas. He is currently vice president of ATM Systems, a Chicago-based counseling firm. He has published articles in The Washington Post *and* Civil Rights Digest. *Rendón also wrote a film script,* El Chicano. *In 1971 he published* Chicano Manifesto, *which outlined his views of the place of Mexicans in American society.*

Kiss of Death

In this section of Chicano Manifesto, *Rendón argues the importance of Hispanics to resist assimilation into mainstream American society and maintain their language and culture to avoid being "sucked into the vacuum of the dominant society."*

1 I nearly fell victim to the Anglo. My childhood was spent in the West Side barrio of San Antonio. I lived in my grandmother's house on Ruiz Street just below Zarzamora Creek. I did well in the elementary grades and learned English quickly.

2 Spanish was off-limits in school anyway, and teachers and relatives taught me early that my mother tongue would be of no help in making good grades and becoming a success. Yet Spanish was the language I used in playing and arguing with friends. Spanish was the language I spoke with my *abuelita*, my dear grandmother, as I ate *atole* on those cold mornings when I used to wake at dawn to her clattering dishes in the tiny kitchen; or when I would cringe in mock horror at old folk tales she would tell me late at night.

3 But the lesson took effect anyway. When, at the age of ten, I went with my mother to California, to the San Francisco Bay Area where she found work during the war years, I had my first real opportunity to strip myself completely of my heritage. In California the schools I attended were all Anglo except for this little mexicanito. At least, I never knew anyone who admitted he was Mexican and I certainly never thought to ask. When my name was accented incorrectly, Rén-don instead of Rendón, that was all right; finally I must have gotten tired of correcting people or just didn't bother.

4 I remember a summertime visit home a few years after living on the West Coast. At an evening gathering of almost the whole family—uncles, aunts, nephews, nieces, my *abuelita*—we sat outdoors through the dusk until the dark had fully settled. Then the lights were turned on; someone brought out a Mexican card game, the *Lotería El Diablito,* similar to bingo. But instead of rows of numbers on a pasteboard, there were figures of persons, animals, and objects on cards corresponding to figures set in rows on a pasteboard. We used frijoles (pinto beans) to mark each figure on our card as the leader went through the deck one by one. The word for tree was called: *Arbol!* It completed a row; I had won. Then to check my card I had to name each figure again. When I said the word for tree, it didn't come at all as I wanted it to; AR-BOWL with the accent on the last syllable and sounding like an Anglo tourist. There was some all-around kidding of me and good-natured laughter over the incident, and it passed.

5 But if I had not been speaking much Spanish up until then, I spoke even less afterward. Even when my mother, who speaks both Spanish and English fluently, spoke to me in Spanish, I would respond in English. By the time I graduated from high school and prepared to enter college, the break was nearly complete. Seldom during college did I admit to being a Mexican-American. Only when Latin American students pressed me about my surname did I admit my Spanish descent, or when it proved an asset in meeting coeds from Latin American countries.

6 My ancestry had become a shadow, fainter and fainter about me. I felt no particular allegiance to it, drew no inspiration from it, and elected generally to let it fade away. I clicked with the Anglo mind-set in college, mastered it, you might say. I even became editor of the campus biweekly newspaper as a junior, and editor of the literary magazine as a senior—not bad, now that I look back, for a tortillas-and-beans Chicano upbringing to beat the Anglo at his own game.

7 The point of my "success," of course, was that I had been assimilated; I had bought the white man's world. After getting my diploma I was set to launch out into a career in newspaper reporting and writing. There was no thought in my mind of serving my people, telling their story, or making anything right for anybody but myself. Instead I had dreams of Pulitzer Prizes, syndicated columns, foreign correspondent assignments, front-page stories—that was for me. Then something happened.

8 A Catholic weekly newspaper in Sacramento offered me a position as a reporter and feature writer. I had a job on a Bay Area daily as a

copyboy at the time, with the opportunity to become a reporter. But I'd just been married, and there were a number of other reasons to consider: there'd be a variety of assignments, Sacramento was the state capital, it was a good town in which to raise a family, and the other job lacked promise for upward mobility. I decided to take the offer.

9 My wife and I moved to Sacramento in the fall of 1961, and in a few weeks the radicalization of this Chicano began. It wasn't a book I read or a great leader awakening me, for we had no Chávezes or Tijerinas or Gonzálezes at the time; and it was no revelation from above. It was my own people who rescued me. There is a large Chicano population in Sacramento, today one of the most activist in northern California, but at the time factionalized and still dependent on the social and church organizations for identity. But together we found each other.

10 My job soon brought me into contact with many Chicanos as well as with the recently immigrated Mexicans, located in the barrios that Sacramento had allocated to the "Mexicans." I found my people striving to survive in an alien environment among foreign people. One of the stories I covered concerned a phenomenon called Cursillos de Cristiandad (Little Courses in Christianity), intense, three-day group-sensitivity sessions whose chief objective is the re-Christianization of Catholics. To cover the story properly I talked my editor into letting me take a Cursillo.

11 Not only was much revealed to me about the phony gilt lining of religion which I had grown up believing was the Church, but there was an added and highly significant side effect—cultural shock! I rediscovered my own people, or perhaps they redeemed me. Within the social dimension of the Cursillo, for the first time in many years I became reimmersed in a tough, *macho ambiente* (an entirely Mexican male environment). Only Spanish was spoken. The effect was shattering. It was as if my tongue, after being struck dumb as a child, had been loosened.

12 Because we were located in cramped quarters, with limited facilities, and the cooks, lecturers, priests, and participants were men only, the old sense of *machismo* and *camarada* was revived and given new perspective. I was cast in a spiritual setting which was a perfect background for reviving my Chicano soul. Reborn but imperfectly, I still had a lot to learn about myself and my people. But my understanding deepened and renewed itself as the years went by. I visited bracero camps with teams of Chicanos; sometimes with priests taking the sacraments; sometimes only Chicanos, offering advice or assistance with badly needed food and clothing, distributed through a bingo-game

technique; and on occasion, music for group singing provided by a phonograph or a guitar. Then there were barrio organization work; migrant worker programs; a rural self-help community development project; and confrontation with antipoverty agencies, with the churches, with government officials, and with cautious Chicanos, too.

13 In a little San Francisco magazine called *Way,* I wrote in a March 1966 article discussing "The Other Mexican-American":

> 14 The Mexican-American must answer at the same time: Who am I? and Who are we? This is to pose then, not merely a dilemma of self-identity; but of self-in-group-identity. . . . Perhaps the answer to developing a total Mexican-American concept must be left in the hands of the artist, the painter, the writer, and the poet, who can abstract the essence of what it is to be Mexican in America. . . . When that understanding comes . . . the Mexican-American will not only have acculturized himself, but he will have acculturized America to him.

15 If anyone knew what he was talking about when he spoke of the dilemma of who he was and where he belonged, it was this Chicano. I very nearly dropped out, as so many other Mexican-Americans have, under the dragging pressure to be someone else, what most of society wants you to be before it hands out its chrome-plated trophies.

16 And that mystique—I didn't quite have it at the time, or the right word for it. But no one did until just the last few years when so many of us stopped trying to be someone else and decided that what we want to be and to be called is Chicano.

17 I owe my life to my Chicano people. They rescued me from the Anglo kiss of death, the monolingual, monocultural, and colorless Gringo society. I no longer face a dilemma of identity or direction. That identity and direction have been charted for me by the Chicano—but to think I came that close to being sucked into the vacuum of the dominant society.

Understanding Meaning

1. What kind of childhood did Rendón have?
2. What represented his early success? What does Rendón mean with the statement "I had bought the white man's world"? What were his goals?
3. What is the "Anglo kiss of death"?

4. How did Rendón respond to people who mispronounced his name?
5. What led to Rendón's "radicalization"?
6. The Chicanos Rendón encountered were the poor of the barrios and bracero camps. Would his sense of identity be different if the Mexicans he encountered in California were affluent professionals and entrepreneurs?
7. *Critical Thinking:* Rendón describes the Gringo society as "monolingual, monocultural, and colorless." Does he overlook the diversity of cultures in mainstream America, which includes Jews, the Irish, Italians, Germans, Greeks, Russians, and the French? Is this the perception that immigrants have of any culture, such as that all Mexicans or Nigerians seem alike?

Evaluating Strategy

1. What tone is established in the first sentence? Does the use of the word "victim" indicate hostility?
2. Rendón includes a quote from one of his articles. Is this an effective device? Would it be better to simply restate his ideas within "Kiss of Death"?
3. *Other Modes:* How does Rendón use *narration, description,* and *comparison* in developing "Kiss of Death"?

Appreciating Language

1. What does the term "kiss of death" mean to you? Do you associate it with the Bible or Hollywood images of the Mafia?
2. Rendón uses several Spanish words without providing definitions in English. What does this suggest about his idea of America becoming "acculturized" to the Mexican American?
3. Rendón uses both "Mexican-American" and "Chicano." What definitions of these terms are you familiar with? Do "Latino" and "Hispanic" have different meanings and connotations?
4. What does Rendón mean by "cautious Chicanos"?

Connections across the Disciplines

1. How do Rendón's attitudes toward his ethnic identity and the Spanish language differ from Richard Rodriguez's acceptance of Anglo society (page 673)? How do the two Mexican Americans respond to Americanized pronunciations of their Spanish names? How does Rendón's concept

of "self-in-group-identity" contrast with Rodriguez's view of a public individuality?
2. How might Rendón view the Chicano police officer described by Ramon "Tianguis" Pérez in "The Fender-Bender" (page 58)? Might he see this officer as a "cautious Chicano"?
3. How does Rendón's concept of cultural identity compare with the concerns of William Raspberry (page 320) and of Leonce Gaiter (636), who questions the stereotypes offered of "genuine African-Americans"? Does Rendón assume that "real" Chicanos live in the barrio and not in suburbs?

Writing Suggestions

1. Write your own version of a "kiss of death" you have escaped in your own life. Perhaps you nearly lost yourself or compromised your future by taking a job or entering a relationship you found initially appealing but now view as an error. Your essay should emphasize how you altered your sense of identity.
2. Write a short essay analyzing your role in society. Do you see yourself as an individual in a collective society or as part of a group within society? Do others view you as a member of an ethnic group, one of the handicapped, or a product of your neighborhood or generation? Does an in-group identity provide support or heighten your sense of alienation from the greater society?
3. *Collaborative Writing:* Discuss Rendón's essay with a group of students, and ask each one to briefly respond to the notion of an "Anglo Kiss of Death." How do members of the group define this? Do they feel it is appropriate or unnecessarily harsh? Does it presume that mainstream American society is a malevolent force? Work together to write a few paragraphs expressing the views your group raises. You may organize your statement by using *comparison* or *division/classification.*

RICHARD RODRIGUEZ

Richard Rodriguez (1944–) was born in San Francisco of Mexican parents. Though he grew up in a non-English-speaking family, he embraced English and attended Stanford, Columbia, and Berkeley. He received a doctorate in English and was awarded a Fulbright fellowship to study English in London. Rodriguez is best known for Hunger of Memory, *a collection of essays examining the immigrant experience. Since the book's publication in 1982, Rodriguez has become a noted journalist and frequent commentator on public television.*

The Tongue That Had to Be Tied

In this passage from Hunger of Memory, *Rodriguez argues that immigrants should learn English. One does not lose an identity by losing a language, Rodriguez argues; one assumes a public identity. Those who advocate that immigrants should retain their heritage, he argues, confuse "mere separateness with individuality."*

1 Today I hear bilingual educators say that children lose a degree of 'individuality' by becoming assimilated into public society. (Bilingual schooling was popularized in the seventies, that decade when middle-class ethnics began to resist the process of assimilation—the American melting pot.) But the bilingualists simplistically scorn the value and necessity of assimilation. They do not seem to realize that there are *two* ways a person is individualized. So they do not realize that while one suffers a diminished sense of *private* individuality by becoming assimilated into public society, such assimilation makes possible the achievement of *public* individuality.

2 The bilingualists insist that a student should be reminded of his difference from others in mass society, his heritage. But they equate mere separateness with individuality. The fact is that only in private—with intimates—is separateness from the crowd a prerequisite for individuality. (An intimate draws me apart, tells me that I am unique, unlike all others.) In public, by contrast, full individuality is achieved, paradoxically, by those who are able to consider themselves members of the crowd. Thus it happened for me: Only when I was able to think

of myself as an American, no longer an alien in *gringo* society, could I seek the rights and opportunities necessary for full public individuality. The social and political advantages I enjoy as a man result from the day that I came to believe that my name, indeed, is *Rich-heard Road-ree-guess.* It is true that my public society today is often impersonal. (My public society is usually mass society.) Yet despite the anonymity of the crowd and despite the fact that the individuality I achieve in public is often tenuous—because it depends on my being one in a crowd—I celebrate the day I acquired my new name. Those middle-class ethnics who scorn assimilation seem to me filled with decadent self-pity, obsessed by the burden of public life. Dangerously, they romanticize public separateness and they trivialize the dilemma of the socially disadvantaged.

3 My awkward childhood does not prove the necessity of bilingual education. My story discloses instead an essential myth of childhood—inevitable pain. If I rehearse here the changes in my private life after my Americanization, it is finally to emphasize the public gain. The loss implies the gain: The house I returned to each afternoon was quiet. Intimate sounds no longer rushed to the door to greet me. There were other noises inside. The telephone rang. Neighborhood kids ran past the door of the bedroom where I was reading my schoolbooks—covered with shopping-bag paper. Once I learned public language, it would never again be easy for me to hear intimate family voices. More and more of my day was spent hearing words. But that may only be a way of saying that the day I raised my hand in class and spoke loudly to an entire roomful of faces, my childhood started to end.

Understanding Meaning

1. What does Rodriguez mean by "public individuality"?
2. Why does Rodriguez see the acquisition of English as being part of obtaining a "public" identity?
3. What does Rodriguez mean when he says bilingualists confuse "separateness" with "individuality"? Does "separation" from mainstream society leave a person without a sense of individual identity but with a mere connection with an outcast group?
4. How does Rodriguez react when his name is Anglicized and pronounced differently?
5. *Critical Thinking:* Rodriguez describes a "public gain" by being assimilated and accepting English as his own language. What does he or any

other immigrant gain by assimilation? How does this notion of "public individuality" contrast with Rendón's assertion of an "in-group" identity? How important is language to cultural identity? Would more Polish Americans, for example, have stronger ties to their heritage if most of them spoke the language? How important was the revitalization of Hebrew and Gaelic to Jewish and Irish identity earlier in this century?

Evaluating Strategy

1. What is the dominant appeal used in this essay?
2. What kind of support for his argument does Rodriguez offer readers?
3. *Other Modes:* How does Rodriguez use *narration* and *comparison* to develop his argument?

Appreciating Language

1. How does the tone and style of this piece compare to Rendón's article?
2. How does Rodriguez's depiction of bilingualists differ from Rendón's view of his opponents?

Connections across the Disciplines

1. Compare these two articles with Leonce Gaiter's (page 636). What do these writers say about minority attitudes toward mainstream culture?
2. Review Amy Tan's essay "The Language of Discretion" (page 277). How does knowing more than one language affect the way we view the world?

Writing Suggestions

1. Write a persuasive, narrative essay about your own experience with languages other than English. How have you felt when you have encountered people you could not talk to? Have you felt uncomfortable in the presence of people speaking to each other in a language you did not understand?
2. *Collaborative Writing:* Discuss Rodriguez's idea of separateness versus individuality in a small group. Does one lose or deny a culture by "blending in"? Does remaining separate cause alienation and hostility? Have your group write a persuasive essay on this topic. If conflicts arise, consider writing a pair of opposing statements.

WRITING BEYOND THE CLASSROOM

ALBERT EINSTEIN

Albert Einstein (1879–1955) was born in Ulm, Germany. He completed a doctorate at the University of Zurich in 1905. He developed his noted theory of relativity at this time and held several teaching positions in physics. His work soon received international attention. In 1921 Einstein was awarded the Nobel Prize in Physics. Nazi persecution forced him to leave Germany, and he took a teaching position at Princeton. As noted in the Introduction, Einstein's reputation led Leo Szilard to ask him to alert the United States government about the possibility of nuclear weapons.

Letter to President Roosevelt, August 2, 1939

As you read the letter, consider the problem Einstein and the other scientists, for whom English was a second language, faced in explaining an abstract scientific theory to a political official.

1 Albert Einstein
Old Grove Rd.
Nassau Point
Peconic, Long Island

August 2nd, 1939

2 F. D. Roosevelt,
President of the United States,
White House
Washington, D.C.

Sir:

3 Some recent work by E. Fermi and L. Szilard, which has been communicated to me in manuscript, leads me to expect that the element uranium may be turned into a new and important source of energy in the immediate future. Certain aspects of the situation which has arisen seem to call for watchfulness and, if necessary, quick action

on the part of the Administration. I believe therefore that it is my duty to bring to your attention the following facts and recommendations:

4 In the course of the last four months it has been made probable—through the work of Joliot in France as well as Fermi and Szilard in America—that it may become possible to set up a nuclear chain reaction in a large mass of uranium, by which vast amounts of power and large quantities of new radium-like elements would be generated. Now it appears almost certain that this could be achieved in the immediate future.

5 This new phenomenon would also lead to the construction of bombs, and it is conceivable—though much less certain—that extremely powerful bombs of a new type may thus be constructed. A single bomb of this type, carried by boat and exploded in a port, might very well destroy the whole port together with some of the surrounding territory. However, such bombs might very well prove to be too heavy for transportation by air.

6 The United States has only very poor ores of uranium in moderate quantities. There is some good ore in Canada and the former Czechoslovakia, while the most important source of uranium is Belgian Congo.

7 In view of this situation you may think it desirable to have some permanent contact maintained between the Administration and the group of physicists working on chain reactions in America. One possible way of achieving this might be for you to entrust with this task a person who has your confidence and who could perhaps serve in an inofficial capacity. His task might comprise the following:

8 a) to approach Government Departments, keep them informed of the further development, and put forward recommendations for Government action, giving particular attention to the problem of securing a supply of uranium ore for the United States;

9 b) to speed up the experimental work, which is at present being carried on within the limits of the budgets of University laboratories, by providing funds, if such funds be required, through his contacts with private persons who are willing to make contributions for this cause, and perhaps also by obtaining the co-operation of industrial laboratories which have the necessary equipment.

10 I understand that Germany has actually stopped the sale of uranium from the Czechoslovakian mines which she has taken over. That she should have taken such early action might perhaps be understood on the ground that the son of the German Under-Secretary of State,

von Weizäcker, is attached to the Kaiser-Wilhelm-Institut in Berlin where some of the American work on uranium is now being repeated.

11 Yours very truly,
Albert Einstein

Understanding Meaning

1. What does Einstein want the president to realize?
2. What specific recommendations does Einstein urge Roosevelt to carry out?
3. *Critical Thinking:* How does Einstein end the letter? Does the mere mention of Germany and nuclear research appear alarming? Remember that in August 1939 Hitler had already taken the Rhineland and Czechoslovakia. That month he was stepping up pressures on Poland. Within a month World War II would begin.

Evaluating Strategy

1. What appeals does Einstein use?
2. How does Einstein suggest that the president accept his recommendations?
3. Does Einstein assume his name alone will command attention? Is that why he uses first person in the letter?

Appreciating Language

1. What level of language does Einstein use? How does he explain physics in common terms?
2. Is the tone of this letter alarmist?

Connections across the Disciplines

1. How would this letter provide added support to Carl Sagan's "Why We Need to Understand Science" (page 642)?
2. Compare this letter to the fund-raising ad on page 680. How are they similar in attempting to make a persuasive argument in a brief statement?

Writing Suggestions

1. Write a persuasive letter to the president or other official to persuade him or her to follow your recommendations on a subject you feel important.
2. *Collaborative Writing:* Discuss the letter with some students. Did Einstein manage to communicate effectively? Is this a lost art today? Work together to write a persuasive essay on the need for experts to communicate with the public and officials.

THE IRISH AMERICAN PARTNERSHIP

The Irish American Partnership is a nonprofit organization supported by Irish American politicians and business executives. Tip O'Neill, former Speaker of the House, and the retired commandant of the U.S. Marine Corps, General Paul X. Kelley, were among the founding members. The organization raises funds to support job training and business development programs in both the Republic of Ireland and Northern Ireland.

Irish Need Apply

This advertisement appeared in Irish American magazines and newspapers. The headline is a variation of the infamous "No Irish Need Apply" notices that greeted many Irish immigrants seeking work. Well into the twentieth century, want ads in American newspapers included this statement as a standard feature, often abbreviating it to "N.I.N.A."

1 **Irish need apply.**

2 Ireland needs us.

3 Unemployment above 20 percent. Young people forced to leave their homeland to find hope and work. Parents saying good-bye to their children everyday.

4 Ireland is a small island of abundant beauty but scarce financial resources. To survive and grow, this land of 5 million needs our help.

5 There are 44 million of us of Irish descent in America. We overcame our own struggles, and found comfort and prosperity in our new land.

6 Now it is time for us to apply that same determination to help those back home. Through the Irish American Partnership. The Partnership is a unique organization committed to peace and economic recovery in Ireland, North and South.

7 The Partnership needs you to support its work. Work like 600 jobs for people in Tralee, Ballymun, and West Belfast. Financial aid for graduate students in science and technology. Management training for Irish youth in U.S. companies.

(Continued)

(Continued from previous page)

8 Ireland has much to build on. Breathtaking beauty. A proud, educated, motivated work force. Some 375 American companies on its soil.

9 Above all, Ireland has us deeply loyal Irish Americans able to help those in need.

10 Just fill out the coupon, and return it with a contribution to the Irish American Partnership. The needs are too great to ignore. Apply yourself.

❑ Yes, I want to apply. I want to support the Irish American Partnership.
Enclosed is my contribution for
❑ $35 ❑ $50 ❑ $100 $______ (amt.)
❑ I am not ready to contribute. Please send me more information.
Call toll-free 1-800-722-3893 or fill out and mail to:
Irish American Partnership, 4 Faneuil Hall Marketplace, Boston, MA 02109

Name (please print)

Address

City State Zip

The Irish American Partnership is a non-profit organization supported by American business executives and endorsed by political, religious and business leaders in Ireland, North and South. Its mission is a strong, healthy, peaceful Ireland through economic development, job creation and education

11 **The Irish American Partnership**

Understanding Meaning

1. How effective is the headline in getting attention? Would people of other ethnic groups recognize the historical allusion?
2. What appeals are used?
3. How much factual support is included in the ad? Why is factual support needed?
4. Is an emotional appeal evident, to an ethnic loyalty to the "Old Sod"?

Evaluating Strategy

1. Ads must communicate in a glance. How effective is this ad?
2. *Critical Thinking:* How does this ad fit a problem/solution pattern?

Appreciating Language

1. What level of language is used? What words would strike the reader?
2. How does word choice reinforce the use of appeals?

Connections across the Disciplines

1. How does this ad compare to the 3M ad on page 158?
2. How does an ad such as this, calling on Irish Americans to support Irish causes, relate to the issues of cultural identity raised by Rendón, Rowan, Pérez, Rodriguez, and others you may have read in this book?

Writing Suggestions

1. Invent a similar organization raising money to help a group you identify with. Consider your readers carefully in devising your appeal.
2. *Collaborative Writing:* Working with a group of students, discuss the implied ethical appeal in this ad—that those who have achieved prosperity have an obligation to help others. Do middle-class African Americans or prominent Hispanics have a similar obligation? Work together to write a persuasive letter or ad urging people to "take care of their own."

GUIDELINES FOR WRITING ARGUMENT AND PERSUASION

1. **Determine your purpose.** Clearly establish your thesis, and define what ideas you want readers to accept and what actions you want them to take. Do not try to communicate too many separate actions in one document.
2. **Evaluate your readers carefully.** Examine the perceptual world of your audience. Do barriers to your message exist that must be overcome? What information do your readers need to accept your ideas?
3. **Determine which appeals will be effective.** Recognize the advantages and disadvantages of each appeal, and consider blending more than one.
4. **Craft your introductions and conclusions carefully.** Your opening paragraphs must arouse interest and prepare readers for your argument or appeal. Your conclusion should end with a statement that will reinforce acceptance of your ideas or the taking of recommended action.
5. **Present factual detail in ways readers can understand.** In presenting facts and statistics, use methods such as analogies and narratives to dramatize their significance.
6. **Do not mistake propaganda for persuasion.** Do not assume that hurling accusations, using questionable facts, or employing shock tactics will make your argument or appeal successful. People dislike feeling manipulated, and often potential supporters will find overstated appeals objectionable and offensive.

SUGGESTED TOPICS FOR WRITING ARGUMENT AND PERSUASION

General Assignments

Write a persuasive argument to a general audience on one of the following topics. You may use one or more appeals. You can frame your paper in the form of an essay, a letter, a flyer, or an advertisement.

- Community and police relations
- The drinking age
- The way colleges prepare or fail to prepare graduates for the job market
- Censorship
- Affirmative Action
- Labor unions
- Welfare programs

- Out-of-wedlock births
- Sexual harassment
- A national sales tax

Select one of the following issues, and craft a persuasive essay targeted to one of the audiences listed.

Issues: Medicare reform, distribution of condoms in public schools, school prayer, bilingual education, recycling, gun control, legalization of drugs
Audiences: Suburban residents, retired schoolteachers, small-business owners, an organization of minority police officers, inner-city health care providers

Writing in Context

1. Imagine you have become close to a highly respected member of your community. This person is well regarded by your family and may have a key role in your future. He or she invites you to join an organization that actively supports a view on abortion that is opposite to yours. Write a letter persuading this person to accept your reasons for declining the offer. Try to make your disagreement known without creating animosity.
2. Write a letter to the editor of the campus newspaper about an issue you have heard discussed but that no one else seems willing to raise. Urge the community to pay attention.

ARGUMENT AND PERSUASION CHECKLIST

1. Is your message clearly defined?
2. Does your paper meet reader needs?
3. Do you counter alternative conclusions?
4. Does evidence logically support your views?
5. Do you anticipate objections?
6. Do you avoid overstated, sentimental, or mawkish emotional appeals?
7. Do you avoid preaching to the converted? Will only those who already share your views agree with your arguments?
8. Do you make it easy for undecided readers to accept your position without feeling manipulated or patronized?

ACKNOWLEDGMENTS

Abbey, Edward, "The First Morning." From *Desert Solitaire* by Edward Abbey. Reprinted by permission of Don Congdon Associates, Inc. Copyright © 1968 by Edward Abbey, renewed 1996 by Clarke Abbey.

Ackerman, Diane, "Why Leaves Turn Color in the Fall." From *A Natural History of the Senses* by Diane Ackerman. Copyright © Diane Ackerman 1990. Reprinted by permission of Random House, Inc.

Austin, James, "Four Kinds of Chance." From *Chase, Chance, and Creativity* by James H. Austin. Copyright © 1978 by Columbia University Press. Reprinted by permission of the publisher.

Bauerlein, Monika, "Plutonium Is Forever: Is There Any Sane Place to Put Nuclear Waste?" From *The Utne Reader,* July/August 1992. Reprinted by permission of the author.

Biden, Joseph, "Domestic Violence: A Crime, Not a Quarrel." Reprinted with permission of *Trial* (June 1993). Copyright 1993 the Association of Trial Lawyers of America.

Burciaga, José Antonio, "My Ecumenical Father." From *Drink Cultura: Chicanismo,* by José Antonio Burciaga published by Joshua Odell Editions, Santa Barbara, California. Copyright 1993. Reprinted by permission.

Capote, Truman, "Out There." From *In Cold Blood* by Truman Capote. Copyright © 1965 by Truman Capote and renewed 1993 by Alan U. Schwartz. Originally appeared in the *New Yorker* in a slightly different form. Reprinted by permission of Random House.

Catton, Bruce, "Grant and Lee." Copyright U.S. Capitol Historical Society, all rights reserved. Reprinted with permission.

Ciardi, John, "What Is Happiness?" Reprinted with permission of the Ciardi Family Publishing Trust.

Connelly, Joel, "A Growing Awareness: Environmental Groups and the Media." From *Aperture* 120 Late Summer 1990. Copyright 1990 Aperture Foundation. Reprinted by permission of Aperture Foundation.

Crawford, Kimberly, "Surreptitious Recording of Suspects' Conversations." Originally published in *FBI Law Enforcement Bulletin* (September 1993). Reprinted with permission.

"Depression." From *The Encyclopedia of Psychology,* 2nd ed. vol 1, ed. Raymond Corsini. Copyright John Wiley and Sons, 1994. Reprinted by permission.

Didion, Joan, "The Metropolitan Cathedral in San Salvador." From *Salvador* by Joan Didion. Copyright © 1983 by Joan Didion. All rights reserved. Originally published in 1983. Reprinted by permission of author.

Dillard, Annie, "Living like Weasels." From *Teaching a Stone to Talk* by Annie Dillard. Copyright © 1982 by Annie Dillard. Reprinted by permission of HarperCollins Publishers, Inc.

Dobson, James, "Biology Determines Gender Differences." From *Straight Talk to Men and Their Wives* by James Dobson. Copyright 1980 Word, Inc., Dallas, Texas. All rights reserved.

Dolnick, Edward, "Deafness as Culture." Originally appeared in *The Atlantic Monthly,* September 1993. Copyright Edward Dolnick. Reprinted by permission of author.

Drakulić, Slavenka, "Pizza in Warsaw, Torte in Prague." From *How We Survived Communism and Even Laughed* by Slavenka Drakulić. Copyright © 1991 by Slavenka Drakulić. Reprinted by permission of W. W. Norton & Company, Inc.

Ehrenreich, Barbara, ". . . Or Is It Creative Freedom?" Copyright © Time Inc. Reprinted by Permission.

Ehrlich, Gretel, "A Storm, the Cornfield, and Elk." From *The Solace of Open Places* by Gretel Ehrlich. Copyright © 1985 by Gretel Ehrlich. Used by permission of Viking Penguin, a division of Penguin Books USA Inc.

Einstein, Albert, "Letter to President Roosevelt, August 2, 1939." Reprinted with permission of the National Archives and Records Administration/ Franklin D. Roosevelt Library, Hyde Park, New York.

Elbow, Peter, "Desperation Writing." From *Writing Without Teachers* by Peter Elbow. Copyright ©

1973 by Peter Elbow. Reprinted by permission of Oxford University Press, Inc.

Fried, Lisa, "A New Breed of Entrepreneur—Women." Reprinted by permission of publisher, from *Management Review,* December 1989 © 1989. American Management Association, New York. All rights reserved.

Gaiter, Leonce, "The Revolt of the Black Bourgeoisie." *New York Times Magazine,* June 26, 1994. Copyright 1994 by the New York Times Company. Reprinted by permission.

Gale, Robert Peter and Thomas Hauser, "Final Warning." From *Final Warning: The Legacy of Chernobyl* by Robert Peter Gale and Thomas Hauser. Copyright © 1988 by Robert Peter Gale. All rights reserved. Reprinted by permission of Warner Books, Inc. New York, New York, USA.

Goodall, Jane, "First Observations." From *In the Shadow of Man* by Jane Goodall. Copyright © 1971 by Hugo and Jane van Lawick-Goodall. Reprinted by permission of Houghton Mifflin Company. All rights reserved.

Goodman, Ellen, "The Company Man." Copyright 1976 The Boston Globe Newspaper Co./ Washington Post Writers Group. Reprinted with permission.

Greenfield, Meg. "Why Nothing Is Wrong Anymore." From *Newsweek,* June 28, 1986 © 1986 Newsweek, Inc. All rights reserved. Reprinted by permission.

Grinslade, Liz, "Evaluating a Job Opportunity." From *Healthcare Financial Management,* June 1993. Copyright © 1993 Healthcare Financial Management Association. Reprinted by permission.

Harris, Marvin, "How Our Skins Got Their Color." From *Our Kind* by Marvin Harris. Copyright © 1989 by Marvin Harris. Reprinted by permission of HarperCollins Publishers, Inc.

Hayakawa, S. I., "Reports, Inferences, Judgments." From *Language in Thought and Action,* Fourth Edition by S. I. Hayakawa. Copyright © 1978 Harcourt Brace and Company, reprinted by permission of the publisher.

"The Heimlich Maneuver." From *The American Red Cross First Aid and Safety Handbook.* Copyright © 1992 The American Red Cross. Reprinted with permission.

Hentoff, Nat, "Should This Student Have Been Expelled?" reprinted by permission of the author and *The Village Voice.*

Hilbert, Betsy, "Disturbing the Universe." From *Orion Magazine* Summer 1987. Copyright 1987 The Myrin Institute. Reprinted with permission.

Holt, John, "Three Kinds of Discipline." From *Freedom and Beyond* by John Holt. E. P. Dutton. Copyright © 1972 John Holt. Reprinted by permission.

"Homicide." From *Black's Law Dictionary,* 6th edition. Reprinted with permission of West Publishing Company.

hooks, bell, "Straightening Our Hair." From *Z Magazine* (September 1988). Copyright © 1988 by the Institute for Social and Cultural Communications. Reprinted by permission of *Z Magazine.*

Huff, Darrell, "How to Lie with Statistics." Copyright 1950 by *Harper's Magazine.* All rights reserved. Reproduced from the August issue by special permission.

"Irish Need Apply." Reprinted by permission of Irish American Partnership.

Ivins, Molly, "A Short Story about the Vietnam War Memorial." From *Molly Ivins Can't Say That Can She?* by Molly Ivins. Copyright © 1991 by Molly Ivins. Reprinted by permission of Random House, Inc.

Jacobson, Jodi, "Swept Away." Originally published in *World Watch.* Copyright 1989 by World Watch Institute. Reprinted by permission.

Jamison, Charles, "Why My Business Failed." Originally published in *Black Enterprise,* June 1994. Copyright 1994 Black Enterprise. Reprinted by permission.

Kenna, Peggy and Sondra Lacy, "Communications Styles: United States and Taiwan." From *Business Taiwan* by Peggy Kenna and Sondra Lacy. Copyright 1994 NTC Publishing Group. Reprinted with permission.

Kincaid, Jamaica, "Alien Soil." Copyright © 1993 by Jamaica Kincaid, reprinted with the permission of Wylie, Aitken & Stone, Inc. First published in the *New Yorker.*

"Kinds of Sentences." From *Rinehart Guide to Grammar Usage,* Third Edition by Bonnie Carter and Craig Skates, copyright © 1993 by Holt, Rinehart and Winston, Inc., reprinted by permission of the publisher.

King, Martin Luther, Jr., "The Ways of Meeting Oppression." From *Stride Toward Freedom.* Copyright 1957 by Martin Luther King, copyright renewed 1985 by Coretta Scott King. Reprinted with arrangement with the Heirs to the Estate of Martin Luther King, Jr., c/o Writers House, Inc.

Korda, Michael, "What Makes a Leader?" Originally appeared in *Newsweek.* Copyright © 1985 Michael Korda. Reprinted by permission of the author.

Lerner, Gerda, "Biology Does Not Determine Gender Differences." From *The Creation of Patriarchy.* Copyright © 1986 by Gerda Lerner. Reprinted with permission of Oxford University Press.

Lord, Walter, "The Reconstructed Logbook of the *Titanic.*" From *A Night to Remember* by Walter Lord. Copyright 1955 by Walter Lord. Reprinted by permission of Henry Holt & Co., Inc.

McCall, Nathan, "The Lesson." From *Makes Me Wanna Holler.* Copyright © 1994 by Nathan McCall. Reprinted by permission of Random House.

Martin, Fran, "Documentation Tips." From *Nursing* June 1994. Used with permission from Springhouse Corporation ®.

Mathabane, Mark, "At the Mercy of the Cure." From *Kaffir Boy in America* by Mark Mathabane. Copyright © 1989 by Mark Mathabane. Reprinted with the permission of Scribner, A Division of Simon & Schuster.

Mebane, Mary, "Black Wasn't Beautiful." From *Mary* by Mary Mebane. Copyright © 1981 by Mary Elizabeth Mebane. Used by permission of Viking Penguin, a division of Penguin Books USA Inc.

Momaday, N. Scott, "The Way to Rainy Mountain." From *The Way to Rainy Mountain* by N. Scott Momaday. First published in *The Reporter,* January 26, 1967. Copyright © 1969 University of New Mexico Press. Reprinted with permission by the publisher.

Mundell, Helen, "How the Color Mafia Chooses Your Clothes." From *American Demographics* magazine, © 1993. Reprinted with permission.

Noda, Kesaya, "Growing Up Asian in America." From *Making Waves by Asian Women.* Copyright © AWR. Reprinted with permission of the author.

Orwell, George, "Pleasure Spots." From *The Collected Essays, Journalism and Letters of George Orwell,* vol. IV. Copyright © 1968 Sonia Brownell Orwell. Reprinted by permission of Harcourt Brace.

Ouchi, William, "Japanese and American Workers: Two States of Mind." From *Theory Z* by William Ouchi. Copyright © 1981 by Addison Wesley Publishing Company, Inc. Reprinted by permission of Addison-Wesley Publishing Company, Inc.

Paulos, John Allen, "Innumeracy." From *Innumeracy.* Copyright © 1988 by John Allen Paulos. Reprinted with permission of Hill and Wang, a division of Farrar, Straus & Giroux, Inc.

Pérez, Ramon "Tianguis," "The Fender-Bender." From *The Diary of An Undocumented Immigrant* by Ramon "Tianguis" Pérez is reprinted with permission from the publisher (Houston: Arte Publico Press University of Houston 1989).

Pilipp, Frank and Charles Shull, "TV Movies of the First Decade of AIDS." From *Journal of Popular Film and TV,* Spring 1993 vol. 21, no. 1, pp. 19–26. Reprinted with permission of the Helen Dwight Reid Educational Foundation. Published by Heldref Publications, 1319 Eighteenth St. N.W., Washington, DC 20036–1802. Copyright © 1993.

Raspberry, William, "The Handicap of Definition." © Copyright 1982 Washington Post Writers Group. Reprinted with permission.

Rataan, Suneel, "Why Busters Hate Boomers." Originally appeared in *Fortune,* October 4, 1994. Copyright 1994 Fortune Magazine. Reprinted by permission.

Raudsepp, Eugene, "Seeing Your Way Past Interview Jitters." From *Machine Design,* April 9, 1994. Copyright 1994 Eugene Raudsepp. Reprinted with permission of Eugene Raudsepp, president of Princeton Creative Research, Inc., Princeton, New Jersey.

Rendón, Armando, "Kiss of Death." From *Chicano Manifesto.* Macmillian Company. Copyright © 1971 by Armando Rendón. Reprinted by permission of the author.

Rideau, Wilbert, "Why Prisons Don't Work." Copyright © Time, Inc. Reprinted by permission.

Rodriguez, Richard, "The Tongue That Had to Be Tied." From *Hunger of Memory* by Richard Rodriguez. Copyright © 1982 by Richard Rodriguez. Reprinted by permission of David R. Godine, Publisher, Inc.

Rosenberg, Donald, "What Is Depression?" Copyright © 1996 by Donald Rosenberg. Reprinted by permission of the author.

Rowan, Carl, "Unforgettable Miss Bessie." From *Reader's Digest* March 1985. Copyright © 1985 by The Reader's Digest Association, Inc. Reprinted with permission.

Sacks, Oliver, "The Man Who Mistook His Wife for His Hat." From *The Man Who Mistook His Wife for His Hat* by Oliver Sacks. Copyright © 1985 by Oliver Sacks. Reprinted with permission of Summit Books, a division of Simon & Schuster, Inc.

Sagan, Carl, "Why We Need to Understand Science." Originally published in *Parade* September 10, 1989. Copyright © 1989 by Carl Sagan. Reprinted with permission of author and *Parade.*

Schor, Juliet B., "The Overworked American." From *The Overworked American: The Unexpected Decline of Leisure* by Juliet Schor. Copyright © 1991 by BasicBooks, a Division of HarperCollins Publishers, Inc. Reprinted by permission of BasicBooks, a Division of HarperCollins Publishers, Inc.

Simpson, Eileen, "Dyslexia." From *Reversals* by Eileen Simpson (The Noonday Press). Copyright © 1979, 1991 by Eileen Simpson. Reprinted by permission of George Borchardt, Inc. for the author.

"Solving Printer Operation Problems." From *The LaserJet 4 User's Manual.* Copyright 1993 by Hewlett-Packard. Reprinted with permission of Hewlett-Packard.

Sommers, Christina Hoff, "Figuring Out Feminism." From *Who Stole Feminism* by Christina Hoff Sommers. Copyright © 1994 by Christina Hoff Sommers. Reprinted with the permission of Simon & Schuster.

Steinem, Gloria, "Words and Change." From *Outrageous Acts and Everyday Rebellions,* 2nd edition by Gloria Steinem. Copyright © 1995 by Gloria Steinem. Reprinted with permission of Henry Holt and Company.

Tan, Amy, "The Language of Discretion." Copyright 1989 by Amy Tan. Reprinted by permission of author/Sandra Dijkstra Literary Agency.

Tomkin, Jocelyn, "Hot Air." Used with permission. From the March 1993 issue of *Reason* Magazine. Copyright 1993 by the Reason Foundation, 3415 S. Sepulveda Blvd, Suite 400, Los Angeles, CA 90034.

Tuan, Yi-Fu, "Chinese Space, American Space." Reprinted by permission of author.

"TV Movies of the First Decade of AIDS" Abstract. Copyright © 1996 Information Access Company, *Expanded Academic Index*™. Reprinted with permission.

"3M Pharmaceutical Sales Representative Want Ad." Copyright 1994 by 3M. Reprinted with permission of 3M.

Urrea, Luis Alberto, "Border Story." From *Across the Wire: Life & Hard Times* by Luis Alberto Urrea. Copyright 1993. Used by permission of Doubleday, a division of Bantam Doubleday Dell Publishing Group, Inc.

Walker, Alice, "The Civil Rights Movement: What Good Was It?" From *In Search of Our Mothers' Gardens: Womanist Prose,* copyright © 1967 by Alice Walker, reprinted by permission of Harcourt Brace & Company.

Weisbord, Anne, "Resumes That Rate a Second Look." From *Nurse Extra,* August 1, 1994. Copyright © 1994 Philadelphia Newspapers Inc. Reprinted with permission.

West, Cornel, "Black Political Leadership." From *Race Matters* by Cornel West. Copyright © 1993 by Cornel West. Reprinted by permission of Beacon Press.

White, E. B., "Three New Yorks." From *Here is New York* by E. B. White. Copyright 1949 by E. B. White. Copyright renewed. Reprinted by permission of HarperCollins Publishers, Inc.

Williams, Terry Tempest, "Yucca." From *Pieces of White Shell: A Journey to Navajoland.* Copyright © 1983, 1984 by Terry Tempest Williams. Reprinted with the permission of Scribner, a Division of Simon & Schuster.

Winn, Marie, "Television and Reading." From *The Plug-In Drug,* revised edition by Marie Winn. Copyright © 1977, 1985 by Marie Winn Miller. Used by permission of Viking Penguin, a division of Penguin Books USA Inc.

Zinsser, William, "The Transaction." From *On Writing Well,* Fifth Edition. HarperCollins. Copyright 1994 by William Zinsser. Reprinted with permission of the author.

INDEX